06/08 £1.50

GW00906461

# CHARLESW
# &
# MORSE

# COMPANY LAW

Companies order 1986

Partnership Act

Insolvency Act.

## AUSTRALIA
The Law Book Company
Brisbane ● Sydney ● Melbourne ● Perth


## CANADA
Carswell
Ottawa ● Toronto ● Calgary ● Montreal ● Vancouver


## AGENTS
Steimatzky's Agency Ltd., Tel Aviv;
N.M. Tripathi (Private) Ltd., Bombay;
Eastern Law House (Private) Ltd., Calcutta;
M.P.P. House, Bangalore;
Universal Book Traders, Delhi;
Aditya Books, Delhi;
MacMillan Shuppan KK, Tokyo;
Pakistan Law House, Karachi, Lahore

# CHARLESWORTH
# &
# MORSE

# COMPANY LAW

## FIFTEENTH EDITION

By

**Geoffrey Morse**, LL.B.
**Barrister, Head of the Department of Law
at the University of Nottingham**

Scottish Editor

**Enid A. Marshall**, M.A., LL.B., Ph.D.
**Solicitor, Reader in Business Law
at the University of Stirling**

Accounting Editor

**Richard Morris**, B.A., M.Sc., F.C.A.
**Professor of Accounting
at the University of Liverpool**

Insolvency Editor

**Letitia Crabb**, LL.B., LL.M.
**Solicitor, Lecturer in Law
at the University of Reading**

**LONDON
SWEET & MAXWELL
1995**

| First Edition | (1932) | By His Honour Judge Charlesworth |
|---|---|---|
| Second Edition | (1938) | ,,        ,,        ,,         ,, |
| Third Edition | (1940) | ,,        ,,        ,,         ,, |
| Fourth Edition | (1946) | ,,        ,,        ,,         ,, |
|   Second Impression | (1947) | |
|   Third Impression | (1948) | |
| Fifth Edition | (1949) | ,,        ,,        ,,         ,, |
|   Second Impression revised | (1950) | ,,        ,,        ,,         ,, |
| Sixth Edition | (1954) | ,,        ,,        ,,         ,, |
|   Second Impression revised | (1956) | ,,        ,,        ,,         ,, |
| Seventh Edition | (1960) | By T. E. Cain |
|   Second Impression | (1962) | |
| Eighth Edition | (1965) | ,,        ,,        ,,         ,, |
| Ninth Edition | (1968) | ,,        ,,        ,,         ,, |
| Tenth Edition | (1972) | ,,        ,,        ,,         ,, |
| Eleventh Edition | (1977) | ,,        ,,        ,,         ,, |
|   Second Impression | (1980) | |
| Twelfth Edition | (1983) | By Geoffrey Morse |
| Thirteenth Edition | (1987) | ,,        ,,        ,,         ,, |
| Fourteenth Edition | (1991) | ,,        ,,        ,,         ,, |
| Fifteenth Edition | (1995) | ,,        ,,        ,,         ,, |
|   Second Impression | (1997) | ,,        ,,        ,,         ,, |

Published by
Sweet & Maxwell Limited of
100 Avenue Road,
London NW3 3PF
Phototypeset by LBJ Enterprises Ltd. of
Aldermaston and Chilcompton
Printed in England by Clays Ltd.,
St Ives plc

*No natural forests were destroyed to make this product; only farmed timber was used and replanted*

A CIP catalogue record for this book is available from the British library

ISBN 0421–53060X

# PREFACE

Yet another four years have elapsed since the previous edition of this book. During that period there have been several changes to company law brought about primarily as the result of amendments to the Companies Act 1985. These have been made by a number of statutory instruments, implementing, in the main, a variety of E.C. directives. Primary legislation for such implementation seems to be out of fashion at the moment so that only Part V of the Criminal Justice Act 1993, implementing the insider dealing directive, can be truly so regarded. The various changes made by these statutory instruments range from the introduction of the single member private company (recognising reality) to technical amendments to the share disclosure rules. Implementation of the directives by means of secondary legislation, apart from being messy, can create problems in that the statutory instruments are made under the European Communities Act 1972 and so can only validly implement the directive and no more. This hardly provides for a comprehensive reform of the area of law in question.

A further complication in ascertaining the statutory framework of company law is that specific provisions, including whole parts of the statutes, still remain in limbo, never having been brought into force. Thus Part IV of the Companies Act 1989 on the registration of charges languishes in the shadows and, since it now appears that it will never be introduced as it stands, I have reverted to the 1985 Act provisions in this edition, having been unduly optimistic in including the 1989 Act version in the previous edition. Part V of the Financial Services Act 1986, relating to offers of unlisted securities has been included in the last two editions. That at least has now been put out of its misery and repealed, again never having come into force. It has been replaced by the Public Offers of Securities Regulations 1995, implementing the E.C. prospectus directive. Similarly, section 159A of the 1985 Act, introduced by the 1989 Act into the redemption of shares provisions at the last moment of the latter's Parliamentary passage, in case it was needed, has also suffered the fate of apparently never being brought into force.

The process of company law reform by statute could therefore best be described as uneven. Although it has now been brought within the ambit of the Law Commission, current proposals are

piece-meal and have all the appearance of patching a leaking ship
rather than designing a new and improved vessel. There are over
20 disparate topics under consideration at the present time. It is
now over 30 years since there was any systematic attempt to look
at the system as a whole. The present system is perhaps too much
driven by the complaints of practitioners on matters of detail,
frequently on provisions introduced by the 1989 Act, and by
political dogma so that a dispassionate overview is impossible.

The courts continue to grapple with the complexities and
absurdities thrown up by the legislation. In two particular areas
there have been a plethora of cases, mostly difficult to reconcile
and sometimes simply contradictory, which almost defy any
logical presentation. In the field of minority protection, the
concept of unfairly prejudicial conduct continues to be dealt with
almost on a case by case basis, whilst in the area of directors'
disqualification following an insolvency, the judges' approach
seems almost schizophrenic at times—perhaps the Chancery
Division is simply ill-equipped to deal with what amounts to a
quasi-criminal process. In other areas the courts are reluctant to
spell out a general solution—for example in the area of disclosure
of directors' interests. There have, however, been major decisions in the fields of shareholder agreements, maintenance of
capital, class rights and charges on book debts amongst others.
The City Panel on Take-overs, on the other hand, have been less
active as a result of the downturn in that area during the
recession. Nevertheless, a revised version of the City Code
appeared in 1993.

The result of all this is that there is even more company law
than there was four years ago. The existence of two specialised
series of law reports on company law puts many more cases into
the public domain than in times past; not all of these cases are
concerned with principles and some might have been better left
in obscurity. In this edition I have tried to incorporate this
growth in the law without extending the book's compass beyond
its aims and strengths—i.e. as a guide to the complexities of the
law, indicating the paths to be followed and the pitfalls to be
avoided. It is not, and never has been, a work of reference. In
attempting this I have omitted some material from the previous
edition which seemed particularly dated in modern company
practice. Hopefully the result is a book which achieves its aims
within a manageable length.

In preparing this edition I have again been fortunate in having
the assistance of the three people who worked on the previous

edition. Dr Enid Marshall, as ever, provided not only a detailed and comprehensive brief on developments in Scotland (where the courts continue to produce a more realistic system of judgments) but also found the time to correct many of my errors of transcription from the word processor to the page and several infelicities of style for which the word processor cannot be blamed. Professor Richard Morris simply carried on his excellent work on chapters 20 to 22 in the accounting and related fields. I expected no less and I was not disappointed. Letitia Crabb who edited chapters 24 to 29 on insolvency had to bear a substantial part of the burden of assimilating the myriad of cases now available in the law reports whilst maintaining reason in both the length and clarity of the book. That she has succeeded speaks volumes for her skill as a legal writer. To all three of my collaborators I owe a great debt for their work and they have my gratitude for their efforts.

My colleagues at Nottingham including, but not limited to, those who teach the company law course with me, have contributed much to this book by their time and patience in discussions over various aspects of the subject. In particular I would like to thank Stephen Girvin, who also read the page proofs, for his constant support and advice, and Michael Bridge for his help in preparing Chapter 23 on debentures. I would also like to thank my secretary, Claire Jennings, who assisted at all stages of the work, and frequently rescued me from an impasse with the word processor. She was particularly valuable in keeping some of the burdens of my being a head of department at bay so that I was able to complete the book within the time allowed.

Finally I would as ever like to record my often unspoken debt to my wife, son and daughter who tolerate the moods of an author with well disguised resignation and provide support when it is really needed, and to the two household Burmese cats who were on hand to demand attention whenever I needed a break. As ever, the final responsibility for all errors and omissions is mine alone. This edition is prepared on the law as known to the editors on March 10, 1995.

Nottingham                                        Geoffrey Morse
March 1995

# CONTENTS

# TABLE OF CASES

lii TABLE OF CASES

lxx TABLE OF CASES

# TABLE OF STATUTES

# TABLE OF STATUTORY INSTRUMENTS

# TABLE OF RULES OF THE SUPREME COURT

# SCOTLAND

# REFERENCES TO CITY CODE ON
# TAKEOVERS/MERGERS

## Chapter 1

## NATURE OF REGISTERED COMPANIES

This book is mostly concerned with registered companies, whether public or private, limited by shares.[1] The term "registered company" means a company incorporated or formed by registration under the Companies Acts. The major Act is the Companies Act 1985, which consolidated the various Acts passed between 1948 and 1983. Although this Act has itself been amended, principally by the Companies Act 1989, and in one area reconsolidated,[2] it may still be regarded as the principal Act and in this book, unless it is otherwise stated or the context otherwise requires, references to sections and Schedules are to those of the Companies Act 1985 and references to the ";Act" are to the Companies Act 1985. This approach is facilitated by the fact that most of the changes made by the 1989 Act and subsequent legislation have been effected by the substitution of sections into the 1985 Act.

The Act provides[3] that for the purpose of the registration of companies under the Act there shall be offices (Companies Registration Offices in England and Scotland) at such places as the Secretary of State (for Trade and Industry) thinks fit, and that he may appoint such registrars, assistant registrars, clerks and servants as he thinks necessary for the registration of companies and may make regulations with respect to their duties.

Section 1(1) enables two or more persons associated for any lawful purpose[4] to form an incorporated company with or without limited liability, by complying with the requirements of the Act in respect of registration. As is explained later in this chapter, the requirements are that certain documents be delivered to the appropriate Registrar of Companies and certain fees paid. Under

---

[1] In general terms commercial companies.
[2] This is the area of insolvency and liquidation generally.
[3] s.704.
[4] A private company may be formed by one person only: s.1(3A).

section 10, for example, a memorandum of association and, usually, articles of association must be delivered to the Registrar, who must retain and register them.

The rest of this chapter attempts first of all to give a simple answer to the question "what is a registered company?" and then to trace briefly the history of the registered company. After that there is a note on the current legislation applicable to companies in particular, including the ever increasing influence of the measures of the European Union. Finally, the following topics are dealt with: the procedure to obtain the registration of a company; the effect of the registration of a company—this is that the company is a corporation with a legal existence separate from that of its members, who usually have limited personal liability; the liability of a registered company, *i.e.* of this separate artificial legal person; and the contrast between registered companies and partnerships—a partnership is not a corporation and the partners do not have limited liability.

## WHAT IS A REGISTERED COMPANY?

A registered company, *i.e.* a company incorporated by registration under the Companies Acts, is regarded by the law as a person, just as a human being is a person. This artificial or juristic person can own land and other property, enter into contracts, sue and be sued, have a bank account in its own name, owe money to others and be a creditor of other people and other companies, and employ people to work for it. The company's money and property belong to the company and not to the members or shareholders, although the members or shareholders may be said to own the company. Similarly, the company's debts are the debts of the company and the shareholders cannot be compelled to pay them, although if, for example, the company is being wound up and its assets do not realise a sum sufficient to pay its debts, a shareholder whose liability is limited by shares is liable to contribute to the assets up to the amount, if any, unpaid on his shares. A company, of course, can only act through human agents, and those who manage its business are called directors. The directors are agents of the company and transact business, etc., on behalf of the company. They may authorise other agents to act on the company's behalf, *e.g.* the company secretary. The company will be bound by any transaction entered into on its behalf if the agent is acting within his authority. The company is also liable for torts[5] and crimes committed by its servants and agents within the scope of their employment or authority. This concept of the company as a corporation, *i.e.* a person separate and distinct from the other persons who are its members and directors, is the fundamental principle of company law.

A company must have members, otherwise it would never exist at all, and in the case of a company with a share capital these members are called shareholders (or, if the shares have been converted into stock, stockholders). The shareholder's position with regard to the company itself and to his fellow shareholders is regulated by the Act, by the memorandum and the articles of association and by any agreement between the shareholders, and also by the principle that controlling shareholders, *i.e.* those with sufficient votes to pass a resolution in general meeting, must act bona fide for the benefit of the company as a whole. The memorandum and articles vary considerably among different companies, but in every case the shareholder's position is that of the owner of one or more shares in the company, which shares usually carry a right of voting at general meetings, and, if profits are made, he may receive dividends on his shares. His shares are something which he has bought—perhaps from the company, or perhaps from somebody else—and something which he can sell or give away, either in his lifetime or by his will.

The general rule is that he cannot get his money back from the company so long as the company is in existence, because his position is not that of a person who has lent money to the company or has deposited his money as with a bank or a building society—it is that of the owner of property, namely, his shares, which can only be turned into money if a buyer can be found to pay for them. Shares may be fully paid or partly paid. When the shares are only partly paid the shareholder can be compelled to pay them up fully if called upon by the company or, if the company is being wound up and its debts exceed its assets, by the liquidator. In any event it is the general policy of the Act to see that the issued share capital is maintained intact, except for losses in the way of business, so that it may be available to satisfy the company's debts. Accordingly, while the company is a going concern the general rule is that no part of the paid-up capital may be returned to the shareholders without the consent of the court, or by following strict procedures intended to protect creditors.

---

[5] Or, in Scots law, delicts.

A company may be formed to acquire and carry on an existing business, which may or may not belong to the promoters, or to start some new business. However, a company is commonly formed as a private company to acquire the promoters' business. In this case a price is put on the business and paid by the issue to the promoters of shares credited as fully or partly paid in the company. Most of the price will be left owing to the promoters so that if the company is later wound up they will rank for repayment of it as unsecured creditors; otherwise if they take the whole price in the form of shares credited as fully paid they will rank for repayment of capital after the unsecured creditors. If a company is formed to acquire a business which does not belong to the promoters they may provide the necessary funds for the company by taking shares in the company for each.

A company can also raise money by borrowing.[6] Persons who lend money to a company may be issued with debentures to show that they have lent money and are entitled to interest on their loans. Unlike shareholders, they are not members of the company and they have no right to vote at general meetings. Creditors may take a charge over the company's property by way of security for repayment of their debt. Such charges must be registered with the Registrar of Companies.

Shares in, and debentures of, public companies are extensively bought as an investment by people who want to derive an income from their capital but who are unable, for reasons of inclination, business, age, health or lack of opportunity, to take any part in the management of the company. To protect investors from dishonest or incompetent people who form companies in which the investors are likely to lose their money, disclosure of such things as the company's past financial record and the benefits of being a director, is required in the document on the strength of which the public is invited to subscribe for shares or debentures of the company. Provision is also made for a company's accounts and the balance sheet and profit and loss account to be audited every year by auditors appointed by the shareholders and for the balance sheet and the profit and loss account and certain other documents to be circulated to every shareholder and debenture holder. With the exception of unlimited companies a copy of the balance sheet and the other documents must also be lodged with the Registrar of Companies.

---

[6] Money borrowed by a company is sometimes called "loan capital". It should not be confused with "share capital": Chap. 9.

The directors of a company, who are usually appointed by the members at their annual general meeting, have wide powers to manage the company's business conferred upon them by the articles. The members cannot control the exercise of these powers, although they can, *e.g.* alter the articles. The directors, in turn, owe certain duties of good faith and care to the company.

The Acts have increasingly required disclosure by companies, their directors and substantial shareholders of many financial and other particulars. Usually this will be to the Registrar who will keep the information on the company's file. Such information is then available to anyone who makes a search of that file and is seen as one of the prices of incorporation. There is no constructive notice of such information, however.

A registered company is capable of perpetual succession but it may become insolvent or it may decide to retire from business. In such a case it is wound up, *i.e.* it is put, or it goes, into liquidation, and a person, called a liquidator, is appointed to wind up its affairs. He sells the company's property and pays as much of its debts as he can do out of the proceeds of sale. If there is a surplus, he distributes it among the shareholders. When the liquidation is completed the company is dissolved and ceases to exist.

## THE DEVELOPMENT OF MODERN COMPANY LAW

The modern commercial company, incorporated by registration under the Act, is the result of the fusion of two different legal principles. A registered company, like a statutory company or a chartered company, is a "corporation",[7] *i.e.* in the eyes of the law it is a person, capable of perpetual succession and quite distinct from the natural persons who are its members at any given moment.[8] However, the expression "company" is not confined to a corporation but includes a parternship, which is not a corporation but, at least in the case of an English partnership,[9] is merely the relationship between the individual partners. The present-day registered company represents the fusion of the principle of incorporation with that of partnership.

[7] s.13(3), *post*, p. 23.
[8] *Salomon v. Salomon & Co. Ltd* [1897] A.C. 22, *post*, p. 24.
[9] A Scottish partnership, although not a corporation, is a legal person distinct from the partners of whom it is composed: Partnership Act 1890, s.4(2).

At common law the Crown has always had the right of granting charters of incorporation.[10] Non-trading companies, such as the Law Society and the Institute of Chartered Accountants, are the kind of company now incorporated by charter but trading companies have in the past been formed in this way. The right was first used for creating commercial corporations at the end of the sixteenth and the beginning of the seventeenth centuries, when such companies as the Levant Company, the East India Company, the Hudson's Bay Company and the notorious South Sea Company (afterwards incorporated by special Act of Parliament) were incorporated. As these corporations were legal entities quite distinct from their members, it followed that at common law the members were not liable for the debts of the corporation, and, indeed, the Crown had no power to incorporate persons so as to make them liable for the debts of the corporation.[11] In a partnership, on the other hand, the partners were always liable for all the debts of the firm and their liability was unlimited.

In England trading companies were originally regulated companies, that is, companies in which each member traded with his own stock subject to the rules of the company, but towards the end of the seventeenth century the joint-stock company emerged,[12] and this is the form of the company in common use today. In a joint-stock company, the company trades as a single person with a stock which is jointly contributed by its members. Such companies could only be formed by special Act of Parliament or by charter but, as the advantages of the joint-stock form of trading became better known, these methods proved too expensive and dilatory to meet the growing commercial needs of the nation. Accordingly there grew up a new type of company based upon contract. This contract took the form of an elaborate deed of settlement containing provisions regulating the relations of the members among themselves and providing for the transfer of shares. A body formed in this way was only a partnership in the eyes of the law and the liability of the members was unlimited. This type of unincorporated company fell into disfavour with the legislature, largely owing to the activities of fraudulent promoters and unscrupulous share dealers, and in 1720 the Bubble Act was passed to deal with it. Unfortunately, that Act had the effect of

[10] A chartered company is sometimes referred to as "a common law corporation."
[11] *Per* Lindley L.J. in *Elve v. Boyton* [1891] 1 Ch. 501 at p. 507 (C.A.).
[12] Holdsworth, *History of English Law*, Vol. 8, pp. 206–222.

suppressing unincorporated companies without satisfying the want which had given rise to their existence, so that "joint-stock" enterprises had to wait till the middle of the nineteenth century before incorporation "for any lawful purpose" could be obtained by the simple process of registration, and personal liability be limited by "one magic word".[13]

The origins of company law in Scotland were distinct from those in England, although regulated companies and joint-stock companies did exist from at least the later years of the seventeenth century. The common law of Scotland sanctioned formation of companies with transferable shares and under the management of directors, and recognised such companies as having a personality separate from that of their members.[14] In Scotland common law companies constituted under contracts of co-partnership corresponded to the English deed of settlement companies. The 1720 Bubble Act extended to Scotland but, because of the common law companies, probably had no legal effect there.[15]

In 1825, by the Bubble Companies, etc., Act, the 1720 Bubble Act was repealed and the Crown was empowered in grants of future charters to provide that the members of the corporation should be personally liable for the debts of the corporation to such extent as the Crown should think proper. This was the beginning of "limited liability." By the Chartered Companies Act 1837 the Crown was empowered to grant letters patent, *i.e.* to grant the advantages of incorporation *without* granting a charter, to a body of persons associated together for trading purposes. The persons in question had to register a deed of partnership dividing the capital into shares and providing for transfers, and satisfy the other requirements of the Act; limited liability was then granted to them. The association to which the letters patent were granted did not become a body corporate and the grant of limited liability was an advantage to which they would otherwise not have been entitled.

---

[13] Carr, *Select Charters of Trading Companies*, Selden Society, Vol. 28, p. xx.

[14] The decision in *Stevenson & Co. v. Macnair and others* (1757) M. 14,560 and 14,667; 5 Brown's Supp. 340 suggests that Scottish courts might even, under continental influence, have developed a principle of limited liability in relation to these companies.

[15] An Act of 1825 (6 Geo. 4, c. 131) mentioned with approval the practice which had prevailed in Scotland of forming joint-stock companies with transferable shares.

By the Joint Stock Companies Registration, etc., Act 1844 provision was made in England for the incorporation of companies by registration without the necessity of obtaining a Royal Charter or a special Act of Parliament. The peculiarity of this statute was, however, that, instead of allowing the usual common law consequences of incorporation to follow, it proceeded on the lines of the Chartered Companies Act 1837 and merely gave a corporate existence to a body which it still evidently regarded as a partnership, because it imposed much the same liability on the members for the debts of the company as they would have had for the debts of a parternship. This Act also made it compulsory to register as companies all partnerships with more than 25[16] members. Liability limited by shares, *i.e.* where a member's liability is limited to the amount, if any, unpaid on his shares, was introduced in the case of registered companies by the Limited Liability Act 1855, and the Joint Stock Companies Act 1856 substituted two documents, the memorandum of association and articles of association, for the deed of settlement.

In Scotland the registered company was not introduced until the Act of 1856: neither the 1844 Act nor the 1855 Act applied to Scotland.

The Companies Act 1862 repealed and consolidated the previous Acts. It also established liability limited by guarantee and, in general, prohibited any alteration in the objects clause[17] of the memorandum of association. This prohibition remained until the Companies (Memorandum of Association) Act 1890 enabled the objects to be altered for some purposes with the leave of the court, after a special resolution[18] had been passed by the members in general meeting. The Companies Act 1867 contained a power to reduce share capital. The Directors' Liability Act 1890 introduced the principle of the liability of the directors to pay compensation to persons who have been induced to take shares on the strength of false statements in a prospectus. The Companies Act 1900 contained the first provisions relating to the contents of prospectuses, the compulsory audit of the company's accounts and the registration of charges with the Registrar. The Companies Act 1907 made provision for the private (as opposed

---

[16] The maximum number of members for a partnership is now 20, but there are exceptions for most professional firms: s.716 *post*, p. 35.

[17] Dealt with *post*, p. 67.

[18] *Post*, p. 68.

to the public) company, *i.e.* a company which is prohibited from inviting the public to subscribe for its shares or debentures.[19] Modern company law was taking shape.

## The 1948 Act and its successors

The 1948 Companies Act made far-reaching changes in the law relating to company accounts. As the Cohen Report[20] (on which the 1948 Act was based) said, "The history of company legislation shows the increasing importance attached to publicity in connection with accounts. The Act of 1862 contained no compulsory provisions with regard to audit or accounts, though Table A[21] to that Act did include certain clauses dealing with both matters. In 1879 provision was made for the audit of the accounts of banking companies, but it was not until 1900 that any such provision was made generally applicable. It was only on July 1, 1908, when the Companies Act 1907 came into force, that provision was made for including a statement in the form of a balance sheet in the annual return to the Registrar of Companies, and that provision exempted private companies from this requirement." The Companies Act 1929 required a balance sheet and a profit and loss account to be laid before the company every year, while the present Acts set out in great detail the contents of those accounts, with stringent provisions for their audit. The 1948 Act also for the first time required the auditor of a public or a private company to have a professional qualification.[22]

A number of the recommendations contained in the Jenkins Report[23] were given effect in the 1967 Act which amended the 1948 Act in a number of respects, including new provisions in connection with a company's accounts. Other important new provisions were: (1) The provisions in connection with the directors' report. For example, the principal activities of the company and its subsidiaries during the year were required to be

---

[19] *Post*, p. 42.
[20] (1945) Cmd. 6659, para. 96.
[21] A model set of articles of association.
[22] For a fuller treatment of the history of company law, see Gower, *Modern Company Law* (5th ed. 1992), Chaps. 2 and 3.
[23] (1962) Cmnd. 1749. This is still the latest report covering the whole of company law. It has never been implemented in full or dealt with in any consistent manner although certain of its recommendations were implemented by the 1989 Act after a gap of 27 years.

stated. The idea was to ensure that shareholders were kept more fully informed of the company's activities. (2) The provisions penalising the dealing by directors, their spouses or children, in certain options to buy or sell shares or debentures of the company or associated companies quoted on a stock exchange, and for securing the disclosure of certain material facts concerning directors. (3). The provisions for securing the disclosure of a person's beneficial ownership of 10 per cent. or more of the shares in the company carrying unrestricted voting rights. Part III of the 1967 Act gave the Department of Trade wide powers to compel companies to produce books and papers for inspection. Many of these provisions have since been amended or replaced but the principle thereby established remain.

1972 saw the European Communities Act, section 9 of which related solely to company law since the U.K. was obliged on accession to comply with an existing EC Directive of 1968 on the harmonisation of company law.[24] This section's principal change was to modify the law relating to *ultra vires* and the problems of agency in relation to companies.[25] In Scotland, the Companies (Floating Charges and Receivers) (Scotland) Act 1972 modified the law of Scotland in relation to floating charges and made provision for the appointment of receivers.

The Companies Act 1976 enacted, amongst other things, some but not all of the clauses and Schedules of the abortive Companies Bill 1973. The 1976 Act amended the law relating to the filing of company accounts and the keeping of accounting records. It provided for the disqualification of persons taking part in the management of companies if they were persistently in default in complying with the requirements to deliver documents to the Registrar. The Act also made new provision with respect to the qualifications, appointment, resignation and powers of auditors. It also required a statement of the first directors and secretary and of the intended situation of the registered office to be delivered to the Registrar on an application for registration of a company, and provided for the regulation of the names of oversea companies.

---

[24] The impact of EC Directives on company law is one of the modern features of the law. See p. 16, *post*.
[25] This worked along the lines of the Jenkins Committee recommendations in para. 42 of the Report. It proved to be defective in many ways, however, and was rewritten by the 1989 Act.

The Companies Act 1980 was inspired by an EC Directive of 1976 regulating the control of public companies. It provided for the first time a major distinction between public and private companies, including minimum financial requirements for the former. It also contained new provisions relating to the issuing of shares and the payment for them. Payment of dividends became the subject of statutory rules. Tighter restrictions on directors were imposed following the many "unacceptable faces of capitalism" which manifested themselves in the 1970s. Insider dealing[26] one of the most obvious of those, became a criminal offence.

The 1981 Companies Act was likewise prompted by an EC Directive, this time of 1978, on company accounts. It provided a new format for accounts and for the public disclosure of them. In addition, however, new rules for company names, the purchase and redemption by a company of its own shares and for more stringent disclosure of shareholders were included. Various other reforms were also appended. The technical nature of much of this recent legislation was so complex that mistakes were made. One particularly embarrassing one, the accidental prohibition of many employee share and pension trusts had to be corrected, in haste, by the Companies (Beneficial Interests) Act 1983.

### The 1985 consolidation and after

In 1981 proposals were made for a consolidation of the various Acts from 1948 onwards. There were two joint Reports of the Law Commission and the Scottish Law Commission[27] which recommended many technical amendments to the existing law in order to assist consolidation. These amendments were effected by the Companies Acts (Pre-Consolidation Amendments) Order 1984[28] and the Companies Acts (Pre-Consolidation Amendments) (No. 2) Order 1984[29] which, by virtue of section 116 of the Companies Act 1981, only took effect on the consolidation itself coming into force. After consultation it was decided to produce a single main Act, the Companies Act 1985, with 747 sections and 25 Schedules (up to seven separate Acts had been canvassed) with three small satellite Acts. The 1981 Act provisions relating

---

[26] See Chap. 19.
[27] (1983) Cmnd. 9114, (1984) Cmnd. 9272.
[28] S.I. 1984 No. 134.
[29] S.I. 1984 No. 1169.

to the use of business names by all traders, including companies, were separated into the Business Names Act 1985, and those of the 1980 Act relating to insider dealing were also hived off into a separate Act, the Company Securities (Insider Dealing) Act 1985, since those rules applied to securities other than those belonging to companies. The fourth Act, the Companies Consolidation (Consequential Provisions) Act 1985, dealt with transitional matters, savings provisions, repeals and consequential amendments to other Acts. In one area, however, it was not consequential: section 28 repealed, rather than consolidated, the existing provisions on cost book companies.

Whilst the consolidation was proceeding through Parliament the Companies (Accounts and Audit) Regulations 1984 and the Companies (Share Premium Account) Regulations 1984 were passed and had to be taken into account. The resulting consolidation, taking into account the various amendments referred to above and the need to harmonise legislative styles and phrases over a 30 year period, was by no means a "scissors and paste" consolidation. In the main it used short subsections and many of the pre-existing sections were divided. It was a triumph of draftsmanship in what was then the largest consolidation ever undertaken. By way of departure from previous practice, Tables A to F, the model forms of memorandum and articles etc., are now contained in separate regulations, the Companies (Tables A to F) Regulations 1985,[30] rather than in a Schedule to the Act. Table A itself was redrafted for this purpose. The whole consolidation came into effect on July 1, 1985.

But it proved to be a short-lived oasis of calm as a unified source of company legislation. Two more EC Directives, the third (on mergers)[31] and the sixth (on divisions),[32] were implemented by the Companies (Mergers and Divisions) Regulations 1987,[33] which added a new section and Schedule to the 1985 Act in the area of schemes of arrangement.[34] More importantly, the Insolvency Act 1985, implementing some of the recommendations of the Cork Committee (Insolvency Law and Practice— Report of the Review Committee)[35] repealed many of the sec-

[30] S.I. 1985 No. 805.
[31] Dir. 78/855/EC, [1978] O.J. L295/36.
[32] Dir. 82/89/EC, [1982] O.J. L378/47.
[33] S.I. 1987 No. 1991.
[34] See Chap. 30, *post.*
[35] (1982) Cmnd. 8558.

tions of the 1985 Act relating to liquidation and other aspects of corporate insolvency and replaced them with several new concepts, *e.g.* administration orders, as well as making several amendments to the rules governing insolvent liquidations. The Act was based on a White Paper,[36] itself based on the Cork Report. The resulting *pot pourri* of legislation on corporate liquidation and insolvency was itself consolidated into the Insolvency Act 1986, apart from the provisions relating to directors' disqualification which were consolidated into the Company Directors Disqualification Act 1986. The result is that some of the 1948 Act winding up provisions were consolidated in 1985, amended in that year and re-consolidated in 1986.

In addition the reform of the law governing the investment industry, prompted by a report by Professor Gower commissioned by the Department of Trade and Industry, was suggested by a White Paper, "Financial Services in the United Kingdom: A New Framework for Investor Protection"[37] and implemented by the Financial Services Act 1986. Whilst this Act is largely concerned with regulating the City and the investment industry generally it has had a double impact on company law. The first is indirect in that company securities are investments for this purpose and those who deal in them are, therefore, subject to the Act's new regulatory system. The second is direct. The Financial Services Act provided new rules for the public issue of shares whether listed on the Stock Exchange or otherwise. It also recast the provisions in the Companies Act 1985 relating to the compulsory acquistion of shares on a take-over and amended the rules relating to insider dealing in the Company Securities (Insider Dealing) Act 1985. The Financial Services Act thus repealed many of the 1985 Act sections relating to the public issue of shares and the Stock Exchange (Listing) Regulations 1984.[38] (The latter were passed to implement yet another set of EC directives, on listing particulars, the admission of securities to listing and the continuing disclosure of information by listed companies,[39] These lay alongside the 1985 Act provisions in a totally obscure manner and may usefully be consigned to history).

[36] (1984) Cmnd. 9175.
[37] (1985) Cmnd. 9432.
[38] S.I. 1984 No. 716.
[39] Dir. 80/390/EC, [1980] O.J. L100/7; Dir. 79/279/EC, [1979] O.J. L66/21; Dir. 82/121/EC, [1982] O.J. L48/26.

More substantial changes were made by the Companies Act 1989 which was occasioned by the need to implement two further EC directives, the seventh on group accounts (Dir. 83/349/EC, [1983] O.J. L193/7) and the eighth on the qualification of auditors (Dir. 84/253/EC, [1984] O.J. L126/20). Opportunity was taken, however, to amend and extend the 1985 Act provisions relating to investigations (together with investigations under the Insolvency Act 1986 and the Financial Services Act 1986), the doctrine of *ultra vires* and application of the agency law to corporate transactions and in several other largely unrelated areas, some of which were recommended by the Jenkins Committee in 1962. It also made several amendments to other Acts, most importantly to the Financial Services Act 1986. Most of the 1989 Act changes were effected by adding, substituting or amending sections in the earlier Acts.

Although there has been no primary companies legislation since 1989 there have been several changes and additions to the text of the 1985 Act as the result of the implementation of EC directives by statutory instrument effected under the power to amend legislation in that way for such purposes under section 2(2) of the European Communities Act 1972.[40] These include the directive amending the fourth and seventh directives on company accounts[41]; the eleventh directive on disclosure requirements for branches of oversea companies[42]; and the major shareholdings directive relating to disclosure of such interests in listed companies.[43] The most fundamental of these changes, however, has been the introduction of the single member company, *i.e.* whereby one person may form a private company, as the result of the implementation of the twelfth directive on single member private limited companies[44] by the Companies (Single Member Private Limited Companies) Regulations 1992.[45] Other changes to the 1985 Act have come from other sources, including the Welsh Language Act 1993.

[40] See p. 16, below.
[41] Dir. 90/604, [1990] O.J. L317/57; implemented by the Companies Act 1985 (Accounts of Small and Medium-Sized Enterprises and Publication of Accounts in ECUS) Regulations (S.I. 1992 No. 2452).
[42] Dir. 89/666, [1989] O.J. L395/36; implemented by the Overseas Companies and Credit and Financial Institutions (Branch Disclosure) Regulations 1992 (S.I. 1992, No. 3179).
[43] Dir. 88/629, [1988] O.J. L348/62; implemented by the Disclosure of Interests in Shares (Amendment) Regulations 1993 (S.I. 1993 No. 1819).
[44] Dir. 89/667, [1989] O.J. L395/40.
[45] S.I. 1992 No. 1699.

One directive has led to primary legislation, however. Implementation of the directive co-ordinating regulations on insider dealing[46] has led to the repeal of the Company Securities (Insider Dealing) Act 1985, part of the 1985 consolidation, and its replacement by Part V of the Criminal Justice Act 1993. Nor can it be supposed that this is the end of the reform process. In addition to the further proposals from the European Union for company law harmonisation, the DTI is actively examining specific areas for reform, such as financial assistance and directors' dealings with their companies. Further, as part of the Government's deregulation policy, it has taken wide powers to remove statutory burdens from small businesses, including companies, under section 1 of the Deregulation and Contracting Out Act 1994, by delegated legislation. That Act also amends the 1985 Act in relation to the removal of non-trading private companies from the register of companies.

On the other hand some parts of the legislation already passed have not actually been brought into force, despite the time period which has elapsed since they were enacted. The two major examples of this are Part V of the Financial Services Act relating to issues of unlisted securities and Part IV of the 1989 Companies Act on the registration of company charges. The first of these will not be brought into force. The previous law has been replaced by a new regime under the Public Offers of Securities Regulations 1995 (see Chapter 7, *post*) whilst the second is the subject of consultation. Accordingly the prior law on that topic has been reinstated in this edition.[47]

To sum up, current company law can be found partly in the 1985 Act and its two remaining satellite Acts, as amended and substituted by three major Acts (the Insolvency Act 1985, the Financial Services Act 1986 and the Companies Act 1989) and several statutory instruments, partly in the Insolvency Act 1986, which contains both the 1985 Companies Act and the Insolvency Act 1985 provisions on corporate insolvency and liquidations, partly in the Company Directors Disqualification Act 1986, partly in the Financial Services Act 1986 and partly in the Criminal Justice Act 1993.

No attempt, however, has ever been made to codify company law, *i.e.* to reduce to a code all the statute law and common law

[46] Dir. 89/592, [1989] O.J. L334/30.
[47] See Chaps. 7 and 23, below.

on the topic. Unlike Acts such as the Partnership Act 1890 the various major Companies Acts have generally simply consolidated provisions previously in several other Acts. Consequently a significant part of company law is still comprised of decided cases. The 1980, 1981, 1986 and 1989 legislation on the other hand contain many technical and complex provisions replacing case-law decisions, often of long standing. This trend, from cases to statutes, is now firmly established and likely to continue in the future. The legislation, unlike case-law, applies in general to both England and Scotland.

One final development has been the emergence of self-regulating bodies such as the City Panel on Take-overs and Mergers. The City Panel operates a code without the force of law but of great significance in certain areas such as the acquisition of shares and take-overs in the public company sphere.

## Impact of the European Union

There are a number of measures of the European Union aimed at the harmonisation of the company laws of the Member States. In general this programme consists of a series of directives issued under Article 58 of the European Treaty. These prescribe common standards for areas of company law which require Member States to amend their law, if necessary, to comply with them.[48] We have already seen that the need to implement these directives has produced several changes to U.K. company law and is likely to go on doing so for the foreseeable future. Implementation by primary legislation creates no domestic problems but the more recent tendency to implement directives by means of delegated legislation under section 2(2) of the European Communities Act 1972 is subject to the difficulty that such measures may only alter a statute in so far as it is necessary for the implementation of the directive. This can lead to problems as to whether the changes go further than was needed[49] and the difficulties of adapting the changes into the existing law which

---

[48] Whether or not other Member States have done so: *Ministère Public v. Blangvernon* [1991] BCLC 635 (ECJ).

[49] There is an argument that the implementation of the third and sixth directives on mergers and divisions by delegated legislation has gone further than was needed by applying in part to private companies which are not within the terms of the directive.

may apply to a wider spectrum of companies than those covered by the directive, thus creating a two-tier system of law.[50]

A further consequence of the existence of these directives arises when either they have not been implemented by the due date or the implementing legislation does not propertly comply with the terms of the directive. The European Court has held that in such cases the directives have vertical *direct effect*, that is to say that as between the Member State and an individual or company their provisions must be given precedence over the national law.[51] Although this is said not to apply as between two companies and/or individuals (so-called horizontal direct effect), that court has stated that in applying national law, whether passed before or after the date for implementing the directive, the national court must interpret its law so far as possible in the light of the wording and purpose of the directive in order to achieve the result required by the directive.[52] It has even, in another area of the law, allowed a claim for damages against a Member State for non-implementation of a directive.[53]

Two further EU inspired developments are not, however, part of the harmonisation programme as such. They are both aimed at establishing cross-frontier entities which may operate throughout the Community—they will not have a purely national existence. These are the European Economic Interest Grouping (in existence since July 1989) and the proposed European Company.

### The European Economic Interest Grouping

This new entity, an E.E.I.G., was created by an EU regulation (*i.e.* a document which has direct legislative effect in the U.K. unlike a directive which must in general terms be implemented by the U.K. Parliament to be effective), Council Regulation 2173/85,[54] as supplemented by the European Economic Grouping

---

[50] For example the implementation of the major shareholdings directive required changes to the share disclosure provisions of the 1985 Act which apply to all public companies, whereas the directive only applies to listed companies so that unlisted public companies are still governed by the old law. See Chap. 12, below.

[51] *Karellas v. Greek Ministry for Industry, Energy and Technology* [1993] BCC 677 (ECJ).

[52] *Marleasing S.A. v. La Commercial Internacional de Alimentation SA* [1993] BCC 421 (ECJ).

[53] *Francovich v. Italian Republic* [1992] IRLR 84 (ECJ).

[54] [1985] O.J. L199/1.

Regulations 1989.[55] The intention is to allow the creation of a separate legal entity for cross-border co-operation between businesses in different Member States. These may or may not be companies. Formation is by contract, registered with the registrar of companies. This contract must include the objects of the E.E.I.G.—since making profits in its own right is not allowed, these must require the E.E.I.G. to enhance the activities of its members, e.g. by joint research or development. The members of the E.E.I.G. will have unlimited liability for its debts, no public investment is allowed and the maximum number of employees is limited to 500. An E.E.I.G. can be formed in any Member State and is subject to some aspects of the national law in which it is registered, e.g. as to the use of name, certain winding-up rules etc. U.K. law must equally recognise an E.E.I.G. registered in another Member State.

**Proposed statute for a European Company**

There is a proposal for a regulation establishing a new cross-border entity to be known as a European Company.[56] This is not a new idea, being originally suggested in 1970, but interest in it has been revived within the Union. In essence it will be formed by the merger of two or more public companies of different EU nationality or the conversion of a public company having a subsidiary in another Member State, and would be subject to a new range of EU company law, although it would still remain subject to national law in certain key areas. The relevant national law would be that of the country in which it was registered. There are different views as to the need for such a transnational company and as to the contents of the supranational law to which it should be subject, e.g. as to the contentious issue of employee participation. If this proposal is implemented, however, it will provide a parallel but not identical system of company law to U.K. domestic company law, available in practice to all public companies.

## PROCEDURE TO OBTAIN REGISTRATION OF A COMPANY

To obtain the registration of a company certain documents must be delivered to the appropriate Registrar of Companies and

[55] S.I. 1989 No. 638.
[56] [1991] O.J. C176/1.

certain fees must be paid. If the registered office is to be situate in England or in Wales,[57] the appropriate registrar is the Registrar of Companies for England,[58] and his address is now Companies Registration Office, Crown Way, Maindy, Cardiff CF4 3UZ.[59] If the registered office is to be situate in Scotland[60] the appropriate registrar is the Registrar of Companies for Scotland[61] and his address is Companies Registration Office, Exchequer Chambers, 102 George Street, Edinburgh EH2 3DJ.

**Documents which must be delivered to the Registrar**

The following documents must be delivered to the Registrar of Companies:

(1) A memorandum of association[62] stating, *inter alia*, the objects of the company and if, as is common, the company is a limited company with a share capital, the amount of share capital with which the company proposes to be registered and its division into shares of a fixed amount,[63] *e.g.* £10,000 divided into 10,000 shares of a nominal amount of £1 each. If the company is a public company this figure must be not less than the authorised minimum,[64] currently £50,000.[65]

(2) Usually, printed articles of association[66] providing for such matters as the transfer of shares in the company, the holding of general meetings, *i.e.* meetings of the members or shareholders, the directors' powers of management and the extent to which they can delegate their powers to a managing director, and the payment of dividends.

(3) If the memorandum states that the registered office is to be situated in Wales and the memorandum and articles are in Welsh, a certified translation in English.[67]

[57] See *post*, p. 62.
[58] s.10.
[59] The main part of the Companies Registration Office is now in Cardiff. There are microfilm reading room facilities in London at Companies House, 55–71 City Road, London EC1Y 1BB.
[60] *Post*, p. 62.
[61] s.10.
[62] s.10. The memorandum is dealt with in Chap. 3.
[63] s.2.
[64] s.11.
[65] s.118.
[66] s.7. Articles are dealt with in Chap. 4.
[67] s.710B. For the meaning of a certified translation see the Companies (Welsh Language Forms and Documents) Regulations 1994 (S.I. 1994 No. 117).

(4)  A statement in the prescribed form of the names of the intended first director or directors, and first secretary or joint secretaries, and the particulars specified in Schedule 1.[68] Such statement must be signed by or on behalf of the subscribers of the memorandum and must contain a consent to act signed by each of the persons named in it. Where the memorandum is delivered for registration by an agent for the subscribers, such statement must specify that fact and the name and address of that person.[69] The statement must also specify the intended situation of the company's registered office.[70]

(5)  A statutory declaration, by a solicitor engaged in the formation of the company or by a person named as director or secretary of the company in the statement delivered under (4) *ante*, of compliance with the requirements of the Acts in respect of registration.[71]

(6)  A statement of capital (Form PUC1), unless the company is to have no share capital.

For the purpose of ensuring that documents delivered to the Registrar are of standard size, durable and easily legible, the Secretary of State may prescribe such requirements as he considers appropriate. If a document delivered to the Registrar does not, in his opinion, comply with such requirements, he may serve a notice on the person or persons by whom the document was required to be delivered, whereupon, for the purposes of any enactment which enables a penalty to be imposed in respect of an omission to deliver a document to the Registrar, the duty to deliver is not discharged but the person subject to the duty has 14 days after the date of service of the notice in which to discharge it.[72]

The Registrar may, if he thinks fit, accept, under any provision of the Companies Acts requiring a document to be delivered to him, such material is a non-legible, *i.e.* electronic, form.[73]

The duty of the Registrar on receiving the above-mentioned documents is to examine them to see whether the statutory

[68] *Post*, pp. 317, 386.
[69] s.10(4).
[70] s.10(6).
[71] s.12(3).
[72] s.706.
[73] s.707.

requirements have been complied with, but in exercising his duty he has no power to hold a judicial inquiry on evidence.[74] Among the statutory requirements to be observed are:

(1) That the memorandum is signed by either one or two persons, and, if the memorandum is accompanied by articles, that the articles are signed by the same person(s).[75]

(2) That the company is being formed for a lawful purpose.[76]

If the company is being formed for a purpose prohibited by law,[77] the Registrar will decline to register it. If the Registrar does register a company with illegal objects the court will cancel the registration on an application by the Attorney General.[78]

(3) That the other requirements of the Act, *e.g.* as to the contents of the memorandum and articles, are complied with.[79]

(4) That the proposed name is not one which is absolutely, or conditionally, prohibited[80]

(5) That the memorandum and articles are in the statutory form.[81]

Any person may inspect a copy[82] of the documents or other material kept by the Registrar relative to individual companies on payment of a fee, and may require a copy or extract of them on payment of the current fee. Such copies may be furnished in an electronic form.[83]

**Registration fees**

Section 708 empowers the Secretary of State, by regulations made by statutory instrument, to require payment to the

---

[74] *R. v. Registrar of Companies, ex p. Bowen* [1914] 3 K.B. 1161.
[75] ss.1(1)(3A), 2, 7, *post*, pp. 51, 80.
[76] s.1(1).
[77] *R. v. Registrar of Companies, ex p. More* [1931] 2 K.B. 197 (C.A.).
[78] *R. v. Registrar of Companies, ex p. Attorney General* [1991] BCLC 476.
[79] ss.1(1)(3A), 2, 7, 11; *post*, pp. 51, 52, 80.
[80] s.26, *post*, p. 53.
[81] ss.3, 8 *post*, pp. 52, 80.
[82] s.709.
[83] s.710A.

Registrar of such fees as may be specified in the regulations in respect of the performance by the Registrar of such functions under the Companies Acts as may be specified, including the receipt by him of any notice or other document which the Acts require to be given or delivered to him.

## CERTIFICATE OF INCORPORATION

On the registration of a company the Registrar gives a certificate, either authenticated by a seal prepared under section 704(4) or under his hand, that the company is incorporated, in the case of a limited company that it is limited and, if it is a public company, that the company is a public company: section 13. The certificate of incorporation, which may be described as the company's birth certificate, is in the following form for private companies.[84]

### CERTIFICATE OF INCORPORATION

I HEREBY CERTIFY that          , Limited, is this day Incorporated under the Companies Act 1985, and that the Company is Limited.
Given under my hand at Cardiff this          day of

Section 711(1)(a) requires the Registrar to publish in the appropriate *Gazette*[85] notice of the issue of a certificate of incorporation.

Section 13(7) provides that the certificate is conclusive evidence that all the requirements of the Act in respect of registration and of matters precedent and incidental thereto have been complied with, and that the association is a company authorised to be registered and duly registered. If the certificate states that the company is a public company it is conclusive evidence that it is such a company.

It is thought that the subsection means that it cannot be argued that a company is not validly incorporated except where a statutory provision as to substance invalidates the registration.[86]

---

[84] Public companies would have a different name and the additional declaration that it is a public limited company.

[85] This amounts to official notification. The appropriate Gazette is either the London or the Edinburgh Gazette depending upon the company's domicile.

[86] *Per* Megarry J. in *Gaiman v. National Association for Mental Health* [1971] Ch. 317, at p. 329. See also *R. v. Registrar of Companies, ex p. Central Bank of India* [1986] BCLC 465 as to judicial review of the registrar's powers in another context.

In *Cotman v. Brougham*[87] Lord Wrenbury criticised[88] "the pernicious practice of registering memoranda of association which, under the clause relating to objects,[89] contain paragraph after paragraph not specifying or delimiting the proposed trade or purpose, but confusing power with purpose and indicating every class of act which the corporation is to have power to do." He went on to say: "Such a memorandum is not, I think, a compliance with the Act" but that if the Registrar registers the memorandum the court "must assume that all requirements in respect of matters precedent and incidental to registration have been complied with and confine [itself] to the construction of the document." The certificate of incorporation has also been held to be conclusive as to the date of incorporation.[90] The reason for this section is that once a company is registered and has begun business and entered into contracts it would be disastrous if any person could allege that the company was not duly registered.[91]

The certificate will not, however, be conclusive if a trade union should be registered as a company[92] as the registration of a trade union under the Companies Acts is void by statute.[93] Again, the certificate is not conclusive as to the legality of a company's objects—proceedings may be brought to have the registration cancelled where objects are illegal.[94]

The Registrar will allocate each registered company a registered number, *i.e.* a sequence of letters and numbers, which must be disclosed on all its business letters and order forms.[95]

## EFFECT OF REGISTRATION OF A COMPANY

From the date of incorporation mentioned in the certificate of incorporation, the subscribers of the memorandum, together with

[87] [1918] A.C. 514.
[88] At p. 523. The "pernicious practice" referred to is now of historical interest only. See p. 69, *post*.
[89] *Post*, p. 66.
[90] *Jubilee Cotton Mills Ltd v. Lewis* [1924] A.C. 958, where it was also held that "From the date of incorporation" in s.[13(3)] included any portion of the day on which the company was incorporated.
[91] *Per* Lord Cairns in *Peel's Case* (1867) L.R. 2 Ch.App. at p. 682.
[92] *British Association of Glass Bottle Manufacturers Ltd v. Nettlefold* (1911) 27 T.L.R. 527.
[93] Trade Union and Labour Relations (Consolidation) Act 1992, s.10(3)(a).
[94] *R. v. Registrar of Companies, ex p. Attorney General* [1991] BCLC 476, adopting the words of Lord Parker of Waddington in *Bowman v. Secular Society Ltd* [1917] A.C. 406, at p. 439.
[95] ss.705; 351(1)(a).

such other persons as may from time to time become members of
the company, form a body corporate by the name contained in
the memorandum, capable forthwith of exercising all the functions of an incorporated company, but with such liability on the
part of the members to contribute to the assets of the company as
is mentioned in the Act: section 13(3).

The registered company is a body corporate, *i.e.* a legal person
separate and distinct from its members.

> S. had for many years carried on business as a boot manufacturer. His
> business was solvent when it was converted into a company, *i.e.* a
> company limited by shares was formed, the subscribers to the memoran-
> dum of which were S. and his wife, daughter and four sons (for one
> share each), and the business was sold to the company at a price of
> £39,000. The terms of sale were approved by all the shareholders. £9,000
> was paid in cash. £20,000 fully paid shares of £1 each were allotted to S.
> so that S.'s wife and children held one share each and S. held 20,001
> shares. S. left the rest of the price on loan to the company and for this
> sum of £10,000 he was given debentures secured by a charge on the
> company's assets. It seems that the directors were S. and his sons and
> that S. was appointed managing director. After a depression the
> company went into liquidation. The assets were sufficient to satisfy the
> debentures, but the unsecured creditors, with debts amounting to
> £7,000, received nothing. *Held*, that the proceedings were not contrary
> to the true intent and meaning of the Companies Act; that the company
> was duly registered and was not a mere "alias" or agent of or trustee for
> the vendor; that he was not liable to indemnify the company against
> creditors' claims; that there was no fraud upon creditors (or share-
> holders); that the company (or the liquidator) was not entitled to
> rescission of the contract of purchase: *Salomon v. Salomon & Co. Ltd*
> [1897] A.C. 22.[96]

"The company is at law a different person altogether from the
subscribers to the memorandum; and, though it may be that after
incorporation the business is precisely the same as it was before, and the
same persons are managers, and the same hands receive the profits, the
company is not in law the agent of the subscribers or trustee for them.
Nor are the subscribers as members liable, in any shape or form, except
to the extent and in the manner provided by the Act"; *per* Lord
Macnaghten at p. 51.

One effect of this is that the property of the company belongs
to the company itself and not to the individual members, so that

---

[96] Although *Salomon's* case is now generally accepted in Scots law, the Scottish
courts were, about the same time and independently of that authority, giving
effect to the same principle, *e.g. Henderson v. Stubbs' Ltd* (1894) 22 R. 51,
*Grierson, Oldham & Co. Ltd v. Forbes, Maxwell & Co. Ltd* (1895) 22 R. 812
and *John Wilson & Son Ltd v. Inland Revenue* (1895) 23 R. 18.

even the largest shareholder has no insurable interest in the property of the company.[97] The managing director, even if he owns all the shares except one, cannot lawfully pay cheques to the company into his own banking account or draw cheques for his own purposes upon the company's banking account,[98] and two sole shareholder/directors can be convicted of theft from "their" company.[99]

*This principle of the independent corporate existence of a registered company is of the greatest importance in company law.* As we shall see, it is this which mainly distinguishes a registered company from a partnership, which is the relation which subsists between persons carrying on a business in common with a view of profit. A partnership is not a corporation and, at least in the case of an English partnership,[1] is only a description of the relationship between the partners, *i.e.* a partnership has no legal existence but is merely the association of two or more persons carrying on business together. The property of the firm belongs to the partners and the firm's debts are the debts of the partners, *i.e.* the partners are personally liable for the firm's debts, whereas in a registered company the assets and liabilities are those of the corporation and not of the members.

This separation of the corporation and its members so that the members are not liable for the company's debts was reaffirmed by the House of Lords in *J. H. Rayner (Mincing Lane) Ltd v. Department of Trade and Industry.*[2] This case arose out of the collapse of the International Tin Council in 1985 which left it owing millions of pounds to a number of metal traders and banks. The Council had been formed by several states and the Council's creditors sought to recover its debts from those member states. The House of Lords first decided that the Council was a corporate body with its own separate legal personality distinct from its members and it followed therefore that only the Council and not its members could be liable for the debts. Under English

---

[97] *Macaura v. Northern Assurance Co. Ltd* [1925] A.C. 619.
[98] *A. L. Underwood Ltd v. Bank of Liverpool & Marine Ltd* [1924] 1 K.B. 775 (C.A.).
[99] *Att.-Gen.'s Reference (No. 2 of 1982)* [1984] Q.B. 624; *R. v. Phillipou* (1989) 5 BCC 33.
[1] A Scottish partnership or firm has a separate legal existence and is not merely the association of two or more persons. The property of the firm belongs to the firm, and the firm's debts are primarily those of the firm, although each partner may ultimately be made personally liable for the firm's debts.
[2] [1990] 2 A.C. 418.

law only the party to a contract can be liable on that contract and
the only contracting party here was the Council. It would be for
Parliament to provide otherwise in any given case.[3]

Lord Oliver expressed the decision thus:

> "Once given the existence of the I.T.C. as a separate legal person and
> given that it was the contracting party in the transactions upon which
> the appellants claim . . . there is no room for any further inquiry as to
> what type of legal person the contracting party is. The person who
> can enforce contracts and the persons against whom they can be
> enforced in English law and the parties to the contract and in
> identifying the parties to the contract there are no gradations of legal
> personality.[4]

The liability of a member of a company limited by shares to
contribute to the company's assets (for the purpose of enabling
its debts to be paid) is limited to the amount, if any, unpaid on
his shares.[5] Thus if he has taken one thousand shares of £1 each
in the company and the shares are fully paid up he is normally
under no further liability to contribute to the assets. In the case
of a partnership every partner is jointly liable with the other
partners for all the firm's debts.[6]

A registered company is capable forthwith of exercising all the
functions of an incorporated company, *e.g.* it can hold land and
other property, and it can sue and be sued. If the company is a
public company it cannot commence business until the requirements of section 117 have been complied with.[7]

## The veil of incorporation

It was established in *Salomon v. Salomon & Co. Ltd, ante,* that
a registered company is a legal person separate from its members. This principle may be referred to as "the veil of incorporation". In general, the law will not go behind the separate
personality of the company to the members, so that, *e.g.* in
*Macaura v. Northern Assurance Co. Ltd,*[8] it was held that the

---

[3] See, *e.g.* n. 1, above.
[4] [1990] 2 A.C. 418 at 508.
[5] s.1(2).
[6] Further differences between registered companies and partnerships are dealt
with later in this chapter.
[7] *Post,* p. 153.
[8] [1925] A.C. 619.

largest shareholder had no insurable interest in the property of the company. However, there are exceptions to the principle in *Salomon's* case, where the veil is lifted and the law disregards the corporate entity and pays regard instead to the economic realities behind the legal facade. In these exceptional cases "the law either goes behind the corporate personality to the individual members, or ignores the separate personality of each company in favour of the economic entity constituted by a group of associated concerns."[9]

Instances of the veil being lifted may be classified into those expressly provided by statute and those under judicial interpretation.[10]

One example of a case where "the veil is lifted" by statute is where a public company carries on business for more than six months with less than the statutory minimum of members (two), in which event every person who is a member during any part of the time that business is so carried on after the end of the six-month period and who knows that business is being so carried on, is jointly and severally liable for all the company's debts contracted during such time and may be severally sued therefor (s.24, intended to ensure that the number of members does not fall below the statutory minimum). This is exceptional because the general rule is that the company's debts cannot be enforced against the members.

Again, where an officer of a company signs, on behalf of the company, a bill of exchange, promissory note, cheque or order for money or goods in which the company's name is not mentioned, the officer is personally liable to the holder of the bill of exchange, etc., for the amount thereof unless it is paid by the company (s.349(4)).[11]

The grounds upon which the courts will lift the corporate veil are more difficult to define. Initially there were a number of fairly random examples. Thus, a company registered in England was held to be an alien enemy if its agents or the persons in *de facto* control of its affairs were alien enemies, and in determining whether alien enemies have such control, the number of alien enemy shareholders and the value of their holdings were mater-

---

[9] Gower, *Modern Company Law*, 5th. ed., 1992, p. 108.
[10] See also Ruthven, *Lifting the Veil of Incorporation in Scotland*, 1969 Juridicial Review, p. 1.
[11] *Post*, p. 57.

ial.[12] Another example was that in cases such as *Re Express Engineering Works Ltd*,[13] the decision of all the shareholders was held to be the decision of the company, *e.g.* something less formal than a resolution, even a special resolution, duly passed at a general meeting was regarded as the act of the company. Further, it was held in *Re Bugle Press Ltd*[14] that if A Ltd makes an offer for the shares in B Ltd and in substance A Ltd is the same as the majority shareholding in B Ltd, A Ltd will not be able to invoke section 429[15] and compel the minority shareholders in B Ltd to sell their shares to A Ltd. In these circumstances the law goes behind the corporate personality of A Ltd to the individual members. The court will not allow that section to be invoked for an improper purpose.

More recently, some judges have adopted an approach based on the interests of justice as being the guiding light. Thus, Lord Denning M.R. was prepared to lift the veil in *Wallersteiner v. Moir*[16]—he said that in that case the plaintiff was also in breach of what is now section 330 (which in general prohibits a company making a loan to a director) because the company of which he was a director made a loan to another company which was his puppet, so that the loan should be treated as made to him. In 1985 the Court of Appeal lifted the veil when a defendant in a company fraud case took elaborate steps to conceal his assets by a complex network of companies and trusts. The court allowed the veil to be lifted in order to establish exactly what he owned and where it was located. They stated that this could be done in the interests of justice irrespective of the legal efficacy of the corporate structure provided he either substantially or effectively controlled the company concerned. The network of companies had been set up in an attempt to confuse and conceal.[17]

The case of *Gilford Motor Co. Ltd v. Horne*[18] shows that the courts will not allow a company to be used as a device to mask the carrying on of a business by a former employee of another person and to enable the former employee to break a valid covenant in restraint of trade contained in the contract under

[12] *Daimler Co. Ltd v. Continental Tyre etc. Ltd* [1916] 2 A.C. 307.
[13] [1920] 1 Ch. 466 (C.A.), *post*, p. 289.
[14] [1961] Ch. 270 (C.A.), *post*, p. 846.
[15] Chap. 31, *post*.
[16] [1974] 1 W.L.R. 991 (C.A.).
[17] *Re A Company* [1985] BCLC 333 (C.A.).
[18] [1933] Ch. 935 (C.A.).

which he was formerly employed. In that case the employee convenanted that after the termination of the employment he would not solicit his employer's customers. Soon after the termination of his employment he formed a company of which the two directors and shareholders were his wife and one other person and which sent out circulars to customers of his former employer. An injunction was granted against the ex-employee and the company.[19]

The interests of justice approach was also applied in *Creasey v. Breachwood Motors Ltd*[20] where an employee who had a claim for unfair dismissal against a company found that, after that claim had arisen, all the assets of the company had been transferred to another company owned by the same individuals and the first company had been dissolved. The second company was added as a defendant to the action. In doing so the judge had to distinguish the decision of the Court of Appeal in *Adams v. Cape Industries plc*[21] where that court refused to pierce the veil of incorporation with respect to an action brought against one company in a group with respect to liability for another company in that group in another country. He did so on the basis that the cause of action had not accrued at the time in that case whereas it had done so at the time of the actions of the defendants in the present case.

Instead of relying on the interests of justice approach, the Court of Appeal in *Adams* applied the test as stated by Lord Keith in the Scottish case of *Woolfson v. Strathclyde Regional Council*[22] that the veil would only be pierced where special circumstances exist indicating that it is a mere facade concealing the true facts. That case, like *Adams*, concerned the question as to whether a group of companies could be regarded as a single entity for legal purposes. In *Woolfson*, the issue was whether a subsidiary and parent company could be regarded as a single entity in order to enable them to claim compensation for disturbance on a compulsory purchase. The issue had previously arisen in *D.H.N. Food Distributors Ltd v. Tower Hamlets London Borough Council*[23] where the Court of Appeal in England

---

[19] See also *Jones v. Lipman* [1962] 1 W.L.R. 832.
[20] [1993] BCLC 480.
[21] [1990] Ch. 433; [1990] BCLC 479.
[22] 1978 S.L.T. 195, H.L.
[23] [1976] 1 W.L.R. 852 (C.A.).

allowed the claim on the basis that D.H.N. was in a position to control its subsidiaries in every respect. The House of Lords in *Woolfson* distinguished the *D.H.N.* case on its facts but also doubted whether it was a correct application of the general principle, stated above, that the veil should only be pierced where special circumstances exist indicating that it is a mere façade concealing the true facts. In *City of Glasgow District Council v. Hamlet Textiles Ltd,*[24] the Scottish Court of Session allowed inquiry as to the true ownership of property in Glasgow where the formal title was held by an English wholly-owned subsidiary of a Scottish company and whose sole function was the holding of that formal title.

The approach taken by the House of Lords in the *Woolfson* case (above) has since been applied, however, in England in *National Dock Labour Board v. Pinn & Wheeler Ltd.*[25] The judge refused to regard three related companies as being a single entity for the purposes of a demarcation dispute. Only where there was a mere facade concealing the true facts would the corporate veil be pierced. In this case the companies had been retained for good commercial reasons. The test was also applied by Lightman J. in *Acatos & Hutcheson plc v. Watson*[25a] in relation to the purchase by a company of another company whose principal asset was shares in the purchaser. Since this was neither a facade nor a sham he regarded the purchaser as having acquired shares in the second company and not its own shares.

The position is therefore far from clear. It may best be summarised by the judge in *Creasey v. Breachwood Motors Ltd,* when he said[26]:

> "The power of the court to lift the corporate veil exists. . . . The authorities provide little guidance as to the circumstances in which this power is to be exercised."

## LIABILITY OF REGISTERED COMPANIES

One consequence of the concept of a company's separate personality is that it can be liable for breaches of contract, torts (in Scots law, delicts), crimes etc. But for obvious reasons it can only

---

[24] 1986 S.L.T. 415.
[25] (1989) 5 BCC 75.
[25a] *The Times,* December 30, 1994.
[26] [1993] BCLC 480, 491.

act through human agents or employees, so that, as a general principle, a company can only be liable either where a principal would be liable for the acts of an agent or an employer liable for the acts of an employee. In Chapter 6 the concept of agency, which is central to an understanding of company commercial transactions, is discussed but sometimes the law only imposes obligations or affords benefits to those who actually do the act and since a company cannot physically do anything there can be a problem assimilating companies into the general law. The answer is that in certain circumstances the acts and mind of the governing body of the company are regarded as the acts and mind of the company—thus, for example, if they intend to defraud, so does the company. Sometimes known as the *alter ego* doctrine this is the antithesis of the doctrine of separate corporate personality.

The doctrine was first laid down by the House of Lords in *Lennards Carrying Co. v. Asiatic Petroleum*[27] where the major shareholder's negligence in navigating the company's ship was held to be the negligence of the company for the purposes of assessing liability. Viscount Haldane L.C. said: "For if Mr Lennard was the directing mind of the company, then his action must, unless a corporation is not to be liable at all, have been an action which was the action of the company itself."[28] This doctrine has been applied in various areas of the law[29] but for some years it remained unclear as to exactly whose acts and intentions could be attributed to the company. In *Bolton (Engineering) Co. Ltd v. Graham & Son*,[30] Lord Denning drew a distinction between the acts of those directors and managers who control what the company actually does and the acts of mere servants who simply carry out the course of action prescribed by those in control.

The leading case is *Tesco Supermarkets Ltd v. Nattrass*,[31] where the supermarket chain was prosecuted under section 11(2) of the Trade Descriptions Act 1968 for carrying an incorrect advertisement as to the availability of a brand of washing powder at a reduced price. Their defence was that provided by section 24(1) of the 1968 Act, *i.e.* that the commission of the offence was due

[27] [1915] A.C. 705 (H.L.).
[28] *ibid.* p. 717.
[29] See, *e.g. Green v. Green* [1993] 1 FLR 326 for an example in family law.
[30] [1957] 1 Q.B. 159 (C.A.).
[31] [1972] 2 All E.R. 127 (H.L.). As to the position in Scotland, see *Purcell Meats (Scotland) Ltd v. McLeod*, 1987 S.L.T. 528.

to the act or default of another person and that they had taken all reasonable care, etc., to avoid the commission of the offence. The relevant question was whether the manager of the particular branch, who had failed to check the stock, was "another person" for this purpose, or whether his default was that of the company. The House of Lords held that he was "another person"; a branch manager of his type was not sufficiently senior to be the *alter ego* of the company. Such an *ego* would be found amongst the directors, managers, secretary or other officers of the company, or someone to whom they had delegated control and management, with full discretionary powers, of some sections of the company's business. In *El Anjou v. Dollar Land Holdings plc*,[32] the Court of Appeal, in determining whether the chairman and non-executive director of the company could have the requisite knowledge to be imputed to the company so as to make it liable for knowing receipt of trust money, applied the test as to whether he was the company's directing mind and will in relation to the specific transactions rather than as to its management generally. They further held that the fact that he had since ceased to be a director did not alter the position.

On the other hand the *alter ego* doctrine does not apply to misappropriations *from* the company by those in control of its affairs. Such misappropriations are not the act of the company, however, as there is no consensus between the controller and the company.[33] Nor does the doctrine apply to offences of strict liability such as pollution offences where it is only necessary to show that the company's employees were acting within the scope of their employment in committing the offence to make the company liable.[33a]

The doctrine has also been applied to decide the procedural question of discovery of documents, *i.e.* to determine whether a company and an individual can be regarded as one person so that a document held by the company can be said to be in the possession of the individual. In *Re Tecnion Investments Ltd*[34] the Court of Appeal held that the company would only be the *alter*

---

[32] [1994] 1 BCLC 464 (C.A.) reversing [1993] BCLC 735. See also *Woodhouse v. Walsall MBC* [1994] 1 BCLC 435.

[33] *Stephens v. T. Pittas Ltd* [1983] S.T.C. 376; *Att.-Gen.'s Reference (No. 2 of 1982)* [1984] Q.B. 624; *R. v. Phillipou* (1989) 5 BCC 33.

[33a] *National Rivers Authority v. Alfred McAlpine Homes East Ltd* [1994] 4 All E.R. 286.

[34] [1985] BCLC 434 (C.A.).

*ego* of the individual for this purpose if it was under his unfettered control. It was not enough to show that he was the dominant figure in running the company's business.

## REGISTERED COMPANIES AND PARTNERSHIPS CONTRASTED

### Advantages of a registered company

A registered company has many advantages over a partnership, which is defined in the Partnership Act 1890[35] as the relationship which subsists between persons carrying on a business in common with a view of profit, and which is not, *e.g.* the relation between members of a company registered under the Companies Acts or incorporated by or in pursuance of any other Act of Parliament or Royal Charter. A registered company has the same advantages over an individual trader. These advantages include the following:

(1) A registered company is a corporation,[36] *i.e.* a separate legal person distinct from the members, whereas an English partnership is merely the aggregate of the partners (although a Scottish partnership has one of the attributes of a corporation in that it is "a legal person distinct from the partners of whom it is composed")[37]. Consequently:

(a) The debts and contracts of a registered company are those of the company and not those of the members, whereas in the case of an English firm every partner is jointly and severally liable with the other partners for all the firm's debts and obligations incurred while he is a partner.[38] (In Scotland the firm's debts are those of the firm but, if the firm fails to pay, each individual partner may be made liable. Again, the firm's contracts are those of the firm but the individual partners may be made liable for them.)

(b) Unless it is dissolved a registered company continues in existence[39] so that it is not affected by the death,

---

[35] s.1. See generally on partnerships, Morse, *Partnership Law* (1995).
[36] s.13(3); *Salomon v. Salomon & Co. Ltd* [1897] A.C. 22, *ante*, p. 24.
[37] Partnerships Act 1980, s.4(2).
[38] *ibid.*, s.9.
[39] See *ante*, p. 5.

bankruptcy, mental disorder or retirement of any of its members. In the case of a partnership, on the other hand, on the death or bankruptcy of a partner, subject to any agreement between the partners the partnership is dissolved as regards all the partners.[40] In practice the share of a partner who dies or retires has to be found out of the business or provided for by the other partners, and this may cause serious financial embarrassment to the firm.

(c) The property of a registered company belongs to and is vested in the company, so that there is no change in the ownership of, or in the formal title to, the property on a change in the ownership of shares in the company. In an English partnership, the property belongs to the partners and is vested in them. Consequently there are changes in the ownership of, and in the formal title to, the firm's property from time to time on the death or retirement of a partner or trustee. (In a Scottish partnership, while the partnership property belongs to the firm as a separate *persona*, the formal title to that property may be, and in the case of heritable property must be, in the names of the partners or of other persons in trust for the firm.)

(d) A registered company can contract with its members and can sue and be sued on such contracts. In England a partner cannot contract with the firm. (In Scotland, by virtue of the firm's separate personality, a partner can contract with the firm and can sue and be sued on such contracts.)

(e) Each partner is normally an agent for the firm for the purpose of the business of the partnership[41] and, subject to any agreement to the contrary between the parties, may take part in the management of the partnership business.[42] The members of a registered company as such are not its agents and have no power to manage its affairs—the directors are agents and managers, *i.e.* they have the powers given to them by the articles.

---

[40] Partnership Act 1890, s.33(1). As to dissolution by the court in the event of the mental disorder of a partner, see 1890 Act, s.35, and Mental Health Act 1959, s.103 (the latter is not applicable to Scotland). As to dissolution by notice by a retiring partner, see 1890 Act, s.32.

[41] Partnership Act 1890, s.5.

[42] *ibid.*, s.24(5).

(f) Subject to any restrictions in the articles, which there may be in the articles of a private company,[43] shares in a registered company can be transferred or mortgaged[44] without the consent of the other shareholders. Subject to any agreement to the contrary, a person cannot be introduced as a partner without the consent of all the existing partners[45] and if in England a partner charges his share of the partnership for his separate debt the other partners normally have the option to dissolve the partnership.[46]

(2) The liability of a member of a registered company to contribute to its assets may be, and usually is, limited, *e.g.* limited, in the case of a company limited by shares, to the amount unpaid on his shares[47] (although the person controlling a private company may have to give a personal guarantee of the company's bank overdraft) but the members of a partnership are jointly and severally liable for all the debts of the firm.[48] This advantage can be secured in a partnership by a person's being a limited partner in a limited partnership formed under the Limited Partnerships Act 1907, but few such partnerships have been formed, owing to the superior advantages of the private limited company.

(3) There is no limit to the number of members of a company, but, except in the case of, *e.g.*, certain professional partnerships such as solicitors, a partnership with more than 20 members for the purpose of carrying on any business which has for its object the acquisition of gain is prohibited.[49]

(4) A registered company has greater facilities for borrowing than a partnership, *e.g.* the company may borrow on debentures.[50]

(5) Floating charges can be created by a registered company but not by a partnership.[51]

---

[43] These have not been compulsory for private companies since 1980.
[44] In Scots law "transferred in security."
[45] Partnership Act 1890, s.24(7).
[46] *ibid.*, s.33(2) (not applicable to Scotland: see s.23(5)).
[47] s.1.
[48] Partnership Act 1890, s.9, *ante.*
[49] s.716.
[50] *Post*, Chap. 23.
[51] *Post*, Chap. 23.

**Advantages of a partnership**

A partnership or an individual trader has certain advantages over a registered company (although these are normally outweighed by the advantages of the latter over the former):

(1) There are fewer formalities to be observed, and therefore there is less publicity and less expense involved in forming a partnership, *e.g.* there is no need to be registered, or to file a memorandum and articles, with the Registrar, and therefore there are no registration fees, and legal costs are less. A partnership agreement may be oral or even inferred from conduct.

(2) There are fewer formalities and therefore less publicity and less expense in running a partnership, *e.g.* returns do not have to be delivered to a Registrar.

(3) A partnership's accounts are never open to public inspection. Except in the case of certain unlimited companies,[52] those of a registered company are, as are the other documents which any registered company must lodge with the Registrar.[53]

(4) A partnership is not subject to the rules in connection with raising and maintenance of share capital, to which a registered company which is not an unlimited company is subject.[54]

(5) A partnership can make any arrangement with creditors that the partners think fit. A registered company can make only those authorised either by the Act or by the Insolvency Act 1986.[55]

[52] *Post*, Chap. 20.
[53] s.426.
[54] *Post*, Chap. 9.
[55] 1985 Act, s.425; Insolvency Act 1986, ss.1, 165, 167.

## Chapter 2

## CLASSIFICATION OF REGISTERED COMPANIES

THIS chapter deals first with the two main legal classifications of registered companies. The first classifies registered companies as being limited by shares, limited by guarantee or unlimited. The second classifies them as being either public companies or private companies. (Any limited company with a share capital may be either a public or a private company.) Secondly, something is said of holding companies and subsidiary companies, which in turn defines the concept of a group.

## COMPANIES LIMITED BY SHARES, COMPANIES LIMITED BY GUARANTEE AND UNLIMITED COMPANIES

A registered company may be—

(1) a company limited by shares, in which case the liability of a member to contribute to the company's assets is limited to the amount, if any, unpaid on his shares; or

(2) a company limited by guarantee, in which case the liability of a member is limited to the amount which he has undertaken to contribute *in the event of its being wound up*; or

(3) an unlimited company, in which case the liability of a member is unlimited: section 1(2).[1]

The vast majority of registered companies are companies limited by shares. Such companies must have a share capital, whereas unlimited companies may or may not have a share capital. Companies limited by guarantee cannot have a share capital if they were formed after December 22, 1980 and are

---

[1] This section provides the statutory rules for the liability of the members of a company for its debts. The common law position is that there is otherwise no liability at all: see *J. H. Rayner (Mincing Lane) v. D.T.I.* [1990] 2 A.C. 418 (H.L.), p. 25, *ante*.

instead supported by subscriptions or fees paid by the members: section 1(4).

## Companies limited by guarantee

A company limited by guarantee is a registered company in which the liability of members is limited to such amount as they respectively undertake to contribute to the assets of the company in the event of its being wound up: section 1(2)(b). The members are not required to contribute whilst the company is a going concern. The memorandum of a company limited by guarantee, in addition to containing the clauses normally contained in a memorandum,[2] must state that each member undertakes to contribute to the assets of the company in the event of its being wound up while he is a member, or within one year after he ceases to be a member, for payment of its debts contracted before he ceases to be a member, and of the costs of winding up, and for adjustment of the rights of the contributories, such sum as may be required, not exceeding a specified amount: section 2(4). The sum specified in Table C, *post*, is £100. Whatever the amount of the guarantee specified in the memorandum, it cannot be increased or reduced.

The amounts which the members have agreed to contribute in a winding up cannot be mortgaged or charged by the company whilst it is a going concern.[3] They are not assets of the company whilst it is a going concern.

Prior to the 1980 Act a company limited by guarantee could be formed either with or without a share capital, but was usually formed without a share capital, in which event money to acquire such things as premises may be raised by loans from the members. Since the 1980 Act no such company can be formed with, or acquire, a share capital: section 1(4). The majority of companies limited by guarantee are formed to incorporate professional, trade and research associations, or clubs supported by annual subscriptions. Many will be able to take advantage of section 304 and omit the word "Limited" from their names.[4]

---

[2] *Post*, p. 51.
[3] *Re Irish Club* [1906] W.N. 127; *Robertson v. British Linen Co.* (1890) 18 R., 1225 (O.H.), approved *obiter* in *Lloyds Bank Ltd v. Morrison & Son*, 1927 S.C. 571.
[4] *Post*, p. 56.

Every company limited by guarantee is obliged to register articles of association with the memorandum: section 7. If the company has no share capital, the memorandum and articles must be in the form set out in Table C, or as near thereto as circumstances admit: sections 3 and 8. Table C is a model form of memorandum and articles for such a company and is set out in the Companies (Tables A to F) Regulations 1985.

An article of a company limited by guarantee with no share capital is not invalid just because it is not contained in Table C. Section 8 is concerned with the form of the articles of such a company and the word "form" here does not embrace contents. Provided that the draftsman of such articles follows the general form of Table C he is free to add, subtract or vary as the needs of the case suggest.[5]

Every provision in the memorandum or articles of a company limited by guarantee and not having a share capital, or in any resolution of the company, purporting to give any person a right to participate in the divisible profits of the company otherwise than as a member is void, and every provision in the memorandum or articles, or in any resolution, purporting to divide the undertaking of the company into shares or interests is treated as a provision for share capital notwithstanding that the nominal amount or number of the shares or interests is not specified: section 15. The object of this section is to prevent the registration of companies with shares of no par value.[6]

Because of the strict régime applied to public companies few companies limited by guarantee can be registered as such companies. In practice they will be private companies.[7]

Apart from what has been said in this chapter, most of what is said elsewhere in this work applies to companies limited by guarantee as it does to companies limited by shares.

**Unlimited companies**

A company may be registered as an unlimited company, in which case there is no limit on the members' liability to contribute to the assets: section 1(2)(c). In the years immediately

---

[5] *Gaiman v. National Association for Mental Health* [1971] Ch. 317.
[6] Companies of the kind involved in *Malleson v. General Mineral Patents Syndicate Ltd.* [1894] 3 Ch. 538.
[7] *Post*, p. 42.

preceding 1967 comparatively few such companies were formed, although they are the oldest class of registered company, but the exemption from publication of accounts[8] given by the 1967 Act, made them more popular.

The memorandum and articles of an unlimited company with a share capital must be in the form set out in Table E, or as near thereto as circumstances admit: sections 3 and 8. Table E is a model form of memorandum and articles set out in the Companies (Tables A to F) Regulations 1985. The company is obliged to register articles with the memorandum: section 7(1). The articles must state, if the company is to have a share capital, the amount of the share capital: section 7(2). There is no requirement that the division of the share capital into shares of a fixed amount be stated. The name will not, of course, include the word "Limited," and there will be no limitation of liability clause in the memorandum. Since 1980 unlimited companies cannot be public companies: section 1(3).

An unlimited company is exceptional in that its members may be associated on the terms that they may withdraw in the mode pointed out by the memorandum and articles, so as to be free from liability in the event of a winding up,[9] and it seems that such a company may validly provide by its memorandum and articles for a return of capital to its members, *i.e.* without the consent of the court. Similarly an unlimited company may purchase its own shares if its constituent documents authorise it to do so.[10]

## Re-registration of unlimited company as limited private company

Section 51 provides that an unlimited company (not registered by virtue of section 49, *post*) may be re-registered as a private company limited either by shares or by guarantee if a special resolution to that effect and complying with the requirements set out below is passed, and the application for re-registration is in the prescribed form, signed by a director or the secretary and lodged with the Registrar, together with certain documents, not earlier than the day on which the copy of the resolution filed under section 380 is received by him.

---

[8] *Post*, Chap. 20.
[9] *Re Borough Commercial and Building Socy.* [1893] 2 Ch. 242.
[10] See, *e.g. Nelson Mitchell v. City of Glasgow Bank* (1879) 6 R. (H.L.) 66; (1878) 6 R. 420. See Chap. 10, *post*.

The resolution—

(1) must state the manner in which the liability of members is to be limited and the share capital if the company is to be limited by shares;
(2) must provide for the appropriate alterations in and additions to the memorandum and articles according to whether the company is to be limited by shares or by guarantee and so with or without a share capital.

The documents which must also be lodged are printed copies of the memorandum and articles as altered.

The Registrar must issue an appropriate certificate of incorporation, whereupon the status of the company is changed and the alterations in and additions to the memorandum and articles take effect. Such a certificate is conclusive evidence of compliance with the requirements of the section with respect to re-registration and of re-registration.[11]

### Re-registration of unlimited company as a public company

No unlimited company can be a public company: section 1(3). Since such a company is therefore a private company, conversion of an unlimited company to a public company requires two steps. First, the acquisition of limited liability and a share capital and second, the acquisition of public company status. Both steps may be achieved in one process under sections 43 to 48. The procedure for re-registration of a private company as a public company is modified to include the appropriate requirements for the acquisition of limited liability; *i.e.* a special resolution similar to that required by section 51: section 48. Following a pre-consolidation amendment[12] it is no longer possible to re-register a company which has already been re-registered as an unlimited company as a public company under section 43.[13]

The Registrar must issue a certificate stating that the company has been incorporated as a company limited by shares and is a public company. Such a certificate is conclusive evidence of the fact that it is a public company: sections 47, 48(3).

---

[11] s.52. As to the meaning of conclusive evidence, see p. 22, *ante.*
[12] The Companies Acts (Pre-Consolidation Amendments) Order 1984, para. 39.
[13] s.43(1). See *post*, p. 46.

**Re-registration of limited company as unlimited**

Section 49 enables a limited private company (not registered in pursuance of section 51, *ante*) to be re-registered as unlimited with the unanimous consent of its members. The application for re-registration must be in the prescribed form, signed by a director or the secretary and lodged with the Registrar together with certain documents. A public company cannot be re-registered as an unlimited company— it must attain private company status first; nor can a company which has previously been re-registered or unlimited: section 49(3).

The application must set out the appropriate alterations in and additions to the memorandum and, if articles have been registered, the articles according to whether or not the company is to have a share capital. If articles have not been registered the application must have annexed to it, and request the registration of, appropriate printed articles.

The Registrar must issue an appropriate certificate of incorporation, which will be conclusive evidence of proper re-registration: section 50.[14]

## PUBLIC AND PRIVATE COMPANIES

A registered limited company may be a public company or a private company.

By section 1(3) a public company is a limited company with a share capital which has a memorandum stating that it is a public company and which has been registered or re-registered as such.

A company which is not a public company is a private company. Thus the private company is the residual class of companies, without any special requirements. This is a complete reversal of the position prior to 1980 whereby all companies were public companies unless their articles contained certain restrictions, *e.g.* as to the transferability of shares.

There are three requirements for the registration of a company as a public company:

    (1)  it must state that it is a public company both in its memorandum and by its name. There must be a clause to that effect in the memorandum[15] and its name must end

---

[14] For the meaning of conclusive evidence, see p. 22, *ante*.
[15] s.1(3).

with the words "public limited company" (frequently abbreviated to "plc").[16] A private company uses the traditional "Limited" or "Ltd" at the end of its name;

(2) the memorandum must be in the form specified in Table F of the Companies (Tables A to F) Regulations 1985[17];

(3) the company must have an authorised capital figure (the amount of shares it may issue to the public) of at least the *authorised minimum*, currently £50,000[18]: section 11.

There are substantial differences in the capital requirements as applied to public and private companies. In particular a public company cannot commence business or exercise any borrowing powers unless it has actually allotted shares up to the authorised minimum and has received at least one quarter of that amount: sections 101 and 117.[19]

Private companies are no longer required to restrict the transferability of their shares, although they are perfectly at liberty to do so, *e.g.* to preserve family control of a company; nor need they limit their membership to 50. A private company cannot issue or cause to be issued any advertisement offering any of its securities to the public. However, by regulations the Secretary of State may allow advertisements of a private character as between the issuer and the recipients, advertisements dealing with investments only incidentally, or those issued only to investors expert enough to understand any risks involved: Financial Services Act 1986, section 170.[20] Contravention of this provision will be regarded as a breach of the conduct of business rules made under that Act, and so have civil consequences. It will also consititute a criminal offence: Financial Services Act 1986, section 171. To use the Stock Exchange, a company must be a public company.

The minimum number of members for a public company is two but one will suffice for a private company[21] and a public company must have at least two directors whereas a private company need only have one.[22]

---

[16] *Post*, p. 53.
[17] s.3.
[18] s.118.
[19] *Post*, p. 153.
[20] The Secretary of State has power to extend these categories by delegated legislation.
[21] ss.1(1)(3A).
[22] s.282.

A private company needs no minimum capital either for registration or the commencement of business.

A private company with only one member is known as a single member company. The fact that it only has one member must be recorded in the company's register of members, but not on the public register.[23] In general terms, the provisions of the Act are to apply to single member companies in the same way as to other companies, with such modifications as are necessary.[24] There are, however, special provisions for meetings and resolutions of such companies.[25]

## Disadvantages of a private company

The effective embargo on access to the capital markets preserved by section 170 of the Financial Services Act 1986 may be regarded as the only disadvantage of a private company as compared with a public company.

## Advantages of a private company

A private company has a number of advantages over a public company. These advantages include the following:

(1) A private company need not issue subsequent issues of shares by way of a rights issue: section 89.[26]
(2) A private company does not need an authorised minimum capital either for registration or to commence business under sections 11 and 117. It may commence business (and make binding contracts and exercise its borrowing powers) immediately on incorporation.[27]
(3) A private company is not subject to the majority of the provisions relating to the payment for shares. This enables a private company to issue shares in return for assets other than cash without lengthy and complex valuations: sections 101–116.[28]

---

[23] s.352A.
[24] The Companies (Single Member Private Limited Companies) Regulations 1992 (S.I. 1992 No. 1699), art. 2(1).
[25] See Chap. 14, below.
[26] Post, p. 148.
[27] Post, p. 153.
[28] Post, p. 159.

(4) A private company need not convene an extraordinary general meeting in the event of a serious loss of capital: section 142.[29]

(5) A private company may give itself wider charges on its own shares to recover debts owed to it by its members. Public companies are restricted in this respect: section 150.[30]

(6) A private company need not make provision for unrealised capital losses when distributing a dividend: section 264.[31]

(7) Directors of private companies are much less restricted in their financial dealings with their company and need disclose far less information about such arrangements in the accounts: sections 330–344.[32]

(8) The company secretary does not need to be specially qualified or experienced: section 286.[33]

(9) Private companies may be excused from publication of some or all of their accounts, depending on their size: sections 247–251.[34]

(10) Private companies may provide financial assistance for the purchase of their own shares by following the statutory procedure: sections 155–158.[35]

(11) Private companies may purchase or redeem their own shares out of capital: sections 170–177.[36]

(12) There is no obligation to disclose the true ownership of private company shares, however substantial the holding: sections 198–211.[37]

(13) Private companies can use the written resolution procedure instead of holding a formal meeting.[38]

(14) Private companies may by passing elective resolutions dispense with the need to comply with certain internal requirements of the Act.[39]

[29] *Post*, p. 183.
[30] *Post*, pp. 277, 279.
[31] *Post*, Chap. 22.
[32] *Post*, p. 339.
[33] *Post*, p. 386.
[34] *Post*, Chap. 20.
[35] *Post*, Chap. 11.
[36] *Post*, Chap. 10.
[37] *Post*, p. 222.
[38] *Post*, p. 308.
[39] *Post*, p. 306.

(15) Private companies may have only one member.[40]

Other differences between a private company and a public company are:

(1)  At a general meeting of a private company a motion for the appointment of two or more directors may be made by a single resolution: section 292.[41]

(2)  A proxy can speak at a meeting of a private company: section 372.[42]

## Re-registration of a private company as a public company

A private company[43] may be re-registered as a public company if it complies with the three conditions set out in sections 43 to 47.

(1)  It must pass a special resolution that it be so re-registered and that its memorandum and articles be amended accordingly (*e.g.* to provide for a change of name).

(2)  It must send an application in the prescribed form signed by a director or secretary of the company to the Registrar together with a printed copy of the amended memorandum and articles, a copy of the latest balance sheet and an unqualified report by the auditors on that balance sheet, a copy of another report by the auditors that the company's net assets are not less than its capital as stated in that balance sheet, and a declaration of compliance by a director or secretary and that the company's position *vis-à-vis* its net assets is unchanged since the last balance sheet.

(3)  It must comply with the necessary financial criteria both for a public company to be able to commence business[44] and as to the payment for shares in public companies.[45]

---

[40] *Ante*, p. 44.
[41] *Post*, p. 314.
[42] *Post*, p. 300.
[43] Other than one without a share capital or one that has previously been re-registered as a private company.
[44] *Post*, p. 153.
[45] *Post*, p. 159.

This applies equally to shares issued since the last balance sheet and before the application; in particular it must have the *authorised minimum* capital.

If the Registrar is satisfied he must issue a certificate of incorporation stating that the company is a public company. This is conclusive evidence that the company is a public company and that all the procedures as to re-registration have been complied with.[46]

### Re-registration of a public company as a private company

A public company may be re-registered as a private company if it complies with the conditions in sections 53 to 55.

(1) It must pass a special resolution that it be so re-registered and that its memorandum and articles be amended accordingly (*e.g.* to remove the statement in the memorandum that it is a public company).

(2) It must send an application in the prescribed form signed by a director or secretary of the company to the Registrar together with a printed copy of the amended memorandum and articles.

(3) 28 days must have elapsed from the passing of the resolution and, either, no application has been brought under section 54 to have the resolution set aside, or the court has confirmed the resolution despite such an application. A minority action may be brought for the cancellation of the resolution to re-register by, either, the holders of five per cent. or more of the issued share capital or any class of capital, or not less than 50 members, within 28 days of the passing of the resolution. No-one who voted for the resolution can make such an application. The court has extensive powers on hearing such an application including confirming or cancelling the resolution, adjourning the proceedings for an arrangement to be made, altering the memorandum and articles, and, if necessary, providing for the purchase by the company of the shares of the dissentient members. This is

---

[46] For the meaning of "conclusive evidence", see p. 22, *ante*.

one of several minority protection sections which occur throughout the Act.

If the Registrar is satisfied he must issue a certificate of incorporation "appropriate to a company that is not a public company." This is conclusive evidence that the requirements as to re-registration have been complied with and that the company is a private company.[47]

### Re-registration of public companies by law

If a public company reduces its capital under section 135[48] so that its allotted share capital is less than the *authorised minimum* the court is empowered to order that the company be re-registered as a private company and that its memorandum and articles be amended accordingly. In such a case no special resolution is necessary and no application by a minority is possible: section 139.

## HOLDING AND SUBSIDIARY COMPANIES

It is sometimes important to know whether a registered company is a subsidiary or a holding company. One reason is that section 23[49] generally prevents a subsidiary from being a member of its holding company. Another reason is that the financial assistance regulations apply as between holding and subsidiary companies.[50] The meaning of the terms "subsidiary" and "holding company" is given in sections 736 and 736A and it is convenient to deal with those definitions here.

Sections 736 and 736A were introduced by the 1989 Act to provide a redefinition of holding and subsidiary companies for company law purposes. The 1989 Act introduced another, additional definition of a group purely for the purposes of the group accounting requirements introduced by that Act, as required by the seventh EC directive.[51] The need to redefine the general concept of a group of companies was made more imperative by

[47] For the meaning of conclusive evidence, see p. 22, *ante*.
[48] *Post*, Chap. 9.
[49] *Post*, p. 213.
[50] *Post*, Chap. 11.
[51] *Post*, Chap. 20.

the planned programme of EU legislation specifically aimed at groups.

Under section 736 there are three ways of establishing that a company (B) is a subsidiary of another company (A):

(i) where A holds a majority of the voting rights in B (this may be called *voting control*);

(ii) where A is a member of B and can appoint or dismiss a majority of its directors (this may be called *director control*);

(iii) where A is a member of B and controls alone or under an agreement with others a majority of the voting rights in B (this may be called *contract control*).

If C is a subsidiary of B and B is a subsidiary of A, then C is also regarded as being a subsidiary of A.

A wholly-owned subsidiary is one whose shares are all owned by one company, its wholly-owned subsidiaries and their and its nominees.

Section 736A expands upon this basic framework. When calculating the voting rights (for voting control or contract control) it is the rights attached to the shares which count. For the purposes of calculating a majority of the board (for director control) it is the majority of the voting rights on the board on all, or substantially all, matters which must be taken into account and not a numerical majority. A company is deemed to be able to control the appointment or dismissal of the director of another company if either that director's appointment follows necessarily from his appointment as a director of the first company or the directorship is held by the first company itself. Rights to appoint or dismiss a director which require another's consent do not count unless there is no-one else who has those rights under the new criteria.

The final aspect of the definition is to discover which *rights*, either as to voting or as to the appointment or dismissal of directors, should be attributed to whom for the purpose of establishing any of the three methods of control. The following rules will apply:

(a) rights which are applicable at all times will count. Restricted rights, *i.e.* ones which only apply in certain circumstances, will only count if they are in fact exercisable at the relevant time. On the other hand a general right which is in a temporary abeyance will still count;

(b) fiduciary rights (*i.e.* held only as a trustee) do not count against the trustee;

(c) nominee rights (*i.e.* those exercisable only on instructions or with consent) are to be attributed to the beneficial owner;

(d) where shares are mortgaged, the rights attached to those shares count as those of the lender and not the borrower only if, apart from normal creditor protection rights, they are exercisable only by or with the lender's, or the lender's subsidiaries', instructions;

(e) the rights of a subsidiary count as those of its holding company and rules (c) and (d) above must not be read as applying to the contrary;

(f) any voting rights held by a company in itself must be discounted when making the calculation; and

(g) rights held under (b)–(f) are cumulative if necessary.

The above, complex, definition may be amended by regulations made by the Secretary of State under section 736B of the Act.

# Chapter 3

# MEMORANDUM OF ASSOCIATION

EVERY registered company must have a memorandum of association, which is the registered company's charter.[1] In general the memorandum regulates the company's external affairs, whilst the articles regulate its internal affairs. The purpose of the memorandum is to enable persons who invest in or deal with the company to ascertain what its name is, whether it is a public company, whether it is an English or a Scottish company, what its objects are, whether the liability of its members is limited and what share capital it is authorised to issue. The memorandum may contain other matters apart from those just referred to. It must also contain an association clause and be properly subscribed. The provisions of the memorandum can be altered in certain specified cases.

Section 2 provides that the memorandum of every company must state:

(1) The name of the company.
(2) Whether the registered office of the company is to be situated in England, Wales or Scotland.
(3) The objects of the company.
(4) That the liability of the members is limited, if the company is limited by shares or by guarantee.
(5) In the case of a limited company having a share capital, the amount of share capital with which the company proposes to be registered and the division thereof into shares of a fixed amount.

Section 1(3) provides that the memorandum of a public company must state, in addition, the fact that the company is a public company.

[1] See *per* Lord Cairns, L.C., in *Ashbury Railway Carriage Co. Ltd v. Riche* (1875) L.R. 7 H.L. 653, at pp. 667, 558.

In the case of a company limited by guarantee the memorandum must also state that each member undertakes to contribute to the assets of the company in the event of its being wound up while he is a member, or within one year after he ceases to be a member, such amount as may be required, not exceeding a specified amount.

Where the memorandum states that the registered office is to be in Wales, the memorandum and the articles may be in Welsh but, if they are, they must be accompanied by a certified translation into English; section 710B.[2]

### Subscription of the memorandum

The memorandum must state the desire of the subscribers to be formed into a company and the agreement of each to take a specified number of shares in the company. Two or more persons must subscribe their names to the memorandum: section 1(1), unless the company is being formed as a single member private limited company: section 1(3A).[3] The form of a memorandum of association of a private company must be that set out in Table B, and, for a public company, that set out in Table F, of the Companies (Tables A to F) Regulations 1985 or as near thereto as circumstances admit: section 3.

No subscriber may take less than one share and each subscriber must write opposite to his name the number of shares he takes and each subscriber must sign the memorandum in the presence of at least one witness, who must attest the signature: section 2.

## The Name

The memorandum must state the name of the company: section 2. The general rule is that any name may be selected. However, a company cannot be registered by a name which is prohibited, either absolutely or conditionally: section 26.[4] Further, the last word of the name of a private limited company must be the word "Limited" (section 25(2)), unless the company is able to comply with the criteria in section 30 and dispenses with the word. The

---

[2] See also the Companies (Welsh Language Forms and Documents) Regulations 1994 (S.I. 1994 No. 117).
[3] See p. 44, *ante.*
[4] *Post,* p. 53.

last words of a public company must be "public limited company" (section 25(1)).[5] Where the memorandum of a limited company states that its registered office is to be in Wales, the last word of the name of the company may be "Cyfyngedig" if the company is a private company, or "Cwmni cyfyngedig cyhoeddus" if it is a public company. In all cases the appropriate abbreviations may be used: section 27. These are Ltd, plc, cyf, and ccc, respectively. In selecting a name, it is not necessary to use the word "Company", and the modern tendency is to omit it. A short name is an obvious practical convenience.

The word "Limited" is a misnomer. The company's liability for its own debts is not limited, but it is the members of the company who are not liable for the company's debts (except to the limited extent provided by section 24),[6] because the company is a legal entity separate and distinct from its shareholders. The important thing about the name is that it should show to others that the company is a body corporate, and not a mere unincorporated partnership. It is too late now to reserve the word "Company" for the exclusive use of incorporated companies, because that is in common use by persons who are not incorporated, e.g. by partnerships. The American term "Incorporated" expresses the true idea, and that or some synonymous word is to be preferred to "Limited."

The use of the word "Limited" or "Cyfyngedig," or any contraction or imitation of it, as the last word of the name under which any person carries on business without being incorporated with limited liability, is prohibited: section 34. Similarly, the use of the words "Public limited company" or its Welsh equivalent or any abbreviation of it by any person who is not a public limited company is an offence: section 33.

## Prohibited and controlled names

Section 26(1) provides five grounds upon which the registration of a name or change of name is absolutely prohibited.

(1) A name including "limited," "unlimited" or "public limited company," or their Welsh equivalents otherwise than at the end of the name;

---

[5] Below.
[6] *Ante,* p. 27.

   (2) A name including any abbreviation of those words other-
       wise than at the end of the name;

   (3) A name which is *the same as* a name appearing in the
       index of registered names kept by the Registrar;

   (4) A name, the use of which would, in the opinion of the
       Secretary of State, constitute a criminal offence;

   (5) A name which in the opinion of the Secretary of State is
       offensive.

The important prohibition is (3)—a name which is *the same as*
one already on the index of registered names kept by the
Registrar under section 714. This includes the names of all
registered companies, limited partnerships and industrial and
provident societies, and so registration of a company name
confers a partial monopoly of the use of that name. The onus of
checking the index is on those who wish to register the name.
There is no control on registration of names similar or "too like"
those already on the index but such a name may be compulsorily
altered within one year of registration under section 28—so called
"post registration control."[7] When deciding whether one name is
*the same as* another for this purpose minor differences are to be
disregarded under section 26(3). Accents, type and case of letters
and the word "the" if it is the first word of the name, are
examples of such minor differences.

Section 26(2) provides for the controlled use of certain words
and expressions either on the registration of a company or a
change of name. The use of any name which in the opinion of the
Secretary of State would be likely to give the impression that the
company is connected in any way with Her Majesty's Government or with any local authority or includes any name or
expression specified in the appropriate regulations cannot be
registered without his consent. The appropriate regulations are
the Company and Business Names Regulations 1981.[8] These
regulations specify 90 separate words or expression, including
their plural and possessive forms, which require consent before
use. These include: "Abortion", "Building Society", "Chamber
of Commerce", "Duke", "English", "Health Visitor", "Insur-

---

[7] *Post,* p. 59.

[8] S.I. 1981/1685. See also the Company and Business Names (Amendment)
Regulations 1982 (S.I. 1982 No. 1653) and the Company and Business Names
(Amendment) Regulations 1992 (S.I. 1992 No. 1196).

ance", "National", "Royal", "Stock Exchange", "Trade Union", "Trust", and "Windsor".

When a company wishes to use such an expression it must request the "relevant body", if one is specified, to indicate whether (and if so why) it has any objections to the proposal. Relevant bodies include the Home Office and the Scottish Home and Health Department. The reply of the relevant body must be sent to the Registrar by the applicant when registration or the change of name is applied for: section 29. The Secretary of State will then make his decision.

Since similar names can be registered there is a possibility of passing-off actions being brought against registered companies, even though such names can be compulsorily changed within one year of registration.[9] Under the general law, the court has jurisdiction to grant an injunction[10] to restrain a company from using a trade name colourably resembling that of the plaintiff if the defendant's trade name, though innocently adopted, is calculated , *i.e.* likely,[11] to deceive, either by diverting customers from the plaintiff to the defendant or by occasioning confusion between the two businesses, *e.g.* by suggesting that the defendant's business is in some way connected with that of the plaintiff.

In *Ewing v. Buttercup Margarine Co. Ltd*,[12] the plaintiff, who carried on business under the trade name of the Buttercup Dairy Company, was held entitled to restrain a newly registered company from carrying on business under the name of the Buttercup Margarine Company Ltd on the ground that the public might reasonably think that the registered company was connected with his business.

However, if the company's business is or will be different from that of the complaining party, confusion is not likely to arise, and an injunction will not be granted.[13]

A company having a word in ordinary use as part of its name cannot prevent another company from using the same word.

---

[9] Post, p. 59.
[10] The Scottish equivalent is interdict.
[11] *Per* Earl of Halsbury L.C. in *The N. Cheshire and Manchester Brewery Co. Ltd v. The Manchester Brewery Co. Ltd* [1899] A.C. at p. 84.
[12] [1917] 2 Ch. 1 (C.A.).
[13] *Dunlop Pneumatic Tyre Co. Ltd v. Dunlop Motor Co. Ltd*, 1907 S.C.(H.L.) 15, where the respondents carried on a motor-repairing company; similarly an interdict was refused in *The Scottish Union and National Insurance Co. v. The Scottish National Insurance Co. Ltd*, 1909 S.C. 318.

So, Aerators Ltd were unable to prevent the registration of Automatic Aerators Patents, Ltd because the word "aerator" was a word in common use in the English language and Aerators Ltd had no monopoly of it: *Aerators Ltd v. Tollitt* [1902] 2 Ch. 319.

## Exemption from using the word "Limited"

Under section 30 a private company limited by guarantee has a right to exclude the word "Limited" from the end of its name if certain criteria are met and certified. Prior to the 1981 Act such exemption was available to all private companies if they were so licensed by the Department of Trade. Such licensed companies continue to enjoy their exemption under the present section.

The present criteria are that the company is to be formed for the promotion of commerce, art, science, education, religion, charity or any profession and anything incidental or conducive to any of those objects; that by its memorandum or articles it must apply its income solely for the promotion of those objects, prohibit the payment of dividends to its members, and require all its surplus assets on a winding up to be transferred to a similar body rather than to its members.[14] A statutory declaration either by the solicitor engaged in the formation, or by a director or secretary of the company, that the company is one to which the section applies will suffice to obtain the exemption: section 30(4), (5).

There is an absolute ban on any alterations of such a company's memorandum or articles so as to breach the criteria— there are fines in default: section 31(1), (5). Any purported alteration will thus be void. If there is a breach of any of the criteria without any such change the Secretary of State can require the addition of the word "Limited" to the company's name and a resolution of the directors to that effect will suffice for the change of name: section 31(2). Such a company cannot again acquire the exemption without the express approval of the Secretary of State: section 31(3).

Any company which obtains exemption under section 30 is relieved of the necessity of (1) having "Limited" as part of its name, (2) publishing its name[15] and (3) sending lists of members to the Registrar,[16] although section 351 requires the fact that it is

---

[14] This requirement was always insisted on by the Department under the previous system.

[15] Under ss.348, 349, 350, *post*.

[16] Under s.363, *post*.

a limited company to be mentioned in its business letters and order forms.

Associations taking advantage of this exemption are typically chambers of commerce, schools and colleges, research associations, learned societies, professional qualifying bodies and charitable bodies doing social work.

## Publication of name by company

The Act provides that every company must:

(1) paint or affix its name on the outside of every office or place in which its business is carried on, in a conspicuous position, in letters easily legible: section 348;

(2) mention its name in legible characters in all business letters of the company and in all notices and other official publications, and in all bills of exchange, promissory notes, endorsements, cheques and orders for money or goods, bills of parcels, invoices, receipts and letters of credit: section 349,[17]

(3) engrave its name in legible characters on its seal, if it has one: section 350.

An exception is that by section 30(7) a company entitled to dispense with the word "Limited" as part of its name[18] is excepted from the provisions of the Act relating to the publishing of its name, although as noted above, section 351 requires the fact that it is a limited company to be mentioned in legible characters in all its business letters and order forms.

Fines are imposed on the company and its officers for non-compliance with the above requirement.

## Company names and company cheques, etc.

If an officer of the company or any person on its behalf, signs or authorises to be signed on behalf of the company any bill of exchange, cheque or order for money or goods in which the company's name is not correctly mentioned,[19] he is liable to a fine

[17] There are additional requirements for charitable companies: Charities Act 1993, s.63, in England and by s.112(6) C.A. 1989 for Scotland.

[18] *Ante,* p. 56.

[19] Abbreviation of 'Company' to 'Co' is not a breach of the section, however: *Banque de l'Indochine et de Seuz S.A. v. Euroseas Finance Co. Ltd* [1981] 3 All E.R.

and, in addition, he is personally liable to the holder of the bill of exchange, cheque or order, for its amount, unless it is paid by the company: section 349(4). Such personal liability is a secondary liability, arising only if the company itself fails to pay, *e.g.* because of liquidation.

The courts have long established that liability under section 349(4) will be imposed upon such an officer when the words "limited" or "plc" are not included on the face of the bill or cheque.[20] The original intention was that third parties should not be misled into thinking that they were dealing with an unlimited organisation when they were dealing with a limited company. There need be no element of deceit involved, however, and the courts will not order rectification of the cheque simply on the basis that "everybody was aware of what the situation was". Rectification cannot be used by an individual simply to avoid a statutory liability.[21]

The situation is less clear where there is a mistake as to the spelling of the name of the company. In one case, *Durham Fancy Goods Ltd v. Michael Jackson (Fancy Goods) Ltd,*[22] where the third party had prepared and specified the form of acceptance of the bill which it required and which misdescribed the company's name as "M. Jackson (Fancy Goods) Ltd," the court refused to allow the third party to enforce the personal liability of the officer who signed the bill on the basis of estoppel. The authority of this decision has since been doubted,[23] however, and it has been distinguished in subsequent cases where the third party had not actually prepared the bill or cheque involved,[24] and more recently where although the third party had prepared the bill it had not *prescribed* the form of wording, but had simply put forward bills which it used for the officer to accept in the proper form.[25] Until recently it was assumed therefore that any mistake in the spelling of the name gave rise to personal liability,[26] but in *Jenice Ltd v.*

---

[20] *Penrose v. Martyr* (1858) 120 E.R. 595, *Atkin v. Wardle* (1889) 5 T.L.R., 734, *British Airways Board v. Parish* [1979] 2 Lloyds Rep. 361 (C.A.).
[21] *Blum v. O.C.P. Repartition SA* (1988) 4 BCC 771 (C.A.); *Rafsanjan Pistachio Producers Co-operative v. Reiss* [1990] BCC 730.
[22] [1968] 2 Q.B. 839.
[23] *Blum v. O.C.P. Repartition SA, ante.*
[24] *Barber & Nicholls v. R. & G. Associates (London) Ltd* (1982) 132 NLJ 1076.
[25] *Linholst & Co. A/S v. Fowler* (1988) 4 BCC 766 (C.A.).
[26] See the cases cited above, and *Bonding Ltd v. Rolloway Shower Blinds* [1986] BCLC 177; *John Wilkes (Footwear) Ltd v. Lee International (Footwear) Ltd* [1985] BCLC 444.

*Dan,*[27] it was held that since the purpose of the section was to ensure that third parties knew they were dealing with a limited company, a minor spelling mistake on the printed cheque in which one letter of the company's name was omitted did not give rise to any liability on the part of the person signing it.

An officer cannot be liable for authorising a signature, as distinct from the signature itself, unless he authorises the making of the order etc. on an incorrectly named document.

A company, Lee International (Footwear) Ltd, ordered several moccasins from the plaintiffs on an old order form which gave the company's former name. The order was signed by one director. The other director, being unaware of the fact that an old order form was being used, was held not to be liabile under the section: *John Wilkes (Footwear) Ltd v. Lee International (Footwear) Ltd* [1985] BCLC 444.

What amounts to a signature may vary according to the context. It is possible that a signature in the company's name alone will suffice, but there must be an individual affixation of that name in confirmation of the order concerned by the officer for him to authorise that signature and so be liable under the section. Merely authorising the filling up of a form with an incorrect name printed on it will not suffice.[28]

**Change of name**

Companies may change their registered names voluntarily or under compulsion. The latter gives the Department of Trade and Industry control over names similar to those already registered even though they cannot prevent registration of such names.

(1) A company may change its name at any time by a special resolution which takes effect from the issue of a new certificate of incorporation by the Registrar: section 28(1). Such a change of name is subject to the same restrictions as are applicable to the choice of name for a new company registering a name for the first time.[29] The only exception to this freedom to change a name applies where it is proposed to remove the word "limited" from a company's name and there had been a direction of the Secretary of State to the contrary.[30]

[27] [1993] BCLC 1349.
[28] *Oshkosh B'Gosh Incorporated v. Dan Marbel Incorporated Ltd* (1988) 4 BCC 795.
[29] *Ante,* p. 53.
[30] s.31(3). See *ante*, p. 56.

(2) If a name has been registered which is *the same as* one already on the index of registered names or one that ought to have appeared on the index at the time of registration or is in the opinion of the Secretary of State *too like* any such name, the name must be changed on the direction of the Secretary of State: section 28(2). Such a direction must be given within 12 months of the original registration and must be complied with within such period as is specified.

Names are *the same* as existing ones as defined by section 26(3).[31] The Registrar has published notes for guidance as to what will be considered *too like* names, *e.g.* phonetically identical names or where two names have a distinctive element in common, or where because of a similarity of the name and operations of two companies there is likely to be some confusion. These are not conclusive criteria however.

(3) When a company has applied to have a controlled name or expression as part of its name it will furnish information to the relevant body and the Department in order to obtain permission under section 26(2).[32] If misleading information has been given or undertakings or assurances have not been fulfilled the Secretary of State may by direction require the company to change its name: section 28(3). Such a direction may be given up to five years from the original registration and must be complied with within such period as is specified.

(4) If the Secretary of State considers that a name gives a misleading indication of the nature of the company's activities so as to be likely to cause harm to the public, he may direct a change. A direction must normally be complied with within six weeks. Within three weeks the company may apply to the court to have the direction set aside: section 32. Failure to comply with any direction renders the company liable to fines.

When a company changes its name a new certificate of incorporation will be issued by the Registrar (sections 28(6), 32(5)) and the new name takes effect from the date of issue of the new certificate.[33]

---

[31] See note 29, above.

[32] *Ante,* p. 54.

[33] The old name continues until then. See *Shackleford, Ford & Co. Ltd v. Dangerfield* (1868) L.R. 3 C.P. 407. In *Lin Pac Containers (Scotland) Ltd v. Kelly,* 1982 S.L.T. 50 (O.H.), a contract entered into in the new name was held valid even though the new certificate was issued three days later.

A change of name does not affect any rights or obligations of the company or any legal proceedings by or against the company: sections 28(7), 32(6).

## Business names

If a company which has a place of business in Great Britain, whether or not incorporated here, carries on business in Great Britain under a business name which does not consist of its corporate name without any addition other than one which indicates that the business is being carried on in succession to the former owner, it becomes subject to the Business Names Act 1985.

The first consequence of this is that the company's business name may not without permission of the Secretary of State include any of the words or expressions subject to control on registration of a corporate name; *i.e.* those within section 26(2) and its regulations: Business Names Act, section 2. An identical procedure to obtain permission must be followed: Business Names Act, section 3. There is a 12 month period of grace where a business has been transferred to a company which then uses the previous permitted business name.

The second consequence is that a company using a business name distinct from its corporate name must disclose its corporate name and an address for the service of any document on all its business letters, written orders for goods or services, invoices and receipts, and written demands for payment arising in the course of the business, and display a statutory notice of such particulars in each of its business premises (to which either its customers or suppliers have access). Further it must supply such particulars to anyone who asks for them and with whom anything is done or discussed in the course of the business. This must be done by giving him notice "immediately" on request: Business Names Act, section 4.

In default of these obligations the company and its officers may be liable to fines. In addition, failure to comply with the disclosure provisions is subject to some civil consequences under section 5 of the Business Names Act 1985. If a company seeks to enforce any action arising out of a contract made at a time when it was in breach of the disclosure obligations, the court must dismiss the action if the other party can show that he either has a course of action against the company which he was unable to pursue because of the breach or has suffered some financial loss in respect of that contract by reason of the company's breach. The section however has no application either to proceedings brought by such a company on counter-claim or to the right of set-off if it is sued by the other party.

## THE REGISTERED OFFICE

A company must at all times have a registered office to which communications and notices may be addressed: section 287(1). The memorandum must state whether the registered office is to be in England and Wales, Wales or Scotland: section 2. The actual address of the registered office need not be set out in the memorandum, but notice of the address must be given to the Registrar in the statement which, under section 10, *ante*,[34] must be delivered for registration with the memorandum. That address is thus the initial address on incorporation of the company: section 287(2).

The statement as to the registered office in the memorandum fixes the company's nationality and domicile, *e.g.* if the memorandum states that the office is to be in England the company is an English company with British nationality and an English domicile. A corporation is domiciled where it is incorporated and cannot change this domicile,[35] except by Act of Parliament, and the law of a corporation's domicile governs all questions of its status, *e.g.* is it duly incorporated, what are its powers, has it been dissolved? The nationality of a corporation, seldom relevant in private international law, also depends on the place of incorporation.

The reason for requiring a company to have a specific registered office is that, since the company has a legal existence but does not have a physical existence, it is necessary to know where the company can be found, where the communications and notices may be addressed and where documents can be served on it. A company need not, and very frequently does not, carry on its business at its registered office. There is nothing, for example, to prevent a company with a registered office in England from carrying on its business abroad.

[34] p. 20.
[35] *Gasque v. I.R.C.* [1940] 2 K.B. 80.

A document can be served on a company by leaving it at or sending it by post to the registered office of the company: section 725(1). It is not necessary to send it by registered post.[36]

If a company registered in Scotland carries on business in England, the process of any court in England can be served at the principal place of the company's business in England, a copy being posted at the same time to the registered office: section 725(2), (3).

Section 351 requires every company to mention its place of registration and registered number, and the address of its registered office, in legible characters on all its business letters and order forms. A company which fails to comply with the subsection, or an officer of a company or other person on its behalf who issues or authorises the issue of a letter or form which does not comply, is liable to a fine. The phrase "order forms" means forms which the company makes available for other persons to order goods or services from the company and includes, *e.g.* coupons in newspapers which the public fill in when asking for goods to be supplied.

### Change of address of the registered office

A company may change the address of its registered office on giving proper notice to the registrar. The new address takes effect on the entry of that address on the register but the company has 14 days after giving due notice in which to use the new address and to transfer the registers, etc., required to be kept there before it commits any offences for using the wrong address, etc. This is because the company will not be able to discover the actual date of registration without making a specific search of the register: section 287(3)(4)(5).

Persons dealing with the company may, on the other hand, validly serve any document on the company at the old address within 14 days of the registration of the new address: section 287(4). This is because the new address will in practice appear on the company's registered file a few days after registration.

If a company is unavoidably unable to keep its registers, etc., at its registered office in circumstances in which it was impracticable to give the registrar prior notice, the company and its officers

---

[36] *T.O. Supplies (London) Ltd v. Jerry Creighton Ltd* [1952] 1 K.B. 42.

will not be liable if it can show that it resumed performance of that duty at other premises as soon as practicable and notified the registrar of that new address within 14 days of doing so: section 287(6)(7).

Section 711 provides that the Registrar must publish in the *Gazette* notice of the receipt by him of notice of a change in the situation of a company's registered office; *i.e.* he must officially notify it. The point being that section 42 provides that a company cannot then rely against other persons (as regards service of any document on the company) on any change in the situation of the company's registered office if either it was not officially notified (under s.711) at the material time and is not shown by the company to have been known at that time to the person concerned, or if the material time is less than 16 days after official notification and it is shown that the person concerned was unavoidably prevented from knowing of the event at that time.[37]

## Items which must be kept at the registered office

The following must be kept at the registered office of a company:

(1) The register of members and, if the company has one, the index of members, unless the register is made up at another office of the company, when they may be kept at that office, or is made up by an agent, when they may be kept at the agent's office: sections 352–354.

(2) The minute books of general meetings: section 383.

(3) The register of interests in the notifiable percentage or more of the shares carrying unrestricted voting rights and, if there is one, the index of names, unless the register of directors' interests is not kept at the registered office, when it must be kept where the register of directors' interests is kept: sections 211, 213.

(4) The register of directors and secretaries: section 288.

(5) The register of directors' interests in shares in, or debentures of, the company or associated companies, together with, if the company has one, the index of names in the

---

[37] On the other hand official notification does not constitute notice of such a change to anyone: *Official Custodian of Charities v. Parway Estates* [1985] Ch. 151 (C.A.).

register, unless the register of members is not kept at its registered office, when they may be kept where the register of members is kept: section 324.

(6) A copy of each director's contract of service or a memorandum thereof, unless kept where the register of members is kept or kept at the company's principal place of business: section 318.

(7) If the company has one, the register of debenture holders, unless the register is made up at another office, when it may be kept where it is made up, or is made up by an agent, when it may be kept at the agent's office: section 190.

(8) A copy of every instrument creating or evidencing any charge requiring registration under Part XII of the Act.

(9) The company's register of charges affecting property of the company: section 407.

(10) Any proposed contract or option for an off-market purchase by a company of its own shares, for 15 days prior to the resolution to approve it: sections 164, 165.

(11) Any proposed release by a company of its rights under an off-market purchase contract or option to purchase its own shares: section 167.

(12) Any contract for the purchase by a company of its own shares approved by the company must be kept at the registered office for 10 years from the purchase of the shares or the determination of the contract: section 169.

(13) The requisite statutory declaration of solvency and auditors' report where a private company intends to purchase or redeem its own shares out of capital: section 175.

Under section 723A the Secretary of State is empowered to prescribe by regulations for the inspection and copying of these documents kept at the company's registered office. Under the current regulations[38] companies must make the documents available for inspection for not less than two hours between 9am and 5pm on each business day (excluding weekends and bank holidays) and allow anyone making such an inspection to copy the information by the taking of notes or the transcription of the information (but are not obliged to provide any other facilities).

[38] The Companies (Inspection and Copy of Registers) Regulations 1991 (S.I. 1991 No. 1998).

Inspection of all documents is free to members of the company and the fees for non-members are fixed at a maximum of £2.50 per hour. The register of charges and documents creating a charge may also be inspected free by debenture holders: section 412.

## THE OBJECTS

The memorandum must state the objects of the company: section 2. As Lord Parker of Waddington said in *Cotman v. Brougham*,[39] the statement of the objects in the memorandum was originally intended to serve a double purpose:

(1) to protect the subscribers who learn from it the purposes to which their money can be applied;[40]
(2) to protect persons dealing with the company, who can discover from it[41] the extent of the company's powers.

At common law, a corporation has the same legal capacity as a human being[42] but, in order to protect the shareholders and those who deal with the company, the courts evolved the *ultra vires* doctrine to the effect that since a registered company is an artificial person incorporated by Parliament for the objects stated in the memorandum, it has power only to carry out such objects together with anything incidental thereto. Anything done which is outside the scope of the objects clause was therefore *ultra vires* and void. The result of this doctrine was that objects clauses became very lengthy because companies took all the objects they could conceivably require and the original short form envisaged by the model memorandum in the Companies (Tables A to F) Regulations was rarely used. Nevertheless the *ultra vires* doctrine continually caused unnecessary hardship for innocent third parties and introduced extreme complexity into the law. An additional "protection" for shareholders and third parties was

---

[39] [1918] A.C. 514 at p. 520. See also *per* Lord Wrenbury at pp. 522, 523.
[40] A member can require the company to send him a copy of the memorandum on payment of a fee: s.19.
[41] They can inspect the memorandum and the other documents kept by the Registrar, s.709.
[42] *Case of Sutton's Hospital* (1612) 10 Co.Rep. 23a; Blackstone Comm. 1, 593; *University of Glasgow v. Faculty of Physicians and Surgeons* (1834) 13 S. 9; (1835) 2 S. & M. 275: (1837) 15 S. 736; (1840) 1 Rob. 397.

provided by the original rule that the objects clause could not be altered except by a special Act of Parliament or a reconstruction. Later, the objects could be altered but only for specified purposes, initially with the court's consent.

The first EC directive required a change in the law of *ultra vires* and this was implemented by section 9(1) of the European Communities Act 1972 which became section 35 of the Companies Act 1985. That section proved to have serious defects, however, and in 1985 Professor Prentice, of Oxford University, was commissioned by the DTI to write a report on the *ultra vires* rule. This report led to major reforms by the 1989 Act. These reforms have effectively abolished the *ultra vires* rule so far as third parties are concerned, allowed for a catch-all short-form objects clause, given companies a general power of alteration of all such clauses, and limited even their internal effects. Most of the old law has been swept away and readers are referred to the thirteenth edition of this work for a detailed analysis of the *ultra vires* rule, etc., prior to 1991. In this edition only a summary of the pre-1991 position is given.

### Form and alteration of the objects clause

Companies are still required to have an objects clause: section 2(1)(c). As the result of the legacy of the *ultra vires* doctrine contemporary objects clauses are, as stated above, usually very long and have general clauses at the end, *e.g.* that every object is a separate main object[43] or that the company may do, in addition to the objects listed, anything which the directors consider can be carried on in conjunction with its other objects.[44] Such clauses, developed in response to the court's attempts to limit long objects clauses by discovering main objects and winding up a company for failure of that main object, are perfectly valid.

The first change in the law relating to the objects clause introduced by the 1989 Act is contained in section 3A of the 1985 Act. This section relates to the form of the objects clause and provides that where the memorandum states that the object of the company is to carry on business as a general commercial company, that company is deemed to be able to carry on any trade or business whatsoever and have the power to do anything

---

[43] See, *e.g. Cotman v. Brougham* [1918] A.C. 514.
[44] See, *e.g. Bell Houses Ltd v. City Wall Properties Ltd* [1966] 2 Q.B. 656.

which is incidental or conducive to the conduct of any trade or business by it. This new short form of objects clause is therefore available to any commercial company and if used will considerably shorten company memoranda. It is not clear, however, whether companies may adopt the wording of section 3A as part of a wider objects clause and still retain the benefit of that section. The section speaks only of *the* object of the company being set out as stated and not of one of the objects, etc.

The 1989 Act also substantially changed the power of a company to alter its objects. Section 4 of the 1985 Act now allows a company to alter its objects clause by a special resolution at any time and for any reason. Previously any alteration had to be for a specified purpose. The important point to note, however, is that any such change must be effected by a special resolution. This has consequences for the effects of the objects clause both on third parties[45] and internally on the directors and shareholders.[46]

The new general right of alteration remains, however, subject to section 5 of the 1985 Act. That section provides that certain dissentients may, within 21 days after the passing of the special resolution, apply to the court for an alteration of the objects to be cancelled, and then the alteration is of no effect unless it is confirmed by the court. The application for cancellation can be made by the holders of not less than 15 per cent in nominal value of the company's issued share capital or any class thereof or, if the company is not limited by shares, not less than 15 per cent of the members. An application cannot be made by a person who consented to or voted for the alteration.

Section 5 also provides that on an application for cancellation the court may confirm the alteration of objects wholly or in part and on such terms as it thinks fit, and may adjourn the proceedings to enable an arrangement to be made for the purchase, other than by the company, of the interests of dissentient members. Alternatively, the court may provide for the purchase of the dissentient members' shares by the company or make any alterations to the memorandum or articles of the company. Such alterations have the same effect as one duly authorised by the company. If the court orders that no specified or general alterations be made to the memorandum or articles this overrides any power in the Act to the contrary.[47]

---

[45] *Post,* p. 69.
[46] *Post,* p. 72.
[47] *Post,* Chap. 18.

A company exempt from using the word "Limited" at the end of its name cannot alter its objects so as to take them outside the conditions for such exemption: section 31.

When the objects are altered, a printed copy of the special resolution, or a copy in some other form approved by him, must be delivered to the Registrar within 15 days: section 380; and, if no application is made for cancellation of the alteration, section 6 requires that a printed copy of the memorandum as altered must be delivered to the Registrar between 21 and 36 days after the date of the resolution. If an application for cancellation is made to the court, the company must forthwith give notice in the prescribed form thereof to the Registrar and, on the alteration being cancelled or confirmed, an office copy of the court order must be delivered within 15 days. In the case of confirmation, a printed copy of the memorandum as altered must also be delivered: section 6(1).

### Effect of the objects clause on corporate transactions—corporate capacity

As has been explained above the objects clause by virtue of the doctrine of *ultra vires* severely restricted the capacity of a company to make contracts, donations, etc. Any act which was outside the objects clause was *ultra vires* and void. A company could not be sued on any such act[48] and probably could not enforce it.[49] A company was, however, allowed to do things which were reasonably incidental to its stated objects.[50] Above all an *ultra vires* act could not be ratified even by all the members.[51] A further restriction on third parties was that they were deemed to have constructive notice of the contents of the objects clause. An example of the potential injustice caused by a combination of these restrictions is *Re Jon Beauforte Ltd.*[52]

A company, authorised by its memorandum to carry on business as costumiers and gown makers, started the business of making veneered panels. This was *ultra vires*. They ordered and received

---

[48] *Ashbury Railway Carriage Co. Ltd v. Riche* (1875) L.R. 7 H.L. 653.
[49] *Bell Houses Ltd v. City Wall Properties Ltd, ante; Cabaret Holdings Ltd v. Meeance Sports & Radio Club Inc.* [1982] N.Z.L.R. 673.
[50] *A.G. v. Great Eastern Railway Co.* (1880) 5 App.Cas. 473.
[51] See note 48, above.
[52] [1953] Ch. 131.

coke for this business from coke merchants. Correspondence showed that the coke suppliers had actual notice that the coke was required for the business of veneered panel manufacturers, and since they had constructive notice of the objects clause that this was an *ultra vires* activity. *Held*, they could not prove for their debts in the company's liquidation. Nor in practice could they recover the coke, which legally remained theirs, since it had been consumed.

It would have been different if the coke merchant had not known that the coke was to be used for an *ultra vires* purpose because he could have assumed that it was for an *intra vires* business.

The *ultra vires* doctrine therefore proved to be both unduly restrictive on shareholders and a trap for unwary third parties. In 1986, however, its operation was restricted by the Court of Appeal in *Rolled Steel Products Ltd v. British Steel Corporation*,[53] so that it only applied to the capacity of the company strictly construed. Earlier cases had decided that a company had no capacity to exercise any of its powers, *e.g.* to borrow or lend money, otherwise than for the authorised objects of the company. This approach was rejected in the *Rolled Steel* case. If the company has a power in its objects clause, *e.g.* to give guarantees, then it has the capacity to give a guarantee for any purpose. Thus, the common law doctrine of *ultra vires* was finally refined so that a transaction or act would only be void for lack of corporate capacity if it was not capable of falling within the terms of the objects clause either as an object or as a power.[53a]

It is important to note that the objects clause is important in relation to corporate transactions outside the area of corporate capacity because it could limit the authority of the company's agents to bind the company even though the company itself has capacity. Questions of agency are dealt with in Chapter 6, *post*. In this chapter we are concerned only with the company's own capacity.

*Statutory amendments to the ultra vires doctrine*

Section 9(1) of the European Communities Act 1972, which became the original section 35 of the 1985 Act, provided that in

---

[53] [1986] Ch. 246 (C.A.). See also *James Finlay Corporation Ltd v. R. & R.S. Mearns,* 1988 S.L.T. 302 (O.H.).

[53a] For a modern example of this approach see *Halifax Building Society v. Meridian Housing Association Ltd* [1994] 2 BCLC 540.

favour of a person dealing with a company in good faith any transaction decided upon by the directors was deemed to be within the capacity of the company. Good faith was presumed in the absence of evidence to the contrary and the third party was not bound to enquire as to the company's capacity (thus reversing the concept of constructive notice). This section proved to be defective in several areas—it did not protect the company, it was limited to dealings and so arguably not to gratuitous transactions,[54] it required a transaction decided on by the directors (all of them?) and finally no definition was provided of good faith. In *International Sales & Agencies Ltd v. Marcus*[55] it was suggested that good faith would be destroyed if the third party had actual knowledge that the transaction was *ultra vires* or could not in all the circumstances have been unaware of the *ultra vires* nature of the transaction. It was also suggested that a decision by a sole director or managing director would suffice if the full board had properly delegated the appropriate powers to him.[56]

As a result of the general dissatisfaction with the *ultra vires* concept and the perceived inadequacies of section 35, the 1989 Act substituted a new section 35 into the 1985 Act. Section 35(1) now reads:

> "The validity of an act done by a company shall not be called into question on the ground of lack of capacity by reason of anything in the company's memorandum."

This subsection effectively abolishes the *ultra vires* doctrine insofar as it affects the capacity of the company. It is actually framed so as to exclude any limits on corporate capacity in the whole memorandum but for practical purposes this will mean the objects clause.[57] Unlike its predecessor the new section 35 applies to all acts and for all purposes whatever the status of the third party.[58] An argument that the section is defective because any lack of corporate capacity is caused by what is *not* in the memorandum rather than what is included, must presumably fail

---

[54] See, *e.g. Re Halt Garage (1964) Ltd* [1982] 3 All E.R. 1016, 1024, *per* Oliver J.
[55] [1982] 3 All E.R. 551.
[56] Agreement by all the directors individually would also suffice: *T.C.B. Ltd v. Gray* [1987] Ch. 458.
[57] It is possible that the capital clause could be infringed by a corporate transaction.
[58] In any event the third party no longer has any constructive notice of the memorandum: s.711A C.A. 1985. See Chap. 6 below.

on the basis that since this section is implementing an EC directive it must be construed so as to give effect to that directive's purpose.[59] However, the section only applies to an act done by a company. It begs the question therefore as to whether those acting on the company's behalf have the power to bind the company to an act in question; *i.e.* have they the authority to act on the company's behalf so that it is an act of the company? The fact that the company has the necessary capacity is therefore only the first element in deciding whether the company is bound by an act. All these and other issues relating to corporate transactions and third parties are discussed in Chapter 6. One consequence is, however, that the company will now always have the ability to ratify any act which is contrary to its objects clause. Since such a ratification would amount to a *de facto* alteration of the objects clause it must be effected by a special resolution (new section 35(3), *post*) in the same way as any actual alteration of the clause under section 4.

Section 35 is subject to section 322A of the Companies Act 1985 where the third party is a director of the company concerned. That section is dealt with in Chapter 6, *post*.

## Effect of the objects clause on shareholders' rights and directors' duties

A company's objects clause has, in addition to its effects on corporate transactions *vis-à-vis* third parties, always fulfilled a role in the internal aspects of company law. The memorandum binds the company and its members to the same extent as if they had been signed and sealed by each member, and contained covenants on the part of each member to obseve all the provisions of the memorandum, especially the objects clause: section 14(1). The effect of this section is that generally there is a contract between the company and its members that the memorandum will be complied with.[60] One consequence of this is that any member has a personal right to seek an injunction to prevent the commission of any act which is outside the objects clause,[61]

---

[59] Following the European Court's ruling in *Marleasing S.A. v. La Commercial Internacional de Alimentacion S.A.* [1993] BCC 421; *ante* p. 17.

[60] Section 14 also applies to the articles of association. For a detailed analysis of this contract and its effects see p. 80, *post*, where what is said applies equally to the memorandum.

[61] *Colman v. Eastern Counties Railway* (1846) 10 Beav. 1.

*i.e.* the investor is entitled to see that the objects for which he invested are adhered to. Since this is a personal right no question of a derivative action arises.[62]

The 1989 Act reforms expressly preserved this right to seek an injunction but it is now subject to two major limitations, one express and one implied.

New section 35(2) of the 1985 Act provides:

> "A member of a company may bring proceedings to restrain the doing of an act which but for subsection (1) would be beyond the company's capacity; but no such proceedings shall lie in respect of an act to be done in fulfilment of a legal obligation arising from a previous act of the company."

Thus there can be no right to an injunction if the company is legally bound to the act complained of, *i.e.* if the third party can relty on the validity of the act. In deciding that, the new rules as to corporate capacity (set out above) and corporate agency (see Chapter 6, *post*) will operate. It follows that if the directors have effectively bound the company to an act outside its objects clause no action for an injunction will lie. Since, in practice, members will probably only discover the existence of the act or transaction after it has been concluded, it is unlikely, as the result of section 35(2), that they will be able to prevent it happening by an injunction.

The second, implied, limitation on the granting of injunctions stems from the fact that the objects clause is now freely alterable by a special resolution under section 4 and any action outside the objects clause can be ratified by such a resolution under section 35(3). Since an injunction is a discretionary remedy it is unlikely that one would be granted if either of the above were imminent or likely. One alternative possibility for an aggrieved minority shareholder may be to petition under section 459 of the Act on the basis of unfairly prejudicial conduct, but he would need to show in that case that acting outside the objects clause was in breach of his legitimate expectations.[63] Alternatively such a shareholder could petition under section 122(1)(g) of the Insolvency Act 1986 for a winding up on the just and equitable ground.[64]

---

[62] *Post*, p. 400.
[63] *Post*, p. 417.
[64] *Post*, p. 409.

There remains, however, a second internal consequence of the objects clause. The directors, acting in the exercise of their powers, are under a duty to act both within the limits of the objects clause and bona fide for the benefit of the company.[65] These duties are owed to the company and not to individual members *per se* so the rules as to derivative actions will apply and in general only the company may enforce them. In this connection section 35(3) provides that, notwithstanding the new rules as to corporate capacity:

"It remains the duty of the directors to observe any limitations on their powers flowing from the company's memorandum."

Since the duties of the directors are owed to the company, the company may ratify such a breach and accordingly section 35(3) allows ratification of any act which would otherwise be contrary to the limitations imposed by the memorandum by a special resolution. However, such ratification is not to affect the liability of the directors, *e.g.* to make good any losses incurred as the result of the act, unless there is a separate resolution to that effect. Special resolutions are required since such ratification will amount to a *de facto* alteration of the objects clause.

If the directors act in breach of their duties in this respect, other persons involved in the breach may well become liable to the company as constructive trustees, if they have the requisite knowledge of the situation. Again the company may only excuse their liability by a special resolution: section 35(3).[66]

## THE LIMITATION OF LIABILITY

Whether the liability of the members is limited by shares or by guarantee it is enough if the memorandum merely states that the liability of the members is limited: section 2(3).

Even though a company is exempted under section 30 from using the word "Limited" as part of its name, the memorandum must contain a statement that the liability of the members is limited.

We saw earlier that under section 24[67] a member who knows that a public company is carrying on business with less than the

---

[65] See generally, Chap. 15, *post.*
[66] The position of such third parties is discussed in Chap. 6, *post.*
[67] *Ante,* p. 27.

statutory minimum of members may become severally liable for its debts and may be sued therefor, *i.e.* not only does he lose the privilege of limited liability but the veil of incorporation is lifted and he can be sued by the creditors of the company.

## THE SHARE CAPITAL

In the case of a limited company with a share capital, section 2 provides that the memorandum must state the amount of share capital with which the company proposes to be registered and its division into shares of a fixed amount, *e.g.* one hundred thousand pounds divided into one hundred thousand shares of one pound each. This capital, called the "nominal capital" or the "authorised capital," is that which the company is authored to raise by the issue of shares. This figure is, however, purely nominal. It is important only in that it represents the aggregate amount of shares which the company may issue. The actual or allotted capital will depend on how many shares are issued. The stated amount of each share is called its nominal amount or par value. Today it is usual to have shares of a nominal amount of £1 or less each because of their marketability.[68]

It is perfectly legal to have an authorised capital expressed in more than one currency, *e.g.* £3m and 3m US dollars. There is no requirement to state the culmulative total. Similarly, individual shares can be expressed in any currency, although only one currency per share is allowed. The shares will still be of a fixed amount for the purposes of the Act, even though they may fluctuate in value owing to the exchange rates.[69]

A public company, however, cannot be registered unless its memorandum has an authorised capital figure of not less than the *authorised minimum*: section 11. This is currently £50,000, (section 118), which is a low figure in practical terms. Other financial requirements must be met by public companies before they commence business.[70] The present requirement merely relates to the shares it *may* issue.

The shares into which the nominal capital is divided may be divided into classes, *e.g.* preference and ordinary shares, but it is usual to do this in the articles rather than in the memorandum.[71]

---

[68] The 1985 Tables B and F use the figure of £1. The former Table B used the figure of £200.

[69] *Re Scandinavian Bank Group plc* [1988] Ch. 87. There are in fact several multi-currency companies on the register.

[70] *Post*, p. 153.

[71] See *Andrews v. Gas Meter Co.* [1897] Ch. 362 (C.A.).

## OTHER CLAUSES

The matters set out *supra* must be stated in the memorandum: section 2. The contents of the memorandum, however, are not restricted to these and may include any other provisions which the framers desire to insert. Sometimes the memorandum contains provisions dealing with the rights attaching to particular classes of shares such as preference shares, *e.g.* dividend and voting rights and the right to participate in the asserts on a winding up. When this is so, the articles cannot be referred to for the purposes of ascertaining the rights of the shareholders, unless there is some ambiguity to be explained or some omission to be supplemented.[72] However, the rights of the holders of particular classes of shares are now usually contained in the articles.

## THE ASSOCIATION CLAUSE AND SUBSCRIPTION

The association clause is the clause by which the subscribers (or subscriber in the case of a single member private company) to the memorandum declare that they desire to be formed into a company in pursuance of the memorandum and agree to take the number of shares set opposite their respective names. The subscription contains their names, addresses and descriptions and the number of shares which each subscribes for. The subscribers must take at least one share each. Each subscriber must write opposite his name the number of shares he takes and must sign in the presence of at least one witness. The signatures must be attested but one witness may attest all or both signatures: section 2. The Registrar requires the date of execution to be given.

In England, a minor[73] may sign the memorandum because, the contract being voidable and not void, any subsequent avoidance by him will not invalidate the registration.[74]

## ALTERATION OF THE MEMORANDUM GENERALLY

A company may alter its memorandum of association only in the cases, in the mode and to the extent for whch express provision is

---

[72] *Re Duncan Gilmour & Co. Ltd* [1952] 2 All E.R. 871.
[73] *i.e.* a person under the age of 18; see *post*, p. 210.
[74] *Re Laxon & Co. (No. 2)* [1892] 3 Ch. 555. And see s.13, *ante*, p. 22.

made in the Act: section 2(7). It has been seen that the name and objects clauses may be altered under section 28 and section 4 of the Act respectively, *ante*. The capital clause can be altered under sections 121 and 135.[75] In addition, by section 17 subject to the provisions of sections 16 and 459, *infra*, any condition in the memorandum which could have been in the articles (*i.e.* not such things as the name, the objects or the share capital, which must be in the memorandum) can be altered by special resolution, unless the memorandum itself provides for or prohibits the alteration of the condition, or it relates to class rights, *i.e.* the special rights of any class of members.

Since provisions concerning class rights are the only important provisions which may be in either the memorandum or the articles, and they cannot be altered under section 17 if they are in the memorandum, it follows that the section is unimportant in practice. Further, as was stated earlier, class rights are normally contained in the articles. The methods of varying class rights are explained later.[76]

Section 17 contains the same provisions as to application to the court for cancellation of an alteration as sections 5 and 6,[77] except that there is no equivalent of section 6(4).

Section 16 provides that neither the memorandum nor the articles can be altered so as to require a member to take up more shares, or in any way increase his liability to contribute to the share capital or otherwise pay money to the company, unless he consents in writing. Section 16 is, therefore, a "minority section," *i.e.* a section intended to prevent the minority of the members being oppressed by the majority.[78] Under section 459 the court can make an order to relieve any part of the members who are being unfairly prejudiced and such an order may alter the memorandum or the articles, in which event the company cannot make a further alteration, inconsistent with the order, without the leave of the court: section 461(3).

Section 351 provides that where a company is required to send to the Registrar any document making or evidencing an alteration in the company's memorandum or articles (other than a special resolution under section 4) the company must send with it a printed copy of the memorandum or articles as altered.

[75] See Chap. 9, *post.*
[76] *Post,* Chap. 12.
[77] *Ante,* p. 68.
[78] *Post,* Chap. 18.

Section 711 requires the Registrar to publish in the *Gazette* notice of the receipt by him of any document making or evidencing an alteration in the memorandum or articles of a company. Section 42 provides that a company cannot rely against other persons on any alteration to the memorandum or articles if it had not been officially notified (under section 711) at the material time and is not shown by the company to have been known at that time to the person concerned, or if the material time is less than 16 days after official notification and it is shown that the person concerned was unavoidabaly prevented from knowing of the event at that time.[79]

---

[79] Official notification does not, however, constitute notice to anyone; *Official Custodian of Charities v. Parway Estates Ltd* [1985] Ch. 151 (C.A.).

## Chapter 4

## ARTICLES OF ASSOCIATION

WHEREAS the memorandum is the company's charter, indicating its nationality, the nature of its business and its capital, the articles of association are the regulations for the internal arrangements and the management of the company. The articles deal with the issue of shares, transfer of shares, alteration of share capital, general meetings, voting rights, directors (including their appointment and powers), managing director, secretary, dividends, accounts, audit of accounts, winding up and various other matters which will be referred to later.

As between the memorandum and the articles, the memorandum is the dominant instrument so that in so far as their provisions conflict, the memorandum prevails,[1] although, apart from matters which by statute must be in the memorandum, reference may be made to the articles to explain an ambiguity in the memorandum or to supplement it where it is silent.[2] Section 7 provides that articles *may*, in the case of a company limited by shares, and *must* in the case of a company limited by guarantee[3] or an unlimited company,[3] be registered with the memorandum.

Table A in the Companies (Table A to F) Regulations 1985 is a model form of articles for a public company limited by shares. Any company limited by shares however may (1) adopt Table A in full, (2) adopt Table A subject to modifications, or (3) register its own articles and exclude Table A: section 8(1).

In the case of a company limited by shares, if articles are not registered, or, if articles are registered, in so far as they do not modify or exclude Table A, Table A will automatically be the company's articles: section 8(2).

A private company should register its own articles adopting all or any of the regulations in Table A as are appropriate. Min-

[1] *Re Duncan Gilmour & Co. Ltd* [1952] 2 All E.R. 871.
[2] *Liquidator of The Humboldt Redwood Co. Ltd v. Coats*, 1908 S.C. 751.
[3] Chap. 2.

imum requirements for the articles of a private company were abolished in 1980,[4] although it may still be thought desirable to indicate whether and how the transfer of shares is restricted.[5] Articles must—

(1) be printed (typewriting is not admissible);
(2) be divided into paragraphs numbered consecutively;
(3) be signed by each subscriber to the memorandum of association in the presence of at least one witness, who must attest the signature. Such attestation is sufficient in Scotland as well as in England: section 7(3).

If the memorandum states that the registered office is to be situated in Wales, the memorandum and articles to be delivered for registration under section 10 may be in Welsh but, if they are, they must be accompanied by a certified translation into English: section 710B.

## Effect of memorandum and articles

Subject to the provisions of the Act, the memorandum and articles, when registered, bind the company and the members as if they had been signed and sealed by each member, and contained convenants on the part of each member to observe their provisions: section 14. The result is:

(1) The articles (and the memorandum) form a contract binding the members to the company. Presumably the rule in *Foss v. Harbottle*[6] applies, *i.e.* an action to enforce the contract must be brought in the name of the company, except where a personal right is infringed.

The articles provided for the reference of differences between the company and any of the members to arbitration. H., a shareholder, brought an action against the company in connection with a dispute as to his expulsion from the company, *i.e.* a dispute between the company and him in his capacity, as a member. *Held*, the company was entitled to have the action stayed, as the articles constituted a contract between the

---

[4] s.28 of the 1948 Act was repealed by the 1980 Act.
[5] This was formerly one of the minimum requirements for forming a private company.
[6] Chap. 18, *post*.

company and its members in respect of their ordinary rights as members: *Hickman v. Kent or Romney Marsh Sheep-Breeders' Assocn.* [1915] 1 Ch. 881.[7]
". . . articles regulating the rights and obligations of the members generally as such do create rights and obligations between them and the company respectively": *per* Astbury J. at p. 900.
A dispute as to a director's right to inspect the company's books, and accounts, including minutes of board meetings, *i.e.* a dispute between the company and the director in his capacity as director, is not within the terms of articles like those in *Hickman's* case *supra*, even though the director is also a member. The plaintiff sued for, *inter alia*, a declaration in a representative capacity as a shareholder. It was then claimed that a director had recieved remuneration to which he was not entitled. He asked for a stay but was refused it: *Beattie v. E. & F Beattie Ltd* [1938] Ch. 708 (C.A.).

(2) Although section 14 does *not* provide that the memorandum and articles shall bind the company and the members as if they had been signed and sealed *by the company*, and contained convenants *on the part of the company* to observe their provisions, the articles constitute a contract binding the company to members.

A company declared a dividend and passed a resolution to pay it by giving to the shareholders debenture bonds bearing interest and redeemable at par, by an annual drawing, over 30 years. The articles empowered the company to declare a dividend "to be paid" to the shareholders. *Held*, the words "to be paid" meant paid in cash, and a shareholder could restrain the company from acting on the resolution on the ground that it contravened the articles: *Wood v. Odessa Waterworks Co.* (1889) 42 Ch.D. 636.

On the other hand the fact that the articles are not so executed by the company limits the time for enforcing such a contract against the company to six years and not the 12 years allowed for contracts under seal: *Re Compania de Electricidad de la Provincia de Buenos Aires Ltd.*[8]
The courts will imply two terms into this contract insofar as it relates to the powers of the directors: (a) they must be exercised in good faith and in the interests of the company; and (b) they must be exercised fairly as between shareholders (which does not mean identically).[9]

---

[7] An article prohibiting any member from taking legal proceedings against his company is contrary to public policy and not binding: *St. Johnstone Football Club Ltd v. Scottish Football Assocn. Ltd*, 1965 S.L.T. 171 (O.H.).
[8] [1978] 3 All E.R. 668. In Scotland the corresponding periods are five years and 20 years under the Prescription and Limitation (Scotland) Act 1973.
[9] *Mutual Life Insuance Co. of New York v. The Rank Organisation Ltd* [1985] BCLC 11

(3) Members are only bound by and entitled on the above mentioned contract *qua* members, *i.e.* in their capacity as members: *Beattie v. E. & F. Beattie Ltd, ante; Eley v. Positive Life Assurance Co. Ltd, post.*

(4) The articles (and the memorandum) constitute a contract between each individual member and every other member but in most cases the court will not enforce the contract as between individual members,[10] it is enforceable only through the company or, if the company is being wound up, the liquidator.

"It is quite true that . . . there is no contract in terms between the individual members of the company; but the articles . . . regulate their rights *inter se*. Such rights can only be enforced by or against a member through the company, or through the liquidator representing the company; but . . . no member has, as between himself and another member, any right beyond that which the contract with the company gives": *per* Lord Herschell in *Welton v. Saffery* [1897] A.C 299 at p. 315.

It seems that it is the rule in *Foss v. Harbottle*[11] which prevents an individual member enforcing the contract. However, the rule is irrelevant where the articles give a member a personal right. In such a case the contract is directly enforceable by one member against another *without* the aid of the company.

Articles of a private company provided that if a member intending to transfer his shares should inform the directors, the *directors* "will take the said shares equally between them at a fair value." *Held*, the articles bound the defendant directors to buy the plaintiff's shares and related to the relationship between the plaintiff as a member and the defendant, not as directors, but as members of the company,[12] and it was not necessary for the company to be a party to the action: *Rayfield v. Hands* [1960] Ch. 1.

(5) The provisions of the articles and the memorandum do not constitute a contract binding the company or any member to an outsider,[13] *i.e.* a person who is not a

---

[10] *Per* Farwell L.J. in *Salmon v. Quin and Axtens Ltd* [1909] 1 Ch. 311 (C.A.).

[11] *Post*, Chap. 18.

[12] As is usual, the directors had shares in the company and so were members.

[13] See *per* Astbury J. in *Hickman's* case at p. 900. A prospective purchaser of shares, being an outsider, cannot found on a breach of a restriction on transfer contained in the articles so as to obtain reduction of his purchase and repayment of the price: *Williams v. MacPherson*, 1990 S.L.T. 279 (O.H.).

member of the company,[14] or to a member in a capacity other than that of member, *e.g.* that of solicitor, promoter or director of the company.[15]

This is on the general principle that a person who is not a party to a contract has neither rights nor liabilities under it.

The articles provided that E. should be the solicitor to the company. He was employed as such for a time but subsequently the company ceased to employ him. *Held*, E. was not entitled to damages for breach of contract against the company. The articles did not create a contract between E. and the company: *Eley v. Positive Life Assurance Co. Ltd* (1876) 1 Ex.D. 88 (C.A.).[16]

However, if a director takes office on the footing of an article providing for remuneration for the director, although the article is not in itself a contract between the company and the director, its terms may be implied into the contract between the company and the director.

An article provided that the remuneration of the directors should be the annual sum of £1,000. The directors were employed and accepted office on the footing of the article. For some time the directors, who were also members, acted as directors but were not paid. The company went into liquidation. *Held,* the article was embodied in the contract between the company and the directors and they were entitled to recover the arrears of remuneration: *Re New British Iron Co.* [1898] 1 Ch. 324.

(6) Because of the words "Subject to the provisions of this Act" in section 14, the contract constituted by the memorandum and articles can be varied to the extent that those documents can be altered in accordance with the provisions of the Act. The extent to which the memorandum may be altered has been dealt with already.[17] It will be seen shortly that, subject to a number of restrictions, the company may always alter the articles by special resolution.

### Alteration of articles

Subject to the provisions of the Act and to the conditions in its memorandum, a company may by special resolution alter or add

---

[14] A Scots illustration is *National Bank of Scotland Glasgow Nominees Ltd v. Adamson*, 1932 S.L.T. 492 (O.H.); see also *Scottish Fishermen's Organisation Ltd v. McLean*, 1980 S.L.T.(Sh.Ct.) 76.

[15] See note 14, above.

[16] A comparable Scottish case is *Muirhead v. Forth etc. Steamboat Mutual Insce. Assocn.* (1893) 21 R. (H.L.); (1893) 20 R. 442.

[17] *Ante*, p. 83.

to its articles. An alteration or addition so made is as valid and can be altered in the same way as if originally contained in the articles: section 9. Thus a provision in the articles purporting to deprive the company of its power to alter them is void,[18] *e.g.* a provision that no alteration of the articles shall be effective without the consent of X, or that on a proposed alteration only the shares of those opposed shall have a vote.[19]

(1) By section 9 the power to alter articles is subject to the provisions of the Act, *e.g.* sections 16, 459[20] and 127.[21]

If, as is common, special rights are attached to a class of shares by the articles then the "modification of rights clause" which is either express or implied by the Act[22] (which provides for alteration of the class rights only with the consent of a specified proportion or the sanction of a specified resolution of the shareholders of the class), ensure that those class rights can only be altered with such consent or sanction.[23] Further, by section 127 dissentient holders of not less than 15 per cent of the issued shares of the class may, within 21 days after the consent was given, apply to the court to have the variation cancelled.[24] This restriction on the alteration of the articles has been held in one case to apply not only to rights actually attached to a specific class of shares, *e.g.* preference shares, but also to rights given by the articles to certain members in their capacity as members. This means that a group of shareholders can enjoy the protection of the variation of a class rights procedure if they *qua* shareholders enjoy different rights, *e.g.* of pre-emption of other shares, even though the shares they own are in no way distinguished from other shares; *i.e.* if their class rights attach to them as shareholders and not specifically to the shares themselves.[25]

[18] *Malleson v. National Insurance Corporation* [1894] 1 Ch. 200.
[19] *Per* Russell L.J. in *Bushell v. Faith* [1969] 2 Ch. 438 (C.A.) at p. 448.
[20] *Post*, Chap. 18.
[21] *Post*, p. 243.
[22] *Post*, p. 242.
[23] *Post*, p. 244.
[24] See note 22, above.
[25] *Cumbrian Newspapers Group Ltd v. Cumberland and Westmorland Herald Newspaper & Printing Co. Ltd* [1987] Ch. 1. See also *Harman v. BML Group Ltd* [1994] 2 BCLC 674.

(2) A company's power to alter its articles is subject to the conditions in the memorandum: section 9. Consequently an alteration of articles must not conflict with the memorandum.

(3) Under the general law the power to alter articles must be exercised bona fide for the benefit of the company as a whole.

Articles gave the company a lien on partly paid shares for all debts and liabilities of a member to the company. Z., on his death, owed money to the company (arrears of calls on partly paid shares), and was the only holder of fully paid shares. The articles were altered so as to give the company a lien on fully paid shares. *Held*, the alteration was valid and, as from the date of the alteration, gave the company a lien on Z.'s fully paid shares in respect of the debts contracted before the date of the alteration: *Allen v. Gold Reefs of West Africa Ltd* [1900] 1 Ch. 656 (C.A.).[26]

The power conferred on companies to alter articles "must, like all other powers, be exercised subject to those general principles of law and equity which are applicable to all powers conferred on majorities and enabling them to bind minorities. It must be exercised, not only in the manner required by law, but also bona fide for the benefit of the company as a whole, and it must not be exceeded. These conditions are always implied, and are seldom, if ever expressed": *Per* Lord Lindley M.R. at p. 671. "The fact that Zuccani's executors were the only persons practically affected at the time by the alterations made in the articles excites suspicion as to the bona fides of the company. But, although the executors were the only person who were actually affected at the time, that was because Zuccani was the only holder of paid-up shares who at the time was in arrear of calls. The altered articles applied to all holders of fully paid shares, and made no distinction between them. The directors cannot be charged with bad faith": *Per* Lord Lindley M.R. at p. 675.[27] "Further, I may say that the alteration of the articles giving the extended lien was, in my opinion, in no true sense retrospective. The lien giving was not made to take effect before the date of the alteration. It operated only from and after that date": *Per Romer* L.J. at p. 682.

It is for the shareholders, and not for the court to say whether an alteration of articles is for the benefit of the company, unless no reasonable man could so regard it.

The articles provided that S. and four others should be permanent directors of the company, unless they should become disqualified by any

---

[26] cf. *Liquidator of W. & A. M'Arthur Ltd v. Gulf Line Ltd*, 1909 S.C. 732. For comments on *Allen's* case, see *Moir v. Thomas Duff & Co. Ltd* (1900) 2 F. 1265.

[27] On this point see also *Mutual Life Insurance Co. of New York v. The Rank Organisation* [1985] BCLC 11.

one of six specified events. None of the six events had occurred. S. on 22 occasions within 12 months failed to account for the company's money he had recieved, and the articles were accordingly altered by adding a seventh event disqualifying a director, namely, a request in writing signed by all the other directors that he should resign. Such a request was made to S. who was also a shareholder. *Held*, the contract, if any, between the plaintiff and the company contained in the original articles was subject to the statutory power of alteration, and the alteration was bona fide for the benefit of the company as a whole and valid: *Shuttleworth v. Cox Bros. & Co. (Maidenhead) Ltd* [1927] 2 K.B. 9 (C.A.).

"Then the first thing to be considered is whether, in formulating the test I have mentioned, Lindley M.R. [In *Allen's* case *supra*] had in mind two separate and distinct matters; first, bona fides, the state of mind of the persons whose act is complained of, and secondly, whether the alteration is for the benefit of the company, apart altogether from the state of mind of those who procured it. In my opinion this view of the test has been negatived by this Court in *Sidebottom's* case.[28] So the test is whether the alteration of the articles was in the opinion of the shareholders for the benefit of the company. By what criterion is the Court to ascertain the opinion of the shareholders upon this question? The alteration may be so oppressive as to cast suspicion on the honesty of the persons responsible for it, or so extravagant that no reasonable man could really consider it for the benefit of the company": *per* Bankes L.J. at p. 18. See also *per* Scrutton L.J. at p. 23.

The expression "bona fide for the benefit of the company as a whole" means that the shareholders must proceed upon what, in his honest opinion, is for the benefit of the company as a whole. The phrase "the company as a whole" does not mean the company as a commercial entity, distinct from the corporators; it means the corporators as a general body. It may be asked whether what is proposed is, in the honest opinion of those who voted in its favour, for the benefit of an individual hypothetical member. Looking at the converse, an alteration of articles is liable to be impeached if its effect is to discriminate between the majority shareholders and the minority so as to give the former an advantage of which the latter are deprived. It is not necessary that persons voting for an alteration of articles should dissociate themselves altogether from their own prospects.[29]

It has been said that the phrase "corporators as a general body" means both present and future members of the company.[30]

---

[28] *infra.*

[29] *Per* Lord Evershed M.R. in *Greenhalgh v. Arderne Cinemas* [1951] Ch. 286 (C.A.) at p. 291.

[30] *Per* Megarry J. in *Gaiman v. National Association of Mental Health* [1971] 1 Ch. 317 at p. 330.

If an alteration of articles is bona fide for the benefit of the company, it is immaterial that it prejudices a minority of the members.

A private company, in which the directors held a majority of the shares, altered its articles so as to give the directors power to require any shareholder who competed with the company's business to transfer his shares, at their fair value to nominees of the directors. S., who had a minority of the shares and was in competiton with the company, brought an action for a declaration that the special resolution was invalid. *Held*, (1) as a power to expel a shareholder by buying him out was valid in the case of original articles it could be introduced in altered articles, provided that the alteration was made bona fide for the benefit of the company as a whole; (2) the alteration was so made and was valid: *Sidebottom v. Kershaw, Leese & Co.* [1920] 1 Ch. 154 (C.A.).[31]

> "I think . . . that it is for the benefit of the company that they should not be obliged to have amongst them as members persons who are competing with them in business and who may get knowledge from their membership which would enable them to compete better": *Per* Lord Sterndale M.R. at p. 166.

The principles of natural justice are not applicable in this field.[32]

It has been held that the members of a compay, acting in accordance with the Act and the constitution of the company, and subject to any necessary consent on the part of the class affected, can alter the relative voting powers attached by the articles to various classes of shares, provided that the special resolution is passed in good faith for the benefit of the company as a whole.

The issued capital of S. Ltd comprised 400,000 management shares, which under the articles carried eight votes each, and 3,600,000 ordinary shares. On the acquisition by S. Ltd of the shares in B. Ltd in consideration of the issue of 8,400,000 ordinary shares in S. Ltd, the articles were altered so as to double the votes carried by management shares in order to ensure continuity of management. The special resolution was passed by a large majority at an extraordinary general meeting of the company. The holders of management shares, directors of S. Ltd, did not vote in respect of these shares or their ordinary shares. Nor did they vote at a separate class meeting of the ordinary shareholders which sanctioned the special resolution. *Held*, the alteration was valid: *Rights and Issues Investment Trust Ltd v. Stylo Shoes Ltd* [1965] Ch. 250.[33]

---

[31] See also *Crookston v. Lindsay, Crookston & Co. Ltd*, 1922 S.L.T. 62 (O.H.).
[32] *Per* Megarry J. in *Gaiman's case, ante*, at p. 335.
[33] A comparable Scottish case is *Caledonian Insurance Co. v. Scottish American Invest. Co. Ltd*, 1951 S.L.T. 23 (O.H.).

In the absence of a prohibition in the memorandum the articles can be altered so as to authorise the issue of preference shares taking priority over existing shares although no power to issue preference shares is conferred by the memorandum or the original articles.[34]

(4)   A company cannot agree not to alter its articles.[35] The members can, however, as between themselves agree not to vote in favour of an alteration unless they all consent, provided that this does not bind future members.[36]

In *Russell v. Northern Bank Development Corp. Ltd*,[37] the House of Lords upheld an agreement between the four shareholders of a company not to vote in favour of an increase in the company's share capital unless they and the company agreed in writing. In doing so they emphasised that the company could not be bound by this agreement and only allowed the agreement to stand because it was valid as between the shareholders without the company's involvement. An agreement involving the company would have been void if it had been included in the company's articles and an extraneous agreement such as this would involve the company effectively fettering its statutory power. The agreement between the shareholders was personal to them and did not bind their successors.

(5)   If a company alters its articles in breach of a contract to which it is a party, such an alteration is valid but it may give rise to an action for damages against the company for breach of contract.

Although there were earlier decisions which suggested that a third party could obtain an injunction to prevent a company altering its articles in breach of a contract,[38] the above statement was made by Lord Porter in *Southern Foundries (1926) Ltd v.*

[34] *Andrews v. Gas Meter Co.* [1897] 1 Ch. 361 (C.A.).
[35] *Southern Foundries (1926) Ltd v. Shirlaw* [1940] A.C. 701, at p. 739, *per* Lord Porter; *Allen v. Gold Reefs of West Africa Ltd* [1900] 1 Ch. 656, at p. 671, *per* Lindley M.R.
[36] *Welton v. Saffery* [1987] A.C. 299, at p. 331, *per* Lord Davey.
[37] [1992] BCLC 1016.
[38] *Bailey v. British Equitable Assurance Co.* [1904] 1 Ch. 374; *British Murac Syndicate v. Alperton Rubber Co.* [1915] 2 Ch. 186.

*Shirlaw*[39] and approved by Scott J. in *Cumbrian Newspaper Group Ltd v. Cumberland and Westmorland Herald Newspaper and Printing Co. Ltd.*[40] It is perfectly possible for a contract to incorporate the articles as a term in the contract but any such clause is subject to alteration in the normal way.

## Inspection of articles

A company is required to furnish a copy of its memorandum (embodying any alterations) and of its articles to its members on request, on payment of not more than five pence a copy: section 19, 20.

Any person, whether a member of the company or not, may inspect a copy of the memorandum and articles of association of any company at the office of the Registrar of Companies. He may also have a copy or extract of them: section 709, 710A.

## Rectification of articles

The court has no inherent jurisdiction to rectify the articles, even if it is proved that they were not in accordance with the intention of the original signatories.[41] Similarly, the court will not imply any terms into the articles other than those which are needed to give effect to the language of the articles themselves. No question of business efficacy arises.[42]

[39] [1940] A.C. 701, at p. 740.
[40] [1987] Ch. 1.
[41] *Scott v. Frank F. Scott (London) Ltd* [1940] Ch. 794 (C.A.).
[42] *Bratton Seymour Service Co. Ltd v. Oxborough* [1992] BCLC 693.

## Chapter 5

## PROMOTERS

BEFORE a company can be formed there must be some persons who have an intention to form a company, and who take the necessary steps to carry that intention into operation. Such persons are called "promoters." Promoters stand in a fiduciary position towards the company and, as a result, they owe certain duties.

### MEANING OF TERM "PROMOTER"

The term promoter was originally defined in the Act by reference to the preparation of a prospectus only for the purposes of liability for a misstatement in a prospectus. The part of the Act was repealed by the Financial Services Act 1986 which uses the term "promoter" but does not define it.[1] However, a promoter has been described, for example, as "one who undertakes to form a company with reference to a given project and to set it going, and who takes the necessary steps to accomplish that purpose."[2]

A company may have several promoters and, as is shown by cases such as the *Leeds Theatres* case, *post*, one existing company may promote another new company.

Persons who give instructions for the preparation and registration of the memorandum and articles of association are promoters. So, too, are persons who obtain the directors (very often a promoter is himself a prospective director), issue a prospectus, negotiate underwriting contracts or a contract for the purchase of property by the company, or procure capital.

A person may become a promoter after the company is incorporated, *e.g.* by issuing a prospectus or preparing listing particulars, or by procuring capital to enable the company to

[1] F.S.A. 1986 s.150(6). The former definition was in s.67 of the 1985 Act.
[2] *Per* Cockburn C.J. in *Twycross v. Grant* (1877) 2 C.P.D. 469 (C.A.) at p. 541.

carry out a preliminary agreement. Whether a person is actually a promoter and, if so, the date when he became one and whether he is still one, are questions of fact.

A person who has taken no active part in the formation of a company and the raising of the necessary share capital but has left it to others to get up the company on the understanding that he will profit from the operation is a promoter.[3]

Anyone who acts merely as the employee or agent of a promoter is not himself a promoter. A solicitor, therefore, who merely does the legal work necessary to the formation of a company is not a promoter.[4]

At one time the business of a company promoter was almost a separate business in itself but this is not so today. Further, the increasingly strict provisions of successive Companies Acts, culminating in the Financial Services Act 1986, in relation to the issue and contents of listing particulars or a prospectus have almost eliminated the fraudulent company promoter.

## POSITION AND DUTIES OF PROMOTERS

A promoter is not an agent for the company which he is forming because a company cannot have an agent before it comes into existence.[5] Furthermore, he is usually not treated as a trustee for the future company.[6] However, from the moment he acts with the company in mind, a promoter stands in a fiduciary position[7] towards the company and therefore he must not make any secret profit out of the promotion, *e.g.* a profit on a sale of property to the company. These liabilities are independent of any liability for misstatements etc. in listing particulars or a prospectus (see Chapter 7).

A promoter must disclose a profit which he is making out of the promotion to either—

---

[3] See *per* Lindley J. in *Emma Silver Mining Co. Ltd v. Lewis* (1879) 4 C.P.D. 396 at p. 408, and *Tracy v. Mandalay Pty. Ltd* (1952–53) 88 C.L.R. 215.

[4] *Re Great Wheal Polgooth Ltd* (1883) 53 L.J.Ch. 42.

[5] *Kelner v. Baxter* (1866) L.R. 2 C.P. 174, *post*, p. 97; *Tinnevelly Sugar Refining Co. Ltd v. Mirrlees, Watson & Yaryan Co Ltd* (1894) 21 R. 1009.

[6] *Omnium Electric Palaces Ltd v. Baines* [1914] 1 Ch. 332, *post*; *Edinburgh Northern Tramways Co. v. Mann* (1896) 23 R. 1056, *post*.

[7] *Henderson v. The Huntington Copper etc. Co. Ltd* (1877) 5 R. (H.L.) 1; (1877) 4 R. 294; the fiduciary relationship was regarded as arising from agency rather than from trust in *Edinburgh Northern Tramways Co. v. Mann* (1896) 23 R. 1056.

(1)　an *independent* board of directors[8], or
(2)　the existing and intended shareholders, *e.g.* by making disclosure in a prospectus.[9]

The requirement of an independent board of directors is one which, in most cases, cannot be complied with, as the promoters, or some of them, are usually the first directors of the company. In the formation of a private company, the promoter usually sells his business to a company, of which he is managing director, and in which he is the largest shareholder, but, nevertheless, the transaction cannot be impeached on the ground that there is no independent board of directors.[10]

> "After *Salomon's Case* I think it is impossible to hold that it is the duty of the promoters of a company to provide it with an independent board of directors, if the real truth is disclosed to those who are induced by the promoters to join the company.[11]

If there is no disclosure to an independent board, there must be *full* disclosure of the profit made by the promoters to the existing and intended shareholders, either in a prospectus or in some other way.

**Remedies for breach of duty**

If a promoter fails to make full disclosure of a profit made by him out of the promotion the following remedies may be open to the company. Since the promoter's duties are owed to the company the rule in *Foss v. Harbottle*[12] is relevant to their enforcement.

(1)　Where the promoter has, *e.g.* sold his own property to the company, the company may rescind the contract and recover the purchase-money paid.

A syndicate, of which E. was the head, purchased an island in the West Indies said to contain valuable mines of phosphates for £55,000. E.

---

[8] *Erlanger v. New Sombrero Phosphate Co.* (1878) 3 App.Cas. 1218 (P.C.) *post*; *Tracy v. Mandalay Pt. Ltd, ante.*
[9] *Lagunas Nitrate Co. v. Lagunas Syndicate* [1899] 2 Ch. 392 (C.A.); *Scottish Pacific Coast Mining Co. Ltd v. Falkner, Bell & Co.* (1888) 15 R. 290.
[10] *Salomon v. Salomon Co. Ltd* [1897] A.C. 22, *ante*, p. 24.
[11] *Per* Lindley M.R. in the *Lagunas* case, above, at p. 426.
[12] *Post*, Chap. 18.

formed a company to buy this island, and a contract was made between X., a nominee of the syndicate, and the company for its purchase at £110,000. *Held,* as there had been no disclosure by the promoters of the profit they were making, the company was entitled to rescind the contract and recover the purchase-money from E. and the other members of the syndicate: *Erlanger v. New Sombrero Phosphate Co.* (1878) 3 App.Cas. 1218 (P.C.).

The right of rescission may be lost in a number of ways. For example, it will be lost if the parties cannot be restored to their original positions, as where the property has been worked so that its character has been altered.[13] However, even if restitution is strictly not possible, rescission may be allowed if restitution is substantially possible. The right to rescind will also be lost if third parties have acquired rights for value, by mortgage or otherwise, under the contract.[14]

(2)  The company may compel the promoter to account for any profit he has made.

Intending to buy property and to form a company and resell the property to the company or another purchaser, a syndicate of four persons bought charges on the property at a discount. They afterwards bought the property for £140,000, formed a company of which they were the first directors and resold the property to the company for £180,000. As a result of this, they made a profit of £40,000 on the property and one of £20,000 on the charges which were paid off in full with the £140,000 received for the property. A prospectus was issued, disclosing the profit of £40,000 but not that of £20,000. It appears that rescission had become impossible. *Held,* the £20,000 was a secret profit made by a syndicate as promoters of the company and they were bound to pay it to the company: *Gluckstein v. Barnes* [1900] A.C. 240.

(3)  The company may sue the promoter for damages for breach of his fiduciary duty.

The F. Co. contracted to purchase two music-halls for £24,000 and had the property conveyed to its nominee, R., intending to sell it to the T. Co. when formed. The F. Co. then promoted the T. Co. and agreed to sell the music-halls to it for £75,000 and directed R. to convey them. The board of directors of T. Co. was not an independent board. A prospectus was issued to the public by the T. Co., giving R. as the vendor, and not disclosing the interest of F. Co. or the profit it was

---

[13] As in *Lagunas Nitrate Co. v. Lagunas Syndicate* [1899] 2 Ch. 392 (C.A.).
[14] As in *Re Leeds and Hanley Theatres of Varieties Ltd* [1902] 2 Ch. 809, *post*, where the mortgagee of the property had sold it.

making. *Held,* the prospectus should have disclosed that F. Co. was the real vendor and the amount of profit it was making. For breach of their fiduciary duty to those invited to take shares the promoters were liable in damages to the company and the measure of damages was the promoters' profit: *Re Leeds and Hanley Theatres of Varieties Ltd* [1902] 2 Ch. 809 (C.A.).

Where promoters sell their own property to the company, the company cannot affirm the contract and at the same time ask for an account of profits or for damages as this would be, in effect, asking the court to vary the contract of sale and order the defendants to sell their assets at a lower price.[15]

## PAYMENT FOR PROMOTION SERVICES

A promoter has no right against the company to payment for his promotion services in the absence of an express contract with the company. In England such a contract will normally have to be under seal since the company cannot make a valid contract before incorporation and when the contract can be made the consideration by the promoter will normally be past.[16] In the absence of such a contract he cannot even recover from the company payments he has made in connection with the formation of the company.

The rule that consideration must not be past is not part of Scots law, and the promoter of a Scottish company might be entitled to found on a suitably worded provision in the memorandum or articles to the effect of recovering from the company payments made by him in connection with the formation of the company.[17] The success of a promoter's claim against the company seems to depend on his establishing that the relevant provision creates a *jus quaesitum tertio* in his favour. Where such a right is established, a promoter is entitled to remuneration for professional services rendered.[18] If no such right is established, neither promoters nor experts employed by them have a right to remuneration from the new company; such experts have no claim except against the persons who employed them, namely the promoters.[19]

---

[15] *Re Cape Breton Co.* (1885) 29 Ch.D. 795 (C.A.); *Jacobus Marler Estates Ltd v. Evatt* 1[1971] A.C. 793 (P.C.).

[16] *Clinton's Claim* [1908] 2 Ch. 515 (C.A.).

[17] *Scott v. Money Order Co. etc. Ltd* (1870) 42 Sc. Jur. 212.

[18] See, *e.g. Edinburgh Northern Tramways Co. v. Mann* (1896) 23 R. 1056.

[19] *Per* Lord M'Laren in *J. M. & J. H. Robertson v. Beatson, M'Leod & Co. Ltd,* 1908, S.C. 921 at p. 928.

Any amount or benefit paid or given within the two preceding years, or intended to be paid or given, to a promoter must normally be disclosed in a prospectus or listing particulars.[20]

## SUSPENSION OF PROMOTERS

A person who has been convicted on indictment of any offence in connection with the promotion or formation of a company may have an order made against him by the court that he shall not, without leave of the court, be a director, liquidator, receiver or take part in the management of a company for a period of up to 15 years: Company Directors Disqualification Act 1986, section 2.[21]

---

[20] F.S.A. 1986, ss.144. See Chap. 7, *post.*
[21] *Post,* p. 373.

## Chapter 6

## CORPORATE TRANSACTIONS

THIS chapter deals, first, with contracts and other transactions made on behalf of a company before it is formed, and secondly, with those made after the company has been formed. Since a company is an artificial person it cannot physically enter into a transaction but must always do so either through a human agent or in writing under its common seal. This chapter is therefore also concerned with the impact of company law on the rules of agency as to the making of such transactions and the law relating to contracts under seal involving companies. Finally, the chapter concludes with a note on a procedural rule which may prevent a company from enforcing its contracts if it is unable to provide security against having to pay the defendant's costs if the action is unsuccessful.

## CONTRACTS MADE BEFORE INCORPORATION OF COMPANY

### Effect on company

If, before the formation of a company, some person purports to make a contract on its behalf, or as trustee for it, *e.g.* a contract for the sale of property to the company, the contract, or "preliminary agreement" as it is sometimes called, is not binding on the company when it is formed, even if the company takes the benefit of the contract. Before incorporation the company lacks capacity to make the contract[1] and an agent cannot contract on behalf of a principal who is not in existence.[2]

---

[1] "If somebody does not exist they cannot contract," *per* Harman J. in *Rover International Ltd v. Cannon Film Sales Ltd* [1987] 1 W.L.R. 1597, at p. 1599.

[2] This does not apply to a company which contracts in a new name prior to the change of name becoming operative. Such a company is at all times in existence: *Oshkosh B'Gosh Incorporated Ltd v. Dan Marbel Inc. Ltd* (1988) 4 BCC 795; *Vic Spence Associates v. Balchin,* 1990 S.L.T. 10 (O.H.).

Solicitors, on the instructions of persons who afterwards became directors of the company, prepared the memorandum and articles of association of the company, and paid the registration fees. *Held*, the company was not liable to pay their costs: *Re English and Colonial Produce Co. Ltd* [1906] 2 Ch. 435 (C.A.).[3]

Similarly, a company cannot, after incorporation, enforce a contract made in its name before incorporation, or sue for damages for breach of such a contract since it was not a party to that contract.

N. Co. agreed with a person acting on behalf of a future company, P. Co., that N. Co. would grant a mining lease to P. Co. P. Co. discovered coal whereupon N. Co. refused to grant the lease. *Held*, P. Co. could not compel N. Co. to grant the lease: *Natal Land etc. Co. Ltd v. Pauline Colliery Syndicate Ltd* [1904] A.C. 120 (P.C.).[4]

Further, such a contract cannot be ratified by the company after it is incorporated—the company was not a principal with contractual capacity at the time when the contract was made—although, as is explained later, the contract may be novated.[5]

The Gravesend Royal Alexandra Hotel Company Ltd was being formed to buy an hotel from K. At a time when all concerned knew that the company had not been formed, a written contract was made "on behalf of" the proposed company by A, B and C for the purchase of £900 worth of wine from K. The company was formed, and the wine handed over to it and consumed, but before payment was made the company went into liquidation. *Held*, A, B and C were personally liable on the contract, and no ratification could release them from their liability: *Kelner v. Baxter* (1866) L.R. 2 C.P. 174.

"Where a contract is signed by one who professes to be signing 'as agent,' but who has no principal existing at the time, and the contract would be altogether inoperative unless binding on the person who signed it, he is bound thereby; and a stranger cannot by a subsequent ratification relieve him from that responsibility": *per* Erle C.J. at p. 183.

---

[3] For Scots law *cf.* Lord President Dunedin in *Welsh & Forbes v. Johnston* (1906) 8 F. 453 at p. 457, and Lord M'Laren in *J. M. & J. H. Robertson v. Beatson, M'Leod & Co. Ltd*, 1908 S.C. 921 at p. 928 *ante* p. 94. See also *F. J. Neale (Glasgow) Ltd v. Vickery*, 1971 S.L.T. (Sh.Ct.) 88.

[4] *Molleson and Grigor v. Fraser's Trustees* (1881) 8 R. 630 is a Scottish authority.

[5] *Kelner v. Baxter*, below; *Tinnevelly Sugar Refining Co. Ltd v. Mirrlees, Watson & Yaryan Co. Ltd* (1894) 21 R. 1009. See also *Cumming v. Quartzag Ltd*, 1980 S.C. 276, in which, following the *Tinnevelly* case, the Court of Session held that an agreement made on behalf of a company to be incorporated could not give rise to a *jus quaesitum tertio* in favour of the company when incorporated; Hector L. MacQueen, *Promoters' Contracts, Agency and the Jus Quaesitum Tertio*, 1982 S.L.T. (News) 257.

This situation cannot be remedied by the operation of the doctrine of estoppel by convention. That requires an assumption of fact, *i.e.* that the company would be bound, by both parties to a contract prior to the "agreement". Since the company was not then in existence it could make no such assumptions.[6]

### Effect on individuals

At common law, if an individual contracts as "agent"[7] for a future company, whether there is a contract between him and the other person involved depends upon whether the agent was intended to be a party to the contract.[8] That is a question of construing the terms of the written contract and does not depend simply upon the way that the individual signed the contract.[9]

In *Kelner v. Baxter,* above, it was intended that A, B and C should contract personally. In the *Newborne* case, the intention was that only the future company should contract.

Tinned ham was sold to S. Ltd. The contract was "We have this day sold to you . . . (Signed) Leopold Newborne (London) Ltd." The signature was typed and underneath was written "Leopold Newborne." The market price of ham fell and S. Ltd. refused to take delivery. When an action was brought it was found that Leopold Newborne (London) Ltd had not been incorporated at the time of the contract and Leopold Newborne tried to enforce the contract in his own name. *Held,* neither Leopold Newborne (London) Ltd nor Leopold Newborne could enforce the contract. It was not a case of an agent undertaking to do certain things himself as agent for somebody else. It was a contract in which a company purported to sell. Leopold Newborne did not purport to contract as principal or agent—the contract purported to be made by Leopold Newborne (London) Ltd, on whose behalf it was signed by a future director. "This company was not in existence and . . . the signature on that document, and indeed, the document itself . . . is a complete nullity": *Newborne v. Sensolid (Great Britain) Ltd* [1954] 1 Q.B. 45.[10]

The position of the individual was, however, changed substantially by section 9(2) of the European Communities Act 1972,

---

[6] *Rover International Ltd v. Cannon Film Sales Ltd* [1987] 1 W.L.R. 1597.

[7] Strictly, one cannot be agent for a principal not yet in existence.

[8] *Phonogram Ltd v. Lane* [1982] Q.B. 938 at 945, *per* Oliver L.J. Approved in *Cotronic (UK) Ltd v. Denozie* [1991] BCLC 721 (C.A.) and *Badgerhill Properties Ltd v. Cottrell* [1991] BCLC 805 (C.A.).

[9] *e.g.* whether he signs "per pro" the company or "for and on behalf of the company". See note 8 above.

[10] See also *Cotronic (UK) Ltd v. Denozie* [1991] BCLC 721 (C.A.) and *Badgerhill Properties Ltd v. Cottrell* [1991] BCLC 805 (C.A.).

which became section 36(4) of the 1985 Act. That section was repealed by the 1989 Act and replaced by section 36C of the 1985 Act.[11] The latest section retains, however, the same concepts as its predecessor.

Section 36C(1) provides:

> "A contract which purports to be made by or on behalf of a company at a time when the company has not been formed has effect, subject to any agreement to the contrary, as one made with the person purporting to act for the company or as agent for it, and he is personally liable on the contract accordingly."[12]

This means that in circumstances like those in *Newborne's* case, *ante,* today, unless there is an agreement to the contrary, there will be a contract between the individual who purports to act for the company and the other person involved. Presumably such individuals will be entitled to sue on the contract as well as being liable to be sued on it. The words "subject to any agreement to the contrary" allow for the case where there is a novation.

In *Phonogram Ltd v. Lane*[13], the Court of Appeal considered the effect of old section 36(4) which was identical in all relevant respects to section 36C. They held that it rendered the individual "agent" liable even though the company was not at the time in the course of formation.[14] Further a contract can be "purported" to be made by a company even though both parties to the contract knew that the company had not then been formed. They also considered that signing the contract as an agent, or as in the *Newborne* case, *ante,* would not amount to an agreement to the contrary so as to avoid personal liability. Lord Denning M.R. considered that only a clear exclusion of personal liability would suffice.

Section 36C only applies, however, to a contract made on behalf of a company which has not been formed. Thus it has been held not to apply to a contract made on behalf of a company

[11] Introduced by s.130(4) C.A. 1989.
[12] Subs. 36C(2) extends this liability to deeds in England and obligations in Scotland. The section applies equally to companies incorporated outside Great Britain: the Foreign Companies (Execution of Documents) Regulations (S.I. 1994 No. 950).
[13] [1982] Q.B. 938.
[14] A contrary argument based on the French text of the Directive implemented by the 1972 Act was rejected.

which no longer existed[15] or on behalf of a company which had been formed but was not properly named in the contract.[16]

## New contract after incorporation—novation

Of course, a company may, after incorporation enter into a new contract with the other party to the same effect as a contract made on its behalf before incorporation, in which event there is a novation, *i.e.* the old contract is discharged and replaced by the new. Such a new contract may be inferred from the acts of the parties after incorporation.

J. had agreed with W., acting on behalf of a company about to be formed, to sell certain property to the company. After the company's incorporation, the directors resolved to adopt the agreement, and to accept J.'s offer to take part of the purchase-money in debentures instead of cash. *Held,* a contract was entered into by the company with J. to the effect of the previous agreement as subsequently modified: *Howard v. Patent Ivory Mfg. Co.* (1888) 38 Ch.D. 156.[17]

However, such a new contract will not be inferred if the acts of the company after incorporation are due to the mistaken belief that it is bound by the contract made before incorporation.

A contract was made between W. and D., who was acting on behalf of an intended company, for the grant of a lease to the company. The company, on its formation, entered on the land the subject of the lease and began to erect buildings on it but did not make any fresh agreement with respect to the lease. *Held,* the agreement, being made before the formation of the company, was not binding on the company, and was incapable of ratification; and the acts of the company were done in the erroneous belief that the agreement was binding on the company and not evidence of a fresh agreement between W. and the company: *Re Northumberland Avenue Hotel Co.* [1886] 33 Ch.D. 16 (C.A.).

## Modern practice

Agreements to sell property to a company about to be formed are not now, as a rule, made with a person expressed to be acting

---

[15] *Cotronic (UK) Ltd v. Denozie* [1991] BCLC 721.
[16] *Badgerhill Properties Ltd v. Cottrell* [1991] BCLC 805.
[17] *cf. James Young & Sons Ltd and Liquidator v. Gowans (James Young & Sons' Trustee)* (1902) 10 S.L.T. 85 (O.H.) and *Park Business Interiors Ltd v. Park,* 1991 S.L.T. 818 (O.H.) (shares allotted for pre-incorporation expenses where company after incorporation had accepted liability to pay those expenses).

on behalf of the company, because of the liability incurred by such person, and the absence of liability incurred by the company unless there is a novation. Although the other party will not be bound before the company is formed, the modern practice is for the promoters[18] to have prepared, before the company is incorporated, a draft agreement to which the company is expressed to be a party, and for the agreement to be executed by the other party and on behalf of the company after incorporation, pursuant to a clause in the company's memorandum to that effect. If, as is common, a company is being formed to acquire the promoters' business,[19] it does not matter that the promoters are not bound.

## Contracts Made Prior to Commencement of Business

Any contract made by a public company after it is incorporated but before it is entitled to commence business[20] is nevertheless valid, but in such cases if the company fails to comply with its obligations within 21 days of being asked to do so the directors are liable to compensate the other party for any loss or damage consequent on its inability to commence business: section 117(8).

## Form of Contracts

A company may make contracts either in writing under its common seal or by an agent acting within his authority on the company's behalf: section 36.[21] The rules as to the form of contracts for companies are the same as those for individuals, *e.g.* as to whether the contract needs to be in writing or under seal or can be made orally.

### Execution of documents—England and Wales

A company may execute any document by affixing its common seal in accordance with the articles (see below). However, a company is not required to have a common seal and whether it

---

[18] *Ante*, Chap. 5.
[19] *Ante*, p. 92.
[20] See *post*, p. 153.
[21] This section together with sections 36A and 36B, below, applies with modifications to overseas companies: the Foreign Companies (Execution of Documents) Regulations (S.I. 1994 No. 950).

has one or not it may execute a document in such a way that it will have the same effect as one made under the seal: section 36A.[22] That section provides that any document signed by a director and the company secretary or by two directors, and expressed, in either case, to be executed by the company (by any form of words) will be treated as if the seal had been affixed.

Further, it they intend the document to be a deed and that is made clear on the face of the document, it will take effect as a deed upon delivery. Such delivery will also be execution of the deed unless a contrary intention is proved.[23]

To protect third parties acting in good faith for valuable consideration,[24] a document which *purports* to be signed by a director and secretary or two directors will be as valid as if it was signed by actual directors and/or the actual secretary provided the other conditions are fulfilled. Thus third parties need not investigate the validity of the appointment of those signing the document.[25]

### Execution of documents—Scotland

Under Scots law a document is validly executed by a company if it is signed on behalf of the company by a director or the secretary or by a person authorised to sign the document on its behalf, except that where authentication is required a document is validly executed by a company, and is probative, if it is subscribed on behalf of the company by—

(a) two of the directors;
(b) a director and the secretary ; or
(c) two persons authorised to subscribe the document on behalf of the company.

The document need not be witnessed or sealed with the company's common seal (which a company is no longer required to have): section 36B as substituted by the Law Reform (Miscellaneous Provisions) (Scotland) Act 1990.

### Use of the seal

Table A, article 101 provides: "The seal shall only be used by the authority of the directors or of a committee of directors authorised by

---

[22] This section only applies to England and Wales.
[23] Similar provisions apply to deeds executed by individuals: see s.1 of the Law of Property (Miscellaneous Amendments) Act 1989.
[24] Including lessees and mortgagees.
[25] This is similar to the general protection given to conveyancers generally in s.74 Law of Property Act 1925.

the directors. The directors may determine who shall sign any instrument to which the seal is affixed and unless otherwise so determined it shall be signed by a director and by the secretary or by a second director."

A company which continues to have a common seal and whose objects comprise the transaction of business in foreign countries may, if authorised by its articles, have for use in any place outside the United Kingdom, an official seal. The official seal must be a facsimile of the company's common seal, with the addition on its face of the name of every place where it is to be used: section 39.

Section 40 allows a company which continues to have a common seal to have an official seal for use in sealing securities issued by the company and for sealing documents creating or evidencing securities issued by the company. This official seal must be a facsimile of the common seal of the company with the addition on its face of the word "Securities".

A document requiring *authentication* by a company is sufficiently authenticated by the signature of a director, secretary or other authorised officer, and need not be under seal: section 41.

**Bills of exchange**

Bills of exchange and promissory notes can be drawn, accepted or indorsed on behalf of a company by any person acting under the company's authority: section 37. Officers who sign their own names without making it clear that they are signing on behalf of the company may incur personal liability.[26] But when a director signs the modern form of company cheque with the company name and account number printed on it, he has been held to be signing only as an agent and is not personally liable on the cheque, even though he has not expressly signed on behalf of the company or as its agent.[27]

## Transactions by Agency

Unless a company contracts in writing using its common seal, or the equivalent procedures discussed in the previous section, it can

---

[26] *Brebner v. Henderson*, 1925 S.C. 643; contrast *McLean v. Stuart and Others*, 1970 S.L.T. (Notes) 77 (O.H.).
[27] *Bondina Ltd v. Rollaway Shower Blinds* [1986] 1 W.L.R. 517 (C.A.).

only enter into a transaction through the medium of agency, *i.e.* by a transaction made by an agent acting on behalf of the company who either has authority to bind the company to that transaction at the time or whose actions are subsequently validly ratified by the company. In general, therefore, the central question is whether the agent has the requisite authority to bind the company (his principal), and in this respect companies are in many ways no different from individuals—the ordinary rules of agency apply as to establishing authority. But companies are artificial persons with a constitution laid down by the memorandum and articles. We have already seen, in Chapter 3, that the objects clause in the memorandum used to restrict the capacity of the company itself to enter into transactions which were outside that clause and a company clearly cannot authorise an agent to do what it itself had no capacity to effect. Section 35 of the Act has removed any such constitutional restrictions based solely on corporate capacity[28] but the memorandum and articles may equally restrict the authority of a company's agents to act on its behalf. In such a case any person dealing with the company would not be able to rely on an agent having authority if the transaction was contrary to the company's constitution, *e.g.* if it was contrary to a restriction in either the memorandum or articles.

## Limitations under the company's constitution—the position prior to 1991

The effect of company law on the general law of agency therefore has been that even if an agent is otherwise acting within his authority to bind the company, a third party will not be able to enforce the transaction if the agent was acting contrary to the company's constitution. Since a third party was deemed to have constructive notice of all the company's registered documents, including the memorandum and articles, he could not rely on the agent having authority where the act was contrary to such documents. This doctrine was, however, subject to an exception, known as the rule in *Royal British Bank v. Turquand*,[29] whereby if an agent was acting apparently consistently with the company's constitution, the third party was not affected by any internal

---

[28] *Ante*, p. 69.
[29] (1856) 6 El. & Bl. 327.

irregularity, *e.g.* the lack of disclosure of a director's interest in a contract to the board as required by the articles, since he could not have discovered whether such disclosure had or had not been made.[30] Third parties did not have constructive notice of matters not on the register.[31] Only actual notice of the irregularity would affect him.[32]

This situation was substantially changed, however, in 1972 by section 9(1) of the European Communities Act 1972, which became section 35 of the 1985 Act. That section, which attempted to remove the limits on corporate capacity,[33] also restricted the effect of limitations on the authority of the company's agents arising from the company's constitution. It suffered from serious defects, however, which have already been noted in Chapter 3, and was repealed by the 1989 Act. That Act substituted a new section 35 and added new sections 35A and 35B into the 1985 Act. These new sections apply as to the effects of the company's constitution on the authority of a company's agents as from 1991 onwards. For a detailed discussion of the position prior to 1991, readers are referred to the thirteenth edition of this work.

### Limitations under the company's constitution—the position from 1991

We have already seen in Chapter 3 that, from 1991 onwards, nothing in a company's memorandum can affect the capacity of a company to enter into a transaction, following the new section 35, and further that no one has constructive notice of any entry on the company's register, *e.g.* of the memorandum and articles, by virtue of section 711A. In addition, new section 35A removes any constitutional limitations on the powers of the directors and others to act on behalf of the company so far as bona fide third parties are concerned, whilst preserving the existing internal rights of members to control the directors if they do act contrary to the company's constitution. The position is substantially dif-

---

[30] *Cowan de Groot Properties Ltd v. Eagle Trust plc* [1991] BCLC 1045.
[31] Thus whether or not an ordinary resolution had been passed would not matter since there is no requirement to register an ordinary resolution, whereas the lack of a required special resolution authorising the deal would destroy the agent's authority—special resolutions must be registered.
[32] But see p. 118, *post.*
[33] *Ante*, p. 68.

ferent, however, if the third party is himself a director of the company concerned (see below).

Section 35A(1) provides that:

> "In favour of a person dealing with a company in good faith, the power of the board of directors to bind the company, or authorise others to do so, shall be deemed to be free of any limitation under the company's constitution."

This therefore removes any restrictions imposed upon the authority of the directors, either to act themselves or to empower others to act, by the company's constitution if the third party is dealing in good faith. If section 35A(1) applies then the sole question is whether the agent was acting within his authority apart from the company's constitution. What amounts to authority is considered below.

It is necessary to analyse section 35A(1). First, the section only applies in favour of a third party and not the company. This is a distinction more apparent than real, however, since the company, like any other principal, may always ratify any agent's acts, unless they are illegal, and then enforce the transaction. Such ratification will need to be by special resolution only if the transaction is contrary either to a provision in the memorandum or articles since a special resolution would be required to alter such a provision.[34]

Second, that person must be "dealing with a company." Section 35(2)(a) provides that anyone who is a party to any transaction[35] or other act to which the company is a party is dealing with that company.[36] The use of the words "transaction" and "act" seem to indicate that gratuitous acts will be included.

Thirdly, the person dealing with a company must be acting in good faith. Section 35A(2)(b) provides that bad faith is not to be assumed simply because the third party knew that the act was contrary to the directors' powers under the constitution. This was

---

[34] Under ss.4 and 9 respectively. S.35(3) makes the position clear with respect to the memorandum, but it must equally apply to the articles. Ratification of a breach of the articles cannot be by anything less than a special resolution which must be registered.

[35] See *T.C.B. Ltd v. Gray* [1986] Ch. 621 for the court's views as to what constitutes a transaction in this context.

[36] This clarifies earlier judicial statements on a similar phrase in the former section 35, see, *e.g. International Sales and Agencies Ltd v. Marcus* [1982] 3 All E.R. 551, *Re Halt Garage (1982) Ltd* [1982] 3 All E.R. 1016, *International Factors (N.I.) Ltd v. Streeve Construction Ltd* [1984] N.I.J.B.

intended to reverse the judicial interpretation of the phrase in the previous section 35 that good faith would be defeated if the third party actually knew or could not in all the circumstances have been unaware of the defect.[37] Something more than mere awareness is now required, presumably understanding, although it is unclear whether this is to be subjectively or objectively tested. What was intended no doubt was a distinction between notice and knowledge, with only the latter counting, as it does for liability under constructive trusts.[38] The wording of the section is such, however, that a third party may on the one hand be able to plead the validity of the transaction against the company under section 35A on the basis that, although he has objective but not subjective knowledge of the defect, that is not enough to defeat a presumption of good faith, whilst on the other hand he may be liable to the company as a constructive trustee under the knowing receipt category because he has such objective knowledge of the defect.

The position of the third party with respect to good faith is further strengthened by section 35A(2)(c) which requires a presumption of good faith until the contrary is proved, and section 35B which provides that the third party is not bound to enquire whether a transaction[39] is either contrary to the memorandum or is subject to any constitutional limitations on the powers of the directors.

In favour of such a third party, the powers of the directors to bind the company or authorise others to do so are to be free of any limitations under the company's constitution. A company's constitution includes its memorandum and articles and under section 35A(3) any resolution of the company or of a class of shareholders and any shareholder agreement.[40] The freedom given by section 35A(1) thus applies to any acts of the directors as a whole or of any agent to whom they have delegated the transaction expressly or impliedly. The section is not intended to extend the authority of an agent, simply to remove fetters if he

---

[37] *International Sales and Agencies Ltd v. Marcus (supra)*, approved in *International Factors (N.I.) Ltd v. Streeve Construction Ltd (supra)*.

[38] *Re Montague's S.T.* [1987] Ch. 264. For the liability of third parties as constructive trustees, see *Hanbury and Martin, Modern Equity* (14th ed., 1993), pp. 300 *et seq*.

[39] But not in this case an act.

[40] All but special resolutions were covered by the rule in *Turquand's* case (see n.29 above) which is still valid, in any event.

would otherwise have authority to bind the company. It is possible, however, that in one respect at least it has extended the ordinary rules of agency.[41]

If the third party is not acting in good faith, the company may always ratify the transaction either by an ordinary resolution, or by special resolution if the defect relates to the memorandum or articles.[42]

## Directors as third parties

The general rule, discussed above, that if the third party dealing with the company is in good faith no restrictions imposed upon the company's directors by the company's constitution will affect him, is modified where that third party is himself a director of that company or of its holding company.[43] In such a case if the board exceed any limitation on their powers under the company's constitution then the transaction[44] is voidable at the instance of the company whether or not the director is dealing in good faith: section 322A(1)(2). The transaction remains valid, however, until it is avoided by the company, unless it is void for some other reason (*e.g.* if it is illegal under the Act): section 322A(4).

The company will lose the right to rescind (avoid) the transaction in any of the following circumstances:

(i)    restitution of property supplied is no longer possible;
(ii)   the company is indemnified against any loss or damage arising from the transaction;
(iii)  bona fide purchasers without actual notice of the defect have acquired rights which would be affected by the avoidance, *e.g.* if the subject matter has been deposited as security with a bank; or
(iv)   the transaction is ratified by the company either by an ordinary or special resolution[45] as necessary.

It is important to remember that to be valid the transaction does not need to be ratified in this way, it is valid unless avoided by

[41] See p. 113, *post.*
[42] See note 34 above.
[43] The modification also applies to persons connected with such a director or an associated company of such a director, as defined in s.346.
[44] Defined so as to include any "act".
[45] A special resolution will be needed if the defect arises from limitations in the memorandum or articles. See note 34 above.

the company. The right to rescind or avoid a transaction may be limited under the general law, *e.g.* by undue delay.

Where there are two (or more) persons dealing with a company, one of whom is a director and the other is neither a director nor connected with one, and where that second person is dealing in good faith then he may continue to rely on the protection given by section 35A, above, although the director will be subject to section 322A. To avoid the difficult situation of a transaction which is valid for one person under section 35A but voidable against another (the director) under section 322A, either the third party or the company may apply to the court to settle the matter. The court may then affirm the transaction as a whole, set it aside on just terms or sever it: section 322A(6)(7).

Finally, section 322A provides that whether or not the transaction is avoided the director who deals with the company and any director of the company who authorised the transaction must account to the company for any gain arising from the transaction and indemnify the company against any loss. The company may, however, waive this right by the appropriate resolution.

**Internal consequences**

Just as with the memorandum, any limitations on the powers of the directors, etc., contained in the company's constitution remain binding on the directors as a limitation on their powers and a contractual right for the members.[46] The liberalisation of the effects of such limitations on third parties under section 35A does not affect any right of the members to petition for an injunction preventing any breach of their powers by the directors or the liability of the directors and others for such breaches: section 35A(4)(5). No injunction can be granted, however, if the company is already legally obliged to carry out the transactions. This is identical to the equivalent provision in section 35 and what has been said on that section applies equally here.[47]

**Agency—persons acting in good faith**

If the outsider is dealing with the company in good faith, as defined in section 35A, *ante*, he will be able to enforce any

---

[46] See the discussion at p. 72, *ante*.
[47] *Ante*, p. 73.

contract made by an agent on the company's behalf if that agent was acting within his authority, irrespective of any limitations on his powers under the company's constitution. If the outsider is not acting in good faith, the position is different.[48] An agent may bind his principal (in this case the company) if he has acted within his actual, implied or apparent authority.

As to actual authority, an individual director or committee of the board may be specifically authorised by the board of directors to make a particular contract on behalf of the company.[49] In *Rolled Steel Products (Holdings) Ltd v. B.S.C.*[50] Slade L.J. stated that the directors had no actual authority to exercise any express or implied power of the company other than for the purposes of the company as set out in the memorandum; although if the shareholders unanimously consented this might not be so. Browne-Wilkinson L.J. expressed no opinion on this point and it would seem that on agency principles a simple majority will suffice to give the directors such actual authority. Whether the directors are then acting in breach of their fiduciary duties is a separate question which does not *per se* affect the outsider.[51]

As to implied authority, a director may, under a power in the articles, be appointed to an office, *e.g.* that of managing director, whch carries with it authority to make certain contracts on behalf of the company.[52] However, the question of implication does not stop there and authority may be implied from the conduct of the parties and the circumstances of the case.[53] A person with actual authority to obtain quotations of prices has no implied authority to communicate acceptance of such quotes where no decision to purchase has been made by his principal—at most such a person may have apparent authority.[54]

[48] *Post*, p. 114.
[49] Or a board of directors may pass a resolution authorising two of their number to sign cheques: *per* Lord Denning M.R. in *Hely-Hutchinson v. Brayhead Ltd* [1968] 1 Q.B. 549 (C.A.), at p. 583.
[50] [1986] Ch. 246 (C.A.).
[51] *Post*, Chap. 15.
[52] *Per* Willmer L.J. in *Freeman & Lockyer v. Buckhurst Park Properties (Mangal) Ltd* [1964] 2 Q.B. 480 (C.A.) at pp. 488, 489. Diplock L.J. agreed. And see *Paterson's Trustees v. Caledonian Heritable Security Co. Ltd* (1885) 13 R. 369 (manager borrowed money for purposes of company, and used money to purchase heritable property the title to which was taken in his own name).
[53] As in *Hely-Hutchinson's* case, *ante.*
[54] *Crabree-Vickers Pty. Ltd v. Australia Direct Mail Advertising Co. Pty. Ltd* (1976) 50 A.L.J.R. 203, following the *Freeman & Lockyer* case and *Turquand's* case.

A company is also bound by the acts of an agent acting within his apparent authority[55] where he lacks actual authority (although actual authority and apparent authority are not mutually exclusive and generally co-exist). Thus an outsider may be protected where an individual director acts on behalf of the company without actual authority but with apparent authority, which apparent authority may arise from a representation that he has authority made by the board of directors or such a representation contained in the company's public documents. In *Rolled Steel Products (Holdings) Ltd v. B.S.C.*,[56] Slade L.J. thought that the directors would have such authority in relation to any transaction which falls within the company's express or implied powers.

In such a case the company will be bound if the other party can prove—

(1) that he was induced to make the contract by the agent being held out as occupying a certain position in the company;

(2) that the representation, which is usually by conduct, was made by the person with actual authority to manage the company, generally or in respect of the matters to which the contract relates, who are usually the board of directors[57]; and

(3) that the contract was either one which a person in the position which the agent was held out as occupying would usually have actual authority to make or one which the company had by its conduct as a whole represented that he had authority to make.[58]

Condition (2), *ante*, is due to the fact that the principal, the company, is not a natural person. It follows from the condition that the outsider cannot as a rule[59] rely on the agent's own representation that he has authority.[60]

---

[55] *Panorama Developments (Guildford) Ltd v. Fidelis Furnishing Fabrics Ltd* [1971] 2 Q.B. 711 (C.A.), *post*, p. 388, where the secretary had apparent authority to hire cars on behalf of the company.

[56] [1986] Ch. 246.

[57] But occasionally the shareholders: *Mahony v. East Holyford Mining Co.* (1875) L.R. 7 H.L. 869, *post*.

[58] *Ebeed v. Soplex Wholesale Supplies Ltd* [1985] BCLC 404 (C.A.). Usually these will be the same.

[59] See the *Crabtree-Vickers* case, *ante*.

[60] *Per* Diplock L.J. in the *Freeman & Lockyer* case, *ante*, at p. 505 and Lord Pearson in the *Hely-Hutchinson* case, *ante*, at p. 593.

R., the chairman of the directors of the defendant company, B. Ltd, acted as its *de facto* managing director. The board knew of and acquiesced in that and the articles of B. Ltd empowered the board to appoint a managing director. H. was the chairman and managing director of a public company, P. Ltd, which needed financial assistance. B. Ltd was prepared to help and accordingly in January, 1965 B. Ltd bought shares in P. Ltd from H. for £100,000 and proposed to inject £150,000 into P. Ltd. H. became a director of B. Ltd but never saw its memorandum and articles and did not attend board meetings until May 19, 1965. After that meeting R. and H. agreed that H. would put more money into P. Ltd if B. Ltd would secure his position. R., on behalf of B. Ltd, signed letters to H. in which B. Ltd purported to indemnify H. against loss on his guarantee of a bank loan of £50,000 to P. Ltd and to guarantee a loan by H. to P. Ltd. H. then advanced £45,000 to P. Ltd. When P. Ltd went into liquidation H. had to honour his guarantee and he claimed the £50,000 and the £45,000 from B. Ltd. B. Ltd denied liability and said that R. had no authority to sign the letters (and that the contracts were unenforceable for non-disclosure of H.'s interest in accordance with s.317). *Held*, that on the facts R. had actual authority implied from the conduct of the parties and the circumstances of the case to enter into the contracts with H. (and that it was too late to avoid them for non-disclosure of H.'s interest as required by the articles): *Hely-Hutchinson v. Brayhead Ltd* [1968] 1 Q.B. 549 (C.A.),[61] applying the *Freeman & Lockyer* case, below.

The articles of a company formed to purchase and resell an estate empowered the directors to appoint one of their body managing director. K., a director, was never appointed managing director but, to the knowledge of the board, he acted as such. On behalf of the company he instructed architects to do certain work in connection with the estate. *Held*, the company was bound by the contract and liable for the architects' fees. K. had apparent authority because he had been held out by the board as managing director and, therefore, as having authority to do what a managing director would usually be authorised to do on behalf of the company, and this act was within the usual authority of a managing director. Accordingly, the plaintiffs could assume that he had been properly appointed: *Freeman & Lockyer v. Buckhurst Park Properties (Mangal) Ltd* [1964] 2 Q.B. 480 (C.A.).[62]

The persons who signed the articles of a company, and who under the articles were entitled to appoint directors, treated some of themselves as directors although there was no proper appointment. The articles

---

[61] And see *post*, p. 359. A corresponding Scots case in *Allison v. Scotia Motor etc. Co. Ltd.* (1906) 14 S.L.T. 9 (O.H.), where a *de facto* managing director engaged a works manager of the company for a period of five years.

[62] Applying *Biggerstaff v. Rowatt's Wharf Ltd* [1896] 2 Ch. 93 (C.A.) and *British Thomson-Houston Co. v. Federated European Bank Ltd* [1932] 2 K.B. 176 (C.A.). See also *Clay Hill Brick Co. Ltd v. Rawlings* [1938] 4 All E.R. 100; *Rhodian River Shipping Co. S.A. v. Halla Maritime Corp.* [1984] BCLC 139.

provided that cheques should be signed as directed by the board. The person acting as secretary informed the company's bank that the "board" had resolved that cheques should be signed by two of three named directors and countersigned by the secretary. The bank acted on the communication and honoured cheques so signed. *Held*, the bank was entitled to honour the cheques and was not liable to refund the money paid. The rule in *Turquand's* case applied; *Mahony v. East Holyford Mining Co.* (1875) L.R. 7 H.L. 869.

The requirement appears to be that the representation was made by a person with "actual" authority to manage the business. Thus if the representation is made by someone with no such authority the outsider cannot rely on it.

A sales representative, with the title of "unit manager," purported to bind his company to repay sums advanced by the bank to another company. He had no actual or apparent authority to do so. The bank sought confirmation from the company's "general manager" of its City branch. He confirmed the "unit manager's" authority, but he himself had no authority to make loans. *Held*, the bank could not rely on the general manager's statements as to the unit manager's authority: *British Bank of the Middle East v. Sun Life Assurance of Canada (U.K.) Ltd* [1983] BCLC 78 (H.L.).[63]

Where the outsider relies on a representation by the board of directors it is of course not necessary that he should actually have inspected the company's public documents but where he is seeking to rely on a representation in the public documents it is essential that he inspected them. A party seeking to set up an estoppel (or, in Scots law, a personal bar) must show that he relied on the representation which he alleges, be it a representation in words or a representation by conduct.

A director purported to make, on behalf of the company, an agreement whereby an outsider was to sell on commission goods imported by the company and to retain the proceeds as security for a debt due from another company. The outsider had not inspected the company's public documents and did not know of the power of delegation contained in the articles. Further, the agreement was so unusual as to put the outsider upon inquiry to ascertain whether the director had authority in fact. *Held*, the company was not bound: *Houghton & Co. v. Nothard, Lowe and Wills Ltd* [1927] 1 K.B. 246 (C.A.); affirmed on other grounds [1928] A.C. 1.

---

[63] *Quaere* the effect of the wording of section 35A on this situation? Now the power of the director to authorise others to act on behalf of the company is free of any limitation under the company's constitution. Does this allow any representation to bind the company in such situations?

R. Co., by their principal director, A., purported to enter into an oral contract with B., who was a director of and purported to act for P. Co. but had no actual authority. The alleged contract was that the two companies should finance the sale of a telephone directory holder produced by a third company. R. Co. claimed repayment of money paid by them to B. as agent for P. Co. in pursuance of the contract. R. Co. alleged that P. Co. were estopped from denying B.'s authority because the P. Co.'s articles provided that the directors could delegate their powers to a committee of one or more directors. However, A. had not inspected the articles until after the action began (and even if A. had inspected the articles a single director would not normally have authority to act for the company). *Held*, because A had not inspected the articles when the contract was made, they could not be relied on as conferring ostensible or apparent authority on B., and the action failed: *Rama Corporation Ltd v. Proved Tin, etc., Ltd* [1952] 2 Q.B. 147.

### Agency—persons acting otherwise than in good faith

If the third party is not acting in good faith he cannot rely on section 35A and will by definition have knowledge of the express limitation in the company's constitution. Unless the transaction is ratified therefore the company will not be bound. In addition, the rule in *Turquand's* case has never applied in four situations, which in effect provide that an outsider acting in bad faith will be bound by internal irregularities as well. In such cases even if the agent is otherwise acting within his implied or apparent authority the outsider will be bound by the irregularity and the company will not be liable.

The rule in *Turquand's* case does not apply, *i.e.* the company is not bound and the outsider is not protected, in the following cases—

(1) Where the outsider knows of the irregularity or lack of actual authority.

Under the articles the directors had power to borrow up to £1,000 on behalf of the company without the consent of a general meeting and to borrow further money with such consent. The directors themselves lent £3,500 to the company without such consent, and took debentures. *Held*, the company was liable, and the debentures were valid, only to the extent of £1,000: *Howard v. Patent Ivory Manufacturing Co.* (1888) 83 Ch.D. 156.

(2) Where the outsider purported to act as a director in the transaction, *i.e.* to act for and on behalf of the company in the transaction. On the other hand, if a director, acting

in his private capacity, contracts with his company, acting by another director, the former director is not automatically to be treated as having constructive knowledge of any defect in the latter's authority, so as to exclude the rule.[64]

(3) Where there are suspicious circumstances putting the outsider on inquiry.

The sole director of and main shareholder in a company paid cheques, drawn in favour of the company, into his own account. *Held*, the bank was put upon inquiry and not entitled to rely on his ostensible authority, and could not rely on the rule: *A. L. Underwood Ltd v. Bank of Liverpool & Martins* [1924] 1 K.B. 775 (C.A.).[65]

The articles of a company carrying on business as forwarding agents empowered the directors to determine who should have authority to draw bills of exchange on the company's behalf. C., the company's Manchester manager, drew bills on the company's behalf in favour of K., who took them, believing C. to be authorised to draw them. C. had no such authority, and it was unusual for a branch manager to have such authority. *Held*, the company was not liable to the holders on the bills because (1) K. did not know of the power of delegation in the articles and therefore could not rely on its supposed exercise; (2) the bills were forgeries; (3) even if K. had known of the power of delegation, he was not entitled to assume that a branch manager had ostensible authority to draw bills on behalf of his company: *Kreditbank Cassel GmbH v. Schenkers Ltd* [1927] 1 K.B. 826 (C.A.).

(4) Where a document is forged so as to purport to be the company's document, unless, perhaps, it is held out as genuine by an officer of the company acting within the scope of his authority.[66]

**Validity of acts of directors—procedural defects in appointment**

Where there is a defect in the appointment of a director who has acted for the company, the outsider may be protected by section 285 and an article like Table A, regulation 92. The section provides that the acts of a director or manager are valid notwithstanding any defect that may afterwards be discovered in

---

[64] *Morris v. Kanssen* [1946] A.C. 459; *Hely-Hutchinson v. Brayhead Ltd* [1968] 1 Q.B. 549 (Roskill J.).

[65] Followed in *Rolled Steel Products (Holdings) Ltd v. B.S.C.* [1986] Ch. 246 (C.A.).

[66] *Ruben v. Great Fingall Consolidated* [1906] A.C. 439, *post*, p. 258, particularly *per* Lord Loreburn L.C. at p. 443.

his appointment or qualification. Table A, regulation 92, provides that all acts done by any meeting of the directors or of a committee of directors or by any person acting as a director shall, notwithstanding that it be afterwards discovered that there was some defect in the appointment of any such director or person acting as aforesaid, or that they or any of them were disqualified, be as valid as if every such person had been duly appointed and was qualified and had continued to be a director.

The effect of these provisions is to validate the acts of a director who has not been validly appointed because there was some procedural slip or irregularity in his appointment. Thus, an outsider dealing with the company, *or a member*, is entitled to assume that a person who appears to be a duly appointed and qualified director is so in fact.

The articles included an article like Table A, article 92. T., N. and S., *de facto* directors, made a call, payment of which was resisted by some shareholders on the ground that T., N. and S. were not *de jure* directors. For example, unknown to his co-directors, N. had vacated office by parting with his qualification shares, although he later acquired a share qualification and continued to act as a director. *Held*, the article operated not only as between the company and outsiders but also as between the company and its members, and covered the irregularities alleged, so that the call was valid: *Dawson v. African Consolidated Land etc. Co.* [1898] 1 Ch. 6 (C.A.).

It is immaterial that it is clear from the company's public documents that a director is not duly qualified to act.[67]

The provisions do not validate acts where there has been no appointment at all.[68] Thus they have no effect on substantive rather than procedural defects. So they cannot validate acts which could not have been done even by a properly qualified director. In *Craven-Ellis v. Canons Ltd*,[69] for example, what is now section 285 did not empower improperly qualified directors to do what properly qualified directors could not do, namely, appoint an improperly qualified director as managing director.

## Security for costs

In the last resort a company can only enforce a contract by taking legal proceedings. Since it is the general practice for the

---

[67] *Per* Farwell J. in *British Asbestos Co. Ltd v. Boyd* [1903] 2 Ch. 439 at p. 444. In this case a director vacated office on becoming secretary.

[68] *Morris v. Kanssen* [1946] A.C. 459, applied in *Grant v. John Grant & Sons Pty. Ltd* (1950) 82 C.L.R. 1.

[69] [1936] 2 K.B. 403 (C.A.), *post*, p. 343.

loser in legal proceedings to pay the costs of the winner, a defendant who successfully defends an action brought by a company which is in doubtful financial circumstances may find that it is unable to recover its costs from that company. Section 726(1) therefore provides that:

> "Where in England and Wales,[70] a limited company is plaintiff in an action or other legal proceedings, the court . . . may, if it appears by credible testimony that there is reason to believe that the company will be unable to pay the defendant's costs if successful in his defence, require sufficient security to be given for those costs, and may stay all proceedings until the security is given."

There are two questions for the court in such cases. First, does it have the power to make such an order for security for costs. The section applies to any legal proceedings and these have been held to apply to a petition under section 459 of the Act[71] and where the company is bringing a counterclaim when it is itself the defendant in the main action.[72] To make such an order the court has to be satisfied on the evidence that the company would, and not merely might, be unable to pay the defendant's costs. This would be established if the company had a deficit on its current account even though it had a small balance sheet surplus.[73]

The second question relates to the amount of the required security. The cases establish that the court has a complete discretion in this area and that there are no set rules.[74] This must be done in relation to all the facts of the case, including the conduct of the company and the defendant. The court must achieve a balance between protecting the defendant and preventing the abandonment of a genuine claim by the company.[75] The court must award a sufficient security which in the circumstances is just, and not necessarily a complete security.[76] The wealth of the defendant and whether or not he has indemnity insurance are in most cases irrelevant to this equation.[77]

---

[70] The position in Scotland is governed by a similar rule in s.726(2).

[71] *Re Unisoft Group Ltd (No. 1)* [1993] BCLC 1292 (C.A.).

[72] *Hutchison Telephone (UK) Ltd v. Ultimate Response Ltd* [1993] BCLC 307 (C.A.).

[73] *Europa Holdings Ltd v. Circle Industries (UK) plc* [1993] BCLC 320 (C.A.)

[74] *Roburn Construction Ltd v. William Irwin (South) & Co. Ltd* [1991] BCC 726 (C.A.), applying the majority reasoning in *Sir Lindsay Parkinson & Co. Ltd v. Triplan Ltd* [1973] Q.B. 609.

[75] *ibid.*

[76] *Innovare Displays plc v. Corporate Broking Services Ltd* [1991] BCC 174 (C.A.).

[77] *Croft Leisure Ltd v. Gravestock & Owen* [1993] BCLC 1273.

# Chapter 7

# PUBLIC OFFERS OF SHARES

THE division of companies into public and private companies is based on economic criteria, *i.e.* a minimum capital requirement for public companies,[1] and it is clear that the law envisages that public companies are those which intend to seek finance from the investing public, since private companies are in general forbidden to raise capital in that way.[2] The most common way for companies to raise public finance is to issue shares or debentures to the public[3] and the 1985 Act contained provisions which controlled the document which a company was required to issue if it wished to invite the public to buy its shares. This document is known as a prospectus.

In practice, however, companies who wish to have their shares, or other securities, quoted on the Stock Exchange have always had, in addition to legal constraints, to comply with the Stock Exchange's own rules—the Admission of Securities to Listing, which were more stringent than those in the Companies Act. The advantage of a Stock Exchange listing is that the shares are freely marketable—which in turn enhances their initial value to an outside investor. Until 1984 listing on the Stock Exchange was not regulated by law, but three European Community directives, which were implemented in that year, brought about significant changes. These directives were the Admissions Directive,[4] which covered the conditions for admission to a stock exchange listing, the Listing Particulars Directive,[5] which set out the requirements for drawing up, scrutiny and distribution of listing particulars to be published as a pre-requisite for admission, and the Interim Reports Directive,[6] which required information to be published on a regular basis by listed companies.

---

[1] *Ante,* p. 43
[2] See ss.143(3) and 170(1) of the Financial Services Act 1986.
[3] The methods available are set out *post,* p. 142.
[4] Dir. 79/279/EEC.
[5] Dir. 80/390/EEC.
[6] Dir. 82/121/EEC.

These directives were implemented in the U.K. by the Stock Exchange (Listing) Regulations 1984,[7] which directly incorporated the text of the three directives. The result of these regulations was to produce two sets of rules: the Companies Act provisions which applied to prospectuses where no listing was required and the Listing Regulations, together with certain of the Companies Act provisions, which applied to listed securities. The result was not entirely a happy one and many problems of construction arose.[8]

With the introduction of a new legal regulation for the investment industry by the Financial Services Act 1986 the intention was for both of those existing provisions, the Companies Act prospectus rules and the Listing Regulations, to be repealed and replaced by Parts IV and V of the 1986 Act. Shares and debentures are investments for the purposes of that Act[9] and the issue of shares to the public is clearly an important aspect of investment law.

The new provisions were intended, in part, to implement the three EC directives and so they adopted different rules for listed and unlisted securities. Part IV of the Act relates to listed securities and Part V to unlisted securities (since the latter are not subject to the directives). However, Part V of the Financial Services Act was never brought into force. Nine years later, however, the relevant parts of the Companies Act relating to unlisted securities were finally repealed and replaced by the Public Offers of Securities Regulations 1995.[10] These Regulations have also made some amendments to the Financial Services Act following the EC Prospectus Directive.[10a]

It is now appropriate to consider the two regimes separately, although, as will be seen, there is now a third category, viz unlisted securities which are vetted under the listing procedure in order to obtain recognition in the EU.

*In the following part of this chapter all references to sections are to sections of the Financial Services Act 1986 and all references to regulations are to the Public Offers of Securities Regulations 1995 unless otherwise stated.*

[7] S.I. 1984 No. 716.
[8] See Professor Robert Pennington: *Stock Exchange Listing—the new requirements,* Butterworths, 1985.
[9] F.S.A. 1986, Sched. 1, paras. 1 and 2.
[10] S.I. 1995.
[10a] Dir. 89/298/EEC.

## OFFICIAL LISTING OF SECURITIES

### Scope of the provisions

Section 142(1) provides that no investments can be admitted to the Official List (of the Stock Exchange), *i.e.* quoted, unless Part IV of the Act is complied with. Investments for this purpose include shares, debentures, instruments entitling the holders to subscribe for shares and certificates which represent property rights or contractual rights in shares.[11]

### *The competent authority*

The Act envisages that, following the directives, the legal requirements of an admission to listing are to be under the control, not of the Department of Trade and Industry, but of the "competent authority." Section 142(6) specifies the latter as the International Stock Exchange of the United Kingdom and the Republic of Ireland Ltd, although it may act through any of its committees, sub-committees, officers or employees: section 142(8). In practice the Stock Exchange operates in this area through its quotations department. In matters outside the scope of the Act the Stock Exchange remains free to act as it pleases.[12]

Following the directives, the Act also delegates the rule-making power for these purposes to the Stock Exchange. Rules made by the Stock Exchange under this power are known as the listing rules. Such rules must either be made by the Stock Exchange itself or confirmed by them within 28 days if they are made by a committee or sub-committee: section 142(6), (8).

### *The listing rules*

The Stock Exchange may make listing rules for the purpose of any of the matters dealt with below. Section 155 allows the rules to prescribe fees payable to the Stock Exchange. The rules must be in writing, printed and made available to the public and there are provisions for ensuring that the rules can be properly admitted as evidence in legal proceedings: section 156(3), (4), (8).

---

[11] s.142(2), (3), Sched. 1, paras. 1, 2, 4 and 5.
[12] s.142(9).

It is a defence to any action for contravention of any of the listing rules to show that at the time of the breach the particular rule had not been made available to the public. However, a certificate signed by the authorised officer of the Stock Exchange that the rule was so available is prima facie evidence of that fact: section 156(5), (6).[13]

The listing rules may make different provisions for different cases and allow the Stock Exchange to take powers to dispense with or modify their application in particular cases or circumstances: section 156(1), (2).

### Applications and admissions to listing

Applications for listing are governed by the listing rules except that all such applications require the consent of the issuer of the securities[14] and it is provided that no private company may so apply: section 143.

No securities may be admitted to listing (*i.e.* quoted) unless the listing rules and any other requirements of the Stock Exchange are complied with: section 144(1). Until 1995, the major requirement of the listing rules for this purpose was the approval by the Stock Exchange of "listing particulars" and the publication of those particulars or some other document. Following the prospectus directive, amendments were made to the Act by the regulations, so that section 144(2) now makes those requirements applicable either to a prospectus or to listing particulars. In effect, whenever the prospectus directive requires it there must be a prospectus, whereas in other cases listing particulars are required. In general, a prospectus is required whenever an application for listing is made and the securities are to be offered to the public prior to admission to listing: section 144(2A). Further, section 156B prohibits invitations, prior to the publication of a prospectus, to acquire the securities offered, except conditionally on the publication of a prospectus, where an application for admission to listing is pending.

Under section 142(7A) an offer is defined as including an invitation to treat and an offer to the public includes an offer to

---

[13] Such a certificate is deemed to have been duly signed unless the contrary is proved: s.156(7).

[14] If the securities are certificates representing shares, the relevant consent is that of the issuer of the shares: s.142(7).

any section of the public, however defined. A number of specific cases are, however, excluded from the prospectus requirement by Schedule 11A to the Act. Since these are identical to those cases where a prospectus need not be issued in the case of unlisted securities, reference should be made to the next part of this chapter where they are set out in full.[14a] It is important to remember, however, that in such cases if admission to listing is required, listing particulars must be issued, etc. Section 154A provides that Part IV of the Act applies equally to prospectuses as it does to listing particulars.

Once securities have been admitted to the Official List of the Stock Exchange, their admission cannot be challenged on the ground that any requirement or condition for their admission has not been complied with: section 144(6).

*Prospectuses and Listing particulars—publication and advertisements*

The publication of prospectuses and listing particulars is as laid down in the listing rules, but section 154 provides that where an application for listing has been made and a prospectus or listing particulars either have been or are to be published, no advertisement or any other information relating to that application, as specified by the listing rules[15] shall be issued in connection with that application, unless the Stock Exchange has either seen and approved its contents or authorised publication without such approval. Any breach is a criminal offence, although there is a defence for someone who whilst acting in the ordinary course of non-investment business[16] can prove that he believed on reasonable grounds that its issue had been approved or authorised.

Where the advertisement or other document has been so approved or authorised for publication neither the publisher nor the person responsible for a prospectus or the listing particulars shall be liable under any civil remedy or to the rescission or repudiation of any subsequent agreement by reason of any misstatement or omission if the document and a prospectus or the listing particulars, taken together, would not be likely to mislead persons of the kind likely to consider the acquisition of the securities in question: section 154(5).

---

[14a] See *post,* p. 127.
[15] Thus the Stock Exchange itself can specify the information it requires to see.
[16] *i.e.* not within Part II of Sched. 2 to the Act.

*Prospectuses and Listing particulars—content*

The listing rules specify the content of a prospectus and listing particulars: section 144(2)(a). However, section 146 imposes a general duty of disclosure in addition to that required by the rules. The prospectus or listing particulars must disclose all the information with respect to the assets and liabilities, financial position, profits and losses, and prospects of the issuer of the securities, and the rights attaching to those securities as an investor and his professional advisers would reasonably require in order to make an informed assessment.

This general duty of disclosure is limited by the section to the information which the persons responsible for the prospectus or listing particulars either knew about or could reasonably have discovered by making enquiries: section 146(2).

The section also lays down four criteria to assist in determining the information to be supplied under this general duty of disclosure. These are designed to cover the various forms of offer available in the market and are: (i) the nature of the securities and the issuer; (ii) the nature of the prospective buyers (*e.g.* the general public or professional investment managers); (iii) that professional advisers who may reasonably be expected to have been consulted will have professional knowledge of certain matters; and (iv) any information provided by the interim reports required or listed companies or under any other statutory provision or that required by recognised exchanges (including the Stock Exchange) to determine the value of the securities: section 146(3).

The Stock Exchange may grant an exemption from the general duty of disclosure for any information if disclosure of that information would be contrary to the public interest, seriously detrimental to the issuer of the securities, or, in the case of certain specialised debt securities, unnecessary for the potential specialised market: section 148(1). The Secretary of State or the Treasury may certify that the disclosure of information would not be in the public interest: section 148(3). Information detrimental to the issuer must still be published, however, if non-disclosure would be likely to mislead a potential buyer as to any knowledge which would be essential for him to have in order to make an informed decision: section 148(2).

In addition the Stock Exchange can under the listing rules dispense with or modify the content of the listing particulars as required by the rules: section 156(2).

*Refusal to list*

The Stock Exchange may refuse an application even if made in due form if the admission to listing would be detrimental to the interests of investors by reason of any matter relating to the issuer: section 144(3)(a). An alternative ground for refusal is failure to comply with the listing requirements in another EU country in respect of securities quoted there: section 144(3)(b). Any such decision should be notified to the applicant within six months although if no such notification is made the Stock Exchange is assumed to have rejected the application: section 144(4), (5).

## Discontinuance and suspension of listings

The Stock Exchange may discontinue a listing of securities in accordance with the listing rules if there are special circumstances which preclude normal regular dealings in the securities.[17] Alternatively a listing may be temporarily suspended, also in accordance with the listing rules: section 145.

## Supplementary prospectus or listing particulars

In two cases the issuer of the securities must, under the listing rules, submit supplementary listing particulars to the Stock Exchange for its approval and if they are approved must publish them.

These cases are where, in the time between the submission of the original listing particulars and the commencement of dealings on the Stock Exchange:

(i)   there is a significant change in any matter which was required to be disclosed in the listing particulars, either under the rules or under the general duty of disclosure; or

(ii)  a significant new matter arises which would have had to have been disclosed if it had arise at the time of application.

---

[17] *i.e.* where there is a false market in the shares, *e.g.* in a take-over bid—see Chap. 31, *post.* Ordinary shareholders, as distinct from the company cannot challenge such a decision: *R. v. International Stock Exchange of the United Kingdom and the Republic of Ireland, ex p. Else (1982) Ltd* [1993] BCLC 834.

If the issuer is unaware of the change or new matter he is under no duty to submit a supplementary prospectus or listing particulars. However, any person responsible for the prospectus or listing particulars (as defined in section 152 below) who is aware of such a matter is under a duty to notify the issuer of it: section 147. Failure to comply with these requirements renders the appropriate person liable to compensate any person who has acquired the securities and suffered loss as a result: section 150(3).[18]

### Registration of prospectus or listing particulars

The prospectus or listing particulars must be registered with the registrar on or before the date of publication. A statement that a copy has been delivered to him must appear in the particulars. There is a criminal sanction in default: section 149.

### Continuing obligations

The listing rules require certain continuing obligations of issuers of listed securities. These relate to half-yearly disclosures of certain matters. Contravention can be made public. The Stock Exchange itself may publish any such information if the issuer fails to do so: section 153. In addition, the company must make public any major new developments in the company's sphere of activity which are not publicly known and which may have a substantial effect on the value of its shares.[19]

### Misrepresentation and omissions

Civil and criminal liability for misrepresentations and omissions in listing and supplementary prospectus and listing particulars are dealt with later in this chapter.[20]

## OFFERS OF UNLISTED SECURITIES

Offers of unlisted securities *i.e.* those where no application is to be made for listing on the Stock Exchange, are subject to Part II

---

[18] See *post*, p. 132.
[19] The Traded Securities (Disclosure) Regulations 1994 (S.I. 1994 No. 188).
[20] *Post*, p. 131.

of the Public Offers of Securities Regulations 1995. However, if the offeror wishes to take advantage of the Mutual Recognition of Prospectuses Directive for an application for listing in another Member State, he will need to follow a different course of having the prospectus pre-vetted by the Stock Exchange. That procedure is set out in the next part of this chapter. The following provisions apply therefore only to offers of unlisted securities where that facility is not required.

### The prospectus requirement—publication and registration

The Regulations impose three requirements on offerors of unlisted securities relating to the need for a prospectus relating to the offer. The first is that when such securities are offered to the public for the first time a prospectus complying with the Regulations must be published by the offeror by making it available to the public, free of charge, at an address in the U.K. during the whole of the period during which the offer is open: regulation 4(1). The meaning of offered to the public is considered below. The second requirement is that before publishing such a prospectus it must be registered with the registrar: regulation 4(2). Finally, any advertisement, notice, poster or other document, other than the prospectus itself, announcing a public offer of securities where a prospectus is required under the Regulations must state that a prospectus is or will be published, giving an address in the U.K. from which it can be obtained: regulation 12. Breach of any of these provisions is a criminal offence and can also give rise to civil liability, *e.g.* for breach of statutory duty: regulation 16.[21]

### *Offered to the public*

A prospectus is not required to be published, etc., under the Regulations unless the securities are being offered to the public. This concept is defined in the Regulations, which then go on to provide a large number of exceptions where, even if there is an offer of securities to the public, there need be no prospectus. An offer, and thereby an offeror, is defined by regulation 5 so as to

---

[21] If the breach is as to the content of the prospectus rather than as to its being published, etc., then there is no contravention of regulation 16. Instead there are specific remedies which are set out *post* at p. 131.

mean either an offer, which if accepted, would give rise to a binding contract to issue or sell the securities (a contractual offer) or an invitation to a person to make such an offer (an invitation to treat).

Such an offer is made to the public if it is made to any section of the public, whether selected as members or debenture holders of a company, or as clients of the person issuing the prospectus or in any manner, and not just to the public at large: regulation 6. This wording was used in the Companies Act under the previous regime which then excluded only two types of such offers. The new regime, however, taking advantage of the exceptions allowed for in the directive, specifies no less than 20 such exceptions. Cases decided under the old law must therefore be treated with some care before applying them to the new rules.[22]

### Exceptions to the prospectus requirement

Because of the wide definition of an offer to the public, regulation 7 sets out 20 situations where there is no need to publish or register a prospectus under the Regulations. These exceptions, which are cumulative, are as follows:

(i)    offers to persons in connection with their trades, professions or occupations;

(ii)    offers to no more than 50 persons (including any previous offers of the same securities in the previous twelve months);

(iii)    offers to members of a club or association where they have a common interest in its affairs and to what is to be done with the proceeds of the offer;

(iv)    offers to a restricted circle of people whom the offeror reasonably believes to be sufficiently knowledgable to understand the risks involved;

(v)    offers made in connection with a bona fide underwriting agreement[23];

(vi)    offers by private companies to existing members, employees or their families,[24] or debenture holders of the company;

---

[22] For such cases see the 13th edition of this work.
[23] See *post*, p. 144.
[24] Defined as to include spouses, children and their decendants and certain trustees for those people.

(vii)   offers to the government or a local or public authority;

(viii)  offers of a total value of less than 40,000 ecus (including any previous offers of the same securities in the past twelve months);

(ix)    offers whereby each person acquiring the securities must pay at least 40,000 ecus or equivalent;

(x)     offers of securities with a value of at least 40,000 ecus each;

(xi)    offers made in connection with a takeover offer[25];

(xii)   offers made in connection with a merger[26];

(xiii)  shares offered free of charge to existing shareholders (bonus shares)[27];

(xiv)   shares offered in exchange for shares in the same company if there is no increase in the company's share capital[28];

(xv)    offers limited to employees, former employees and their spouses and children (under 18);

(xvi)   offers arising from the conversion of convertible debentures or warrants where the original issues were accompanied by a prospectus or listing particulars;

(xvii)  offers by charities and certain other non-profit making bodies;

(xviii) certain shares issued by building societies and industrial and provident societies;

(xix)   offers of Euro-securities (within s.207 of the Act);

(xx)    offers of securities which are of the same class and were issued at the same time as securities which were accompanied by a prospectus in accordance with the regulations.

## Form and content of a prospectus

A prospectus published under the Regulations must contain all the information specified in Schedule 1 to the Regulations presented in as easily analysable and comprehensible form as possible: regulations 8(1)(3). This requirement is subject to a dispensation in regulation 8(2) whereby if a particular item in the

---

[25] As defined in s.428 C.A. 1985. See Chap. 31, *post*.
[26] See Chap. 30, *post*.
[27] See *post*, Chap. 22.
[28] See Chap. 9, *post*.

Schedule is inappropriate to the issuer's business the prospectus must contain equivalent information if that is appropriate. The Schedule provides detailed requirements relating to the issuer and the persons responsible for the prospectus, if different, and the securities on offer. The prospectus must be dated and give the names and functions of the directors of the issuing company.

In addition, regulation 9 imposes a general duty of disclosure over and above that required by the Schedule. This is similar to that imposed by section 146 of the Act for listed securities. Thus the prospectus must disclose all the information with respect to the assets and liabilities, financial position, profits and losses, prospects of the issuer of the securities and the rights attaching to the securities as an investor would reasonably require in order to make an informed assessment, having regard to the nature of both the issuer and the securities.

This general duty of disclosure is limited by regulation 9(2) to the information which the persons responsible for the prospectus (not necessarily the issuer) either knew about or could reasonably have discovered by making enquiries.

The Regulations contain various derogations from the need to publish a prospectus in accordance with the Schedule. Where the shares are to be admitted to an approved exchange (e.g. the Unlisted Securities Market) on a pre-emptive basis[29] certain information can be omitted by the governing body of the exchange if it is available as a result of the disclosure requirements of that exchange; regulation 8(4). Similarly, where an offer relates to shares of a class which are already admitted to an approved exchange, the governing body of that exchange may allow the offer to proceed without a prospectus if they amount to no more than a 10 per cent increase in the shares already admitted and the disclosure rules of the exchange provide the necessary information: regulation 8(5).

Regulation 8(6) provides that where the same issuer makes an offer of securities within twelve months of a previous offer of different securities for which a prospectus was issued, the issuer may simply append a copy of that first prospectus with a second prospectus detailing the changes which have taken place since the first offer. Finally, regulation 11(1) empowers the Treasury or the Secretary of State to authorise the omission of material which if

[29] See post, p. 148.

disclosed would be contrary to the public interest, and regulation 11(2) applies a relaxation in the case of a genuine secondary offer, *i.e.* one not by the issuer of the securities or anyone acting on his behalf. Where the secondary offeror does not have the specified information available and has not been able to obtain it by making reasonable efforts to do so, then there is no obligation to include it.

## Supplementary prospectus

If, during the currency of an offer, there is any significant change in any material in the prospectus, or a significant inaccuracy in the prospectus is discovered, or if a significant new matter arises which would have been included in the prospectus either under the Schedule or the general duty of disclosure had it arisen when that was prepared, a supplementary prospectus must be published and registered at the same time but otherwise in the same way as the prospectus: regulation 10. A significant matter, change or error is one which would affect an informed assessment by a prospective purchaser. Where the person who delivered the prospectus for registration is unaware of the change, etc., there is no duty on him to issue a supplementary prospectus unless he was notified of it by a person responsible for the prospectus who is under a duty to notify him of any such change, etc. Failure to comply with these requirements may lead to civil liability.[30]

## Misrepresentations and omissions

Civil and criminal liability for misrepresentations and omissions in a prospectus and supplementary prospectus are dealt with later in this chapter.[31]

# OFFERS OF UNLISTED SECURITIES WHERE MUTUAL RECOGNITION IS SOUGHT

Where an offeror of securities does not seek a listing of those securities on the U.K. Stock Exchange but wishes to take advantage of the Mutual Recognition Directive to use the offer

---

[30] See *post,* p. 132.
[31] *Post,* p. 131.

document for admission to listing in another Member State he must still publish a prospectus on offering those securities to the public for the first time under regulation 4(1), *i.e.* by making it available to the public free of charge at an address in the U.K.[32]

However, regulation 4(3) provides that instead of registering a prospectus under regulation 4(2), complying with the form and content of the Regulations, the prospectus should be submitted for approval in accordance with the listing rules made by the Stock Exchange under the Act. Thus the prospectus will be pre-vetted by the Stock Exchange (for a fee) as if a U.K. listing were required and the form and content of the prospectus will be governed by those rules and not by the Regulations.

Section 156A of the Act accordingly provides that the listing rules may provide for such a pre-vetting procedure including rules relating to the form and content of such a prospectus. Part IV of the Act is adapted by section 156A(3) in connection with such offers so that the provisions applicable to offers of listed shares will apply to these offers.

## MISREPRESENTATIONS AND OMISSIONS IN LISTING PARTICULARS OR PROSPECTUS

### Statutory right to compensation

Sections 150 to 152 of the Financial Services Act provide a statutory remedy for misrepresentations and omissions in a prospectus or listing particulars and supplementary prospectus or listing particulars subject to Part IV of that Act (*i.e.* offers of listed securities and those unlisted securities subject to pre-vetting). Regulations 13 to 15 of the Public Offers of Securities Regulations 1995 provide an identical remedy for prospectuses relating to other offers of unlisted securities. In the following text, therefore, the remedies are taken together. This remedy is available in addition to other common law and statutory remedies which are set out below[32a]: section 150(4); regulation 13(4).

There are two basic heads of liability, followed by six defences, and finally the Act and Regulations detail those deemed to be

---

[32] *Ante,* p. 126.
[32a] *Post,* p. 135.

responsible for the listing particulars who can be sued for compensation.

## Heads of liability

(a) Any person responsible for a prospectus or listing particulars or supplementary prospectus or listing particulars (as defined above) *shall be liable* to compensate anyone who has acquired relevant securities (or an interest therein) and has suffered loss as a result of any untrue or misleading statement in the particulars or the omission of anything required to be included by virtue of the general duty of disclosure under section 146(1)[33] or regulation 9[33a] or the duty to publish particulars of any significant new matter or change under section 147[34] or regulation 10[35]: section 150(1); regulation 14(1).

Omission of any matter required by the rules to be included, even in the negative, is to be regarded as a statement that there is no such matter for this purpose: section 150(2); regulation 14(2).

The plaintiff need only prove a misstatement or omission and loss as a result to establish liability. Once established it is for the defendant to establish a defence. There must be causation, however, between the misstatement/omission and the loss. Unlike the former provision, section 67 of the Companies Act 1985, there is no need to show that the securities were acquired "on the faith of the prospectus." Subsequent purchasers may therefore be able to claim if they acquire their shares within a reasonable time.[36]

(b) Anyone who fails to issue supplementary listing particulars when required to do so or is otherwise in breach of section 147[37] or regulation 10[37a] is liable to compensate any person who has acquired those securities (or an interest in them) and suffered loss as a result of the failure.

Section 150(6), but not the Regulations, provides that no-one, whether as promoter or otherwise, is to be liable for failing to

---

[33] *Ante,* p. 123.
[33a] *Ante,* p. 129.
[34] *Ante,* p. 124.
[35] *Ante,* p. 130.
[36] The defence, under section 151(1)(c) and (d) and regulation 15(1)(c) and (d) would otherwise be irrelevant. See *post,* p. 133.
[37] See note 34.
[37a] *Ante,* p. 130.

disclose any information which he would not be required to disclose or would be exempt from disclosing in a prospectus or listing particulars. This exemption extends to any civil liability and to any action for rescission or repudiation of any subsequent agreement. These words do not lie easily with section 150(4) which provides that the section cannot affect any liability outside that section. The main effect will be to ensure that information which has been withheld under section 148 (*e.g.* on public interest grounds) and which then makes the information given misleading, will not give rise to civil liability.

## Exemptions from liability

There are six defences available to anyone who has been sued for compensation under section 150 or regulation 14. The first four are applicable to the general liability (a) above, the next to both that liability and the specific liability for failing to submit supplementary listing particulars, and the sixth to the latter liability only.

(1) *Reasonable Belief* (s.151(1); reg. 15(1)). It is a defence to show that the defendant, having made reasonable enquiries, believed at the time when the particulars or prospectus was submitted (or the prospectus sent for registration as appropriate) either that the statement was true and not misleading or that the omission was a proper one, provided that he can also show one of four additional facts: (i) that he still held the belief when the securities were acquired; (ii) that they were acquired before he could bring the matter to the attention of potential investors; (iii) that before they were acquired he had taken all reasonable steps to bring a correction to the attention of potential investors; or (iv) that he held that belief until dealings commenced (in the case of offers of listed securities) and (in both cases) that the securities were so acquired after such a lapse of time that he ought fairly to be excused.

(2) *Expert's Statements* (s.151(2); reg. 15(2)). Where the offending statement is made by or on the authority of an expert with his consent, the defendant (other than the expert) will be excused if he can show reasonable belief in the expert's competence and consent to the statement's inclusion in that form and context. This belief must be held at the time when the prospectus or particulars were submitted and maintained until the securities have been acquired, unless either they were acquired before he

could reasonably bring the matter to potential investors' attention, or he took reasonable steps before they were acquired to bring a correction to the attention of potential investors, or that he continued in that belief until after dealings were commenced on the Stock Exchange or approved exchange, if relevant, and the securities were acquired after such a lapse of time that he ought in the circumstances to be excused.

(3) *Reasonable Steps to Correct Defect* (s.151(3); reg. 15(3)). If the defendant takes reasonable steps to bring a correction or a defect in an expert's competence or consent to the attention of potential investors before the securities were acquired there is no liability. This defence is complementary to (1) and (2) above.

(4) *Official Statements and Documents* (s.151(4); reg. 15(4)). There is no liability for any loss resulting from the accurate and fair reproduction of a statement by official persons or contained in an official document.

(5) *Plaintiff's Knowledge* (s.151(5); reg. 15(5)). If the defendant can prove that the person suffering the loss acquired the securities "with knowledge" of the misrepresentation or omission in listing particulars or of any change or new matter giving rise to the obligation to publish supplementary particulars, he will not be liable under the appropriate head of liability. In practice such knowledge would probably destroy the causation between the statement and the loss so that no liability would arise.

(6) *Reasonable Belief and Supplementary Listing Particulars/ Prospectus* (s.151(6); reg. 15(6)). Reasonable belief that the change of new matter was not such as to call for supplementary listing particulars is a defence to liability under head (b) above.

*Persons responsible for the particulars/prospectus*

Section 152(1) and regulation 13 detail those persons who are deemed to be responsible for the listing or supplementary listing particulars or prospectus or supplementary prospectus and so liable for misrepresentations and omissions. The five groups are:

(a) the issuer of the securities involved;
(b) the directors of the issuer;
(c) anyone who is named, and has authorised himself to be named in the document as a director of the issuer or as having agreed to become a director at some future time;
(d) those who accept and are stated as having accepted responsibility for all or any part of the document;

(e) anyone else who has authorised the contents of all or part of the document; and
(f) for offers of unlisted securities only, the offeror of the securities where he is not the issuer of those securities.

Those liable under (d) or (e) are only so liable for those parts of the document which they have accepted responsibility for or authorised: section 152(3), regulation 13(3).

If the issuer becomes liable to pay compensation no account is to be taken of that liability in deciding the amount due or to be due for those shares. This is because it would otherwise affect the principle of capital maintenance: section 152(9); regulation 13(5).

The basic principle is that all directors of the issuer are responsible for the prospectus or particulars and liable as such under paragraph (b) above. This liability extends to those who have authorised themselves to be described either as a director or as having agreed to become a director in the particulars under paragraph (c) above. These directors may, of course, rely on the defences under section 151 or regulation 15 but section 152(2) and regulation 13(2) provide an exemption from liability for those in category (b) and section 152(5) provides two further exemptions for those in categories (b) and (c) with regard to offers of listed securities.

Section 152(2) and regulation 13(2) provide that no director under category (b) is to be regarded as being responsible if the document was issued without his knowledge or consent provided that when he became aware of its publication he gave reasonable public notice of that fact. Such notice must be given "forthwith".

The second exemption, available to those under (b) or (c) above where a listing or pre-vetting is sought, applies to directors of issuers of specialised international debt securities which is a specialist market: section 152(5)(6). The third is of more general application. Liability under category (b) above can be excluded in advance by any director who is certified by the Stock Exchange as being exempted by reason of his having an interest, or any other circumstances, which makes it inappropriate for him to be responsible for the particulars: section 152(5).

**Other civil liability**

Since a company is liable for the misrepresentations of its directors and other agents acting within the scope of their authority, a person induced to subscribe for shares or debentures by a misrepresentation in a prospectus or listing particulars may have other remedies under the general law against the individual or the individuals responsible, *e.g.* promoters, directors or experts.[38] The remedy may be available under the general law or it may be statutory. It should be remembered that persons protected under sections 150(6)[39] and 154(5)[40] are protected from all civil liability, including actions for rescission or repudiation of a subsequent agreement, if those sections apply.

The main remedy against the *company* is rescission[41] of the contract of allotment, with or without an action for damages. At common law it was held that a shareholder cannot recover damages for fraud against the company without rescission, because that would be inconsistent with the contract between him and the other shareholders.[42] The same was true of a claim for damages, *e.g.* for breach of contract, which a shareholder *qua* shareholder may seek to enforce against the company.[43] These prohibitions were removed by section 111A of the Act, and there is nothing in principle to prevent such actions now. Damages in lieu of rescission may be recovered in England and Wales under the Misrepresentation Act 1967, s.2(2), which states that where a person has entered into a contract after a misrepresentation made to him *otherwise than fraudulently*, and he would be entitled to rescind, then if rescission is claimed the court may award damages in lieu of rescission, if of opinion that it would be equitable to do so. Damages for *negligent* misrepresentation may be recovered from the company under section 2(1) of the Misrepresentation Act, which provides that where a person has entered into a contract after a misrepresentation made to him by another party thereto and as a result has suffered loss, then the

---

[38] As in *Frankenburg v. Great Horseless Carriage Co.* [1900] 1 Q.B. 504 (C.A.).
[39] *Ante,* p. 132.
[40] *Ante,* p. 122.
[41] The representee may elect to repudiate the contract, and legal proceedings are not essential, in the event of misrepresentation. However, if, as it usual, he wishes to recover money or property transferred by him under the contract he may have to initiate proceedings for rescission.
[42] *Houldsworth v. City of Glasgow Bank* (1980) 7 R. (H.L.) 53; (1880) 5 App. Cas. 317, where it was too late to rescind since the company had gone into liquidation. See also *Western Bank v. Addie* (1867) 5 M. (H.L.) 80.
[43] *Re Dividend Fund Incorporated (In Liquidation)* [1974] V.R. 451, where an unlimited company failed to repurchase shares in accordance with the articles and the shareholder had to pay calls in a liquidation.

representor is liable in damages unless he proves that on reasonable grounds he believed up to the time when the contract was made that the representation was true. A similar provision to section 2(1) applies to Scotland under section 10(1) of the Law Reform (Miscellaneous Provisions) (Scotland) Act 1985.

It may also be possible to claim damages for negligent misrepresentation under the principle in *Hedley Byrne & Co. Ltd v. Heller & Partners Ltd*,[44] which is that a negligent, although honest, misrepresentation, spoken or written, may give rise to an action for damages for financial loss caused thereby. The law implies a duty of care where one party seeks information or advice from another party, trusts the other to exercise due care, it is reasonable for him to do so, the other knows or ought to know that reliance is being placed on his skill or judgment or ability to make careful inquiry and he does not expressly disclaim responsibility for his representation. In *Mutual Life and Citizens' Assurance Co. Ltd v. Evatt*[45] the Privy Council advised that the party from whom information or advice is sought must carry on the business of giving advice or in some other way he must have let it be known that he claims to possess the necessary skill and competence to do so and is prepared to exercise the necessary diligence to give reliable advice.

. The restrictive nature of this liability was affirmed by the House of Lords in *Caparo Industries plc v. Dickman*,[46] where their Lordships stressed that the defendant's liability was limited to those whom he knew would receive the statement and would rely upon it for the purposes of a particular transaction. Thus reliance for another purpose, *e.g.* a subsequent purchase on the market, will not suffice for liability on a prospectus issued in respect of original purchases only.[47]

*Rescission of the contract of allotment*

In order to obtain rescission of a contract of allotment on the ground that it was induced by misrepresentation, the allottee must prove (1) a material false statement of fact, (2) which induced him to subscribe.[48]

---

[44] [1964] A.C. 465.
[45] [1971] A.C. 793 (P.C.).
[46] [1990] 2 W.L.R. 358.
[47] *Al-Nakib Investments (Jersey) Ltd v. Longcroft*, [1991] BCLC 7. See also *Morgan Crucible Co. v. Hill Samuel Bank Ltd*, [1991] BCLC 178.
[48] The right to rescind is qualified by ss.150(6) and 154(5) F.S.A. 1986.

(1) There must be a material false statement of fact.

A prospectus stated: "a large number of gentlemen in the trade and others have become shareholders." When the register of members was made up there were 55 shareholders, of whom 10 or 12 were connected with the trade. *Held,* there was not a sufficiently material misrepresentation to entitle a person who had taken shares on the faith of the prospectus to have his name deleted from the register: *City of Edinburgh Brewery Co. Ltd v. Gibson's Trustee* (1869) 7 M. 886.

A statement of fact must be distinguished from a statement of opinion.[49] A statement that the property of the company is worth a certain sum of money, or that the profits are expected to reach a certain figure, is only opinion and gives no right to rescission except where it can be shown that the maker of the statement did not hold the opinion. Statements, on the other hand, that "the surplus assets, as appear by the last balance sheet, amount to upwards of £10,000"[50] that £200,000 of share capital has been subscribed,[51] and that certain persons have agreed to be directors,[52] are all material statements of fact and, if false, will give rise to a right to rescission.

Where the facts are not equally well known to both sides a statement of opinion by one who should know the facts often implies a statement of fact, *i.e.* that there are reasonable grounds for his opinion, and if it can be proved that he could not as a reasonable man honestly have had the opinion, there is misrepresentation of fact.[53] Again, a statement of intention does not amount to a representation of fact unless it can be proved that the alleged intention never existed.[54]

If a prospectus refers to a report which contains inaccurate statements of fact, the contract can be rescinded if the company has vouched for the accuracy of the report, but otherwise it cannot. Thus, if the company employs an accountant to go

---

[49] *Liverpool Palace of Varieties Ltd v. Miller* (1896) 4 S.L.T. 153 (O.H.).

[50] *Re London and Staffordshire Fire Insurance Co.* (1883) 24 Ch.D. 149.

[51] *Arnison v. Smith* (1889) 41 Ch.D. 348 (C.A.); where the share capital had only been allotted *as* fully paid up. But see *Akerhielm v. De Mare* [1959] A.C. 789 (P.C.), *post,* p. 141.

[52] *Re Scottish Petroleum Co.* (1883) 23 Ch.D. 413 (C.A.); *Blakiston v. London and Scottish Banking etc. Corpn. Ltd* (1894) 21 R. 417; contrast *Chambers v. Edinburgh etc. Aerated Bread Co. Ltd* (1891) 18 R. 1039.

[53] *Per* Bowen L.J. in *Smith v. Land, etc., Corpn.* (1884) 28 Ch.D. 7 (C.A.) at p. 15.

[54] *Edgington v. Fitzmaurice* (1885) 29 Ch.D. 459 (C.A.).

through the books and make a report, and then sets out the report in a prospectus, it will not be liable for any inaccuracy in the report.[55] But if the company makes statements of its own, although they are expressed to be based upon a report, it will be liable for an inaccuracy unless in clear and unambiguous terms it has warned intending applicants that it does not vouch for the accuracy of the report, or of any statement based on it.

A company issued a prospectus inviting subscriptions for the purpose of buying a rubber estate in Peru. The prospectus contained extracts from the report of an expert on the spot, which gave the number of mature rubber trees on the estate, and other information. The report was false. *Held,* the accuracy of the report was prima facie the basis of the contract and, therefore, if the company did not intend to contract on that basis, it should have dissociated itself from the report in clear and unambiguous terms, and warned the public that it did not vouch for the accuracy of the report. As there was no such warning the contracts to take shares could be rescinded: *Re Pacaya Rubber and Produce Co. Ltd* [1914] 1 Ch. 542.[56]

An *innocent* misrepresentation is a sufficient ground for rescission. It is not necessary to prove knowledge of the untruth of the statement.[57]

Non-disclosure of a material fact amounts to misrepresentation if the omission makes what is stated misleading. It has been said[58] that "It is not that the omission of material facts is an independent ground for rescission, but the omission must be of such a nature as to make the statement actually made misleading.[59]"

(2) The allottee must have been induced to subscribe by the false statement.

Whether or not an allottee was induced to subscribe by reason of the misrepresentation is a question of fact depending on the circumstances of each case. It is not sufficient that the prospectus has been widely advertised in the locality if there is proof that the applicant relied, not on the prospectus, but on independent advice.[60] He is entitled to rely upon the prospectus, and is not

---

[55] *Bentley & Co. v. Black* (1893) 9 T.L.R. 580 (C.A.).
[56] An earlier Scottish case which went to the House of Lords is *Mair v. Rio Grande Rubber Estates Ltd,* 1913 S.C. (H.L.) 74.
[57] *Per* Lord Shaw of Dunfermline in *Mair v. Rio Grande Rubber Estates Ltd,* 1913 S.C. (H.L.) 74 at p. 81.
[58] *Per* Rigby L.J. in *McKeown v. Boudard Peveril Gear Co. Ltd* (1896) 74 L.T. 712 at p. 713.
[59] *Coles v. White City (Manchester) Greyhound Assn. Ltd* (1929) 4S T.L.R. 230(C.A.).
[60] *M'Morland's Trustees v. Fraser* (1896) 24 R. 65.

bound to verify the statements it contains. Where, therefore, a prospectus simply gave the dates of and parties to contracts and stated where they could be inspected, without indicating that they were material contracts, the omission of the applicant to inspect them did not fix him with notice of their contents.[61]

The false statement need not have been the decisive inducing cause of the contract. It is enough that it was one of the contributory causes.[62]

Rescission enables the allottee to recover what he paid for the shares or debentures, plus interest.[63]

The right to rescind is lost—

(1) If, after discovering the misrepresentation, the allottee does an act which shows that he elects to retain the shares and so affirms the contract; for example, he attends and votes at general meetings,[64] receives dividends,[65] or attempts to sell the shares.[66]

(2) If he fails to act within a reasonable time of discovering the true facts.

The right to rescind must be exercised promptly if the company is a going concern, and even a delay of a fortnight has been held to be too long in such a case.[67] When a shareholder was put on inquiry in June, but took no steps to make any investigation until November, his delay prevented him from rescinding the contract.[68]

(3) If restitution is impossible[69] e.g. because he sells the shares.

(4) If the company goes into liquidation.[70]

---

[61] *Aaron's Reefs Ltd v. Twiss* [1896] A.C. 273.
[62] *Edgington v. Fitzmaurice* (1885) 29 Ch.D. 459 (C.A.)
[63] *cf.* the damages available for actions in tort, *post,* p. 141.
[64] *Sharpley v. South and East Coast Ry. Co.* (1876) 2 Ch.D. 663 (C.A.).
[65] *Scholey v. Central Ry. of Venezuela* (1868) L.R. 9 Eq. 266n.
[66] *Ex p. Briggs* (1866) L.R. 1 Eq. 483.
[67] See *Re Scottish Petroleum Co.* (1883) 23 Ch.D. 413 (C.A.).
[68] *Re Christineville Rubber Estates Ltd* [1911] W.N. 216; *cf. Caledonian Debenture Co. Ltd v. Bernard* (1898) 5 S.L.T. 392 (O.H.). See also Lord President Inglis in *City of Edinburgh Brewery Co. Ltd v. Gibson's Trustee* (1869) 7 M. 886 at p. 891.
[69] *Western Bank v. Addie* (1867) 5 M. (H.L.) 80.
[70] *Oakes v. Turquand* (1867) L.R. 2 (H.L.) 325; *Western Bank v. Addie, ante; Houldsworth v. City of Glasgow Bank* (1880) 7 R. (H.L.) 53; (1879) 6 R. 1164.

## Damages for fraud

Fraud is difficult to prove. Nevertheless, promoters, directors, experts or the persons making an offer for sale, are liable for fraud if it can be shown that they signed, or authorised the issue of, a prospectus or listing particulars containing a false statement which they did not honestly believe to be true[71] with the intention that another person should act upon it, and that he acted on it to his detriment. The test is subjective, *i.e.* did they honestly believe the statement to be true according to its meaning as understood *by them*, albeit erroneously, when it was made.[72] If they cannot be proved to have made a false representation knowingly, or without belief in its truth, or recklessly, careless whether it be true or false, they may have to pay compensation under the statutory provisions, *ante,* the predecessor of which[73] was first enacted as a result of the decision in *Derry v. Peek.*[74]

A tramway company by a special Act had power to move trams by animal power and, with the consent of the Board of Trade, by steam power. A prospectus was issued by the the directors stating that the company, under its special Act, had the right to use steam power instead of horses. P. subscribed for shares on the strength of this statement. The Board of Trade afterwards refused its consent, and the company was wound up. P. sued the directors for damages for fraud. *Held,* the directors were not liable, the statement as to steam power having been made in the honest belief that it was true: *Derry v. Peek* (1889) 14 App.Cas. 337.

The measure of damages for fraud is prima facie the difference between the actual value of the shares at the time of allotment and the sum paid for them.[75] The plaintiff recovers for all the actual damage directly flowing from the fraudulent misrepresentation.[76] It is not an action for breach of contract and therefore no damages in respect of prospective gains can be recovered.

---

[71] *Per* Lord Herschell in *Derry v. Peek* (1889) 14 App. Cas. 337 at p. 374.
[72] *Akerhielm v. De Mare* [1959] A.C. 789 (P.C.).
[73] Directors' Liability Act 1890.
[74] The explanation of fraud given in that case was referred to with approval in the Scottish case of *Boyd & Forrest v. Glasgow etc. Rlwy. Co.,* 1912 S.C. (H.L.) 93. See also *Lees v. Tod* (1882) 9 R. 807.
[75] *McConnel v. Wright* (1903) 1 Ch. 546 (C.A.); *Davidson v. Tulloch* (1860) 3 Macq. 783; 22 D. (H.L.) 7.
[76] *Doyle v. Olby (Ironmongers) Ltd* [1969] 2 Q.B. 158 (C.A.); *c.f. Smith New Court Securities Ltd v. Scrimgeour Vickers (Asset Management) Ltd* [1994] 2 BCLC 212 (C.A.).

## Direct Invitations, Offers For Sale, Placings

Shares or debentures may be offered to the public by means of—

(1) a direct invitation to the public; or
(2) an offer for sale; or
(3) a "placing".

### Offers for sale

An offer for sale is the usual way in which shares or debentures are offered to the public. It occurs when an issuing house (either a specialised concern or a department of a merchant bank) subscribes for an issue of shares or debentures and then invites the public to purchase from it at a higher price.

Where it is difficult to fix the issue price of the shares or debentures being offered to the public, because it is uncertain what the public response to the offer will be, an offer for sale by tender may be made. In this event, a minimum price is fixed and the issue price is determined by the prices tendered in the applications. Thus, where 250,000,000 ordinary 25p shares are offered, a minimum price of 80p a share may be fixed. The prices tendered may range from 80p to £2 and the shares may all be sold at 87p. The object is to ensure that the company receives what the shares are worth to the public, and to defeat stags who, by taking shares and then immediately selling them at a higher price, would otherwise receive the difference between the issue price of a share and its worth to the public.

### Placings

An issue of shares or debentures may be placed in one of two ways. An issuing house may subscribe for the issue and then invite its clients (*e.g.* insurance companies and pension funds) to purchase from it at a higher price.

Alternatively, an issuing house or stockbrokers or a bank may, without subscribing, act as agents for the company and invite their clients to take from the company. In this case the agents will be paid a commission called "brokerage" for their services.

## COMMISSIONS AND DISCOUNTS

In order to procure capital a company frequently desires to pay a commission or discount to a person introducing capital.

Section 97(1) of the Companies Act 1985 allows a company to pay a commission to a person in consideration of his subscribing or agreeing to subscribe, absolutely or conditionally, or procuring or agreeing to procure subscriptions, for *shares* in the company if, in addition to complying with any conditions in rules made by the Secretary of State under section 169 of the Financial Services Act 1986 *(ante)*:

(1)  the payment is authorised by the articles (authority in the memorandum is insufficient[77]);

(2)  the commission does not exceed either (a) any limit imposed by such rules or, if there are no such limits, 10 per cent. of the price at which the shares are issued, or (b) the amount or rate authorised by the articles, whichever is the less.

This subsection applies as well to private as to public companies.[78] It enables a company to pay underwriting commission or brokerage, which commissions are dealt with later.[79]

Section 98 of the 1985 Act provides that, except as allowed by subsection (1), no company shall apply any of its shares or capital money, either directly or indirectly, in payment of any commission, discount or allowance to any person in consideration of his subscribing or agreeing to subscribe, whether absolutely or conditionally, or procuring or agreeing to procure subscriptions, absolute or conditional, for any *shares* in the company, whether the shares or money be applied by being added to the purchase money or any property acquired by the company or to the contract price of any work to be done for the company, or the money be paid out of the nominal purchase money or contract price, or otherwise.

An agreement to pay commission in contravention of section 98 is invalid.

The company agreed to pay A. a commission of 10 per cent. on any sum accepted by the company on A.'s introduction. No statement in

[77] *Re Republic of Bolivia Exploration Syndicate Ltd* [1914] 1 Ch. 139.
[78] *Dominion of Canada General Trading Syndicate v. Brigstocke* [1911] 2. K.B. 648.
[79] pp. 144, 145.

prescribed form, as required by section 53, was registered with the Registrar. A. was the means of introducing £4,600 to the company, and was paid £200 on account. A. sued for £260, the balance of commission. *Held,* A. was not entitled to recover, as the commission was unlawful, but the company could not recover the £200 already paid to A.: *Andreae Zinc Mines of Great Britain Ltd* [1918] 2 K.B. 454.

An agreement by a company to apply some of its shares partly for underwriting services and partly for other services is caught by section 98, *ante,* and the whole agreement is invalid.[80]

If shares are allotted at par to persons who are given an option to subscribe for further shares at par within a certain time, an allotment of such further shares at par is not subject to the provisions of section 98 of the 1985 Act, even though the market value of the shares has risen to a premium, because it does not involve the payment of a commission or discount.[81]

## UNDERWRITING

Before an issue of shares is made to the public, it is usual to insure the success of the issue by having it underwritten. Underwriting means "agreeing to take so many shares, more or less in number, as are specified in the underwriting letter if the public do not subscribe for them."[82] Another definition is, an agreement "to take up by way of subscription in a new company or new issue a certain number of shares if and so far as not applied for by the public.[83] An underwriter does not guarantee that the public will take up the shares; he agrees with the company to subscribe for them himself on the happening of an event, *i.e.* the failure of the public to subscribe them fully. The underwriter may be, for example, a broker, a bank or an issuing house.

The consideration for underwriting usually takes the form of an underwriting commission which the underwriter receives whether or not the public take up all the shares underwritten. The commission may be in the form of shares or it may be a payment

---

[80] *Banking Service Corporation Ltd v. Toronto Finance Corporation Ltd* [1928] A.C. 333 (P.C.).

[81] *Hilder v. Dexter* [1902] A.C. 474; *cf. Cameron v. Glenmorangie Distillery Co. Ltd* (1896) 23 R. 1092.

[82] *Per* Lindley L.J. in *Re Licensed Victuallers' Mutual Trading Association* (1889) 42 Ch.D. 1 (C.A.), at p. 7.

[83] *Per* Lord Tomlin in *Australian Investment Trust Ltd v. Strand and Pitt Street Properties Ltd* [1932] A.C. 735 (P.C.) at p. 745.

out of the money derived from the issue of shares underwritten. Again, it is thought that it may be a payment out of the company's profits, if the company has profits in hand and they have not been capitalised. In any case, section 97 of the 1985 Act, above, must be complied with.

## Sub-underwriting

It is a common practice for underwriters to relieve themselves from some of their risk by entering into sub-underwriting contracts. In such cases a sub-underwriter, in return for a commission, becomes bound to take and pay for his proportion of the shares sub-underwritten which are not allotted to the public.

By the nature of a sub-underwriting contract the sub-underwriter authorises the underwriter to apply for shares on his behalf if the public do not apply for them and he cannot revoke the authority so given, whether or not the sub-underwriting letter contains a formal grant of authority to the underwriter. The authority is coupled with an interest.[84]

## BROKERAGE

Brokerage is a payment made to an issuing house or brokers in return for their placing shares or debentures without subscribing.[85] It differs from underwriting commission in that it is a payment made to a person for placing shares or debentures without involving him in any risk of having to take them. Section 98(3) of the Companies Act 1985 provides that nothing in the section affects the power of any company to pay such brokerage as was previously lawful. It was previously held in *Metropolitan Coal Consumers' Association v. Scrimgeour*[86] that brokerage of a reasonable amount payable in the ordinary course of business was legal.

A payment is brokerage only if it is paid to "stockbrokers, bankers and the like, who exhibit prospectuses and send them to their customers, and by whose mediation the customers are induced to subscribe."[87] The person to whom it is paid must be

[84] *Re Olympic etc. Reinsurance Co. Ltd* [1920] 2 Ch. 341 (C.A.); *cf. Premier Briquette Co. Ltd v. Gray,* 1922 S.C. 329.
[85] *Ante,* p. 142.
[86] [1885] 2 Q.B. 604 (C.A.).
[87] *Per* Bailhache J. in *Andreae v. Zinc Mines of Great Britain Ltd* [1918] 2 K.B. 454, at p. 458.

one who, in some way, carries on the business of a broker. A
payment, therefore, to a lady of a percentage on the amount of
capital which she induced third parties to subscribe for shares in a
company—such a transaction being an isolated one, and not in
the ordinary course of the lady's business—was held not to be
brokerage.[88]

---

[88] *Andreae v. Zinc Mines of Great Britain Ltd, ante.*

## Chapter 8

# ALLOTMENT AND COMMENCEMENT OF BUSINESS

THIS chapter deals first with the powers of the directors and the company to allot shares, then with the contract of allotment under which shares are allotted by a company to a person who has applied for them, certain statutory restrictions on allotment by a public company, and the return which the company usually must deliver to the Registrar after it has allotted shares. Finally, the chapter deals with certain statutory restrictions on the commencement of business by a public company.

## Power to allot shares

Prior to the 1980 Act directors generally had the power to allot shares up to the limit of the authorised capital.[1] This led to several abuses by directors allotting shares to their allies in order to forestall take-over bids.[2] Under what is now section 80 of the 1985 Act, however, the directors of any company may not allot shares, or any right to acquire shares, without express authority being given either in the articles or by a resolution in general meeting.

Such authority may be given for a specific allotment or generally and must state the maximum amount of the shares which may be issued. Even if the authority is given by the articles it cannot last for more than five years, and, in any case, it can be varied, revoked or renewed by an ordinary resolution. Thus the articles may actually be altered, on this one occasion, by an ordinary resolution.[3] A copy of any resolution either conferring, revoking, varying or renewing the authority must, however, be registered with the Registrar as if it were a special resolution,

[1] *Ante,* p. 75.
[2] See, *e.g. Hogg v. Cramphorn* [1967] Ch. 254; *Bamford v. Bamford* [1970] Ch. 212; *post,* p. 351.
[3] *cf.* s.9; *ante,* p. 83.

under section 380,[4] and notice of it must be put in the appropriate Gazette under section 711.[5]

A private company may by elective resolution[6] decide that section 80A shall apply. In such a case the directors can be given either an indefinite authority to allot shares or one for any fixed period, rather than for the five year maximum period. The only restrictions are that the authority must state the maximum amount of shares which may be allotted under it and, if it is for a fixed period, the date on which it is to expire. Such authority may still be varied or revoked by an ordinary resolution. If the election itself is revoked (by an ordinary resolution) then the authority under section 80A will be construed as one for five years only. Thus for example if it has been in existence for six years it will cease immediately.

Nothing in section 80 affects the validity of any allotment, but any director who knowingly and wilfully contravenes it may be prosecuted and fined. It has no application to employee share schemes.[7]

## Pre-emption rights

The 1980 Act introduced further restrictions on the allotment of ordinary, "equity", shares by companies for cash other than those subject to employee share schemes. This basic restriction is, however, subject to wide exemptions.

Under section 89 of the 1985 Act, ordinary shares issued for cash must first be offered to existing,[8] ordinary shareholders in proportion to the nominal value of their existing holdings. The articles may go further and provide for such pre-emption rights to apply with each class of ordinary shares. Such rights are not given by the Act to the holders of preference shares or shares to be paid for, in whole or in part, otherwise than by cash. Any offer must be open for 21 days.[9] Any shares not taken up on the *pro rata* basis must then be offered to the ordinary shareholders generally. Any contravention of the statutory or other pre-emption rights renders the company and any officer in default

---

[4] *Post,* p. 307.
[5] *Post,* p. 307.
[6] Elective resolutions must be unanimous. See p. 306, *post.*
[7] *Post,* p. 246.
[8] Including those who held shares 28 days before the offer made.
[9] s.90.

liable to compensate any existing shareholders who have suffered a loss as a result.

Private companies may exclude the effects of section 89 by a provision to that effect in their articles: section 91. Such exclusions must be clear, however, and where the articles can be read consistently with the sections, the latter will apply.[9a] In addition, both public and private companies may qualify or exclude pre-emption rights if their directors have the authority to issue shares under section 80.[10] If the directors have a general authority to allot shares under that section the company, either by its articles, or by a special resolution, may vary or exclude section 89 altogether. On the other hand, if the directors only have authority to make a specific allotment, section 89 can only be modified or excluded by a special resolution recommended by the directors and supported by a circular sent out with the notices of the meeting, setting out the directors' reasons for making the recommendation, the amount to be paid to the company on the allotment, and the directors' justification for that amount. Directors who issue a misleading, false or deceptive circular in support of such a resolution may be convicted and fined or imprisoned. The exclusion or modification of pre-emption rights in this way may be renewed or revoked by a special resolution: section 95.[11]

## AGREEMENT FOR ALLOTMENT

The ordinary law of contract, which usually requires an offer and an acceptance if there is to be an agreement, applies to agreements to take shares in a company. Where a prospectus or listing particulars are issued by the company, otherwise than on a rights issue, the document is not an offer—it is merely an invitation to the public to make offers. An offer is made by the applicant in sending a form of application for shares to the company and it is accepted by the allotment of shares to the applicant. Under normal articles the power to allot shares is vested in the board of directors. Shares will be allotted when the board passes the

[9a] *Re Thundercrest Ltd* [1994] BCC 857.
[10] *Ante,* p. 147.
[11] This procedure is modified by Sched. 15A, para. 3 if the written resolution procedure is used by a private company (see *post,* p. 308). The circular must be sent to each member prior to his signature.

appropriate resolution. They will not actually be issued, however, until they are entered into the register of members.[12]

An acceptance must be unconditional[13] and correspond with the terms of the offer. If, therefore, the application was for 100 shares and only 25 were allotted, the allotment would be a counter-offer and the applicant could refuse to take any shares. An issue may be over-subscribed, and the company unable to make an allotment in full to every applicant. In order to obviate these difficulties the form of the application usually runs, "I agree to accept such shares or any smaller number that may be allotted to me."

To constitute a binding contract, an acceptance must be communicated to the offeror.[14] If the parties must have contemplated that the post might be used to communicate acceptance, the posting of a letter of allotment is sufficient communication to the applicant.

> G. applied for shares in the H. company. A letter of allotment was posted, but never reached G. *Held*, G. was a shareholder in the company: *Household Fire Insurance Co. v. Grant* (1879) 4 Ex.D. 216 (C.A.).[15]

Communication, however, may be made in any way which shows the applicant that the company has accepted his offer,[16] *e.g.* by a letter demanding payment of an instalment on the shares,[17] or by receipt of a notice calling a general meeting and notification given orally by the secretary that shares have been allotted.[18] The applicant must, however, have *agreed* to take shares and not merely have expressed a "willingness" to take them.[19] The sending to a person who has not so agreed of notices of meetings and of letters making calls on the shares does not of itself make the recipient a shareholder.[20]

---

[12] *National Westminster Bank plc v. I.R.C.* [1994] 2 BCLC 239 (H.L.).

[13] *Liquidator of the Consolidated Copper Co. etc. Ltd v. Peddie* (1877) 5 R. 393.

[14] See *Entores Ltd v. Miles Far East Corporation* [1955] 2 Q.B. 327 (C.A.).

[15] Doubted in Scotland: *Mason v. Benhar Coal Co. Ltd* (1882) 9 R. 883, *per* Lord Shand at p. 890.

[16] *Chapman v. Sulphite Pulp Co. Ltd* (1892) 19 R. 837.

[17] *Forget v. Cement Products Co. of Canada* [1916] W.N. 259 (P.C.)

[18] *Chapman v. Sulphite Pulp Co. Ltd* (1892) 19 R. 837; see also *Curror's Trustee v. Caledonian Heritable Security Co. Ltd* (1880) 7 R. 479 and *Nelson v. Fraser* (1906) 14 S.L.T. 513 (O.H.).

[19] *Mason v. Benhar Coal Co. Ltd* (1882) 9 R. 883.

[20] *Goldie v. Torrance* (1882) 10 R. 174; and see *Liquidator of the Florida etc. Co. Ltd v. Bayley* (1890) 17 R. 525.

An offer can be revoked at any time before acceptance is communicated.

H. applied for shares in a company. Shares were allotted to him, and the letter of allotment sent to the *company's* agent to deliver by hand to H. Before the letter was delivered H. withdrew his application. *Held*, H. was not a shareholder in the company: *Re National Savings Bank Association* (1867) L.R. 4 Eq. 9.

To be effective, revocation of an offer must be communicated to the offeree. Thus notice of the revocation of an application must reach the company before the letter of allotment is posted.[21] If the revocation is communicated by post it is not effective until the letter is received by the company.

An offer lapses if it is not accepted within the time prescribed or, if none is prescribed, within a reasonable time. Thus an allotment must be made within a reasonable time after the application, otherwise the application will lapse and the applicant will be entitled to refuse to take the shares.

On June 8 M. offered to take shares in the R. company. He heard nothing until November 23, when he received a letter of acceptance. M. refused to take the shares, *Held*, M. was entitled to refuse, as his offer had lapsed: *Ramsgate Victoria Hotel Co. Ltd v. Montefiore* (1866) L.R. 1 Ex. 109.

An offer is also terminated by the failure of a condition subject to which it was made. Thus if an application for shares is conditional, *e.g.* on the applicant having a contract to supply goods to the company,[22] or on all capital being subscribed,[23] and the condition is not fulfilled when shares are allotted to him, the applicant is under no liability to take the shares.

A conditional application must be distinguished from an application for shares coupled with a collateral agreement, *e.g.* where £10 shares are to be paid up to the extent of £1.50 in cash on allotment, that the balance is to be set-off against goods to be supplied to the company by the allottee. In the latter case, when shares are allotted the applicant becomes a shareholder with the right merely of suing the company on the collateral agreement.[24]

---

[21] *Byrne v. Van Tienhoven* (1880) 5 C.P.D. 344; *Thomson v. James* (1855) 18 D. 1.

[22] *Shackelford's Case* (1866) L.R. 1 Ch.App. 567.

[23] *Swedish Match Co. Ltd v. Seivwright* (1889) 16 R. 989.

[24] *Elkington's Case* (1867) L.R. 2 Ch.App. 511; *cf. Liquidator of the Pelican etc. Insurance Co. Ltd v. Bruce* (1904) 11 S.L.T. 658 (O.H.), and see opinions in *National House etc. Investment Co. Ltd v. Watson*, 1908 S.C. 88.

## RESTRICTIONS ON ALLOTMENT

Sections 84, 85, 88 and 101 contain restrictions on allotment by *public* companies. Section 84 provides that no allotment can be made unless either the capital is subscribed for in full or the offer states that if it is not so subscribed the allotment will nevertheless take place subject to any specified conditions.

If any of the above conditions are not satisfied within 40 days of the first issue of the prospectus, all money received must be forthwith returned to the applicants without interest. If it is not returned within 48 days of the issue of the prospectus, the directors are jointly and severally liable to repay it with interest at five per cent. per annum. A director is not liable, however, if he proves that the default in repayment was not due to any misconduct or negligence on his part.

A sum is, for the purposes of this section, deemed to have been paid to and received by the company if a cheque for the sum has been received in good faith by the company and the directors have no reason to suspect that it will not be paid. Any condition requiring an applicant to waive compliance with any of these requirements is void.

### No allotment unless minimum payment paid up

Under section 101 no share may be allotted unless one quarter of the nominal value and the whole of any premium on the share has been paid up. In breach the share will be regarded as having been so paid up but the allottee and any subsequent holder will be liable to pay that amount together with interest. A bona fide purchaser without actual notice of the breach is not liable nor any successor to such a person. In addition the court may grant relief under section 113. Contravention by the company and any officer in default is a criminal offence; section 114.

### Effect of irregular allotment

When an allotment is made which does not satisfy the provisions of section 84, *ante,* section 85 gives the applicant two remedies, one against the company and the other against the directors.

As against the *company*, the allotment is *voidable* by the allottee within one month after allotment, even if the company is being wound up. Legal proceedings need not be taken within a month. Notice of avoidance within the month, followed by prompt legal proceedings after the month, is sufficient.[25]

As against the *directors*, the allottee can sue such of them as have knowingly contravened or authorised the contravention of the provisions for any loss, damages or costs he may have sustained or incurred thereby. Any such proceedings against directors must be brought within two years after allotment. The company has a similar remedy against the directors for any loss, damages or costs sustained or incurred by it.

## RETURN AS TO ALLOTMENTS

Section 88 provides that whenever a limited company with a share capital makes any allotment of its *shares*, it must, within a month, deliver to the Registrar—

(1) A return of the allotments, stating the number and nominal amount of the shares, the names, addresses and descriptions of the allottees and the amount paid or payable on each share, whether on account of the nominal value of the share or by way of premium.

(2) In the case of shares allotted *otherwise than for cash*, a contract constituting the title of the allottee to the allotment, together with any contract of sale or for services or other consideration for the allotment, and a return stating the number and nominal amount of shares so allotted, the extent to which they are to be treated as paid up, and the consideration for the allotment.

## RESTRICTIONS ON COMMENCEMENT OF BUSINESS

A private company can commence business, exercise any borrowing power[26] which it has and make binding contracts immediately on incorporation.

By section 117 a public company must do none of these things until it has either obtained a certificate from the Registrar that it may do so or is re-registered as a private company.

---

[25] *Re National Motor Mail-Coach Co. Ltd* [1908] 2 Ch. 228.
[26] *Post,* Chap. 23.

To obtain a certificate under this section the company must make a declaration to the Registrar in the prescribed form signed by a director or secretary of the company:

(1) Stating that the nominal value of the company's *allotted* share capital is not less than the authorised minimum (£50,000)[27];

(2) Disclosing the amount of such allotted share capital actually paid up at that time (at least 25 per cent. of the nominal value and the whole of any premium is necessary[28],

(3) Stating the amount, or estimated amount, of the preliminary expenses of the company and the persons by whom any of those expenses have been paid or are payable; and

(4) Detailing any amount or benefit paid or given or intended to be paid or given to any promoter of the company, and the consideration for the payment or benefit.

This declaration may be accepted by the Registrar as sufficient evidence of the matters stated therein.

If the Registrar issues a certificate under this section it is conclusive evidence that the company is entitled to do business and exercise any borrowing powers.

If a public company enters into a transaction without a certificate under section 117, the transaction remains valid, but if the company fails to comply with any obligations under it within 21 days of being called upon to do so, the directors are liable to indemnify the other party for any loss suffered as a result. In addition, the company and any officer in default will be guilty of a criminal offence.

Finally, if more than a year after the incorporation of a public company it has not been issued with a section 117 certificate, the Secretary of State may petition the court for the company to be wound up under section 122 of the Insolvency Act 1986.[29]

---

[27] s.118.
[28] s.101, *post,* p. 159.
[29] *Post,* Chap. 27.

**Chapter 9**

# SHARE CAPITAL

THE topics dealt with in this chapter are the rules that a company's share capital must be raised and, once raised, must be maintained for the benefit of creditors, and the consequent need to control the reduction of share capital. The associated topics of the purchase and redemption by a company of its own shares and the giving of financial assistance by a company for the acquisition of its own shares are dealt with in the following two chapters.

## MEANING OF "CAPITAL"

The word "capital" used in connection with a company has several different meanings, thus it may mean the nominal or authorised share capital, the issued or allotted share capital, the paid-up share capital or the reserve share capital of the company.

The *nominal* or *authorised capital* is merely the amount of share capital which the company is authorised to issue, not what it has actually issued. As we have seen,[1] in the case of a limited company the amount of potential share capital with which it proposes to be registered, and the division thereof into shares of a fixed amount, must be set out in the memorandum of association, but this amount may be increased or reduced as explained later.[2] Companies may fix on any figure, which is large enough for its potential requirements. In earlier times, stamp duty was payable on this figure which had the effect of keeping it as low as possible, but that no longer applies. It must be remembered that public companies must have at least £50,000 authorised capital; sections 11 and 118.

The *issued* or *allotted capital* is that part of the company's nominal capital which has been issued or allotted to the shareholders. The company is not bound to allot all its capital at once,

---

[1] *Ante*, p. 75.
[2] *Post*, pp. 166, 173.

although a public company must allot at least £50,000 nominal value of shares before it may commence business (section 117). Allotments of capital are made as they are needed by the directors, if properly authorised under the Act,[3] up to the amount allowed by the authorised capital figure. The restrictions and controls imposed by the Act relate in general to the *allotted* shares. In certain cases, such as taxation, it may be important to distinguish between the allotment and issue of shares. In *National Westminster Bank plc v. I.R.C.*,[4] the House of Lords by a majority decided that a share is allotted when the company and shareholder are contractually bound and it is only issued when the shareholder is registered as such on the register of members.[5]

The *paid-up capital* is that part of the issued capital which has been paid up by the shareholders. The company may, for example, have a nominal capital of £500,000 divided into 500,000 shares of a nominal amount of £1 each, of which £400,000 is issued, *i.e.* 400,000 of the shares have been issued, and only £100,000 has been paid up, *i.e.* the company has so far required only 25p. to be paid up on each share. The *uncalled capital* is the remainder of the issued capital and can be called up at any time by the company from the shareholders in accordance with the provisions of the articles. Section 101 requires public companies to call up at least one quarter of the nominal value of a share and all the premium on allotment.

The *reserve capital,* or reserve liability, is that part of the uncalled capital which a limited company has by special resolution determined shall not be called up except in the event and for the purposes of the company's being wound up and which cannot otherwise be called up: section 120. This capital is not under the control of the directors and cannot be reconverted into ordinary uncalled capital, or charged by the company, *e.g.* as security for debentures.[6] It is available only for the creditors on the winding up of the company, although it will be seen that it can be reduced with the consent of the court under section 135.[7] Reserve capital must be distinguished from capital reserves, a capital redemption reserve, revenue reserves, and a reserve or a general reserve, all of which will be dealt with later.[8]

[3] *Ante,* p. 147.
[4] [1994] 2 BCLC 239 (H.L.)
[5] *Post,* p. 214.
[6] *Re Mayfair Property Co.* [1898] 2 Ch. 28 (C.A.).
[7] *Re Midland Rlwy. Carriage Co.* (1907) 23 T.L.R. 661.
[8] *Post,* Chap. 22.

Section 351 provides that if, in the case of a company having a share capital, there is on the stationery used for any business letters, or on the order forms of the company, a reference to the amount of the share capital, the reference must be to paid-up share capital.

The paid-up share capital includes the nominal value of the shares paid-up and any premium on such shares.[9] For example if 10,000 £1 shares are sold for £2 each the paid up capital will be £20,000. This will however be expressed as £10,000 share capital and £10,000 share premium account in the balance sheet.

## RAISING OF SHARE CAPITAL

The issued share capital of a company is the fund to which creditors of the company can look for payment of their debts, and so, to protect the creditors, it has been held that the issued share capital must be raised. This means that shares can be treated as paid up only to the extent of the amount actually received by the company in cash or in kind, and must not be issued at a discount, i.e. must not be issued as fully paid for a consideration less than payment or the promise of payment of the nominal amount of each share,[10] although the company may not necessarily require payment in full of the nominal amount on allotment. There is no objection to shares being issued at a premium, i.e. at more than the nominal value.[11] The rule that the share capital must be raised is intended to ensure that money or assets equal in amount or value to the paid-up capital on paper is or are received by the company. Certain sections of the Act, e.g. section 98, which generally prohibits the payment of commissions and discounts out of a company's shares or capital money,[12] and section 23, which provides that a subsidiary company generally may not be a member of its holding company,[13] also have the effect of ensuring that the capital is raised. The provisions relating to payment for share capital are also intended to strengthen this rule.[14]

[9] Post, p. 164.
[10] Ooregum Gold Mining Co. v. Roper [1892] A.C. 125, codified by s.100, post, p. 158.
[11] Post p. 164.
[12] Ante, p. 143.
[13] Post, p. 214.
[14] Post, p. 160.

## ISSUE OF SHARES AT A DISCOUNT

The general rule has always been that shares must *not* be issued at a discount, *i.e.* must not be issued as fully paid for a consideration less than the nominal amount. This is now expressly stated in section 100. The shareholder must pay the full nominal value of his shares, whether he pays in cash or in kind, together with interest on the discount. Any subsequent holder of the shares may also be held liable for the discount unless he is a bona fide purchaser for value without actual notice of the discount issue or a subsequent transferee of the shares from such a person. The court may grant relief in appropriate circumstances under section 113. Contravention of section 100 is a criminal offence by the company and any officer in default (section 114). The general principle was first established in England by the House of Lords in 1892.

> The market value of the £1 ordinary shares of a company was 2s 6d. The company thereupon issued preference shares of £1 each with 15s. credited as paid, leaving a liability of only 5s. a share. A contract to this effect was registered under what is now s.52. *Held,* the issue was *ultra vires,* and allottees were liable to pay for the shares in full: *Ooregum Gold Mining Co. of India Ltd v. Roper* [1892] A.C. 125.[15]
>
> "The dominant and cardinal principle of [the Companies] Acts is that the investor shall purchase immunity from liability beyond a certain limit on the terms that there shall be and remain a liability up to that limit": *per* Lord Macnaghten at p. 145.

There is no issue at a discount where shares are issued at par, *e.g.* after the exercise of an option to take them up at par, even though they could otherwise be issued at premium,[16] or where shares are issued at a lesser premium than that at which they might have been paid.[17]

There is nothing to prevent debentures being issued at a discount. However, in the case of convertible debentures, if the debentures are issued at a discount, with a right to exchange them for fully paid shares equal in nominal amount to the par

---

[15] An earlier Scottish case to the same effect is *Klenck v. East India Co. etc. Ltd* (1888) 16 R. 271, where the memorandum contained a power to issue shares at a discount.

[16] *Hilder v. Dexter* [1902] A.C., *post,* p. 164.

[17] *Cameron v. Glenmorangie Distillery Co. Ltd* (1986) 23 R. 1092.

value of the debentures, the right has been held void as being a right to an issue of shares at a discount.[18] The right will be valid if it is a right to fully paid shares equal in nominal amount to the issue price of the debentures—the shares will not then be issued at a discount.

The general rule is subject to the following exceptions:

(1) There is in effect a discount when shares are issued by a private company for an overvalued non-monetary consideration, as in *Re Wragg Ltd, post*[19]

(2) Similarly where, under section 97, *ante*[20] commission is paid to a person who agrees to subscribe, or to procure subscriptions, for shares in a company.

## CONSIDERATION FOR ALLOTMENT

The general rule is therefore that an allottee must pay for his shares in full. Under section 99(1) shares are only treated as paid up to the extent that the company has received money or money's worth (including goodwill and know-how) in return for them. Section 99(2) further prohibits a public company from accepting an undertaking by any person to do work or perform services in return for shares. Such an undertaking may nevertheless be enforced by the company (section 115), and the holder of shares issued in return for such undertaking becomes liable to pay any shortfall in the value for the shares (section 99(3)).

Any subsequent holder of shares not regarded as fully paid up as a result of a breach of section 99, may be liable for the amount due, unless he is either a bona fide purchaser of the shares without actual notice of the defect, or an immediate subsequent transferee from such a person (section 112). The court may grant relief in appropriate circumstances (section 113). Contravention of section 99 by a company and any officer in default is a criminal offence (section 114).

Under section 101 public companies are further prevented from allotting shares unless at least one quarter of the nominal value and the whole of any premium has actually been paid. This is a restriction on allotment and has been dealt with in chapter 8.

---

[18] *Mosely v. Koffyfontien Mines Ltd* [1904] 2 Ch. 108 (C.A.).
[19] p. 162.
[20] p. 143.

Shares taken by any subscriber to the memorandum of a public company in pursuance of an undertaking of his in the memorandum must be paid up in cash (section 106).

## Payment of non-cash consideration—public companies

Section 102 prohibits a public company[21] from accepting as consideration for shares any undertaking, *e.g.* to transfer property, which is to be or may be performed more than five years after the date of the allotment. Any variation of a valid undertaking (*i.e.* within five years) taking it outside the five year period is void. Any allotment in contravention of this requirement, or a failure by the purchaser to fulfil a valid undertaking within the contract period, renders the allottee liable to pay the company the amount owed on the shares, together with interest. Any subsequent holder of the shares is also liable subject to the bona fide purchaser exemption noted above.[22]

Section 103 provides that a public company, and not just a quoted company, may not allot shares for any non-cash consideration unless a report on the value of the consideration had been made by an independent person qualified to be an auditor of the company. His report must be sent to the company within six months prior to the allotment and to the proposed allottee. He may accept another's valuation if it is reasonable to do so, provided that that person is also independent and appears to be qualified and such facts are disclosed in the report. The company's auditor may be so used: section 108.

The report must state the amount payable on the shares, a description of the consideration and the valuation methods used, the date of valuation and the extent to which the shares are to be treated as paid up by the consideration and in cash. It must be filed with the Registrar: section 111.

In making his report the expert may require from the officers of the company such information and explanation as he thinks necessary to enable him to carry out the valuation or to make the report. False, misleading or deceptive statements made in this context constitute criminal offences: section 110.

There is a general exemption for shares issued generally to shareholders in another company on a take-over or merger with

---

[21] The 2nd EC Directive which instigated these sections does not apply to private companies.
[22] *Ante*, p. 159.

the other company: section 103(5). Such issues are, however, subject to the extra-statutory rules on take-overs: see Chapter 31, *post*.

In default of such a report the allottee will be liable to pay any amount owed on the shares in cash if either he did not receive a copy of the report or he knew or ought to have known of the breach; section 103(6). Subsequent holders may also be liable subject to the bona fide purchaser exemption. Relief may again be given by the court if it is just and equitable to do so, taking into account the actual amount received for the shares and other liabilities of the allottee under the contract: section 113.[23] It is for the allottee to show that the company has actually received assets to the value of the nominal value and premium of the shares in order to obtain this relief.[24]

These provisions only apply if the shares are issued "otherwise than for cash." Issues for cash are defined in section 738(2) so as to include payment by a cheque received by the company in good faith, or the release of liability of the company for a defined sum (*i.e.* a set-off)[25] or an undertaking to pay cash at a future date. This may be thought to cover a multitude of sins although it does not include the assignment of a debt.[26]

It is convenient to note here that similar provisions apply, by virtue of sections 104 and 109, to the acquisitions by public companies of non-cash assets from any subscriber of the memorandum, within two years of the issue of the certificate entitling it to commence business, if the consideration to be given by the company is not less than 10 per cent of the nominal value of the company's issued shares at that time.[27]

**Payment of non-cash consideration—private companies**

Sections 102–112 do not apply to private companies, but where shares are allotted as fully or partly paid up otherwise than in cash, a contract constituting the title of the allottee to the allotment together with any contract of sale, or for services or

---

[23] See, *e.g. Re Ossory Estates plc* (1988) 4 BCC 460. In *Re Bradford Investments plc* [1991] BCLC 224 the failure to obtain a report led to the shareholders losing their right to vote under the articles.

[24] *Re Bradford Investments plc (No. 2)* [1991] BCLC 688.

[25] Thus preserving the decision in *Spargo's Case* (1873) L.R. 8 Ch.App. 407.

[26] *Systems Control plc v. Munro Corporate* [1990] BCC 386.

[27] *Ante*, p. 155.

other consideration for the allotment, or, if such a contract is not
in writing, particulars of the contract, must, with the return as to
allotments, be delivered to the Registrar, usually within a month
after the allotment: section 88.[28] Default renders the officers of
the company liable to penalties but does not make the allotment
void.

Any such contract must be supported by consideration. Provided there is some consideration, however, the courts will not
inquire into the adequacy of that consideration unless it is merely
colourable or manifestly inadequate. Thus provided property is
transferred to the company in return for shares the court will not
examine whether that property is actually worth the value of the
shares.[29] In England, however, past consideration is no
consideration.[30]

A private company decided to turn itself into a public company. Before
doing so it resolved to allot £6,000 of fully paid shares to the existing
directors and shareholders, and a contract was made agreeing to allot the
shares in consideration of their past services and expenses in forming the
company and establishing the business. The contract was registered and
the shares were allotted. The company afterwards went into liquidation.
*Held*, the director and shareholders were liable to pay for the shares, as
there was no consideration in money or money's worth for the allotment,
past services being no consideration: *Re Eddystone Marine Insurance
Co.* [1893] 3 Ch. 9 (C.A.).

An agreement by a private company to allot shares in consideration of services to be performed in the future also renders the
allottee liable to pay for the shares.[31] "It is not open to a
company to agree with the holder or proposed holder of its
shares to replace the statutory liability by a special contract
sounding in damages only".[32] However, a private company may
agree to pay a fixed sum immediately for services to be performed in the future, *e.g.* for the erection of a building, and to
satisfy that debt by the allotment of shares.[33]

[28] *Ante*, p. 153.
[29] *Re Wragg Ltd* [1897] Ch. 796; *Park Business Interiors Ltd v. Park* [1992] BCLC
1034.
[30] In Scotland past consideration is valid consideration so that, e.g., shares can be
issued in return for the past services of the company's promoters: *Park Business
Interiors Ltd v. Park* [1992] BCLC 1034.
[31] *National House etc. Investment Co. Ltd v. Watson*, 1908 S.C. 888.
[32] *Per* Parker J. in *Gardner v. Iredale* [1912] 1 Ch. 700, at p. 716.
[33] *Gardner v. Iredale*, above.

If there is a contract for the acceptance by a private company of specified property or services of substantial value in payment for shares, the court will not, whilst the contract stands, inquire into the adequacy of the consideration, as it it for the parties to make their own bargain.

The goodwill, stock-in-trade and property of a business was sold to a company for £46,000, of which £20,000 was to be paid in fully paid shares. The stock-in-trade was shown in the company's books at a figure of £11,000 less than the sum allocated to it in the agreement. On the company's going into liquidation, a misfeasance summons was taken out to obtain payment for the shares. *Held,* since the agreement could not be impeached, the adequacy of the consideration could not be gone into: *Re Wragg Ltd* [1897] 1 Ch. 796 (C.A.).

Where the contract is fraudulent or shows on the face of it that the consideration is illusory, the allottee is liable to pay for the shares.

G. agreed to sell a concession to a company which agreed to allot him as fully paid 400 shares forthwith and also one-fifth of any future increase of capital. *Held,* the agreement was good so far as it obliged the company to allot one-fifth of any future increase of capital but void so far as it relieved G. from paying for the shares. It was apparent that the value of the concession bore no relation to the amount of the shares: *Hong Kong and China Gas Co. Ltd v. Glen* [1914] 1 Ch. 527.
"If the agreement were that the property to be purchased should be valued, and that against this property shares should be issued as fully paid to an extent exceeding the amount of the valuation by one-third, the arrangement would ... be bad as to this excess of one-third. It would to this extent be apparent on the face of the contract that the attempted discharge of a part of the liability was illusory": *per* Sargant J., at p. 539.

When shares are issued in pursuance of a contract registered under section 88, and the allottee also subscribes the memorandum for the same number of shares, care should be taken to see that the agreement makes it clear that the shares for which the memorandum is signed are the same as those referred to in the agreement; otherwise both lots of shares will have to be paid for.[34] To prevent this from happening, it is usual for the allottee under the agreement not to subscribe the memorandum.

---

[34] *Fothergill's Case* (1873) L.R. 8 Ch.App. 270.

## ISSUE OF SHARES AT A PREMIUM

Where a company's issued shares have a market value greater
than the amount paid up up on them, when further shares are
being issued the company may require applicants to agree to pay
more than the nominal amount of the new shares, *i.e.* to pay a
premium.

A company may, without any special power in its articles, issue
its shares at a premium, *i.e.* for a consideration in cash or in kind
which exceeds the nominal amount of the shares, although there
is no law which obliges a company to issue its shares above par
because they are saleable at a premium in the market.[35] However,
by section 130, where shares are issued at a premium, whether
for cash or otherwise, a sum equal to the aggregate amount or
value of the premiums must be transferred to the "share premium account".

As will be seen later, section 130 extends the principle that the
share capital of a company must be maintained[36] to a share
premium account, because the section goes on to provide that the
provisions of the Act relating to reduction of capital apply to this
account, *i.e.* it cannot be reduced without leave of the court
except where it is applied in—

(1)  paying up unissued shares of the company to be issued to
     members as fully paid bonus shares[37], or
(2)  writing off (*a*) the preliminary expenses, or (*b*) the
     expenses of, or the commission paid or discount allowed
     on, an issue of shares or debentures of the company; or
(3)  providing for the premium payable by the company on
     the redemption of shares[38] or debentures.[39]

The object of the provision relating to the share premium
account is to prevent dividends being paid out of premiums
received on an issue of shares.[40] When, therefore, any part of the

---

[35] *Per* Lord Davey in *Hilder v. Dexter* [1902] A.C. 474, at p. 480, *Cameron's* case,
*ante.*
[36] *Re Moorgate Mercantile Holdings Ltd* [1980] 1 All E.R. *Post,* p. 174.
[37] Other ways in which bonus shares can be paid for are dealt with *post,* Chap. 22.
[38] *Post,* Chap. 10.
[39] *Post,* Chap. 23.
[40] As in *Drown v. Gaumont-British Picture Corporation Ltd* [1937] Ch. 402, where
there was a trading loss in one year but a dividend was paid out of the reserve
fund, part of which consisted of premium on issues of shares.

share premium account is otherwise distributed among the share-holders it is to be treated as if the company were reducing its capital by repaying paid-up share capital.[41] Although share premiums are regarded as capital, it is not capital belonging to any individual shareholder. The shareholder paying the premium has no dividend rights in respect of it and has no right to repayment of it in a winding up.

The issue of shares at a premium accentuates the unreality of the nominal or par value of a share. The capital in the share premium account is an anomalous form of capital because it is capital on which no dividend is paid, which is not attributable to the ownership of any class of shares, which is not part of the company's nominal capital, and which the ordinary investor may not realise is part of the company's actual capital.

## Share premium account and issues other than for cash

Shares can be issued at a premium not only for cash but also for consideration other than cash. If, in the latter case, the value of the consideration received, *e.g.* of land, exceeds the nominal value of the shares issued there is an issue of shares at a premium and section 130 applies.

In two cases this principle was applied where a company acquired shares in another company by virtue of an exchange of shares, *e.g.* on a merger or take-over, and the value of the shares acquired exceeded the value of the shares issued. The excess had to be transferred to the share premium account, with the result that the pre-acquisition profits of the acquired company, reflected in the value of its shares, were frozen and could not be distributed as dividends by the acquiring company: *Shearer v. Bercain*[42]; *Head (Henry) & Co. Ltd v. Ropner Holdings Ltd.*[43] Until the decision in *Shearer v. Bercain*, however, this principle was regarded as fallacious by many lawyers and accountants, with the result that few such transfers to share premium accounts had been made. Following that decision, the Act provides two forms of relief from the obligations of section 130 in certain defined

---

[41] *Re Duff's Settlements* [1951] Ch. 923 (C.A.).
[42] [1980] 3 All E.R. 295.
[43] [1952] Ch. 124.

circumstances.[44] The basic rule, however, remains valid in other circumstances.

## Merger relief

Where the issuing company acquires a 90 per cent. holding in another company by way of a share for share exchange no transfer to the share premium account need be made: section 131. In fact this is a wide relief as it applies whether or not the issuing company owned any shares in the other company e.g., it applies to a company owning 60 per cent. of the shares of a subsidiary acquiring another 30 per cent. There is no obligation in such cases to disclose any "premiums" in the balance sheet. It also applies if the consideration provided by the acquired company is a cancellation of its issued shares rather than an issue—a frequent practice in schemes of reconstruction.

## Group reconstruction relief

Where a wholly-owned subsidiary acquires a shareholding (not necessarily 100 per cent.) in a fellow subsidiary (not necessarily wholly-owned) in return for an allotment of its own shares or other non-cash assets to its holding company or another of its wholly-owned subsidiaries, relief from section 130 is available: section 132.[45] Only the lower of the cost or book value to the issuing company of the acquired shares need be taken into account.

Where both sections 131 and 132 could apply only the latter relief can be claimed.[46]

## ALTERATION OF SHARE CAPITAL

Section 121 provides that a limited company with a share capital, if so authorised by its articles, may alter the conditions of its memorandum relating to share capital by—

[44] These reliefs can be extended or varied by subsequent regulations: s. 134. In fact this has been done with respect to the second relief—see note 45 below. A general amnesty for pre-February 1981 mergers can be found in s.12 of the Companies Consolidation (Consequential Provisions) Act 1985.
[45] The present form of this relief originates from the Companies (Share Premium Account) Regulations 1984 (S.I. 1984 No. 2007), which substituted the new section into the 1981 Act and so the 1985 Act. The original form of the relief, which operated until December 1984, can be found in Sched. 25 to the 1985 Act.
[46] For the effect on group accounts see Chap. 22, post.

(1) increasing its share capital by new shares; or
(2) consolidating and dividing all or any of its share capital into shares of larger amount than its existing shares; or
(3) converting all or any of its paid-up shares into stock, or reconverting stock into paid-up shares of any denomination; or
(4) subdividing all or any of its shares into shares of smaller amount than is fixed by the memorandum; or
(5) cancelling shares which have not been taken or agreed to be taken by any person. (This is called "diminution of capital" and it should not be confused with reduction of capital which will be explained later.[47])

All these powers require for their exercise a resolution of the company in general meeting.

### Increase of capital

Every increase of capital, *i.e.* nominal capital, must be effected by the company in general meeting: section 121. If the articles authorise the increase of capital, whether an ordinary or a special resolution is required depends on the articles.

Table A, regulation 32, provides: "The company may by ordinary resolution—(a) increase its share capital by new shares of such amount as the resolution prescribes; . . ."

If the articles do not give authority to increase capital, the articles must be altered by special resolution so that they do give authority but the one special resolution can both authorise and effect an increase.[48]

The notice convening the meeting must specify the amount of the proposed increase.[49] Within 15 days after the passing of the resolution effecting the increase, a notice in the prescribed form of the amount of the increase must be filed with the Registrar. A printed copy of the resolution effecting the increase, or a copy in some other form approved by him, must also be filed with the Registrar (section 123).

The conditions on which the new shares are held are set out in the terms of issue. The articles usually provide that they shall be

---

[47] s.121(5). See *post,* p. 173.
[48] *Campbell's Case* (1873) I.R. 9 Ch.App. 1.
[49] *MacConnell v. E. Prill & Co. Ltd* [1916] 2 Ch. 57.

subject to the same provisions with reference to the payment of
calls, lien, transfer, transmission, forfeiture, and otherwise as the
shares in the original capital.

## Consolidation of shares

This takes place when several shares are consolidated into one,
*e.g.* when twenty 5p shares are consolidated into one £1 share.
Consolidation is effected in the same way as an increase of capital
under section 121, *i.e.* if the articles authorise consolidation, the
resolution specified in the articles must be passed. If the articles
are silent, a special resolution to give authority and to effect the
consolidation is necessary. Table A, regulation 32(b), requires an
ordinary resolution. Notice must be given to the Registrar within
a month of the consolidation (section 122).

## Conversion of shares into stock

The difference between stock and shares was described by
Lord Hatherley as follows: "Shares in a company, as shares,
cannot be bought in small fractions of any amount, fractions of
less than a pound,[50] but the consolidated stock of a company can
be bought just in the same way as the stock of the public debt can
be bought, split up in as many portions as you like, and
subdivided into as small fractions as you please." He also
referred to stock as "simply a set of shares put together in a
bundle.[51]

A company *cannot issue stock directly* but can only convert
shares into stock under section 121, although there seems to be
no reason for this rule today. The conversion can only be made if
the shares are fully paid. The conversion of shares into stock (or
a reconversion of stock into shares) is effected in the same way as
an increase of capital under section 121. Notice must be given to
the Registrar within a month (section 122).

Although in theory stock can be transferred in fractional
amounts, in practice the articles usually confer on the directors
power to fix the minimum amount transferable.

When shares are converted into stock the register of members
must show the amount of stock held by each member: section

---

[50] This only refers to the shares of the particular company under discussion. The
nominal value of shares may be less than a pound.
[51] In *Morrice v. Aylmer* (1875) L.R. 7 H.L. 717 at pp. 724, 725.

352. Stock certificates similar in form to share certificates must be issued except that stock warrants transferable by delivery may be issued if the articles so provide.[52] When shares have been converted into stock the annual return must state the amount of stock held by each member: section 364A(8).

The advantage of converting shares into stock was that the work caused by the fact that each share had a separate number was obviated. However, this advantage is now minimised by the proviso to section 182(2), under which shares need not have a distinguishing number.[53] In practice stock is now rare and Table A no longer contains any reference to it.

## Subdivision of shares

This is the division of shares into shares of smaller amount, e.g. the division of one £1 share into twenty 5p. shares, and it is often resorted to for the purpose of improving the marketability of expensive shares. Subdivision is effected in the same way as an increase of capital: section 121. Table A, regulation 32(c), requires an ordinary resolution. If the shares are not fully paid up, the proportion between the amount paid and the amount unpaid on each reduced share must be the same as it was in the case of the share from which the reduced share is derived (section 121(3)). The subdivision of shares must be registered with the Registrar within a month (section 122).

## Cancellation of unissued shares

A company can cancel shares which have not been taken or agreed to be taken[54] by any person, and *diminish* the amount of its nominal share capital by the amount of the shares so cancelled. This is not to be deemed a reduction of share capital (section 121(5)). Cancellation is effected in the same way as an increase of capital: section 121. Table A, regulation 32(d), requires an ordinary resolution. Notice of cancellation must be registered with the Registrar within a month (section 122).

[52] *Pilkington v. United Railways of The Havana etc. Warehouses Ltd* [1930] 2 Ch. 108.
[53] *Post,* p. 234.
[54] Where a person offers to take unissued shares but that has not been accepted, there is no agreement to take shares for this purpose: *Re Swindon Town Football Co. Ltd* [1990] BCLC 467.

### Effect of an alteration of share capital on an option to purchase shares

When a company has issued options to take up its shares and that company then chooses to alter its share capital under section 121, such an alteration may effect the option holders' rights. An increase of capital or a sub-division of shares may dilute the option rights since there will simply be more potential shares and thus the option will relate to a proportionately smaller percentage of the total. On the other hand, a consolidation of shares can result in a proportionate increase in the amount of share capital represented by an option when it is exercised. It is common therefore to include an express term in the option contract to meet such situations, *e.g.* for the terms of the option to be adjusted either by agreement or, failing that, as certified by a third party, say a nominated accountant. If there are no such express terms, however, the courts will allow the original option terms to stand despite the alteration, at least if this will benefit the option holder.

In *Forsayth Oil & Gas NL v. Livia Pty. Ltd* [1985] BCLC 378 (P.C.) options had been issued for shares at $ Aus 1 nominal value. The company then wrote down its capital from $1 to 0.025 cents and then consolidated every ten shares into one share, with nominal value of 25 cents. The Privy Council held that in the absence of any express term the option holders' rights had not been modified by the consolidation.

## MAINTENANCE OF SHARE CAPITAL

It is a fundamental principle of company law that the share capital must be maintained. It has been said that "a company cannot, without the leave of the court or the adoption of a special procedure, return its capital to its shareholders. It follows that a transaction which amounts to an unauthorised return of capital is ultra vires and cannot be validated by shareholder ratification or approval."[55] This is not affected by section 35 of the Act since it is not derived from the company's memorandum.[56] Capital may be lost as a result of ordinary business risks and, as we shall see, it

---

[55] *Per* Hoffman J. in *Aveling Barford Ltd v. Perion Ltd* [1989] 1 W.L.R. 360 at p. 364; approved by Harman J. in *Barclays Bank plc v. British Commonwealth Holdings plc* [1995] BCC 19.
[56] See Chap. 3, *ante*.

may be returned to the shareholders with the consent of the court under section 135, but otherwise, subject to the certain carefully controlled exceptions,[57] it must be maintained since it is the fund to which creditors of the company look for payment of their debts.[58]

The principle that the share capital of a company must be maintained boils down to this—paid up share capital must not be returned to its members, even indirectly,[58a] and their liability in respect of capital not paid up on shares must not be reduced.

The principle has the following consequences—

(1) A company generally must not purchase its own shares unless it follows the strict procedures laid down by the Act.[59]

(2) A subsidiary company generally must not be a member of its holding company and any allotment or transfer of shares in a holding company to its subsidiary is void: section 23.[60]

(3) It is generally unlawful for a company to give any kind of financial assistance for the acquisition by any person of its own shares or those of its holding company. There are, however, exceptions to this rule: section 151–158.[61]

(4) Dividends must not be paid to the shareholders except out of distributable profits as defined by the Act, *i.e.* in general not out of capital.[62]

(5) Where a public company suffers a serious loss of capital, *i.e.* of more than half the subscribed capital, a meeting of the company must be called to discuss the issue.[63]

There are certain exceptions to the principal—

(1) A company may reduce its share capital with the consent of the court under section 135, *post.*[64]

---

[57] See Chaps. 10 and 11, *post.*
[58] See, *e.g. Jenkins v. Harbour View Courts Ltd* [1966] N.Z.L.R. 1 (C.A.).
[58a] *Barclays Bank plc v. British Commonwealth Holdings plc* [1995] BCC 19.
[59] *Post,* Chap. 10
[60] *Post,* p. 214.
[61] *Post,* Chap. 11.
[62] *Post,* Chap. 22.
[63] *Post,* p. 183.
[64] p. 173.

(2) A company may purchase or redeem its shares under the Act.[65]

(3) A company may purchase its own shares under a court order made either under section 459 to relieve an unfairly prejudiced minority[66] or section 54 to relieve a minority on the conversion of a public company to a private company.

(4) Capital may be returned to the members, after the company's debts have been paid, in a winding up.

Other apparent exceptions are forfeiture of shares and surrender to avoid a forfeiture, although here the amount paid on the shares remains with the company when the shareholder unable to pay a call is relieved of liability for future calls, and the shares revert to the company, bear no dividend and must either be reissued or cancelled.[67]

Finally, the principle as to maintenance of share capital has been extended—

(1) By section 170, to a capital redemption reserve set up when redeemable shares are redeemed or other shares purchased by the company out of profits.[68]

(2) By section 130, to a share premium account.[69]

A company limited by guarantee and not having a share capital is subject to the principle of raising and maintenance of capital as far as the guarantee fund is concerned. The principle as applied to such a company is stricter than as applied to the company limited by shares, since in the latter type of company the principle does not prevent the creation of security over called or uncalled capital.[70]

The principle does not apply to an unlimited company.[71]

[65] *Post,* Chap. 10.
[66] *Post,* Chap. 18.
[67] *Per* Lord Herschell at p. 417, and Lord Watson at p. 424, in *Trevor v. Whitworth* (1887) 12 App. Cas. 409.
[68] *Post,* p. 191.
[69] *Ante,* p. 165.
[70] *Robertson v. British Linen Co.* (1890) 18 R. 1225 (O.H.); approved *obiter* in *Lloyds Bank Ltd v. Morrison & Son,* 1927 S.C. 571.
[71] *Nelson Mitchell v. City of Glasgow Bank* (1879) 6 R. (H.L.) 66; (1878) 6 R. 420.

## REDUCTION OF CAPITAL

The share capital of the company must be subscribed in money or money's worth. This capital may be lost or diminished according to the fluctuations of the business, but otherwise, subject to the Act,[72] it cannot be reduced without the sanction of the court.[72a] Thus any agreement which has the effect of returning capital to a shareholder is void, however indirect that effect might be.[72b] The object of requiring the court's sanction is threefold—(1) to protect persons dealing with the company, so that the fund available for satisfying their claims shall not be diminished except by ordinary business risks; (2) to ensure that the reduction is equitable as between the various classes of shareholders in the company; (3) to protect the interests of the public.[73]

**Reduction procedure**

Section 135 provides that, subject to the confirmation by the court, a limited company with a share capital may, if authorised by its articles, by *special* resolution, reduce its share capital and, if and so far as is necessary, alter its memorandum by reducing the amount of its share capital and of its shares.

"The court," in relation to a company, means the court with jurisdiction to wind up the company: section 744. The courts with jurisdiction to wind up a company are set out in sections 117 and 120 of the Insolvency Act 1986 and will be dealt with later.[74] The application for confirmation is by petition: R.S.C., O: 102, r. 5 (England); R.C. 190 (Scotland).[75]

---

[72] See Chaps 11 and 12, *post.*
[72a] This is generally known as the rule in *Trevor v. Whitworth* (1887) 12 App.Cas. 409 (H.L.).
[72b] For a complex agreement which had this effect see *Barclays Bank plc v. British & Commonwealth Holdings plc* [1995] BCC 19.
[73] *Per* Lord Watson in *Trevor v. Whitworth* (1887) 12 App.Cas. 409, at p. 423; *per* Lord MacNaghten in *British and American Finance Corporation Ltd v. Couper* [1894] A.C. 399 at p. 411.
[74] *Post,* Chap. 27.
[75] In Scotland the petition is presented to the Inner House of the Court of Session and, as a rule, a remit is made by the court to a "reporter" (a man of business, usually a solicitor of standing) who scrutinises the proposed reduction and draws the attention of the court to any doubtful points; the court may dispense with a remit to a "reporter," as in *Fowlers (Aberdeen) Ltd, Petitioners,* 1928 S.C. 186, and *Scottish Stamping etc. Co. Ltd, Petitioners,* 1928 S.C. 484, but only on sufficient cause being shown for departure from the ordinary practice: *J. Hay & Sons Ltd, Petitioners,* 1928 S.C. 622.

Power to reduce must be given in the articles; power in the memorandum is not effective.[76] The power must be a specific power to reduce.[77]

Table A, regulation 34, provides: "subject to the provisions of the Act, the company may by special resolution reduce its share capital, any capital redemption reserve and any share premium account in any way."

If the articles do not authorise the reduction of capital, *two* special resolutions—one to alter the articles so as to give authority and the other to effect the reduction—will be necessary, in addition to the consent of the court.[78]

The court cannot condone a reduction which has been carried out without its prior approval.[79] The resolution must be in the correct form and comply with the requirements of section 378 as to the exact notice required.[80] In *Re Barry Artist Ltd*[81] the court exceptionally allowed a resolution signed by all the members authorising the reduction to suffice instead of a special resolution, but confirmed that it would not be prepared to do so in any similar case in the future. Reductions must also comply with the company's articles.[82]

Stock[83] may be reduced without being first converted into shares.[84] Reserve liability, *i.e.* capital which can only be called up on a winding up of the company, may also be reduced.[85]

## Cases of reduction

The power to reduce capital given by section 135 is general, *i.e.* if the proper procedure is adopted a company can reduce its

[76] *Re Dexine Rubber Co.* [1903] W.N. 82.
[77] *John Avery & Co. Ltd, Petitioners* (1890) 17 R. 1101.
[78] *Re Patent Invert Sugar Co.* (1885) 31 Ch.D. 166 (C.A.); *Oregon Mortgage Co. Ltd, Petitioners,* 1910 S.C. 964.
[79] *Alexander Henderson Ltd, Petitioners,* 1967 S.L.T. (Notes) 17.
[80] *Re Moorgate Mercantile Holdings Ltd,* [1980] 1 All E.R. 40. However, if there is an error in the actual resolution as passed which is so insignificant that no one would be prejudiced by its correction the court will allow the reduction to proceed: *Re Williams Systems plc* (1987) BCLC 67. See also *Re European Homes Products plc* (1988) 4 BCC 779.
[81] [1985] BCLC 283.
[82] But see *Re M.B. Group plc* (1989) 5 BCC 684.
[83] *Ante* p. 168.
[84] *Re House Property and Investment Co.* [1912] W.N. 10; *cf. Doloi Tea Co. Ltd, Petitioners,* 1961 S.L.T. 168.
[85] *Re Midland Rlwy. Carriage Co.* (1907) 23 T.L.R. 661.

share capital in any case. However, the section specifies three particular cases of reduction—

(1) the extinction or reduction on shares in respect of capital not paid up;
(2) with or without the extinction or reduction of liability on shares, the cancellation of paid-up share capital which is lost or unrepresented by available assets;
(3) with or without the extinction or reduction of liability on shares, the payment off of any paid-up share capital which is in excess of the wants of the company.

For example, if a company has more than enough capital, it may reduce the nominal amount of shares by repaying paid-up capital, as where fully paid shares of a nominal amount of £5 each are reduced to £2 fully paid shares and £3 is paid back on each share. This would reduce the company's nominal, issued and paid-up capital and, so far as the nominal capital and the nominal amount of the shares are concerned, alter the memorandum. In one case 10 per cent. of the capital was returned on the footing that the amount returned could be called up again.[86]

A return of capital may be at a premium.

A reduction of capital involved repaying the capital paid-up on each of the company's preference shares of 10s. each plus a premium of 5s. per share. The court confirmed the reduction: *Re Saltdean Estate Co. Ltd* [1968] 1 W.L.R. 1844.

A reduction may involve the company paying off part of its share capital not with money but by transferring to its shareholders shares of another company.[87] Alternatively it can be used to create a reserve out of the share premium account arising on an acquisition which will then be available to set off against that "surplus" on consolidated account.[88]

Moneys withdrawn from the capital and set free by the reduction can be employed in the purchase of the company's own

---

[86] *Scottish Vulcanite Co. Ltd, Petitioners* (1894) 21 R. 752; *cf. William Brown Sons & Co. Ltd, Petitioners,* 1931 S.C. 701, and *Stevensons, Anderson & Co. Ltd, Petitioners,* 1951 S.C. 346.

[87] *Westburn Sugar Refineries Ltd, Petitioners,* 1951 S.C. (H.L.) 57; [1951] A.C. 625.

[88] *Per* Lord Macnaghten in *British and American Finance Corporation v. Couper* [1894] A.C. 399 at p. 414.

shares which it is intended to extinguish. The procedure can also be used to convert ordinary shares into redeemable shares, at least where there is a specific date for the redemption.[89]

The reduction procedure cannot be used as a device to raise new capital to replace capital which has disappeared, e.g. by the conversion of £1 fully paid shares into £1 shares with only 75p. paid, thus imposing an additional liability on shareholders.[90] On the other hand it can be used as a method of varying the type of capital. In such cases the reduction resolution will be contingent on the corresponding increase of capital taking place. This practice was approved in Re TIP-Europe Ltd[91] provided the increase has taken place prior to the court's approval being given. In this way shares may be converted into a different currency, e.g. from sterling into dollars, by cancelling the sterling shares and immediately issuing dollar shares.[92]

### Questions for the court on reduction

Subject to the discretion conferred on the court by section 135 and the statutory provisions for the protection of creditors, post, the question whether there should be a reduction of capital and, if so, how it should be effected, is a domestic question for the prescribed majority of the shareholders to decide.[93] The court should sanction a reduction unless what is proposed to be done is unfair or inequitable in the interests of (1) the creditors, (2) the shareholders or (3) the public who may have dealings with the company or may invest in its securities.[94] When creditors are not concerned (because the reduction does not involve the diminution of any liability in respect of unpaid capital or the payment to any shareholder of any paid-up capital) the questions to be considered by the court are:

(1)  ought the court to refuse its sanction to the reduction out of regard to the interest of those members of the public who may be induced to take shares in the company?

---

[89] Forth Wines Ltd, Petitioner 1993 S.L.T. 170.
[90] See s.16 and also W. Morrison & Co. Ltd, Petitioners (1892) 19 R. 1049.
[91] (1987) 3 BCC 647. See also Re M.B. Group plc (1989) 5 BCC 684.
[92] Re Anglo-American Insurance Co. Ltd [1991] BCLC 564.
[93] British and American Finance Corpn. v. Couper [1984] A.C. 399. See Lord President Inglis in Hoggan v. Tharsis Sulpher etc. Co. Ltd (1882) 9 R. 1191 at p. 1212.
[94] Westburn Sugar Refineries Ltd, Petitioners, 1951 S.C. (H.L.) 57; [1951] A.C. 625.

(2) is the reduction fair and equitable as between the different classes of shareholders.[95]

In considering what is fair as between different classes of shareholders, the court proceeds upon the basis that a reduction is a sort of anticipation to a limited extent of what would take place in a winding up, *i.e.* the various classes of shareholders[96] have the rights which they would have in a liquidation. Accordingly, if capital is lost, the loss should, prima facie, fall upon all the shareholders equally if their rights in respect of capital are equal. If, therefore, preference shareholders are only preferential as to dividend and not as to capital, a reduction of capital should be borne rateably by the preference and the ordinary shareholders.[97] On the other hand, if on a winding up the preference shareholders are entitled to preference as to capital, the ordinary shares should normally bear the loss first.[98]

When liability on shares is being extinguished or reduced, the proper capital to reduce in the first instance, is the unpaid capital (if any).[99]

## Reductions due to over capitalisation

When capital is being returned as surplus to the company's requirements, it should normally[1] be returned first to the class of shareholders with priority as to capital in a winding up,[2] at any rate where preference shares are not entitled to participate in surplus assets.[3]

A coal company with a capital of £400,000, half of which was in ordinary shares and half in 6 per cent. preference shares, had a surplus

---

[95] *Poole v. National Bank of China Ltd* [1907] A.C. 229. See Lord Parker of Waddington in *Caldwell & Co. Ltd v. Caldwell,* 1916 S.C. (H.L.) 120 at p. 121.

[96] See p. 235 *post.*

[97] *Bannatyne v. Direct Spanish Telegraph Co.* (1886) 34 Ch.D. 287 (C.A.).

[98] *Re Floating Dock Co. of St. Thomas Ltd* [1895] 1 Ch. 691. For exceptional circumstances where a different scheme of reduction was held just and equitable see *Balmenach-Glenlivet Distillery Ltd v. Croall* (1906) 8 F. 1135.

[99] Per Lord President Inglis in *Hoggan v. Tharsis Sulpher etc. Co. Ltd* (1882) 9 R. 1191 at p. 1211.

[1] But not always: see *William Dixon Ltd, Petitioners,* 1948 S.C. 511.

[2] *Wilsons and Clyde Coal Co. Ltd v. Scottish Insurance Corporation Ltd,* 1949 S.C. (H.L.) 90; 1948 S.C. 360; *Prudential Assurance Co. Ltd v. Chatterley-Whitfield Collieries Ltd* [1949] A.C. 512.

[3] Per Lord Greene M.R. in the *Prudential* case, *supra,* in the Court of Appeal [1948] 2 All E.R. 593 at pp. 596, 600.

of capital as a result of nationalisation. A special resolution was passed reducing the capital by paying off the preference shares. By the articles, the preference shareholders in the event of a winding up had a right to priority of repayment of capital *but no further right to participate in the surplus assets. Held,* the reduction should be confirmed as fair and equitable, the preference shareholders having no right to a continuance of their rate of dividend during the life of the company if the company desired and had the means to pay them off. The preference shareholders were being treated in accordance with their rights and it was immaterial that the elimination of their shares extinguished any hopes which they had of obtaining some additional advantage as a result of regulations to be made under the Coal Industry Nationalisation Act 1946, s.25: *Prudential Assurance Co. Ltd* v. *Chatterley-Whitfield Collieries Ltd* [1949] A.C. 512.

It is not necessary for the company to show by how much its capital is surplus to its requirements. "Public policy" is not a ground for the court's refusing to confirm a reduction which is otherwise unobjectionable, *e.g.* reduction may be confirmed although the motive for it may have been avoidance of the consequences of possible future nationalisation,[4] or minimisation of tax liability.[5]

A modification of rights clause in the articles has no application to a cancellation of shares on a reduction of capital which is in accord with the rights attached to the shares under the articles.[6] It follows that if such a reduction of capital of a class of shares is made a class right by the articles, any reduction will be subject to the modification procedure, usually approval by three quarters of that class, before it can be confirmed by the court.[7] If the necessary approval has been obtained, the reduction will be approved unless it is unfair or has been sanctioned by the influence of some improper or extraneous consideration.[8] The burden of proving that the reduction is unfair lies on those who oppose it.[9] (If the proper sanction is not obtained the burden of proving that the reduction is fair lies on those in favour.[10])

---

[4] See note 90, *ante.*
[5] *David Bell Ltd, Petitioners,* 1954 S.C. 33.
[6] *Re Saltdean Estate Co. Ltd* [1968] 1 W.L.R. 1844; *House of Fraser v. A.C.G.E. Investments Ltd* [1987] A.C. 387; 1987 S.C. (H.L.) 125; *cf. Re Old Silkstone Collieries Ltd* [1954] Ch. 169 (C.A.).
[7] *Re Northern Engineering Industries plc.* [1994] 2 BCLC 704 (C.A.).
[8] *Re Welshbach Incandescent Gas Light Co. Ltd* [1904] Ch. 87 (C.A.). A scheme of arrangement is not necessary: *Oban and Aultmore-Glenlivet Distilleries Ltd, Petitioners* (1903) 5 F. 1140, and *Marshall, Fleming & Co. Ltd, Petitioners,* 1938 S.C. 873 (O.H.).
[9] *Carruth v. I.C.I. Ltd* 1937) A.C. 707.
[10] *Re Holders Investment Trust Ltd* [1971] 1 W.L.R. 583, *post,* p. 243.

In one case, where there were special circumstances, a reduction involving a variation of class rights was confirmed although no class meeting of the class of shareholders (the preference shareholders) had been held—no one objected, there was no prospect of liquidation (when the preference shareholders had the right to participate in surplus assets after repayment of capital), and the preference shareholders received more, than they would have received by selling.[11]

When one part of a class of equity shareholders is treated differently from another, the usual practice is to proceed by a scheme of arrangement under section 425, under which the interests of the minority are better protected.[12]

*Reductions due to loss of capital*

In England, where reduction is sought on the ground that capital has been lost or is not represented by available assets, evidence of the loss or that the available assets do not represent the capital must be given.[13] A reduction may be confirmed where capital has been lost but it is still represented by available assets.

A company had built up a reserve fund. It had incurred a loss arising from the depreciation in the value of its public-houses below the amount stated in the balance sheet, and it proposed to reduce its capital by apportioning the loss between its capital account and the reserve. *Held,* the loss ought to be rateably apportioned between the capital account and the reserve, and the company was not bound to apply the whole of its reserve to wipe out the loss: *Re Hoare & Co. Ltd* [1904] 2 Ch. 208 (C.A.).

Capital is not lost unless it is permanently lost.[14] If the evidence is therefore that the loss might not be permanent the courts will not allow a reduction unless the company gives an undertaking to protect the creditors in the event of the loss being made good. In one case[15] the judge required an undertaking to place any sums recovered in respect of the loss (by way of compensation) into

[11] *Re William Jones & Sons Ltd* [1969] 1 W.L.R. 146.
[12] *Re Robert Stephen Holdings Ltd* [1968] 1 W.L.R. 522.
[13] *Per* Lord Parker of Waddington in *Caldwell & Co. Ltd v. Caldwell,* 1916 S.C. (H.L.) 120 at p. 121. Scottish courts dispense with such evidence where there is no reason to suspect the bona fides of the parties: *Caldwell's* case.
[14] *Re Haematite Steel Co.* [1901] 2 Ch. 746 at 749 *per* Romer L. J.; *Re Walsbach Incandescent Gas Light Co. Ltd* [1904] 1 Ch. 87.
[15] *Re Jupiter House Investments (Cambridge) Ltd* [1985] 1 W.L.R. 975.

# SHARE CAPITAL

capital reserve so that it could not be distributed as dividend. But in a subsequent case[16] Nourse J. refused to accept that such an undertaking must always require a reserve to be set aside indefinitely to safeguard the interests of future creditors and shareholders. The undertaking in most cases need only safeguard the interests of creditors at the time of the reduction.

This approach was followed in *Quayle Munro Ltd, Petitioners*,[17] where the court confirmed a petition to cancel the share premium account to allow for past losses leaving a credit balance as a special reserve fund. Undertakings were only needed for present creditors with respect to that reserve, and could allow for the writing off of future losses irrespective of any creditors.

## Creditors' rights to object to reduction

If a proposed reduction of share capital involves either (1) diminution of liability in respect of unpaid share capital, or (2) payment to any shareholder of any paid-up capital,[18] and (3) in any other case where the court so directs, creditors who, if the company were being wound up, would be able to prove against it, are entitled to object to the reduction. For this purpose the court must settle a list of creditors, with the nature and amount of their claims, and may publish notices fixing a day by which creditors not entered on the list are to claim to be entered. Such of the creditors as do not consent to the reduction must be paid off or the company must secure payment of their claims by appropriating such amount as the court directs: section 136. In special circumstances the court may dispense with these requirements: section 136(6). The court might dispense with the requirements where the company has sufficient cash, trustee securities and good sundry debtors[19] to more than cover any capital to be returned to shareholders and the company's debts, or if the discharge of the debts is guaranteed to the court's satisfaction, or if a simultaneous increase in capital results in the paid-up capital being the same as it was before the reduction.[20]

[16] *Re Grosvenor Press plc* [1985] 1 W.L.R. 980.
[17] 1993 S.L.T. 723, [1994] 1 BCLC 410.
[18] Replacement of preference shares with loan stock, which became a common practice for the purposes of reducing liability to corporation tax, counts as such payment, although the loan stock does not fall to be repaid by the company until a future date: *Lawrie & Symington Ltd, Petitioners*, 1969 S.L.T. 221.
[19] *Anderson, Brown & Co. Ltd, Petitioners*, 1965 S.C. 81.
[20] *New Duff House Sanitarium, Petitioners*, 1931 S.L.T. 337 (O.H.); cf. *Cadzow Coal Co. Ltd, Petitioners*, 1931 S.C. 272.

Before dispensing with a list of creditors under section 136(6) the court must be satisfied that no creditor who might be entitled to object to the reduction would be prejudiced by it.[21]

In cases not within (1) and (2) above, the creditors have, prima facie, no right to object to the proposed reduction of capital, because no asset out of which their claims could be satisfied is being given up or returned to the shareholders.

A company had a paid-up share capital of £1,000,000, and had also issued £1,000,000 debentures secured by a trust deed constituting a floating charge. In 1904 losses to the extent of £800,000 were incurred and no dividends had since been paid, any profits being applied in reduction of the deficiency. By 1917 the deficiency had been reduced to £640,000, and the company proposed to reduce its capital to £360,000 by writing off the lost capital. The latest balance sheet showed assets worth £1,500,000. The debenture holders objected. *Held,* as the reduction involved no diminution of unpaid capital or repayment to shareholders of paid-up capital, creditors were not entitled to object unless a strong case was made out, and the debenture holders had not made out any such case: *Re Meux's Brewery Co. Ltd.* [1919] Ch. 28.

The object of reducing capital, where capital has been lost or is not represented by available assets, is to enable the accounts to present a realistic picture of the company's financial position, which may permit the company to pay dividends. To safeguard the creditors in the case of an application by a company to write off capital not lost or unrepresented by available assets, thereby setting free capital which might be distributed among the shareholders, the court is empowered by section 136 to give effect to a creditor's objection "in any other case".

**Order for reduction; Minute of reduction**

Confirmation by the court must precede the actual reduction of capital.[22] On making an order confirming the reduction, the court may direct:

(1) for special reasons, that the company add the words "and reduced" to its name for a specified time.
(2) that the reasons for reduction and the causes leading to the reduction be published, with a view to giving proper information to the public (section 137).

[21] *Re Luconia Temperance Billiard Halls (London) Ltd* [1966] Ch. 98.
[22] *Alexander Henderson Ltd, Petitioners,* 1967 S.L.T. (Notes) 17.

These powers are rarely used today and the Jenkins Report recommended their repeal.[23]

Section 138 provides that a copy of the order for reduction and a minute approved by the court showing the amount of the share capital, the number of shares into which it is divided, the amount of each share and the amount, if any, deemed to be paid up on each share, must be registered with the Registrar.[24] The Registrar then grants a certificate of registration, which is conclusive evidence of the reduction and that all the requirements of the Act with respect to reduction have been complied with—even if it is afterwards discovered that the special resolution for a reduction was not properly passed,[25] or that there was no power in the articles to reduce capital.[26] The reduction takes effect as from the date of registration. By section 380,[27] a copy of the special resolution must be forwarded to the Registrar within 15 days.

## Reduction below authorised minimum capital

Where the court confirms a reduction of capital of a public company which has the effect of bringing the nominal value of the company's allotted share capital below the authorised minimum capital[28] this will only be registered (and so will only be effective) if the company is first re-registered as a private company: section 139.

To ease this process the court may authorise the company to re-register as a private company under section 53[29] without passing a special resolution and will also specify the necessary alterations to the company's memorandum and articles. In practice many public companies prohibit any reduction of capital below the authorised minimum in their articles.[30]

---

[23] Paras. 159, 187.
[24] Where the reduction takes the share capital to nil for a split second and new shares are then issued, this fact can be included in the minute of reduction: *Re Anglo-American Insurance Co. Ltd* [1991] BCLC 564.
[25] *Ladies' Dress Association v. Pullbrook* [1900] 2 Q.B. 276 (C.A.).
[26] *Re Walker and Smith Ltd* [1903] W.N. 82.
[27] *Post*, p. 307.
[28] £50,000: s.118.
[29] *Ante*, p. 47.
[30] But see *Re M.B. Group plc* (1989) 5 BCC 684; *Re Anglo-American Insurance Co. Ltd*, [1991] BCLC 564.

## SERIOUS LOSS OF CAPITAL

Following the EC Second Directive,[31] under section 142 the directors of a *public* company are obliged to call an extraordinary meeting of the company within 28 days from the earliest date on which any director knew that the company had suffered a serious loss of capital.

A serious loss of capital occurs where the net assets of the company are half or less of the amount of the company's called up share capital. In other words if it has lost half or more of its called up share capital.

The meeting must be fixed for a date not later than 56 days from when the obligation arose. It is to consider whether any, and if so what, measures should be taken to deal with the situation. Directors who knowingly and wilfully authorise or permit a failure to convene such a meeting are liable on conviction to a fine.

There is some ambiguity as to what may actually be discussed. Section 142(3) provides that the meeting may not be used to discuss anything "which could not have been considered at that meeting apart from this section." Does this include a resolution to dismiss or censure the directors? Such a resolution may fall within the ambit of the section.

---

[31] Art. 17.

# Chapter 10

# THE ACQUISITION AND REDEMPTION BY A COMPANY OF ITS OWN SHARES

THE principle that a company cannot reduce its capital except in accordance with the Act, discussed in the previous chapter, means that it is unlawful for a company to buy or redeem its own shares without statutory authorisation, irrespective of how far such a purchase is in the interests of the company or its shareholders as a whole.[1] This rule does not, however, prevent a company from buying the shares of another company even if that second company's assets consist entirely of a holding of shares in the purchaser—the court will not pierce the corporate veil. The purchaser is buying shares in the second company and not its own shares.[1a] Companies were, however, able to issue redeemable preference shares under section 58 of the 1948 Act; *i.e.* preference shares which were expressly redeemable at a future date. The 1981 Act replaced that narrow power with a general power to issue redeemable shares of any type and gave companies the additional power for the first time to purchase their own shares.

This chapter is mainly concerned with these powers of purchase and redemption, covering a company's ability to do so, the mechanisms involved, the funds available and the capital consequences of so doing. The powers were originally part of a "package" designed to assist small companies in finding outside investors who might wish to be able to withdraw such investment at will. To this end it will be seen that private companies may in some cases fund the acquisition or redemption out of capital. The effect is that subject to certain procedures and authority all shares are now potentially redeemable either by the terms of their issue or by subsequent agreement.

---

[1] See *Trevor v. Whitworth* (1887) 12 A.C. 409.

[1a] *Acatos & Hutcheson plc v. Watson, The Times,* December 30, 1994. The judge suggested that it might be different if the second company was formed expressly for the purpose of avoiding the rule. Under s.23, *post*, p. 214, the purchaser's own shares so acquired can be retained by the newly acquired subsidiary although the voting rights attached to them are suspended.

## ACQUISITIONS—THE GENERAL RULE

Section 143 also prohibits a company from acquiring its own shares. However, this does not apply in the following cases:

(i) gifts of shares to the company[2],

(ii) acquisitions on a reduction of capital under section 135[3];

(iii) the redemption or purchase of its shares under the Act[4];

(iv) purchases authorised by the court under sections 54,[5] 461[6] or 5[7];

(v) the forfeiture of shares or acceptance of any shares surrendered in lieu for failure to pay for them.[8]

(vi) the acquisition of a company which owns shares in the acquiring company.[8a]

### Acquisitions by nominees

Section 144 provides that if a person subscribes for shares in a company or buys them for a third party partly-paid up, apparently in his own name, but in reality as a nominee for the company, he is to be regarded as the full owner of the shares to the exclusion of the company. He thus becomes personally liable for the amount owed on the shares. If he fails to pay within 21 days of being asked to do so the other subscribers, or the directors, whichever is appropriate, will be liable to pay, subject to a defence that they acted honestly and reasonably and ought fairly to be excused.

Section 145, however, provides that the company retains the ownership of such shares in two cases:

(i) if a public company provides financial assistance for the purchase of such shares. This topic is dealt with in the following chapter. Here we are only concerned with

---

[2] Following *Re Castiglione's W.T.* [1958] Ch. 549; *cf. Gill v. Arizona Copper Co. Ltd* (1900) 2 F. 843.

[3] *Ante*, p. 173.

[4] *Post*, p. 186.

[5] *Ante*, p. 47.

[6] *Post*, p. 425.

[7] *Ante*, p. 68.

[8] *Post*, p. 277.

[8a] *Acatos & Hutcheson plc v. Watson*, The Times, December 30, 1994.

assistance given to a nominee. Such shares must be cancelled or disposed of within one year under section 146;

(ii) where the company is a trustee only of the shares and has no beneficial interest in them. Thus a company acting as a trustee may accept shares issued by itself in the name of a nominee on behalf of a trust fund. Beneficial interests for this purpose do not include certain residential interests commonly found in trust deeds, corporate pension funds or employee share schemes, as defined in Schedule 2.

Of course the company retains the beneficial ownership of shares to which section 144 does not apply—e.g. fully paid up shares acquired from a third party.

## Consequences of an acquisition

Apart from purchases and redemptions under the Act, shares acquired by a company or its nominee must be treated as follows:

(i) shares acquired by the company as gifts, or by forfeiture or surrender for non-payment of calls, shares acquired by a nominee without financial assistance from the company and in which the company has a beneficial interest (e.g. gifts of fully paid up shares to a company's nominee)— disposal or cancellation of the shares within three years: section 146;

(ii) shares acquired by a nominee of a public company with financial assistance from the company—disposal or cancellation of the shares within one year: section 146. Cancellation may be achieved by a resolution of the directors reducing the capital by the nominal amount of the shares acquired without complying with section 135: section 147. If necessary a public company must apply to be re-registered as a private company.[9]

### REDEMPTION AND PURCHASE OF SHARES

#### Redeemable shares

Section 159 allows companies to issue redeemable shares of any class, i.e. shares which are specifically redeemable under the terms of their issue.

[9] i.e. because it ceases to comply with the authorised minimum capital under s.118.

To issue redeemable shares a company must have power to do so by its articles. No company may issue only redeemable shares[10] but one non-redeemable share will technically be enough. Shares issued under section 159 may be issued either as redeemable at a fixed date or event, or as redeemable at the option of the company or the shareholder; but any shares redeemed must be fully paid up at the date of redemption—there must be no incidental reduction of capital, and the terms of redemption must provide for payment on redemption. In one case, the court allowed a company to issue redeemable shares on a reduction of capital as a replacement for ordinary shares which were cancelled under the scheme.[11]

Apart from those basic requirements, the terms and conditions of redemption are to be as specified in the company's articles. Further restrictions, set out in section 159A, contained in the 1989 Act, have never been brought into force and the government has indicated that they are not likely to be.[12]

When redeemable shares are redeemed they must be cancelled at once and the issued share capital figure reduced accordingly. A company must not be a member of itself: section 160(4). There is no option, as in section 146 noted above, for their re-issue within a limited time.

Replacement issues of shares can be made prior to the redemption without any increase in the authorised capital figure being necessary, so that if the new issue would take the nominal capital temporarily above the authorised figure, section 121 will not apply: section 160(5).[13]

The funds available for redemption of shares are discussed below.

**Purchase by a company of its own shares**

Section 162 allows companies to purchase their own shares by following one of three procedures contained in sections 164 to 166 of the Act. The power to purchase must be included in the articles—it can include the purchase of redeemable shares, *e.g.* if

---

[10] Nor can a company purchase its own shares if that would leave only redeemable shares in existence: s.162. See below.
[11] *Forth Wines Ltd, Petitioner* 1993 S.L.T. 170.
[12] DTI Consultative Document 1993.
[13] *Ante*, p. 166.

the date for redemption has not been reached. There is nothing in the Act which either allows or prohibits the *compulsory* purchase by a company of its own shares. It is doubtful whether a majority of the shareholders can be given this power because of the doctrine of a fraud on the minority[14] but the point remains open *vis-à-vis* the company itself.

Subject to the rule that a company cannot buy itself out completely or leave only redeemable shares, the power in the articles can be framed as desired.

The funds available to a company for the purchase of its own shares are dealt with below.[15] The power to purchase its own shares can only be implemented, however, by one of the following three procedures:

*Off-market purchases.* A purchase of unquoted shares,[16] *i.e.* in general, those of private companies, is governed by section 164. Such a purchase requires a special resolution of the company authorising it to make the contract to purchase (*N.B.* not the purchase itself). In the event of a public company buying its own unquoted shares such approval must then be limited to a contract made within a period of no more than 18 months from the granting of approval.

Such authority to contract may be varied, renewed or revoked by a special resolution.

The proposed contract, or a memorandum of its terms, must be available for inspection for at least 15 days ending with the date of the meeting at the company's registered office and at the meeting itself.[17] The name of the proposed vendor(s) must be made clear. That is because such vendors may not vote with the shares concerned on the resolution if such a vote would affect the result. In such circumstances failure to abstain with those votes will invalidate the resolution.[18] The vendor(s) can however vote

---

[14] *Brown v. British Abrasive Wheel Co.* [1919] 2 Ch. 290; *Dafen Tinplate Co. Ltd v. Llanelly Steel Co.* [1920] 2 Ch. 124; *cf. Sidebottom v. Kershaw, Leese and Co.* [1920] 1 Ch. 154.

[15] *Post*, p. 190.

[16] *i.e.* shares which are not traded on a recognised investment exchange within the meaning of the F.S.A. 1986: s.163.

[17] The documents must be sent to each member prior to his signature if the written resolution procedure is being used: Sched. 15A, para. 5, see *post*, p. 308.

[18] In the case of a written resolution the vendor's signature is irrelevant provided all the other shareholders sign the resolution: Sched. 15A, para. 5. See p. 308 *post*.

with any other shares owned and can demand a poll[19] to exercise those votes.

Any variation of the contract itself, as distinct from the authority to enter into it, must be authorised in the same way as the original contract except that both contracts must be available for inspection.

It has been decided in Scotland that a contract to purchase shares which has not complied with the statutory requirements for approval cannot be enforced.[20]

*Contingent purchase contracts.* Companies may purchase options to acquire their own shares under the terms of section 165. The procedure involved is that for an off-market purchase, *i.e.* a special resolution authorising each such option. Such a procedure means that listed companies cannot purchase traded options to acquire their own listed shares so as to speculate against the value of such shares.

*Market purchases.* Public companies may, however, purchase their quoted shares under the procedure laid down by section 166. In essence the company needs the prior approval of an ordinary resolution[21] for the purchase of a number of shares within a specified price band and within a specified time, not greater than 18 months. The maximum and minimum figures in the price band may be settled by reference to a formula.

The need for a general rather than a specific authority to purchase is dictated by the Stock Exchange rules on trading. It is difficult to see, however, why only an ordinary resolution should be required.

The Stock Exchange has its own rules covering such purchases.

## Disclosure of purchases

Under section 169 details of all purchases must be registered within 28 days. A purchase may be effected by a surrender of shares so that no transfer document will be necessary.

All contracts of purchase or options to purchase must also be kept at the company's registered office for 10 years from the date

---

[19] *Post*, p. 299.
[20] *Western v. Rigblast Holdings Ltd*, 1989 G.W.D. 23-950 (Sh.Ct.).
[21] This resolution must, however, be registered as if it was a special resolution.

of completion of the purchase or expiry of the options, as appropriate. These must be open to inspection. Option contracts need only be registered if activated.

### Assignment and release of a company's rights to purchase

Under section 167 any assignment by a company of its rights under a contract to purchase its own shares is totally prohibited. Companies are not allowed to speculate against their own share price by buying and selling rights to purchase.

Companies with rights under an off-market purchase or option, however, may release such rights if such a release is approved by a special resolution. The vendor shareholders are, however, prohibited from voting with those shares if it would affect the result.

### Funds available for redemption or purchase

The rules relating to the funding of a redemption or purchase of a company's own shares are the same. They are set out in sections 160(1) and (2).

The nominal value of the redeemed or purchased shares may be paid for either out of the company's distributable profits[22] or the proceeds of a specific fresh issue of shares made for the purpose. In the event there will be no reduction of capital—in the latter case a fresh amount of capital will replace that used.

The premium on any such shares may, however, only be paid for out of distributable profits unless the shares themselves were originally issued at a premium. In that case the proceeds of a fresh issue may be used up to the amount of the company's share premium account at the time. In effect the share premium account may be used to fund the purchase or redemption and then be replaced by a fresh issue of shares.

Under section 168 any payment to acquire an option to purchase shares, or to obtain any variation or release from a contract to purchase, as distinct from the purchase itself, must be found from distributable profits.

In so far as the company uses distributable profits for such payments the funds available for dividends[23] are thereby reduced:

---

[22] *Post*, Chap. 22. These include a non-capital reserve created on a reduction of capital: *Quayle Munro Ltd, Petitioners* 1993 S.L.T. 723, [1994] 1 BCLC 410.
[23] *Post*, Chap. 22.

section 274. Further, in such a case an amount equal to the amount of profits used must be transferred on the company's balance sheet to a fund known as the *capital redemption reserve*: section 170. This is a capital fund to which the rules relating to reduction of capital apply. The object of this section is to prevent the balance sheet showing a paper profit which might be distributed by way of dividend. The profit would otherwise arise through the current assets being reduced by the amount necessary to redeem or purchase the shares, and both the share capital[24] and the revenue reserves being reduced.

### Failure by a company to redeem or purchase its own shares

If a company has issued redeemable shares under section 159 and fails to redeem them, or agrees to purchase its own shares and fails to honour that agreement, the shareholder has a right of action for breach of contract under section 178.

However, the shareholder is prevented by that section from suing for damages for breach of contract,[24a] and specific performance will only be granted if the company is able to fulfil its obligations out of distributable profits.

If the company goes into liquidation after the obligation to redeem or purchase has arisen the shares are regarded as being cancelled on the liquidation but the vendor/shareholder may prove (apply for) any loss suffered as a creditor in the liquidation unless the company could not have fulfilled its obligations out of distributable profits at any time between the date of redemption or purchase and the date of liquidation. Such a vendor/shareholder is a deferred creditor[25] and, as such, will be paid after all the other creditors but before the shareholders.

## REDEMPTION OR PURCHASE OF SHARES OUT OF CAPITAL

Sections 171 to 177 allow private companies to purchase or redeem their own shares out of capital. These sections do not increase the powers of redemption or purchase themselves—

---

[24] Because of the need to cancel the redeemed or purchased shares.

[24a] This does not apply, however, to a claim for damages by a person other than the shareholder for a breach of contract even if those damages have been caused by the company's failure to redeem or purchase its shares: *Barclays Bank plc v. British & Commonwealth Holdings plc* [1995] BCC 19.

[25] *Post*, Chap. 29.

sections 159 to 166 must first be complied with[26]—but they extend
the funds available beyond distributable profits and proceeds of a
fresh issue of shares. In essence, if those funds prove to be
insufficient, *private* companies may resort to "capital."

"Capital" in this context is any fund other than distributable
profits and the proceeds of a fresh issue, whether or not it is
technically capital for the rules relating to reduction of capital
etc.[27] Thus undistributable profits[28] may be used. Section 171
however, makes it clear that private companies must first utilise
distributable profits before resorting to "capital."

To use the power a private company must have authority to do
so in its articles. Secondly there must be a shortfall in the funds
available to all companies (distributable profits and issue proceeds). In reality this means distributable profits as there is no
obligation to make a special issue of shares to provide any
proceeds: section 171.

To ascertain whether there is a genuine shortfall the company
must calculate its available distributable profits under section
263[29] by reference to accounts drawn up at any date within the
three months immediately preceding the date on which the
directors make the required declaration of solvency, which initi-
ates the procedure. The accounts must enable a reasonable
judgment to be made: section 172. The shortfall between available profits and the amount needed for purchase or redemption is
known as the *permissible capital payment* (P.C.P.).

If the P.C.P. and the proceeds of any issue used for the
redemption or purchase are together less than the nominal value
of the shares redeemed or purchased, the remainder must have
come from distributable profits. In that case section 171(4)
provides that an equivalent amount to those profits must be
transferred to the *capital redemption reserve* as in the general
funding power and for the same reasons.[30]

However if the P.C.P. and the proceeds of any issue used for
the redemption or purchase amount to more than the nominal
value of the shares redeemed or purchased, part of those capital
funds must have been used to cover the redemption or purchase

---

[26] *Ante*, p. 186.
[27] *Ante*, p. 170. See also *Quayle Munro Ltd, Petitioners* 1993 S.L.T. 724.
[28] *e.g.* the revaluation reserve.
[29] *Post*, Chap. 22.
[30] *Ante*, p. 191.

of the premium on those shares. In such a case section 171(5) provides that the excess must be deducted either from the capital redemption reserve, the share premium account, share capital figure or unrealised profits of the company. If such profits are subsequently realised they cannot then be used for dividends.

**Exercise of the power**

Section 173 makes it unlawful for a company to use its *permissible capital payment* (P.C.P.) unless the procedure laid down in that section is followed. This procedure is in addition to that required for the approval of the purchase; it is to approve the redemption or purchase *out of capital.*

Just as a specific off-market purchase requires the prior authority of a special resolution so does the use of capital. However in this case it must be preceded not by details of the contract but by a statutory declaration of solvency by the directors. This declaration must relate both to the company's immediate ability to pay its debts after using its P.C.P. and its ability to do so for the following year, taking into account the company's resources and the directors' management intentions.[31] It must be accompanied by an auditors' report that the P.C.P. has been properly ascertained and that the declaration of solvency itself is not unreasonable: section 173.

That declaration must be followed on the same day or within one week by the necessary special resolution.[32] After it has been passed no payment can be made for five weeks. (This is to enable any objection to the payment to be made to the court—see below.) The resolution must then be implemented within two further weeks: section 174.

The proposed vendor will invalidate the resolution if he votes with the shares in question in such a way as to affect the result.[33]

The requirement of a special resolution will put the shareholders on notice as to what is intended. But since this involves

---

[31] A similar procedure applies to the rules allowing financial assistance to be given by private companies for the purchase by others of these shares. See Chap. 13, *post.*

[32] The written resolution procedure may be used (*post,* p. 308). In such a case the documents must be supplied to each member prior to his signature of the resolution: Sched. 15A, para. 6.

[33] If the resolution is a written resolution the signature, or otherwise, of the vendor is irrelevant: Sched. 15A, para. 6.

"capital," the company's creditors need to know. It will affect their guarantee fund. Accordingly section 175 requires the company to place a notice both in either the London or the Edinburgh Gazette, as appropriate[34], and in a national newspaper.[35] The latter can, theoretically, be avoided by giving a notice to each creditor of the company.

The notice must state that the resolution has been passed and what its effect is. It must also specify the P.C.P. and the date of the resolution and state first that the statutory declaration of solvency and auditors' report are available for inspection at the company's registered office and second that a creditor may apply to the court, within five weeks of the date of the resolution, to have the resolution set aside.

The declaration of solvency and the auditors' report must be available both for shareholders at the meeting, and subsequently, for either shareholders and creditors at the registered office during the five week holding period: section 174. Further, they must be registered with the Registrar by the first notice date—*i.e.* the date of publication in the Gazette or the newspaper, whichever is earlier.

### Objections by members and creditors

Under section 176, any member who did not vote for the special resolution authorising the use of capital, or any creditor[36] may petition the court to have the resolution set aside within five weeks of the date of the resolution. For a creditor the effective time limit may be four weeks since the advertisements putting him on notice can be put in up to a week after the resolution.

On such a petition the court has all the powers available to it as on a petition to prevent a public company re-registering as a private company under section 54.[37] Thus it may order a compulsory purchase of the shareholder's shares by the company, alter the company's constitution, cancel, amend or confirm the resolution or impose new time scales for its implementation: section 177.

If either there are no objections, or the court overrides them, the P.C.P. may be used by the company for the purchase or redemption as appropriate.

---

[34] Depending on the location of the company's registered office.
[35] In England and Wales, or Scotland as appropriate.
[36] There appears to be no minimum debt required.
[37] *Ante*, p. 47.

**Liability of shareholders and directors**

Where a private company which has made a payment out of capital under section 173 for the purchase or redemption of its own shares is wound up as being unable to pay its debts within one year of the payments being made, section 76 of the Insolvency Act 1986 applies.

In such a case the recipient of the payment, known as the relevant payment, and any director who signed the statutory declaration of solvency without having reasonable grounds for doing so, are liable to repay the amount of the relevant payment up to the amount needed to cover the company's insolvency.

This liability is linked to the amount of the relevant payments needed to cover the company's outstanding debts. Liability is joint and several so that any of the recipients or directors may be sued for the whole amount leaving him to recover a contribution from the others.

By way of protection anyone who might be liable to make payment under this section may petition to wind up the company on the grounds of its insolvency or on the just and equitable ground under section 122(1)(f) or (g) of the Insolvency Act 1986.[38]

---

[38] *Post,* Chap. 27.

## Chapter 11

# FINANCIAL ASSISTANCE BY A COMPANY FOR THE PURCHASE OF ITS OWN SHARES

UNDER section 54 of the 1948 Act it was unlawful for a company to give any person financial assistance for the purchase of, or subscription for, its own shares or those of its holding company. The motives were to preserve the share capital, to prevent the misuse of assets by these in control of a company[1] and to prevent the creation of a false market in that company's shares—*i.e.* by artificially stimulating demand for the shares at a time when the share price may be particularly important, *e.g.* in a take-over situation.[2]

Section 54 of the 1948 Act was repealed by the 1981 Act and replaced by what are now sections 151 to 158 of the 1985 Act. Section 151 re-enacts the basic prohibition in a much modified form and applies to all companies. Section 153 contains many exceptions to that prohibition. Private companies are, however, allowed to give such assistance generally, subject to safeguards for creditors and minority shareholders, under sections 154 to 158.[3]

## The basic prohibitions

Section 151 applies two basic prohibitions on the giving of financial assistance—one when the assistance precedes the acquisition and the other when it follows it. In both cases a breach is a criminal offence, both for the company and any

---

[1] By using corporate funds to assist in the acquisition of the controlling interest, see, *e.g. Selangor United Rubber Estates Ltd v. Cradock (No. 3)* [1968] 1 W.L.R. 1555.

[2] Other provisions are now aimed at controlling this—see Financial Services Act 1986, s.47.

[3] Article 23 of the Second Directive which requires some limited restrictions does not apply to private companies. This whole area is under consideration by the DTI which issued a consultative document in 1994.

officer in default, which can lead to a term of imprisonment, or a fine, or both.[4] There are differences from the original 1948 prohibition brought about by the apparently very wide scope of the earlier section.

(1) *Financial assistance given before or at the time of the acquisition.* It is unlawful[5] for a company or any of its subsidiaries to give financial assistance[6] directly or indirectly for the purpose of an acquisition or proposed acquisition by any person of its own shares or those of its holding company, either before or at the same time as the acquisition took place: section 151(1).

Thus assistance may be direct or indirect. It applies to all acquisitions of shares so that it includes all transfers of shares. The most important phrase is that the assistance must be given *for the purpose* of an acquisition, etc. This is an attempt to narrow the scope of the section and is important to remember when the exceptions are considered below.

(2) *Financial assistance given after the acquisition.* It is also unlawful for a company or any of its subsidiaries to give financial assistance[7] directly or indirectly for the purpose of reducing or discharging any liability incurred by any person for the purpose of an acquisition of that company's own shares or those of its holding company, provided that the acquisition took place prior to the assistance being given: section 151(2).

Again the important phrases concern the word *purpose*. This liability must be incurred by the acquirer or another for the purpose of the acquisition, and the financial assistance given by the company to the person who has incurred that liability must be for the purpose of reducing that liability.

For this prohibition a person incurs a liability if he changes his financial position by making any agreement of any type: section 152(3)(a). That liability is reduced or discharged by the company if the financial assistance is given wholly or partly *for the purpose of* restoring that person's financial position to what it was before the acquisition took place: section 152(3)(b).

---

[4] Originally under section 54 of the 1948 Act the only sanction was a £100 fine. For the civil consequences see below.
[5] Subject to the exemptions set out below.
[6] *infra.*
[7] *infra.*

*Financial assistance* for the purposes of both these prohibitions is very wide. It is defined in section 152(1) and clearly includes direct financing by the company and the more common indirect financing whereby a take-over bidder purchases the shares of a cash-filled company by means of a loan and then uses the assets of the company to repay the loan.[8] Guarantees, provision of security to cover a loan,[9] gifts, an indemnity,[9a] any form of credit are also included—in fact anything which reduces the net assets of a company to a material extent.

In *Carney v. Herbert*,[10] the Privy Council decided that the fact that shares in a company were purchased by means of a cheque drawn on that company's account did not constitute evidence of financial assistance for the purposes of the equivalent New South Wales provisions. There were a number of ways that such a transaction could have been effected without breaching the section. It was also held that the release of the two vendor/directors from liability on their loan account with the company and a proportionate reduction in the purchase price of the shares did not amount to financial assistance, since the reduction was more than offset by a credit balance in the purchaser/director's loan account. Since that could be reduced to the extent of the release it would leave the company in an identical position to that prior to the transactions. The definition of financial assistance in section 152(1) now includes assistance given by waiver or release—the court in that case seems to have been prepared to adopt the best construction so as to validate the transaction.

## Subsidiaries

The prohibitions apply equally to a subsidiary providing financial assistance for the acquisition of shares in its holding company. In *Arab Bank plc v. Mercantile Holdings Ltd*[11] it was held that the mere fact that a subsidiary provides such assistance does

---

[8] See, *e.g. Selangor United Rubber Estates Ltd v. Cradock* (No. 3) [1968] 1 W.L.R. 1555; *Wallersteiner v. Moir* [1974] 1 W.L.R. 991.

[9] *Carney v. Herbert* [1985] A.C. 301 (P.C.). For the meaning of security generally see *Singer v. Williams* [1921] 1 A.C. 41 (H.L.).

[9a] In *Barclays Bank plc v. British and Commonwealth Holdings plc* [1995] BCC 19 this was taken to mean only an agreement whereby one person agrees to keep another free of loss.

[10] [1985] A.C. 301 (P.C.).

[11] [1994] 1 BCLC 330.

not mean that the assistance has been provided by the holding company, although there may be circumstances, *e.g.* where the holding company transfers an asset to the subsidiary which the latter then uses to provide the assistance, where the holding company may do so indirectly. That case also decided that the prohibitions do not apply to foreign subsidiaries providing assistance in relation to the shares of a U.K. holding company.

**The purpose exceptions**

One of the reasons for the revision of the rule on financial assistance in 1981 was the judgment of the Court of Appeal in *Belmont Finance Corporation v. Williams Furniture Ltd (No. 2).*[12] The case was concerned with the situation whereby a company enters into a commercial transaction, *e.g.* buying goods from X, and, at the same time, X uses the proceeds of sale to buy shares in the company. Buckley L.J. said[13] that in such a case if the company genuinely needed those goods there might be no breach of section 54 of the 1948 Act. On the other hand if the company made the purchases solely to provide X with the means to buy its shares then there was a breach, even if the company paid a fair price for the goods. More difficult is the middle case, *i.e.* when the company enters into the transaction genuinely in its own commercial interests but it is done partly to put X in funds to buy shares in that company. The Court of Appeal left that point open.[14]

It was also decided that financial assistance could be given in breach of section 54 of the 1948 Act if it was made not to the purchaser but to the vendor of the shares *e.g.* when the company made a payment to the owner of some of its shares which persuaded him to sell them to a purchaser, even when the purchaser then paid the full price for them.[15]

As a result of these and other cases two new exceptions were introduced by the 1981 Act. They can be found in section 153(1) in relation to financial assistance given before or at the same time as the acquisition and section 153(2) for post-acquisition assist-

[12] [1980] 1 All E.R. 393.
[13] [1980] 1 All E.R. 393, 402.
[14] See also *Charterhouse Investment Trust Ltd v. Tempest Diesels Ltd* [1986] BCLC 1.
[15] *Armour Hick Northern Ltd v. Whitehouse* [1980] 3 All E.R. 833.

ance. However both contain the same two exceptions based on the purpose for which the assistance was given.

(1) *Where the principal purpose of giving the financial assistance was not for the purpose of the acquisition[16] and was given in good faith in the interests of the company.* The exception was designed to protect groups of companies with relevance to the post-acquisition assistance prohibition. For example where, following the acquisition of a new subsidiary company, the acquiring company has to charge the assets of that subsidiary to comply with a prior debenture which requires all the assets of the group to be charged on security. In such a case the security would not be given for the principal purpose of reducing a liability incurred for the purpose of acquiring the subsidiary.

(2) *Where even if the principal purpose of giving the financial assistance was for the acquisition of shares it was an incidental part of some larger purpose and was given in good faith in the interests of the company.* This exception was also defined with reference to post-acquisition financial assistance within a group of companies. For example, when a subsidiary company provides funds to its parent company some years after it has been acquired to effect a more efficient deployment of assets within the group, the proviso may relieve the parent company of indebtedness incurred for the purpose of acquiring the subsidiary but if the larger purpose can be established it will be exempt.

These two purpose exceptions contain an inherent difficulty. They could be interpreted very widely so that if there is any overall scheme, *e.g.* a take-over bid, which involves financial assistance being given for the purpose of the acquisition of shares, the overall scheme will serve as the principal or larger purpose for the exceptions to apply, even though the narrow purpose of giving the assistance was the acquisition (the latter is necessary for the prohibition to apply in the first place). On the other hand if the purpose of giving the assistance is the acquisition of shares (as above, the starting point) how can the giving of that assistance (as distinct from the acquisition of the shares) ever be part of a larger or principal purpose? In either extent what is meant by good faith in this context?

---

[16] Or reducing a liability as appropriate.

In *Brady v. Brady*,[17] a group of private companies, which ran two businesses, was controlled by two brothers who quarrelled with a resulting deadlock. The proposed solution was a division of the businesses between them, but one was more valuable than the other. To equalize the division, a complex series of transactions followed, one of which involved the transfer of a large proportion of one company's assets to pay off loan stock which had been issued as the purchase price of that company's shares. This was clearly a breach of section 151. The question arose as to whether the transaction could be saved under either of the purpose exceptions. The Court of Appeal was prepared to allow that the division of the group was a larger purpose of which the giving of the financial assistance was but an incidental part, but refused to apply the exception on the grounds that it was not given in good faith in the interests of the company, apparently on the basis that in the context of financial assistance the company includes the creditors as well as the shareholders, and the former had never been taken into consideration.

The House of Lords reversed the Court of Appeal on that point. Without deciding whether the interests of the creditors had to be considered, since at all times the group was solvent so that the creditors were not at risk and, in other respects, since the division of the group had prevented deadlock and expensive winding up petitions, it was in the interests of the company.

But on the main issue, the House decided that the assistance had not been given either as subsidiary to a principal purpose or incidental to a larger purpose. The key, according to Lord Oliver, was to distinguish between motive and purpose. The reason or motive was the division of the group but the only purpose of the assistance was to allow the shares to be acquired. "Larger" is not the same as "more important" nor is "reason" the same as "purpose". Thus the House of Lords has come down on the restrictive interpretation of the purpose exceptions. Indeed, since the financial assistance must be given for the purpose of the acquisition for a potential breach of section 151 to occur, how can the purpose exceptions ever apply on Lord Oliver's analysis?

As a result of this decision the scope of section 151 remains potentially very wide. It would apply to any transaction in which

---

[17] [1989] A.C. 755 (H.C.); [1988] BCLC 20 (C.A.). See also *Plaut v. Steiner* (1989) 5 BCC 352, where it was held that it could never be in the interests of the company if it became insolvent as a result of giving the assistance.

a company is involved and which puts someone in funds who around that time acquires shares in the company. Many innocent transactions may well be caught as a result of the decision in *Brady*. This has led the Department of Trade and Industry to publish a consultation document in which it is suggested that an exception based on the predominant reason for the assistance should be adopted. At present, however, it seems that there must be evidence of a corporate purpose, *i.e.* one for the company's benefit, rather than for the benefit of the shareholders as in the case itself, before the purpose exceptions can apply. There are, however, other specific exceptions, set out below, which are of limited effect.

## Authorised transaction exceptions

Section 153(3) sets out nine specific transactions permitted under company law which are not to be subject to the prohibition. These are as follows:

(i) the distribution of lawful dividends.[18] The rules relating to the funds available for dividends are considered strong enough to protect companies. One of the old abuses was to extract unusually large dividends from a company to repay a loan used by the borrower to gain control of the company.

(ii) distributions made in the course of a winding-up[19];

(iii) the allotment of bonus shares[20];

(iv) anything done under a court order under section 425[21];

(v) anything done under an arrangement between a company and its creditors under section 1 of the Insolvency Act 1986[22];

(vi) anything done under an arrangement made in pursuance of section 110 of the Insolvency Act 1986[23];

(vii) any reduction of capital confirmed by the court under section 137[24];

---

[18] *Post*, Chap. 22.
[19] *Post*, Chap. 29.
[20] *Post*, Chap. 22.
[21] *Post*, Chap. 30.
[22] *Post*, Chap. 24.
[23] *Post*, Chap. 30.
[24] *Ante*, Chap. 9.

(viii) a redemption of shares under section 159[25];

(ix) a purchase of its own shares by a company under sections 162–178.[25]

## Loans and employee share scheme exceptions

The following three exceptions were, in general, available in the former section 54. They are only available to public companies if the book value of the net assets is not reduced as a result, or, if it is, the assistance is paid out of distributable profit[26]: section 154.

(1) *Lending as part of the ordinary course of business.* If the lending of the money is in the company's course of business *and* the loan itself is within the ordinary course of that business section 151 does not apply. Banks may use this exception but an unusual loan will not qualify for exception[27]: section 153(4)(a).

(2) *Employee share schemes.* There is no prohibition on the provision of financial assistance by a company for the purposes of an employees' share scheme[28] if it is given in good faith in the interests of the company: section 153(4)(b). This exception was widened by the 1989 Act to allow companies, for example, to guarantee loans made to such schemes. Before, assistance was limited to the provision of money for the acquisition of such shares. The good faith criteria was added, however, and as we have seen this is by no means easy to define in such a context[29]. Directors can be included. This exception also applies to the provision of assistance by the company or another company in the same group to allow beneficiaries under a scheme and their families to trade between themselves: section 153(4)(b)(5).

(3) *Loans to employees to purchase shares.* A company may lend money to those employed in good faith by the company in order for them to purchase shares in that company or its holding company for their own benefit. It does not apply to directors: section 153(4)(c).

---

[25] *Ante,* Chap. 10.
[26] *Post,* Chap. 22.
[27] *Steen v. Law* [1964] A.C. 287. A loan deliberately made by a bank with the purpose of an acquisition in mind is unlikely to be regarded as a usual loan.
[28] Defined in s.743.
[29] *Ante,* p. 201.

## Validity of the transaction

Section 151, like its predecessor, creates only a criminal offence. What then is the validity of a loan or the provision of any security given to cover a loan which is in breach of the section? The judges have provided an answer.

Any security given to provide financial assistance is void.[30] It cannot be enforced by the lender. So is any guarantee supporting the invalid agreement.[31] In most of the cases the action has simply sought to enforce the security but in other cases the wider issue as to the validity of the whole agreement to buy the shares has been considered.

In *South Western Mineral Water Co. v. Ashmore*[32] Cross J. suggested that the agreement might be saved if the parties proceeded with the acquisition of the shares in a manner dissociating the purchase from the invalid security—*e.g.* by the seller/lender waiving his rights in the security or by the buyer paying the price at once. In the absence of this, however, the whole agreement was in his opinion void. In *Lawlor v. Gray*,[33] however, the controller of a company agreed to sell his shares. The agreement could have been carried out in many ways but the controller chose one which was in breach of the financial assistance rules. The court allowed the purchaser to enforce the agreement.

In *Carney v. Herbert*,[34] the Privy Council decided that if the unlawful elements in the transaction could be severed from the overall transaction and their elimination would leave the sale of the shares unchanged, the remainder of the agreement could be enforced. Only the unlawful elements would be void. The fact that the vendor might have refused to enter into the transaction unless the unlawful elements had been included was *not* a relevant factor in determining their severability. The effect of this is to allow a contract of sale to be enforced where there is no damage to the company.

---

[30] *Selangor United Rubber Estates Ltd v. Cradock* (No. 3) [1968] 1 W.L.R. 1555; *Heald v. O'Connor* [1971] 1 W.L.R. 497; *Carney v. Herbert* [1985] A.C. 301 (P.C.); *cf. Victor Battery Co. Ltd v. Curry's Ltd* [1946] Ch. 242.

[31] *Heald v. O'Connor* [1971] 1 W.L.R. 497.

[32] [1967] 1 W.L.R. 1110.

[33] [1984] 3 All E.R. 345.

[34] [1985] A.C. 301 (P.C.) This decision was approved in *Neilson v. Stewart* 1991 S.L.T. 523 (H.L.). See also *Motor & General Insurance Co. Ltd v. Gobin* (1987) 3 BCC 61.

H, A and J were directors of A Ltd and of its subsidiary N Ltd C was the fourth director of these companies and he decided to buy the shares of the other directors. They agreed to sell their shares to I Ltd, a company controlled by C, the purchase price to be payable in three instalments by I Ltd. C guaranteed I Ltd's payments, which were also secured by mortgages executed over N Ltd's property. I Ltd failed to pay for the shares and H, A and J sued C on his guarantee. C alleged that the whole transaction was void for unlawful financial assistance. The Privy Council held that the only unlawful financial assistance was the mortgage over N Ltd's property and that this could be severed so as to leave the sale and guarantee intact and enforceable: *Carney v. Herbert* [1985] A.C. 301 (P.C.).

## Liability of those partipating in the breach

It has been held that section 54 of the 1948 Act was passed to protect the company from having its assets misused and not merely to protect its creditors[35] and this must also apply to section 151. Thus any director who is knowingly a party to a breach of this section will be in breach of duty to the company and liable to repay the loss.[36]

In addition anyone who receives the funds of the company so misapplied is liable to it as a constructive trustee if he knew or ought to have known of the breach. Anyone who assists in the breach is also liable but only if he actually knew of the breach or was deliberately blind to it.[37]

It appears from the *Belmont* case that the company may also recover in the tort of conspiracy if it can prove: (1) that the conspirators combined to partipate in a common agreement with a common purpose; (2) that the combination was to carry out an unlawful purpose; *i.e.* the provision of financial assistance contrary to section 151; (3) that the company suffered damages as a consequence. Damage must be proved.

## General exemption for private companies

Private companies may obtain complete exemption from the prohibitions regarding the provision of financial assistance for the

---

[35] *Wallersteiner v. Moir* [1974] 1 W.L.R. 991, 1014, *per* Lord Denning M.R.
[36] *Belmont Finance Corp. v. Williams Furniture Ltd* (No. 2) [1980] 1 All E.R. 393; *Wallersteiner v. Moir*, above; *Karak Rubber Co. v. Burden* (No. 2) [1972] 1 W.L.R. 602.
[37] *Belmont Finance Corp. v. Williams Furniture Ltd*, above.

acquisition of their own shares provided that they comply with a set procedure and timetable under sections 154 to 158. This general exemption is in addition to the exceptions already mentioned which are applicable to all companies. It is not available, however, for the acquisition of shares in a holding company unless that is itself a private company: section 155.

A general restriction on the use of this exemption is that the assistance must either leave the book value net assets of the company untouched or be made out of distributable profits, section 155(2). The idea is to protect creditors by ensuring that only funds available under section 263 for distribution as dividend are used.[38] That section, however, does not require companies to make provision for unrealised losses, so section 155(6) requires the directors to make a statutory declaration of the company's solvency prior to giving the assistance. If the shares to be acquired are in the company's holding company the directors of that company must also make a declaration.

*Statutory declaration.* Section 156 prescribes the form of the declaration. First, it must set out the assistance to be given[39], the business of the company and the identity of the recipient. Secondly the directors must state that *in their opinion* the company will be able to pay its debts both immediately after giving the assistance and as they fall due during the following year.[40]

Attached to the declaration must be an auditors' report to the effect that they are not aware of anything to indicate that the opinion of the directors is unreasonable.[41]

*Special resolution.* To protect shareholders rather than creditors the financial assistance must be approved by a special resolution of each of the companies (holding, subsidiary) involved: section 155(4).

---

[38] *Post*, Chap 22.

[39] The obligation is to provide particulars of the form and principal terms of the financial assistance so that an omission of the identity of property to be charged and the kind of charge taken did not invalidate the declaration. The solvency declaration is, however, regarded as the more important: *Re S.H. & Co. (Realisations) 1990 Ltd* [1993] BCC 60.

[40] If it is intended to wind up the company during this time the declaration must state that the company will be able to pay its debts within 12 months of the winding up.

[41] Provided that the relevant particulars are provided it is not necessary to use the official form: *Re N.L. Electrical Ltd* [1994] 1 BCLC 22.

The statutory declaration and auditors' report must be available at the meeting at which the special resolution is passed. The meeting must take place on the same day as, or within one week of, the date on which the declaration is made: section 157.[42] The declaration, auditors' report and resolution must be registered with the Registrar within 15 days of the passing of the resolution: section 156(5).[43]

After passing the resolution the company may not act upon it for four weeks unless all the members voted in favour. This allows a dissenting minority to petition the court to have the resolution set aside (see below). If more than one company is involved the period runs from the date of the last resolution to be passed: section 158.

Assuming that there are no minority shareholder objections the company must then implement the authority within eight weeks of the making of the declaration of solvency. In general therefore companies will have between three and four weeks to implement the authority after the four week delay, depending on how soon the resolution followed the declaration: section 158.

*Minority protection.* Holders of at least 10 per cent. of the nominal share capital of any class, who did not vote for the authorising resolution, may apply to the court to have the resolution set aside. Such applications must be made within 28 days of the passing of the resolution—which corresponds to the waiting period for the company: section 157(2)(3).

The court has wide powers on such an application—those which are available to it on a petition under section 54[44] to prevent the re-registration of a public company as a private one. One of these powers is to order that the minority be bought out. The court may otherwise cancel, confirm or vary the resolution. Whilst the petition is being considered the resolution cannot be implemented unless the court orders otherwise: s.158(3).

The existence of this exemption procedure persuaded the House of Lords in *Brady v. Brady,*[45] to allow the company to adopt the procedure and so rectify the illegality.

---

[42] If the written resolution procedure (*post,* p. 308) is used then the relevant documents must be sent to each member prior to his signature: Sched. 15A para. 4.
[43] Breach of this obligation does not, however, invalidate the procedure: *Re N.L. Electrical Ltd* [1994] 1 BCLC 22.
[44] *Ante,* p. 47.
[45] [1989] A.C. 755 (H.L.), *ante,* p. 201.

## Chapter 12

## MEMBERSHIP

THIS chapter is concerned with the members of a company, *i.e.* in the case of a company limited by shares, the shareholders. In addition to the ways in which a person can become a member and the persons who can become members, the following topics are dealt with: the register of members which every company must keep, disclosure of substantial shareholdings in public companies, and the annual return which every company must make to the Registrar.

### WAYS OF BECOMING A MEMBER

The members of a company consist of:

(1) The subscribers of the memorandum.[1] These are deemed to have agreed to become members, and on the registration of the company they must be entered as members in its register of members: section 22.

(2) Directors who have signed and delivered to the Registrar an undertaking to take and pay for their qualification shares.[2]

(3) All other persons who have agreed to become members of the company *and* whose names are entered in the register of members: section 22.

#### Subscribers of the memorandum

A subscriber of the memorandum becomes a member on registration of the company, and an entry in the register of members is not necessary to make him a member of the company. It is the duty of the directors to enter his name at once in the register, but

---

[1] *Ante,* pp. 76.
[2] *Post,* p. 317.

their failure to do this will not enable him to escape liability for calls on the shares for which he has signed the memorandum.[3]

The subscribers to the memorandum of a company limited by shares are liable, by virtue of their subscription, to pay up the full amount of their shares, in cash if it is a public company,[4] as and when called up. Until the commencement of winding up the times and amounts of payment depend, apart from express agreement between the company and the signatories, on the articles.[5]

A subscriber's obligation to take the shares for which he has subscribed is not satisfied by the (later) allotment of shares credited as fully paid and to which someone else is entitled.

M. signed the memorandum for five shares. The company had agreed to allot paid up shares to C., as the purchase price of property sold to the company, and C. directed the company to allot five of these shares to M. This was done and the company was afterwards wound up. *Held,* M. was liable to pay for the five shares for which he had signed the memorandum: *Migotti's Case* (1867) L.R. 4 Eq. 238.

If, however, the entire share capital has been allotted to others, the subscriber is under no liability to take shares.[6]

A subscriber of the memorandum cannot rescind the contract to take shares on the ground of a misrepresentation made by a promoter, because (*a*) the company could not appoint an agent before it came into existence and it is therefore not liable for the promoter's acts, and (*b*) by signing the memorandum the subscriber became bound, on the registration of the company, not only as between himself and the company, but also as between himself and the other persons who should become members on the footing that the contract existed.[7]

Non-cash assets supplied by a subscriber to a public company in return for consideration from the company may require a valuation report from an independent valuer.[8]

In Scotland, specific implement is available as a remedy to enforce an undertaking to subscribe for shares.[9]

[3] *Evans's Case* (1867) L.R. 2 Ch.App. 427.
[4] s.106
[5] *Per* Lindley M.R. in *Alexander v. Automatic Telephone Co.* [1900] 2 Ch. 56 (C.A.) at p. 63.
[6] *Mackley's Case* (1875) 1 Ch.D. 247.
[7] *Lord Lurgan's Case* [1902] 1 Ch. 707.
[8] *Ante,* p. 160.
[9] *Beardmore & Co. v. Barry,* 1928 S.C. 101; affirmed 1928 S.C. (H.L.) 47.

## Other members

A person, other than those mentioned above, who has agreed to become a member of the company does not actually become one until his name is entered in the register of members. Section 22 "makes the placing of the name of a shareholder on the register a condition precedent to membership."[10] Registration is essential for membership.[11] A member agrees to become a member, however, if he consents to do so even though there is no contract between him and the company that he should be entered on the register: *Re Nuneaton Borough A.F.C. Ltd.*[12]

Such a person may take an allotment of his shares direct from the company,[13] or may purchase shares from an existing member,[14] or he may succeed to shares on the death or bankruptcy of a member.[15]

## WHO CAN BE MEMBERS

### Minors

In English law a minor, *i.e.* a person under the age of 18,[16] may be a member unless this is forbidden by the articles. However, a minor's contract to take shares is voidable by him before or within a reasonable time after he attains the age of 18. If he avoids he cannot recover the money paid for the shares unless there has been a total failure of the consideration for which the money was paid.

S., an infant,[17] agreed to take 500 £1 shares from a company, and paid 10s. on each share. She received no dividend on the shares. While still an infant she repudiated the shares, and brought an action (a) for a declaration that she was entitled to avoid the contract, and (b) to recover the money she had paid. *Held,* (a) S. was entitled to rescind and so was not liable for future calls, but (b) there was no total failure of

---

[10] *Per* Fry L.J. in *Nicol's Case* (1885) 29 Ch.D. 421 (C.A.), at p. 447; *per* Lord Deas in *Macdonald v. City of Glasgow Bank* (1879) 6 R. 621 at p. 633.

[11] See *Re Baku Consolidated Oilfields Ltd* [1994] 1 BCLC 173.

[12] [1989] BCLC 454.

[13] *Ante,* p. 149.

[14] *Post,* p. 246.

[15] *Post,* p. 266.

[16] Family Law Reform Act 1969, s.1.

[17] The age of majority was formerly 21 and persons under that age were called "infants."

consideration and S. could not recover money already paid because she had got the thing for which the money was paid, a thing of value: *Steinberg v. Scala (Leeds) Ltd* [1923] 2 Ch. 452 (C.A.).

If the company is wound up the minor member loses his right to avoid unless the liquidator agrees.[18]

In Scotland the capacity of young persons is governed by the Age of Legal Capacity (Scotland) Act 1991. The general rules are:

(1) A person under the age of 16 years has no legal capacity to enter into any transaction; his guardian may act on his behalf.

(2) A person of or over 16 years but under 18 years has legal capacity to enter into any transaction, but such a person is entitled up to the age of 21 to apply to the court to have the transaction set aside if it is "prejudicial", *i.e.* if it is a transaction which—

    (a) an adult, exercising prudence, would not have entered into in the circumstances, and

    (b) has caused, or is likely to cause, substantial prejudice to the young person.

This provision might make another party reluctant to enter into a transaction with a person between 16 and 18, and so the Act provides that all the parties to a proposed transaction may make a joint application to the court to have the transaction ratified by the court. The court must not grant such an application if it considers that an adult, exercising reasonable prudence and in the circumstances, would not enter into the transaction. If a proposed transaction is ratified by the court, the transaction cannot afterwards be set aside as a prejudicial transaction.

A person of 18 years of age or over has full legal capacity.

**Personal representatives**

Ownership of the shares of a deceased member is transmitted to his executors[19] or administrators. They must produce to the company the grant of probate of the will, or of letters of

---

[18] *Symons' Case* (1870) L.R. 5 Ch. 298.

[19] In Scots law the term "executors" is used whether there is a will or not, and "confirmation" is the equivalent of both probate and letters of administration.

administration of the estate, or, in Scotland, of confirmation and, notwithstanding anything in the articles, such document must be accepted by the company as sufficient evidence of the grant: section 187.[20] Production to the company does *not*, however, make the representatives members of the company.[21] The deceased member's estate is the member for some purposes, such as an article providing that on an increase of capital the new shares are to be divided among the existing members in proportion to their existing shareholdings.[22]

The personal representatives are liable for calls[23] on partly paid shares only to the extent of the deceased's assets in their hands, and if in England the personal representatives make default in paying calls, the company can obtain an order for administration of the estate of the deceased member: section 81 of the Insolvency Act 1986.

The personal representatives are entitled to transfer the shares without being registered as members (s.183(3)),[24] and to receive all dividends, bonuses or other benefits from the shares, but the articles usually prevent them from voting at general meetings.

Table A, regulation 31, provides: "A person becoming entitled to a share in consequence of the death or bankruptcy of a member shall have the rights to which he would be entitled if he were the holder of the share, except that he shall not, before being registered as the holder of the share, be entitled in respect of it to attend or vote at any meeting of the company or at any separate meeting of the holders of any class of shares in the company."

Personal representatives may, however, be entitled to be given notice of general meetings, even though they have no right to attend and vote at the meetings. Table A, regulation 38, gives them a right to be given notice of general meetings.

Personal representatives are entitled, if they so choose and there is no contrary provision in the articles, to be registered as members.[25] The articles may give the directors, the same power

---

[20] For foreign personal representatives, see *Re Baku Consolidated Oilfields Ltd* [1994] 1 BCLC 173.

[21] *Macdonald v. City of Glasgow Bank* (1879) 6 R. 621.

[22] Per Lord Herschell in *James v. Buena Ventura Nitrate Grounds Syndicate Ltd* [1896] 1 Ch. 456 (C.A.), at p. 464.

[23] *Post,* p. 247.

[24] See also *Buchan v. City of Glasgow Bank* (1879) 6 R. (H.L.) 44; (1879) 6 R. 567.

[25] *Edwards v. Ransomes and Rapier Ltd* [1930] W.N. 180.

to decline to register personal representatives as members as the directors would have had in the case of a transfer by the deceased shareholder before his death.[26]

If personal representatives are registered as members, they become personally liable for calls, although they have a right of indemnity against the deceased's estate.[27]

## Trustees in bankruptcy

A bankrupt may be a member of a company, although the beneficial interest in his shares will be vested in his trustee in bankruptcy as from the time when he is adjudged bankrupt.[28] Unless the articles provide to the contrary, a shareholder does not cease to be a member of the company on becoming bankrupt. Accordingly, as long as he is on the register he is entitled to exercise any vote conferred by his shares at the meetings of the company, even though the articles provide—as does regulation 38 of Table A—that notice of meetings is to be sent to the trustee in bankruptcy and not to the bankrupt.[29] The bankrupt must vote in accordance with the directions of the trustee.

## Other companies

1. A company may, if authorised by its memorandum, take shares in and be a member of another company. It attends meetings of the other by a representative authorised by resolution of its directors: section 375.[30]

2. A company may in certain circumstances purchase or acquire its own shares. Under the Act companies may redeem or purchase their own shares but they must cancel the shares so acquired. It cannot be a member of itself as this would amount to a false statement of its capital. Companies may also forfeit or accept the surrender of their shares. This topic has been covered in Chapter 10.

---

[26] See, *e.g. Shepherd's Trustees v. Shepherd,* 1950 S.C. (H.L.) 60. See also *post,* p. 272.

[27] *Per* Cotton L.J. in *Duff's Executors' Case* (1886) 32 Ch.D. 301 (C.A.), at p. 309.

[28] Insolvency Act 1986, s.306. In Scots law, a debtor's estate vests as at the date of sequestration in the permanent trustee: Bankruptcy (Scotland) Act 1985, s.31.

[29] *Morgan v. Gray* [1953] Ch. 83.

[30] *Post,* p. 302.

3. For the same reason that a company cannot be a member of itself, section 23[31] provides that, subject to certain exceptions, a subsidiary company[32] cannot be a member of its holding company[32] and any allotment or transfer of shares in a holding company to its subsidiary is void.[33] This prohibition cannot be evaded by having a nominee for the subsidiary. On the other hand there is no rule to prevent a company acquiring the shares of another company, which thereby becomes its subsidiary, even where that second company owns shares in the first company.[33a] There are exceptions where the subsidiary is concerned (a) as a personal representative, or (b) as a trustee, unless the holding company or a subsidiary of it is beneficially interested under the trust otherwise than by way of security for the purposes of a transaction entered into in the ordinary course of a business which includes the lending of money.

For example, as regards (a), Y, who holds shares in X Bank Ltd, appoints its subsidiary, X Bank (Executor & Trustee) Ltd, as his executor and on Y's death the subsidiary is registered in respect of the shares.

As to (b), Y transfers his shares to the subsidiary on trust for a beneficiary, Z, who borrows money from X Bank Ltd and secures repayment by mortgaging his interest in the shares to X Bank Ltd.

The definition of beneficial interest for this purpose excludes those detailed in Schedule 2. These are minor and residual interests under company pension and employee shares schemes. Otherwise a subsidiary's pension fund could not invest in its parent company.

## REGISTER OF MEMBERS

Section 352 provides that every company must keep a register of its members containing;

(1) the names and addresses of the members, and, if the company has a share capital, a statement of the shares held by each member, distinguishing each share by its

---

[31] This section was redrafted and expanded by s.129 C.A. 1989.

[32] *Ante,* p. 48.

[33] In Scotland this does not prevent a company from arresting its subsidiary's shares to found jurisdiction, at least where the shares are marketable: *Stenhouse London Ltd v. Allwright,* 1972 S.L.T. 255.

[33a] *Acatos & Hutcheson plc v. Watson, The Times,* December 30, 1994. See *ante,* p. 184.

number[34] so long as it has one and by its class if there is more than one class of shares, and the amount paid or agreed to be considered as paid on the shares of each member. If the company has converted shares into stock, the register must show the amount of stock held by each member. In any other case where the company has more than one class of members the register must show the class to which each member belongs.[35]

(2) the date at which each person was entered in the register as a member;

(3) the date at which any person ceased to be a member.

In addition, section 352A provides that where a private company's number of members falls to one then, in addition to the name and address of the sole member, the register must state: (a) that the company only has one member; and (b) the date on which the company became a single member company. If the number of members subsequently increases to two or more the register must state both the fact that the company has ceased to have only one member and the date of the change.[36]

Default renders the company and every officer in default liable to a fine.

The register may be kept by making entries in a bound book or by recording the required information in any other manner, including a computer, so long as adequate precautions are taken to guard against falsification: sections 722 and 723. Any entry relating to a former member may be removed from the register after 20 years from the date on which he ceased to be a member: section 352(6).

A company with more than 50 members must, unless the register of members constitutes an index, keep an index (which may be a card index) of the names of its members, and must alter the index within 14 days after any alteration in the register. The index must be kept at the same place as the register and must contain sufficient information to enable the account of each member in the register to be readily found: section 354.

---

[34] *Post*, p. 234.

[35] This applies therefore to guarantee companies without a share capital. It was added by 1981 Act, s.101 and reverses the decision in *Re Performing Right Society Ltd* [1978] 3 All E.R. 972 (C.A.).

[36] This is the only formal requirement as to a single member company's existence as such.

The register of members is prima facie evidence of any matters directed by the Act to be inserted in it: section 361.

## Inspection of register

The register is to be kept at the company's registered office, but if the register is made up at another office of the company, it may be kept there, and if it is made up by an agent, it may be kept at his office. If the company is registered in England, the register must not be kept outside England, and it the company is registered in Scotland, the register must not be kept outside Scotland. When the register has not always been kept at the registered office, notice must be given to the Registrar of the place where it is kept: section 353.

The register and index are to be open to the inspection of any member without charge, and of any other person on payment of the appropriate charge.[37] Within 10 days after being required to do so, the company is bound to furnish, either to a member or to any other person, a copy of any part of the register on payment of the appropriate charge[38]: section 356. The right of inspection terminates on the company going into liquidation.[39]

The company may, on giving notice by advertisement in some newspaper circulating in the district in which its registered office is situate, close the register for any time or times not exceeding 30 days in each year: section 358. This is to enable the company to prepare a list of members entitled to payment of a dividend.

## Importance of register

The importance of the register as a public representation of who the members are and what their liability is has often been emphasised in Scottish cases, and a company has no power to create a right of pledge or lien over the register, since that would deprive the public of their statutory right of access and inspection.[40] The register and not the share certificate is the document of title to shares, the share certificate being merely an acknow-

---

[37] See *ante* p. 65.
[38] *Re Kent Coalfields Syndicate Ltd* [1898] 1 Q.B. 754 (C.A.).
[39] *e.g. per* Lord Curriehill in *Liquidator of the Garpel etc. Co. Ltd v. Andrew* (1866) 4 M. 617 at p. 623.
[40] *Liquidator of the Garpel etc. Co. Ltd v. Andrew* (1866) 4 M. 617.

ledgement on the part of the company that, at the time of its issue, the name of the person mentioned in it is duly recorded in the register.[41]

Any liability incurred by a company as the result of making or deleting an entry in its register, or failing to do either, cannot be enforced against it more than 20 years after the date of first default: section 352(7). This is a final limitation provision; earlier ones may well apply.

**Power of court to rectify register**

Section 359 gives the court a discretion to rectify the register of members in two cases, namely—

(1) if the name of any person is, without sufficient cause, entered in or omitted from the register;
(2) if default is made or unnecessary delay takes place in entering on the register the fact of any person having ceased to be a member.

Application to the court for rectification may be made by the person aggrieved,[41a] or any member of the company, or the company. The application is made in a summary way—by originating summons or originating motion in England: R.S.C. O. 102, r. 3, and by petition in Scotland: R.C. 189.

The court may order rectification of the register by deleting a reference to some only of the registered shareholder's shares. It need not delete his name entirely. Thus when an existing shareholder was registered as the holder of an additional number of shares issued in breach of the then Exchange Control Regulations the court deleted the reference to those shares only: *Re Transatlantic Life Assurance Co. Ltd.*[42]

Rectification of the register is the only procedure available for the settlement of disputes as to the legal ownership of shares.[43] The respondents to the application for rectification will therefore

[41] *Re Baku Consolidated Oilfields Ltd* [1994] 1 BCLC 173.
[41a] This includes a person who is alleging that the shares ought to have been allotted to him and that another has been registered in respect of those shares, even though he does not yet have a right to be registered: *Re Thundercrest Ltd* [1994] BCC 857.
[42] [1979] 3 All E.R. 357.
[43] Where the company has been wound up it is not necessary for the liquidator to apply for rectification: *Re Baku Consolidated Oilfields Ltd* [1994] 1 BCLC 173.

be the company and those shareholders whose title is disputed. It is not necessary to join the directors unless the applicant is seeking to have the costs awarded against them rather than the company. Costs may be awarded against those responsible for the error in the register rather than the company.[44] The court has exclusive jurisdiction as to the rectification of the registers of British registered companies, irrespective of the nationality of the parties.[45]

The court may order not only rectification of the register but also payment by the company of any damages sustained by any party aggrieved. However, the applicant must show for subsection (1) that he was improperly entered in or omitted from the register. If the true complaint is that he was never allotted any shares at all and if instead they were validly allotted to a third party, the applicant will only be entitled to an action for damages for breach of contract. The applicant has never been entitled to be on the register and so has no remedy under section 359.[46]

If an order is made in the case of a company required to send a list of members to the Registrar[47] notice of the rectification must be given to the Registrar: section 359(4).

The period of two months specified in section 183(5) for giving a transferee of shares notice of the company's refusal to register the transfer is the outside limit after which there is normally unnecessary delay.[48]

An order for rectification may be made even if the company is being wound up.

B, a transferee of shares in a company, sent in his transfer for registration but, by mistake, registration of the transfer was omitted. The company then went into liquidation with a view to reconstruction and B, thinking that he was on the register of members, served the liquidator with notice of dissent to the scheme. The liquidator disregarded the notice on the ground that B was not a member. *Held,* there was such "default or unnecessary delay" in registration as entitled B to rectification of the register: *Re Sussex Brick Co.* [1904] 1 Ch. 598 (C.A.)[49]

[44] *Morgan v. Morgan Insurance Brokers Ltd* [1993] BCLC 676.
[45] *Re Fagin's Bookshop plc* [1992] BCLC 118; *International Credit and Investment Co. (Overseas) Ltd v. Adham* [1994] 1 BCLC 66.
[46] *Re BTR plc* (1988) 4 BCC 45.
[47] See *post.*
[48] *Re Swaledale Cleaners Ltd* [1968] 1 W.L.R. 1710 (C.A.), *post,* p. 283.
[49] See also *Stocker v. Liqdrs. of the Coustonholm Paper Mills Co. Ltd* (1891) 19 R. 17; *Barbor v. Middleton,* 1988 S.L.T. 288 (O.H.) (petitioner declared never to have been a member).

Section 359 does not exhaust the court's power to order rectification and does not prevent the court from altering the register in cases other than those specified. Accordingly where shares were registered in the names of two joint holders, and under the articles the first alone could vote and if the first was ill or absent the second could not vote or be appointed a proxy, an order was made to have the holding split into two holdings with the names of the shareholders in different order.[50] Rectification is, however, always a discretionary remedy and not one available as of right.[51]

**Trusts not to be entered on register in England**

Section 360 provides that no notice of any trust shall be entered on the register, or be received by the Registrar, in the case of companies registered in England (which, for this purpose, includes Wales). This means that, subject as below, the company is entitled to treat every person on the register of members as the beneficial owner of shares, even if in fact he holds them on trust for another, *i.e.* the company need not take notice of equitable interests in shares. If, therefore, the company registers a transfer of the shares held by a person as trustee, it is under no liability to the beneficiaries even if the sale was a breach of trust and in fraud of the beneficiaries.

X's shares were, on his death, registered in the name of his executors. They subsequently transferred the shares to Y in breach of the terms of X's will, and the transfer was registered by the company. The company had a copy of the will in its possession, and its president was one of X's executors. *Held,* the company did not act wrongfully, as it was only bound to satisfy itself from the will that the executors were executors, and was not concerned with the disposition by X of his property: *Simpson v. Molson's Bank* [1895] A.C. 270.

A further result is that the company is not a trustee for persons claiming the shares under an equitable interest. For example, if A, the owner of shares, makes an equitable mortgage of his shares by depositing his share certificate and a blank transfer with B as security for a debt and afterwards makes another equitable mortgage of the same shares by depositing another blank transfer

---

[50] *Burns v. Siemens Brothers Dynamo Works Ltd* [1919] 1 Ch. 225.
[51] *Re Piccadilly Radio plc* [1989] BCLC 683.

of them with C as security for another debt, saying that he has
lost his share certificate, C cannot by giving notice to the
company affect the company with notice of his interest in
the shares or gain any priority of B.[52] As will be seen later,[53] the
proper way to protect the interest of a beneficiary in shares is to
serve a stop notice. As a rule, if a company receives notice of an
equitable claim it should allow the person giving the notice to
apply for a restraining order, if he makes a request to that effect,
before registering a transfer to his prejudice.[54]

The articles frequently deal with notice of trusts, as does Table
A, regulation 5:

> Except as required by law, no person shall be recognised . . . as
> holding any share upon any trust, and (except as otherwise provided
> by the articles or by law) the company shall not be bound by or
> recognise any interest in any share except an absolute right to the
> entirety thereof in the holder."

It is doubtful whether this adds anything to the effect of section
360, although the section deals only with entries on the register
while the article is not limited to entries on the register.[55]

A trustee of shares who is entered on the register is entitled to
exercise any vote conferred by the shares although he may be
bound to vote in accordance with the directions of the beneficiary. The trustee is personally liable to the company for any calls
or other obligations attaching to the shares but is entitled to an
indemnity from the beneficiary, not only out of the trust property
but to the full extent of his indebtedness in respect of the shares.[56]
The company cannot put the beneficiary on the list of contributories but it can, through the trustee, enforce the trustee's right to
an indemnity.[57]

A purchase of shares in the name of a nominee, even if a
minor or a man of straw, is legal. In such a case the company
cannot go behind the nominee to the beneficial owner.

M. and G., a firm of stockbrokers, bought shares which were registered
in the name of L., their clerk. L. was an infant. On the company's going

---

[52] *Société Générale de Paris v. Walker* [1885] 11 App. Cas. 20.
[53] *Post,* p. 269.
[54] *Per* Lindley L.J. in *Société Générale de Paris v. Tramways Union Co.* (1884) 14
Q.B.D. 424 (C.A.) at p. 453.
[55] See *post,* p. 269.
[56] *Hardoon v. Belilios* [1901] A.C. 118 (P.C.).
[57] *Per* James L.J. in *Re European Society Arbitration Acts* (1878) 8 Ch.D. 679
(C.A.) at p. 708.

into liquidation, the liquidator applied that M. and G.'s names might be substituted for that of L. in the register of members and the list of contributories. *Held,* the application failed, as there was no contractual relation between the company and M. and G.: *Re National Bank of Wales Ltd* [1907] 1 Ch. 582.

If a person applies for shares in a fictitious name, or in the name of a person who has never agreed to accept the shares, rectification of the register can be obtained so as to place the name of the real owner upon the register.[58]

## Trusts may be entered on register in Scotland

It has always been competent for companies registered in Scotland to enter notices of trusts on their registers.[59]

Entry of a notice of trust does *not* have the effect of limiting the liability of the trustees to the amount of the trust estate in their hands.[60]

The legal position of trustees is distinct from that of executors.[61]

On the assumption of a new trustee by deed of assumption his name may be entered on the register without any transfer being executed, and the trustee will then be a member and liable as such.[62] A trustee who duly resigns his office by minute registered in the Books of Council and Session, and intimated to his co-trustees and to the company, is entitled to have his name removed from the register; no deed of transfer is necessary.[63] When one of several trustees dies, shares registered in the names of the trustees vest in the surviving trustees, and the executors of the deceased trustee are not liable as members even though no intimation of the death has been given to the company.[64] The last surviving trustee, however, is in a different position from the

---

[58] *Pugh and Sharman's Case* (1872) L.R. 13 Eq. 566; *Richardson's Case* (1875) L.R. 19 Eq. 588.

[59] As to the purpose of such entry, see, *per* Cairns L.C. in *Muir v. City of Glasgow Bank* (1879) 6 R. (H.L.) 21 at p. 26.

[60] *Muir v. City of Glasgow Bank* (1879) 6 R. (H.L.) 21 (1878) 6 R. 392, following *Lumsden v. Buchanan* (1865) 3 M.(H.L.) 89.

[61] *Per* Lord Selborne in *Buchan v. City of Glasgow Bank* (1879) 6 R. (H.L.) 44 at p. 50.

[62] Trusts (Scotland) Act 1921, s.21; *Bell v. City of Glasgow Bank* (1879) 6 R. (H.L.) 55; (1879) 6 R. 548.

[63] 1921 Act, s.19(1); *Dalgleish v. Land Feuing Co. Ltd* (1885) 13 R. 223.

[64] *Oswald's Trustees v. City of Glasgow Bank* (1879) 6 R. 461.

other trustees in that his death does not automatically terminate
his liability as a member.[65]

The liability of trustees to the company is *in solidum*, not *pro
rate*, *i.e.* the company may hold any one of the several trustees
liable for the full amount due on shares.[66]

Trustees who have been made liable for calls in respect of
shares forming part of the trust estate are entitled to full relief
from the trust estate without reference to their own payments or
ability to pay; the trust estate may be made liable beyond what
the trustees can personally pay, and the company may by
diligence compel the trustees to make the right of relief available
to the company.[67]

The persons for whom shares are held in trust are *not* members
of the company, although their names may appear on the
register.[68]

## DISCLOSURE OF SUBSTANTIAL SHAREHOLDINGS

Sections 198–220 contain provisions for securing the disclosure
and registration of substantial individual interests in share capital
carrying unrestricted voting rights. The aim is to ensure that
directors,[69] shareholders and employees of a public company may
ascertain the identity of, for instance, any person who may be in
the process of buying shares in the company through nominees,
who will only appear on the register, to gain control of it or of
any person who is in a position to veto a special resolution of the
company not only at the date of the request but also in respect of
the previous three years.[70] In addition they allow companies to
carry out their own investigations into such matters without
necessitating intervention by the Secretary of State under sections
442–444.[71] These provisions have been subjected to amendment

---

[65] *Low's Executors v. City of Glasgow Bank* (1879) 6 R. 830.
[66] *Cuninghame v. City of Glasgow Bank* (1879) 6 R. 98; (1879) 6 R. 679.
[67] *Cuninghame v. Montgomerie* (1879) 6 R. 1333; contrast *Brownlie v. Brownlie's
Trustees* (1879) 6 R. 1233.
[68] *Gillespie & Paterson v. City of Glasgow Bank* (1879) 6 R. (H.L.) 104; (1879) 6
R. 714.
[69] For the provisions relating to directors' shareholdings, see *post*, p. 319 and
sections 324, 732 of and Schedule 13, parts I, II and III to the 1985 Act.
[70] *Re Geers Gross* [1987] 1 W.L.R. 837.
[71] *Post*, p. 437.

by various statutory instruments, including the implementation of Directive 88/27/EEC which applies only to listed companies.[72]

## Disclosure obligations—public companies

Section 198 requires any person who acquires or disposes of a notifiable interest in shares to inform the company of that and of any significant change in the number of shares in which he is or was interested. A notifiable interest is currently defined[73] either as a material interest in "relevant share capital" amounting to three per cent. or more, or any interests in shares amounting to ten per cent. or more of the "relevant share capital". A material interest is any interest in shares other than an interest as the manager of an investment scheme or unit trust.[74] "Relevant share capital" is defined as the voting shares of any public company. On adding up any individual's interest to ascertain whether he has passed the disclosure threshold, sections 204–208 provide for the attribution to individuals of interests in shares. These attributed interests are added to those already clearly held by the person to ascertain whether or not he is obliged to make disclosure of his interest in shares under this part of the Act.

Under section 202 any person obliged to disclose must within two days of the date upon which the obligation arose make the appropriate disclosure of his interest, material or otherwise as relevant, in writing to the company specifying the share capital to which it relates. He must also state either the number of shares in that public company in which he knows he was interested immediately after the time his obligation to notify arose together with the names of the registered holder(s) of those shares and the number of shares for each registered holder,[75] or state that he no longer has a notifiable interest if that is the case. Any known changes in those particulars must be subsequently notified by him to the company within two days of the day upon which he became aware of them and this obligation continues until he notifies the company that he has no longer any interest in those shares.

[72] See the Disclosure of Interests in Shares (Amendment) Regulations 1993 (S.I. 1993 No. 1819); the Disclosure of Interests in Shares (Amendment) (No. 2) Regulations 1993 (S.I. 1993 No. 2689).
[73] The figure may be changed by statutory instrument: s.210A.
[74] For the details of a notifiable interest, see p. 226 below.
[75] This is defined so as to include options held by nominees.

Section 198(4) states that the time an obligation arises is either the time the event or change of circumstances occurred or the time when the person becomes aware of those facts.

Sections 203 and 208 aim to make subject to the disclosure provisions interests in shares which arise indirectly. The notifiable interests in shares defined in section 208 include interests in shares on which a person has an option or a right to call for delivery or to acquire an interest in them. Section 203 specifies various instances where a person is attributed with the interests which are ostensibly held by other persons and which are to be taken into account in ascertaining whether or not he is obliged to make notification under sections 198–202. Other persons' interests which come into this category as defined in section 203 include those of his spouse or any infant child or stepchild and 203(2), (3) includes those interests, of any company which is accustomed to acting in accordance with his directions or in which he is entitled to control one third or more of the voting power at general meetings; and where that company which he "controls" itself has a one-third shareholding in another company, the interest in shares of that other company is also attributable to him. The same is true where a person is entitled to exercise or control the exercise of one-third or more of the voting power at general meetings and that company has the same right or control of the voting power at general meetings of another company.

Further important attributions of interests in shares are contained in sections 206 and 207 which deal with so-called "concert parties,"[76] i.e. those combinations of persons with agreements for the purpose of acquiring interests in shares. The aim is to prevent control in concert, in other words avoidance of the disclosure provisions by groups of persons secretly agreeing that while each acquires openly less than the disclosure threshold level they will secretly use the combined interests to gain control or to ensure a takeover or a special resolution at the meeting of the company. Sections 204 and 205 provide that each person involved in any such agreement is to be attributed with the interests of all the other parties to it even though some of those persons' interests may have been acquired before or outside of the so-called "concert party" agreement. The effect is that in ascertaining the

[76] cf. the City Code on Take-overs and Mergers, post, Chap. 31.

obligation of each member of a concert party individually to notify his interests, the interests of all the other members are added to his interest or interests and if the total exceeds three per cent or ten per cent., as appropriate, he must make notification in accordance with section 204. In addition, under section 205 that person shall state that he is a party to such an agreement, the names and if known to him, the addresses of the other parties to the agreement, which, if any, of the shares to which the notification relates are shares in which he is interested by reason of attribution under section 204 and if that is the case, he must also notify the number of those shares.

In addition to the obligation to notify the company, section 206 obliges all the persons involved in a concert party to keep each other informed of facts relevant to their shareholding. This provision aims to give each and every member of a concert party the ability to know whether or not the interests attributed to him under section 204 (alone or together with any other interest he might have) are such as to necessitate his making a notification under sections 198–201. To do this he must know all the interests attributable to him and any changes in those interests.

Section 204, for example, may impose an obligation to disclose where two or more persons agree that one or more of them acquire interests in relevant shares of a particular "target" company. Once such interests have been acquired the obligation to disclose is not affected by any further acquisition under it or by a variation of or alteration in the membership of, the agreement. Section 205 states that each party to the agreement is deemed interested in all the shares in the target company held by any other party to the agreement irrespective of whether or not they were acquired pursuant to the agreement. Section 204(5) and (6) widely define an agreement to include any agreement, arrangement, undertaking, expectation or understanding whether express or implied, conditional or absolute which is legally binding except agreements to underwrite any offer of shares. An agreement which is not legally binding may give rise to the obligations to disclose if it involves mutuality in the undertakings, expectations or understandings of the parties to it.

Therefore all the concert party members must inform every other member of their existing interests, acquisitions and disposals of shares in that company and this obligation comes into being with the first acquisition of shares in that company in pursuance of the "concert party" agreement: section 206. Each party to the agreement has three days from the day on which the obligation arose within which to notify the other parties in writing of his interests in target company shares and of his current address. Failure to meet these obligations is made a criminal offence by section 210(3)(c).

*Notifiable interests*

Section 208 defines for the purpose of the duty to disclose the interests to be notified. Most significant is that a person is deemed to have an interest in shares if he enters into a contract for their purchase or where, even though he is not the registered holder, he is entitled to exercise or control the exercise of any right conferred by holding those shares or (trust aside) he has a right to call for delivery of the shares to himself or his order or he has a right to acquire an interest in shares or is under an obligation to take an interest in shares whether or not in any case that right or obligation is conditional or absolute. Joint interests are attributed equally to each person who has an interest and it is immaterial that the shares in which a person has an interest are unidentifiable. In this way contingent agreements which otherwise might be used to conceal an interest requiring disclosure are exposed.

Section 209 lists various interests in shares which do not give rise to the disclosure obligation under sections 198–202, for example an interest in shares as a security is an exempt security interest and disregarded if it is held by specified bodies which lend money in the course of business. Criminal liability for failure to meet the obligations imposed under this part of the Act is contained in section 210. Under section 210(3) failure to comply with sections 198–202 is made a criminal offence.

The Secretary of State may by regulations amend the notifiable percentage, the definition of relevant share capital, the time limits for notification and the definition of and exclusions from notifiable interests: section 210A.

Shares which are the subject of an offence may have imposed on them by the Secretary of State all the restrictions of Part XV of the Act.[77]

### Register of substantial shareholders

By section 211 every public company must maintain a register of interests in shares notified to it in accordance with sections

[77] *Post,* p. 230.

198–202. It must record the relevant information against the name of the person obliged to provide such information together with the date of the entry and where the company is notified that a person has ceased to be party to an agreement to which section 204 applies it must record that fact against that person's name wherever his name appears in the register as a party to that agreement. These obligations must be fulfilled by the company within three days of notification. Section 211(5) and (6) prescribe the form that the register and the index to the register are to take and specifies that the company must make any necessary alterations in the index within 10 days of a name being entered on the register.

Any company that ceases to be a public company must keep the register and index to it for six years from the date it ceases to be a public company and in any case the register must, according to section 325 and Part IV of Schedule 13, para. 25, be kept together with the register of directors' interests[78] either at the company's registered office (if that is where its register of members is kept) or at the place where its register is kept in compliance with the terms set out in section 219. Section 211(10) states that the company and every officer[79] in default is made criminally liable to a fine for either failing to keep the register or failing to keep it in the manner prescribed and to a daily default fine for continued contravention.

## Company's power to require information

Under section 212 a public company can require information from existing members about the capacity in which they hold their shares, and it is further empowered to make enquiries of any person who it has been informed is or who its investigations reveal to be, interested in shares in the company. Members may be asked whether or not any voting rights on their shares are controlled by another person under some agreement and if that is the case, particulars of the parties and terms of the agreement may be required. Members and persons who also indicated that they were interested in shares during the three years prior to the date of notice under this section must disclose details of their present interests or any past interests in shares held within the

[78] *Post*, p. 317.
[79] *Post*, p. 313.

previous three years or of any other past or present interest not referred to in a notice issued under this section. Such information, known to a member, must be disclosed to the company. Likewise the company may require similar information from any person named or revealed as a party to such an agreement as will enable it to cross check the information it receives concerning interests in shares. Section 212 is subject to change by regulations made by the Secretary of State under section 210A.

A public company is entitled to use section 212 to probe and discover the true beneficial owner, of its shares.[80] It is a failure to comply with the section if the person required fails to give a full and truthful answer so far as it lies within his knowledge, and this can include failure to disclose the precise nature of his interest in the shares.[81]

However, such a person must be given time not only to collect the information but to take legal advice to ensure that it is complete. In the case of U.K. residents the same day ought to suffice but two days would be needed for non-residents.[82]

The company, in turn, is obliged by section 213 to register the information received in response to an inquiry under section 212 including an indication of the fact and date of the requirement imposed by the company under section 212. Thus not only the company but the public has a right to know of the true owners of the shares.

Furthermore the company may be compelled to investigate and, under the power given in section 212, report on persons who hold the controlling interest in the company. This power of compulsion is provided by section 214 to a 10 per cent. minority of shareholders at the date of making the requisition provided they comply with the procedures laid down in the section, such as specifying the manner in which the company is to exercise its power and the giving of reasonable grounds for their request. There is, however, nothing to stop the members making the request, applying to the court if the company is slow in responding to a good request or to the Department of Trade and Industry in terms of sections 442–445, 454–457 and 732. Also if the company fails to comply with a valid requisition to exercise its powers of investigation then both it and every officer of it who is

---

[80] *Re Lonrho plc (No. 2)* (1988) 4 BCC 234.
[81] *Re TR Technology Trust plc* (1988) 4 BCC 244.
[82] *Lonrho plc v. Edelman* (1989) 5 BCC 68.

in default is liable to a fine specified in Schedule 24 to the Act. Likewise should any person validly[83] requested by the company fail to provide the requisite information in terms of section 212 he becomes subject to the penalties imposed by section 216. Under this provision the company can ask the court to impose restrictions set out in Part XV of the Act, including putting a stop on dividend payments to or the exercise of voting rights by that person.[84] Also persons who fail to comply or who knowingly or recklessly give false information are liable to imprisonment and/or a fine as shown in Schedule 24. But no offence justifying such an order or such other penalties would be committed if the person can prove that the notice seeking information is frivolous or vexatious.

The company is empowered by section 217 to remove out-of-date entries from the register of interests in shares which it is required to keep under section 211[85] if these entries are six years old and also if a person has ceased to be a member or it is that old and has been superseded by a later entry against the name of that person.

Section 217(2) imposes on the company the obligation to notify within 15 days any person whose name has been provided to it as a member and state what entries in consequence have been made against his name on the register of interests in shares and inform him of his right to apply to have the entry removed in accordance with the procedures in section 217. A person whose name appears in the register of share interests as a party to an agreement to which section 204 applies and who ceases to be a party to that agreement may apply in writing to the company to record that fact (if satisfied) in every place where his name appears as a party to the agreement in the register. If a company refuses such a request the applicant may apply to the court for an order to remove the entry or to enter the fact that it is incorrect or that he has ceased to be a party to any such agreement. The company having removed any name from the register on request or under an order to do so must within 14 days make the necessary alterations to any associated index. Failure to comply with any of the obligations imposed by this section exposes the

---

[83] An invalid notice will have no effect: *Malaga Investments Ltd, Petitioners*, 1987 S.L.T. 603 (O.H.)
[84] See below
[85] *Ante*, p. 226.

company and officers in default to a fine and a daily default fine for a continued contravention as set out in Schedule 24. According to section 218 the same applies where any deletion not authorised by section 217 occurs and in addition it requires the company to restore any improperly removed name to the register as soon as reasonably practicable.

Both the section 211 register of interests and the section 215 report on investigation must by virtue of section 210 be kept available for inspection without charge to members and non-members during business hours at either the company's registered office or the place where the register of members is kept. Again, failure to do so makes both the company and any officer in default criminally liable and the court may by order compel an immediate inspection or order that a copy be sent to the person requiring it.

### Restrictions for non-disclosure of interests in shares

If there is a breach of the compulsory notification provisions under sections 198 to 202[86] the Secretary of State may order that all or any of the restrictions set out in Part XV of the Act shall apply to those shares: section 210. Similarly if there is a failure to provide information as requested by a company under section 212[87] the company may go to court to ask for such restrictions to be imposed upon the shares: section 216. In either case, the Secretary of State or the court may protect third parties who might be unfairly affected by the restrictions, by providing that certain acts by those parties shall not constitute a breach of Part XV or by otherwise varying the order.

Part XV of the Act contains sections 454 to 457.[88] Under section 454 the restrictions are that:

(a) any purported transfer of the shares will be void;
(b) no voting rights may be exercised in respect of the shares;
(c) no further shares may be issued in respect of them (*e.g.* on a rights issue); and
(d) no dividends or other payments are to be made in respect of them.

---

[86] *Ante,* p. 222.
[87] *Ante,* p. 227.
[88] As amended by the Companies (Disclosure of Interests in Shares) (Orders imposing restrictions on shares) Regulations 1991 (S.I. 1991 No. 1646).

Section 455 provides penalties for evasion or attempted evasion of the restrictions.

Subject to the protection of third parties who have been unfairly affected by the restrictions, who may seek an order from the court exempting them from the restrictions, the restrictions may only be lifted by the Secretary of State or the court as appropriate if either:

(i)   the relevant facts about the shares have been disclosed and no unfair advantage has accrued to anyone as the result of non-disclosure[89], or

(ii)  the shares are transferred for valuable consideration, under a transfer approved or ordered by the court, in which case the court may pay the proceeds to those beneficially interested in the shares: sections 456, 457.

Under (ii) the transfer, *i.e.* a sale or exchange, must be approved by the court: it is not enough that the applicant is proposing to sell the shares at arm's length. It is always a matter for the court's discretion, but if the relevant facts have not been disclosed it is less likely to be exercised.[90]

Similarly, in any case the question of costs is a matter for the court's discretion. In general the court will consider each party upon whom a notice has been served, or against whom an obligation has arisen, and ascertain whether that party has provided full information within its power and whether its default has caused or contributed to the costs incurred.[91]

## ANNUAL RETURN

Every company must make a return (called the annual return) to the Registrar each year made up to a date not later than the company's "return date." That date is fixed initially at one year from the date of the company's incorporation, and subsequently it is one year from the date when the last return was made up. Because the only restriction is that an annual return must not be

---

[89] See, *e.g. Re Ricardo Group plc* (1989) 5 BCC 388.
[90] *Re Geers Gross plc* [1987] 1 W.L.R. 837.
[91] *Re The Bestwood plc* (1989) 5 BCC 620; *Re Ricardo Group plc (No. 2)* [1989] BCLC 766.

made up to a period of more than 12 months from the previous one, the return date may be brought forward so as to harmonise return dates within a group of companies. The return date concept allows a "shuttle system" for annual returns. Under this system the Registrar sends out a completed annual return based on last year's information to the company in advance of its return date. The company need only amend it, have it signed by a director or the secretary and return it to the Registrar within 28 days of the return date. It is an offence for any director or officer of the company to fail to comply with these obligations: section 363.

The contents of the annual return for all companies are specified by section 364. The following information is required:

(a) address of the registered office;
(b) the type of company it is, according to a classification scheme laid down by the Registrar;
(c) its principal business activities, according to a prescribed classification;
(d) the name and address of the company secretary (if that is a firm, the name and principal officer of the firm may be used; if it is a company its corporate name and registered office will suffice);
(e) the name and address of all directors, including shadow directors;
(f) details of nationality, date of birth, business occupation, other directorships held and former names of all directors and shadow directors[92];
(g) details of corporate directors;
(h) location of the register of members[93] if it is not at the registered office;
(i) location of the register of debenture holders if it is not at the registered office; and
(j) notification of any election by a private company to dispense with the laying of accounts[94] or the holding of an annual general meeting.[95]

In addition, if the company has a share capital, section 364A requires the annual return to contain details of shares allotted or

[92] *Post*, p. 313.
[93] *Ante*, p. 214.
[94] *Post*, Chap. 22.
[95] *Post*, p. 285.

subscribed for, of each class of share, of current shareholders and those who have ceased to be shareholders since the previous return was made up, including details as to which class of share is so held or has ceased to be held. Once a list of such shareholders has been given, subsequent returns need only specify any changes.

The required contents of an annual return can be amended by regulations made by the Secretary of State: section 365.

# Chapter 13

# SHARES

A SHARE has been defined as "the interest of a shareholder in the company measured by a sum of money, for the purpose of liability in the first place, and of interest in the second, but also consisting of a series of mutual covenants entered into by all the shareholders *inter se* in accordance with [the Companies Act, s.14[1]]. The contract contained in the articles of association is one of the original incidents of the share."[2] The share is measured by a sum of money, namely, the nominal amount of the share, and also by the rights and obligations belonging to it as defined by the Companies Acts and by the memorandum and articles of the company. The undivided profits form an integral part of the shares to which they appertain.[3]

Each share in a company must be distinguished by its appropriate number, provided that it need not have a number if all the issued shares, or all the issued shares of a particular class, are fully paid up and rank *pari passu* for all purposes: section 182(2). Numbers are often dispensed with today under the proviso to section 182(2).

A share certificate, which specifies the shares held by the member and which is prima facie evidence of his title to the shares (section 186), is usually issued to a shareholder.

Shares in a company are personal[4] estate, transferable in the manner provided by the articles of the company: section 182(1). Shares are intangibles, *i.e.* choses in action, and are located in the country in which the register of members is kept.[5]

A shareholder may borrow money on the security of his shares, *i.e.* in England, he may give the lender a mortgage over the

---

[1] *Ante,* p. 80.
[2] *Per* Farwell J. in *Borland's Trustee v. Steel Bros. & Co. Ltd* [1901] 1 Ch. 279 at p. 288. See also *Whittome v. Whittome (No. 1)* 1994 S.L.T. 114 (O.H.).
[3] *Carron Co. v. Hunter* (1868) 6 M (H.L.) 106.
[4] The Scottish equivalent of "personal" is "moveable".
[5] *International Credit and Investment Co. (Overseas) Ltd v. Adham* [1994] 1 BCLC 66.

shares to secure the payment of interest and repayment of the principal sum.[6]

## CLASSES OF SHARES

A company is not bound to issue all its shares with the same rights but may confer different rights on different classes of shares. Such classes may be described as ordinary shares and preference shares but the name by which a class of shares is called gives only an indication of the rights attaching to it in any particular company, and to ascertain the rights reference must be made to the articles or the terms of issue of the shares.

Although the memorandum of association is required to set out the division of the nominal capital into shares of a fixed amount, it is not required to set out, and in practice it will not usually set out, the different classes of shares into which the capital is divided. However, the articles will normally give the company power to issue different classes of shares.

Table A, regulation 2, provides: "Subject to the provisions of the Act and without prejudice to any rights attached to any existing shares, any share may be issued with such rights or restrictions as the company may by ordinary resolution determine."

Where a company issues shares with rights which are not stated in its memorandum or articles or in any resolution or document which must be registered with the Registrar,[7] or varies the rights attached to shares otherwise than by amendment of its memorandum or articles or by resolution or document requiring registration, section 128 requires the company to deliver particulars to the Registrar unless the shares are uniform with shares previously issued.

### Preference shares

Preference shares are shares the issue of which was authorised by the memorandum or the articles and which are entitled to some priority over the other shares in the company. They usually carry a right to preference in payment of dividend (if a dividend is declared) at a fixed rate, and a right to preference in the

[6] See below. In Scotland shares may be assigned in security.
[7] See s. 380.

repayment of capital in a winding up. There may be several classes of preference shares, first, second and third, ranking one after the other.

The rights attached to preference shares are always a question of construction of the memorandum, the articles or the terms of issue of the shares. However, unless the articles, etc., otherwise provide, the rights which attach to preference shares are as described below. These prima facie rights differ according to whether the company is a going concern or in liquidation.

## When the company is a going concern

1. When a right to a preferential dividend is given without more, it is a right to a *cumulative* dividend, *i.e.* if no preference dividend is declared in any year the arrears of dividend are carried forward and must be paid before a dividend is paid on the other shares.[8] If, however, the shares are declared to be non-cumulative preference shares, or the preferential dividend is to be paid out of the yearly profits,[9] or out of the net profits of each year,[10] the dividend will not be cumulative.

2. Preference shares are *non-participating, i.e.* they do not confer any right to a participation in the surplus profits of the company, after payment of a specified rate of dividend on the ordinary shares, in the absence of anything to that effect in the articles, etc. Where a special resolution that the holders of preference shares were entitled to a cumulative preference dividend at the rate of 10 per cent. per annum and that such shares should rank, both as regards capital and dividend in priority to the other shares, the holders were only entitled to a 10 per cent dividend in the distribution of profits—the provision defined the whole terms of the bargain between the shareholders and the company.[11] Sometimes, however, cumulative and participating preference shares are created, conferring a right to participate in surplus profits up to a fixed percentage, *e.g.* a right to a preferential dividend of seven per cent. may be given, together

---

[8] *Webb v. Earle* (1875) L.R. 20 Eq. 556; *Ferguson & Forrester Ltd v. Buchanan,* 1920 S.C. 154. Interest is not payable on the arrears: *Partick etc. Gas Co. Ltd v. Taylor* (1888) 15 R. 711.
[9] *Adair v. Old Bushmills Distillery* [1908] W.N. 24.
[10] *Staples v. Eastman Photographic Materials Co.* [1896] 2 Ch. 303 (C.A.); contrast *Miln v. Arizona Copper Co. Ltd* (1899) 1 F. 935.
[11] *Will v. United Plantations Co. Ltd* [1914] A.C. 11.

with a further right, after seven per cent has been paid on the
ordinary shares, to participate in the surplus profits equally with
the ordinary shares until an additional seven per cent has been
paid, but no more.

3. Unless the articles, etc., otherwise provide, preference
shares carry the *same voting rights* at general meetings as the
other shares.[12] However if, as is common, the preference shareholders are expressly given a right to vote in certain specified
circumstances, *e.g.* when their preference dividend is in arrears[13]
or the rights attached to the preference shares are being varied,
prima facie they have no right to vote in other circumstances.

*When the company is being wound up*

1. In the absence of a provision in the articles, etc., arrears of
cumulative preference dividend are not payable out of the assets
in a liquidation, unless the dividend has been declared.[14] If,
however, as is usual, the articles provide for the payment of
arrears, such arrears are payable out of the surplus assets after
payment of the company's debts, whether or not any
undistributed profits are included in the assets.[15] If the articles
provide only for payment of all arrears "due" at the date of
winding up, no arrears will be payable unless dividends have
been declared, because a dividend is not due until it has been
declared.[16]

2. Prima facie, preference shares have no priority in the
repayment of capital in a winding up. However, such a right may
be, and usually is, given by the articles, and its effect is that after
the company's debts and liabilities, and any arrears of preference
dividend which are payable, have been paid, the preference
shareholders are entitled to repayment of their capital in full
before the ordinary shareholders are repaid their capital.[17]

[12] See s.370(6), *post*, p. 299.
[13] Preference dividend is in arrears if it has not been paid even though that is
because there are no available profits: *Re Bradford Investments plc* [1991]
BCLC 224.
[14] *Re Crichton's Oil Co.* [1902] 2 Ch. 86 (C.A.); *Re Catalinas Warehouses & Mole
Co. Ltd* [1947] 1 All E.R. 51; *Robertson-Durham v. Inches*, 1917, 1 S.L.T. 267
(O.H.).
[15] *Re Springbok Agricultural Estates Ltd* [1920] 1 Ch. 563; *Re Wharfedale Brewery
Co. Ltd* [1952] Ch. 913. The rules as to the payment of dividends (*post*, Chap.
22) have no application to the surplus assets in a winding up.
[16] *Re Roberts and Cooper Ltd* [1992] 2 Ch. 383.
[17] See, *e.g. Re Walter Symons Ltd* [1934] Ch. 308; *Re E. W. Savory Ltd* [1951] 2
All E.R. 1036.

3. Where there are surplus assets available after the discharge
of all the company's liabilities and the repayment of the capital to
the shareholders, such surplus assets are divisible rateably among
all classes of shareholders in the absence of any provision in the
articles etc. to the contrary.[18] But, if, as is common, the articles
set out the rights attached to a class of shares to participate in
profits while the company is a going concern or to share in the
property of the company in liquidation, prima facie those rights
are exhaustive. Thus, articles giving preference shareholders
priority in the repayment of capital in a liquidation but containing
no reference to any further rights in the capital do not entitle the
preference shareholders to participate in such surplus assets.[19]

The colliery assets of a coal mining company had been transferred to
the National Coal Board under the Coal Industry Nationalisation Act
1946 and the company was to go into voluntary liquidation. Meanwhile
the company proposed to reduce its capital by returning their capital to
the holders of the preference stock. The articles provided that in the
event of a winding up the preference stock ranked before the ordinary
stock to the extent of repayment of the amounts, called up and paid
thereon. *Held*, the proposed reduction was not unfair or inequitable.
Even without it, the preference shareholders would not be entitled in a
winding up to share in the surplus assets or to receive more than a return
of their paid up capital. Accordingly, they could not object to being
paid, by means of the reduction, the amount which they would receive in
the proposed liquidation: *Wilsons and Clyde Coal Co. Ltd v. Scottish
Insurance Corpn. Ltd,* 1949 S.C. (H.L.) 90; [1949] A.C. 462.

It follows from this decision that where the preference shareholders have priority as to repayment of capital on a winding up
they should also be repaid first on a reduction of capital due to
over-capitalisation,[20] and have no right to complain about any
variation of their class rights,[21] since it is in accord with their
rights[22] unless the articles expressly make such a reduction a class

[18] *Monkland Iron etc. Co. Ltd v. Henderson* (1883) 10 R. 494; *Liquidators of
Williamson-Buchanan Steamers Ltd, Petitioners,* 1936 S.L.T. 106 (O.H.).;
*Town and Gown Assocn. Ltd, Liquidator, Petitioner,* 1948 S.L.T. (Notes) 71
(O.H.).
[19] *Wilsons and Clyde Coal Co. Ltd v. Scottish Insurance Corpn. Ltd,* 1949 S.C.
(H.L.) 90; 1948 S.C. 360; *Re The Isle of Thanet Electricity Supply Co. Ltd*
[1950] Ch. 161 (C.A.).
[20] *Ante,* p. 177.
[21] *Prudential Assurance Co. Ltd v. Chatterley-Whitfield Collieries Ltd* [1949] A.C.
512 (H.C.). See *post,* p. 240.
[22] *Re Saltdean Estate Co. Ltd* [1968] 1 W.L.R. 1844; *House of Fraser plc v.
A.C.G.E. Investments Ltd* [1987] A.C. 387 (H.L.), 1987 S.C. (H.L.) 125.

right, in which case the variation of class rights procedure must be used.[23]

If articles expressly give preference shareholders a right to share in surplus assets after the repayment of capital, they are entitled to share in accumulated profits in a liquidation even if the articles give the ordinary shareholders a right to exclusive enjoyment of accumulated profits not required for the preference dividend—the right of the ordinary shareholders depends on the appropriate resolutions being passed before a winding up.[24]

### Preference shares contrasted with ordinary shares

Preference shares are more like debentures than ordinary shares in that, if profits are available and if a dividend is declared on preference shares, it will be at a fixed rate just as debentures carry a fixed rate of interest (whether profits are available or not), whereas the rate of dividend on ordinary shares varies according to the amount of profits available.

Further, in the case of preference shares the right of the holders to vote at general meetings is usually restricted to when their special rights are being varied, or their dividend is in arrear,[25] and debentures normally confer no right to vote at general meetings, whereas ordinary shares usually confer a full right of voting.

The above may be said to be, at least in times of inflation when profits are high, the main disadvantages of preference shares. Another disadvantage is that in a prosperous business the preference shareholder is now regarded as a temporary member of the company, whose rights are limited to his preferential dividend and to priority in the return of capital on a winding up, and whose capital is liable to be returned to him whenever the company can raise the necessary money at a lower dividend rate.[26] The advantage of preference shares is that they are a safe investment. In particular, in a winding up, under normal articles the preference capital is repayable after payment of the company's debts and before the ordinary capital is returned.

---

[23] *Re Northern Engineering Industries plc* [1994] 2 BCLC 704 (C.A.).
[24] *Dimbula Valley (Ceylon) Tea Co. Ltd v. Laurie* [1961] Ch. 353.
[25] *Ante*, p. 236.
[26] *Ante*, p. 177.

## Variation of class rights

1. Where a company's shares are divided into classes, "class rights" are special rights of a class of shares, *e.g.* a preferential right as to dividend attached to preference shares where a company's shares are divided into preference shares and ordinary shares.

It has been said that the term "class" must be confined to those persons whose rights are not so dissimilar as to make it impossible for them to consult together with a view to their common interest.[27]

Section 125 applies to alterations governing the rights attaching to any class of shares in a company whose share capital is divided into shares of different classes.[28] It has been held in one case that it is not necessary for those rights to be attached to particular types of shares as long as they are given to a class of members in their capacity as members or shareholders, *e.g.* a right of pre-emption over other shares. For the purposes of section 125 therefore the share capital of a company is to be regarded as being divided into different classes, if shareholders, *qua* shareholders, enjoy different rights. It follows that the shares could come into or go out of a particular class on their acquisition or disposal by a particular individual.[29] Class rights cannot be overridden by an order under section 371 to hold a meeting with a reduced quorum.[30]

Class rights are usually given to preference shareholders and if the articles give the *ordinary* shareholders a right to the distributed profits after payment of a dividend on the preference shares, and a right to surplus assets on a liquidation, these are *not* class rights—they are no more than would be implied if the articles did not refer to them.[31] However, if seems that the

---

[27] *Per* Bowen L.J. in *Soverein Life Assurance Co. v. Dodd* [1892] 2 Q.B. 573 (C.A.) at p. 583. (This case concerned a forerunner of s.425, *post*, Chap. 30. An arrangement was made between a company in course of being wound up and its creditors. Insured persons whose policies had matured formed a distinct class of creditors from those whose policies had not.) See also *Re Hellenic and General Trust Ltd* [1979] 1 W.L.R. 123.

[28] See *post.*

[29] *Cumbrian Newspaper Group Ltd v. Cumberland and Westmorland Newspaper and Printing Co. Ltd* [1987] Ch. 1; *Harman v. BML Group Ltd* [1994] 2 BCLC 674 (C.A.).

[30] *Harman v. BML Group Ltd* [1994] 2 BCLC 674 (C.A.). See p. 286, *post.*

[31] *Hodge v. James Howel & Co., The Times,* December 13, 1958 (C.A.).

original ordinary shares in *Greenhalgh v. Arderne Cinemas*,[32] *post*, formed a class of shares within the meaning of an article providing for variation of the rights attached to a class of shares. Again, in *Lord St. David's v. Union-Castle Mail Steamship Co. Ltd*,[33] where under the articles the large number of preference shares carried a right to vote when the preference dividend was in arrears and, such dividend being in arrears, the preference shareholders proposed to alter the articles so as to give themselves a right to vote on all resolutions, it was held that the proposed resolution would not affect the rights of the small number of ordinary shares unless the ordinary shareholders approved in accordance with an article providing for variation of class rights, *i.e.* class rights were attached to the ordinary shares.[34]

Class rights may be attached to a class of shares by the memorandum or the articles of the company, by the terms of issue of the shares, by a special resolution of the company in general meeting as in *Re Old Silkstone Collieries Ltd*,[35] or by a shareholders' agreement.[36] They are usually concerned with voting, dividend, and the distribution of assets in the event of the company's being wound up but if the wider definition in the *Cumbrian Newspapers*[37] case is adopted they can be much wider than that.[38]

2. If class rights are set out in the memorandum, or incorporated therein by reference to the articles,[39] they are only alterable if all the members of the company agree[40] unless the memorandum itself provides a method of alteration which must be complied with, or a method of alteration is provided by articles which were included at the time of the original incorporation of the company,[41] or the consent of the court is obtained to a scheme of arrangement under section 425.[42]

---

[32] [1946] 1 All E.R. 512 (C.A.).
[33] *The Times*, November 24, 1934.
[34] See too, *Rights and Issues Investment Trust Ltd v. Stylo Shoes Ltd* [1965] Ch. 250, *ante*, p. 87.
[35] [1954] Ch. 169, *ante*, p. 178.
[36] *Harman v. BML Group Ltd* [1994] 2 BCLC 674 (C.A.).
[37] *Ante*, p. 240.
[38] *e.g.* a right to be a necessary part of a quorum at any meeting of the company: *Harman v. BML Group Ltd* [1994] 2 BCLC 674 (C.A.)
[39] *Dimbula Valley (Ceylon) Tea Co. Ltd v. Laurie* [1961] Ch. 353.
[40] s.125(5).
[41] s.125(4).
[42] *Post*, Chap. 30.

An alteration by a method provided by the memorandum will probably be subject to section 127, *post*. If the proposed variation relates to the authority to issue shares[43] or a reduction of capital,[44] the specified majority will be three quarters whatever the procedure provided by the memorandum or articles might say; section 125(3).

Any meeting held to vary the class rights must comply with the Act as to notice and conduct of meetings with a minimum quorum of the holders of at least one third of the nominal value of the class being at least two in number: section 125(6).

Under section 425 a company may make a binding compromise or arrangement with a class of members. Application must be made to the court to order a meeting of the class. Then the compromise or arrangement must be approved at the meeting by a simple majority in number representing three-fourths in value of those voting in person or by proxy. Finally, the court must approve it.

The power to alter the memorandum conferred by section 17[45] does not authorise any variation or abrogation of the special rights of any class of members.

3. The rights of different classes of shares are usually set out in the articles[46] and the articles often provide for the variation of class rights. In any event the Act now implies such a variation procedure.

If the articles attach class rights to a class of shares and contain a "modification of rights clause" the class rights may in general be varied, with the consent of the specified proportion or resolution of the holders of shares of the class, by a valid alteration of the articles by a special resolution of the company in general meeting.[47] In two cases, *viz.* a variation relating to the directors' powers to issue shares[48] and one connected with a reduction of capital,[49] the required majority is three quarters whatever the articles may say: section 125(3).

---

[43] *Ante*, p. 147.
[44] *Ante*, p. 173.
[45] *Ante*, p. 76.
[46] Class rights set out in a shareholders' agreement have the same affect as if they were contained in the articles: *Harman v. BML Group Ltd* [1994] 2 BCLC 674 (C.A.).
[47] *Ante*, p. 83.
[48] *Ante*, p. 147.
[49] *Ante*, p. 173.

Such modification of rights clauses must be complied with: section 125(4). Any meeting held must comply with the Act as to the notice and conduct of meetings with a minimum quorum of the holders of at least one third in nominal value of the class being at least two in number: section 125(6).

If the articles do not set out a modification of rights clause, the rights can nevertheless be varied either by the written consent of the holders of three quarters of the issued shares of that class or by an extraordinary resolution to that effect passed at a separate meeting of that class: section 125(2). Again the meetings provisions in the Act must be complied with: section 125(6). This implied procedure may eventually replace express clauses—Table A no longer contains one.[50]

There is no effective compliance with a modification of class rights unless those holding a sufficient majority of the shares of the class vote in favour of the modification in the bona fide belief that they are acting in the interests of the general body of members of the class, *i.e.* at the class meeting the majority shareholders must consider what is best for the shareholders as a class, not what is best in their own interests.

A reduction of capital was to be effected by cancelling the five per cent. £1 cumulative preference shares and allotting the holders an equivalent amount of six per cent. unsecured loan stock repayable 1985/90. The majority of the preference shareholders, who supported the reduction, were also holders of 52 per cent. of the company's ordinary stock and non-voting ordinary shares. Minority preference shareholders opposed the reduction. The court refused to confirm it. The majority preference shareholders had considered what was best in their own interests, based on their large equity shareholding, without considering what was best for preference shareholders as a class. Further, the reduction was unfair[51] —the advantages of the exchange into unsecured stock did not compensate for the disadvantages: *Re Holders Investment Trust Ltd* [1971] 1 W.L.R. 582.

4. Where there is in the articles (or the memorandum) an express or implied power to vary class rights, the exercise of the power is subject to section 127. This section provides that if, in the case of a company with a share capital divided into different classes of shares, provision is made by the articles (or memorandum) for the variation or abrogation of the rights attached to any

[50] This implemented para. 198 of the Jenkins Committee Report.
[51] *Ante,* p. 178.

class of shares, subject to the consent of a specified proportion of the holders of the shares of the class or the sanction of a resolution passed at a separate meeting of the holders of such shares, and in pursuance of such provision the rights attached to any such class of shares are varied, an application can be made to the court to have the variation cancelled, whereupon it has no effect unless and until it is confirmed by the court. The section also applies to variations under the procedure implied by section 125(2): section 127(1)(b).

Those who can apply are the holders of not less than 15 per cent. of the issued shares of the class who did not consent to or vote for the variation. The application must be made within 21 days after the giving of the consent or the passing of the resolution. In England it is made by petition by one or more of the dissenting shareholders authorised in writing by the 15 per cent.: R.S.C., Ord. 102, r. 5. For Scotland, see R.C. 189.

The court may disallow the variation if, after hearing the various parties interested, it is satisfied that the variation would unfairly prejudice the shareholders of the class in question. If the court is not so satisfied it must confirm the variation.

The company must, within 15 days, send a copy of the order made by the court to the Registrar of Companies: section 127(5).

The object of the section is to protect shareholders from being prejudiced by the voting of other shareholders who hold shares of another class in addition to those of the class affected by the variation.

For example, if a variation reduces the dividend on preference shares from seven per cent. to six per cent. per annum, and 80 per cent. of the preference shareholders are also ordinary shareholders, the requisite consent of the preference shareholders is likely to be obtained, since the variation will leave more profits for a dividend on the ordinary shares. This would be unfair to the 20 per cent. of the preference shareholders who are not ordinary shareholders and they could apply under section 127.

A variation of class rights, includes an abrogation of those rights: section 125(8).[52] However, it has been held that class rights are *not* "varied" by the subdivision of other shares, under a

---

[52] Preference shareholders' rights are not abrogated by being repaid first on a reduction of capital: *House of Fraser plc v. A.C.G.E. Investments plc* [1987] A.C. 387, 1987 S.C. (H.L.). 125, unless such a reduction is made a specific class right: *Re Northern Engineering Industries plc* [1994] 2 BCLC 704 (C.A.).

power in the articles, which results in the holders of the shares with the class rights being outvoted by the holders of the other shares.

2s. ordinary shares, as regards voting, ranked *pari passu* with the 10s. ordinary shares. Each 10s. share was sub-divided into five 2s. ordinary shares. *Held*, the voting rights of the original 2s. shares had not been varied. The only voting right attached to that class was one vote per share, and that right remained: *Greenhalgh v. Arderne Cinemas Ltd* [1946] 1 All E.R. 512 (C.A.).[53]

Again, class rights are *not* "affected" by the creation or issue of new shares of the class ranking equally with the old.

Capital was being increased by the issue of 600,000 £1 preference shares ranking *pari passu* with the existing 600,000 £1 preference stock, and 2,640,000 ordinary shares of 10s. each ranking *pari passu* with the existing £3,300,00 ordinary stock. The new shares were to be issued to the ordinary stockholders and paid for out of the reserve fund. *Held*, the proposed issue of new capital did not "affect" the rights of the existing preference shareholders. Only the enjoyment of the rights was affected, the rights themselves were not: *White v. Bristol Aeroplane Co. Ltd* [1953] Ch. 65 (C.A.).[54]

A modification of rights clause in the articles cannot be altered by special resolution without the appropriate consent of shareholders of the class under that procedure: section 125(7).

**Deferred shares**

Deferred shares, which are sometimes called founders' or management shares, are usually of small nominal amount with a right to take the whole or a proportion of the profits after a fixed dividend has been paid on the ordinary shares. The rights of the holders of deferred shares depend on the articles or the terms of issue.

Deferred shares are rarely issued now and the modern tendency is to convert existing deferred shares into ordinary shares.

**Non-voting ordinary shares**

In recent years some companies have issued non-voting ordinary shares. The purpose of such issues is to enable the com-

---

[53] And see the *Dimbula* case, *ante*, p. 241.
[54] And see *Re John Smith's Tadcaster Brewery Co. Ltd* [1953] Ch. 308.

panies concerned to raise money and at the same time enable those with the majority of the existing voting shares to retain control. However, with the idea of ensuring that the public is not misled, the Stock Exchange requires non-voting shares to be designated as such. This is usually done by describing the shares as A Ordinary shares, etc.

## No par value shares

The memorandum of a limited company with a share capital must state the amount of share capital with which the company proposes to be registered and its division into shares of a fixed amount (s.2(5)(a)), and any provision in the memorandum or articles, or in any resolution, of a company limited by guarantee purporting to divide the undertaking into shares or interests is treated as a provision for a share capital, notwithstanding that the nominal amount or number of the shares or interests is not specified thereby (s.15(2)). The requirement that the nominal share capital must be divided into shares of a fixed amount means that *shares of no par value cannot be issued.*

## Employees' shares

Some companies issue special shares to their employees. Modern tax legislation, however, in general only provides tax incentives for companies who provide their employees with ordinary shares, *i.e.* those not specifically available only to employees.

## TRANSFER OF SHARES

There is a distinction between a transfer of shares and a transmission of shares. A transfer is by the act of the member, while a transmission occurs by operation of law on the death or the bankruptcy of a member.[55] The procedure on transfer is set out below,[56] but there must be a valid agreement of transfer, either by gift or contract. In *Harvela Investments Ltd v. Royal Trust Company of Canada (C.I.) Ltd*[57] the House of Lords held that the holder of shares in a private company could not validly

[55] *Post,* p. 266.
[56] *Post,* p. 248.
[57] [1986] A.C. 207 (H.L.).

invite other parties to submit sealed bids for those shares and
then accept a bid which is referential, *i.e.* one which is given as
an amount above that submitted by the other bidder. If such bids
were allowed one party could not lose and the other party could
not win.

**Form of transfer**

Section 183(1), which was passed to make sure that there is an
instrument which can be stamped with stamp duty, provides that
it is unlawful for a company to register a transfer of shares, and
so complete the legal title, unless a "proper instrument of
transfer" has been delivered to the company. Consequently it is
illegal to have an article that upon the death of a shareholder his
shares shall be deemed to have passed to his widow, without any
transfer.[58]

The form of the transfer may be that prescribed by the articles
but a "proper instrument" for the purposes of section 183(1) does
not necessarily mean an instrument complying with the formalities prescribed by the articles—it means an instrument such
as will attract stamp duty.[59] Thus a transfer document which
failed to state the consideration for the transfer was held to be
valid since it was still appropriate for stamping purposes — the
Revenue could go behind the form to ascertain that amount.[60]

> Table A, regulation 23, provides: "The instrument of transfer of
> a share may be in any usual form or in any other form which
> the directors may approve and shall be executed by or on behalf of
> the transferor and, unless the share is fully paid, by or on behalf of
> the transferee."

Where the shares are only partly-paid it is essential that the
transferee signs the transfer document to accept the liability on
the shares.[61]

In the case of a company limited by shares, if shares are fully
paid they may be transferred by a simplified form of transfer,
namely a stock transfer under hand in the form set out in

[58] *Re Greene* [1949] Ch. 333.
[59] *Re Paradise Motor Co. Ltd* [1968] 1 W.L.R. 1125 (C.A.); *Dempsey v. Celtic
Football and Athletic Co. Ltd* [1993] BCC 514; *Nisbet v. Sheperd* [1994] 1 BCLC
300.
[60] *Nisbet v. Shepherd* [1994] 1 BCLC 300.
[61] *Dempsey v. Celtic Football and Athletic Co. Ltd* [1993] BCC 514.

Schedule 1 to the Stock Transfer Act 1963.[62] Such a transfer need
be executed only by the transferor and need not be attested: 1963
Act, s.1. Additional permitted forms were introduced for the
computerised system of transfers on the stock exchange; *i.e.*
where the transfer is to or from a stock exchange nominee.[63]

**Procedure on transfer**

If a shareholder has sold or given all his shares comprised in
one share certificate[64] to one person,[65] the transfer is effected as
follows:

(1) the transferor sends the transferee the "proper instrument
of transfer" required by section 183(1) and executed by
the transferor, together with the share certificate relating
to the shares comprised in the transfer;

(2) the transferee then executes the transfer[66] if it is in
accordance with the articles, and forwards it, with the
share certificate[67] and the registration fee, to the company
for registration;

(3) within two months[68] after the transfer is lodged the
company must either issue a new share certificate to the
transferee or, where the directors are exercising a power
to refuse registration, send *him* notice of its refusal to
register the transfer: sections 183(5), 185(1). In the case
of transfers on the stock exchange where a stock exchange
nominee is the transferee, the company is exempt from
the obligation to prepare the new share certificate: section
185(4).

A transfer may also be registered, at the request of the
transferor, in the same manner and subject to the same condi-

---

[62] As amended by the Stock Transfer (Amendment of Forms) Order 1974 (S.I.
No. 1214).

[63] Introduced by the Stock Transfer (Addition of Forms) Order 1979 (S.I. No.
277).

[64] As to shares comprised in a share warrant, see *post*, p. 280.

[65] As to the procedure when, *e.g.* part only of the holding is being sold, see
Certification of transfer, *post*.

[66] If he is required to do so under the articles.

[67] See *post*, p. 255.

[68] Fourteen days if the shares are quoted on a stock exchange: Admission of
Securities to Listing.

tions as if registration were applied for by the transferee: section 183(4).

## Certification of transfer

If a holder of shares sells or gives some only of his shares comprised in a share certificate, *e.g.* 250 shares out of 1,000, it will be unsafe for him to deliver his share certificate for 1,000 shares to the purchaser. Similarly if he sells some of the shares to one person and the rest to another. The usual procedure in such cases is, therefore:

(1) the transferor executes the transfer and sends it, with the share certificate, to the company;
(2) the secretary indorses on the transfer the words "certificate lodged" or similar words, and returns the transfer so certificated to the transferor;
(3) the transferor hands over this certificated transfer to the transferee against payment of the price;
(4) the transferee executes the transfer[69] if it is in the form prescribed by the articles, and forwards it to the company for registration;
(5) within two months[70] the company either issues new share certificates or, where a power to refuse registration is being exercised, informs the *transferee* of its refusal to register him: sections 183(5), 185(1), *ante.* This does not apply to transfers to a stock exchange nominee, *ante.*

The certification of a transfer by the company is a representation by the company to any person acting on the faith of the certification that there have been produced to the company such documents as show a prima facie title to the shares in the transferor, but it is not a representation that the transferor has any title: section 184(1). However, if a company *fraudulently or negligently* makes a false certification the company is liable in damages to a person who acts on the faith of it to his detriment: section 184(2).

Suppose that P transferred all his shares to X and his certificate was lodged by X with the company. Before registration was completed, P

[69] If required to do so by the articles.
[70] See note 68, *ante.*

executed a transfer of some of the shares to Y, who sold them to B. Y's transfer to B was negligently certificated by the company and, on the strength of this, B paid Y. The company registered X and refused to register B. The company is liable in damages to B.

A certification is deemed to be made by the company if it is made by a person, such as the secretary, authorised to issue certificated transfers on the company's behalf, and if it is signed by a person authorised to certificate transfers on the company's behalf: section 184(3).

When a transfer is certificated the company destroys the original certificate and issues new certificates. But if it *negligently* returns the original certificate with the certified transfer to the transferor and the transferor then fraudulently deals with the original certificate so as to inflict loss on a third party, *e.g.* the transferor purports to transfer *all* the shares comprised in the original certificate to the third party, the company is not liable to the third party. The reason is that the share certificate is neither a negotiable instrument nor a statement that the transferor is still the owner on the part of the company issuing it[71] and the company owes no duty to the public as to the custody of the certificate. Further, the company is not estopped from denying the validity of the transferor's title to the shares *previously* transferred, because the proximate cause of the third party's loss is the fraud of the transferor and not the negligence of the company.[72]

## Rights as between vendor and purchaser

On a sale of shares the ordinary contract between the parties is that the vendor shall give to the purchaser a valid transfer and do all that is required to enable the purchaser to be registered as a member in respect of the shares, the purchaser's duty being to get himself registered.[73] The vendor's duty is not only to give a genuine transfer but also, where the vendor is not the transferor,

---

[71] See *post*, p. 256.

[72] *Longman v. Bath Electric Tramways Ltd* [1905] 1 Ch. 646. The Scottish equivalent of "estoppel" is personal bar, but, in the absence of Scottish authority on certification, it seems doubtful whether a company would be entitled to deny the validity of a share certificate in the circumstances mentioned: *cf. Clavering, Son & Co. v. Goodwins, Jardine & Co. Ltd* (1891) 18 R. 652.

[73] *Skinner v. City of London Marine Insce. Corpn.* (1885) 14 Q.B.D. 882 (C.A.).

one which is signed by a transferor willing that the transfer shall be registered.

Solicitors instructed stockbrokers to sell stock and enclosed the certificate and a blank transfer (*i.e.* a transfer in which the transferee's name had still to be inserted)[74] signed by the stockholder. The stockbrokers sold the stock but the stockholder repudiated the contract and the company, on her instructions, refused to register the transfer. The stockbrokers replaced the stock by a purchase on the Stock Exchange and sued the solicitors for an indemnity. *Held,* (1) the solicitors were principals of the stockbrokers as regards the sale, (2) it was the solicitor's duty to deliver a transfer executed by a transferor willing that it should be registered, and (3) the solicitors were liable. *Hichens, Harrison, Woolston & Co.* v. *Jackson & Sons* [1943] A.C. 266.

If the directors, in pursuance of a power in the articles,[75] decline to register the transfer, the purchaser, unless he bought "with registration guaranteed", will be unable to sue the vendor for damages or rescind and recover the price from the vendor— there is no implied condition subsequent to such effect.[76] In such a case the vendor will be a trustee of the shares for the purchaser.[77] The vendor is, of course, under a duty to the purchaser not to prevent or delay the registration of the transfer.[78]

As from the time of the contract of sale the equitable or beneficial interest in the shares passes to the purchaser, and the vendor holds the legal title as quasi-trustee for the purchaser.[79] The purchaser does not obtain the legal or complete title until his name is entered on the register of members.[80]

Until the transfer is registered, the vendor will receive any dividends or other benefits declared on the shares and, in the case of partly paid shares, calls may be made on him. As between the vendor and the purchaser the rights and liabilities depend on the terms of the contract. The shares may be bought "cum" or

---

[74] Such a transfer may be invalid in Scots law: *post*, p. 270.

[75] See *post*, p. 264.

[76] *London Founders Assocn. Ltd* v. *Clarke* (1888) 20 Q.B.D. 576 (C.A.).

[77] *Stevenson* v. *Wilson*, 1907 S.C. 445; this quasi-trust would not, however, defeat a subsequent arrestment of the shares by a creditor of the transferor: *per* Lord Moncrieff (Ordinary) in *National Bank of Scotland Glasgow Nominees Ltd* v. *Adamson*, 1932 S.L.T. 492 (O.H.) at p. 495.

[78] *Hooper* v. *Herts* [1906] 1 Ch. 549 (C.A.)

[79] See note 77, *ante.*

[80] See *per* Lord Gifford in *Morrison* v. *Harrison* (1876) 3 R. 406 at p. 411; see also *Tennant's Trustees* v. *Tennant*, 1946 S.C. 420.

"ex" dividends or rights, or with a specified sum paid. In the absence of any such agreement, the purchaser is entitled to dividends or other benefits declared after the *date of the contract.*[81]

> In September 1935, R. sold shares privately to W. In April 1936, the company declared a dividend for the year ending December 31, 1935. *Held,* the sale being by private bargain and not governed by Stock Exchange rules, W. was entitled to the whole dividend and it was not apportionable between W. and R.: *Re Wimbush* [1940] Ch. 92.

Subject to contrary agreement, the purchaser must indemnify the vendor against calls made after the date of the contract.[82]

Again, until the transfer is registered, the vendor is entitled to exercise any vote conferred by the shares but he must vote as directed by the purchaser.[83]

An unpaid vendor of shares who remains on the register of members after the contract of sale retains *vis-à-vis* the purchaser the right to vote in respect of those shares. Where the contract expressly provides for delay in payment and makes alternative arrangements as to voting then the unpaid vendor will lose his right to vote[84], but not where the purchaser defaults in payment even though the voting rights have passed to the purchaser under the contract.[85]

**Priorities**

*English law*

The general rules are:

(1) The party who is on the register of members and therefore has the legal title has priority.

---

[81] *Black v. Homersham* (1878) 4 Ex.D. 24; *Re Kidner* [1929] 2 Ch. 121.
[82] *Spencer v. Ashworth, Partington & Co.* [1925] 1 K.B. 589 (C.A.).
[83] *Dempsey v. Celtic Football and Athletic Co. Ltd* [1993] BCC 514.
[84] *Musselwhite v. C.H. Musselwhite & Son Ltd* [1962] Ch. 964, where a contract for the sale of shares provided that the transfer and share certificate should be held by a third party until the price was paid by instalments over a period of years.
[85] *JRRT (Investments) Ltd v. Haycroft* [1993] BCLC 401.

(2) If neither party is on the register, the party whose equitable title is first in time has priority.

For example, if X, the registered owner, is trustee of the shares for Y and, in breach of trust sells the shares to Z, who buys without notice of the trust and becomes registered as owner before the company knows of the trust, Z will have priority over Y. A company, however, is entitled to a reasonable time for the consideration of every transfer before it registers the transfer,[86] and therefore if Y, in the example just given, had given notice of his claim to the company before Z was actually registered as owner, he would have been entitled to priority over Z, as his equitable title would have been first in time.

C. assigned all his property to P. as trustee for C.'s creditors. The property included some shares. P. asked for the share certificates but was unable to obtain them from C.; he then gave notice of the assignment to the company. C., after the date of the assignment to P., sold the shares to X, who applied for registration. *Held*, P., having an equitable title which was prior in time, was entitled to registration: *Peat v. Clayton* [1906] 1 Ch. 659.

Entry on the register after notice of a prior equitable claim will not give priority.

In 1893 X transferred debentures of a private company to Y on trust for X for life with remainder to X's sons. The transfer was not registered. In 1894 one son sold his share of the debentures to Z. In 1911 X deposited the debentures with the bank as security for the company's overdraft. In 1914 the bank, on learning of the settlement and transfer to Y, took a transfer of the debentures from X, and were registered as owners. *Held*, Z was entitled to priority over the bank: *Coleman v. London County and Westminster Bank Ltd* [1916] 2 Ch. 353.

It has been said[87] that even if a complete legal title has not been obtained, a person who has, as between himself and the company, a present, absolute, unconditional right to registration before the company learns of a better title, has the same priority as if he were actually registered. It is doubtful, however, whether anything short of registration will give priority, except perhaps in very special circumstances. Directors should refuse to register a transfer after receiving notice of an adverse equitable claim to the

[86] *Re Ottos Kopje Diamond Mines Ltd* [1893] 1 Ch. 618 (C.A.)
[87] *Per* Romer J. in *Moore v. North Western Bank* [1891] 2 Ch. 599 at pp. 602, 603.

shares, unless the transfer has already been passed for registration.[88]

Delay in obtaining registration is dangerous to a transferee for two reasons: a later transferee may gain priority by obtaining registration first, or an earlier equity may come to light.

A husband mortgaged shares of which he was trustee for his wife. Before the mortgagee was registered the wife successfully claimed that her equitable title prevailed over that of the mortgagee: *Ireland v. Hart* [1902] 1 Ch. 522.

To protect himself such a transferee should issue a stop notice.[89]

*Scots law*

If there are competing claims for membership of a company, the person preferred is the one who first completes his title to the shares by having his name entered on the register; a mere assignation of shares, even though intimated to the company, does not make the assignee a member.[90] Where a competition arises between a transferee and an arrester, the transferee is preferred to the arrester as soon as the transfer has been registered.[91] In a question between a transferee whose transfer has been duly intimated to the company but not registered and a subsequent arrester, the intimation of the transfer has been held to cut out the arrestment.[92]

Directors may delay registration where they suspect that a transfer is effected by fraud or dishonesty[93] but, if they receive intimation of a competing interest in the shares from some party other than the transferee, they are entitled to register the transfer unless the intimation is followed up by a legal measure such as interdict.[94] The company must be made a party to any such interdict process, and interdict has been refused where it was alleged that share transfers, bearing that the beneficial interest

[88] *Per* Joyce J. in *Ireland v. Hart* [1902] 1 Ch. 522 at p. 529.
[89] See p. 269, *post.*
[90] *Morrison v. Harrison* (1876) 3 R. 406.
[91] *National Bank of Scotland Glasgow Nominees Ltd v. Adamson*, 1932 S.L.T. 492 (O.H.).
[92] *Jackson v. Elphick* (1902) 10 S.L.T. 146 (O.H.).
[93] *Property Investment Co. of Scotland Ltd v. Duncan* (1887) 14 R. 299.
[94] *Per* Lord M'Laren in *Shaw v. Caledonian Rlwy. Co.* (1890) 17 R. 466 at p. 482.

remained in the transferors, had been executed by a body of trustees to certain of their own number and another person in order to give the transferees a qualification to act as directors; the possibility that the shares had been transferred in breach of trust was not, the court held, a matter which concerned the company or which made the registration of the transferees invalid.[95]

## SHARE CERTIFICATES

Every company must complete the share certificates and have them ready for delivery within two months[96] after the allotment of any of its shares or after the date on which a transfer of its shares is lodged for registration, unless the conditions of issue otherwise provide, under a penalty of a default fine: section 185. The form of the certificate is governed by the articles. Table A, regulation 6, gives the right to a certificate without payment and provides that it shall be under the seal of the company,[97] and shall specify the shares to which it relates and the amount paid up thereon.

If shares, debentures or debenture stock are allotted to a stock exchange nominee (SEPON Ltd), or a transfer of shares, debentures or debenture stock to a stock exchange nominee is lodged with the company, the company is exempt from the obligation to prepare certificates under section 185: section 185(4). This is to facilitate the computerised system of transfers on the stock exchange.

The certificate is a formal statement by the company under its common seal if it has one, or its official seal under section 40, or is otherwise signed in accordance with section 36A or 36B,[98] that the person named therein is the holder of the number of shares in the company specified in the certificate at the date of issue. It is prima facie evidence of the title of that person to the shares: section 186.[99] It is not, however, a document of title (as the register of members is).[1] The object of the certificate is to facilitate dealings with the shares, whether by way of sale or

---

[95] *Elliot v. J. W. Mackie & Sons Ltd*, 1935 S.C. 81.
[96] Fourteen days if the shares are quoted on the Stock Exchange: Admission of Securities to Listing.
[97] This can include the official seal for this purpose authorised under s.40.
[98] *Ante,* p. 101.
[99] See *Re Baku Consolidated Oilfields Ltd* [1994] 1 BCLC 173.
[1] See *International Credit and Investment (Overseas) Co. Ltd v. Adham* [1994] 1 BCLC 66; and see *ante*, p. 214.

security, and so make them more valuable to their owner. On the other hand, a share certificate is not a negotiable instrument, so that its accidental loss or destruction is not a matter of great moment. The articles usually make provision for the granting of a new certificate in such a case.

Table A, regulation 7, provides: "If a share certificate is defaced, worn out, lost or destroyed, it may be renewed on such terms (if any) as to evidence and indemnity and payment of the expenses reasonably incurred by the company in investigating evidence as the directors may determine but otherwise free of charge, and (in the case of defacement or wearing out) on delivery up of the old certificate."

In England a share certificate is not a deed for the purposes of the Law of Property Act 1925, s.74,[2] which might otherwise validate it.[3]

## Estoppel[4] as to statements in a certificate

The issue of a share certificate may give rise to an estoppel against the company. The company cannot deny the truth of the certificate against a person who has relied on the certificate and in consequence has changed his position.

T., the registered holder of shares, left the share certificate with her broker. T.'s signature was forged to a transfer in favour of S. T. did not reply to notice of the transfer sent to her by the company and a new certificate in the name of S. was issued by the company. A. bought from S. and paid for the shares on delivery of the share certificate and a new share certificate was issued to A. The fraud was subsequently discovered and T.'s name was restored to the register. *Held*, the company was liable to indemnify A. The giving of the certificate to S. amounted to a statement by the company, intended to be acted upon by purchasers of shares in the market, that S. was entitled to the shares, and A. having acted on the statement, the company was estopped from denying it. A. was entitled to recover from the company as damages the value of the shares at the time when the company first refused to recognise him as a shareholder, with interest: *Re Bahia and San Francisco Rlwy. Co.* (1868) L.R. 3 Q.B. 584.

---

[2] *Per* Clauson J. in *South London Greyhound Racecourses Ltd v. Wake* [1931] 1 Ch. 496, at p. 503. *Quaere* whether it is a deed for the purposes of s.36A, *ante*, p. 101.

[3] If attested in the presence of a director and secretary.

[4] Personal bar is the Scottish equivalent of "estoppel". See Lord Kyllachy (Ordinary) in *Clavering, Son & Co. v. Goodwins, Jardine & Co. Ltd* (1891) 18 R. 652 at p. 657.

There is no estoppel in favour of a person, such as S. in the above case, who procures the granting of a certificate on a forged transfer[5] or forged power of attorney,[6] even if he has acted in good faith. In fact the company may be able to claim an indemnity from such a person.[7] There is no estoppel either in favour of a person who relies on the certificate to establish that the person named is still the owner, only to someone relying on the fact that that person was the owner at the date of issue.[8]

The company may be estopped from denying the title to shares of the person to whom it has issued a share certificate.[9]

D. bought 30 shares through a broker, L., who was also secretary of the company, and paid L. She received and returned to L. a transfer of shares executed to L.'s direction by his clerk, P., who was never a man of substance and who did not hold any shares. The transfer, which did not specify the numbers of the shares, was put before the board by L. and passed without production of P.'s certificate being required, and a new certificate prepared by L. was issued to the effect that D. held 30 shares, numbers 115—144 inclusive. The chairman, who did not sign the certificate, did not notice that the shares were part of his holding (numbers 1-133). The board properly relied on the secretary to check transfers and certificates with the register. Two years later the board notified D. that P.'s transfer was invalid and declined to recognise her as a shareholder. L. was bankrupt by then and the company could not prove that he could not have reimbursed D. if, when the certificate was issued, the company had refused to issue it. *Held,* D. was entitled to damages: *Dixon v. Kennaway & Co.* [1900] 1 Ch. 833.

The company may be estopped from denying the amount stated to be paid up on shares.

B. lent money to a company on the security of fully paid shares in the company and was handed by the company share certificates for 10,000 shares of £1 each which the certificates stated to be fully paid up. No money had been paid on the shares, which had been issued direct by the company to B., but B. did not know this. On the company's going into liquidation, B. was placed on the list of contributories in respect of these shares. *Held,* the company was estopped by the certificate from denying that the shares were fully paid up and B. was entitled to have his name

---

[5] *Sheffield Corporation v. Barclay* [1905] A.C. 392, *post*, p. 259.
[6] *Starkey v. Bank of England* [1903] A.C. 114.
[7] *Post*, p. 258.
[8] *Longman v. Bath Electric Tramways Ltd* [1905] 1 Ch. 646; *International Credit and Investment Co. (Overseas) Ltd v. Adham* [1994] 1 BCLC 66.
[9] *Balkis Consolidated Co. Ltd v. Tomkinson* [1893] A.C. 396.

removed from the list of contributories: *Bloomenthal v. Ford* [1897]
A.C. 156.[10]

The company may be made liable in damages to the person
who has relied on the statement in the share certificate.[11]

If B., in the *Bloomenthal* case, had known that the shares were
not fully paid up, there would have been no estoppel— there is
no estoppel in favour of a person who knows the untruth of
statements in a share certificate.[12] An original allottee, therefore,
will seldom be in a position to benefit from the principle.[13]

The company is not estopped where a certificate is a forgery.

R. lent money to the secretary of a company for his own purposes on
the security of a share certificate issued to R. by the secretary and
certifying that R. was registered as transferee of the shares. The
secretary issued the share certificate without authority, affixed the
common seal and forged the signatures of two directors, so that the
certificate apparently complied with the articles. R. sued the company
for damages for refusal to register him. *Held,* in the absence of evidence
that the company had held out the secretary as having authority to do
more than the mere ministerial act of delivering share certificates, when
duly made, to those entitled to them, the company was not estopped
from disputing the claim or responsible for the secretary's act: *Ruben v.
Great Fingall Consolidated* [1906] A.C. 439.

## Forged transfers

A forged transfer of shares is a nullity and cannot affect the
title of the shareholder whose signature is forged. If the company, therefore, has registered the forged transfer and removed
the true owner of the shares from the register, it can be
compelled to replace him.[14] It can then claim an indemnity from
the person who sent the forged transfer for registration if it has
sustained loss through acting thereon. No estoppel in favour of

[10] *cf. Waterhouse v. Jamieson* (1870) 8 M (H.L.) 88, in which it was held that
statements in the memorandum and articles, which also appeared in share
certificates, as to the amount paid up on shares could not be contradicted by the
liquidator.
[11] *Clavering, Son & Co. v. Goodwins, Jardine & Co. Ltd* (1891) 18 R. 652.
[12] See *Crickmer's Case* (1875) L.R. 10. Ch.App. 614. In England, if the shares
had been transferred to a purchaser without notice that they were not fully paid
up he could give a good title to a purchaser from him without notice: *Barrow's
Case* (1880) 14 Ch.D. 432 (C.A.).
[13] *Liquidator of Scottish Heritages Co. Ltd* (1898) 5 S.L.T. 336 (O.H.): contrast
*Penang Foundry Co. Ltd v. Gardiner*, 1913 S.C. 1203 (O.H.).
[14] *Barton v. N. Staffordshire Rlwy. Co.* (1888) 38 Ch.D. 458.

such a person arises from a share certificate issued to him even though he knows nothing of the forgery—he has not relied on the act of the company in issuing the certificate.

B. sent to the corporation for registration a transfer of stock which stood in the names of T. and H. The transfer was a forgery, T. having forged H.'s signature to the transfer, but B. was ignorant of this. The corporation registered the transfer. B. transferred the stock to third parties to whom certificates were issued. The corporation was estopped from denying that those registered were the stockholders entitled. H. subsequently discovered the forgery and compelled the corporation to buy him an equivalent amount of stock and to pay him the missing dividends with interest. *Held,* B. was bound to indemnify the corporation upon an implied contract that the transfer was genuine: *Sheffield Corporation v. Barclay* [1905] A.C. 392.[15]

This right extends to an indemnity from a stockbroker who makes the application on behalf of the person with the forged transfer. The company may not, however, be able to claim a complete indemnity if it is guilty of negligence in failing to spot the forgery. In such a situation it has been suggested that section 2(1) of the Civil Liability (Contribution) Act 1978 may prevent complete recovery.[16]

In an effort to prevent the registration of a forged transfer, companies usually, on a transfer being lodged for registration, write to the shareholder informing him of the transfer and of their intention to register it unless by return of post they hear that he objects. The neglect of the shareholder to reply to this communication does not estop him from proving that the transfer is a forgery.[17]

## RESTRICTIONS ON TRANSFER

Every shareholder has a right to transfer his shares to whom he likes, unless the articles provide to the contrary.[18]

---

[15] *cf.* Lord Kyllachy (Ordinary) in *Clavering, Son & Co. v. Goodwins, Jardine & Co. Ltd* (1891) 18 R. 652 at p. 657.
[16] *Yeung v. Honk Kong and Shanghai Bank Ltd* [1980] 2 All E.R. 599 (P.C.). In Scotland see Law Reform (Miscellaneous Provisions) (Scotland) Act 1940, s.3.
[17] *Re Bahia and San Francisco Rlwy Co.* (1868) L.R. 3 Q.B. 584, *ante*, p. 256, *Barton v. L. & N.W. Rlwy Co.* (1890) 24 Q.B.D. 77 (C.A.).
[18] *Weston's Case* (1868) L.R. 4 Ch.App. 20: *O'Meara v. The El Palmar Rubber Estates Ltd.*, 1913, 1 S.L.T. 383 (O.H.). It is otherwise, *e.g.* where the company is being wound up and a transfer is prevented by I.A. 1986, s.127, *post,* Chap. 29.

By the Companies Acts "it is provided that the shares in a company under these Acts shall be capable of being transferred in manner provided by the regulations of the company. The regulations of the company may impose fetters upon the right of transfer. In the absence of restrictions in the articles the shareholder has by virtue of the statute the right to transfer his shares without the consent of anybody to any transferee, even though he be a man of straw, provided it is a bona fide transaction in the sense that it is an out-and-out disposal of the property without retaining any interest in the shares—that the transferor bona fide divests himself of all benefit. . . . In the absence of restrictions it is competent to a transferor, notwithstanding that the company is *in extremis* to compel registration of a transfer to a transferee notwithstanding that the latter is a person not competent to meet the unpaid liability upon the shares. Even if the transfer be executed for the express purpose of relieving the transferor from liability, the directors cannot upon that ground refuse to register it unless there is in the articles some provision so enabling them": *per* Buckley L.J. in *Lindlar's Case* [1910] 1 Ch. 312 (C.A.) at p. 316.[19]

In the case of a private company, the articles may, and usually do, restrict the right to transfer its shares.[20] In the case of a public company, shares must normally be free from restrictions on the right of transfer if a stock exchange quotation is to be obtained.[21]

Any restrictions on the transfer of shares are a derogation from the common law right of free transfer. It follows that: any rights conferred by the articles will not be extended to situations not covered by them[22], the procedure laid down in the articles for the exercise of the rights must be strictly followed[23], and if the rights are not actively exercised the right of free transfer will revive.[24]

If there has been a registered transfer in breach of the articles the only remedy available to an aggrieved shareholder is rectification of the register. This is a discretionary remedy, however, and will not be granted to third parties for extraneous purposes.[25]

[19] See also *Borland's Trustee v. Steel Bros. & Co. Ltd* [1901] 1 Ch. 279. For Scottish authority to the same effect, see, *e.g.* Lord Kincairney (Ordinary) in *Stewart v. James Keiller & Sons Ltd* (1902) 4 F. 657 at p. 667.

[20] Until the 1980 Act such restrictions were obligatory for private companies: *ante*, p. 42. The restriction on the transfer of shares in a private company is one reason why such shares are not dealt in on stock exchanges.

[21] Admission of Securities to Listing. The main advantage of a stock exchange quotation is that it makes the securities more marketable.

[22] *Furness & Co. v. Liquidators of "Cynthiana" Steamship Co. Ltd* (1893) 21 R. 239.

[23] *Neilson v. Ayr Race Meetings Syndicate Ltd,* 1918, 1 S.L.T. 63 (O.H.).

[24] *Shepherd's Trustees v. Shepherd*, 1950 S.C. (H.L.) 60 (application for registration granted, the two directors having failed to agree to refuse registration); *Re New Cedos Engineering Co. Ltd* [1994] 1 BCLC 797.

[25] *Re Piccadilly Radio plc* [1988] BCLC 683. For rectification of the register, see p. 217, *ante*.

Such restrictions usually fall within one of two categories: pre-emption clauses and refusal clauses.

## Pre-emption clauses

The articles of a private company usually contain a pre-emption clause, *e.g.* to the effect that no shares shall be transferred to any person not a member of the company so long as a member can be found to purchase them at a fair price to be determined in accordance with the articles.[26] Such a pre-emption clause does not entitle the company to refuse to register a transfer of shares from one member to another member of the company.[27] Where the value of shares for the purpose of such a clause falls to be fixed by the directors, the court will not review the directors' valuation provided that they have acted fairly and honestly.[28]

Sometimes the articles provide that a member desiring to sell any of his shares must inform the directors of the number of shares, the price and the name of the proposed transferee, and the directors must first offer the shares at that price to the other shareholders. In such a case, any member to whom the shares are offered cannot buy part only of the shares, and if none of the members is willing to buy all the shares the proposed transfer can be carried out.[29]

A member whose shares have been offered to other members under a pre-emption clause has been held entitled to withdraw his offer at any time before its acceptance.[30]

Articles provided that no transfer of shares should take place so long as any other shareholder was willing to purchase at a price to be ascertained by agreement between the intending transferor and the directors, or, failing agreement, at a price to be fixed by the auditors, and that any shareholder who was "desirous of transferring" his shares should inform the secretary of the number of shares which he desired to transfer. *Held*, shareholders who, on a take-over bid accepted an outside offer to buy their shares, received the price, gave the purchaser general proxies, and agreed to execute transfers and deliver up the share

---

[26] *Post*, p. 282.
[27] *Delavenne v. Broadhurst* [1931] Ch. 234.
[28] *Stewart v. James Keiller & Sons Ltd* (1902) 4 F. 657.
[29] *The Ocean Coal Co. Ltd v. The Powell Duffryn Steam Coal Co. Ltd* [1932] 1 Ch. 654.
[30] *J. M. Smith Ltd v. Colquhoun's Trustees* (1901) 3 F. 981.

certificates when called upon to do so, were "desirous of transferring" their shares and had to comply with the pre-emption clause, unless they gave notice that they had changed their minds before the other shareholders exercised their pre-emption rights: *Lyle & Scott Ltd v. Scott's Trustees*, 1959 S.C. (H.L.) 64; [1959] A.C. 763.[30a] Such a dispute between the company and its members has been distinguished from a case involving a third party: *Williams v. MacPherson*, 1900 S.L.T. 279 (O.H.).

Where the pre-emption clause requires the directors to find a purchaser for the shares, they may be under a duty to disclose all relevant facts to the shareholders.[31]

Many pre-emption clauses provide a machinery whereby the shares may be offered to the existing members, *e.g.* by making the company secretary agent for their sale. In *Tett v. Phoenix Property and Investment Co.*[32] the articles simply provided that there should be no transfer if any member indicated that he was willing to purchase the shares. The Court of Appeal, reversing Vinelott J., implied a term into the articles requiring a transferor to take reasonable steps to give the other members a reasonable opportunity to offer to purchase the shares at a fair value. Strictly speaking such a clause is not a pre-emption clause since it simply forbids a transfer to outsiders where a member has indicated his willingness to buy.

Pre-emption clauses on the other hand do not necessarily prevent a shareholder declaring himself a trustee for a proposed transferee, or even on death allowing the executors to hold the shares on trust for a beneficiary. Unless the pre-emption clause expressly applies to such situations the other shareholders may not invoke it. Thus in *Safeguard Industrial Investments Ltd v. National Westminster Bank plc*,[33] the executor bank holding shares on trust was held not to be a "proposing transferor" for the purposes of the clause. It is a question of fact, however, as to whether the clause applies in any given case. For example, in *Re Macro (Ipswich) Ltd*,[33a] a shareholder who had agreed to sell the legal title to his shares and had provided the purchaser with executed transfer forms was a member "desiring to sell his

---

[30a] See also *Safeguard Industrial Investments Ltd v. National Westminster Bank plc* [1982] 1 W.L.R. 62 (C.A.) and *Re Macro (Ipswich) Ltd* [1994] 2 BCLC 354.
[31] *Munro v. Bogie* [1994] 1 BCLC 415 CS (O.H.).
[32] [1986 BCLC 149 (C.A.).
[33] [1982] 1 W.L.R. 62 (C.A.).
[33a] [1994] 2 BCLC 354.

shares" and so caught by the pre-emption clause. On the other hand, in *Theakston v. London Trust plc*,[34] one member agreed to sell his shares to another member but in fact the purchase price was paid by a non-member, in whose name the shares were charged and according to whose directions the "purchaser" was to vote. Harman J. held that this was a transfer from one member to another and so outside the pre-emption clause. The fact that the transferee had equitable obligations to an outsider did not affect that position.

If the provision in the articles relating to the offer of the shares to the existing shareholders before a transfer is made is disregarded, the directors cannot validly register the transfer since it is a transfer in breach of the articles.[35] In England the same is true in the case of a sale, in disregard of the articles, by a mortgagee under his power of sale.[36] However, a transfer by a shareholder, in breach of the pre-emptive rights given by the articles, to a person who has paid for the shares operates as a transfer of the *beneficial interest* in the shares, so that the transferee takes priority over a judgment creditor who subsequently obtains a charging order[37] on the shares.[38] There must be substantial compliance with the pre-emption procedure before a transfer outside its terms can be effective. If there is no such compliance the court can award an injunction to prevent such transfer.[39]

Articles may provide that the other members are bound to buy the shares of a member who wishes to transfer them.[40]

It has also been held that a company enforcing a power of sale under a lien on its own shares must itself comply with the pre-

---

[34] [1984] BCLC 390.
[35] *Tett v. Phoenix Property and Investment Co. Ltd* [1986] BCLC 149 (C.A.).
[36] *Hunter v. Hunter* [1936] A.C. 222.
[37] *Post*, p. 270.
[38] *Hawks v. McArthur* [1951] 1 All E.R. 22. In *Tett v. Phoenix Investment and Property Co. Ltd supra*, Vinelott J. upheld *Hawks v. McArthur* and rejected any general argument to the contrary based on *Hunter v. Hunter, supra*. This part of his judgment was not challenged in the Court of Appeal.

Similarly, in Scotland, in a competition between a transferee and an arrester, the arrester was held not to be entitled to found on an alleged failure on the part of the company to observe the proper procedure relating to pre-emption and registration of transfers, with the result that the court declared that the shares had vested in the transferee: *National Bank of Scotland Glasgow Nominees Ltd v. Adamson*, 1932 S.L.T. 492 (O.H.).
[39] *Curtis v. J.J. Curtis & Co. Ltd* [1986] BCLC 86 (N.Z.).
[40] *Rayfield v. Hands* [1960] Ch. 1 *ante* p. 89.

emption clause in its articles in effecting that sale: *Champagne Perrier-Jouet S.A. v. H. H. Finch Ltd.*[41]

Note what is said later as to the duty of care owed by an auditor who values shares in the knowledge that his valuation will determine the price to be paid under a contract.[42]

## Directors' powers to refuse transfers

In addition to containing a pre-emption clause, the articles of a private company usually contain an article that the directors may, in their absolute discretion and without assigning any reason therefor, refuse to register any transfer of any share. If the shares are transferred in breach of the pre-emption clause then the directors have no power to register the transfer—no question of discretion arises.[43] In other cases, if the directors refuse to register a transfer the court will not interfere unless it can be shown that the directors are exercising their discretion improperly.[44]

When directors have power to decline to register a transfer, whether their power is absolute or limited to certain specified grounds, they need not disclose their reasons for refusing registration and if, having considered the questions, they refuse registration without giving any reasons, their refusal cannot be questioned unless there is evidence (which will be hard to come by) that they have not acted in good faith.[45]

The directors' discretionary power is a fiduciary power and must be exercised in good faith, *i.e.* legitimately for the purpose for which it is conferred. In exercising it the directors must act in good faith in the interest of the company and with due regard to the shareholder's right to transfer his shares, and they must fairly consider the question at a board meeting.[46]

Articles gave the directors "an absolute and uncontrolled discretion" to refuse to register any transfer of shares. The two directors each held

---

[41] [1982] 1 W.L.R. 1359.
[42] *Post*, p. 282.
[43] *Tett v. Phoenix Property and Investment Co. Ltd* [1986] BCLC 149 (C.A.).
[44] See *Stewart v. James Keiller & Sons Ltd* (1902) 4 F. 657.
[45] *Re Coalport China Co.* [1895] 2 Ch. 404; *Kennedy v. North British Wireless Schools Ltd*, 1916, 1 S.L.T. 407; 1915, 1 S.L.T. 196 (O.H.).
[46] *Per* Chitty J. in *Re Bell Bros. Ltd* (1891) 65 L.T. 245 at p. 245, and *per* Lawton L.J. in *Heron International Ltd v. Lord Grade* [1983] BCLC 244 at p. 265; and see also Lord Trayner in *Stewart v. James Keiller & Sons Ltd* (1902) 4 F. 657 at p. 678.

4,001 of the 8,002 ordinary shares. F. died and his son, as the executor, applied for the shares to be registered in his name. S. refused, but offered to register 2,001 shares if 2,000 were sold to him at a fixed price. F.'s son applied for rectification of the register but failed. There was nothing to show that the director's power was not exercised in the company's interest: *Re Smith and Fawcett Ltd* [1942] Ch. 304 (C.A.).

There is a presumption that the directors have acted *bona fide* and reasonably.[47]

If the articles empower the directors to decline to register transfers on certain grounds, *e.g.* on the ground that the transferor is indebted to the company, or that the transferee is a person of whom they do not approve, they can be interrogated as to the ground on which they have refused registration, although not as to the reasons for their refusal, unless the articles provide that they shall not be bound to specify the grounds for their refusal, in which case they cannot be interrogated at all.[48]

If the directors give reasons for their refusal, the court can decide whether they are sufficient to justify the refusal.

The articles empowered the directors to refuse the register a transfer if "in their opinion it is contrary to the interests of the company that the proposed transferee should be a member thereof." The directors declined to register transfers of single shares, stating that it was contrary to the interests of the company that shares should be transferred singly or in small amounts to outside persons with no interest in, or knowledge of, shipping. *Held,* this was a bad reason for refusing—refusal should have been on grounds personal to the transferee—and the transfers were directed to be registered: *Re Bede S.S. Co. Ltd* [1917] 1 Ch. 123 (C.A.).

A formal active exercise of the right of refusal to register is required before the company is authorised to refuse to register shares in the names of the transferees. Where directors are equally divided and so come to no decision to decline to register, the transfer must be registered.[49]

Where the articles provided that no share should be transferred to a person not already a member of the company without the consent of the directors and, to prevent a particular transfer from being registered, a director purposely abstained from attending

---

[47] *Per* Lord Anderson (Ordinary) in *Kennedy v. North British Wireless Schools Ltd*, 1916, 1 S.L.T. 407; 1915, 1 S.L.T. 196 (O.H.) at p. 198.
[48] *Berry and Stewart v. Tottenham Hotspur Football Club Co. Ltd* [1935] Ch. 718.
[49] *Shepherd's Trustees v. Shepherd*, 1950 S.C. (H.L.) 60, *per* Lord Porter at p. 66; *Re Hackney Pavilion Ltd* [1924] 1 Ch. 276.

board meetings so that a quorum could not be obtained, it was held that the transferee was entitled to an order directing the company to register the transfer.[50]

In one case the board lost their right to veto a transfer because they were guilty of an unreasonable delay of four months in deciding whether or not to exercise the veto—the period of two months specified in section 183(5) for giving a transferee notice of the company's refusal to register a transfer was considered to be the outside limit after which there is unnecessary delay for this purpose, unless in an exceptional case it is impossible to constitute a board.[51] Where there are no properly appointed directors to constitute a quorum to decide whether to exercise the right of refusal any refusal to register is a nullity,[52] but the transferee has no right to registration until the end of the period within which a properly constituted board could have exercised the power, *i.e.* two months. It follows that any purported registration during that period is invalid.[53]

In a rare case, the remedy of the transferee, or of the transferor, on a refusal to register a transfer is to apply to the court to rectify the register of members by substituting his name for that of the transferor under section 359. Unnecessary delay in registering a transfer does not in itself constitute a ground for rectification, and a transferor applying for rectification must be able to show that he has been prejudiced by the delay.[54] A winding-up petition is not the proper remedy for the transferor where registration of a transfer is refused.[55]

## TRANSMISSION OF SHARES

Section 183(2) provides that section 183(1) *ante*,[56] does not prejudice any power of a company to register as shareholder any person to whom the right to any shares in the company has been transmitted by operation of law. Transmission of shares occurs on the death or the bankruptcy of a member, or, if the member is a company, on its going into liquidation.

---

[50] *Re Copal Varnish Co. Ltd* [1917] 2 Ch. 349.
[51] *Re Swaledale Cleaners Ltd* [1968] 1 W.L.R. 1710 (C.A.).
[52] *Re New Cedos Engineering Co. Ltd* [1994] 1 BCLC 797.
[53] *Re Zinotty Properties Ltd* [1984] 1 W.L.R. 1249.
[54] *Property Investment Co. of Scotland Ltd v. Duncan* (1887) 14 R. 299.
[55] *Charles Forte Investments Ltd v. Amanda* [1964] Ch. 240 (C.A.).
[56] p. 247.

On the death of a sole shareholder the shares vest in his personal representative,[57] *i.e.* his executor or administrator.[58] The company is bound to accept production of the probate of the will or, in the case of an intestacy, letters of administration of the estate, or, in Scotland, the confirmation as executor, as sufficient evidence of the grant: section 187.[59] Subject to any restrictions in the articles, the personal representative may be registered as a member or transfer the shares without himself becoming a member: section 183(3).[60]

Table A, regulation 30, provides: "Any person becoming entitled to a share in consequence of the death or bankruptcy of a member may, upon such evidence being produced as the directors may properly require, elect either to become the holder of the share or to have some person nominated by him registered as the transferee. If he elects to become the holder he shall give notice to the company to that effect. If he elects to have another person registered he shall execute an instrument of transfer of the share to that person. All the articles relating to the transfer of shares shall apply to the notice or instrument of transfer as if it were an instrument of transfer executed by the member and the death or bankruptcy of the member had not occurred."

When shares are jointly held, the surviving holder becomes the sole holder. Under Table A, regulation 29, the estate of the deceased joint holder is not released from any liability in respect of the shares.

## MORTGAGE OF SHARES (ENGLISH LAW)

In England, a shareholder who borrows money on the security of his shares may give the lender either a legal mortgage or an equitable mortgage over the shares.

### Legal mortgage

A legal mortgage of shares is effected by transfer of the shares to the lender (the mortgagee) followed by registration of the transfer by the company. There should also be a document setting out the terms of the loan and containing an agreement to

---

[57] *Re Greene* [1949] Ch. 333.
[58] Executor in Scottish law: see p. 211, *ante.*
[59] See *e.g. Re Baku Consolidated Oilfields Ltd* [1994] 1 BCLC 173.
[60] *Ante,* p. 259.

retransfer the shares on repayment of the amount borrowed with interest. The document will empower the lender to sell the shares in the event of default by the borrower (the mortgagor). When exercising a power of sale the lender is under a duty to take reasonable care to obtain a proper price for the shares. He does not have to wait for a higher price but he must obtain the true market value of the shares. Any clause in the deed which purports to exclude this liability for negligence must be expressly worded to that effect.[61]

This form of mortgage gives the lender complete security up to the value of the shares. He will be entitled to dividends and to exercise any voting rights in respect of the shares, unless it is agreed that the dividends shall be paid to the borrower and that he shall exercise the voting rights as the borrower directs.[62]

However, restrictions on the transfer of shares contained in the articles[63] may prevent this kind of mortgage being made. Further, it might not be advisable where the shares are not fully paid because the lender on the register would be personally liable for calls.

**Equitable mortgage**

1. An equitable mortgage of shares may be made by depositing the share certificate with the lender as security for such a loan. In such a case the lender can enforce his security by applying to the court for a sale of the shares or for an order for transfer and foreclosure.[64]

2. A method more commonly adopted is for the borrower to deposit with the lender the share certificate together with a blank transfer *i.e.* a transfer signed by the borrower with the transferee's name left blank. In such a case the lender has an *implied* power to sell the shares if default is made by the borrower in making repayment at the agreed time or, if no time for repayment is agreed, within a reasonable time after notice.[65] The implied power of sale includes power to insert the name of the buyer in the blank transfer if, as is usual, the articles provide for

---

[61] *Bishop v. Bonham* [1988] BCLC 656 (C.A.)
[62] *Siemens Brothers & Co. Ltd v. Burns* [1918] 2 Ch. 324.
[63] *Ante,* p. 259.
[64] *Harrold v. Plenty* [1901] 2 Ch. 314.
[65] *Hooper v. Herts* [1906] 1 Ch. 549.

transfers to be in writing. The borrower is under an implied obligation not to delay registration of the transfer so filled up.[66]

3. If the articles require transfers to be by deed, the lender cannot fill up a blank transfer unless he is authorised by deed. In such a case an equitable mortgage may be made by deposit of the share certificate plus a transfer by deed to the lender. If the borrower defaults, the lender can lodge the transfer for registration.

No equitable mortgage is in itself absolutely secure because the borrower remains on the register and may sell the shares and procure the registration of the purchaser with priority over the lender, who would have no remedy against the company.

C. deposited his share certificate and a blank transfer with R. as a security for a loan. Upon the certificate was printed: "Without the production of this certificate no transfer of the shares mentioned therein can be registered." C. sold the shares to Y. and induced the company to register Y. as owner of the shares without the production of the share certificate. R. sued the company for wrongfully registering the shares in Y's name. *Held,* the company was not liable as it owed no duty of care to R., and the statement on the certificate was only a warning to the owner of the shares to take care of the certificate and not a statement of fact giving rise to an estoppel: *Rainford v. James Keith & Blackman Co. Ltd* [1905] 1 Ch. 296.[67]

However, the mortgagor must exercise any voting rights as directed by the mortgagee.[68]

## Stop notice

To obtain complete protection, an equitable mortgagee of shares should serve a stop notice. This is done by filing an affidavit setting out the facts, and a notice in the prescribed form, in the Central Office of the Supreme Court or in a District Registry and serving an office copy of the affidavit and a duplicate notice on the company. The effect of the notice is that, whilst it continues in force, if the company receives any request to register a transfer of the shares in question it must give notice

---

[66] *Powell v. London and Provincial Bank* [1893] 2 Ch. 555 (C.A.).
[67] Reversed on the facts [1905] 2 Ch. 147 (C.A.). On the facts the company was affected with notice of R's charge and he was able to recover the price of the shares which had been paid to the company in repayment of a loan made by the company to C.
[68] *Wise v. Landsell* [1921] 1 Ch. 420.

in writing to the person who has served the notice. Within eight days, such person must apply for an injunction restraining the transfer or the company will be at liberty to register the transfer.[69]

## Charging order

A judgment creditor of the registered owner of shares may obtain an order charging the shares with payment of the judgment debt,[70] after which, until the order is discharged, the company cannot permit a transfer except with the authority of the court. A charging order will not have priority over a mortgage created by deposit of the share certificate and a blank transfer before the date of the charging order, as the judgment creditor can be in no better position than the judgment debtor at the time when the order was made.

## ASSIGNATION OF SHARES IN SECURITY (SCOTS LAW)

The only effective way of assigning shares in security is by the execution and registration of a transfer in favour of the lender. See the section headed "Legal mortgage," *ante*.[71]

No form of the equitable mortgage recognised by English law gives the lender any real security in competition with the general creditors of the borrower.[72] Accordingly, where a borrower delivers the share certificate to the lender and undertakes to transfer the shares to the lender when requested to do so, a transfer executed within six months before the borrower's sequestration or his granting of a protected trust deed is reducible as an unfair preference under section 36 of the Bankruptcy (Scotland) Act 1985.[73] For the purposes of that section the day on which a preference was created is the day on which the preference became "completely effectual",[74] and that would only be so when the transfer had been registered. It may be, however, that

---

[69] R.S.C., Ord 50, rr. 11–15. See also the Charging Orders Act 1979.

[70] R.S.C., Ord. 50, rr 2–7.

[71] p. 267.

[72] *Gourlay v. Mackie* (1887) 14 R. 403; *per* Lord Gifford in *Morrison v. Harrison* (1876) 3 R. 406 at p. 411; *cf. Guild v. Young* (1884) 22 S.L.R. 520 (O.H.).

[73] This provision is the successor to the repealed Bankruptcy Act 1696 (Scots Act 1696, c. 5) which made fraudulent preferences reducible on the ground of notour bankruptcy.

[74] Bankruptcy (Scotland) Act 1985, s.36(3).

where a completed transfer has been delivered to the lender along with the share certificate so that the lender is in a position to have himself registered as a member without further interposition of the borrower, registration of the transfer on the eve of the borrower's sequestration is not open to challenge as an unfair preference provided the delivery of the documents to the lender was made more than six months before the borrower's sequestration.[75] A blank transfer may be invalid under the Blank Bonds and Trusts Act 1696 (Scots Act 1696, c. 25) which declares null "bonds, assignations, dispositions or other deeds" subscribed blank in the name of the person or persons in whose favour they are conceived.

Stop notices and charging orders are not part of Scots law. When a company called on to register a transfer receives intimation from some person other than the transferee that that other person has an interest in the shares, the company is entitled to proceed to register the transfer unless the intimation is followed up by an application for interdict or other legal measure.[76]

Shares are subject to arrestment at the instance of the creditors of the shareholder, whether the arrestment is in execution,[77] or merely to found jurisdiction.[78] Where competition arises between a transferee and an arrester the transferee has the preferable right to the shares as soon as his transfer has been lodged, even although it is not registered before the lodging of the arrestment.

> In January S. transferred 200 shares to M. and 1,000 shares to F., and the transfers were received by the secretary of the company on January 19, and February 2, respectively. Because of an arrestment lodged the previous November against S. at the instance of a bank, the transfers were not registered. On March 30, arrestments were executed at the instance of D. against S. *Held,* the transfers to M. and F. were preferable to D.'s arrestments: *Harvey's Yoker Distillery Ltd v. Singleton* (1901) 8 S.L.T. 369 (O.H.).

---

[75] *Guild v. Young* (1884) 22 S.L.R. 520 (O.H.), decided under the 1696 Act, can give at best slender support to the proposition. Whereas the 1696 Act affected only *voluntary* preferences conferred by the bankrupt on favoured creditors, section 36 of the 1985 Act applies to any *transaction entered into* by the debtor. Although section 36 is not restricted to the challenge of voluntary preferences, it is submitted that the registration by the creditor of an already executed transfer in circumstances such as arose in *Guild v. Young* would not be classed as a *transaction entered into* by the debtor.

[76] *Per* Lord M'Laren in *Shaw v. Caledonian Rlwy Co.* (1890) 17 R. 466 at p. 482.

[77] *Sinclair v. Staples* (1860) 22 D. 600.

[78] *American Mortgage Co. of Scotland Ltd v. Sidway*, 1908 S.C. 500.

"An arrestment can only attach property belonging truly and in substance to the common debtor. Now these shares did not belong in substance to Singleton at the time of the arrestment, because he had by that time done all in his power to dispose of them by executing the transfers": *per* Lord Stormonth Darling (Ordinary) at p. 370.

An arrester is not entitled to found on any irregularity in the registration procedure to the effect of defeating the transferee's title.[79] Intimation to the company of a transfer, even without registration, has the effect, in a question between the transferee and a subsequent arrester of cutting out the arrestment.[80]

## CALLS ON SHARES

A call on shares is a demand by the directors that a member pay to the company money which is unpaid on his shares, whether on account of the nominal value of the shares or by way of premium.[81] If, when shares are issued, the full amount of each share is not payable at once as in the privatisation issues, the terms of issue will provide that part is payable on application, part on allotment and the remainder by instalments at fixed dates, in which case the instalments are not calls,[82] as the obligation of the shareholder to pay is not dependent on a call from the company. However, in a rare case, the company may not require all the nominal amount of a share, or the full amount of a premium on a share, to be paid at or soon after allotment but may leave part to be called up in accordance with the provisions of the articles as and when required by the company or, in the event of a winding up, by the liquidator. If so, a shareholder is bound to pay the whole or part of the balance unpaid on his shares "as and when called on", in accordance with the provisions of the articles. Calls must be made in the manner laid down in the articles.

In England a call creates a specialty debt due from the shareholder to the company (s.14(2)), and so the period within

---

[79] *National Bank of Scotland Glasgow Nominees Ltd v. Adamson*, 1932 S.L.T. 492 (O.H.); for an arrestment made effective by the granting by the court of a warrant to sell the shares, see *Valentine v. Grangemouth Coal Co. Ltd* (1897) 35 S.L.R. 12 (O.H.).

[80] *Jackson v. Elphick* (1902) 10 S.L.T. 146 (O.H.).

[81] For Scots *dicta* on the nature of a call see Lord President M'Neill in *Wryght v. Lindsay* (1856) 19 D. 55 at p. 63; affd. (1860) 22 D. (H.L.) 5.

[82] But articles may provide that they shall be *deemed* to be calls: see Table A, reg 16.

which an action can be brought for payment of it is 12 years.[83] In Scotland a call remains enforceable until the expiry of 20 years.[84] Table A, regulation 15, provides for payment of interest from the date fixed for payment until actual payment.

If authorised by the articles, a company may make arrangements on the issue of shares for a difference between the shareholders in the amounts and times of payment of calls: section 119(a). Table A, regulation 17, authorises such an arrangement. Such a power does not entitle directors to make calls on all the shareholders except themselves,[85] at any rate without the knowledge and sanction of the other shareholders— the directors' power to make calls must be exercised bona fide for the benefit of the company as a whole, and not so as to give themselves an advantage over other shareholders.[86]

Any arrangement made under section 119(a) must be made at the time of the issue of shares. If no such arrangement is made, the rule is that "prima facie it is entirely improper for the directors to make a call on some members of a class of shareholders who stand in the same relation to the company as the other members of the class without making a similar call on all the other members of that class."[87]

Table A, regulations 18 to 22, provides for forfeiture for non-payment of a call or an instalment.[88]

## LIEN ON SHARES (ENGLISH LAW)

The articles of a private company may give the company a lien on the shares held by a member for his unpaid call or instalment, or for some other debt due from him to the company. Public companies however may only have a lien on such shares for an unpaid call or instalment on those shares: section 150. By way of exception a money-lending or credit company may have a lien on any of its shares for non-payment of a debt owed by the shareholder in the ordinary course of the company's business.

Such a lien is an equitable charge upon the shares, and gives rise to the same rights as if the shares had been expressly charged by the member in favour of the company.[89]

[83] Limitation Act 1980, s.8(1).
[84] Prescription and Limitation (Scotland) Act 1973, s.7.
[85] *Alexander v. Automatic Telephone Co.* [1900] 2 Ch. 56 (C.A.).
[86] *Post,* p. 351.
[87] *Per* Sargeant J in *Galloway v. Hallé Concerts Society* [1915] 2 Ch. 233 at p. 239.
[88] *Post,* p. 277.
[89] *Everitt v. Automatic Weighing Machine Co.* [1892] 3 Ch. 506.

Table A, regulation 8, provides: "The company shall have a first and paramount lien on every share (not being a fully paid share) for all moneys (whether presently payable or not) payable at a fixed time or called in respect of that share. The directors may at any time declare any share to be wholly or in part exempt from the provisions of this regulation. The company's lien on a share shall extend to any amount payable in respect of it."

The articles of a private company may extend regulation 8 to include any debt owed by a member to the company. Where a director had incurred a debt by virtue of the company paying bills on his behalf, the company was held to have a lien on his shares even though it was also, by virtue of another article, prohibited from making a loan to that director on security of its shares. The company had not made a loan to the director; he had simply become indebted to the company: *Champagne Perrier-Jouet S.A. v. H. H. Finch Ltd* [1982] 1 W.L.R. 1359.

The articles may grant a lien on shares which are fully paid but in such a case an official quotation on the Stock Exchange cannot be obtained.[90] If the lien given by the articles extends only to shares not fully paid, the company can alter its articles so as to give a lien on all shares, even if only one member will be affected by the alteration.[91]

Table A, regulation 24, empowers the directors to decline to register the transfer of a share on which the company has a lien.

A shareholder against whom a lien is to be enforced can compel the company to assign its lien to his nominee who is willing to pay off the amount of the lien.[92]

**How a lien is enforced**

A lien is enforced, like any other equitable charge, by a sale. If the articles do not give the company power to sell the share, an application for an order for sale may be necessary. It is probable that the company has the implied power of sale given by the Law of Property Act 1925, s.101, to a mortgagee whose mortgage is made by deed. However, since it is uncertain that the articles, which create the lien, are a deed for the purposes of section 101,[93] to avoid the necessity of an application to the court the articles usually give an express power of sale.

[90] Admission of Securities to Listing.
[91] *Allen v. Gold Reefs of West Africa Ltd* [1900] 1 Ch. 656 (C.A.), *ante*, p. 85.
[92] See note 89, *ante*.
[93] See s.14, *ante*, p. 80.

Table A provides: "9. The company may sell in such manner as the directors determine any shares on which the company has a lien if a sum in respect of which the lien exists is presently payable and is not paid within 14 clear days after notice has been given to the holder of the share or the person entitled to it in consequence of the death or bankruptcy of the holder demanding payment and stating that if the notice is not complied with the shares may be sold."

Further, articles usually give the company power to nominate someone to execute the transfer.

However the sale of the shares is subject to any restrictions on the transferability of those shares contained in the articles of a private company, e.g. a pre-emption clause requiring them to be offered to existing shareholders.[94]

A lien cannot be enforced by forfeiture even if power to forfeit is contained in the articles.

The articles of a company provided that the company should have a lien on shares for the debts of the shareholder, and also provided that the lien could be enforced by forfeiture. Held, (1) forfeiture for debts generally, as distinct from debts due from the shareholder as a contributory, amounted to an illegal reduction of capital; (2) power to forfeit on failure to redeem after notice amounted to a clog on the shareholder's equity of redemption, and was invalid and *ultra vires: Hopkinson v. Mortimer, Harley & Co. Ltd* [1917] 1 Ch. 646.

**Priority of lien**

When a third party advances money on the security of shares, a question may arise as to whether the third party has priority over the company's lien. In such a case, if the third party gives notice of his security to the company before the company's lien arises, the third party will have priority, but otherwise not.

The articles of a company gave "a first and paramount lien and charge" on shares for debts due from the shareholder. A shareholder created an equitable mortgage of his shares by depositing the share certificate with a bank as security for an overdraft and the bank gave notice of the deposit to the company. The shareholder subsequently became indebted to the company whereupon a lien arose in favour of the company. Held, the bank had priority as the company's lien arose after notice of their equitable mortgage. The notice was not notice of a trust contrary to what is now section 360 but notice affecting the company, in

---

[94] *Champagne Perrier-Jouet S.A. v. H. H. Finch Ltd* [1982] 1 W.L.R. 1359.

its character of trader, with knowledge of the bank's interest: *Bradford Banking Co. v. Briggs & Co.* (1886) 12 App.Cas. 29.

It seems that the position may be different even if the articles contain a clause like Table A, regulation 5,[95] relieving the company of the obligation to take notice of equities in relation to shares.[96]

Similarly, where the shareholder is a trustee, the company's lien will prevail over the claims of the beneficial owners unless the company is given notice, before the lien arises, that the shareholder is a trustee.

A trustee held shares in a company, the articles of which gave the company a lien on shares standing either in a single name or in joint names for any debt due from any of the holders, either separately or jointly with any other person. There was also an article like Table A, regulation 5. Long after the registration of the shares in the trustee's names, one of the trustees incurred a liability to the company. It was *not* alleged that the company had notice of the trust before the lien arose. *Held,* the company's lien prevailed over the title of the *cestuis que trust: New London and Brazilian Bank v. Brocklebank* (1882) 21 Ch.D. 302 (C.A.).

The title of the beneficial owners, however, will have priority if the company has notice, before the lien arises, that the shareholder is a trustee of the shares.[97]

The company has no lien on the shares registered in the name of a trustee for debts due to it from the beneficial owner.[98]

If a lien in favour of the company has arisen and the shareholder sells part only of his shares, the purchaser can require the company to discharge the lien primarily out of the shares not sold.[99]

A lien does not cease on the shareholder's death, but may be enforced against his executors.[1]

[95] *Ante,* p. 220.
[96] *Champagne Perrier-Jouet S.A. v. H. H. Finch Ltd* [1982] 3 All E.R. 713, 720–721.
[97] *Mackereth v. Wigan Coal Co. Ltd* [1916] 2 Ch. 293.
[98] *Re Perkins* (1890) 24 Q.B.D. 613 (C.A.).
[99] *Gray v. Stone* (1893) 69 L.T. 282.
[1] *Allen v. Gold Reefs of West Africa Ltd* [1900] 1 Ch. 656 (C.A.), *ante,* p. 85.

## LIEN ON SHARES (SCOTS LAW)

A company has at common law and independently of any provision in its articles a lien on shares held by a member for debts due by the member to the company.[2] Articles, however, usually make express provision to the same effect. The lien enables the company to refuse to register any transfer of the shares until the transferor's debt to the company has been satisfied.

A company whose articles expressly limit the lien to partly paid shares may alter the articles so as to extend the lien to all shares, but if such an alteration is not made until after a transfer of fully paid shares has been presented for registration the transferee's right to be registered is not affected by that alteration.[3]

A lien can be enforced by a sale only if the power of sale has been conferred by the articles, or a warrant is obtained from the court. A lien in respect of debts other than calls or instalments could not be enforced by forfeiture, since that would be an illegal reduction of capital.

Where X, a shareholder, has assigned his shares in security to Y who has completed his title to the shares by being registered as the holder of them, the company is no longer entitled to a lien on the shares in respect of debts due to it by X, since X is not the registered holder.[4]

For the provisions of section 150 and of Table A on lien, see "Lien (English Law)", above.

## FORFEITURE OF SHARES

Although a forfeiture of a member's shares by the company is recognised by the Act, the directors may forfeit shares only if expressly authorised to do so by the articles and only for non-payment of a call or an instalment: section 143(3)(d).

Table A provides:
Regulation 18 "If a call remains unpaid after it has become due and payable the directors may give to the person from whom it is due not less

---

[2] *Hotchkis v. Royal Bank* (1797) 3 Paton 618; (1797) M. 2673; *Burns v. Lawrie's Trustees* (1840) 2 D. 1348; *Bell's Trustee v. Coatbridge Tinplate Co. Ltd* (1886) 14 R. 246.

[3] *Liquidator of W & A M'Arthur Ltd v. Gulf Line Ltd*, 1909 S.C. 732.

[4] *Paul's Trustee v. Thomas Justice & Sons Ltd*, 1912 S.C. 1303.

than 14 clear days' notice requiring payment of the amount unpaid together with any interest which may have accrued. The notice shall name the place where payment is to be made and shall state that if the notice is not complied with the shares in respect of which the call was made will be liable to be forfeited."

Regulation 19 "If the notice is not complied with any share in respect of which it was given may, before the payment required by the notice has been made, be forfeited by a resolution of the directors and the forfeiture shall include dividends or other monies payable in respect of the forfeited shares and not paid before the forfeiture."

Forfeiture, being in the nature of a penal proceeding, is valid only if the provisions of the articles, *e.g.* as to notice, are strictly followed. Any irregularity will avoid the forfeiture.[5] To protect purchasers of the forfeited shares against possible irregularities in the forfeiture, the articles usually provide, as does Table A, regulation 22, that the title of the purchaser shall not be affected by any invalidity in the proceedings in reference to the forfeiture.

Forfeited shares may be sold or reissued by a private company according to the provisions of the articles. A public company however must cancel the forfeited shares unless they are disposed of within three years. In the interim period the company may not vote with the shares. If this cancellation takes the public company below the authorised minimum capital it must re-register as a private company: section 146.

Forfeited shares can be reissued at less than the amount which has been paid on them.

A company had forfeited a number of shares of £5 5s. each, £2 5s. paid, and proposed to reissue them at the price of 30s. a share. *Held,* the company could do so, as it was not bound to treat the forfeited shares as if nothing had been paid upon them: *Morrison v. Trustees, etc., Corpn. Ltd* (1898) 68 L.J.Ch. 11 (C.A.).

The purchaser of the reissued shares is liable for the payment of all future calls duly made, including one for the amount of the call which occasioned the forfeiture.[6] Consequently, there is no issue of shares at a discount, as the company has already received the amount paid up. The purchaser should be credited with any subsequent payments made by the ex-owner.[7]

---

[5] *Johnson v. Lyttle's Iron Agency* (1877) 5 Ch.D. 687 (C.A.).
[6] *New Balkis Eersteling Ltd v. Randt Gold Mining Co.* [1904] A.C. 165, where the purchaser was to hold the shares "discharging from all calls due prior to such purchase".
[7] *Re Randt Gold Mining Co.* [1904] 2 Ch. 468. *Re Bolton*, below, shows that the converse is true.

The effect of the forfeiture on the former owner of the shares is to discharge him from his liability on the shares.[8] To prevent this position from arising, the articles usually preserve the liability of the former owner.[9]

The company cannot recover more than the difference between the calls due and the amount received on reissue.

B. underwrote two blocks of shares in a company. The issue to the public was a failure and B. was consequently allotted (*inter alia*) 8,200 £1 shares in the company. He was unable to pay the calls on these shares, which were forfeited. They were then reissued so that the company received the balance of the calls in full, but to obtain the new allottees the company had to pay £1,018 by way of commission. B. became bankrupt. The articles provided that the holder of forfeited shares should remain liable for calls notwithstanding the forfeiture and the company attempted to prove for the balance of calls due from B. *Held,* the company could not receive payment of the calls twice over and could only prove for the actual loss sustained *viz.* the £1,018 commission: *Re Bolton* [1930] 2 Ch. 48.

## SURRENDER OF SHARES

The Act does not give a company any express power to accept a surrender of his shares by a member. A company's articles, however, frequently give power to the directors to accept a surrender of shares where they are in a position to forfeit such shares, *i.e.* for non-payment of calls or instalments on those shares: section143(3)(d).

Surrender in these circumstances has been described as an "apparent exception" only to the principle of maintenance of capital,[10] since "the extinction of the obligation of a bankrupt shareholder can injure nobody."[11]

Following section 143 a company may only acquire its own shares in a few cases in addition to a surrender in lieu of forfeiture. These have been considered above.[12] It appears that in all those cases, *e.g.* a purchase by the company, a surrender of

---

[8] *Stocken's Case* (1868) L.R. 3 Ch.App. 412; in *Goldsmith v. Colonial Finance etc. Corpn. Ltd* [1909] 8 C.L.R. 241, Griffith C.J., at p. 249, and Barton J., at p. 253, thought that what Lord Cairns L.J. said in *Stocken* was founded on the particular article there in question.

[9] Table A, reg. 21.

[10] *Ante,* p. 170.

[11] *Per* Lord M'Laren in *Gill v. Arizona Copper Co. Ltd* (1900) 2 F. 843 at p. 860.

[12] *Ante,* Chap. 10.

shares may be used as the method of acquisition. No other forms of surrender appear to be valid.

In particular, a surrender of partly paid shares, not liable to forfeiture, is unlawful, as it (a) releases the shareholder from further liability in respect of the shares, (b) amounts to a purchase by the company of its own shares, and (c) is a reduction of capital without the sanction of the court.

A company sustained a loss of £4,000 and the directors agreed to share the loss between themselves. They therefore surrendered shares to the amount of £4,000. The shares were £11 each, £10 paid, and the intention was that the directors should be released from the remaining £1 a share unpaid. The company subsequently became more prosperous and the directors took proceedings to have the surrender declared invalid. *Held,* the surrender was invalid as amounting to a purchase by the company of its own shares: *Bellerby v. Rowland & Marwood, Steamship Co. Ltd* [1902] 2 Ch. 14 (C.A.).

Shares which have been validly surrendered can be reissued in the same way as forfeited shares, if the articles authorise their reissue.

## Share Warrant

A share warrant is a document issued by a company either under its common seal or otherwise in compliance with section 36A or 36B as appropriate,[13] stating that the bearer of the warrant is entitled to the shares specified therein: section 188.

Before share warrants can be issued the following conditions must be satisfied:

(1) the company must be a company and limited by shares;
(2) there must be authority in the articles (Table A does not authorise the issue of share warrants);
(3) the shares must be fully paid up: section 188.

When the issue of share warrants is authorised, the articles usually provide for such matters as the deposit of the share warrant with the company a certain number of days before any right is exercised, and for the giving of notices of meetings by advertisement.

[13] *Ante,* p. 101.

On issuing a share warrant, the company must strike out of its register of members the name of the holder of the shares as if he had ceased to be a member and make the following entries in the register:

(1)  the fact of the issue of a warrant;
(2)  a statement of shares included in the warrant, distinguishing each share by its number, so long as the share has a number;
(3)  the date of issue of the warrant: section 355(1).

The bearer of a share warrant may, however, if the articles so provide, be deemed to be a member of the company either to the full extent or for any purposes defined in the articles: section 355(1).

A share warrant can, subject to the articles, be surrendered for cancellation, whereupon the holder is entitled to be entered in the register of members: section 355(2).

Stock warrants to bearer can be issued on the same terms as share warrants.[14]

A share warrant differs from a share certificate[15] in the following respects:

(1)  the bearer of a warrant is not entered in a register: section 355;
(2)  he is entitled to the shares specified in the warrant: section 188(1);
(3)  the shares are transferable by delivery of the warrant: section 188(2);
(4)  a warrant is a negotiable instrument and if it is stolen and afterwards gets into the hands of a bona fide purchaser for value without notice of the fraud, he can enforce against the company payment of coupons for dividends due in respect of such share warrant;[16]
(5)  coupons for dividends may be attached to a warrant: section 188(3).

Dividends are advertised, and then collected upon the handing over of the appropriate coupon. This procedure is necessary

[14] *Pilkington v. United Railways of Havana* [1930] 2 Ch. 108.
[15] *Ante*, p. 255.
[16] *Webb Hale & Co. v. Alexandria Water Co. Ltd* (1905) 93 L.T. 339.

because the company does not know to whom to send the dividend;

> (6) holding a share warrant is not enough where the articles require a director to hold a specified share qualification: section 291(2).[17]

Share warrants are not very common. This is because until 1979, they could only be issued with Treasury consent and had to be deposited with an authorised depository, because of the serious consequences of loss or theft, and also because of the heavy stamp duty. Another reason is that the company has to advertise in newspapers to get in touch with the shareholders. With the abolition of exchange controls in 1979 there are fewer restrictions on their use.

Section 189 makes special provision for certain offences in connection with share warrants in Scotland.

## VALUATION OF SHARES

Articles of private companies often provide that a member who wants to sell his shares must first offer them to the existing members at a price to be fixed by the auditors. Similar provisions are often applicable in the case of a member's death.[18] When the auditor or other expert makes a valuation the question arises as to whether either side may validly challenge that valuation. Originally it was held that the valuation could be set aside on the grounds of mistake by the valuer,[19] but later that it could only be so set aside if the valuer had given reasons (a "speaking certificate") but not if no reasons were given ( "a non-speaking certificate").[20] Such a distinction has now been rejected by the Court of Appeal in *Jones v. Sherwood Computer Services plc.*[21] On principle they decided that any valuation could only be set aside if the valuer had departed from his instructions in a material respect, *e.g.* if he valued the wrong number of shares or

---

[17] *Post*, p. 317.
[18] *Ante*, pp. 266, *et seq.*
[19] *Dean v. Prince* [1954] CH. 409 (C.A.)
[20] *Burgess v. Purchase and Son (Farms) Ltd* [1983] Ch. 216; analysing *Campbell v. Edwards* [1976] 1 W.L.R. 403 (C.A.) and *Baber v. Kenwood Manufacturing Co. Ltd* [1978] 1 Lloyd's Rep. 175 (C.A.).
[21] [1992] 1 W.L.R. 277.

failed to employ an expert valuer for a specific item which he was required to do,[22] and not on the basis of mistake. The reason for this change in the courts' approach has been the possibility of the aggrieved party suing the valuer in negligence, which did not exist at the time of the original decisions.

In valuing a minority shareholding a valuer should allow for a discount to reflect that fact.[23] If there is an actual offer by a third party subsequent to the date of valuation the valuer may use that as evidence of value at that date. It would be different if there was a subsequent change in the market conditions.[24] For the purpose of valuing the shares of a private company with high returns but little or no assets, the value of the company is the capitalised sum of the future profits.[25]

A valuer may now therefore be liable in negligence to either party even though the valuation may not be liable to be set aside. To be liable in this way a valuer must be acting as a valuer and not as an arbitrator, *i.e.* settling a dispute between at least two parties which was sent to him to resolve in such a way that he had to exercise a judicial discretion.[26] An auditor of a private company who, on request, values its shares in the knowledge that this valuation will determine the price to be paid under a contract owes a duty of care to both the vendor and the purchaser. An agreement for valuation is not generally one for an arbitration. The function of a valuer is usually to settle a price so that no differences arise between the parties. His function is not to make an award after a difference has arisen. Only in the latter case will no duty of care arise.[27]

Even if a duty of care does arise, the standard of care expected of an ordinary auditor is not that of a specialist valuer. This "auditor standard" will only be displaced by express contrary intention.[28]

Where the directors are required to find a purchaser for shares valued by the auditor they may have a duty to disclose relevant facts to the shareholders.[29]

---

[22] *Jones (M.) v. Jones (R.R.)* [1971] 1 W.L.R. 840.
[23] *Howie v. Crawford* [1990] BCC 330, *cf. Re Bird Precision Bellows Ltd* [1986] Ch. 658.
[24] *Re ESC Publishing Ltd* [1990] BCC 335.
[25] *Buckingham v. Francis* [1986] BCLC 353.
[26] *Sutcliffe v. Thackrah* [1974] A.C. 727.
[27] See *Leigh v. English Property Corporation* [1976] 2 Lloyd's Rep. 298.
[28] *Whiteoak v. Walker* (1988) 4 BCC 122.
[29] *Munro v. Bogie* [1994] 1 BCLC 415.

# Chapter 14

# GENERAL MEETINGS

THIS chapter is concerned with general meetings, *i.e.* meetings of the members or shareholders of a company and certain other persons (the auditors, the personal representatives of a deceased member and the trustee in bankruptcy of a bankrupt member). The various kinds of general meeting are dealt with first, including who may call such meetings. Then the notice that the members must be given of general meetings is explained. Thirdly, proceedings at general meetings are dealt with—how many members must be present to constitute a meeting and enable it to transact business, who take the chair, how a vote is taken and so on. Fourthly, the various kinds of resolution that may be passed at a meeting, including elective resolutions, are explained. Finally, the effects of written resolutions which do not require a meeting at all are discussed.

For obvious reasons, special provisions had to be made for single member private companies. In general, it is possible for the single member either to constitute a meeting or to decide on an issue which requires a resolution, in which case a written record of the decision must be kept.

If a company has more than one class of shares, class meetings, *i.e.* meetings of the holders of the shares of a certain class, may be held. Some of the sections referred to below, *e.g.* section 369 with regard to the length of notice for calling meetings, also apply to meetings of any class of members of a company as they apply to general meetings of the company. Section 125(6) provides that the provisions of the Act and the articles relating to general meetings apply to class meetings, except that a quorum shall be two persons at least holding or representing by proxy one-third of the issued shares of the class and that any holder of shares of the class present in person or by proxy may demand a poll.

## KINDS OF GENERAL MEETING

**Annual general meeting**

By section 366 the general rule is that, subject to an election by a private company to the contrary under section 366A[1], every company must hold an annual general meeting, specified as such in the notice calling it, every year, with an interval of not more than 15 months between one annual general meeting of the company and the next. The word "year" means calendar year, *i.e.* the period January 1 to December 31.[2] A limited exception is that as long as a company holds its first annual general meeting within 18 months of incorporation it need not hold it in the year of incorporation or, sometimes in the following year, *e.g.* a company incorporated on October 1, 1995, might hold its first annual general meeting in March 1997.

The directors must call the annual general meeting. The object of section 366 is to ensure that those members who wish to do so can meet together and confront the directors at least once a year. The usual business at an annual general meeting is: the declaration of a dividend, the consideration of the accounts, balance sheets and the reports of the directors and auditors, the election of directors in place of those retiring, and the appointment of, and the fixing of the remuneration of, the auditors.

If default is made in holding an annual general meeting, the Secretary of State may, on the application of any member of the company, call or direct the calling of a meeting and give such ancillary directions as he thinks expedient, including a direction that one member present in person or by proxy shall be deemed to constitute the meeting: section 367.

Under section 366A a private company may, by an elective resolution,[3] dispense with the holding of an annual general meeting. It may also by such a resolution elect not to lay its annual accounts at the meeting,[4] and not to appoint its auditors annually,[5] which dispenses with a large part of its annual business. Any member may, despite a section 366A election being in

[1] *Infra.*
[2] *Gibson v. Barton* (1875) L.R. 10 Q.B. 329.
[3] *Post*, p. 306.
[4] *Post*, Chap. 22.
[5] *Post*, Chap. 23.

force, require an AGM to be held by giving notice to that effect
to the company at least three months before the end of the year
in question, and section 366 will then apply. If the election is
revoked no meeting need be held in that year, however, if there
are less than three months of the year remaining.

**Extraordinary general meetings**

Any general meeting of a company, other than an annual
general meeting, is an extraordinary general meeting. Table A,
regulation 36, so provides and regulation 37 provides that the
directors *may*, whenever they think fit, convene an extraordinary
general meeting.

Further, by section 368, despite anything in the articles, the
directors are *bound* to convene an extraordinary general meeting
on the requisition of the holders of not less than one-tenth of the
paid-up capital of the company carrying the right of voting at
general meetings or, if the company has no share capital, of
members representing not less than one-tenth of the total voting
rights. The requisition must state the objects of the meeting and
be signed by the requisitionists. If the directors do not, within 21
days of the deposit of the requisition at the registered office of
the company, proceed to convene the meeting fixed for a date
within 28 days of its being summoned, the requisitionists, or the
holders of more than half their voting rights, may convene it
themselves so long as it is held within three months after such
deposit.[6] The reasonable expenses of the requisitionists in convening the meeting must be repaid by the company, which must
retain them out of any remuneration of the directors in default.

Section 142 requires the directors of a public company to call a
general meeting in the event of a serious loss of capital. In such a
case the meeting must be convened within 28 days for a date not
later than 28 days after the notice convening the meeting.[7]

*Powers of the court*

By section 371, if for any reason it is impracticable to call a
meeting in any manner in which meetings may be called, or to

[6] This right may be abrogated if the requisionists are themselves directors who
have, by failing to attend board meetings, been the cause of the directors'
default: *Thyne v. Lauder*, 1925 S.C. 123 (O.H.).
[7] *Ante*, p. 183.

conduct a meeting in the manner prescribed by the articles or the
Act, the court may, either of its own motion or on application by
any director or any member entitled to vote at the meeting, order
a meeting to be called, held and conducted in such manner as the
court thinks fit, and may give such ancillary directions as it thinks
expedient, including a direction that one member present in
person or by proxy shall be deemed to constitute the meeting.
The courts have used this power to prevent a minority shareholder using the quorum provisions as a weapon in a dispute, *i.e.*
by refusing to attend meetings so that no quorum under the
articles can be obtained.[8] This will not apply, however, if the
right of a member to be present for a quorum to be obtained is a
class right of that member.[9]

> E. Ltd had three members, A, B and C. A and B were directors
> and held five per cent. of the shares each. C, who was not a director,
> held 90 per cent. of the shares. No general meetings were held. The
> articles provided that a quorum at a meeting should be two members.
> A and B frustrated C's efforts to call a meeting under section 368 by
> refusing to attend. C gave special notice of his intention to move
> ordinary resolutions to remove the directors at the next extraordinary
> general meeting, and asked the court to call a meeting under section
> 371 and to direct that one member should be a quorum. C's
> application was opposed by the directors. *Held,* the application
> should be granted because (1) otherwise C would be deprived of his
> right to remove the directors under section 303, (2) the directors were
> in breach of their statutory duty by not holding an annual general
> meeting: *Re El Sombrero Ltd* [1958] Ch. 900.[10]
>
> O Ltd had two members, A and B, who were the sole directors. A
> owned 51 per cent. of the votes and B the remainder. They fell out
> and A called a meeting to dismiss B as a director. B refused to attend
> so that the quorum provisions for meetings (two) could not be
> complied with. On A's application under section 371, the court
> ordered a meeting with a quorum of one, otherwise there would be a
> deadlock situation. The quorum provisions did not give B a veto. A's
> conduct in dismissing B was a matter for other proceedings: *Re Opera
> Photographic Ltd* [1989] 1 W.L.R. 634.

The jurisdiction of the court under the section is very wide and
will apply whenever "as a practical matter the desired meeting of
the company can be conducted." Thus it has been used to order a

---

[8] *Re Opera Photographic Ltd* [1989] W.L.R. 684
[9] *Harman v. BML Group Ltd* [1994] 2 BCLC 704 (C.A.).
[10] For a Scottish instance, see *Edinburgh Workmen's Houses Improvement Co.
Ltd, Petitioners*, 1935 S.C. 56.

meeting restricted to a few members to be followed by a postal ballot of all the members, where it was feared that a normal meeting would lead to a riot.[10a]

Where there is a dispute between the shareholders which is the subject of other proceedings[11] and one of the parties seeks an order under section 371 because the other party refuses to attend meetings, the court has a discretion whether to make an order under the section. If the application under section 371 is made prior to the other proceedings it is more likely to be granted then if the application is made after the other proceedings have commenced.[12] In other cases the nature of the dispute may be relevant.[13]

A private company may dispense with meetings for the majority of items by using the written resolution procedure, *post*.

## NOTICE OF GENERAL MEETINGS

### Length of notice for calling meetings

The effect of section 369 is that notwithstanding a provision in the articles providing for shorter notice:

(1) an annual general meeting must be called by not less that 21 days' written notice:

(2) any other general meeting of a limited company must be called by not less than 14 days' written notice, unless a special resolution is to be proposed, in which case, by section 378, not less than 21 days' such notice is required.

Table A, regulation 38, provides that the notice shall be clear notice, *i.e.* exclusive of the day on which it is served or deemed to be served and of the day for which it is given.[14]

A meeting may be called by shorter notice than that specified above or in the articles if that is agreed to by—(1) all the

---

[10a] *Re the British Union for the Abolition of Vivisection, The Times*, March 3, 1995.

[11] Usually a petition under s.459. See *post*, p. 417.

[12] *Re Sticky Fingers Restaurant Ltd* [1992] BCLC 84; *Re Whitchurch Insurance Consultants Ltd* [1993] BCLC 1359; *Re Opera Photographic Group Ltd* [1989] 1 W.L.R. 634.

[13] *Harman v. BML Group Ltd* [1994] 2 BCLC 704 (C.A.).

[14] In Scotland articles may be so worded as not to require *clear* notice, *e.g.* a provision that "days shall be reckoned, excluding the first and including the last of such days," allows the day of the meeting to be counted: *The Aberdeen Comb Works Co. Ltd, Petitioners* (1902) 10 S.L.T. 210.

members entitled to attend and vote in the case of an annual general meeting; or (2) a majority in number of the members holding not less than 95 per cent. of the shares giving the right to attend and vote or, in the case of a company without a share capital, representing not less than 95 per cent. of the total voting rights, in the case of any other meeting. A private company may by an elective resolution[15] reduce the percentage of members required to sanction short notice to 90 per cent: sections 369(3), (4); 378(3).

If a resolution is to be passed on short notice, it must be appreciated that the resolution is being so passed.[16]

Sections 369(3), (4) and 378(3) are derived from cases like *Re Express Engineering Works Ltd*[17] and *Re Oxted Motor Co. Ltd*[18] which established that it is competent for all the shareholders to waive formalities as regards notice of meetings, etc.

In the *Express Engineering* case five persons formed a private company in which they were the sole shareholders. They sold to the company for £15,000 a property which they had just bought for £7,000. The price was to be paid by the issue of debentures for £15,000 by the company. The transaction was carried out at a "board" meeting of the five individuals who appointed themselves the directors. The articles forbade a director to vote in respect of a contract in which he was interested. It was held that there was no fraud and the company was bound in the matter by the unanimous agreement of the members. Consequently the debentures were valid.

In the *Oxted Motor* case both members of a company waived the normal length of notice of a meeting at which an extraordinary resolution for voluntary winding up was validly passed.

The *Express Engineering* case was applied in *Re Bailey, Hay & Co. Ltd*[19] where short notice was given of a meeting to pass an extraordinary resolution for voluntary winding up but all five corporators attended and the resolution was passed by the votes of two shareholders, the other shareholders abstaining from voting. The resolution was deemed to have been passed with the unanimous agreement of all the corporators and those who abstained were treated as having acquiesced in the winding-up.

### Service of notice of meetings

Section 370 provides that, unless the articles provide to the contrary, notice of the meeting of a company is to be served on every member of the company as required by Table A. Section 387(1) requires that notice of every general meeting be given to the auditors.

If notice of a meeting is not given to every person entitled to notice, any resolution passed at the meeting will be of no effect.

A committee of a club met and passed a resolution expelling Y from the club. X, a member of the committee, was not summoned to the meeting, as she had previously informed the chairman that she would be unable to attend meetings. *Held,* the omission to summon X invalidated the proceedings of the committee: *Young v. Ladies' Imperial Club Ltd* [1920] 2 K.B. 523 (C.A.).

To obviate this result it is usually provided in the articles, as in Table A, regulation 39, that the accidental omission to give notice to, or the non-receipt of notice by, any person entitled to receive notice shall not invalidate the proceedings at that meeting.

In *Re West Canadian Collieries Ltd* [1962] Ch. 370, the omission to give notice of a meeting to a few members, because the plates for these members were inadvertently kept out of the machine when the envelopes for the notices were being addressographed, was an accidental omission within an article like Table A, article 39.

However, in *Musselwhite v. C. H. Musselwhite & Sons Ltd* [1962] Ch. 964, the omission to give notice of a general meeting to the unpaid vendors of shares who remained on the register of members, because the directors erroneously believed the vendors were no longer members, was due to an error of law and was not an accidental omission within such an article.

## Nature of notice of meetings

The articles of a company will contain provisions dealing with the nature of the notice to be given of meetings. Table A, regulation 38, provides that the notice of a meeting shall state the time and place of the meeting and the general nature of the business to be transacted.

Notice of an annual general meeting was in common form and included in the business was "to elect directors." C., the retiring director, offered himself for re-election, but was not elected. A motion was proposed for the election of three new directors to fill up the places of the retiring director and two vacancies, but the chairman refused to accept it. *Held,* the refusal was wrong, as the notice sufficiently specified the general nature of the business to bring it within the competence of the meeting to elect directors up to the number permitted by the articles: *Choppington Collieries Ltd v. Johnson* [1944] 1 All E.R. 762 (C.A.).

Notice of the business to be transacted must "state the resolution to be passed in such way as fairly to state the purpose for which the meeting is convened, so that every shareholder may make up his mind whether he will or will not attend with knowledge of the result of his act."[20]

Directors of a holding company had from 1907 to 1914 been receiving remuneration as directors of a subsidiary company without the knowledge of the shareholders of the holding company. Special resolutions, authorising the directors to retain the remuneration and altering the articles to allow the directors to receive remuneration as directors of subsidiary companies, were proposed and an extraordinary general meeting summoned to pass them. The notice did not specify the amount of the remuneration, which was £44,876. The resolution was passed. A shareholder brought an action on behalf of himself and all other shareholders of the company against the company and its directors claiming, *inter alia*, a declaration that the resolution was not binding upon the company. *Held*, the resolution was not binding as the notice was insufficient: *Baillie v. Oriental Telephone etc. Co. Ltd* [1915] 1 Ch. 503 (C.A.).

The notice of a general meeting at which a special resolution or an extraordinary resolution is to be proposed must specify the intention to propose the resolution as a special resolution or an extraordinary resolution[21] as the case may be: section 378. There must be complete identity between the substance of the resolution as passed and the substance of the resolution set out in the notice. Thus in a resolution for a reduction of capital a change in the amount proposed to be reduced of £321 out of a total of £1,356,900 as shown in the notice was held to invalidate the notice. Changes because of grammatical or clerical errors or the use of more formal language might however be allowed.[22]

Where a meeting has been requisitioned under section 368, *ante*,[23] it may competently deal with business additional to that

---

[20] Stiebel's *Company Law* (3rd. ed.), p. 335.
[21] Strictly interpreted in *Rennie v. Crichton's (Strichen) Ltd*, 1927 S.L.T. 459 (O.H.), in which a notice of a resolution for voluntary winding up was held invalid because it did not specify the intention to propose the resolution *as an extraordinary resolution*; for *obiter dicta* to the contrary see *North of Scotland etc. Steam Navigation Co. Ltd, Petitioners*, 1920 S.C. 94.
[22] *Re Moorgate Mercantile Holdings Ltd* [1980] 1 All E.R. 40.
[23] p. 286.

specified in the requisition, provided adequate notice of the additional business has been duly given.[24]

Every notice calling a meeting of a company with a share capital must contain a statement, given reasonable prominence, that a member entitled to attend and vote may appoint a proxy to attend and vote instead of him, and that the proxy need not be a member of the company: section 372.

## Notice of members' resolutions and statements

If some of the members of a company themselves wish to move a resolution at an *annual general meeting*, or to circulate to members a statement relating to any proposed resolution or the business to be dealt with at *any general meeting*, they can do so under section 376. The section provides that on the written requisition of members holding not less than one-twentieth of the voting rights of the members entitled to vote at the relevant meeting, or of one hundred members on whose shares there has been paid up an average sum of not less than £100 a member, the company must:

(1) give notice to every member entitled to receive notice of the annual general meeting of any resolution which may properly be moved and is intended to be moved at that meeting;

(2) circulate to every member entitled to receive notice of any general meeting any statement, of not more than 1,000 words, relating to any proposed resolution or the business to be dealt with at the meeting.

The notice of the resolution must be given, and any statement must be circulated, with the notice of the meeting or, if that is impracticable, as soon as possible afterwards. The company is not bound to circulate a statement if, on the application of the company or any aggrieved person, the court is satisfied that the rights given by the section are being abused to secure needless publicity for defamatory matter: section 377(3).

The requisition must be signed by the requisitionists and deposited at the registered office: (1) at least six weeks before the

---

[24] *Per* Lord Hill Watson (Ordinary), in *Ball v. Metal Industries Ltd*, 1957 S.C. 315 (O.H.) at p. 316.

meeting when notice of a resolution is required; and (2) at least one week before the meeting in any other case. A sum reasonably sufficient to meet the company's expenses must be deposited or tendered: section 377(1).

If the directors call an annual general meeting for a date six weeks or less after deposit of the requisition, the requisition is deemed to have been properly deposited.

## Special notice

Section 379 provides that where under the Act special notice is required of a resolution, notice of the intention to move it must be given *to the company* not less than 28 days before the meeting at which it is to be moved, and the company must give notice of the resolution *to the members* when it gives them notice of the meeting (or, if that is not practicable, either by advertisement in a newspaper having an appropriate circulation or in any other mode allowed by the articles, not less than 21 days before the meeting). To close a loophole which would otherwise allow directors to avoid the provision by claiming that the notice had not been given in time, the section also provides that if the directors call a meeting for a date 28 days or less after the notice has been given to the company, the notice is deemed to have been properly given. The notice to the company may be left at or sent by post to the registered office: section 725.[25]

Special notice is only required by sections 293, 303 and 388 (appointment of a director who has attained the age of 70, removal of directors and the appointment and removal of auditors respectively).

Section 379 does not confer any rights on a shareholder to have a resolution to which it applies circulated if he cannot fulfil the requirements of section 376, above. It simply confers a right to receive notice in a special way if the resolution is being proposed in due form.[26]

## PROCEEDINGS AT GENERAL MEETINGS

### Quorum

Under Table A, regulation 40, no business is to be transacted at a general meeting unless a quorum of members is present.

[25] *Ante,* p. 62.
[26] *Pedley v. Inland Waterways Association Ltd*, [1977] 1 All E.R. 209.

Formerly this article only required a quorum when the meeting proceeded to business and so in England was satisfied if a quorum was present at the beginning of the meeting.[27] This was not the law in Scotland, however,[28] and the new wording agrees with that law.

The quorum must be an effective quorum, *i.e.* it must consist of members qualified to take part in and decide upon questions before the meeting,[29] and where articles require a quorum of members to be "present" (without any such addition as "personally or by proxy") that word means "present in person."[30]

By section 370, unless the articles otherwise provide, a quorum, except for a single member private company, is two members present in person for any company. Table A, regulation 40, also fixes two members present in person or by proxy as a quorum. Under section 370A one member present in person or by proxy is a quorum for a single member private company despite any contrary provision in the articles. As to a quorum at a class meeting, see section 125(6), *ante*.[31]

Strictly, since the word "meeting" prima facie means a coming together of more than one person, one person cannot constitute a meeting,[32] even where he attends in more than one capacity or holds proxies for the other persons.[33] However, in *East v. Bennett Bros. Ltd*[34] it was held that one member, who held all the shares of a class, constituted a class meeting. Further, under sections 367[35] and 371,[36] the Secretary of State and the court, respectively, may direct that one member shall be deemed to constitute a

[27] *Re Hartley Baird Ltd* [1955] Ch. 143, distinguished in *Re London Flats Ltd* [1969] W.L.R. 711.
[28] *Henderson v. Louttit & Co. Ltd* (1894) 21 R. 674.
[29] *Henderson's case*, above, *per* Lord President Robertson at p. 676.
[30] *M. Harris Ltd, Petitioners*, 1956 S.C. 207, in which a member represented by an attorney was held not to be "present".
[31] p. 242.
[32] *Sharp v Dawes* (1876) 2 Q.B.D. 26 (C.A.), applied in *Re London Flats*, above; *cf. Souter, Petitioner*, 1981 S.L.T. (Sh. Ct.) 89, in which a single creditor was held not to constitute a committee of inspection.
[33] *James Prain & Sons Ltd, Petitioners*, 1947 S.C. 325. This case was distinguished in *Neil M'Leod & Sons Ltd, Petitioners*, 1967 S.C. 16, in which the requisite quorum of three *members* personally present was held to be constituted by two individuals, one of whom attended in two capacities (*i.e.* as a member holding shares in his own right and as a member entitled to vote in respect of a trust holding).
[34] [1911] 1 Ch. 163.
[35] *Ante*, p. 285.
[36] *Ante*, p. 286.

meeting and the sole member of a single member company may clearly constitute a meeting given the quorum provision in section 370A.

If a quorum is not present within half an hour of the time appointed for the meeting, Table A, regulation 41, provides that the meeting shall stand adjourned to the same day in the next week at the same time and place, or to such time and place as the directors may determine, and if at the adjourned meeting a quorum is not present within half an hour, the members present shall form a quorum. It is thought that a single member can constitute a quorum at an adjourned meeting.[37]

## Chairman

Section 370 provides that, unless the articles otherwise provide, the members present at a meeting may elect any member as a chairman. However, the articles usually provide who is to be chairman. Table A, regulation 42, states that the chairman of the board of directors shall preside at every general meeting of the company, or if there is no such chairman, or if he is not present within 15 minutes after the time appointed for the meeting or is unwilling to act, the directors present shall elect one of themselves to be chairman. Regulation 43 provides that if no director is willing to act as chairman or if no director is present within 15 minutes, the members present may elect one of their number to be chairman of the meeting.[38]

It is the duty of the chairman:

(1) to preserve order,
(2) to see that the proceedings are regularly conducted,[39]
(3) to take care that the sense of the meeting is properly ascertained with regard to any question properly before it,[40]
(4) to decide incidental questions arising for decision during the meeting, e.g. whether proxies are valid.[41]

---

[37] See *Jarvis Motors (Harrow) Ltd v. Carabott* [1964] 1 W.L.R. 1101.
[38] In *Re Bradford Investments plc* [1991] BCLC 224 it was held that where no directors are present and there is a dispute as to who may vote then any member may appoint a chairman. This could later be challenged only if the voting rights were themselves subject to challenge.
[39] *Byng v. London Life Association Ltd* [1990] Ch. 170 (C.A.).
[40] *National Dwellings Society v. Sykes* [1894] 3 Ch. 159.
[41] *Post*, p. 300.

He must allow the minority of the shareholders to have a reasonable time to put forward their arguments, but at the expiration of that time he is entitled, if he thinks fit, to put a motion to the meeting that the discussion be terminated.[42]

The chairman has no casting vote unless expressly given one by the articles.[43] Table A regulation 50, gives him a casting vote.

## Adjournment

A chairman can only adjourn a meeting at his own will in cases of disorder, or where owing to inadequacy of space it is impossible for all those entitled to take part in the debate or vote. In such a case he need not put a motion for an adjournment. If the chairman exercises this common law power of adjournment he must act not only in good faith but also reasonably in deciding when to reconvene the meeting, so that adjourning to another location for the afternoon of a morning meeting was held not to be reasonable since it did not give all members a reasonable opportunity for attending.[44] If, in any other case, he purports to so adjourn the meeting it may elect another chairman and proceed with the business.[45]

The chairman is not bound to adjourn a meeting, even if the majority desire him to do so,[46] unless the articles otherwise provide.

Table A, regulation 45, provides:
"The chairman may, with the consent of a meeting at which a quorum is present (and shall if so directed by the meeting), adjourn the meeting from time to time and from place to place, but no business shall be transacted at any adjourned meeting other than the business which might properly have been transacted had the adjournment not taken place. When a meeting is adjourned for fourteen days or more, at least seven clear days' notice shall be given specifying the time and place of the adjourned meeting and the general nature of the business to be transacted. Otherwise it shall not be necessary to give any such notice."

## Conduct of a meeting

In *Byng v. London Life Association Ltd,*[47] it was held that a meeting could be properly held in more than one room provided

---

[42] *Wall v. London and Northern Assets Corporation* [1898] 2 Ch. 469 (C.A.).
[43] *Nell v. Longbottom* [1894] 1 Q.B. 767.
[44] *Byng v. London Life Association Ltd* [1990] Ch. 170 (C.A.).
[45] See note 40.
[46] *Salisbury Gold Mining Co. Ltd v. Hathorn* [1897] A.C. 268.
[47] [1990] Ch. 170 (C.A.).

that all the rooms are properly provided with audio-visual links so that those in all the rooms can see and hear what is going on in the other rooms and that all due steps are taken to direct to the overflow rooms those unable to get into the main meeting.

Where there are insufficient audio-visual links, as in that case, the main meeting may still constitute a meeting although it will be incapable of proceeding to business. The chairman may therefore validly adjourn this "meeting". There is no rule of law that a meeting at which members are validly excluded is a nullity for that purpose.[48]

Subject to provisions of the Companies Act and the articles, the way in which the business at a meeting is to be conducted is decided by the meeting itself.

"There are many matters relating to the conduct of a meeting which lie entirely in the hands of those persons who are present and constitute the meeting. Thus it rests with the meeting to decide whether notices, resolutions, minutes, accounts, and such like shall be read to the meeting or be taken as read; whether representatives of the Press, or any other persons not qualified to be summoned to the meeting, shall be permitted to be present, or if present shall be permitted to remain; whether and when discussion shall be terminated and a vote taken; whether the meeting shall be adjourned. In all these matters, and they are only instances, the meeting decides, and if necessary a vote must be taken to ascertain the wishes of the majority. If no objection is taken by any constituent of the meeting, the meeting must be taken to be assenting to the course adopted": *per* Lord Russell of Killowen in *Carruth v. I.C.I. Ltd* [1937] A.C. 707[49] at p. 761.

## Voting

### 1. *A show of hands*

The common law rule is that, unless the articles otherwise provide, a resolution put to a meeting is normally decided in the first instance by a show of hands.[50] Further, on a show of hands each member entitled to vote and present in person has one vote only, *i.e.* proxies[51] are not counted. In practice articles do not provide otherwise, *e.g.* Table A, regulation 46, below, provides that a vote shall be by a show of hands unless a poll is demanded

---

[48] Mustill L.J. dissented on this point.
[49] *Ante,* p. 178.
[50] *Re Horbury Bridge Coal Co.* (1879) 11 Ch.D. 109 (C.A.).
[51] *Post,* p. 300.

and regulation 54 provides that subject to any rights or restrictions attached to any class of shares,[52] every member present in person shall have one vote on a show of hands, *i.e.* proxies cannot vote.

Table A provides:
Regulation 57 "No member shall vote at any general meeting or at any separate meeting of the holders of any class of shares in the company, either in person or by proxy, in respect of any share held by him unless all moneys presently payable by him in respect of that share have been paid."

Regulation 58 "No objection shall be raised to the qualification of any voter except at the meeting or adjourned meeting at which the vote objected to is tendered, and every vote not disallowed at the meeting shall be valid. Any objection made in due time shall be referred to the chairman whose decision shall be final and conclusive."

In *Marx v. Estates & General Investments Ltd,*[53] Brightman J. said that there is much to be said for an article like regulation 58. In that case a proxy form, which was liable to stamp duty because it authorised a proxy to vote at more than one meeting but which was unstamped, was not void but a valid authority capable of being stamped, and since the company had accepted it without objection at the meeting the votes cast by the proxy were valid. Further, by virtue of regulation 58 the objection taken several days after the meeting was made too late.

A bankrupt shareholder may vote if he is still on the register.[54] A shareholder, even if he is a director, can vote although he has an interest in the question to be voted on, provided that the majority of the members do not unfairly oppress the minority.[55]

"The shareholder's vote is a right of property, and prima facie may be exercised by a shareholder as he thinks fit in his own interest": *per* Lord Maugham in *Carruth v. I.C.I. Ltd* [1937] A.C. 707 at p. 765.

Table A, regulation 47, provides that, unless a poll is demanded, a declaration by the chairman that a resolution has on a show of hands been carried, or carried by a particular majority, or lost, and an entry to that effect in the minutes, is conclusive evidence of the fact without proof of the number or proportion of the votes recorded for or against.[56]

---

[52] *Ante,* p. 235.
[53] [1976] 1 W.L.R. 380.
[54] *Morgan v. Gray* [1953] Ch. 83.
[55] *Post,* Chap. 18.
[56] Where a show of hands has been taken and the minutes record the passing of the resolution but omit any mention of the show of hands, further evidence may be required to establish the validity of the procedure: *Fraserburgh Commercial Co. Ltd, Petitioners,* 1946 S.C. 444.

## 2. A poll

Although a show of hands can be taken quickly, it is not an accurate method of ascertaining the wishes of the members of a company because the votes of those voting by proxy are not counted. Again, it does not pay due regard to the wishes of a member holding a large number of shares since he has only one vote on a show of hands. Consequently, although the right to demand a poll exists at common law,[57] section 378(4) gives a statutory right to demand a poll in the case of a special or an extraordinary resolution and articles always make provision for taking a poll. The effect of Table A, regulation 46, is that a poll may be demanded before, or on the declaration of the result of, a show of hands, i.e. it is not necessary to have a show of hands before a poll is taken.[58] A proper demand for a poll does away with the need for, or the result of, a show of hands.

The number of votes which a member has on a poll depends upon the articles. Section 370(6) states that unless the articles otherwise provide a member shall have one vote in respect of each share or each £10 of stock held by him, and regulations 54 and 59 of Table A provide that, subject to any rights or restrictions attached to any class of shares, on a poll every member present in person or proxy shall have one vote for each share of which he is the holder, i.e. proxies can be counted.

A poll is complete when the result is ascertained, not on an earlier day when the votes are cast.[59]

Section 373 provides that, on any question other than the election of the chairman or the adjournment of the meeting, any article is void in so far as it excludes the right to demand a poll or requires more persons to demand a poll than (a) five members entitled to vote at the meeting, or (b) members representing one-tenth of the voting rights, or (c) members holding one-tenth of the paid-up capital conferring a right to vote. Further, a proxy has the same right to demand a poll as the member he represents. If articles could require a considerable number of members to demand a poll the right would be worthless. It is essential that a proxy be able to demand a poll—he has no vote on a show of hands.

---

[57] R. v. Wimbledon Local Board (1882) 8 Q.B.D. 459 (C.A.)
[58] Per Jenkins L.J. in Holmes v. Keyes [1959] Ch. 199 (C.A.) at p. 212, although see per Lord Blanesburgh in Carruth's case, ante, at p. 755.
[59] Holmes v. Keyes, post, p. 317.

Table A, regulation 46, provides that in addition to the members in (*b*) or (*c*), *ante*, a poll may be demanded by the chairman or by two members having the right to vote at the meeting, and, by article 48, that the demand for a poll may be withdrawn, but only with the consent of the chairman.

The poll is taken as laid down in the articles. Table A, regulation 51, provides that a poll demanded on the election of a chairman or on a question of adjournment shall be taken forthwith. If demanded on any other question, it shall be taken at such time as the chairman directs. Where, under articles similar to Table A, a poll was demanded on a question of adjournment and taken, but the scrutineers informed the chairman that the result could not be announced within the time during which the meeting hall was available, it was held that the meeting subsequently convened to hear the result was a continuation of the original meeting, with the result that no proxies deposited between the date of the original meeting and the date of the continuation meeting were valid, as the articles required proxies to be deposited 48 hours before the meeting.[60]

On a poll, a member entitled to more than one vote need not cast all his votes or cast them all in the same way: section 374. This provision was introduced to meet the difficulties of a large trust corporation which might hold shares in a company on behalf of two or more different trusts, whose respective interests might well require different exercises of its votes.[61]

## Proxies

Although there is no common law right to vote by proxy,[62] section 372 gives such a right.

The section contains the following provisions: Any member entitled to attend and vote at a company meeting may appoint another person, whether a member of the company or not, to attend and vote as his proxy, and if the company is a private company, to speak as his proxy. The Jenkins Report[63] recom-

---

[60] *Jackson v. Hamlyn* [1953] Ch. 577, applying *Shaw v. Tati Concessions Ltd* [1913] 1 Ch. 292.

[61] *Per* Walton J. in *Northern Counties Securities Ltd v. Jackson & Steeple Ltd* [1974] 1 W.L.R. 1133, at p. 1147.

[62] *Per* Lord Hanworth M.R. in *Cousins v. International Brick Co. Ltd* [1931] 2 Ch. 90 (C.A.) at p. 100.

[63] Para. 468.

mended that a proxy be allowed to speak at a meeting of any company. Every notice calling a meeting must state this right of a member to appoint a proxy. Unless the articles otherwise provide, a proxy can only vote on a poll, a member of a private company cannot appoint more than one proxy to attend on the same occasion, and a member of a company without a share capital cannot appoint a proxy. Articles cannot require the instrument appointing a proxy to be deposited with the company more than 48 hours before a meeting or an adjourned meeting. If articles could require the instrument to be deposited a considerable time before a meeting the right to appoint a proxy would be worthless.

A proxy is appointed by an instrument in writing in accordance with the articles. There are two forms of proxy in use—a general proxy appointing a person to vote as he thinks fit, having regard to what is said at the meeting, and a special proxy appointing a person to vote for or against a particular resolution. A special proxy is often called "a two-way proxy." The Stock Exchange requires two-way proxy forms to be sent to shareholders.[64] The articles usually provide for the form and proof of proxies.[65]

It has been held that directors acting bona fide in the interests of the company are entitled to send out to the shareholders proxy papers in favour of named directors at the expense of the company.[66] However, section 372(6) provides that if invitations to appoint a proxy by a person or one of a number of persons specified in the invitations are issued at the company's expense to some only of the members entitled to vote at a meeting, every officer of the company who knowingly and wilfully authorises or permits their issue is liable to a fine, although an officer is not liable by reason only of the issue to a member, at his written request, of a form of appointment naming the proxy or of a list of persons willing to act as proxy, if the form or list is available to every member entitled to vote. If this were not so the directors might send the proxy papers to friendly shareholders only.

It is the duty of the chairman to decide on the validity of proxies. If the articles provide, as does Table A, regulation 58, that votes tendered at a meeting and not disallowed shall be deemed to be valid, the court will not review the chairman's

[64] Admission of Securities to Listing.
[65] See Table A, regs. 59 to 63.
[66] *Peel v. L & N.W. Rlwy. Co.* [1907] 1 Ch. 5 (C.A.).

decision, even if it is wrong, in the absence of fraud or bad faith on his part.[67] Where articles do not incorporate Table A, a mere misprint or some quite palpable mistake on the face of a proxy form does not entitle the company to refuse to accept the proxy.[68]

Where proxy forms were sent out to all the stockholders in a company and the chairman was named as their proxy, it was held that he was bound to demand a poll in order to ascertain the sense of the meeting, and bound to exercise all the proxies in accordance with the instructions which they contained.[69]

A shareholder who has given a proxy is free to attend the meeting and vote in person, in which case the vote tendered by the proxy may properly be rejected.[70] He does not thereby revoke the proxy and the proxy may, e.g. vote on a second resolution on which the shareholder does not vote.[71]

A corporation, whether a company within the meaning of the Act or not, may, if it is a member of another corporation which is such a company, by resolution of its directors or other governing body authorise such person as it thinks fit to act as its representative at any meeting of the company or any class of members of the company. The representative is entitled to exercise on behalf of the corporation the powers which the corporation could exercise if it were an individual shareholder of the company: section 375. Such a representative is *not* a proxy and may vote on a show of hands as well as on a poll, and may address the meeting even if the company is not a private company.

In one case,[72] where no committee of inspection had been appointed and no directions had been received from the body of creditors or the court, the liquidator in a creditors' voluntary winding up was held to be within the phrase "or other governing body" in section 375, *ante*, and entitled to appoint himself as representative of the company at general meetings of subsidiary companies.

---

[67] *Wall v. Exchange Investment Corporation* [1926] Ch. 143 (C.A.). And see *Marx v. Estates and General Investments Ltd* [1976] 1 W.L.R. 380, *ante*, p. 298.

[68] *Oliver v. Dalgleish* [1963] 1 W.L.R. 1274, where the proxies referred to the "annual general meeting" instead of the "extraordinary general meeting" and there was no other meeting which could be confused with the date which was stated in the proxies.

[69] *Second Consolidated Trust Ltd v. Ceylon, etc. Rubber Estates Ltd* [1943] 2. All E.R. 567.

[70] *Cousins v. International Brick Co. Ltd, ante*, where the proxy had not been revoked under Table A, art. 63. *ante.*

[71] *Ansett v. Butley Air Transport Ltd* (No. 2.) (1958) 75 W.N. (N.S.W.) 306.

[72] *Hillman v. Crystal Bowl Amusements Ltd* [1973] 1 W.L.R. 162 (C.A.).

## Minutes

Every company must keep minutes of all proceedings of general meetings. Such minutes, signed by the chairman of the meeting at which the proceedings were held or of the next succeeding meeting, are evidence of the proceedings: section 382(1), (2). Unless the articles so provide, they are not conclusive evidence, and so, if a resolution has been passed, but is not entered in the minutes, other evidence to prove it will be admitted.[73] However, when the articles provide that the minutes, signed by the chairman, shall be "conclusive evidence without any further proof of the facts therein stated," as between those bound by the articles, namely the company and the members *qua* members,[74] evidence cannot be called to contradict the minutes unless they have been fraudulently written up.[75]

When minutes have been duly made, there is a presumption that all the proceedings were in order, and all appointments of directors, managers or liquidators are deemed to be valid: section 382(4).

The books containing minutes of general meetings are to be kept at the registered office and open to the inspection of any member without charge. A member is entitled to be furnished, within seven days, with a copy on payment of the prescribed fee. If inspection is refused or copies are not sent, the court can compel immediate inspection of the books[76] or direct that copies be sent to those requiring them: section 383. The minute books may be bound, or loose-leaf provided that adequate precautions are taken for guarding against falsification: section 722. Section 723, *ante*, enables the company to use a computer to keep the minutes.

Where the sole member of a single member private company takes a decision which has the effect of a resolution of a general meeting, he must provide the company with a written record of that decision. Failure to do so may lead to a fine being imposed but does not invalidate the decision: section 382B.

---

[73] *Re Fireproof Doors* [1916] 2 Ch. 142; *cf. Fraserburgh Commercial Co. Ltd, Petitioners,* 1946 S.C. 444.
[74] *Ante*, p. 82.
[75] *Kerr v. Mottram* 91940] Ch. 657.
[76] By the member himself or by a named expert on his behalf; *M'Cusker v. M'Rae,* 1966 S.C. 253.

## RESOLUTIONS

**Kinds of resolution**

In the absence of a contrary provision in the Act or in the memorandum or the articles the company in general meeting acts by ordinary resolution. Sometimes, however, the Act or the memorandum or articles require a special resolution, an extraordinary resolution or an elective resolution. Any of these types of resolution may be effected by the written resolution procedure, *post*.

An *ordinary resolution,* which is not defined in the Act, is a resolution passed by a simple majority of the votes of the members entitled to vote[77] and voting in person or, where allowed, by proxy, at a meeting of which notice has been duly given. The length of the notice depends upon a number of factors including the kind of meeting at which the resolution is passed.[78]

Section 378 defines an *extraordinary resolution* as a resolution passed by at least a three-fourths' majority of [the votes of] the members entitled to vote and voting, in person or, where allowed, by proxy, at a general meeting of which notice specifying the intention to propose the resolution as an extraordinary resolution has been duly given. Again the length of the notice depends upon a number of factors including the kind of meeting at which the resolution is passed.

A *special resolution* is defined as a resolution passed by a majority of at least three-fourths of [the votes of] the members entitled to vote and voting, in person or, where allowed, by proxy, at a general meeting of which at least 21 days' notice specifying the intention to propose the resolution as a special resolution has been given: section 378(2).

The words in brackets must be read into section 378 because voting may be on a show of hands, in which case each member will usually have one vote, or on a poll, in which case each member will usually have one vote for each of his shares.

In England a provision in the articles that the day of service is to be included in the number of days' notice to be given does not

[77] *Bushell v. Faith* [1970] A.C. 1099. A shareholders' agreement may, however, prevent a member voting in a particular way on a particular resolution: *Russell v. Northern Bank Development Corp Ltd* [1992] BCLC 1016, *ante,* p. 239.
[78] *Ante,* p. 285.

apply to notice of a special resolution, *i.e.* the period of not less than 21 days prescribed by section 378 is a period of not less than 21 clear days, exclusive of the day of service of the notice and of the day on which the meeting is to be held. Articles cannot curtail the length of time which Parliament has said must elapse between the date on which the notice is served and the date on which the meeting is held.[79] In Scotland the requisite notice under section 378(2) means a notice of not less than 21 days computed by excluding the day on which the notice is received by the shareholder but including the day on which the meeting is to be held.[80] We have seen[81] that less than 21 days' notice of a special resolution may be given if it is so agreed by a majority in number of the members holding not less than 95 per cent. of the shares giving the right to attend and vote at the meeting: section 378(3).

At a meeting at which a special resolution or an extraordinary resolution is submitted to be passed, a declaration of the chairman that the resolution is carried is, unless a poll is demanded, conclusive evidence of the fact without proof of the number or proportion of the votes recorded in favour of or against the resolution: section 378(4). This provision prevents a resolution from being challenged on the ground, *e.g.* that certain shareholders were not qualified to vote.[82] If, however, the declaration of the chairman is fraudulent, or shows on the face of it that the proper majority has not been obtained, it is not conclusive.

A special resolution was put to the meeting. The chairman then said: "Those in favour 6; those against 23; but there are 200 voting by proxy,[83] and I declare the resolution carried." *Held,* the declaration was not conclusive, and the resolution was not passed: *Re Caratal (New) Mines Ltd* [1902] 2 Ch. 498.[84]

Further, the chairman's declaration is not conclusive where the resolution has not been effectively submitted to the meeting, *e.g.* if a show of hands has not been taken as required by the articles.[85]

---

[79] *Re Hector Whaling Ltd* [1936] Ch. 208, applied in *Thompson v. Stimpson* [1961] 1 Q.B. 195.
[80] *Neil M'Leod & Sons Ltd, Petitioners,* 1967 S.C. 16, *per* Lord President Clyde at p. 20.
[81] *Ante,* p. 289.
[82] *Grahams' Morocco Co. Ltd, Petitioners,* 1932 S.C. 269.
[83] Those "voting" by proxy could not vote on a show of hands.
[84] A corresponding Scottish case is *Cowan v. Scottish Publishing Co. Ltd* (1892) 19 R. 437.
[85] *Citizens Theatre Ltd, Petitioners,* 1946 S.C. 14; *cf. Fraserburgh Commercial Co. Ltd, Petitioners,* 1946 S.C. 444.

The chairman can put a resolution to the meeting without its being seconded, unless the articles prohibit it.

## Elective resolution

Section 379A provides for an elective resolution which a private company may use to elect out of any of five internal requirements of the Acts. The Secretary of State has the power to add additional areas of election by regulations: 1989 Act, section 117.

An elective resolution may be made by a private company for any one of the following purposes:

(i)   to apply section 80A in relation to the authority of directors to allot shares[86],

(ii)  to dispense with the laying of accounts and reports before a general meeting[87],

(iii) to apply section 366A to dispense with the holding of an annual general meeting[88],

(iv)  to reduce the percentage required for sanctioning short notice of meetings or special resolutions[89],

(v)   to dispense with the annual appointment of auditors.[90]

An elective resolution requires at least 21 days' notice in writing both of the terms of the resolution and of the meeting. It must then have the unanimous consent of all those entitled to attend and vote at the meeting—one shareholder can therefore prevent it being pursued. The election can be revoked at any time by an ordinary resolution and is automatically revoked if the company is re-registered as a public company. No company may contract out of this elective regime by its articles: section 379A.

An elective resolution and one revoking an elective resolution must be registered in the same way as a special resolution: section 380. Both may be effected by the written resolution procedure, *post*.

## Amendments

If a positive amendment, pertinent to the subject-matter of the resolution, is proposed, it must be voted upon first. If the

---

[86] *Ante,* p. 148.
[87] *Post,* Chap. 20.
[88] *Ante,* p. 285.
[89] *Ante,* p. 289.
[90] *Post,* Chap. 21.

chairman refuses to put a proper amendment to the meeting, the resolution, if passed, is not binding.[91]

An amendment cannot be moved if it goes beyond the notice convening the meeting. Because notice of special business must state the resolution to be passed in such a way as fairly to state the purpose for which the meeting is convened,[92] there is little scope for amendment where a resolution is special business. Where a notice of a meeting stated that it was to pass, with such amendments as should be determined, a resolution that three named persons be appointed directors, an amendment to elect two other directors as well was held valid.[93] Again, there is little scope for amendment of special and extraordinary resolutions since, as we have seen, the notice of a special resolution or an extraordinary resolution must set out in substance the exact wording of the resolution.[94] However, where a notice of a meeting stated that it was to pass special resolutions to wind up voluntarily and to appoint X as liquidator, and the second resolution was dropped and a new one to appoint Y as liquidator was passed, it was held that Y's appointment was valid because as soon as the resolution to wind up was passed a liquidator could be appointed, without notice, under the Act.[95]

### Registration and copies of certain resolutions

A printed copy of certain resolutions and agreements, or a copy in some other form approved by him, must be forwarded to the Registrar within 15 days after they are passed or made and, where articles have been registered, a copy must be annexed to every copy of the articles issued subsequently: section 380(1), (2).

Section 380 applies to, *inter alia,* special and extraordinary resolutions, elective resolutions, written resolutions and other resolutions agreed to by all the members which would otherwise not have been effective unless passed as special resolutions or extraordinary resolutions, and resolutions agreed by all the members of a class of shareholders. This section also applies to certain ordinary resolutions, *e.g.* one to vary or revoke the

[91] *Henderson v. Bank of Australasia* (1890) 45 Ch.D 330 (C.A.).
[92] *Ante,* p. 291.
[93] *Betts & Co. Ltd v. Macnaghten* [1910] 1 Ch. 430.
[94] *Re Swindon Town Football Co. Ltd* [1990] BCLC 467, 468, *per* Harman J.
[95] *Re Trench Tubeless Tyre Co.* [1990] 1 Ch. 408 (C.A.)

authority of the directors to issue shares under section 80, or to revoke an elective resolution: section 380(4).

A resolution passed at an adjourned meeting is treated as having been passed on the date on which it was in fact passed, and is not deemed to have been passed on the date of the original meeting: section 381.

It will be remembered that a printed copy of a resolution effecting an increase of capital, or a copy in some other form approved by the Registrar, must also be filed within 15 days: section 123.

## THE WRITTEN RESOLUTION PROCEDURE

The courts have evolved the doctrine that if all the members assent to a transaction *intra vires* the company, the company is bound and it is not necessary that they should hold a meeting in one room or one place to express that assent simultaneously.

In *Parker & Cooper* v. *Reading*[96] there was no actual meeting but the members individually and at different times informally ratified a debenture granted by the directors, which although *intra vires* the company, was beyond the powers of the directors because two directors had been invalidly appointed.

*Parker & Cooper* was applied in *Re Duomatic Ltd*[97] in which it was held that where it can be shown that all shareholders who have a right to attend and vote at a general meeting of the company assent to some matter which a general meeting of the company could carry into effect, that assent is as binding as a resolution in general meeting. This principle was subsequently applied to such an assent to vary the articles of a company even though no formal special resolution to that effect had been passed. It was held to be a basic principle that all the shareholders acting together could do anything which was *intra vires* the company: *Cane v. Jones*.[98] This principle cannot apply where the assentors could not validly have passed the resolution at a formal meeting.[99]

Further, Table A, regulation 53, provides that a written resolution signed by all the members entitled to attend and vote

---

[96] [1926] Ch. 975.
[97] [1969] 2 Ch. 365.
[98] [1981] 1 All E.R. 533.
[99] *Re New Cedos Engineering Co. Ltd* [1994] 1 BCLC 797.

at general meetings shall be as effectual as if passed at a general meeting of the company duly convened and held. However, Nourse J. in *Re Barry Artist Ltd,*[1] whilst approving the use of such an informal resolution as a special resolution for a reduction of capital, stated that he would not do so again since the reduction of capital procedure requires confirmation by the court.[2] This decision cast doubt on the exact parameters of regulation 53. Could it apply where the resolution is part of a wider process, *e.g.* authorising a private company to give financial assistance for the acquisition of its own shares?

As a result, the 1989 Companies Act added four new sections, 381A, 381B, 381C and 382A and a new Schedule 15A into the 1985 Act to provide for a statutory framework to allow any private company to pass a resolution without holding any meeting, provided all those who could have attended the meeting and voted sign the resolution instead. This basic right is given by section 381A. No notice requirements apply and, provided all the relevant members sign a document which accurately states the resolution, it need not be the same document or even identical wording. Moreover, a signature can be delegated to another. Thus several letters can be sent for signature.

Under section 381A(3) the date of the resolution is the date when the last relevant member signs it; until then the resolution has no validity at all and so is subject to a veto by any member. The date of the resolution is also the date of the passing of the resolution for the relevant provisions of the Act unless, because of the procedure under section 381B, the date when it comes into effect is later (see below). A written resolution under this procedure can be used to effect all types of resolution and is to be deemed to be duly passed for all purposes. Under Schedule 15A, however, the procedure cannot be used to dismiss a director under section 303 or an auditor under section 391. It is also subject to modifications in the case of certain procedural resolutions.

Section 381B requires that a copy of every proposed written resolution must be sent to the auditors who may do one of four things, with the following consequences:

---

[1] [1985] BCLC 283.
[2] *Ante,* p. 173.

(i)    do nothing for seven days from receipt. In that case the resolution will be effective either from that time or the date of the resolution (*i.e.* when the last person signs), whichever is later;

(ii)   within seven days notify the company that it does not concern them as auditors. In that case the resolution will be effective either from the time of notification or the date of the resolution, whichever is later;

(iii) within seven days notify the company that it does concern them as auditors but that no meeting need be held. In that case the consequences are as in (ii) above;

(iv) within seven days notify the company that it does concern them as auditors and that it should be considered by a meeting. In that case the resolution has no effect even if it has already been signed by all the members. At any meeting called the auditor then has a right to attend and speak: section 390(2).

It is apparent from section 381B that it will be politic to send a copy of any written resolution to reach the auditors at least seven days before it is intended to initiate the written resolution procedure.

Under section 382A, written resolutions must be recorded in the same way as ordinary resolutions. If the procedure is being used to effect a special, extraordinary or elective resolution it must be registered as such

It is clear from section 381(2) that nothing in the new written resolution procedure will affect the doctrine laid down in *Re Duomatic*[3] etc., as to informal resolutions being allowed if all the relevant members assent. But its relationship with the articles, and regulation 53 of Table A (*ante*) in particular, is unclear. Regulation 53 allows a company to pass a written resolution without the need to consult the auditors, etc. Is it still possible to use that regulation and so avoid any reference to the auditors under section 381B above, at least where no regulatory process is involved?

Section 381C(1) is ambiguous. It states that:

"Section 381A and 381B have effect notwithstanding any provision of the company's memorandum or articles."

[3] [1969] 2 Ch. 365.

This was intended to prevent companies restricting the new procedure by their articles but it is arguable that it could equally prevent the articles providing a simpler procedure and so could render regulation 53 subject to the new procedure.

The new written resolution procedure is available even on those occasions where a resolution is required as part of a complex authorisation procedure, by adapting that procedure to the written resolution process: Schedule 15A. The six areas affected are: a disapplication of pre-emption rights,[4] exemption by a private company from the financial assistance provisions,[5] approval of off-market purchase contracts and contingent purchase contracts by a company in relation to its own shares,[6] approval by a company for the redemption or purchase of its own shares out of capital,[7] approval of directors' service contracts,[8] and funding of directors' expenditure.[9] These variations are dealt with in relation to their subject area but in general any voting prohibition is lifted in such a way that it becomes irrelevant whether the restricted person signs the resolution or not, and any necessary documents are required to be sent to each relevant member in advance of his signing rather than in advance of the meeting.

---

[4] *Ante*, p. 149.
[5] *Ante*, p. 205.
[6] *Ante*, p. 188.
[7] *Ante*, p. 191.
[8] *Post*, p. 333.
[9] *Post*, p. 339.

# Chapter 15

# DIRECTORS

THE management of a company is usually entrusted to a body of persons called "directors." It will be seen later that the Act requires a public company to have at least two directors and a private company to have at least one. Among other things, this chapter deals with the appointment, remuneration and vacation of office of directors. It also shows that the directors of a company act as a board, that normal articles (*e.g.* Table A, regulation 70) give the directors extensive powers to manage the company's business (and that so long as the directors act within their powers, the company in general meeting cannot overrule them), and that articles usually empower the directors to appoint a managing director and delegate any of their powers to him.

The most important topics dealt with in the chapter are the fiduciary duties and duties of care which a director owes to his company in exercising these powers. Recent statutory developments have further restricted the powers of the directors and provide for disclosure by them of many transactions involving themselves and the company. The chapter concludes with the impact of corporate insolvency on the liability of directors for their conduct prior to the insolvency.

It should be noted that in a private company the directors are usually substantial shareholders. In a public company, the directors normally have few shares, their fees and other emoluments, rather than their dividends, being their main source of profit from the company, with the result that management and ownership of the company are divorced.

The exact name by which a person occupying the position of director is called, is immaterial as, under section 741(1) in the Act, the expression "director" includes any person occupying the position of director by whatever name called. Thus someone who assumes to act as a director, *i.e.* who does things which can only be done by a director, even though not actually appointed as such, will be regarded as a *de facto* director for liability purposes.[1] Section 744 also provides that the expression "officer," which is used in some sections of the Act, in relation to a company includes a director or manager.

## Shadow directors

Several of the statutory provisions relating to directors also apply to "shadow directors." Section 741(2) provides that these are persons in accordance with whose instructions the directors are accustomed to act, excluding purely professional advice. These are different from *de facto* directors because they do not purport to act as directors, on the contrary they claim not to be directors but hide behind those who are. In *Re Hydrodam (Corby) Ltd,*[2] the question arose as to whether two directors of a parent company could be regarded as shadow directors of a subsidiary company. It was said that for someone to be a shadow director four things must be shown: (1) those who are the proper or *de facto* directors of the company; (2) that the person directed those directors as to how to act in relation to the company; (3) that those directors acted in accordance with such directions; and (4) that they were accustomed so to act. The judge was prepared to accept that the parent company may have been a shadow director of its subsidiary[3] but the two directors of the parent company could not be liable as shadow directors of the subsidiary simply because they took part in board meetings of the parent company. Further, if they acted in implementing board decisions with respect to the subsidiary, they were only acting as agents of the parent company. It would have been different if they had acted individually with respect to the subsidiary company.

Similarly, it has been held that the right to appoint two out of five directors does not make the appointer a shadow director, nor was he vicariously liable for their acts[4] and that controlling one director out of several will not make the controller a shadow director.[4a] A more difficult question arises over the position of a "company doctor," *i.e.* someone who is sent into a company to

---

[1] See *Re Hydrodam (Corby) Ltd* [1994] 2 BCLC 180.

[2] [1994] 2 BCLC 180.

[3] This depends upon the wording of the particular statutory provision, many of which negate this possibility.

[4] *Kuwait Asia Bank E.C. v. National Mutual Life Nominees Ltd* [1990] BCLC 868.

[4a] *Re Unisoft Group Ltd (No. 2)* [1994] BCC 766.

attempt to save it from insolvency, *e.g.* by the bank,[5] or the position of a major customer of a company who dictates the production policy of the company.

## NUMBER AND APPOINTMENT OF DIRECTORS

Every public company registered on or after November 1, 1929, must have at least two directors. Companies registered before that date, and every private company, must have at least one director: section 282. Apart from section 282, the number of directors is regulated by the articles.

At to the *first directors,* section 13(5) provides that the persons named in the statement of first directors and secretary, which must be delivered for registration with the memorandum, shall, on the incorporation of the company, be deemed to have been appointed as the first directors and secretary, and any appointment by any articles delivered with the memorandum shall be void unless the person concerned is named as a director or secretary in the statement.

*Subsequent directors* are appointed in the way laid down in the articles, *e.g.* by the company in annual general meeting.

Table A provides:

> "Regulation 73. At the first annual general meeting all the directors shall retire from office, and at every subsequent annual general meeting one-third of the directors who are subject to retirement by rotation or, if their number is not three or a multiple of three, the number nearest to one-third shall retire from office; but, if there is only one director who is subject to retirement by rotation, he shall retire."
>
> "Regulation 74. Subject to the provisions of the Act, the directors to retire by rotation shall be those who have been longest in office since their last appointment or re-appointment, but as between persons who became or were last re-appointed directors on the same day those to retire shall (unless they otherwise agree among themselves) be determined by lot."

The articles also usually contain a clause, as does Table A in regulation 78, providing that casual vacancies, *i.e.* vacancies occurring between two annual general meetings, may be filled by the directors. Regulation 79 also provides that the directors may

---

[5] See *Re A Company* (1988) 4 BCC 424; *Re Tasbian (No. 3) Ltd* [1992] BCLC 358 (C.A.).

appoint additional directors to hold office until the next annual general meeting but so that the total number of directors fixed in accordance with the articles is not exceeded. Where there are articles similar to regulations 78 and 79 the power of appointing additional directors has not been delegated to the directors so as to exclude the inherent power of the company in general meeting to appoint directors.[6]

The appointment of directors at a general meeting, except in the case of a private company, must be voted on individually unless a resolution to the contrary has first been agreed to by the meeting without any vote being given against it. A motion for the appointment of two or more persons as directors of a public company by a single resolution is void (although the operation of section 285,[7] by which the acts of the "directors" are valid, is not excluded and no provision in the articles for the automatic reappointment of retiring directors in default of another appointment applies): section 292.

Table A, regulation 75, provides that if the company at the meeting at which a director retires by rotation does not fill the vacancy, the retiring director, if offering himself for re-election, is deemed to have been re-elected unless (a) another person is elected, (b) a resolution not to fill the vacancy is passed, or (c) a resolution for his re-election is lost. In the absence of a provision like (c), a retiring director will be deemed to be re-elected even though a resolution that he be re-elected is lost.[8] It is also provided, by regulation 76, that no person, other than the retiring director or a person recommended by the directors, is eligible for election as a director unless notice of intention to propose him, signed by a member entitled to vote, is left at the registered office not less than 14 nor more than 35 days before the meeting, together with a signed notice of his willingness to act.

### Assignment of office by directors

If the articles or any agreement contains power for a director to assign his office to another person, an assignment is of no effect unless and until it is approved by a special resolution of the company: section 308.

[6] *Worcester Corsetry Ltd v. Witting* [1936] Ch. 640.
[7] *Ante,* p. 115.
[8] *Grundt v. Great Boulder Proprietary Mines Ltd* [1948] Ch. 145 (C.A.).

## Persons Who Cannot be Directors

Certain persons cannot be appointed or act as directors:

### Age

A person who has reached the age of 70 cannot be *appointed* director *unless* the company is private and not the subsidiary of a public company, *or* the articles otherwise provide, *or* he is appointed or approved by a resolution of which special notice, stating his age, has been given: section 293. The exceptions are such as to make this section ineffective.

A person who is *first* appointed a director of a company, other than a private company which is not the subsidiary of a public company, after he has reached the age at which the directors retire under the Act or the articles, must give notice of his age to the company: section 294.

### Bankruptcy

An undischarged bankrupt must not act as director of, or be concerned in the promotion, formation or management of, a company without the leave of the court by which he was adjudged bankrupt,[9] under penalty of imprisonment or a fine or both: Company Directors Disqualification Act 1986, section 11. Such a person may be personally liable if he acts whilst disqualified—see below.[10]

In England, on an application for leave to act as director, notice must be given to the Official Receiver, who can oppose the application if he is of opinion that it is contrary to the public interest.

### Disqualification

A director who has been disqualified from acting as a director under the Company Directors Disqualification Act 1986 cannot be a director whilst so disqualified. This topic is dealt with at the end of this chapter.[11]

---

[9] For Scotland, substitute "sequestration of his estates was awarded" for "he was adjudged bankrupt."

[10] *Post,* p. 385.

[11] *Post,* p. 373.

## SHARE QUALIFICATION OF DIRECTORS

A share qualification is a specified number of shares which a person must hold in the company to qualify him for appointment as a director of it. There is no share qualification unless the articles otherwise provide, although there is no such requirement in Table A. It should be remembered that in the case of a private company a director will in any event usually be a substantial shareholder.

When a qualification is imposed, a director not already qualified must obtain his qualification within two months of his appointment or the shorter time fixed by the articles: section 291(1).[12] If a director fails to obtain his qualification within the appropriate period, or if he thereafter ceases to hold it, his office is vacated and he is liable to a fine until he ceases to act as director: section 291(3).[13]

Where articles provide that a first director is to "be deemed to have agreed to take" his qualifying shares from the company, a person who has accepted office as one of the first directors and has acted as such is bound to accept an allotment of shares made in accordance with that provision.[14] Shares held jointly with another person are a sufficient qualification, unless the articles otherwise provide.[15]

The holding of a share warrant does not constitute the holding of qualification shares, as the shares can be transferred at any time by delivery of the warrant: section 291(2).

## REGISTER OF DIRECTORS AND SECRETARIES

Section 288(1) provides that a company must keep at its registered office a register of its directors and secretaries. In the case of an individual director, section 289 provides that the register must contain his name[16] and any former name,[17] address,

---

[12] See *Holmes v. Keyes* [1959] Ch. 199 (C.A.).

[13] But see *Liquidator of the Consolidated Copper Co. etc. Ltd v. Peddie* (1877) 5 R. 393.

[14] *The Kingsburgh Motor Construction Co. Ltd v. Scott* (1902) 10 S.L.T. 424 (O.H.).

[15] *Grundy v. Briggs* [1910] 1 Ch. 444.

[16] A corporate director will use its corporate name. A Scottish partnership can use its firm name.

[17] This does not include the maiden name of a married woman, the previous name of a peer or a name changed before the director was 18 or more than 20 years ago.

nationality and business occupation, together with particulars of
any other present or past directorships held by him (except
directorships of companies of which the company is the wholly
owned subsidiary, or which are wholly owned subsidiaries either
of the company or of another company of which the company is
the wholly owned subsidiary) and the date of his birth. The
obligation relating to past directorships only relates to the
previous five years and does not apply to dormant companies,
*post*. The register is open to inspection by members without fee
and by others on payment of the prescribed fee.

Within 14 days of any change in the directors or secretary or in
the particulars contained in the register, the company must notify
the Registrar of the change and the date when it occurred. A
notification of a person having become a director or secretary
must contain his signed consent to act as such: section 288(2).

Section 711 requires the Registrar to publish in the *Gazette*
notice of the receipt by him of any notification of a change among
the directors of a company. Further, section 42 provides that a
company cannot rely against other persons on any change among
its directors if it had not been officially notified at the material
time and is not shown by the company to have been known at
that time to the person concerned, or if the material time is less
than 16 days after official notification and it is shown that the
person concerned was unavoidably prevented from knowing of
the event at that time. Such official notification does not con
stitute notice to anyone—section 42 has a purely negative effect.[18]


## PARTICULARS OF DIRECTORS ON BUSINESS LETTERS


No company may state, in any form, the name of any of its
directors[19] in a business letter, either in the text or as a signatory,
unless is states in legible characters the name of every director of
the company: section 305. Initials or recognised abbreviations of
forenames may be used.

---

[18] *Official Custodian of Charities v. Parway Estates Ltd* [1985] Ch. 151.
[19] This includes shadow directors.

## DISCLOSURE OF DIRECTORS' SHAREHOLDINGS, ETC.

### Obligation of director to notify company of his interests in shares in, or debentures of, it or associated companies

Subject to any exceptions made by the Secretary of State,[20] a person who becomes a director[21] when he is interested in shares in or debentures of the company or its subsidiary, holding company or co-subsidiary, must, within five days[22] (or, if he does not know of the interest, within five days after it comes to his knowledge), give the company written notice of his interests and of the number of shares of each class in, and the amount of debentures of each class of, the company and each of the associated companies: section 324(1).

A director must (within five days, if he knows of the event and that its occurrence gives rise to the obligation; otherwise within five days after he becomes aware that the occurrence of the event gives rise to the obligation) give the company written notice if, while he is a director:

(i)   an event occurs in consequence of which he becomes or ceases to be interested in shares in or debentures of the company or an associated company; or

(ii)  he contracts to sell any such shares or debentures; or

(iii) he assigns a right given to him by the company to subscribe for shares in or debentures of the company; or

(iv)  he is granted by an associated company a right to subscribe for shares in or debentures of that other company, or he exercises or assigns such a right;

stating the number or amount, and class, of shares or debentures involved: section 324(2). Certain other matters such as the price or other form of consideration must be stated too.

Schedule 13 provides detailed rules for determining what amounts to an interest in shares and debentures for the purposes of section 324. These include restricted rights of ownership, rights of control over shares or debentures, interests under a trust but

---

[20] See the Companies (Disclosure of Directors' Interests) (Exceptions) Regulations 1985. (S.I. 1985 No. 802).

[21] Including shadow directors: s.324(6).

[22] Excluding Saturdays, Sundays and bank holidays.

not as a trustee, joint interests and the right to acquire any shares or debentures.

Contravention of section 324, or making to the company a statement known to be false or recklessly making a false statement, gives rise to liability to two years' imprisonment or a fine or both. Proceedings can, in England or Wales, be instituted only by or with the consent of the Secretary of State or the Director of Public Prosecutions.

If it appears that section 324 has been contravened the Secretary of State may order an investigation: section 446.[23]

### Extension of obligation to disclose to interests of spouses and children

For the purposes of section 324, *ante*, an interest of the spouse of, or of a child under the age of majority of, a director (not being himself or herself a director) in shares or debentures is treated as the director's interest, and a contract, assignment or right of subscription entered into, exercised or made by, or a grant made to, such a spouse or child is treated as that of the director: section 328(1)(2).

Within five days after the event in question comes to his knowledge, a director must notify the company in writing if, while he or she is a director—

(a) the company grants the director's spouse or child a right to subscribe for shares in or debentures of the company; or

(b) such spouse or child exercises such a right: section 328(3).

In each case the like information as is required by section 324, *ante*, must be stated: section 328(4). If section 328(4) appears to have been contravened the Secretary of State may order an investigation: section 446.[24]

In section 328, "son" includes step-son and adopted son, and "daughter" includes a step-daughter and adopted daughter.

### Register of directors' shareholdings, etc.

Section 325 contains provisions for securing that information furnished under section 324, and certain other information about directors' interests,[25] is recorded and made available.

---

[23] *Post*, p. 438.
[24] *Post*, p. 438.
[25] Including shadow directors.

Every company must keep a register for the purposes of section 324 and whenever it receives information from a director in consequence of that section, within three days[26] thereafter it must inscribe in the register, against his name, the information and the date of inscription.

When a company grants a director a right to subscribe for shares or debentures it must, within a similar time, inscribe against his name the date of the grant, the period during or time at which it is exercisable, the consideration for the grant, the description of the shares or debentures and the number or amount thereof, and the price to be paid. When such a right is exercised there must be inscribed that fact (identifying the right), the number or amount of shares or debentures involved, the fact that they were registered in his name or the names of the persons in whose names they were registered, together with the number or amount registered in the name of each person.

The entries against the names in the register must appear in chronological order. If a director requires it, the nature and extent of his interest in shares or debentures must also be recorded.

The company is not, by virtue of anything done for the purposes of section 325, affected with notice of, or put upon inquiry as to, the rights of any person in relation to shares or debentures.[27]

## Index of names

Unless the register is in the form of an index the company must also keep an index of the names inscribed therein. The index must give a sufficient indication to enable the information against each name to be readily found and must be altered within 14 days after the date on which a name is entered in the register.

## Contravention of section 325

There are default fines[28] and other fines for contravention of section 325, and the court is empowered to order inspection of the register and delivery of a copy: section 326.

---

[26] Excluding Saturdays, Sundays and bank holidays.
[27] For inspection of the register see *ante*, p. 65.
[28] Sched. 24.

**Duty of company to notify recognised investment exchange of acquisition of its securities by director**

Section 329 provides that when a company, whose shares or debentures are listed on a recognised investment exchange, is notified of any matter by a director under section 324 or section 328 *ante*, and that matter relates to shares or debentures listed on an investment exchange, the company must notify that exchange of the matter before the end of the following day (Saturdays, Sundays and Bank Holidays in any part of Great Britain being disregarded).

If there is default in complying with the section the company and every officer in default is guilty of an offence and liable on summary conviction to a fine and further to a default fine, although proceedings in England and Wales cannot be instituted except by, or with the consent of, the Secretary of State or the Director of Public Prosecutions.

## DEALING BY DIRECTORS IN CERTAIN OPTIONS

To prevent directors from speculating against the value of their company's shares, section 323, as extended by section 327, penalises the dealing by directors,[29] their spouses or children, in options to buy or sell quoted shares in, or quoted debentures of, the company or associated companies. A director who buys a right to call for delivery, or a right to make delivery, or, at his election, a right either to call for or to make delivery, at a specified price and within a specified time of a specified number of relevant shares or a specified amount of relevant debentures, is liable to two years' imprisonment or a fine or both: section 323.

"Relevant shares" and "relevant debentures' mean, respectively, shares in, or debentures of, the company or its subsidiary, holding company or co-subsidiary, as respects which a stock exchange listing has been granted in Great Britain or elsewhere.

Buying a right to subscribe for shares or debentures is not penalised, nor is buying debentures which carry a right to subscribe for or convert into shares.

Section 327 extends section 323 to the spouse of, or child under the age of majority of, a director, not being herself or himself a

---

[29] Including shadow directors.

director of the company, except that it is a defence for such a spouse or child, charged with an offence under section 323, to prove that he had no reason to believe that his spouse or parent was a director of the company in question. "Child" includes step-child and adopted child.

If it appears that section 323 has been contravened the Secretary of State may order an investigation: section 446.[30]

## VACATION OF OFFICE BY DIRECTORS

A director may cease to be such for various reasons, *e.g.* death, dissolution of the company, retirement by rotation under articles like Table A, regulations 73 and 74, *ante,*[31] or retirement under an age limit, disqualification, under the terms of the articles, removal under section 303, or because they are subject to a disqualification order by a court.[32]

### Retirement of directors under age limit

A director must retire at the end of the first annual general meeting after he reaches 70 *unless*:

(1)  the company is a private company which is not the subsidiary of a public company; or
(2)  the articles otherwise provide; or
(3)  he was appointed or approved by the company in general meeting by a resolution, *i.e.* an ordinary resolution, of which special notice, stating his age, was given: section 293.

If a director should have to retire under this section he may be reappointed by an ordinary resolution of which special notice,[33] stating his age, has been given. The result is that the section is a weak one and unimportant in practice. In particular, the articles may alter the age limit or provide that directors shall not be obliged to retire on reaching any age.

[30] *Post,* p. 438.
[31] p. 314.
[32] *Post,* p. 373.
[33] *Ante,* p. 293.

## Vacation of office by directors under the articles

The articles usually provide for the vacation of office by directors on the happening of certain events, *e.g.* bankruptcy or resignation.[34]

When the articles provide that a director shall vacate his office if he absents himself from board meetings for a certain time,[35] the office will not be vacated if the absence is involuntary, as where the director is ill and unable to travel.[36] On the other hand, if the director is absent because his doctor has advised that his health will be benefited by going abroad, the office will be vacated.[37]

On the happening of any of the events mentioned in the articles, the vacation of office is automatic and the board of directors has no power to waive the offence or condone the act.[38] Similarly, on the resignation of a director the office is automatically vacated, so that the resignation cannot be withdrawn without the consent of the company.[39]

In *Lee v. Chou Wen Hsien*[40] the articles provided that a director should vacate his office if he was "requested in writing by all his co-directors to resign." The Privy Council held that a notice in the correct form validly removed the recipient from his directorship even if it was made with an ulterior motive. Any challenge had to be made on the basis that the other directors had acted in breach of their fiduciary duty which was in any event owed to the company and not to an individual director.[41] The clause was so drafted that the dismissal was automatic on the giving of the correct notice.

## Removal of directors

By section 303 a company may by ordinary resolution[42] remove a director before the expiration of his period of office, *notwith-*

---

[34] These matters are distinct from those who cease to be directors because they are subject to a disqualification order made by the court; *post*, p. 373.

[35] See, *e.g.* Table A, reg. 81.

[36] *Mack's Claim* [1900] W.N. 114.

[37] *McConnell's Claim* [1901] 1 Ch. 728.

[38] *Re The Bodega Co. Ltd* [1904] 1 Ch. 276.

[39] *Glossop v. Glossop* [1907] 2 Ch. 370.

[40] [1985] BCLC 45 (P.C.).

[41] *Post*, p. 349.

[42] This is a rare case where the Act *expressly* provides for an ordinary resolution. The written resolution procedure is not available for such a purpose: Sched. 15A para. 1; *ante*, p. 308.

*standing* anything in the articles or in any agreement between him and the company. Special notice[43] must be given of any resolution to remove a director or to appoint another person in place of a removed director at the meeting at which he is removed. On receipt of notice of an intended resolution to remove a director the company must send a copy to the director concerned, who is entitled to have his representations in writing of a reasonable length sent to the members of the company or read out at the meeting and also to be heard on the resolution at the meeting. The director may be deprived of the former right if the court is satisfied that it is being abused to secure needless publicity for defamatory matter.

It has been held that nothing in the Act prevents the articles giving a director's shares special voting rights, *e.g.* three votes per share on a poll, on a resolution to remove him.[44] On the other hand, it appears that the company cannot contract not to remove a director although the shareholders may do so as between themselves.[45]

Subsection (5) provides that nothing in section 303 deprives a removed director of any compensation[46] or damages payable to him in respect of the termination of his appointment as director or of any appointment, *e.g.* as managing director, terminating with that as director; and nothing in the section derogates from any power of removal which may exist apart from the section, *e.g.* a power of removal given by the articles of the company. For example, as will be explained later,[47] he will be entitled to damages if he has a contract of service, outside the articles, appointing him managing director for a specified period which has not yet expired, and his removal is inconsistent with such contract. Section 318, *post,*[48] enables members to inspect the service contract and thus ascertain how much it will cost to remove a director.

A director validly removed from office may, if he is a member, in appropriate circumstances be entitled to an order under section 459 where the affairs of the company have been conducted in an unfairly prejudicial manner,[49] or an order that the

---

[43] See n.33, *ante.*
[44] *Bushell v. Faith* [1970] A.C. 1099.
[45] *Russell v. Northern Bank Development Corp. Ltd* [1992] BCLC 1016.
[46] *e.g.* for unfair dismissal. See *Parsons v. Parsons Ltd* [1978] I.C.R. 456.
[47] p. 333.
[48] p. 334.
[49] *Post,* p. 417.

company be wound up by the court on the ground that winding up is just and equitable.[50]

## PROCEEDINGS OF DIRECTORS

Table A, regulation 88, provides that subject to the articles, the directors may regulate their proceedings as they think fit.

Regulation 88 further provides that a director may, and the secretary on the requisition of a director must, at any time summon a board meeting.

Every director is entitled to have reasonable notice of a meeting except that regulation 88, *ante,* provides that notice need not be given to a director who is absent from the United Kingdom. What is reasonable notice depends on the practice of the company, but if a director wishes to complain of the shortness of the notice he should act promptly, otherwise the court will not interfere.[51]

If notice is not properly given, the proceedings at the meeting are void.

Application was invited for 106,000 shares, and the directors resolved not to allot until 14,000 shares were applied for. A subsequent meeting was held at which two directors, a quorum, were present, when a resolution was passed to allot the shares applied for, about 3,000. The meeting was held at a few hours' notice at 2 o'clock. This was much shorter notice than had ever been given before. One director did not receive notice until next day, and another gave notice that he could not attend until 3 o'clock. *Held,* the allotment was void: *Re Homer District Gold Mines* (1888) 39 Ch.D. 546.

A quorum is that number of directors which must be present to make the proceedings of the board valid. The articles usually fix a quorum. Table A, regulation 89, provides: "The quorum for the transaction of the business of the directors may be fixed by the directors and unless so fixed at any other number shall be two." If the number of directors sinks below the quorum, the directors cannot act unless the articles provide, as they usually do, that the continuing directors can act.

Table A, regulation 90, provides that if the number of directors is less than the number fixed as the quorum, the continuing directors or

---

[50] *Re Westbourne Galleries Ltd* [1973] A.C. 360, *post,* p. 413.
[51] See *Browne v. La Trinidad* (1887) 37 Ch.D. 1 (C.A.).

director may act only for the purpose of filling vacancies or of calling a general meeting.

In ascertaining whether a quorum is present, those directors who are incompetent to vote on the matter under discussion must not be counted.[52] Directors, however, can attend the meeting even if they are unable to vote.[53] One transaction cannot be split up into two resolutions so as to qualify directors to vote.

Y. and D., two directors of a company, had made advances to the company in consideration of receiving debentures. The company had four directors, three of whom were a quorum. A resolution was passed granting a debenture to Y. Y. did not vote on this resolution. Another resolution was then passed granting a debenture to D., on which D. did not vote. The two debentures ranked equally among themselves. *Held*, the issue of the two debentures formed one transaction in which Y. and D. were equally interested and that the two resolutions were invalid for want of a quorum: *Re North Eastern Insurance Co. Ltd* [1919] 1 Ch. 198.

The articles deal with the election of a chairman. By Table A, regulation 91, the directors may elect a chairman of their meetings and determine the period for which he is to hold office.

Table A, regulation 93, provides that a resolution in writing, signed by all the directors entitled to receive notice of a meeting of the directors, shall be as valid as if it had been passed at a board meeting duly convened and held. (The position is the same at common law.[54])

Section 382 provides that minutes of proceedings at directors' meetings must be entered in books kept for the purpose, and such minutes signed by the chairman of the meeting at which the proceedings were had, or by the chairman of the next succeeding meeting, are evidence of the proceedings. Where minutes have been duly made there is a presumption that the meeting was duly held and convened, that all proceedings were duly had and that all appointments of directors and managers were valid.

By section 722 the minutes may be kept in a bound book, or in a loose-leaf book provided that adequate precautions are taken for guarding against falsification. Minutes may also be kept on a computer under section 723. If the minutes are incomplete, a resolution duly passed can be proved by other evidence.[55]

---

[52] *Re Greymouth Point Elizabeth Ry., etc. Co. Ltd* [1904] 1 Ch. 32. See also Table A, reg. 89 as to alternate directors, and reg. 95.

[53] *Grimwade v. B.P.S. Syndicate Ltd* (1915) 31 T.L.R. 531.

[54] *Re Bonelli's Telegraph Co.* (1871) L.R. 12 Eq. 246; *Runciman v. Walter Runciman plc* [1992] BCLC 1084.

[55] *Re Fireproof Doors Ltd* [1916] 2 Ch. 142.

## POWERS OF DIRECTORS

The powers of the directors depend on the articles since, apart from requiring that certain things, *e.g.* alterations to the articles (s.9) or the capital (ss.121, 135) or the delegating of authority to issue shares (s.80), must be done by the members in general meeting, the Act leaves the distribution of powers between the general meeting and the board to the articles, which in practice always give the directors extensive powers.

Table A provides:
Regulation 70: "Subject to the provisions of the Act, the memorandum and the articles and to any directions given by special resolution, the business of the company shall be managed by the directors who may exercise all the powers of the company. No alteration of the memorandum or articles and no such direction shall invalidate any prior act of the directors which would have been valid if that alteration had not been made or that direction had not been given. The powers given by this regulation shall not be limited by any special power given to the directors by the articles and a meeting of directors at which a quorum is present may exercise all powers exercisable by the directors."

If they act within the powers given to them by such an article, directors are not bound to obey resolutions passed by the shareholders at a general meeting; such resolutions cannot override a decision of the directors or control the exercise of their powers in the future.[56]

"A company cannot by ordinary resolution dictate to or overrule the directors in respect of matters entrusted to them by the articles. To do that it is necessary to have a special resolution": *per* Plowman J. in *Bamford v. Bamford* [1970] Ch. 212 at p. 220.

The articles of a company contained an article like the predecessor of Table A, regulation 70, except that it was stated to be "subject to such regulations as might be made by the company by extraordinary resolution." The majority of the shareholders arranged a sale of the company's undertaking and requisitioned a meeting at which an ordinary resolution requiring the directors to seal the contract was passed. *Held,* the directors were not bound to obey the resolution: *Automatic Self-Cleansing Filter Syndicate Co. Ltd v. Cuninghame* [1906] 2 Ch. 34 (C.A.).

[56] *Automatic Self-Cleansing Filter Syndicate Co. Ltd v. Cuninghame* [1906] 2 Ch. 34 (C.A.); *Salmon v. Quin and Axtens Ltd* [1909] 1 Ch. 311 (C.A.); [1909] A.C. 442; *Breckland Group Holdings Ltd v. London and Suffolk Properties Ltd* [1989] BCLC 100; *cf. Marshall's Valve Gear Co. Ltd v. Manning Wardle & Co. Ltd* [1909] 1 Ch. 267.

The articles contained an article like the predecessor of Table A, regulation 70, and also provided that no resolution of the directors to acquire or dispose of premises was to be valid unless neither A nor B dissented. (A and B were the managing directors.) The directors resolved to acquire premises. B dissented. An ordinary resolution to the same effect as the board resolution was passed at an extraordinary general meeting of the company. *Held,* the ordinary resolution was inconsistent with the articles and the company was restrained from acting on it: *Salmon v. Quin & Axtens Ltd* [1909] 1 Ch. 311 (C.A.); [1909] A.C. 442.

"This Court decided not long since, in [the *Automatic Self-Cleansing* case], that even a resolution of a numerical majority at a general meeting of the company cannot impose its will upon the directors when the articles have confided to them the control of the company's affairs": *per* Farwell L.J. in [1909] 1 Ch. 311 at p. 319, quoting Buckley L.J. in *Gramophone & Typewriter Ltd v. Stanley* [1908] 2 K.B. 89 (C.A.).

"Thus, as it seems to me, there is little doubt that the law is that, where matters are confided by articles such as article [70] to the conduct of the business by the directors, it is not a matter where the general meeting can intervene": *per* Harman J. in *Breckland Group Holdings Ltd v. London & Suffolk Properties Ltd* [1989] BCLC 100 at p. 106.

In accordance with the principle set out above, a resolution passed by a company in general meeting that the directors should make an advance of money to the shareholders pending the declaration of a dividend was held to be inoperative.[57]

The powers of the board may also be regulated by a share-holders' agreement. In *Breckland Group Holdings Ltd v. London and Suffolk Properties Ltd,*[58] the company had adopted regulation 70 of Table A and also had a shareholders' agreement that no litigation could be brought without the approval of a director appointed by each of the two shareholders. Harman J. decided that a combination of regulation 70 and the agreement precluded any interference by the general meeting in a decision whether to bring proceedings on behalf of the company.

If directors are unable to exercise one of their powers because of deadlock on the board or because their number has fallen below the number required for a quorum, the company in general meeting may exercise the power.[59]

[57] *Scott v. Scott* [1943] 1 All E.R. 582.
[58] *Supra.*
[59] *Barron v. Potter* [1914] 1 Ch. 895, where the articles gave the board of directors power to appoint an additional director and, owing to differences between the directors, no board meeting could be held for the purpose. *Held,* the company retained power to appoint additional directors in general meeting.

The position is similar if a company has no directors.[60] Where a company has no directors and two individuals, acting without the authority of the company, commence an action in the company's name the company in general meeting or, if the company is being wound up, the liquidator can ratify the proceedings.[61]

If directors exceed or improperly exercise their powers, their action can be ratified by an ordinary resolution of the company in general meeting.[62] If they act contrary to the company's articles or memorandum it must be ratified by a special resolution.[63]

By way of defence to a take-over bid directors allotted 500,000 shares at par for cash to a third company which was the principal distributor of the products of the company to be taken over. The articles provided that the unissued shares were to be at the directors' disposal. Two share-holders brought an action against the three directors, the third company, and the company, claiming a declaration that the allotment was invalid in that the directors had not acted bona fide in the interests of the company. *Held,* assuming that the allotment was *intra vires* the company and the directors but not bona fide in the interests of the company and therefore voidable, it could after full disclosure be ratified by an ordinary resolution at a general meeting: *Bamford v. Bamford* [1970] Ch. 212 (C.A.), approving *Hogg v. Cramphorn Ltd, post.*[64]

If directors improperly refuse to exercise a power to initiate an action in the company's name, a minority shareholders' action may be brought by way of exception to the rule in *Foss v. Harbottle.*[65]

In one case where the directors directed the company to plead guilty to a charge of conspiriacy to defraud, the court granted an injunction to prevent the company so pleading because the company's interests would thereby suffer, *e.g.* the loss of a potential civil action against an individual defrauder: *Re A Company: F.F.I. (U.K. Finance) Ltd v. Lady Kagan* (1982) 132 N.L.J. 830.

Power to manage the business of the company does not as such give directors power to fix their own remuneration.[66] The articles, however, may empower them, or a committee of the board, to do so.[67]

[60] *Per* Lord Hailsham of St. Marylebone in *Alexander Ward & Co. Ltd v. Samyang Navigation Co. Ltd,* 1975 S.C. (H.L.) 26 at p. 47.
[61] *Alexander Ward* case, *ante.*
[62] *Grant v. United Kingdom Switchback Rlwys. Co.* (1888) 40 Ch.D. 135 (C.A.).
[63] ss. 35, 35A; see Chaps. 3 and 6.
[64] p. 352.
[65] *Cook v. Deeks* [1916] A.C. 554, *post,* p. 402.
[66] *Foster v. Foster* [1916] 1 Ch. 532.
[67] See the next section.

The directors cannot delegate their powers unless empowered to do so by the articles. It will be seen later[68] that the articles usually provide for delegation to a managing director. They may also provide for delegation to a committee of directors.[69] However, such a delegation must be validly authorised by the articles or such a committee will have no authority to enter into the transaction. In *Guinness plc v. Saunders,*[70] a committee of the directors set up to conduct a take-over bid had no authority under the articles to authorise special payments to the directors involved. Such payments could only be authorised by the full board. It followed that the payments were unauthorised, and therefore reclaimable from the directors concerned.

## REMUNERATION OF DIRECTORS

### Where the director does not have a service contract

Directors as such are not employees of the company, but managers or controllers of the company's affairs and, in that capacity, are regarded as fiduciaries.[71] Accordingly they have no claim to payment for their services unless, as is usual, there is a provision for payment in the articles.[72]

If there is no authorisation, either in the articles or elsewhere, for payment a director cannot make a claim for payment by way of quantum meruit or in equity for special work performed. Thus in *Guinness plc v. Saunders, ante,* the House of Lords refused such a claim by a director who had successfully negotiated a take-over bid for the company but whose remuneration was not properly authorised either by the directors or the company.[73]

Table A provides:
Regulation 82: "The directors shall be entitled to such remuneration as the company may by ordinary resolution determine and, unless the resolution provides otherwise, the remuneration shall be deemed to accrue from day to day."

---

[68] p. 340.
[69] See Table A, reg. 72.
[70] [1990] 2 A.C. 663 (H.L.).
[71] *Post,* p. 345.
[72] *Per* McCardie J. in *Moriarty v. Regent's Garage Co. Ltd* [1921] 1 K.B. 423, at p. 446; *cf.* Lord President Inglis in *M'Naughtan v. Brunton* (1882) 10 R. 111 at p. 113.
[73] See also *Zemco Ltd v. Jerrom-Pugh* (1993) BCC 275.

Regulation 83: "The directors may be paid all travelling, hotel and other expenses properly incurred by them in connection with their attendance at meetings of directors or committees of directors or general meetings or separate metings of the holders of any class of shares or of debentures of the company or otherwise in connection with the discharge of their duties."

If remuneration is voted to the directors, it constitutes a debt due from the company and is consequently payable not only out of profits but also out of capital.[74]

A director who is entitled to remuneration for his services is not entitled to his travelling and other expenses in attending board and other meetings unless the articles expressly so provide.[75]

Unless authorised by the articles, directors cannot vote remuneration to one of themselves or appoint one of their number to a salaried position with the company. It has been said that "Directors have no right to be paid for their services, and cannot pay themselves or each other, or make presents to themselves out of the company's assets, unless authorised so to do by the instrument which regulates the company or by the shareholders at a properly convened meeting."[76]

The article governing directors' remuneration was the same as the predecessor of regulation 82.[77] The *directors* passed a resolution appointing K., one of the directors, "overseas director" at a salary of £1,800 a year. In pursuance of this appointment K. was obliged to go, and did go, to Australia. He sued for arrears of salary. *Held,* the appointment was *ultra vires* the board, so that K. could not recover the arrears of salary and was liable to refund salary already received: *Kerr v. Marine Products Ltd* (1928) 44 T.L.R. 292.

On the other hand, where the articles do allow a director's fees to be fixed by the board, or a committee of the board, the board (or committee) must act bona fide in the interests of the company in fixing the remuneration. In breach the authorisation for the payment will be invalid.[78] Provided all the board or committee acquiesce in the payments being authorised then no formal meeting need be held.[79]

---

[74] *Re Lundy Granite Co.* (1872) 26 L.T. 673.
[75] *Young v. Naval and Military Society* [1905] 1 K.B. 687.
[76] *Per* Lindley L.J. in *Re George Newman & Co.* [1895] 1 Ch. 674 (C.A.) at p. 686.
[77] *Ante,* p. 331.
[78] *Zemco Ltd v. Jerrom-Pugh* (1993) BCC 275.
[79] *Runciman v. Walter Runciman plc* [1992] BCLC 1084. The position is different if the board is unaware of the payments as in *Guinness plc v. Saunders* [1990] 2 A.C. 663 (H.L.).

A resolution of the directors to forgo fees to which they are entitled is binding on them and on the company if the company is a party to the agreement.[80] Otherwise the directors may rescind the resolution and claim for fees.[81]

When a director ceases to be a director during a year of office, a question arises as to whether he is entitled to have his remuneration apportioned. If, *e.g.* the articles say that he is to be paid "at the rate of" so much a year, he is entitled to be paid for the period during which he was a director.[82] On the other hand, if he is to be paid £1,000 a year, or in a way other than at the rate of so much a year, it has been held that he is entitled to be paid only for each complete year he serves, and not for any broken period.[83]

## Directors' Service Contracts

In addition to being a director a person may be appointed to a post within the company, such as the managing or finance director, in which case he will be given a service contract as an employee of the company. Such persons are often referred to as the executive directors as opposed to the non-executive directors who do not have such contracts. It is usual for the articles to provide that the terms of such contracts be fixed by the board or a commmittee of the board, and they must act bona fide in the interests of the company in exercising this power. Similar rules apply to the variation or renewal of such contracts.[84] It appears that since the director concerned has an obvious interest in such a contract he must still disclose that interest under section 317, although the consequences of not doing so are unlikely to be severe.[85]

Where a director has been paid fees out of the company without proper authorisation he cannot claim a set-off against money owed to him under a service contract. He must repay the

[80] *West Yorkshire Darracq Agency Ltd v. Coleridge* [1911] 2 K.B. 326.
[81] *Re Consolidated Nickel Mines Ltd* [1914] 1 Ch. 883.
[82] *Swabey v. Port Darwin Gold Mining Co.* (1889) 1 Meg. 385, although despite the report, the articles did not contain the words "at the rate of," as pointed out in *Inman's* case, *post.*
[83] *Salton v. New Beeston Cycle Co.* [1899] 1 Ch. 775; *Inman v. Ackroyd & Best Ltd* [1901] 1 Q.B. 613 (C.A.), followed in *Liquidator of the Fife Linoleum etc. Co. Ltd v. Lornie* (1905) 13 S.L.T. 670 (O.H.).
[84] *Runciman v. Walter Runciman plc* [1992] BCLC 1084.
[85] See *post*, p. 356.

money improperly paid, since he is a constructive trustee of it, and sue under his contract for damages.[86]

The Act imposes some controls on directors' service contracts. Section 318 provides that, subject as below, every company must keep a copy of each director's contract of service[87] or of any variation thereof, or a memorandum thereof setting out its terms if it is not in writing, at one place. This obligation extends to the directors of its subsidiary companies, if any. The place may be:

(1) the company's registered office; or
(2) the other place where the register of members is kept; or
(3) its principal place of business in England, if the company is registered in England, or in Scotland if the company is registered in Scotland.

Notice of such place and of any changes in it must be given to the Registrar except where the documents have always been kept at the registered office.

Contracts requiring a director to work wholly or mainly outside the United Kingdom are excluded although a memorandum of the duration of the contract, and, if appropriate, the name and place of the subsidiary company, must be kept. Also excluded are those where the unexpired term of the contract is less then 12 months or the contract can be terminated by the company without payment of compensation within 12 months.

There are default fines[88] for contravention of section 318 and the court is empowered to order an inspection.

To prevent possible abuse by directors granting themselves long-term service contracts in order to obtain large compensation payments in the event of a dismissal, section 319 limits the length of such contracts without the approval of a general meeting at which a copy of the proposed contract is available, and where such a copy has been available for inspection at the registered office for the previous 15 days.[89] Any term in such a contract which entitles a director[90] to employment with the company for

---

[86] *Zemco Ltd v. Jerrom-Pugh* [1993] BCC 275.

[87] This applies also to "shadow directors."

[88] Sched. 24.

[89] Such a resolution may be passed using the written resolution procedure provided the agreement etc. is supplied to each relevant member prior to his signature: Sched. 15A, para. 7; *ante*, p. 311.

[90] This includes a shadow director.

longer than five years must be approved by the company in general meeting.

Any term in breach of this section is void and replaced by one which enables the company to terminate the contract at any time, subject to reasonable notice. This requirement cannot be avoided by negotiating several consecutive five year agreements, since no second contract may succeed the first if that contract has more than six months left to run. Current practice is for contracts to be five year "rolling" contracts, *i.e.* which at any time have five years to run.

In addition to the disclosure rules noted above such contracts are to be set out in the company's accounts (*post*).

## Disclosure of directors' emoluments

Any provision in the articles as to the directors' remuneration must usually be disclosed in a prospectus or listing particulars issued by the company.[91]

By section 232 and Schedule 6, Part I, a note to the accounts which must be laid before the company in general meeting must show certain particulars of directors' salaries, pensions, etc.

The particulars are:

(1) The aggregate amount of the directors' emoluments.
    These include fees, including those paid for accepting the position of director, and percentages, sums paid as expenses allowances which are charged to income tax,[92] contributions paid in respect of the directors under any pension scheme, and the estimated money value of any other benefits received otherwise than in cash. The accounts must distinguish between emoluments in respect of services as directors and other emoluments such as sums received by the directors as salaried employees of the company.

(2) The aggregate amount of directors' or past directors' pensions.
    This does not include pensions paid under a pension scheme where the contributions are substantially adequate for the maintenance of the scheme, but does include a pension paid to a director's widow or other dependant.

(3) The aggregate amount of any compensation paid to directors or past directors for loss of office.
    This includes sums paid on a director's retirement from office.

---

[91] *Ante,* Chap. 7.
[92] See Income and Corporation Taxes Act 1988, ss.153–168.

These amounts must include all relevant sums received from the company, the company's subsidiaries and any other person. The amount shown under (3), above, must distinguish between sums received from the company, the company's subsidiaries and other persons.

(4) With respect to each person who has been chairman of the directors' meetings during the year, his emoluments so far as attributable to his period of office (unless his duties were mainly discharged outside the United Kingdom).
(5) With respect to all the directors (other than any whose duties were mainly discharged abroad), the number whose several emoluments did not exceed £5,000, exceeded £5,000 but not £10,000,[93] and so on in bands of £5,000.
(6) If the emoluments of one or more directors exceed the chairman's emoluments, his emoluments or the greater or, as the case may be, the greatest emoluments.
   Emoluments include all such amounts (other than contributions paid in respect of a person under a pension scheme) as are caught by (1) above.
(7) The number of directors who have waived rights to receive emoluments and the aggregate amount of such emoluments.

Heads (4)–(7) do not apply if the company is a subsidiary company or the aggregate amount of the directors' emoluments for that year does not exceed £60,000.

Each director is under a duty to give notice to the company of such matters relating to himself as may be necessary to enable the above information to be shown in the accounts, under penalty of a fine: section 232.

**Compensation for loss of office**

It is unlawful for a company to make to a director any payment by way of compensation for loss of office, or as consideration for or in connection with retirement, unless particulars of the proposed payment, including the amount, are disclosed to the members and the proposal is approved by the company: section 312. It was held in *Re Duomatic Ltd*[94] that disclosure must be made to *all* members, even those with no right to attend and vote at general meetings, whilst the payment is still a proposed payment, although in *Wallersteiner v. Moir*[95] Lord Denning M.R.

[93] Sched. 6, para. 4.
[94] [1969] 2 Ch. 365.
[95] [1974] 1 W.L.R. 991 (C.A.) at p. 1016.

said that he imagined that payment could be later approved by the company in general meeting. The section does not apply to compensation for breach of a service contract: section 312(3).

It is unlawful for anyone to make to a director a payment by way of compensation for loss of office, etc., in connection with the transfer of the whole or part of the company's undertaking or property unless particulars are disclosed and approved. If such a payment is not disclosed the director holds it upon trust for the company: section 313.

When, in connection with a transfer of all or any of the shares in the company resulting from (a) an offer made to the general body of shareholders, (b) an offer made with a view to the company becoming the subsidiary of another, (c) an offer made with a view to an individual obtaining control of not less than one-third of the voting power at a general meeting, or (d) any other offer conditional on acceptance to a given extent, a payment is to be made to a director as compensation for loss of or retirement from office, he must take reasonable steps to see that particulars of the proposed payment, including the amount, are sent with any notice of the offer for their shares given to the shareholders. If this is not done, or the payment is not, before the transfer of the shares, approved by a meeting of the shareholders summoned for the purpose, the director holds the payment on trust for the persons who have sold their shares as a result of the offer: sections 314 and 315.

Sections 313, 314 and 315 cannot be avoided, *e.g.* by paying more than the market value for a director's shares, because section 316 provides that, in connection with sections 313 and 315, the price paid to a director for any of his shares in the company in excess of the price which could have been obtained by other shareholders, or the money value of any valuable consideration given to him, is deemed to have been a payment to him of compensation for loss of office. References in sections 313 to 315 to payments of compensation for loss of office exclude bona fide payments of damages for breach of contract or of pensions in respect of past services. But these provisions have been held not to protect an *ex gratia* payment in lieu of pension made on the eve of liquidation in the case of a company whose directors had no power to make such payments.[96]

[96] *Gibson's Executor v. Gibson,* 1978 S.C. 197 (O.H.).

## SUBSTANTIAL PROPERTY TRANSACTIONS INVOLVING DIRECTORS

Section 320 is intended to prevent directors abusing their position by stripping the company of its assets. The section provides that no contract may be made without the approval of the general meeting, between a director and his company involving the transfer, either way,[97] of a non-cash asset,[97a] if its value exceeds either £100,000 or 10 per cent. of the company's net assets, provided it is not less than £2,000.[98]

This section applies equally to "shadow directors"[99] and persons "connected with a director."[1]

Any arrangement entered into in breach of this section is voidable by the company (unless restitution of the status quo is impossible). Further, the director concerned and any director who authorised the transaction are liable to account to and indemnify the company for any loss.[1a]

The section does not apply if the director concerned received the assets solely by virtue of being a member (*e.g.* on a general reduction of capital), or the transaction was entered into during the course of the winding-up of an insolvent company. Most transactions within a group of companies are also excluded as are transactions on a recognised investment exchange made through an independent broker by a director of a group which includes the market maker concerned: section 321.

Disclosure of such arrangements in the accounts is required by section 232.

---

[97] Thus applying both to sales to the company by a director, *e.g. Pavlides v. Jensen* [1956] Ch. 565; and sales to a director by his company, *e.g. Daniels v. Daniels* [1978] 2 W.L.R. 73.

[97a] As defined in s.739. This can include the benefit of a contract: *Duckwari plc v. Offerventure Ltd* [1995] BCC 89.

[98] The burden of proof is on those alleging that these monetary limits have been exceeded: *Receivers of Niltan Carson Ltd v. Hawthorne* [1988] BCLC 298.

[99] s.320(3). *Ante,* p. 313.

[1] s.346. This includes his minor children, spouse, partners, or any company in which he and his other associates control one-fifth of the equity share capital or votes.

[1a] It is not yet established as to how this loss is to be calculated. See *Duckwari plc v. Offerventure Ltd* [1995] BCC 89.

## LOANS TO DIRECTORS

Section 330 prohibits various categories of loans and other credit transactions between a company and its directors, "shadow directors"[2] and "persons connected with its directors."[3] A subsidiary is equally restrained as regards its holding company.[4]

All companies are prohibited from making loans to, giving guarantees for and security for loans to, their directors or "shadow directors." The strength of this provision appears, however, to be somewhat weakened by the decision of Walton J. in *Champagne Perrier-Jouet S.A. v. H. H. Finch Ltd,*[5] that where a company paid a great many bills for one of its directors it had not made a loan to that director. "Money paid to B at the request of A is quite definitely not a loan."[6] This would seem to be an obvious loophole in the general embargo on loans.

In addition, however, public companies, and companies forming part of a group which includes a public company, may not make loans, give guarantees or securities to persons connected with such directors. Further, public companies may not make "quasi-loans" to their directors, etc., nor may they provide credit facilities for such persons. A "quasi-loan" is defined (s.331(3)) to include the provision of credit card facilities, *e.g.* where the company is the cardholder and the card is used by the director. A credit transaction is one where goods or services are provided on the undertaking that payment will be made later.

These prohibitions cannot be avoided by directors assigning their liabilities to their company or by "back to back" deals, *i.e.* where two companies each make what appear to be separate provisions for each other's directors.

Sections 332 to 338 provide certain exceptions to the prohibitions of section 330. The effect is to allow all loans up to a total of £5,000 outstanding for each director; to allow all credit transactions, if they are on normal commercial terms; to provide an exemption for loans to cover expenses incurred by a director for company purposes, provided the transaction has the prior

---

[2] See note 99, *supra.*
[3] See note 1, *supra.*
[4] This includes a wholly-owned subsidiary, unlike s.320 above.
[5] [1982] 1 W.L.R. 1359.
[6] *Ibid.,* p. 1364.

approval of the general meeting[7] or is ratified within six months, subject to a maximum of £20,000 for directors of public companies; to allow quasi-loans up to £1,000 outstanding at any one time if the terms require repayment within two months; and to allow credit transactions up to £10,000 outstanding at any one time per director.

In addition moneylending companies[8] may make loans and quasi-loans to directors on normal commercial terms subject to a maximum of £100,000 outstanding at any one time apart from "authorised banks."[9] Directors of such companies may also be allowed to participate in subsidised house purchase schemes up to a limit of £100,000.

The various sums used in sections 334 to 338, *i.e.* £10,000, £20,000 and £100,000, are sums outstanding at any time and are calculated in accordance with section 339.

Section 341 provides that the civil consequences of a breach of section 330 are the same as those for a breach of section 320 (substantial property transactions), *ante*.[10] In addition section 342 provides for a series of criminal offences for public companies and their directors who know or have reasonable cause to believe that section 330 has been breached.

Sections 232 to 237 require particulars of all loans etc., whether prohibited or not, to be disclosed in the accounts unless they are less than £2,000 in total. This includes disclosure of the principal terms of the transaction and the true beneficiary. Authorised banks[11] are subject to special rules. Auditors must disclose any breach of the disclosure requirements in their report.

## MANAGING DIRECTOR

Unless the directors are empowered to appoint a managing director[12] by the memorandum[13] or the articles, the directors

[7] The various amounts and purposes must be disclosed at the relevant meeting: s.337. If the written resolution procedure, *ante*, p. 308, is used such disclosures must be made to each relevant member before he signs the resolution: Sched. 15A.

[8] s.338(2).

[9] s.338(4).

[10] p. 338.

[11] See note 9, *supra*.

[12] For discussion of the general nature of the post of managing director, see *Anderson v. James Sutherland (Peterhead) Ltd*, 1941 S.C. 203, also *Hindle v. John Cotton Ltd* (1919) 56 S.L.R. 625 (H.L.) (managing director held to be an "employee" within the meaning of the articles) and opinions in *Kerr v. Walker*, 1933 S.C. 458.

[13] *Re Scottish Loan & Finance Co. Ltd* (1944) 44 S.R. (N.S.W.) 461.

cannot appoint a managing director.[14] When the articles empower the directors to appoint a managing director, the company in general meeting cannot itself make such an appointment without first altering the articles.[15]

Table A, regulation 84, provides that the directors may appoint *one or more of their number* to the office of managing director for such period and on such terms as they think fit, and, *subject to the terms of any contract of service,* may revoke such appointment; that a director so appointed shall not, whilst holding that office, retire by rotation,[16] but that the appointment shall be automatically determined if he ceases to be a director.

A managing director has two functions and two capacities, those of director and managing director. As managing director he is usually a party to a contract of employment or service with the company.[17] In a family company, however, if there is no express contract of service the managing director may not be regarded as an employee.[18]

Subject to the articles, the powers and duties of a managing director depend upon his contract of service with the company.

C. was appointed a managing director of H. Co. His service agreement provided that he should perform the duties and exercise the powers in relation to the business of H. Co. and the businesses of its existing subsidiary companies which might from time to time be assigned to or vested in him by the directors. Later the directors resolved that C. should confine his attention to a particular subsidiary company. C. sued for damages for breach of contract. C.'s action was dismissed: *Caddies v. Harold Holdsworth & Co. (Wakefield) Ltd,* 1955 S.C. (H.L.) 27; [1955] 1 All E.R. 725 (H.L.).

As has been seen in Chapter 6, a managing director may have implied power to enter into certain agreements on behalf of the company even though there has been no express delegation of the power to him by the board.[19] On the other hand the implied authority of a managing director is not limitless. He has no such

---

[14] *Per* Swinfen Eady J. in *Boschoek Proprietary Co. Ltd v. Fuke* [1906] 1 Ch. 148 at p. 159.

[15] *Thomas Logan Ltd v. Davis* (1911) 104 L.T. 914; 105 L.T. 419.

[16] *Ante,* p. 314.

[17] *Per* Lord Normand in *Anderson v. James Sutherland (Peterhead) Ltd,* 1941 S.C. 203 at p. 218; *per* Jenkins L.J. in *Goodwin v. Brewster* (1951) 32 T.C. 80 at p. 96.

[18] *Parsons v. Albert J. Parsons & Sons Ltd* [1979] I.C.R. 271 (C.A.).

[19] *Allison v. Scotia Motor etc. Co. Ltd* (1906) 14 S.L.T. 9 (O.H.) (implied power to engage a works manager for a period of five years).

implied power to act contrary to the articles and resolutions of the company and/or the board[20] or to use the company's money to bribe someone for the benefit of the company.[21]

Where a managing director is appointed under an article like Table A, regulation 84, above, his appointment may be prematurely determined by his removal from his directorship,[22] *e.g.* under section 303,[23] but the company will be liable in damages if this is in breach of his contract of service, as it usually will be. In fact the company will often have to pay a large sum by way of liquidated damages.

S. was appointed managing director of N. Ltd, a subsidiary of L. Co., for 10 years. The articles of N. Ltd included regulation 68 of Table A in the 1929 Act (which provided that a managing director's appointment should be automatically determined if he ceased to be a director or if the company in general meeting resolved to terminate his appointment). M. Co. bought the shares in L. Co., and at a general meeting of N. Ltd resolutions were passed removing S. from office as a director and terminating his service agreement. S. sued for damages for wrongful dismissal. *Held,* S. succeeded. It was an implied term of the service agreement that N. Ltd would do nothing of its own motion to put an end to the state of circumstances which enabled S. to continue as managing director: *Shindler v. Northern Raincoat Co. Ltd* [1960] 1 W.L.R. 1038 applying *Stirling v. Maitland* (1865) 34 L.J. O.B. 1 and *Southern Foundries (1926) Ltd v. Shirlaw* [1940] A.C. 701.[24]

R. was appointed managing director at £7 a week, the duration of his appointment not being specified. Article 68 of Table A in the 1929 Act was one of the articles. Later, the directors dismissed R. on a month's notice and their action was confirmed by the company in general meeting. R. sued for damages for wrongful dismissal on the ground that he was not given reasonable notice. *Held,* the claim failed, because R.'s

---

[20] *Guinness plc v. Saunders* [1990] 2 A.C. 663 (H.L.).

[21] *E. Hannibal & Co. Ltd v. Frost* (1988) 4 BCC 3.

[22] *Southern Foundries (1926) Ltd v. Shirlaw* [1940] A.C. 701, *ante,* p. 88; *Nelson v. James Nelson & Sons Ltd* [1914] 2 K.B. 770 (C.A.); *Carrier Australasia Ltd v. Hunt* (1939) 61 C.L.R. 534. In the *Nelson* case the articles empowered the board to appoint a managing director and to revoke the appointment. The board appointed the plaintiff managing director, the agreement providing that he was to hold the office so long as, *inter alia,* he efficiently performed the duties. The board revoked his appointment whilst he was still fulfilling the conditions of the agreement and he was held entitled to damages for breach of contract. In the *Carrier Australasia* case the articles empowered the company to remove a director, subject to the provisions of any agreement. The articles were altered so as to delete the words "subject to . . . any agreement" and then the managing director was removed from his directorship. He was to be entitled to damages.

[23] *Ante,* p. 324.

[24] *Ante,* p. 88.

contract incorporated article 68 which empowered the company to dismiss him without notice by a resolution in general meeting. In the absence of any contract independent of article 68 and the directors' resolution appointing him, there was no ground for implying a term as to reasonable notice: *Read v. Astoria Garage (Streatham) Ltd* [1952] Ch. 637 (C.A.).

Where directors have a discretionary power to dismiss a managing director, this power must be exercised in good faith in the interests of the company and not for some ulterior purpose such as appropriation of the managing director's shares.[25]

In practice a managing director's remuneration will be specified in his contract of service which the directors will negotiate on behalf of the company.

If, where the appointment of a managing director is in fact void, he performs services which are accepted by the company, it has been held that he is entitled to reasonable remuneration.

The articles authorised the directors to appoint one of their number managing director. By contract under the company's seal, C. was appointed managing director at a salary. The seal was affixed to the contract by a resolution of the board of directors but none of the directors had acquired his qualification shares. C. himself acted as managing director, but also failed to acquire his qualification shares. *Held,* C.'s contract was void and C. was not properly appointed managing director. His claim for remuneration in contract failed but the alternative claim in quasi-contract succeeded, *i.e.* he was entitled to payment on a *quantum meruit* basis arising from the performance of his services and their acceptance by the company: *Craven-Ellis v. Canons Ltd* [1936] 2 K.B. 403 (C.A.).[26]

## POSITION OF DIRECTORS

As a company has no physical but only a legal existence, the management of its affairs, as we have seen, is entrusted to the directors whose exact position in relation to the company is, however, rather hard to define.[27] Directors as such are not employees of the company, but are rather managers who in some

---

[25] *Hindle v. John Cotton Ltd* (1919) 56 S.L.R. 625 (H.L.).

[26] In *Guinness plc v. Saunders* [1990] 2 A.C. 663 the House of Lords refused a *quantum meruit* claim by a director, but in rather different circumstances, where there was no doubt as to the validity of the appointment.

[27] *Quaere* whether there is any contract between a company and its directors arising out of the appointment alone: *Newtherapeutics Ltd v. Katz* [1990] BCLC 700.

respects may be said to be (1) quasi-trustees or fiduciaries, and
(2) agents for the company. The result is that they owe fiduciary
duties and certain duties of care to the company, as will be
explained later.

> "The Directors are a body to whom is delegated the duty of
> managing the general affairs of the Company. A corporate body can
> only act by agents, and it is of course the duty of those agents so to
> act as best to promote the interests of the corporation whose affairs
> they are conducting. Such agents have duties to discharge of a
> fiduciary nature towards their principal. And it is a rule of universal
> application that no one, having such duties to discharge, shall be
> allowed to enter into engagements in which he has, or can have, a
> personal interest conflicting, or which possibly may conflict, with the
> interests of those whom he is bound to protect": *per* Lord Cranworth
> L.C. in *Aberdeen Rlwy. Co. v. Blaikie Bros.* (1854) 1 Macq. 461 at
> p. 471.
>
> "The directors are the mere trustees or agents of the company—
> trustees of the company's money and property—agents in the trans-
> actions which they enter into on behalf of the company": *per* Lord
> Selborne L.C. in *Great Eastern Rlwy. Co. v. Turner* (1872) L.R. 8
> Ch. 149 at p. 152.
>
> "The director's functions are in one view those of an agent, and in
> another those of trustee. But the former predominate over the
> latter": *per* Lord Johnston in *McLintock v. Campbell*, 1916 S.C. 966
> at p. 980.

Since a director's fiduciary duties only apply to his acts *qua*
director, his acts *qua* shareholder are not so affected. Thus, a
director has the same right as any other shareholder to transfer
his shares to a man of straw in order to avoid payment of a call,[28]
and he may exercise his voting power at general meetings, even
though the effect is to increase his own remuneration[29] or to
prevent the calling up of a loan made by the company to
himself.[30]

On the other hand, the fiduciary nature of a director's position
will not allow a director of a listed company who is negotiating
the sale of his strategic shareholding in the company to insist on a
service contract with the company from the purchasers, nor may
he promise the purchasers the right to appoint directors. Such
matters are for the company, and attempts at such a bargain are
"commercially disreputable".[31]

[28] *M'Lintock v. Campbell*, 1916 S.C. 966.
[29] *Harris v. A. Harris Ltd*, 1936 S.C. 183.
[30] *Baird v. J. Baird & Co. (Falkirk) Ltd*, 1949 S.L.T. 368 (O.H.).
[31] *Wilton Group plc v. Abrams* [1990] BCC 310.

## Directors as fiduciaries

Directors have been described as trustees (1) of the company's money and property,[32] and (2) of the powers entrusted to them. More properly they may be regarded as being in a fiduciary position to the company because the company's money and property are not vested in them but in the company. They are liable as if they were trustees.

Thus they must act as regards the company's property as if they were trustees for the company although of course the company is the legal owner. Such property must be applied for the specified purposes of the company and a misapplication of it is a breach of fiduciary duty.[33] Where a person has improperly profited from his fiduciary position the court has equitable jurisdiction to award interest on the judgment for damages for misfeasance or breach of duty as a director.[34]

In an action to recover moneys of the company misapplied by them, directors can in England rely on the Limitation Act 1980, s.21, as if they were trustees,[35] *i.e.* the action must be brought within six years except where they have been guilty of fraud, or where the property is still in their possession or has been previously converted to their own use.

Directors are fiduciaries of their powers in the sense that, as will be explained later,[36] they must exercise them for the purposes for which they were conferred and bona fide for the benefit of the company as a whole. They must not put themselves in a position where their duty and interest conflict.

Directors had power to issue the unissued shares of the company. The company was in no need of further capital, but the directors made a fresh issue to themselves and their supporters with the object of maintaining control of the company and resisting the election of three additional directors which would have made the two existing directors a

---

[32] *Per* Lord Selborne L.C. in *Great Eastern Rlwy. Co. v. Turner* (1872) L.R. 8 Ch. 149 at p. 152.

[33] *Selangor United Rubber Estates Ltd v. Cradock (No. 3)* [1968] 1 W.L.R. 1555, *post*, p. 366; *Bishopsgate Investment Management v. Maxwell (No. 2)* [1993] BCLC 1282.

[34] *Wallersteiner v. Moir (No. 2)* [1975] Q.B. 373 (C.A.), where the interest awarded was compound interest at one per cent per annum above the official bank rate or minimum lending rate in operation at the time.

[35] *Re Lands Allotment Co.* [1894] 1 Ch. 616 (C.A.), *cf. John S. Boyle Ltd v. Boyle's Trustees*, 1949 S.L.T. (Notes) 45 (O.H.).

[36] p. 351.

# 346

minority on the board: *Held,* the allotment of the shares was invalid and void. Directors are not entitled to use their power of issuing shares merely for the purpose of maintaining their control or the control of themselves and their friends over the affairs of the company, or merely for the purpose of defeating the wishes of the existing majority of shareholders. The power to issue shares is primarily given to directors for the purpose of enabling them to raise capital when required for the company: *Piercy v. S. Mills & Co. Ltd* [1920] 1 Ch. 77.[37]

The extent of the directors' fiduciary position is constantly being tested in the courts. The Court of Appeal has held that there is no rule that directors cannot bind themselves as to the future exercise of their powers in a particular manner if the contract as a whole is substantially for the benefit of the company, *e.g.* where money is paid to a company by a developer and the directors agree to support the latter's application for planning permission,[38] despite strong earlier decisions that in such cases the directors' duty to the company must override any such agreement where the two subsequently became irreconcilable.[39] Again in *Elliott v. Wheeldon,*[40] it was held that it was at least arguable that where there was a joint venture agreement between two people operating through the medium of a company of which they both became directors and one director continued his pre-existing personal guarantee of that company's debts, the other director owed a duty to his fellow director not to act as a director so as to increase the latter's liability under the guarantee. The questions as to whether a director can owe fiduciary duties to a shareholder as distinct from the company and who exactly is the company for this purpose are dealt with below.[41]

The consequence of directors owing fiduciary duties is that liability may arise even if there is no loss or common law fraud involved. Those affected, *i.e.* the company, can recover under the remedy of account which requires simply that the fiduciary, the director, has abused his powers or made a profit out of his position. Unlike the common law remedy of damages no loss need be shown.

[37] *Cook v. Barry, Henry & Cook Ltd,* 1923 S.L.T. 692 (O.H.). See now s.80.
[38] *Fulham Football Club Ltd v. Cabra Estates plc* [1994] 1 BCLC 363 (C.A.).
[39] *Rackham v. Peek Foods Ltd* [1990] BCLC 895; *John Crowther Group plc v. Carpets International plc* [1990] BCLC 460; *Dawson International plc v. Coats Patons plc* 1988 S.L.T. 854 (O.H.).
[40] [1993] BCLC 53.
[41] See *post,* p. 349.

Since directors owe fiduciary duties to the company it follows that if there is a fraudulent or dishonest breach of such a duty and company property is misapplied, anyone who receives such property with knowledge of the breach of duty will be liable to the company as a constructive trustee. Knowledge for this purpose originally meant actual or constructive notice,[42] but in *Re Montague's S.T.*,[43] it was doubted whether anything less than actual notice or deliberate ignorance would suffice. Subsequently, in one case, the required knowledge has been stated as being actual knowledge, or deliberately not knowing, or where the circumstances were such that a reasonable man would have inferred what was going on—in all cases proof of dishonesty or lack of probity was required,[44] and in another case the test has been framed as whether an honest and reasonable man would have realised that the money was trust money and was probably being misapplied.[45] In addition, anyone who assists in the breach will also be liable to account to the company if he has knowledge of the breach. For this purpose knowledge has been defined as either actual knowledge or wilfully shutting one's eye to the obvious or, possibly, wilfully and recklessly failing to make the enquiries which an honest and reasonable man would have made.[46]

### Directors as agents

Directors are agents through whom a company acts,[47] and it is largely because they are agents that they were originally regarded as owing fiduciary duties and certain duties of care to the company.

"Directors of a company are fiduciary agents, and a power conferred upon them cannot be exercised in order to obtain some private

---

[42] *Selangor United Rubber Estates Ltd v. Cradock (No. 3)* [1968] 2 All E.R. 1073, *Belmont Finance Ltd v. Williams Furniture Ltd (No. 2)* [1980] 1 All E.R. 393, *International Sales and Agencies Ltd v. Marcus* [1982] 3 All E.R. 551.
[43] 1987 Ch. 264
[44] *Eagle Trust plc v. SBC Securities Ltd* [1991] BCLC 438.
[45] *El Anjou v. Dollar Land Holdings plc* [1994] 1 BCLC 464 (C.A.).
[46] *Belmont Finance Ltd v. Williams Furniture Ltd, supra, Baden, Delvaux and Lécuit v. Société General etc.* [1983] BCLC 325. Some approval for this classification was given by Fox L.J. in *Agip (Africa) Ltd v. Jackson* [1991] Ch. 547.
[47] See, *e.g. per* Lord Selborne L.C. in *Great Eastern Rlwy. Co. v. Turner* (1872) L.R. 8 Ch. 149 at p. 152. See Chap. 6.

advantage or for any purpose foreign to the power": *per* Dixon J. in
*Mills v. Mills* (1938) 60 C.L.R. 150 at p. 186.

Like other agents, directors incur no personal liability on
contracts made by them on behalf of the company, within the
scope of their authority.[48]

E. contracted to supply goods to a company of which H. was chairman
of directors, payment to be made by the issue of £600 of the company's
debentures. The contract was made at a board meeting at which H. was
chairman. E. constantly pressed for the debentures, but none was issued,
and eventually the company was wound up. *Held,* H. was not liable to
an action at the suit of E.: *Elkington & Co. v. Hürter* [1892] 2 Ch. 452.

If, however, directors exceed the powers given to them by the
memorandum and articles they will be liable for breach of
warranty of authority.[49] Their actions may be ratified by the
company in general meeting even if they have acted contrary to
the company's constitution.[50]

Directors may be *specifically appointed* agents for the shareholders to negotiate a sale of the company's shares. If so, the
shareholders are liable for their fraud.

R., managing director of N. Ltd, by frauds of which the other
directors were ignorant, made N. Ltd profitable, and negotiated with E.
Ltd for the sale of the shares in N. Ltd without disclosing that the profits
were based on dishonest trading. The negotiations were reported to the
shareholders who, in ignorance of R.'s fraud, authorised R. to complete
the sale on the basis of his negotiations. The fraud was subsequently
discovered and the shareholders were sued for damages. *Held,* they were
liable as R. was their agent to negotiate the sale of their shares, and they
were liable for his fraud even though it preceded his appointment as
agent: *Briess v. Woolley* [1954] A.C. 333.

Further, directors may *hold themselves out* to the shareholders
as agents for the shareholders, in which case the directors must
disclose any profit made by them to the shareholders.

Directors entered into negotiations for the amalgamation of the
company with other companies. Before the negotiations were completed
they induced a number of shareholders to give them options on their
shares at par, representing that this was necessary to effect the amal-

[48] Directors may be personally liable under s.349(4), *ante,* p. 57.
[49] *Firbank's Exors. v. Humphreys* (1886) 18 Q.B.D. 54 (C.A.).
[50] See Chap. 6.

gamation. The directors then exercised the option and thereby made a handsome profit. *Held,* they had to account for this profit to the shareholders: *Allen v. Hyatt* (1914) 30 T.L.R. 444,[51] distinguishing *Percival v. Wright,* below.

## DUTIES OF DIRECTORS

**To whom are the duties owed?**

In general, directors owe their fiduciary duties[52] and duties of care[53] to the company. Traditionally this has meant the members as a body to the exclusion of the interests of employees, creditors or individual shareholders. However, the position is changing. The Act itself, in section 309, first introduced in 1980, provides that directors must also have regard to the interests of the employees as a whole. This section has two weaknesses. First it makes no attempt to resolve the position where the interests of the members and those of the employees conflict and second it provides the employees with no means of enforcing this duty. As we shall see in Chapter 18, since the duties of directors are owed to the company only the company may enforce them and this means either a majority of the shareholders or, in exceptional cases, a minority shareholder but not the employees.

The courts have now accepted that the traditional concept of the members' interests being paramount in considering directors' duties may be displaced by the interests of the creditors where the company is operating under doubtful solvency. In *Liquidator of West Mercia Safetywear Ltd v. Dodd,*[54] the Court of Appeal adopted the following statement of Street C.J. in the Australian case of *Kinsela v. Russell Kinsela Pty Ltd*[55]:

> "In a solvent company the proprietary interests of the shareholders entitle them as a general body to be regarded as the company when questions of the duty of directors arise . . . But where a company is insolvent the interests of the creditors intrude. They become prospectively entitled, through the mechanism of liquidation, to displace the

[51] See also *Munro v. Bogie* [1994] 1 BCLC 415 CS (O.H.)
[52] *Per* Lord Cranworth L.C. in *Aberdeen Railway Co. v. Blaikie Bros.* (1854) 1 Macq. 461 at p. 471.
[53] *Per* Romer J. in *Re City Equitable Fire Insurance Co. Ltd* [1925] Ch. 407 at p. 428.
[54] [1988] BCLC 250 (C.A.). See also *Nicholson v. Permakraft (N.Z.) Ltd* [1985] N.Z.L.R. 242.
[55] [1986] 4 N.S.W.L.R. 722 at p. 730.

power of the shareholders and directors to deal with the company's, assets. It is in a practical sense their assets and not the shareholders' assets that, through the medium of the company, are under the management of the directors pending liquidation, return to solvency, or the imposition of some alternative administration."

The importance of this is that in such cases the members would not be able to ratify the acts of the directors so as to excuse them from liability which they could otherwise do if the company was solvent.[56] On the other hand, directors are only required to act in good faith in such situations, they are not to be regarded as liquidators.[57] It has also been held that directors owe no duty of care to individual creditors for economic loss.[58] But in *Brady v. Brady*,[59] the House of Lords left open the question as to whether the interests of the creditors were relevant to the issue of whether financial assistance for the acquisition of its own shares by a company had been given in good faith in the interests of the company.[60]

With regard to individual shareholders the traditional view has been that the directors are not trustees for them so that they may, for example, purchase shares from an individual shareholder without disclosing any information which they may have which affects the value of the shares, such as negotiations for the sale of the company. This is based on the decision to that effect in *Percival v. Wright*[61] but this case has been doubted as creating an absolute rule in both New Zealand[62] and England[63] and distinguished by the Privy Council where there has been a specific finding that the directors were acting as agents for the shareholder in question.[64] The position is perhaps best expressed by Browne-Wilkinson V.-C. in *Re Chez Nico (Restaurants) Ltd.*[65]

"Like the Court of Appeal in New Zealand, I consider the law to be that in general, directors do not owe fiduciary duties to share-

[56] *Re DKG Contractors Ltd* [1990] BCC 903; cf. *Multinational Gas & Petrochemical Co. Ltd v. Multinational Gas & Petrochemical Services Ltd* [1983] Ch. 258 (C.A.). The position may not actually arise because of the statutory liability of directors for wrongful trading, *post,* p. 367.
[57] *Re Welfab Engineers Ltd* [1990] BCLC 833.
[58] *Nordic Oil Services Ltd v. Berman,* 1993 S.L.T. 1168 (O.H.).
[59] [1989] A.C. 755 (H.L.).
[60] *Ante,* p. 201.
[61] [1902] 2 Ch. 421.
[62] *Coleman v. Myers* [1977] 2 N.Z.L.R. 225 (C.A.).
[63] *Re Chez Nico (Restaurants) Ltd* [1992] BCLC 192.
[64] *Allen v. Hyatt* (1914) 30 T.L.R. 444 (P.C.), see *ante,* p. 348.
[65] [1992] BCLC 192 at p. 208.

holders but owe them to the company: however, in certain special circumstances fiduciary duties, carrying with them a duty of disclosure, can arise which place directors in a fiduciary capacity *vis-à-vis* the shareholders."

As the law develops it will become clearer as to what these special circumstances may be. In *Dawson International plc v. Coats Patons plc,*[66] it was said that if the directors chose to give shareholders advice about a take-over offer they must act in good faith but that this was a fiduciary duty owed to the company, *i.e.* the present and future members and not to the current members as vendors of their shares. In *Munro v. Bogie,*[67] the articles, by appointing the directors as agents for shareholders wishing to sell their shares with a duty to find purchasers for those shares, were held to create a duty of disclosure on the directors to the shareholders as to factors affecting the value of those shares, even though the valuation was to be by the auditors.

## Fiduciary duties

The fiduciary duties of directors are:

(1) to exercise their powers within the company's constitution, bona fide for the benefit of the company as a whole,[68] as defined above, and in some cases for their "proper purpose";

(2) not to put themselves in a position in which their duties to the company and their personal interests may conflict.[69]

## Exercise of powers

With regard to the exercise of their wide powers of management it is clear that directors must act bona fide for the benefit of the company and not for any collateral purpose such as to benefit or protect themselves. But with respect to certain powers that will not be enough; it will also be a breach of duty if the directors

---

[66] 1988 S.L.T. 854 (O.H.), affirmed on other grounds 1989 S.L.T. 655; *cf. Re A Company* [1986] BCLC 382.

[67] [1994] 1 BCLC 415, CS (O.H.).

[68] And not, *e.g.* for his fellow directors: *Lee v. Chou When Hsien* [1985] BCLC 45 (P.C.); *ante,* p. 324.

[69] *Guinness plc v. Saunders* [1990] 2 A.C. 633 (H.C.).

do not exercise that power for the purpose for which it was granted even if they are acting bona fide, etc. An example of this is the power to allot new shares, which is a fiduciary power, even though now subject to controls in section 80, *ante*. The purpose of that power is to raise capital for the company and for no other purpose, (*i.e.* the prevention of a take-over bid).[70]

Directors, in an endeavour to secure control in order to forestall a take-over bid, issued unissued shares in the company to trustees to be held for the benefit of employees, the shares being paid for by the trustees out of an interest-free loan from the company. *Held*, the issue exceeded the directors' fiduciary power, it being immaterial that it was made in the bona fide belief that it was in the interests of the company. Since the directors did not hold the majority of the shares before the new issue, the issue could be ratified by the company in general meeting, the votes carried by the shares issued to the trustees not being exercised: *Hogg v. Cramphorn Ltd* [1967] Ch. 254.

The reasoning in *Hogg v. Cramphorn* was criticised and distinguished in Canada in the case of *Teck Corporation Ltd v. Millar*[71] on the basis that it was an exception to the general rule that directors must act bona fide in what they consider to be the best interests of the company. It was not correct to say that issuing shares otherwise than to raise capital was always a breach of duty. Directors were entitled to consider the reputation, experience and policies of anyone seeking to take-over the company. If they decided on reasonable grounds that the take-over would cause substantial damage to the company's interests they were entitled to use their powers to protect the company.

This divergence of view was considered by the Privy Council in the case of *Howard Smith Ltd v. Ampol Petroleum Ltd*[72] where, on similar facts to *Hogg v. Cramphorn,* the judge had established (i) that the primary purpose of the allotment was not to raise money but to destroy the existing majority block of shares and (ii) that the directors were not motivated by self-interest. The Privy Council rejected both extreme arguments—*i.e.* that once no self-interest is discovered there can be no breach of duty, and that an allotment of shares can only be made to raise capital— any other purpose being wrong. Instead they considered that no

---

[70] *Piercy v. S. Mills & Co. Ltd* [1920] 1 Ch. 77; *Hogg v. Cramphorn Ltd* [1967] Ch. 254; *Bamford v. Bamford* [1970] Ch. 212 (C.A.).

[71] (1972) 33 D.L.R. (3d) 288.

[72] [1974] A.C. 821 (P.C.).

limitation can be placed in advance on the exercise of the directors' powers. The court must examine the substantial purpose for which the power was exercised and whether that purpose was proper or not. The court must respect the directors' opinion on questions of management but in other cases it is a question for decision in each case. Although *Teck's* case was concerned with an area of management this was not—it was a question of altering an existing majority shareholding into a minority one. In *Mutual Life Insurance v. The Rank Organisation*,[73] Goulding J. applied this distinction between areas of management and others in upholding a rights issue which was not available to certain U.S. shareholders. Unlike the *Howard Smith* case it did not upset the *status quo* but maintained the investment policy of the company.

In the *Howard Smith* case it was said that it was unconstitutional for the directors to exercise their powers purely for the purpose of destroying an existing majority or creating a new majority which had not previously existed and as such it was not an area of management. The company's constitution is separate and distinct from the powers themselves. Thus it would be a breach of duty for the directors to operate contrary to the memorandum or articles of the company[74] or to enter into a contract on behalf of the company whereby they remained in post as directors so that the shareholders could not exercise their constitutional rights to appoint new directors.[75] In other cases which are regarded as being management areas, however, the courts will simply apply the bona fide test to decide whether the directors have acted in breach of their duty in exercising a power under the articles, *e.g.* to vary the terms of the managing director's service contract.[76] That raises the question as to what is meant by bona fide in the interests of the company.

In *Rolled Steel Products (Holdings) Ltd v. British Steel Corporation*,[77] the Court of Appeal suggested that the question of whether a power had been exercised bona fide for the benefit of the company could be answered by applying the tests laid down by Eve J. in *Re Lee Behrens & Co. Ltd*[78] and formerly applied to determine whether an act was *ultra vires* the company or not.[79] These tests are:

---

[73] [1985] BCLC 11.
[74] See Chaps. 3 and 6.
[75] *Lee Panavision Ltd v. Lee Lighting Ltd* [1992] BCLC 22 (C.A.).
[76] *Runciman v. Walter Runciman plc.* [1992] BCLC 1084.
[77] [1984] BCLC 466 (C.A.).
[78] [1932] 2 Ch. 46.
[79] Chap. 3, *ante*.

(1) is the transaction reasonably incidental to the carrying on of the company's business; (2) is it a bona fide transaction; (3) is it done for the benefit and prosperity of the company.

If directors exercise a power in good faith, their judgment is not open to review by the courts. The duty is for the directors to act bona fide in what they consider—not what a Court may consider—is in the interests of the company.[80] However, although it would be wrong for the courts to question the correctness of the management's decision on a question of management, if bona fide arrived at, when the question is whether directors exercised a power for one purpose or another, the courts are entitled to look at the situation objectively in order to ascertain how substantial an alleged requirement may have been.[81]

A nominee director, e.g. a director appointed by a shareholder, owes the same duties to the company as any other director.[82]

## Undisclosed benefits of directors

Because a director is in a fiduciary position, he must not make an undisclosed profit by reason of that position. If he does, he must account for it to the company. It is immaterial that the company itself could not have obtained the profit. The company in general meeting may, however, consent to such a profit being made or kept.

A. was a director of B. Co. and, on the company's behalf, contracted for the building of fishing smacks. Unknown to the company, he was paid a commission on the contract by the shipbuilders. A. was also a shareholder in an ice company which, in addition to dividends, paid bonuses to shareholders who were owners of fishing smacks and who employed the ice company in supplying ice to the fishing smacks. A. employed the ice company in respect of B. Co.'s fishing smacks and

---

[80] Re Smith and Fawcett Ltd [1942] Ch. 304; Runciman v. Walter Runciman plc. [1992] BCLC 1084.
[81] Howard Smith case, ante.
[82] Per Lord Denning in Meyer v. Scottish C.W.S. Ltd, 1958 S.C. (H.L.) 40 at pp. 67, 68; [1959] A.C. 324 at pp. 366, 367; per Ungoed-Thomas J. in Selangor United Rubber Estates Ltd v. Cradock (No. 3) [1968] 1 W.L.R. 1555, at pp. 1613, 1614; cf., e.g. per Jacobs J. in Re Broadcasting Station 2 GB Pty. Ltd [1964–65] N.S.W.R. 1648; at p. 1663, where he said that so long as the nominee directors believed that the interests of the shareholder who nominated them were identical with those of the company, they could follow the wishes of the shareholder without a close personal analysis of the issues.

received the bonus. *Held,* A. must account to B. Co. for both the commission and the bonus, although the bonus could never have been received by B. Co. as it was not a shareholder in the ice company: *Boston Deep Sea Fishing Co. v. Ansell* (1888) 39 Ch.D. 339 (C.A.).

R. Ltd owned one cinema and wanted to buy two others with a view to selling the three together. R. Ltd formed a subsidiary company to buy the two cinemas, but was unable to provide all the capital required; so all the directors of R. Ltd except one subscribed for some of the shares in the subsidiary themselves. The cinemas were acquired and the shares in R. Ltd and the subsidiary sold at a profit. *Held,* the former directors who subscribed for shares in the subsidiary themselves must account to R. Ltd for the profit they made, because it was only through the knowledge and opportunity they gained as directors of R. Ltd that they were able to obtain the shares. The one former director who did not himself subscribe but merely found someone else to do so was under no liability nor was a solicitor who was invited to subscribe by the directors: *Regal (Hastings) Ltd v. Gulliver*[83]

A director must not divert to his own use a "maturing business opportunity" which his company is pursuing even after his resignation, at least if his resignation is prompted by that desire.[84] There is no breach of duty, however, if a director investigates the possibility of setting up his own business whilst still a director.[85] He may not use confidential information obtained in his capacity as a director for his own use, but this does not apply to general information, *e.g.* as to a particular market.[86]

In the *Regal* case the directors could have protected themselves by a resolution (either antecedent or subsequent) of the Regal shareholders in general meeting,[87] and the case was distinguished in *Lindgren v. L. & P. Estates Ltd*[88] where the directors were released from liability by the company retaining them on the board, after it had knowledge of the facts (the alleged breach of duty was that the directors had merely "rubber-stamped" the decision of other persons).

"The rule of equity which insists on those, who by use of a fiduciary position make a profit, being liable to account for that profit, in no

---

[83] [1967] 2 A.C. 134 (Note), applied in *Phipps v. Boardman* [1967] 2 A.C. 46.
[84] *Industrial Development Consultants Ltd v. Cooley* [1972] 1 W.L.R. 443; *Island Export Finance Ltd v. Umunna* [1986] BCLC 460.
[85] *Balston Ltd v. Headline Filters Ltd* [1990] F.S.R. 385.
[86] *Island Export Finance Ltd v. Umunna (ante).*
[87] *Per* Lord Russell of Killowen at p. 150.
[88] [1968] Ch. 572 (C.A.), in which is was also held that the prospective directors of a company owe no duty to it and that directors of a parent company owe no duty to, and are not debarred from contracting with, a subsidiary with an independent board.

way depends on fraud, or absence of bona fides; or upon such
questions or considerations as whether the profit would or should
otherwise have gone to the plaintiff [*i.e.* the company], or whether
the profiteer was under a duty to obtain the source of the profit for
the plaintiff, or whether he took a risk or acted as he did for the
benefit of the plaintiff, or whether the plaintiff has in fact been
damaged or benefited by his action. The liability arises from the mere
fact of a profit having, in the stated circumstances, been made. The
profiteer, however honest and well-intentioned, cannot escape the
risk of being called upon to account": *per* Lord Russell of Killowen in
the *Regal* case at p. 144.

In a case before the Privy Council the managing director of a
company obtained licences for the company to develop a mine
but it was unable to proceed owing to financial problems. He
resigned and with the knowledge of the directors, he developed
the mine himself. The Privy Council held that he was not liable to
account for his profits since the rejection by the company and the
knowledge of the board excused him: *Queensland Mines Ltd v.
Hudson.*[89] This decision also has some Canadian support,[90] but
seems to be out of line with the established U.K. position as
established by the *Regal* case.[91]

Another example of the principle that a director must not
make a secret profit out of his position is that a director must not,
without the consent of the company, accept from a promoter any
gift, *e.g.* of shares or money, either while any negotiations
between the promoter and the company are still going on or after
they have been completed.[92]

## Disclosure of directors' interests in corporate transactions

It soon became established that the application of fiduciary
principles to directors allowed a company to avoid any contract
which the board entered into on its behalf in which one or more
of the directors had an interest, unless that interest had been

[89] (1978) 18 A.L.R. 1 (PC).
[90] *Peso Silver Mines Ltd v. Cropper* (1966) 58 D.L.R. (2d) 1.
[91] For Scotland see Lord Young in *Great North of Scotland Railway Co. v.
Urquhart* (1884) 21 S.L.R. 377, 382, and *Laughland v. Millar, Laughland &
Co.* (1904) 6 F. 413 (contract for indirect secret benefit of director held
unenforceable).
[92] *Eden v. Ridsdales Railways Lamp Co. Ltd* (1899) 23 Q.B.D. 368 (C.A.);
*Archer's Case* [1892] 1 Ch. 322 (C.A.); *Henderson v. The Huntington Copper
etc. Co. Ltd* (1877) 5 R. (H.L.) 1; *Scottish Pacific Coast Mining Co. Ltd v.
Falkner, Bell & Co.* (1888) 15 R. 290.

disclosed to the company and approved by the general meeting.[93] Any benefit derived by the director from such a contract could also be recovered.[94] This need to disclose an interest was extended to include not only contracts made directly with a director, *e.g.* a service contract, but also those in which he had an interest, *e.g.* as a shareholder[95] or partner[96] of the other contracting party.

It is not surprising that this strict rule was unacceptable to the business community and companies began to modify the application of the principle by clauses in their articles so as to avoid the embarrassment and delay involved in disclosure to and approval by the general meeting. Such articles are now commonplace in modern company constitutions. Regulation 85 of Table A provides:

> Subject to the provisions of the Act, and provided that he has disclosed to the directors the nature and extent of any material interest of his, a director notwithstanding his office:
>
> (a)   may be a party to, or otherwise interested in, any transactions or arrangement with the company or in which the company is otherwise interested;
> (b)   may be a director or other officer of, or employed by, or a party to any transaction or arrangement with, or otherwise interested in, any body corporate promoted by the company or in which the company is otherwise interested; and
> (c)   shall not, by reason of his office, be accountable to the company for any benefit which he derives from any such office or employment or from any such transaction or arrangement or from any interest in any such body corporate and no such transaction or arrangement shall be liable to be avoided on the grounds of any such interest or benefit.

Regulation 86 provides:

> For the purposes of regulation 85—
> (a)   a general notice given to the directors that a director is to be regarded as having an interest of the nature and extent specified in the notice in any transaction or arrangement

---

[93] *Aberdeen Ry. Co. v. Blackie Bros.* (1854) 1 Macq. 461.
[94] *Per* Lord Cairns L.C. in *Parker v. McKenna* (1874) L.R. 10 Ch. App. 96 at p. 118.
[95] *Transvaal Lands Co. v. New Belgium (Transvaal) Land, Co.* [1914] 2 Ch. 488 (C.A.).
[96] *Costa Rica Ry. v. Forwood* [1901] 1 Ch. 746 (C.A.).

in which a specified person or class of person is interested
shall be deemed to be a disclosure that the director has an
interest in any such transaction of the nature and extent so
specified; and

(b)  an interest of which a director has no knowledge and of
which it is unreasonable to expect him to have knowledge
shall not be treated as an interest of his.

Parliament intervened in the 1929 Act to prevent some of the
more excessive clauses in the articles of companies. The modern
provision, in section 317 of the 1985 Act, provides a statutory
duty on a director who is in any way, directly or indirectly,
interested in any actual or proposed contract, transaction or
arrangement with the company to declare the nature of that
interest at a meeting of the board of directors. Loans and other
credit transactions involving directors or connected persons are
specifically included in this.

Disclosure must be made to the board of the nature of the
director's interest, however slight, but the section does not
require any other information.[97] Disclosure under the section
must be made at the first meeting of the board at which the
transaction is discussed or, if the director was not present, at the
next meeting held after he became so interested. If a director
subsequently becomes interested in a transaction after it is made,
disclosure must be made at the next meeting of the board,
whether or not it would be on the agenda. Alternatively a
director may give a general notice to the board to the effect that
he is a member of a specific company or firm and is interested in
any transaction made with that company or firm or that he is
interested in any transaction made with a specific person with
whom the director is connected.

The immediate question which arises is how the statutory duty
of disclosure to the board relates both to the equitable duty of
disclosure to the company and provisions in the articles which
seek to modify that equitable duty such as article 85 above. The
section itself merely imposes a fine on the director for non-
compliance but also provides that nothing in the section "prejudices the operation of any rule of law restricting directors from
having an interest" in corporate transactions.

It is reasonably clear that if a director discloses his interest in
accordance with both the section and article 85, or equivalent,

---

[97] Regulation 85 requires a director to disclose the nature and extent of his
interest.

then he will be liable neither to a fine nor to the effects of the basic equitable doctrine. The validity of article 85 to avoid the latter has always been assumed under the general equitable principle that the beneficiary may waive or modify a breach of fiduciary obligations.[98] It is also clear that if a director fails to disclose his interest at all, either under the section or article 85, then not only is he liable to a fine under the section but the company may avoid the contract and recover any benefits accruing to the director under the conflict of interest and duty principle, since he will not be able to take advantage of the modification clause in the articles. This was the decision both of the Court of Appeal in *Hely-Hutchinson v. Brayhead*[99] and the House of Lords in *Guinness v. Saunders,*[1] although in both cases the company was held for other reasons not to be able to rescind the contract.[2]

A more complex situation arises where there is no disclosure of an interest by a director, either under the section or under the articles, but the articles, unlike article 85, provide that the equitable rules shall not apply even where there is no disclosure. Does non-disclosure under section 317, by itself, allow the company to rescind the contract? All three members of the Court of Appeal in *Hely-Hutchinson v. Brayhead Ltd* stated that the fact of non-disclosure under the section simply brought the normal principles of equity into play. The emphasis of each judge was, however, different. It is arguable that Lord Denning M.R. thought that the contract would be voidable since the articles could not allow the directors to contract out of their statutory duty to disclose. This was also the opinion of Lord Templeman in *Guinness v. Saunders.*[3]

Lord Pearson and, arguably, Lord Wilberforce in *Hely-Hutchinson,* on the other hand, were more inclined to the view that non-disclosure under the section had no effect on the equitable principles which therefore became a matter for the articles alone to decide. The section merely imposed a fine in default. This view has also been taken by two judges in subse-

---

[98] *Movitex Ltd v. Bulfield* [1988] BCLC 104; see *post,* p. 365.
[99] [1968] 1 Q.B. 549 (C.A.).
[1] [1990] 2 A.C. 663 (H.L.).
[2] It was impossible to restore the parties to their original position.
[3] [1990] 2 A.C. 663 at p. 695.

quent cases.[4] On that basis it must be assumed that non-disclosure under the section would not invalidate the contract where the articles absolve the director from disclosing his interest. But it has to be said that in no case has the issue arisen directly since the articles have always required disclosure and that, if directly confronted with the issue, a different conclusion might be reached. The Court of Appeal in *Lee Panavision Ltd v. Lee Lighting Ltd,*[5] expressly refused to discuss the issue.

In addition, there are other difficulties in this area which also await a solution. Article 85 requires disclosure to the board but, unlike section 317, does not specify any method of disclosure. In the *Lee Lighting Ltd* case,[6] Harman J. decided that since article 85 was expressly "subject to the provisions of the Act" the disclosure procedures in section 317 must be read into the article. The Court of Appeal in that case again expressed no opinion on this matter. This solution would give a neater result since it would not then be possible to comply with the Act but not article 85 or vice versa. The alternative would reopen the effect of non-compliance with one provision on the other which raises similar issues to those just discussed. It may, however, depend upon the wording of the particular article in question.

Another difficult area is what amounts to an interest which must be disclosed. In *Cowan de Groot Properties Ltd v. Eagle Trust,*[7] the question arose as to whether in a contract of sale between A Ltd and B Ltd a director of A who was either a creditor of B, or of shareholders of B, had a disclosable interest. The judge was of the opinion that in most cases that would not amount to a disclosable interest but that circumstances could exist where the director would have an interest in B making that contract. He did, however, state that a director who was a bare trustee for another would not have a disclosable interest. On the other hand, it is clear that section 317 applies both to the granting and variation of directors' service contracts. In *Runciman v. Walter Runciman plc,*[8] this was expressly decided despite the "apparent absurdity" of requiring such a disclosure where it is patently obvious that the director has an interest.

---

[4] *Per* Harman J. in *Lee Panavision Ltd v. Lee Lighting Ltd* [1991] BCLC 575 at p. 583; and *per* Knox J. in *Cowan de Groot Properties Ltd v. Eagle Trust plc.* [1991] BCLC 1045 at p. 1113.
[5] [1992] BCLC 22 (C.A.).
[6] [1991] BCLC 575.
[7] [1991] BCLC 1045.
[8] [1992] BCLC 1084.

Such situations, however, raise the further question of whether there can ever be implied disclosure to the board under section 317. This issue arose in the *Lee Lighting* case where the directors all knew of each others' interest in the agreement being discussed by the board. The Court of Appeal, unlike Harman J. at first instance, were reluctant to regard this as a breach of section 317 but that approach might seem to miss the point that a formal declaration would not only require the other directors to expressly consider the conflict of interest position, it would also be recorded in the minutes of the directors and there could be no suspicion of secret dealings.[8a] It remains to be decided what the penalty might be for such a technical non-disclosure.

This issue was considered by Simon Brown J. in the *Runciman* case. In the light of the difference of opinion in the *Lee Panavision* case, the judge again declined to give any definitive view on the matter. Instead he preferred to excuse the, assumed, non-declaration of the director's interest on the basis that it was purely technical and that the facts should not entitle the company (which had been taken over by means of a hostile bid) to rescind the agreement. Rescission is an equitable remedy and so is not available as of right even in cases where the right to rescind has not been lost by delay or acquiescence, etc.

**Directors competing with company**

Under the general law, apart from the case where a director has a service agreement with the company which requires him to serve only the company, there is authority to the effect that he may become a director of a rival company, *i.e.* that in this way he may compete with the first company, provided that he does not disclose to the second company any confidential information obtained by him as a director of the first company, and that what he may do for a rival company he may do for himself[9] or a rival firm. However, it has been said that he must not subordinate the interests of the first company to those of the second and that if he

---

[8a] It has been held that a single director must expressly disclose an interest to a "meeting" of the directors: *Neptune (Vehicle Washing Equipment) Ltd v. Fitzgerald, The Times,* March 2, 1995.
[9] *London & Mashonaland Exploration Co. v. New Mashonaland Exploration Co.* [1891] W.N. 165; *per* Lord Blanesburgh in *Bell v. Lever Bros. Ltd* [1932] A.C. 161 at p. 195.

does so it is at the risk of an application under section 459.[10] (Remedy in case of unfairly prejudicial conduct.)[11]

## Duties of care

Directors' duties of care towards the company were, until recently, defined in three propositions laid down by Romer J. in *Re City Equitable Fire Insurance Co. Ltd.*[12] These were:

(1) A director need not exhibit in the performance of his duties (*i.e.* his functions) a greater degree of skill than may reasonably be expected from a person of his knowledge and experience (*i.e.* the particular director's own knowledge and experience) and not that of the reasonable man. He must take such care, however, in the performance of his duties as an ordinary man might be expected to take on his own behalf.

(2) A director is not bound to give continuous attention to the affairs of his company. His duties are of an intermittent nature to be performed at periodical board meetings.

(3) In respect of all duties that, having regard to the exigencies of business, and the articles of association, may properly be left to some other official, a director is, in the absence of grounds for suspicion, justified in trusting that official to perform such duties honestly.

The first two of these propositions have, however, been substantially qualified by later cases. The standard of care as laid down in proposition (1) was first modified in respect of an executive director, *i.e.* one who has a service contract with the company. There is an implied term in such a contract that he will use reasonable skill in the performance of the duties of the office based on what might reasonably be expected from a person in his position.[13] But, more significantly, the general standard of care has been restated as being the same as the test for establishing wrongful trading under section 214(4) of the Insolvency Act 1986.[14] In *Norman v. Theodore Goddard,*[15] this was stated as

[10] *Per* Lord Denning in *Meyer v. Scottish C.W.S. Ltd,* 1958 S.C. (H.L.) 40 at p. 68; [1959] A.C. 324 at p. 368.
[11] *Post,* Chap. 18.
[12] [1925] Ch. 407, at p. 428.
[13] *Lister v. Romford Ice and Cold Storage Co. Ltd* [1957] A.C. 555.
[14] *Post,* p. 367.
[15] [1991] BCLC 1028. The director was excused liability on the basis of reasonable reliance on another under the third of Romer J.'s propositions.

being that of a reasonably diligent person having the knowledge, skill and experience both of a person carrying out that director's functions and of that person himself. Thus the test is both objective and subjective. This test was also applied in *Re D'Jan of London Ltd*[16] to establish the negligence of a director in signing an inaccurate fire insurance proposal form to insure the company's property.

The attendance duty under proposition (2) has also been tightened up. In *Dorchester Finance Co. Ltd v. Stebbing,*[17] two non-executive directors were held to be negligent in not attending board meetings of a subsidiary company even though it was shown that it was not commercial practice to do so.

Duties of care, as is the case with fiduciary duties, can always be ratified by the company.[18]

## Other liablities

In certain cases a director may be personally liable for some wrong or debt connected with his company. In *C. Evans and Sons Ltd v. Spritebrand Ltd,*[19] the Court of Appeal discussed a director's liability for torts committed by his company. They decided that a director is not automatically liable for such torts even if it is a small company over which he exercised total control. It is necessary to examine the role he played in regard to the commission of the tort. On the other hand it would not always be necessary to prove that the director had acted recklessly or knowing that the company's acts were tortious. If the tort itself required negligence or recklessness then the director's state of mind might well be relevant, but for torts of strict liability different considerations could apply.

On the other hand, a director will be personally liable in tort to a third party if he makes a personal statement in connection with the company's business which is either negligent or deceitful and which he knows is being relied upon by the person receiving it. This is a separate personal liability.[20]

---

[16] [1994] 1 BCLC 561. See *post,* p. 367.
[17] [1989] BCLC 498.
[18] *Pavlides v. Jensen* [1956] Ch. 565.
[19] [1985] 1 W.L.R. 317.
[20] *Thomas Saunders Partnership v. Harvey, The Independent,* May 5, 1989.

## Contribution between directors

The liability of directors for breaches of trust is joint and several,[21] so that where the directors have misapplied the company's funds, as by paying dividends out of capital or advancing money for an unauthorised purpose, a director who has been sued for the misapplication is entitled to contribution from the other directors who were parties to it.[22] If, however, the money misappropriated has been applied for the sole benefit of one of the directors, that director is not entitled to obtain contribution.[23]

## Relief of directors from liability for breach of duty

### By a resolution in general meeting

Since directors' fiduciary duties are owed to the members as a body, the majority of the members in general meeting may, at least while the company is solvent, after full disclosure of all material circumstances, waive a breach of fiduciary duty by a director.[24] If the breach involves acting contrary to the company's memorandum or articles such ratification must be by a special resolution.[25] In any case, however, if his is a member, the director may vote in favour of waiver, provided that there is no fraud on the minority of the members.

The directors of a company contracted to buy a ship from a vendor who was a director. (This was a breach of duty by him since the articles contained no clause authorising a director to contract with the company. Further, there was at the time no section like the present section 199, *post*). At a general meeting a resolution affirming the contract was carried, against the wishes of the minority shareholders, by reason of the fact that the vendor held the majority of the shares in the company. *Held,* the resolution was valid. As a shareholder, the vendor was merely using his voting power to his own advantage, and there was no question of a fraud on the minority—there was no unfairness or impropriety: *N.-W. Transportation Co. v. Beatty* (1887) 12 App.Cas. 589 (P.C.).

Two directors of a construction company negotiated for a construction contract in the usual way in which the company's business was carried

---

[21] *Bishopsgate Investment Management Ltd v. Maxwell (No. 2)* [1993] BCLC 1282.
[22] *Ramskill v. Edwards* (1886) 31 Ch.D. 100; see also (for England) Civil Liability (Contribution) Act 1978, and (for Scotland) Law Reform (Miscellaneous Provisions) (Scotland) Act 1940, s.3.
[23] *Walsh v. Bardsley* (1931) 47 T.L.R. 564.
[24] *Bamford v. Bamford* [1970] Ch. 212 (C.A.), *ante*, p. 330.
[25] ss.35(3), 35A(5). See Chap. 6, *ante*.

on, and then took the contract in their own names. A meeting of the company was called, and by their votes as holders of three-quarters of the shares a resolution was passed declaring that the company had no interest in the contract. *Held,* the benefit of the contract belonged to the company and the directors must account to the company for it, and the purported ratification was a fraud on the minority and ineffective: *Cook v. Deeks* [1916] 1 A.C. (P.C.).

The position will be different if the company is operating under doubtful solvency since the duties may then be owed to the creditors rather than the members of the company.[26]

## Not by a provision in the articles

Under the general law a director can be exempted from liability for breach of duty by a provision in the articles of the company. However, section 310, first introduced in 1929, states that, subject as below, any provision, whether in the articles or in any contract with the company or otherwise, for exempting a director or other officer or the auditor from liability for negligence, default, breach of duty or breach of trust in relation to the company, or indemnifying him against such liability, is void.

One problem with the section is that it appears to be inconsistent with regulation 85 of Table A (and similar articles) which allow a director to have an interest in a transaction etc. subject to disclosure to the board. Insofar as this is an attempt to relieve the director from the conflict of interest rule (*supra*) is it not exempting him from a breach of duty or trust and so void under section 310? In *Movitex Ltd v. Bulfield*[27] Vinelott J. resolved the difficulty by deciding that the conflict of interest rule was a disability imposed by equity and not a duty owed by the director. Thus by modifying the rule the articles are removing a disability and not exempting a breach of duty under section 310.

The section goes on to provide that the company may, in pursuance of a provision in the articles etc., indemnify such a person against any liability, *i.e.* against any costs, incurred by him in defending any proceedings, civil or criminal, in which judgment is given in his favour or in which he is acquitted,[28] or in connection with any application under section 727 in which relief is granted to him by the court.

---

[26] *Re DKG Contractors Ltd* [1990] BCC 903; *ante,* p. 349.
[27] [1988] BCLC 104.
[28] *cf. Tomlinson v. Liquidators of Scottish Amalgamated Silks Ltd,* 1935 S.C. (H.L.) 1.

There is a further exemption provided by the section in
relation to indemnity insurance policies taken out by companies
in favour of their directors as cover for any such liability for
breach of duty. Any such policy must be disclosed in the
Directors' Report however.[29]

## By the court

Section 727 provides that if, in proceedings for negligence,
default, breach of duty or breach of trust against a director or
other officer or auditor of a company, it appears that he has acted
honestly and reasonably, and that, having regard to all the
circumstances, including those connected with his appointment,
he ought fairly to be excused, the court may relieve him, wholly
or partly, from liability on such terms as it thinks fit.[30]

It has usually been held in an action for negligence against a
director that he does not act reasonably unless he does everything
which a normal person would do in the conduct of his own
affairs.

> B. and G., two of the directors of a company were present at a
> finance committee in June at which it was resolved to sell £60,000
> War Bonds and to reinvest the proceeds at B.'s discretion. In
> September, G. inquired about the reinvestment of the proceeds and
> was told that they had been temporarily invested on the Stock
> Exchange. B. misappropriated the proceeds of sale. *Held,* (1) G. was
> negligent in allowing the money to remain in B.'s hands longer than
> was reasonable and in not making inquiries as to its permanent
> investment, and (2) though G. had acted honestly, he had not acted
> reasonably and ought not to be granted relief: *Re City of London
> Insurance Co.* (1925) 41 T.L.R. 521.
>
> In *Selangor United Rubber Estates Ltd v. Cradock (No. 3)*[31]
> directors of a public company who disposed of virtually all its assets
> without regard for minority shareholders, and without consideration,
> but blindly at the behest of the majority shareholder who nominated
> them to the board, did not act reasonably and could not be relieved.
> In *Re Duomatic Ltd*[32] a director dealing with payment to another
> director of compensation for loss of office, who did not seek legal
> advice but dealt with the matter himself without a proper exploration
> of what should be done on the company's behalf, did not act
> reasonably.

[29] See Chap. 20, *post.*
[30] This defence can be raised for the first time at the trial: *Re Kirby's Coaches Ltd*
[1991] BCLC 414.
[31] [1968] 1 W.L.R. 1555.
[32] [1969] 2 Ch. 365.

But in *Re D'Jan of London Ltd*,[33] Hoffmann L.J. held that a director who had acted negligently but "understandably" and who would have suffered a personal loss through his shareholding in the company at the time of the negligence could be excused under the section.

Section 727 only applies to proceedings against a director for breach of duty by, on behalf of, or for the benefit of, the company as a whole or penal proceedings against a director for breach of the Companies Acts. It does not apply to claims against a director by a third party to enforce a debt, *e.g.* arrears of general betting duty.[34] It has no relevance either to a claim by a company for recovery of money paid to a director under an unauthorised and void contract, since that is not founded on a breach of duty,[35] or to a claim for wrongful trading.[36]

## DIRECTORS AND INSOLVENCY

When a company becomes insolvent its directors may face additional liabilities and consequences to those in operation whilst the company is a going concern. In addition to those detailed in Chapter 29 which apply generally, the Insolvency Act 1986 imposes specific liabilities on directors under the headings of wrongful trading; liability for setting up successive companies under the same name, the so-called "Phoenix Syndrome"; and liability for misfeasance. Corporate insolvency may also lead to the directors being disqualified.[37]

### Liability for wrongful trading

One of the principal aims of the Insolvency Act 1986 was to encourage directors to put their company into liquidation when all reasonable expectation of saving it has gone. Before 1986 the only remedy available to a liquidator against a director who had allowed his company to incur debts after all reasonable hope had gone was to institute proceedings for fraudulent trading. This remedy still exists and can give rise to both civil and criminal

[33] [1994] 1 BCLC 561.
[34] *Customs and Excise Commissioners v. Hedon Alpha* [1981] 2 All E.R. 697 (C.A.).
[35] *Guinness plc v. Saunders* [1990] 2 A.C. 633.
[36] *Re Produce Marketing Consortium Ltd* [1989] BCLC 513; *post,* p. 368.
[37] See *post,* p. 373.

consequences.[38] But it requires proof of intent to defraud creditors and in practice that is often difficult to establish. Under
section 214 of the Insolvency Act 1986 there is now an additional
liability on directors and shadow directors[39] for those guilty of
wrongful trading in such circumstances.[40]

To establish wrongful trading the liquidator of a company must
show that the company has gone into an insolvent liquidation,[41]
that the director, prior to the liquidation, knew or ought to have
concluded that there was no reasonable prospect that the company could avoid going into insolvent liquidation, and that he
took insufficient steps in the circumstances to minimise the
potential loss to the company's creditors: Insolvency Act 1986,
section 214(2)(3). Note that no dishonesty need be involved,
simply unreasonable behaviour or negligence.[42] Where the directors have addressed the reality of the situation and have
prepared revised business plans and forecasts that may be taken
as evidence of a reasonable belief that the company will
survive.[42a]

To decide whether a director ought to have concluded that an
insolvent liquidation was unavoidable the court must ask whether
that would have been the conclusion of a reasonably diligent
person having both the general knowledge, skill and experience
that might reasonably be expected of a person carrying out that
particular director's duties with regard to the company (including
those entrusted to him even if he does not actually carry them
out) and the general knowledge, skill and experience which that
director actually has: Insolvency Act 1986, section 214(4)(5).[43]

In construing these provisions Knox J. in *Re Produce Marketing Consortium Ltd (No. 2)*,[44] held that each director had to be
judged by what might reasonably be expected of a person
fulfilling his functions in a reasonably diligent way, always

[38] *Post*, Chap. 27.
[39] *Ante*, p. 313.
[40] No defence under s.727 is available against a claim for wrongful trading: *Re
Produce Marketing Consortium Ltd* [1989] BCLC 513; *ante*, p. 366.
[41] This is defined as where its assets are insufficient for the payment of its debts
and other liabilities and the expenses of winding up.
[42] Becoming aware of pressing creditors will suffice: *Re DKG Contractors Ltd*
[1990] BCC 903.
[42a] *Re Sherborne Associates Ltd* [1995] BCC 40.
[43] This test has also been applied as to the standard of care of directors generally:
*ante*, p. 000.
[44] [1989] BCLC 520.

bearing in mind certain minimum standards such as the preparation of annual accounts, etc. Further such a director must be
judged not only on the facts as known to him but those which he
would have known had the company complied with its obligations
under the Act, *e.g.* as to the publication of accounts, so as to
establish when the wrongful trading began. Where the liquidator
specifies a specific date as to when the wrongful trading began he
cannot subsequently ask the court to make such a finding as at a
later date instead.[44a]

If wrongful trading is established the court may require the
director to make a contribution to the company's assets: Insolvency Act 1986, section 214(1). Such an order is to be compensa-
tory, *i.e.* to provide. an amount equal to that by which the
company's assets were depleted by the directors' conduct, and
not penal.[44b] The absence of fraudulent intent can be taken into
account but is not in itself a reason for fixing a low or nominal
figure. Any amount is payable with interest from the date of
winding up.[45] If the company has failed to keep any records the
court can use its discretion in calculating the period of wrongful
trading for this purpose.[46] Following such an order the court may
also make a disqualification order against the director: Company
Directors Disqualification Act 1986, section 10.[47]

One of the major issues as to liability for wrongful trading
concerns the liability of shadow directors. Who exactly is a
shadow director has been discussed at the beginning of this
chapter. In *Re Hydrodam (Corby) Ltd*[48] the judge accepted for
the purposes of that case that a parent company could be a
shadow director and so liable for wrongful trading of its subsidiaries but that individual directors of the parent company would
not be so liable if they were merely acting as agents of the parent
company in relation to the subsidiary. The judge also accepted
that *de facto* directors, *i.e.* those holding themselves out as
directors, would be liable under the section.

---

[44a] *Re Sherborne Associates Ltd* [1995] BCC 40.
[44b] For this reason the liability survives the death of the director: *Re Sherborne Associates Ltd* [1995] BCC 40. That case also suggested that responsibility for the wrongful trading could be reduced by a defence of reasonable reliance on another.
[45] *Re Produce Marketing Consortium Ltd (No. 2)* [1989] BCLC 520.
[46] *Re Purpoint Ltd* [1991] BCLC 491.
[47] *Post,* p. 373.
[48] [1994] 2 BCLC 180.

## Liability for use of insolvent company's name

Another abuse prior to 1986 was the so-called "Phoenix" company operation. The liquidator would dispose of the company, its name and assets to the existing directors, who would purchase it with other funds and then continue to trade in exactly the same way as before the insolvent liquidation leaving the creditors of the old company stranded. With the new controls on liquidators and extended rights of creditors in the Insolvency Act 1986 it may have been thought that such practices might come to an end. However, sections 216 and 217 of the Insolvency Act 1986 are intended to make sure. Where a company goes into insolvent liquidation,[49] anyone who was a director (or shadow director[50]) of that company at any time in the previous year and becomes a director of a company using the name[51] or trading name of the insolvent company for five years unless he either has leave of the court or comes within limited exceptions under the Insolvency Rules 1994, commits an offence.[52] This prohibition extends to being concerned in the promotion, formation, management or taking part in the business of a company using the insolvent company's name.

The Insolvency Rules allow, *inter alia,* the director to act as such in respect of the new company where the business of the old company has been acquired by the new company[53] under arrangements made with an insolvency practitioner[54] provided notice is given to all the creditors of the old company within 28 days of the completion of the acquisition. The court's residual discretion may allow the director to act as such with respect to the new company but may require certain undertakings as to future conduct of the management of that company.[55]

In addition to the criminal offence under section 216, section 217 imposes personal liability on a director who acts either as such or in the management of a company in breach of section

[49] See note 41, *supra.*
[50] *Ante.*
[51] Or any name which is so similar as to suggest an association with the previous company.
[52] Section 216.
[53] This does not have to include the old company's liabilities: *Re Bonus Breaks Ltd* (1991) BCC 546.
[54] See Chap. 25, *post.*
[55] *Re Bonus Breaks Ltd* (1991) BCC 491.

216, for all debts incurred by that company whilst he is in breach. In *Thorne v. Silverleaf,*[56] the Court of Appeal upheld a director's liability under this section to an investor in the second company, despite the fact that it was alleged that the latter was fully aware of the breach and had encouraged it. Public policy demanded that the liability under section 217 be strict.

**Personal liability of delinquent directors etc.**

Section 212 of the Insolvency Act 1986 provides that if in a winding up it appears that any person who is or has been an officer[57] of the company, or a promoter, or manager, liquidator, administrator[58] or administrative receiver[59] of a company, has misapplied or retained or became accountable for any money or other property of the company, or has been guilty of any misfeasance or breach of trust or other duty to the company the court may on the application of the Official Receiver,[60] the liquidator or any creditor or contributory,[61] examine his conduct and order him to repay or restore the assets or to contribute to the assets of the company as the court thinks just. A contributory can only bring such an action with the leave of the court.

This section replaced section 631 of the Companies Act 1985 which had established a similar summary procedure whereby directors and others could be called to account swiftly for any breach of duty or misfeasance prior to the liquidation. In many ways it is identical with section 631 and many of the cases on that section will still apply. The main differences are that section 212 applies to administrative receivers and includes breaches of duty other than breaches of trust, *i.e.* negligence.[62] Although "misfeasance" is not a Scots law term, the section does apply to Scotland.

Section 631 was held to be procedural only. It gave a summary remedy, not a new cause of action.[63] It has been said that it "did

[56] [1994] 1 BCLC 637.
[57] This includes a director, manager or secretary.
[58] *Post,* Chap. 26.
[59] *Post,* Chap. 25.
[60] Not applicable in Scotland.
[61] *Post,* Chap. 29.
[62] Thus overriding the earlier case law on s.631—see *Re B. Johnson & Co. (Builders) Ltd* [1955] Ch. 634.
[63] *Coventry and Dixon's Case* (1880) 14 Ch.D. 660 (C.A.). See Lord President Inglis in *Liquidators of City of Glasgow Bank v. Mackinnon* (1881) 9 R. 535 at p. 564 and Lord Guest (Ordinary) in *Lord Advocate v. Liquidators of Purvis Industries Ltd,* 1958 S.C. 338 (O.H.), at p. 342.

not create any new liability, any new right, but only provides a summary mode of enforcing rights which must otherwise have been enforced by the ordinary procedure of the Courts." Also, that the applicant "must shew something which would have been the ground of an action by the company if it had not been wound up." Further, that the word "misfeasance" in the section meant "misfeasance in the nature of a breach of trust, that is to say, it refers to something which the officer . . . has done wrongly by misapplying or retaining in his own hands any moneys of the company, or by which the company's property has been wasted, or the company's credit improperly pledged. It must be some act resulting in some actual loss to the company."[64] There seems no reason why all this should not apply equally to section 212 of the Insolvency Act 1986.

A summons[65] was taken out by the liquidator against the secretary of a company for sums overdrawn by him on account of his salary on the instructions of the managing director. *Held,* as this was a claim for repayment of an ordinary debt due from the secretary without any wrongful conduct on his part, no order on the summons ought to be made: *Re Etic Ltd* [1928] Ch. 861.

Instances of misfeasance under section 631 were the improper receipt by a director of his qualification shares from a promoter,[66] the overpayment of a director when he knew the company was insolvent,[67] and of an *ex gratia* payment in lieu of pension on the eve of liquidation.[68] No set-off was allowed to a claim for misfeasance under that section.[69]

The court has a discretion as to the amount to be ordered to be paid on an application under section 212 of the Insolvency Act 1986.

A liquidator negligently admitted a proof, which he should have disallowed, and as a result the company paid £30,000 to a creditor. An attempt to recover this failed, as there was no mistake of fact on the

---

[64] *Per* James L.J. in *Coventry and Dixon's Case* at p. 670.
[65] In Scotland the application to the court would take the form of a note in the petition process (compulsory winding up): R.C. 218M, or a petition (voluntary winding up): R.C. 189.
[66] Which occurred in *Eden v. Ridsdales Railway Lamp Co. Ltd* (1889) 23 Q.B.D. 368 (C.A.).
[67] *Blin v. Johnstone,* 1988 S.L.T. 335.
[68] *Gibson's Executor v. Gibson,* 1978 S.C. 197 (O.H.).
[69] *Ex p. Pelly* (1882) 21 Ch.D. 492 (C.A.).

liquidator's part. *Held,* the liquidator was liable for misfeasance under section 631, but the court, in the exercise of its discretion, ordered him to pay only such a sum as would enable the creditors to be paid in full with interest at five per cent.: *Re Home and Colonial Insce. Co. Ltd* [1930] 1 Ch. 102.

Further, the court's power under section 631 was not merely to specify a sum by way of compensation but to apportion it between co-defendants in such a way and with such priority of liability as the court thought fit.[70] Again there is no reason to suppose that section 212 of the Insolvency Act 1986 has altered this.

An application under section 212 has been held irrelevant where it was an attempt to gain information rather than to obtain a remedy on information already known.[71]

## DISQUALIFICATION OF DIRECTORS

**Disqualification orders other than on insolvency**

The law relating to disqualification orders was consolidated from the Companies Act 1985 and the Insolvency Act 1985 into the Company Directors Disqualification Act 1986.

*Conviction of indictable offence*

A person cannot, without leave of the court, be a director of or be concerned in any way, whether directly or indirectly, in the management of a company if he has been convicted of an indictable offence in connection with the promotion, formation, management or liquidation of a company, or with the receivership or management of a company, or if in a winding up it has appeared that he has been guilty of fraudulent trading[72] or that he has been guilty, while an officer, of fraud or breach of duty in relation to the company, or that he has been persistently in default in relation to the Act,[73] and the court has made a disqualification order that he shall not be a director or be

---

[70] *Re Morcambe Bowling Ltd* [1969] 1 W.L.R. 133.
[71] *Gray v. Davidson,* 1991 S.L.T. (Sh.Ct.) 61.
[72] *Post,* Chap. 27. This applies whether or not he is actually convicted of the offence.
[73] *Infra.*

concerned in management for up to 15 years[74]: sections 1 to 5 of the Company Directors Disqualification Act 1986. An offence is committed in connection with the management of a company if it has some factual connection with the management of a company; it does not have to be committed in the actual management of the company. Thus it includes insider dealing in the relevant company's shares[75] and carrying on an unlawful business through the medium of a company.[76]

The period of disqualification must date from conviction, not, *e.g.* from the convicted person's release from prison.[77] The restriction on taking part in the management of the company is very wide. In particular the words "be concerned in" the management do not mean "take part in," and so include acting as a management consultant.[78]

An application for such a disqualification order may be made by the Secretary of State, the Official Receiver, the liquidator or any past or present member or creditor of the company concerned. Ten days' notice must be given and the person concerned may appear and give evidence or call witnesses.

In *R. v. Young,*[79] the director had had a three and a half year record of successful business after committing the offence before the matter came to court. On the offence he was given a conditional discharge but disqualified for two years. This was quashed by the Court of Appeal (Criminal Division) on the basis of the intolerable delay and his recent record. Disqualification was a punishment which should be linked to the conditional discharge.

## Persistent default

A person may alternatively be disqualified from being a director of or being concerned in the management of a company if he has been persistently in default in relation to any provision of the Companies Acts which requires any document to be delivered, or notice of any matter to be given, to the Registrar.[80]

---

[74] Disqualification orders may run concurrently. For the width of the disqualification, see p. 383, below.
[75] *R. v. Goodman* [1994] 1 BCLC 349.
[76] *R. v. Georgiou* (1988) 4 BCC (C.A.). See also *R. v. Austen* (1985) 1 BCC 99 528.
[77] *R. v. Bradley* [1961] 1 W.L.R. 398 (C.C.A.).
[78] *R. v. Campbell* [1984] BCLC 83 (C.A.).
[79] [1990] BCC 549.
[80] The conditions for application for, and breach of, an order are set out above.

The fact that a person has been persistently in default in relation to any provision of the Companies Acts may be conclusively proved by showing that in the five years ending with the date of the application he has been adjudged guilty (whether or not on the same occasion) of three or more defaults. A person is to be treated as being adjudged guilty of a default if:

(a) he is convicted of any offence by virtue of any contravention of or failure to comply with any provision of the Companies Acts (whether on his own part or on the part of the company); or

(b) a default order is made against him under sections 244 or 713 or sections 41, 170 of the Insolvency Act 1986, *post.*

However, it is not necessary to show three such convictions. In *Re Artic Engineering Ltd*[81] failure to send 35 required returns to the Registrar was held to be sufficient evidence for the making of an order.

An order made on this basis may only last for five and not fifteen years.

*Successive convictions or default orders*

Alternatively a disqualification order may be made if a person is convicted of any offence by virtue of or failure to comply with any provision of the Act and in the five year period up to that conviction he has been convicted of other such offences or received default orders (see above), totalling three in number. In this case the court making the conviction can impose the disqualification order which may last for 5 years.

In *Re Civica Investments Ltd,*[82] the judge said that deciding the length of the disqualification was similar to the passing of a sentence in a criminal case. Elaborate reasoning was therefore unnecessary for, as more of the cases arose, it would be undesirable for the judge to be taken through the facts of previous cases. The five year period was a maximum and should be reserved for serious cases. In the case before him, since most of the defaults had been remedied the judge imposed a one year disqualification only.

[81] [1986] 1 W.L.R. 686.
[82] [1983] BCLC 458.

## Following an investigation by the DTI

The Secretary of State may apply for a disqualification order against a person if it appears to him to be expedient in the public interest following a report by inspectors,[83] or from the production of books and papers[84] or the entry and search of premises.[85] The decision of the Secretary of State not to apply may be challenged by way of judicial review by a person with sufficient interest but only if the decision was perverse or that the only lawful and proper decision would have been to make an application.[86] The court may make an order if it is satisfied that the person's conduct makes him unfit to be concerned in the management of a company: Company Directors Disqualification Act 1986, section 8. This is the same test as is applied in relation to orders made following ·a corporate insolvency[87] and the courts apply similar criteria both as to unfitness and as to the length of the period imposed,[88] although there is no mandatory minimum period.

## Register of disqualification orders

Section 18 of the Company Directors Disqualification Act provides that the prescribed officer of any court which makes an order that a person shall not, without the leave of the court, be a director of or be concerned in the management of a company for a specified period or grants leave in relation to such an order, must furnish the Secretary of State with particulars of the order or the grant of leave where the order is made under that Act.

The Secretary of State must maintain a register of such orders and grants of leave, which register is open to inspection on payment of such fee as may be specified by the Secretary of State in regulations made by statutory instrument.[89]

---

[83] Under s.437, see p. 435.
[84] Under s.447, see p. 440.
[85] Under s.448, see p. 441.
[86] *R. v. Secretary of State, ex p. Lonrho plc* [1992] BCC 325.
[87] See p. 377, below.
[88] *Re Samuel Sherman plc.* [1992] 1 W.L.R. 107; *Re Looe Fish Ltd* [1993] BCLC 1160 (improper allotment of shares to maintain control).
[89] See the Companies (Disqualification Orders) Regulations 1985 (S.I. 1985 No. 829).

## Disqualification orders following corporate insolvency

If the court is satisfied that a person is or has been a director[90] of a company which has become insolvent[91] within the past two years,[92] and that his conduct as such makes him unfit to be concerned in the management of a company,[93] it must make a disqualification order against him for at least two years: Company Directors Disqualification Act, section 6.[94] The conduct may relate to one or more companies as specified.[95] The application for such an order must be made by the Secretary of State (or the Official Receiver if the company is in compulsory liquidation), if it appears to him to be in the public interest, as the result of information received from a liquidator,[96] administrator,[97] administrative receiver[98] or the Official Receiver.[99] Those officials are under a duty to report information about a director's conduct in such matters to the Secretary of State: Company Directors Disqualification Act 1986, section 7. Although the proceedings are civil and not criminal they do involve penal consequences for the director and natural justice requires that he should know the substance of the charges he has to meet. Only if there will be no injustice will a modified charge be allowed during the proceedings.[1] A company becomes insolvent for this purpose: (a) when it goes into liquidation at a time when its assets are insufficient to pay its debts etc[2]; (b) when an administration order is made in respect of the company[3]; (c) when an administrative receiver is appointed: Company Directors Disqualification Act, section 6(2).

---

[90] Including a shadow director or *de facto* director. See *Re Tasbian Ltd (No. 3)* [1993] BCLC 297 (C.A.).
[91] See *infra*.
[92] See *infra*.
[93] See *infra*.
[94] This section applies equally to non-residents and to conduct which occurred outside the U.K.: *Re Seagull Manufacturing Co. Ltd (No. 2)* [1994] 1 BCLC 273.
[95] *Re Bath Glass Ltd* (1988) 4 BCC 130.
[96] See Chaps. 27 and 28, *post*.
[97] See Chap. 26, *post*.
[98] See Chap. 25, *post*.
[99] See Chap. 27, *post*.
[1] *Re Churchill Hotel (Plymouth) Ltd* (1988) 4 BCC 112; *Re Lo-Line Electric Motors Ltd* [1988] Ch. 477.
[2] The effective date here is the making of the winding up order: *Re Walter L. Jacob & Co. Ltd* [1993] BCC 512.
[3] But not an interim order: *Secretary of State for Trade and Industry v. Palmer* [1993] BCC 650; 1993 S.C.L.R. 827.

*Time limit for applications*

The director must be given ten days clear notice before the
institution of proceedings. Failure to do so may make the
proceedings invalid under section 16(1) of the Company Directors Disqualification Act.

However, failure to give such notice will not invalidate proceedings commenced without it unless there has been substantial
prejudice caused to the defendant.[4]

More importantly section 7(2) of the Act provides that no
application for a disqualification may be made after the end of
the period of two years beginning with the day when the relevant
company first became insolvent unless the court gives leave. This
means the earliest of the insolvent acts set out above.[5] In deciding
whether to give leave for an application out of time the courts[6]
have evolved four factors to be taken into consideration: (i) the
length of the delay; (ii) the reasons for the delay[7]; (iii) the
strength of the case against the director; and (iv) the degree of
prejudice caused to the director by the delay. In assessing the
third of those the courts have allowed hearsay evidence to be
used.[8] In general they will not go into the merits of the case in the
same way as in a full trial. If there is a conflict of evidence then
the courts must decide on the supporting evidence but if there is
no conflict but an explanation by the defendant, these can be
taken together.[9] In *Re Cedar Developments Ltd,*[9a] the judge
decided that the four factors were not the only matters to be
taken into account and that in all cases it was for the applicant to
show why leave should be granted and not for the director to
show why it should not be granted. A short delay was not in itself
an automatic ground for leave to be given.

*Unfitness to be concerned in the management*

In deciding whether a person's conduct makes him unfit to be
concerned in the management of a company, section 9 of the

[4] *Secretary of State for Trade and Industry v. Langridge* [1991] BCLC 543.
[5] *Re Tasbian Ltd* [1990] BCC 318.
[6] *Re Probe Data Systems Ltd (No. 3)* [1992] BCLC 405 (C.A.); *Re Polly Peck
International plc (No. 2)* [1994] 1 BCLC 574; *Re Packaging Direct Ltd* [1994]
BCC 213.
[7] See *e.g. Re Noble Trees Ltd* [1993] BCLC 1185; *Re Copecrest Ltd* [1994] 2
BCLC 284 (C.A.).
[8] *Re Polly Peck International plc (No. 2)* [1994] 1 BCLC 574.
[9] *Re Packaging Direct Ltd* [1994] BCC 213.
[9a] [1994] 2 BCLC 714.

Company Directors Disqualification Act 1986 requires the court to have regard to the matters specified in Schedule 1 to that Act. These are: (a) any misfeasance, breach of duty or misapplication of assets[10]; (b) failure to comply with the requirements under the Companies Act relating to books and records, returns and accounts[11]; and, where the company has become insolvent; (c) responsibility for the cause of insolvency or for losses of customers who furnished advance payments and involvement in any transaction (or preference) which can be set aside[12]; and (d) failure to comply with the statutory requirements relating to insolvency.

In addition to such specific criteria the judges have laid down various tests to determine whether a director's conduct is deserving of disqualification. In *Re Dawson Print Group Ltd*[13] Hoffmann J. said:

> "There must, I think, be something about the case, some conduct which if not dishonest is at any rate in breach of standards of commercial morality, or some really gross incompetence which persuades the court that it would be a danger to the public if he were allowed to continue to be involved in the management of companies, before a disqualification order is made."

In *Re Churchill Hotel (Plymouth) Ltd*[14] Peter Gibson J. construed this to mean that gross incompetence without a breach of commercial morality would suffice for a disqualification, whilst the statement was approved by Browne-Wilkinson V.-C. in *Re McNulty's Interchange Ltd*[15] together with his own test in *Re Lo-Line Electric Motors Ltd*[16] that:

> "Ordinary commercial misjudgment is in itself not sufficient to justify disqualification. In the normal case, the conduct complained of must display a lack of commercial probity although I have no doubt

---

[10] *Re Keypack Homecare Ltd (No. 2)* [1990] BCC 117; *Re T. & D. Services Ltd* [1990] BCC 592; *Re Tansoft Ltd* [1991] BCLC 339.

[11] See, *e.g. Re Rolus Properties Ltd* (1988) 4 BCC 446; *Re T. & D. Services Ltd, ante; Re New Generation Engineers Ltd* [1993] BCLC 435 and *Re Firedart Ltd* [1994] 2 BCLC 340.

[12] See *Secretary of State for Trade and Industry v. Gray, The Times*, November 24, 1994 (C.A.) and Chap. 29, *post.*

[13] (1987) 3 BCC 322, 324.

[14] (1988) 4 BCC 112, 117.

[15] (1988) 4 BCC 533, 536.

[16] [1988] Ch. 477, 479. See also *Re Chartmore Ltd* [1990] BCLC 673; *Re Tansoft Ltd* [1991] BCLC 339; *Re Austinsuite Furniture Ltd* [1992] BCLC 1047.

that in an extreme case of gross negligence or total incompetence disqualification could be appropriate."

However, the Court of Appeal in *Re Sevenoaks Stationers (Retail) Ltd*[17] although describing such statements as helpful in identifying particular circumstances in which a person would clearly be unfit warned against treating them as paraphrases of the wording of the section. It is a question of whether particular conduct makes a director unfit to be concerned in the management of a company. They added that incompetence to a marked degree would be sufficient, it need not be total, although it must amount to more than a simple commercial misjudgment, involving some form of lack of probity or abuse of the system. The clearest case where the courts regard the conduct as amounting to unfitness is where successive companies are formed which each become insolvent in turn, often transferring the business from one to the other.[18]

The general intention is to protect the public from abuse of the limited liability given by a company. However, the Court of Appeal in *Secretary of State for Trade and Industry v. Gray*[18a] made it quite clear that no such requirement is needed for an order to be made. It was irrelevant that the judge had decided that the director was no longer such a danger. The same idea is sometimes phrased by reference to the test being whether the director has forfeited the right to enjoy the privileges of limited liability by failing to perform the attendant duties.[19]

Disqualification orders have been refused where the director's conduct was only imprudent and improper[20] and where there was a reasonable reliance on advice which indicated that the director had none of the badges of a man who had exploited limited liability in a cynical way, with disregard for proper responsibility, or by incompetence.[21] On the other hand, an order was made

[17] [1991] BCLC 325.
[18] *Re Travel Mondial Ltd* [1991] BCC 224; *Re Linvale Ltd* [1993] BCLC 654; *Re Swift 736 Ltd* [1993] BCLC 896 (C.A.).
[18a] *The Times,* November 24, 1994 (C.A.).
[19] This test was used by Vinelott J. in *Re Stanford Services Ltd* (1987) 3 BCC 326, Peter Gibson J. in *Re Bath Glass Ltd, ante,* Mervyn Davies J. in *Re Majestic Recording Studios Ltd* (1988) 4 BCC 519, and Hoffmann J. in *Re Ipcon Fashions Ltd* (1989) 5 BCC 773.
[20] *Re Bath Glass Ltd, ibid.* See also *Re ECM (Europe) Electronics Ltd* [1991] BCC 268 and *Re Wimbledon Village Restaurant Ltd* [1994] BCC 753.
[21] *Re Douglas Construction Services Ltd* (1988) 4 BCC 553.

against a director who had assumed a position which could not be
shirked by leaving everything to others, since that indicated that
he was a danger to the public.[22] There is no general rule that
entrusting the running of a company to others is automatically
grounds for disqualification but the owner of a company is not
allowed to walk away from his responsibilities as a director—that
is more than a commercial misjudgment.[23]

The major area of dispute has been the relevance of a director
allowing his company to run up arrears of money which it ought
to have paid over to the tax authorities. The significant point is
that these debts are not trading debts in the ordinary sense since
they arise out of the use for other purposes of money which the
company actually receives on behalf of the Crown, e.g. VAT
collected from suppliers, income tax deducted at source from
employees' wages under the Pay As You Earn system and
national insurance contributions similarly deducted and not
handed over to the correct authorities. In Re Dawson Print
Group Ltd[24] Hoffmann J. rejected the idea that in some way
these sums amounted to quasi-trust moneys so that misappropriation was a serious matter. Failure to pay such debts was not a
sufficient breach of commercial morality as to justify a disqualification. In Re Stanford Services Ltd,[25] Vinelott J., whilst
deciding that failure to set aside sums to cover those debts was
not in itself a breach of commercial morality, stated that the
Crown was nevertheless an involuntary creditor and if a company
went into liquidation with such sums owing and irrecoverable the
directors would be regarded as either being improperly informed
as to the company's financial position or as acting improperly in
using the money to finance the company's current trade.

In Re Sevenoaks Stationers (Retail) Ltd[26] the Court of Appeal
agreeing with Hoffmann J.'s statement, regarded non-payment of
Crown debts as important, not because of the fact that they were
such debts, but because their non-payment indicated that the
director was only paying those creditors who were pressing for
their debts at the time to the detriment of other creditors,

---

[22] ibid.
[23] Re Burnham Marketing Services Ltd [1993] BCC 518.
[24] (1987) 3 BCC 322. See also Re CV Fittings Ltd (1989) 5 BCC 210; Re Keypack
Homecare Ltd (No. 2) [1990] BCC 117.
[25] (1987) 3 BCC 326. This approach was followed in other cases, e.g. in Re
Lo-Line Motors Ltd [1988] Ch. 477.
[26] [1991] BCLC 325.

including the Crown. Viewed in that light such non-payment was a factor to be taken into account when deciding whether a director was unfit to be concerned in the management of a company. This approach has since been adopted by the judges.[27]

In deciding whether a director is unfit to be concerned in the management of a company the court will examine the evidence presented by the Secretary of State or the Official Receiver, and the affidavit evidence of the defendant. The latter has no right to insist on giving oral evidence.[28] On the other hand the court can only act on the charges presented against the director and not those which may be said to emerge during the trial.[29] Evidence can be taken in relation to any company and not the specific one in question and evidence of past conduct is relevant. Where the main charges are agreed between the parties the courts will act on those summarily even though there are disagreements on other aspects of the case if it is satisfied that they would not materially affect the result.[30]

*Period of disqualification*

If the court finds that a director is unfit to be concerned in the management of a company under section 6 of the Company Directors Disqualification Act 1986, it has no choice but to impose a period of disqualification of between two and 15 years.[31] This is the only area where a disqualification order must be imposed; the court has no discretion except as to the length of the order. This has been criticised by Vinelott J. in *Re Pamstock Ltd*[32] as being unduly rigid, especially as no minimum period is required in other areas such as fraudulent trading. There is no equivalent of a conditional discharge.

The Court of Appeal in *Re Sevenoaks Stationers (Retail) Ltd*[33] laid down what, in effect, amounts to sentencing guidelines, which have been adopted in all the cases decided thereafter. The

---

[27] See *e.g. Re City Investment Centres Ltd* [1992] BCLC 956; *Re New Generation Engineers Ltd* [1993] BCLC 435.
[28] *Re Rex Williams Leisure plc* [1994] BCC 551 (C.A.).
[29] *Re Sevenoaks Stationers (Retail) Ltd* [1991] BCLC 325 (C.A.).
[30] *Re Carecraft Construction Co. Ltd* [1993] BCLC 1259; *Re Aldermanbury Trust plc* [1993] BCC 598.
[31] Section 6(4).
[32] [1994] 1 BCLC 716.
[33] [1991] BCLC 325 (C.A.).

15 year ambit should be divided into three bands. The band over 10 years should be used only for very serious cases such as a second disqualification; that between five and 10 years for serious first cases such as misappropriation of assets or deliberate misuse of the corporate form to prejudice creditors, and that from two to five years for less serious first cases such as gross negligence or incompetence. There are many reported examples of this system operating in practice, one may suffice by way of illustration.

In *Re A & C Group Services Ltd*[34] the allegations against three directors included not only responsibility for the company's failure by ineffective stewardship of its affairs such as defective accounting procedures, failure to take into account execessive trading losses and non payment of Crown debts, but also more serious allegations of improper use of company funds, making misleading statements, taking excessive remuneration and illegal use of directors' loan accounts. One of the directors was identified as being responsible for all of these and was disqualified within the middle band, for six years. That took into account the delay in bringing the proceedings and the fact that he had admitted the charges. The other two directors were held not to be primarily responsible for the more serious allegations and to have been influenced by the other at a time of ill health. Nevertheless they were responsible for the poor management and should be disqualified for the minimum period of two years.

Both parties can appeal against the length of the disqualification period and it is possible for the period to be increased on appeal. In *Re Swift 736 Ltd*[35] the defendant had been a director of sixteen insolvent companies. In respect of six of these, which had carried on the same business in succession as the previous one failed, he had not been the principal director. The other directors had already been disqualified for five years in separate proceedings. With regard to the other 10 companies the complaints were of failure to keep proper accounts and to file returns, etc. The judge disqualified him for three years. The Court of Appeal decided that the judge had been over-concerned with the periods given to the other directors and had failed to take into account the other 10 companies. Taken together this was serious misconduct and justified a six year period.

The court has the power when making a disqualification order to make an exception for a particular company. Various factors

[34] [1993] BCLC 1297.
[35] [1993] BCLC 312 (C.A.).

will be taken into account including the seriousness of the conduct, the nature and status of the proposed exempted company, (*e.g.* is it a family company which will fold without him) and others involved in that company, (*e.g.*, are there others who will be able to monitor the defendant). In *Re Chartmore Ltd*[36] such an order was made on a yearly basis, but in *Re Cargo Agency Ltd*[37] the court said that this would only be done in cases of need, *e.g.* the company's survival, and not where it would be nice. In *Re Gibson Davies Ltd*,[37a] the judge allowed an exception to an order where there was a need and, because of the circumstances in the case, there would be no danger to the public in allowing the director to act in respect of one company.

*Costs*

The normal rule is that costs are awarded against the losing party but the court has a discretion and may decide that no costs are to be awarded, *e.g.* where the Secretary of State has brought an application on reasonable grounds but withdrawn it once the defendant has put in his evidence.[38] There has been some dispute as to the basis upon which costs are to be awarded against a disqualified director. Some judges have awarded costs on an indemnity basis, (*i.e.* full costs unless the defendant can prove that they are unreasonable) rather than the normal standard basis (where costs have to be justified) on the grounds that these are public interest proceedings.[39] Others have used the standard basis unless the defendant has acted unreasonably.[40] The matter appears to have been resolved by the Court of Appeal in *Re Dicetrade Ltd*,[41] in favour of the latter approach. These are civil proceedings and the Secretary of State must take his chance. Cases where the indemnity basis would be appropriate include where the defendant makes extravagant claims or a wholly false and futile defence, or defends claims with no conceivable defence.

---

[36] [1990] BCLC 673.
[37] [1992] BCLC 686.
[37a] [1995] BCC 11.
[38] *Re Southborne Sheet Metal Co. Ltd* [1991] BCC 732.
[39] See *e.g. Re Brooks Transport (Purfleet) Ltd* [1993] BCC 766.
[40] See *e.g. Re Synthetic Technology Ltd* [1993] BCC 549.
[41] [1994] 2 BCLC 113 (C.A.). See also *Re Godwin Warren Ltd* [1993] BCLC 80 (C.A.).

**Personal liability of persons acting whilst disqualified through bankruptcy or by a disqualification order**

Any person disqualified by reason of his personal bankruptcy under section 11 of the Company Directors Disqualification Act 1986 or by a disqualification order and who becomes involved in the management of the company[42] is personally liable for all debts incurred whilst he was so involved. This liability extends to those who although not disqualified themselves act or are willing to act on the orders of someone who is so disqualified and whom he knows is so disqualified. Anyone who has so acted is presumed to be willing to act in the future. The liability extends to debts incurred whilst they were so acting or willing to act: Company Directors Disqualification Act 1986, section 15. Liability under this head can also lead to a criminal offence under section 13 of the Act. The offence is one of strict liability so that it is no defence that the defendant thought that he was no longer bankrupt.[43]

---

[42] This includes acting as a director or directly or indirectly taking part in the management of the company: C.D.D.A. 1986 s.15(4). See *R. v. Campbell, supra.*

[43] *R. v. Brockley* [1994] 1 BCLC 606.

# Chapter 16

# THE SECRETARY

EVERY company must have secretary and a sole director cannot also be secretary: section 283(1), (2). The secretary may be an individual or a Scottish firm or a corporation, but a corporation cannot be the secretary if its sole director is also the sole director of the company: section 283(4). A company may have all the partners of a firm as joint secretaries: see section 290. That section also requires disclosure of the identity of the secretary in the register of directors and secretaries to be kept by the company under section 288.

Section 286, first introduced in 1980, requires the directors of a public company to secure that the secretary is a person who appears to them to have the requisite knowledge and experience to be a secretary. In addition a public company secretary must have either been a public company secretary for three out of the five years before his present appointment, or be a barrister, advocate or solicitor, or a member of one of the professional accountancy bodies or of the Institute of Chartered Secretaries and Administrators, or be someone who because of his position or qualifications appears to the directors to be capable of discharging the duties of a public company secretary. A private company secretary need have no such qualifications.

The secretary is usually appointed by the directors, but sometimes he is named in the articles.[1]

Table A, regulation 99, provides: "Subject to the provisions of the Act, the secretary shall be appointed by the directors for such term, at such renumeration and upon such conditions as they may think fit; and any secretaries so appointed may be removed by them."

The position of a company's secretary has changed a great deal in the last 100 years. In 1887 it was said that: "a secretary is a

---

[1] As to which see *Eley v. Positive Life Assurance Co. Ltd* (1876) 1 Ex.D. 88 (C.A.), *ante*, p. 83.

mere servant; his position is that he is to do what he is told, and no person can assume that he has any authority to represent anything at all; nor can anyone assume that statements made by him are necessarily to be accepted as trustworthy without further inquiry."[2] Again in 1902 his duties were described as "of a limited and of a somewhat humble character."[3] Accordingly, it has in the past been held that a company is not liable for the acts of its secretary in fraudulently making representations to induce persons to take shares in the company,[4] or in issuing a forged share certificate.[5] The secretary is, however, the proper official to issue share certificates, and so the company is estopped or barred from denying the truth of genuine share certificates issued by him without the authority of the company.[6] He may also, with a director, validly excute a deed on behalf of the company whether or not that company has a common seal.[7]

It has also been held under the old cases that the secretary has no implied authority to bind the company by contract.[8]

L., a director of N. Co., without any authority from the company, made a contract with H. The contract was confirmed by a letter written by the secretary on behalf of the company. *Held*, the secretary, as such, had no power to bind the company, and N. Co. was not liable on the contract: *Houghton & Co. v. Nothard, Lowe & Wills Ltd* [1928] A.C. 1, *ante*.[9]

Thus, it has been held that he has no implied authority to borrow money on behalf of the company,[10] issue a writ in the company's name[11] or lodge defences in the company's name,[12] and it is not his duty as secretary to instruct the company as to its legal rights.[13]

---

[2] *Per* Lord Esher M.R. in *Barnett, Hoares & Co. v. South London Tramways Co.* (1887) 18 Q.B.D. 815 (C.A.), at p. 817.
[3] *Per* Lord Macnaghten in *George Whitechurch Ltd v. Cavanagh* [1902] A.C. 117, at p. 124.
[4] *Barnett, Hoares & Co. v. South London Tramway Co., ante.*
[5] *Ruben v. Great Fingall Consolidated* [1906] A.C. 439, *ante*, p. 276.
[6] *Clavering, Son & Co. v. Goodwins, Jardine & Co. Ltd* (1891) 18 R. 652.
[7] S.36A. *Ante*, p. 101.
[8] *Williams v. The Chester and Holyhead Ry. Co.* (1851) 15 Jur. 828. He may of course have actual authority to do anything: see *UBAF Ltd v. European Banking Corp.* [1984] Q.B. 713.
[9] Chap. 6.
[10] *Re Cleadon Trust Ltd* [1939] Ch. 286 (C.A.).
[11] *Daimler Co. Ltd v. Continental Tyre, etc., Co. Ltd* [1916] 2 A.C. 307.
[12] *Edington v. Dunbar Steam Laundry Co.* (1903) 11 S.L.T. 117 (O.H.).
[13] *Niven v. Collins Patent Lever Gear Co. Ltd* (1900) 7 S.L.T. 476 (O.H.).

The secretary of a company is not "an official who *virtute officii* can manage all its affairs with or without the help of servants, in the absence of a regular directorate": *per* Lord Parker in *Daimler Co. Ltd v. Continental Tyre Co. Ltd* [1916] 2 A.C. 307 at p. 377.

However, the changed position of the company secretary was taken into account in *Panorama Developments (Guildford) Ltd v. Fidelis Furnishing Fabrics Ltd*[14] where it was said[15] that a company secretary is a much more important person now than he was in 1887. He is the chief administrative officer of the company with extensive duties and responsibilities. This appears not only in the modern Companies Acts but in the role which he plays in the day-to-day business of the company. He is no longer a mere clerk. He regularly makes representations on behalf of the company and enters into contracts on its behalf which come within the day-to-day running of its business. So much so that he may be regarded as held out as having authority to do such things on behalf of the company. He is certainly entitled to sign contracts connected with the administrative side of a company's affairs, such as employing staff and ordering cars. All such matters come within the implied or apparent authority of a company's secretary.

The secretary, purportedly on behalf of the company, fraudulently hired cars, ostensibly for the purpose of meeting customers, and used the cars for his own private purposes. *Held*, the secretary had implied authority to enter into contracts for the hire of cars on behalf of the company and the company was liable to pay the hire charges: *Panorama Developments (Guildford) Ltd v. Fidelis Furnishing Fabrics Ltd* [1971] 2 Q.B. 711 (C.A.).

On the other hand it appears that he still has no ostensible or apparent authority to make representations about the company in relation to a commercial transaction, *e.g.* a syndicated loan.[16]

This new status of the company secretary was recognised by the introduction in the 1980 Act of a qualification standard for public company secretaries: section 286, *ante*.

The duties of the secretary depend on the size and nature of the company, and on the arrangement made with him. In any case he will be present at all meetings of the company, and of the

---

[14] [1971] 2 Q.B. 711 (C.A.).
[15] *Per* Lord Denning M.R. and Salmon L.J., at pp. 716, 717.
[16] *UBAF Ltd v. European American Banking Corp.* [1984] Q.B. 713.

directors, and will make proper minutes of the proceedings. He will issue, under the direction of the board, all notices to members and others. In practice he will usually countersign every instrument to which the seal of the company is affixed. Alternatively, he is one of those whose signature will validate a document as a document under seal by virtue of sections 36A and 36B (Chap. 6, *ante*). He or his department will conduct all correspondence with shareholders in regard to transfers and otherwise, will certify transfers, and will keep the books of the company, or such of them as relate to the internal business of the company, *e.g.* the register of members, the share ledger, the transfer book, the register of charges, etc. He will also make all necessary returns to the Registrar, *e.g.* the annual return, return of allotments, notice of increase of capital, etc.

If a provision requires or authorises a thing to be done by or to a director and the secretary it is not satisfied by the thing being done by or to the same person acting both as director and as secretary: section 284.

If a person is secretary of two companies, a fact which comes to his knowledge as secretary of one company is not notice to him as secretary of another company, unless it was his duty to the first company to communicate his knowledge to the second company.

H. was secretary to two companies, A. Co. and B. Co. B. Co. drew a bill on a third company, C. Co., and indorsed it in favour of A. Co. The bill was dishonoured by C. Co. and no notice of dishonour was given to B. Co. It was claimed that as H., in his capacity of secretary, knew of the dishonour, no notice was necessary. *Held*, notice to H., as secretary of A. Co., was not notice to B. Co.: *Re Fenwick, Stobart & Co.* [1902] 1 Ch. 507.

In England a full-time secretary has been held to be a "clerk or servant" so as to be entitled to preferential payment of his salary on a winding up but a part-time secretary is not.[17] Since that decision the relevant wording has been amended to "employee".

The secretary is an officer of the company: section 744. In some instances therefore he is in the same position as a director so that a provision in the articles or in any contract for relieving him from liability is void: section 310.[18] Again, the court can

[17] *Cairney v. Back* [1906] 2 K.B. 746 *post*, p. 823. Scottish cases in which a secretary was held not be a "clerk or servant" for this purpose are *Scottish Poultry Journal Co.* (1896) 4 S.L.T. 167 (O.H.), *Clyde Football etc. Co. Ltd* (1900) 8 S.L.T. 328 (O.H.) and *Laing v. Gowans* (1902) 10 S.L.T. 461 (O.H.).
[18] *Ante*, p. 365.

relieve him from liability in certain cases: section 727.[19] The disclosure in the accounts of loans etc. to the secretary is less stringent than that for directors.[20] Under Schedule 6 only the aggregate amounts outstanding need to be disclosed together with the number of officers involved.

A secretary has been held to have no lien over the books of the company coming into his possession in the course of his duties.[21]

---

[19] *Ante*, p. 366.
[20] *Ante*, p. 335.
[21] *Gladstone v. M'Callum* (1896) 23 R. 783 (minute book); *Barnton Hotel Co. Ltd v. Cook* (1899) 1 F. 1190 (register of members and other books and documents at secretary's own premises).

# Chapter 17

## CONTROLLING MEMBERS' DUTIES

IN this chapter the term "controlling members" means those members of a company who between them possess sufficient voting power to pass the appropriate resolution in general meeting, usually an ordinary resolution.

We have seen that the company in general meeting may waive a breach of fiduciary duty by a director who contracts with the company as in the *N.W. Transportation* case,[1] or by one who makes a secret profit out of his position as in *Regal (Hastings) Ltd v. Gulliver*,[2] or may waive a breach of a director's duty of care, as in *Pavlides v. Jensen*.[3] It has often been stated that although the directors of a company owe a fiduciary duty[4] to the company, as such, shareholders do not: "When voting, a shareholder may consult his own interests."[5]

Until recently it has thus been accepted that a share is a piece of property which is to be enjoyed and exercised for the owner's personal advantage.[6] Thus a shareholder may bind himself by contract to vote in a particular way:

"When a director votes as a director for or against any particular resolution in a directors' meeting he is voting as a person under a fiduciary duty to the company for the proposition that the company should take a certain course of action. When a shareholder is voting for or against a particular resolution he is voting as a person owing no fiduciary duty to the company and who is exercising his own right of property, to vote as he thinks fit. The fact that the result of the voting at the meeting (or at a subsequent poll) will bind the company cannot affect the position that, in voting, he is voting simply in exercise of his own property rights . . . a director is an agent, who casts his vote to

---

[1] (1987) 12 App. Cas. 589 (P.C.).
[2] [1942] 1 All E.R. 378 (H.L.).
[3] [1956] Ch. 656.
[4] *Ante*, p. 345.
[5] *Per* Megarry V.-C. in *Estmanco (Kilner House) Ltd v. G.L.C.* [1982] 1 All E.R. 437, 444.
[6] See, *e.g. N.W. Transportation v. Beatty, supra.*

decide in what manner his principal shall act through the collective agency of the board of directors; a shareholder who casts his vote in general meeting is not casting it as an agent of the company in any shape or form. His act therefore, in voting as he pleases, cannot in any way be regarded as an act of the company": *per* Walton J. in *Northern Countries Securities Ltd v. Jackson and Steeple Ltd* [1974] 1 W.L.R. 1133, at p. 1144.

In *Greenwell v. Potter*,[7] where executors and trustees of a will who held shares agreed to sell some to G., who stipulated that he should nominate X as a director and that the executors should, when X retired by rotation, vote for his re-election, it was held that the executors were bound by the agreement. It may be mentioned that there was a voting agreement in *Greenhalgh v. Mallard*[8] but it was held that the shareholders who agreed to vote in a certain way were under no obligation to retain their shares and there was no continuing obligation running with the shares.

This right to vote has however always been subject to the doctrine of fraud on the minority so that the majority cannot waive a breach of a director's fiduciary duty by approving a misappropriation by him of the company's property which would be a fraud on the minority. That is what the majority tried to do in *Cook v. Deeks*.[9]

The same is true where there is an attempted confirmation of a share issue made by a director in order to give him control of the company and benefit the majority to the detriment of the minority, *i.e.* the general meeting cannot then waive the director's breach of duty.[10]

Members cannot, by resolution in general meeting, expropriate the company's property.

The shareholders in E. Co., which was formed with the object of constructing a submarine telegraph, were H. Co. with 3,000 shares, M. with 2,000 and thirteen other persons with 325 between them. H. Co. was to make and lay cables for E. Co. The directors of E. Co., who were nominees of H. Co., and H. Co. decided not to pursue an action in which E. Co. was claiming a concession to construct the telegraph, procured the passing of a resolution in general meeting to put E. Co. into voluntary winding up and concealed the fact that they had agreed to end the agreement between E. Co. and H. Co. so that H. Co. could sell the cable to a third company. M. brought an action on behalf of himself and the other shareholders, except those who were defendants, in which he joined E. Co. as a defendant. He claimed, *inter alia*, a declaration

---

[7] [1902] 1 Ch. 530. See also *Puddephatt v. Leith* [1916] 1 Ch. 200.
[8] [1943] 2 All E.R. 234 (C.A.).
[9] [1916] 1 A.C. 554, *post*, p. 402.
[10] *Ngurli v. McCann* (1954) 90 C.L.R. 425.

that H. Co. was a trustee of the resulting profit for M. and the other shareholders in E. Co. *Held*, M. succeeded. The majority shareholder had obtained certain advantages by dealing with something which was the property of the whole company: *Menier v. Hooper's Telegraph Works* (1874) L.R. 9 Ch.App. 350.

As regards the property of other members of the company, we saw in Chapter 4 that, on the authority of *Sidebottom v. Kershaw, Leese & Co.*,[11] an alteration of the articles by special resolution in general meeting in order to enable some members to acquire the shares of other members must be bona fide for the benefit of the company as a whole.

Further, we saw that cases such as *Greenhalgh v. Arderne Cinemas Ltd*,[12] and *Shuttleworth v. Cox Bros. Ltd*,[13] established the rule that in making any alternation to the articles the general meeting must act bona fide for the benefit of the company as a whole. Similarly, a class meeting of preference shareholders sanctioning a modification of the special rights of the preference shares must act bona fide for the benefit of the class as a whole.[14]

It was said in a Scottish case[15] that: "Prima facie, the shareholders are the best judges of their own affairs, and it is only where it appears that some sinister motive has operated, or that interests other than the interest of the company have plainly prevailed, that the Court will entertain a complaint. The test always is—is the thing complained of a thing done in the interest of the company?—or, to put it perhaps more accurately, is the action of the majority irreconcilable with their having proceeded upon any reasonable view of the company's interest?" In the case in question a resolution of a general meeting to issue unissued shares to the managing director at a lower premium than would have been obtained on the market was valid. In another Scottish case it was said[16] that "The question . . . is whether the resolution complained of . . . can be held to be so oppressive and extravagant that no reasonable man could consider it to be for the benefit of the Company."

Thus controlling members do owe a duty to the company, *i.e.* the corporators as a body, to act bona fide for the benefit of the company as a whole and not to commit a fraud on the minority.

It has been said in one case, however, that the controlling members may in fact be subject to more stringent controls than

---

[11] [1920] 1 Ch. 154 (C.A.), *ante*, p. 87.
[12] [1951] Ch. 286 (C.A.), *ante*, p. 86.
[13] [1927] 2 K.B. 9 (C.A.).
[14] *Re Holders Investment Trust Ltd* [1971] 1 W.L.R. 583, *ante*, p. 243.
[15] *Per* Lord Kyllachy (Ordinary) in *Cameron v. Glenmorangie Distillery Co. Ltd* (1896) 23 R. 1092 at p. 1095.
[16] *Per* Lord Wark (Ordinary) in *Harris v. A. Harris Ltd*, 1936 S.C. 183 at p. 192.

the accepted doctrine of a fraud on the minority, although not being subject to the full fiduciary duties of a director.

In *Clemens v. Clemens Bros. Ltd*[17] the defendant owned 55 per cent. of the issued shares of a family company. She was one of five directors and proposed to give the other directors shares and to set up a trust for long-service employees. The plaintiff, who was the defendant's niece, held 40 per cent. of the shares and was not a director. The defendant proposed resolutions to increase the capital so that the plaintiff's shares would fall below 25 per cent. of the total and her right to veto special resolutions would be lost. It was also clear that she would never now obtain control of the company. The judge held that the defendant was not entitled to exercise her majority votes as an ordinary shareholder in any way she pleased. That right was subject to equitable considerations which could make it unjust to exercise them in a particular way. In this case such considerations applied and the resolutions would be set aside.

One interpretation of this case is that it shows that the majority do not have unrestricted voting rights if it is "unjust" in the particular circumstances.

In *Estmanco (Kilner House) Ltd v. Greater London Council*[18] Megarry V.-C., however, accepted the general proposition that the shareholders do not owe any fiduciary duties but affirmed that in altering the articles they are subject to the doctrine of fraud on the minority, *i.e.* they must act in what they believe to be in the best interests of the company as a whole. In that case the majority shareholder wished to deprive the company of a right of action under a contract and proposed, and carried, a resolution to that effect. A minority shareholder sought to bring an action on behalf of the company[19] to prevent this. Megarry V.-C. considered the situation thus[20]:

> "Plainly there must be some limit to the power of the majority to pass resolutions which they believe to be in the best interests of the company and yet remain immune from interference by the courts. It may be in the best interests of the company to deprive the minority of some of their rights or some of their property, yet I do not think that this gives the majority an unrestricted right to do this, however unjust

[17] [1976] 2 All E.R. 268.
[18] [1982] 1 All E.R. 437.
[19] *Post*, p. 402.
[20] [1982] 1 All E.R. 437, 444.

it may be, and however much it may harm shareholders whose rights as a class differ from those of the majority."

More recently, however, in *Re Swindon Town Football Club Ltd*,[21] Harman J. accepted that the general rule that shareholders are entitled to vote in their own interest remains the law and is the correct proposition, even though it has not been followed on every modern occasion, notably in *Clemens v. Clemens Bros. Ltd* (above). The judge also accepted the proposition that: "The company is entitled to consider lawful resolutions, however silly, and, if thought fit, to pass them, and it is not for the court to tell the company that it should not be silly."[22]

On the other hand, the courts do retain an inherent power to grant an injunction to prevent a shareholder from voting with his shares if there would otherwise be substantial injury to the company, or to protect secured creditors from destruction of the secured assets.[23]

[21] [1990] BCLC 467.
[22] *ibid.*, at p. 469.
[23] *Standard Chartered Bank v. Walker* [1992] BCLC 603.

## Chapter 18

# MAJORITY RULE AND MINORITY PROTECTION

## Majority Rule

The members of a company can express their wishes at general meetings by voting for or against the resolutions proposed. However, the will of the majority of the members usually prevails and if the appropriate majority is obtained a resolution binds all the members, including those who voted against it. Sometimes the majority is a simple majority and sometimes it is a three-quarters majority—for example, an ordinary resolution is a resolution passed by a simple majority of the votes of the members entitled to vote and voting; a special resolution is a resolution passed by a three-quarters majority of the votes of such members.[1] This can be said to be the first example of what is called "majority rule."

Further, it should be remembered that, subject to a few restrictions, the articles of a company, which constitute a contract binding the company and the members, can be altered by special resolution.[2]

Another example of majority rule, as we shall see, is the rule in *Foss v. Harbottle,* by which, subject to certain exceptions, if a wrong to a company is alleged, or if there is an alleged irregularity in its internal management which is capable of confirmation by a simple majority of the members, the court will not interfere at the suit of a minority of the members.

## Minority protection

Both under the general law and under the Companies and other Acts there is some protection of the minority.

[1] *Ante,* p. 304.
[2] *Ante,* p. 80.

Examples of minority protection are:—

(1) Under the general law, the doctrine that the majority of the members must not commit a fraud on the minority but must act bona fide for the benefit of the company as a whole.[3]

(2) The other exceptions to the rule in *Foss v. Harbottle,* in which cases an individual member may bring a derivative action.

(3) The various sections intended to protect a minority of members. Some apply on a general basis; thus under sections 122 and 124 of the Insolvency Act 1986[4] a member can petition the court to wind up the company on the ground that it is just and equitable that the company be wound up. Further, under section 459[5] of the Companies Act a member can petition the court for other relief where the company's affairs are being conducted in an unfairly prejudicial manner to some or all of the members, including himself. Other minority sections enable a number of shareholders to challenge the majority on specific issues. For example, under section 5, dissentient holders of 15 per cent of the issued shares can apply to the court for cancellation of an alteration of objects.[6] Again, under section 127, where class rights are varied in pursuance of a clause in the articles, dissentient holders of 15 per cent of the issued shares of the class can apply for cancellation of the variation.[7] Finally, under sections 442 and 443,[8] 200 members or the holders of one-tenth of the issued shares can apply to the Department of Trade and Industry for an investigation of the company's affairs or of the ownership of the company.

## THE RULE IN FOSS V. HARBOTTLE[9]

The rule is that, as one would expect, the proper plaintiff[10] in an action to redress an alleged wrong to a company on the part of anyone, whether director, member or outsider, or to recover

---

[3] *Ante,* p. 393.
[4] *Post,* p. 409.
[5] *Post,* p. 417.
[6] *Ante,* p. 68.
[7] *Ante,* p. 240.
[8] *Post,* p. 437.
[9] "It is common ground between the parties, and those familiar with the complications of the rule in *Foss v. Harbottle* will not find this a matter of surprise, that difficult questions do arise," *per* Knox J. in *Smith v. Croft (No. 2)* [1987] BCLC 206, 208.
[10] The Scots term is "pursuer."

money or damages alleged to be due to it, is prima facie the company and, where the alleged wrong is any irregularity which might be made binding on the company by a simple majority of members, no individual member can bring an action in respect of it.[11]

In other words, the company is normally the proper plaintiff in an action to enforce a duty owed to the company by directors or controlling members, and where the breach of duty can be condoned by an ordinary resolution of the members in general meeting, no individual member or minority of members may sue. A general meeting may be held so that the members may by ordinary resolution decide whether to sue or not. If such a meeting has been held and the breach of duty condoned not only does this prevent a single shareholder from bringing an action it may also prevent the liquidator from subsequently doing so.[12] It also follows that where the wrong may be ratified by a special resolution, and such a resolution is passed, no action will lie.[13] It is for this reason also that the employees of a company to whom the directors now owe a duty following section 309,[14] first introduced in 1980, may find it impossible to enforce such a right. Only the members have the right to enforce it.

It has been said[15] that there are two branches of the rule and these have been described[16] as—

(1) the proper plaintiff principle,
(2) the internal management principle.

Two members took proceedings on behalf of themselves and all other members except those who were defendants against the directors of a company to compel them to make good losses sustained by the company owing to the directors buying their own land for the company's use and paying themselves a price greater than its value. *Held*, as there was nothing to prevent the company from taking the proceedings, if it

[11] See *per* Lord Davey delivering the judgment of the court in *Burland v. Earle* [1902] A.C. 82 (P.C. at pp. 93, 94).
[12] *Multinational Gas and Petrochemical Co. v. Multinational Gas and Petrochemical Services Ltd* [1983] Ch. 258 (C.A.). But see also the dissenting judgment of May L.J. and *Re DKG Contractors Ltd* [1990] BCC 903 to the contrary.
[13] See s.35(3); Chap. 6., *ante*.
[14] *Ante*, p. 349.
[15] *Per* Jordon C.J. in *Australian Coal etc. Employees' Fedn. v. Smith* (1937) 38 S.R. (N.S.W.) 48.
[16] *Per* Street J. in *Hawkesbury Development Co. Ltd. v. Landmark Finance Pty. Ltd* (1970) 92 W.N. (N.S.W.). 199.

thought fit to do so, the action failed: *Foss v. Harbottle* (1843) 2 Ha. 461;
67 E.R. 189.[17]

A minority shareholder sought to bring an action on behalf of himself
and to all other shareholders, save three who were directors, against
those directors and the company for damages, alleging that the directors
had been negligent in selling an asset of the company for less than its
market value. Most of the shares in the company were held by another
company, the directors of which were also directors of the first company.
*Held*, since the sale of the mine was *intra vires* the company, and there
was no allegation of fraud by the directors or appropriation of assets of
the company by the majority shareholders in fraud of the minority, the
action was not maintainable. It was open to the company, on the
resolution of a majority of the shareholders, to sell the mine at a price
decided by the company in that manner, and it was open to the company
by a vote of the majority to decide that, if the directors by their
negligence had sold the mine at an undervalue, proceedings should not
be taken by the company against the directors. *Semble*, it is sometimes
admissible to go behind the apparent ownership of shares to discover
whether a company is in fact controlled by wrongdoers, *e.g.* where the
shares are held by nominees: *Pavlides v. Jensen* [1956] Ch. 565.[18]

The rule avoids multiplicity of suits. The reason for the last
part of the rule is that litigation at the suit of a minority of the
members is futile if the majority do not wish it.

> "If the thing complained of is a thing which in substance the
> majority of the company are entitled to do, or if something has been
> done irregularly which the majority of the company are entitled to do
> regularly, or if something has been done illegally which the majority
> of the comapny are entitled to do legally, there can be no use in
> having litigation about it, the ultimate end of which is only that a
> meeting has to be called, and then ultimately the majority gets its

---

[17] Applied in the *Hawkesbury* case, *ante*. In a corresponding Scottish case, *Orr v.
Glasgow etc. Rlwy. Co.* (1860) 3 Macqueen 799, "the ground of action . . . was
that the directors were also directors of a rival company, and that they had
acted in the interests of this latter company to the prejudice of the shareholders
of the first. The action was dismissed on the ground that although the
transaction complained of was beyond the powers of the directors, it was
competent for the shareholders to sanction it, and therefore that a single
shareholder, or a minority, had no title to sue," *per* Lord Kinnear (Ordinary) in
*Rixon v. Edinburgh Northern Tramways Co.* (1889) 16 R. 653 at p. 656.

[18] Scottish illustrations are *Lee v. Crawford* (1890) 17 R. 1094 (action against
director for payment to the company of funds alleged to have been illegally lent
to officials of the company), *Cameron v. Glenmorangie Distillery Co. Ltd.*
(1896) 23 R. 1092 (directors carrying out shareholders' resolution to allot to
managing director unissued shares at a premium considered by a shareholder to
be inadequate) and *Brown v. Stewart* (1898) 1 F. 316 (claim for damages against
directors on ground that they had acted recklessly in commencing business
when so few shares had been applied for).

wishes": *per* Mellish, L.J. in *MacDougall v. Gardiner* (1875) 1 Ch.D. 13 (C.A.) at p. 25.[19]

Another modern rationale for the rule is that it prevents the company being subjected to a long and expensive litigation to no ultimate purpose if an independent majority of the company do not wish to pursue the claim. As a result the rule is dealt with as a preliminary issue before any full trial is held.[20]

Under this rule, the court will not, for example, interfere with irregularities at meetings at the instance of a shareholder.

> The articles empowered the chairman, with the consent of the meeting, to adjourn a meeting, and also provided for taking a poll if demanded by five shareholders. The adjournment was moved, and declared by the chairman to be carried; a poll was then demanded and refused by the chairman. A shareholder suing on behalf of himself and all other shareholders except those who were directors brought an action against the directors and the company for a declaration that the chairman's conduct was illegal and an injunction to restrain the directors from carrying out certain arrangements without the shareholders' approval. *Held*, the action could not be brought by a shareholder; if the chairman was wrong, the company alone could sue: *MacDougall v. Gardiner* (1875) 1 Ch.D. 13 (C.A.).

> Nor will the court grant a declaration that the accounts are not in the correct form at the instance of a shareholder: *Devlin v. Slough Estates Ltd.* [1983] BCLC 497.

## Derivative actions—exceptions to the rule in *Foss v. Harbottle*

The rule is subject to a number of exceptions, in which case a minority of shareholders, or even an individual shareholder, may bring a minority shareholders' action, usually under R.S.C., Ord. 15, r. 12,[21] *i.e.* the minority shareholders sue on behalf of themselves and all other shareholders except those who are defendants, and may join the company as a defendant. The directors are usually defendants. This action is brought instead of an action in the name of the company.

---

[19] *cf.* Lord Hunter in *Harris v. A. Harris Ltd*, 1936 S.C. 183 at p. 198.

[20] *Prudential Assurance Co. Ltd v. Newman Industries (No. 2) Ltd* [1982] Ch. 204 (C.A.); *Smith v. Croft (No. 3)* [1987] BCLC 355; *post*, p. 404.

[21] Not applicable to Scotland. There is no special form for a "derivative action" in Scots law: the minority shareholder would require to proceed in his own name. For procedural problems in Scotland see Allan L. Mackenzie. *The Problem of Enforcement of Directors' Duties in Scotland*, 1981 S.L.T. (News) 257, and A. A. Paterson, *The Derivative Action in Scotland*, 1982 S.L.T. (News) 205.

"The form of the action is always" A.B. (a minority shareholder) on behalf of himself and all other shareholders of the company' against the wrongdoing directors and the company": *per* Lord Denning M.R. in *Wallersteiner v. Moir (No. 2)* [1975] Q.B. 373 (C.A.) a p. 390.

This type of action is a *derivative action, i.e.* the right to sue derives from that of the company. The shareholders as such have no such right. If their own personal rights are being infringed they may bring a *representative* action, *post.*

The nature of the derivative action is that it is a "procedural device for enabling the court to do justice to a company controlled by miscreant directors or shareholders."[22] It follows that the court is entitled to examine the conduct of whoever intends to start such proceedings—he must be doing so for the benefit of the company and not for some other purpose; *i.e.* he must be a proper person to bring a derivative action. A particular person might not be a proper person because his conduct is tainted in some way which under the rules of equity may bar relief; *e.g.* he might not come with "clean hands" (*e.g.* having participated in the wrong), or he may have been guilty of delay,[23] or be motivated by purely personal motives which are not to the benefit of the company.[24]

A husband was the majority shareholder and his wife the minority shareholder of a company. The husband had appropriated money belonging to the company for his own use, but the wife had previously brought matrimonial proceedings and had been awarded a sum in respect of that money by the court. The Court of Appeal decided that she was not a proper person to bring a derivative action on behalf of the company since she had, with knowledge of the facts, elected to pursue the matrimonial claim, and it would be inequitable to allow a double claim. A defendant to a derivative action can raise any defence which he could have raised had the action been brought by the shareholder personally: *Nurcombe v. Nurcombe* [1985] 1 W.L.R. 370 (C.A.).

It also follows from the nature of a derivative action that if the company has no right to bring an action then no derivative action can be allowed.[25] A minority shareholder[26] cannot have a larger

---

[22] *Nurcombe v. Nurcombe* [1985] 1 W.L.R. 370, *per* Lawton L.J. at p. 376. See also *Wallersteiner v. Moir (No. 2)* [1975] Q.B. 373, *per* Lord Denning M.R. at p. 390.

[23] *Towers v. African Tug Co.* [1904] 1 Ch. 588.

[24] *Barrett v. Duckett, The Times,* July 27, 1994 (C.A.).

[25] See *Watts v. Midland Bank plc* [1986] BCLC 15, 20, *per* Peter Gibson J.

[26] This includes a fifty per cent shareholder: *Barrett v. Duckett, The Times,* July 27, 1994 (C.A.).

right to relief than the company itself would have if it were the plaintiff. If therefore there is a valid reason why the company should not sue, it will equally prevent a minority shareholder suing on its behalf.[27]

A derivative action may be brought in the following cases:—

(1) Where the wrong complained of is a fraud by the majority of the members on the minority and the wrongdoers are in control of the company in general meeting, *i.e.* they control the majority of the shares in the company, and they will not permit an action to be brought in the name of the company. If the aggrieved minority could not bring a minority shareholders' action in this case their grievance would never reach the courts. Where an action is brought under this exception the wrongdoers are usually both directors and controlling shareholders.

In *Cook v. Deeks*[28] a shareholder brought a minority shareholders' action to compel the directors to account to the company for the profits made out of the construction contract which they took in their own names.[29]

In Scotland it has been held that the minority must have first made a definite attempt to obtain the company's co-operation: it is not sufficient for them to plead that the majority had the power to outvote them; *per* Lord Kyllachy (Ordinary) in *Lee v. Crawford* (1890) 17 R. 1094 at p. 1096; *Brown v. Steward* (1898) 1 F. 316.

Recent cases have widened this exception to the rule in two ways and, possibly, narrowed it in others. First as to the meaning of "fraud" in this context:

In *Daniels v. Daniels*[30] the minority shareholders of a company were allowed to bring an action where the directors had authorised the sale of company land to one of them at a price alleged to be well below its market value. The directors objected that since fraud had not been alleged the action should not be allowed.

Templeman J. laid down a wider definition of "fraud" for this purpose: "If minority shareholders can sue if there is fraud, I see no reason why they cannot sue where the action of the majority

[27] *Smith v. Croft (No. 3)* [1987] BCLC 355.
[28] [1916] 1 A.C. 554.
[29] See also *Menier v. Hooper's Telegraph Works* (1874) L.R. 9 Ch.App. 350. For Scotland see also *Rixon v. Edinburgh Northern Tramways* (1889) 16 R. 653 and *Hannay v. Muir* (1898) 1 F. 306.
[30] [1978] Ch. 406.

and the directors, though without fraud, confers some benefit on those directors and majority shareholders themselves."[31] The judge distinguished *Pavlides v. Jensen*, above, on the grounds that in that case the directors had not benefited by their "negligence." It follows from this that there is no exception where the allegation is simply that the directors were acting with a collateral purpose with no benefit to themselves.[32]

In *Estmanco (Kilner House) Ltd v. Greater London Council*[33] the majority shareholder proposed to alter a contract it had with the company in order to deprive the minority shareholders of certain rights. The majority shareholder then proposed a resolution whereby the company should not sue for breach of contract. When a minority shareholder sought to sue on the company's behalf the majority shareholder argued that since it had acted bona fide for the benefit of the company there was no fraud on the minority to allow such an action.

Megarry V.-C, refused to accept that test of fraud on the minority as applicable for the purposes of bringing an action. It only related to the alteration of the company's articles.[34] In this case the action of the majority shareholder injured one category of shareholder to the benefit of another. Fraud in this sense is abuse of a power.

The second development concerns the requisite element of "control" by the majority. It has always been accepted, as stated above, that this means actual voting control. But in *Prudential Assurance Co. Ltd v. Newman Industries Ltd (No. 2)*[35] Vinelott J. was prepared to extend the exception when the alleged fraud was committed by directors who did not exercise actual voting control but who exercised control in *practice*. Large public companies, such as *Newman*, are in fact controlled by less than 50 per cent of the votes. The Court of Appeal in that case did not express any opinion on this point.

It may be, however, that following Knox J.'s decision in *Smith v. Croft (No. 3)*,[36] *infra*, if a majority of the independent shareholders do not wish to sue, then no action may be brought, even when the defendants are in control.

A petition was rejected in *Barrett v. Duckett*[37] on the basis that the alleged wrongdoer had already sought to have the company

---

[31] *ibid.*
[32] *Re Downs Wine Bar Ltd* [1990] BCLC 839.
[33] [1982] 1 All E.R. 437.
[34] *Ante*, p. 85.
[35] [1982] 1 All E.R. 354 (C.A.); [1980] 2 All E.R. 841.
[36] [1987] BCLC 355.
[37] *The Times,* July 7, 1994 (C.A.).

wound up before the petition was presented and that in the circumstances this was a better remedy then the derivative action since the liquidator could decide whether to bring any action on behalf of the company.

(2)   Where the act is one which is illegal, or, prior to the 1989 Act, contrary to the company's constitution.[38]

The members cannot ratify an illegal act. However, if the act is merely contrary to the company's constitution it may be condoned, and any action against the directors waived, by separate special resolutions under section 35(3).[39] An individual shareholder still has the right to seek an injunction to prevent such an act, which is not subject to the rule in *Foss v. Harbottle*, and this is preserved by sections 35(2) and 35A(4)[40] unless the company is already bound. It follows that an act contrary to the company's constitution is better regarded as falling within (3) below following the changes made by the 1989 Act, rather than under this head.

Even if the act is illegal, *e.g.* under the Companies Act, however, the majority may validly resolve to take no action to remedy the wrong done and if that resolution is made in good faith and in what the majority consider to be for the benefit of the company, it will bind the minority.[41]

In *Smith v. Croft (No. 3)*,[42] the action involved alleged payments by the directors in breach of section 151, *i.e.* the financial assistance rules,[43] which if proved would have been illegal. The judge held that an individual shareholder did not have an absolute right to bring a derivative action on that basis to recover the money so spent, as distinct from preventing it beforehand. Such a right of recovery would only be available if the company had such a right. In that case a majority of the independent shareholders[44] did not wish the action for recovery to be brought and the judge regarded that as a sufficient reason to disallow the action.

[38] *Flitcroft's Case* (1882) 21 Ch.D. 519 (C.A.). And see the *Hawkesbury* case, referred to in note 16.
[39] *Ante*, Chap. 6.
[40] *Ante*, Chap. 6.
[41] *Taylor v. National Union of Mineworkers (Derbyshire Area)* [1985] BCLC 237.
[42] [1987] BCLC 355.
[43] *Ante*, p. 196.
[44] That is a question of fact in each case.

"Ultimately the question which has to be answered . . . is: 'Is the plaintiff being prevented improperly from bringing these proceedings on behalf of the company?' If it is an expression of the corporate will of the company by an appropriate independent organ that is preventing the plaintiff from prosecuting the action he is not improperly but properly prevented and so the answer to the question is No. The appropriate independent organ will vary according to the constitution of the company concerned and the identity of the defendants, who will in most cases be disqualified from participating by voting in expressing the corporate will"; *per* Knox J. [1987] BCLC 355, 403.

(3) Where the matter is one which can be validly done or sanctioned, not by a simple majority, but only by some special majority, *e.g.* a special resolution, which has not been obtained. If an action could not be brought in this case the company could, in breach of the memorandum or articles, do *de facto* by ordinary resolution that which according to its regulations can only be done by a special resolution.

Thus in *Baillie v. Oriental Telephone Co. Ltd*,[45] a shareholder was able to bring a minority shareholders' action to restrain the company from acting on a special resolution of which insufficient notice had been given.[46]

Acts contrary to the company's constitution may be ratified by a special resolution, so that the above rule applies in that case. However, it may be that in all such cases, where an action is for recovery of loss to the company, a majority of the independent shareholders may be able to prevent such an action being brought, following the decision in *Smith v. Croft (No. 3), supra.*

(4) It was assumed, although not decided, in *Heyting v. Dupont*[47] that there may be a further exception to the rule in *Foss v. Harbottle*—namely where justice demands that an action be brought, *e.g.* where all that is alleged is damage to the company arising from a director's misfeasance in withholding an asset of the company without fraud or *ultra vires.*

The company was to exploit an invention of the defendant's consisting of a machine for making plastic pipes and the defen-

[45] [1915] 1 Ch. 503 (C.A.), *ante*, p. 291.
[46] And see *Dunn v. Banknock Coal Co. Ltd* (1901) 9 S.L.T. 51 (O.H.).
[47] [1964] 1 W.L.R. 843 (C.A.), *per* Russell and Harman L.JJ. at pp. 851, 854.

dant withheld the company's patent application. However, the company could not have exploited the invention because it was in a state of paralysis owing to discord, so there was no damage to the company and therefore justice did not require that exception be made. Again, there is some authority to the effect that justice may demand that exception be made where the directors are in breach of duty which the company in general meeting could, but will not, condone and, although the directors are not controlling shareholders, they prevent the company suing because an article like Table A, regulation 70, gives them most of the powers of the company.[48]

In the *Prudential* case[49] Vinelott J. based his decision on the derivative action against the directors on the doctrine that a minority action could be allowed if "the interests of justice require that a minority action should be permitted."[50] The Court of Appeal did not need to discuss the rule in *Foss v. Harbottle* because the company had actually adopted the case, but expressed the opinion that any exception based on the justice of the case was not a practical one.

## Procedure

The real difficulty is that the question of whether a minority shareholder should be allowed to bring a derivative action ought to be a preliminary issue tried before the merits of the case, *e.g.* alleged fraud, are debated. If the justice exception is used it will in effect need a full trial of the issues to decide how justice will be best served. The Court of Appeal in the *Prudential* case thought that in such a preliminary action the minority shareholder should be required to establish at least a prima facie case that (a) the company is entitled to the relief claimed, and (b) the action falls within the proper boundaries of the rule restricting members' actions on behalf of the company.

This procedure was approved by Knox J. in *Smith v. Croft (No. 2)*[51] as a half way house between assuming for procedural purposes either that all allegations are true or requiring the

---

[48] See *per* Hudson J. in *Kraus v. J.G. Lloyd Pty. Ltd* [1965] V.R. 232 at pp. 236, 237.
[49] *Ante*, p. 404.
[50] [1980] 2 All E.R. 841 at p. 877.
[51] [1987] BCLC 206.

plaintiff to prove everything as a preliminary issue, as happened in the *Prudential* case.

On the other hand, the court may now authorise civil proceedings to be brought on behalf of the company by such persons and on such terms as it shall direct, as the result of a petition under section 459, *post*.

The minority shareholders' action is called a derivative action[52] to indicate that the right being enforced is that of the company. If the company is in liquidation such an action should be taken over by the liquidator if he is willing to do so.[53] The Legal Aid Act 1988 makes no provision for legal aid in a minority shareholders' action but it is open to the court in such an action to order the company to indemnify the plaintiff against the costs of the action. The minority shareholder should apply for the sanction of the court soon after issuing his writ. If granted he will be given such indemnity. It would be unlawful as being contrary to public policy for a solicitor to accept a retainer for the plaintiff(s) to conduct the action on a contingency fee basis (*i.e.* he is paid the fee if he wins but not if he loses).[54]

It has been held that applications for indemnity should be made *inter partes* and that the court will apply the same criteria as when deciding whether there is a triable case. Further it was said in that case that costs should not be awarded unless financially necessary.[55] This contradicts an earlier case,[56] where an indemnity order was granted on the basis of whether an honest, independent and impartial board would have authorised the action and the fact that the minority shareholder was not impecunious was held not be a ground for refusing the indemnity order.

### Representative actions

In *Hogg v. Cramphorn*[57] the plaintiff was held to be justified in suing in a representative capacity in respect of the alleged

---

[52] *Per* Lord Denning M.R. at p. 390 and Scarman L.J. at p. 406 in *Wallersteiner v. Moir (No. 2)* [1975] Q.B. 373 (C.A.). Scarman L.J. said that the American description of a minority shareholders' action brought to obtain redress for the company, as a stockholders' derivative action, is apt.

[53] *Fargo Ltd v. Godfroy* [1986] BCLC 370.

[54] *Wallersteiner* case, *ante*.

[55] *Smith v. Croft* [1986] 1 W.L.R. 580.

[56] *Jaybird Group Ltd v. Greenwood* [1986] BCLC 319.

[57] [1967] Ch. 254, *ante*, p. 352.

wrongful disposition of the company's money by the directors
which could be condoned by a resolution in general meeting, so
that the action should have been dismissed unless it was not a
*derivative* representative action but an individual rights *representative* action.

A member of a company may enjoy a right alone or in
common with other members of the company and the rule in *Foss
v. Harbottle* has no application where individual members sue,
not in right of the company, but in their own right to protect their
*individual* rights as members[58]—in such a case a member can
bring an action in his own name and may sue on behalf of himself
and other members, and the breach of duty owed to an individual
shareholder cannot be ratified by a majority of shareholders.
Thus in *Pender v. Lushington*[59] a shareholder was able to enforce
the article giving him a right to vote at meetings and compel the
directors to record his vote.[60] Similarly, actions for damages by
shareholders in their own right do not come within the rule. Thus
where the defendant owes a duty to the shareholder personally,
no restrictions apply.[61]

Circumstances in which an individual member can sue in his
own name include actions to prevent:

(1) the company from acting illegally or contrary to the
    memorandum[62];
(2) proposed acts where a special majority is required and has
    not been obtained[63];
(3) the company from acting contrary to its articles.

It used to be thought that where the wrong complained of
damaged the rights of individual members, in the sense of
lowering the value of their shares, as well as being a breach
of duty to the company, the individual members could sue for the

---

[58] *Per* Sir Geo. Jessel M.R. in *Pender v. Lushington* (1877) 6 Ch.D. 70 at pp. 80, 81.
[59] (1877) 6 Ch.D. 70.
[60] See also *Ngurli v. McCann* (1954) 90 C.L.R. 425, as explained in *Provident International Corpn. v. International Leasing Corpn. Ltd* (1969) 89 W.N. (Pt. 1) (N.S.W.) 370.
[61] *R.P. Howard Ltd v. Woodman, Matthews & Co.* [1983] Com.L.R. 100.
[62] *Per* Lord Campbell L.C. in *Simpson v. Westminster Palace Hotel* (1860) 8 H.L.C. 712, 11 E.R. 608 at p. 610; *Russell v. Wakefield Waterworks Co.* (1875) L.R. 20 Eq. 474, at p. 481. See also ss.35(3) and 35A(4), *ante*, Chap. 6.
[63] *Edwards v. Halliwell* [1950] 2 All E.R. 1064 (C.A.).

damage to themselves as proper plaintiffs and so avoid the rule in
*Foss v. Harbottle.* One member could thus sue on behalf of
the others in a *representative action.* In the *Prudential* case[64] the
minority shareholder used this form of action in addition to the
derivative action. The claim was based on the loss suffered by
the shareholders as a result of the directors' alleged fraud on the
company. Because the company had lost money, the shareholders' profit expectations had been diminished. This argument
failed, however, in the Court of Appeal. The alleged loss to the
shareholders was neither separate nor distinct from that suffered
by the company. Only one loss had occurred and only one action
could be allowed. Such actions would "subvert" the rule in *Foss
v. Harbottle.* However, if the payment of damages to the
company would not compensate the shareholders for the loss
they have suffered, *e.g.* because as a result of the directors'
breach of duty the shareholders' former company has been
acquired by another at a lower value than would otherwise have
occurred, a representative action may still be brought.[65]

The rule does not apply where a shareholder relies on a
statutory right, *e.g.* a right to have the register of members
rectified under section 359.

## Winding up by the Court on the "Just and Equitable" Ground

Under sections 122 and 124 of the Insolvency Act 1986 a
contributory may petition that a company be wound up by the
court and where the court is of opinion that it is just and
equitable that the company should be wound up, the court may
order winding up.

### Who may bring a petition

A member of a company is a contributory, and it has been held
that a holder of fully paid-up shares is a contributory.[66] Thus in
appropriate circumstances even a single member can petition for
a winding up. We shall see[67] that section 124 of the 1986 Act

---

[64] *Ante,* p. 403.
[65] *Heron International Ltd v. Lord Grade* [1983] BCLC 244, 262 *per* Lawton L.J.
[66] *Re National Savings Bank Assocn.* (1866) L.R. 1 Ch.App. 547; *Walker and Others, Petitioners* (1894) 2 S.L.T. 230 and 397 (O.H.).
[67] *Post,* Chap. 27.

generally prevents a contributory from petitioning unless he has held his shares for at least six months.

In petitioning for a winding up on the just and equitable ground a member is not confined to such circumstances as affect him as a shareholder, *i.e.* he is not confined to cases where his position as a shareholder has been worsened by the action of which he complains; he is entitled to rely on any circumstances of justice or equity which affect him in his relations with the company or with the other shareholders,[68] although it may be otherwise on a petition under section 459. The relationship between petitions for winding up and those under section 459 is dealt with *post.*[69]

The court will not, as a rule, order a winding up on a contributory's petition unless he alleges in the petition, and proves at the hearing, at least to the extent of a prima facie case, that there will be assets for distribution among the shareholders or that some disadvantage would accrue to him by virtue of his membership which could be avoided or minimised,[70] a purely private advantage will not suffice.[71] The reason is that unless there are such assets the contributory has no interest in a winding up. The courts will not normally strike out a petition before the hearing on that basis, however, unless it has no doubts about the matter. Thus even where the company's only asset was a non-assignable lease with no clear market value the judge let the petition go to trial since it might have been of some value to the company.[72] Similarly, where the petition is based on the fact that there has been a failure to provide accounts and information so that it is impossible for the petitioner to be able to tell whether or not there will be a surplus available to the contributories, the courts will allow the petition to proceed.[73]

Further, a contributory's petition which is opposed by the majority of the contributories will usually not be granted except

---

[68] *Ebrahimi v. Westbourne Galleries Ltd* [1973] A.C. 360.

[69] p. 430.

[70] *Re Rica Gold Washing Co.* (1879) 11 Ch.D. 36 (C.A.); *Re Martin Coulter Enterprises Ltd.* [1988] BCLC 12; *Re Instrumentation Electrical Services Ltd* (1988) 4 BCC 301.

[71] *Re Chesterfield Catering Co. Ltd* [1976] 3 All E.R. 294. If the petitioner is also a creditor and the company is insolvent the petition may be amended to one seeking a winding up on the grounds of insolvency: *Re Commercial and Industrial Insulations Ltd* [1986] BCLC 19.

[72] *Re Martin Coulter Enterprises Ltd* [1988] BCLC 12.

[73] *Re Wessex Computer Stationers Ltd* [1992] BCLC 366.

where the conduct of the majority is something of which the minority have a right to complain,[74] or the main object of the company has failed.[75] The petitioner need not establish that the other members have not acted bona fide in the interests of the company.[76] If the directors who are not contributories wish to bring a petition they must be acting unanimously.[77]

**Meaning of just and equitable**

An order for winding up on the just and equitable ground will be made in the following circumstances, some of which do not involve oppression of the minority:

(1) Where the main object of the company has failed or the company is engaging in acts which are entirely outside what can fairly be regarded as having been within the general intention or common understanding of the members when they became members.[78]

A company was formed to acquire the English portion of the aircraft business of M. Blériot, a well-known airman. M. Blériot refused to carry out the contract. *Held*, the company should be wound up because its substratum had gone: *Re Blériot Aircraft Co.* (1916) 32 T.L.R. 253.

A company formed to purchase, charter and work ships and to carry on the business of shipowners lost its only vessel. Its remaining asset was a balance of £363 in the bank. A majority in number and value of shareholders petitioned for compulsory winding up, but a minority of shareholders desired to carry on the business as charterers. *Held*, it was just and equitable that the company should be wound up: *Pirie v. Stewart* (1904) 6 F. 847.

(2) If the company is a "bubble," *i.e.* there is no bona fide intent on the part of the directors to carry on business in a proper manner.[79]

The court will not order a solvent company to be wound up merely because it is making a loss or is deeply indebted if the

---

[74] *Re Middlesborough Assembly Rooms Co.* (1880) 14 Ch.D. 104 (C.A.); *Re Tivoli Freeholds Ltd* [1972] V.R. 445.

[75] *Re German Date Coffee Co.* (1882) 20 Ch.D. 169; *Pirie v. Stewart* (1904) 6 F. 847; *Re Perfectair Holdings Ltd* (1989) 5 BCC 837; contrast *Cox v. "Gosford" Ship Co. Ltd.* (1894) 21 R. 334 and *Galbraith v. Merito Shipping Co. Ltd*, 1947 S.C. 446.

[76] See note 68.

[77] *Re Instrumentation Electrical Services Ltd* (1988) 4 BCC 301.

[78] See note 75.

[79] *Re London and County Coal Co.* (1866) L.R. 3 Eq. 355.

majority of the shareholders are against a winding up,[80] or if no
meeting of shareholders has been held to consider winding up.[81]
A company was wound up, however, where it had a contract
damages claim against it to which it was defenceless and which
the petitioner could have invoked at any time.[82]

    (3)  Where the company was formed to carry out a fraud, or
           to carry on an illegal business.

    T.E.B. and his sons were relatives of, and had been employed by,
persons who carried on the business of piano manufacturers under the
name of J. B. & Sons. They left J. B. & Sons and formed a company
called T. E. B. & Sons Ltd for carrying on a similar business. A
prospectus was issued which stated that the price paid for the business
was £76,650, when it was really only £1,000 in cash together with £5,000
in shares in the company. Money was subscribed by the public and most
of this money found its way into the hands of the persons who were the
real, though not the ostensible, promoters. J. B. & Sons obtained an
injunction restraining the company from using the name B., and it was
found that the company was formed to filch as much trade as possible
from J. B. & Sons. Numerous actions were brought against the company
for fraud in the prospectus. *Held*, the company should be wound up: *Re
Thomas Edward Brinsmead & Sons* [1897] 1 Ch. 45; 406 (C.A.).

Fraudulent misrepresentation in the listing particulars or prospectus[83] or fraud in the course of business with the outside world[84]
are not, by themselves, grounds for winding up the company, as
the majority of the shareholders may waive the fraud, or there
may be a change of management; but fraud in the real, though
not the ostensible, object of the company will be such a ground.

    (4)  Where the mutual rights of the members are not
           exhaustively defined in the articles, *e.g.* where they
           entered into membership on the basis of a personal
           relationship involving mutual confidence or an under-
           standing as to the extent to which each is to participate in

---

[80] *Re Suburban Hotel Co.* (1867) L.R. 2 Ch.App. 737 (company making a loss),
*Black v. United Collieries Ltd* (1904) 7 F. 18 (company deeply indebted). See
also *Galbraith v. Merito Shipping Co. Ltd,* 1947 S.C. 446, *per* Lord Mackay, at
p. 458.
[81] *Cox v. "Gosford" Ship Co. Ltd* (1894) 21 R. 334; *Scobie v. Atlas Steel Works
Ltd* (1906) 8 F. 1052.
[82] *Re Dollar Land Holdings plc* [1994] 1 BCLC 404.
[83] *Re Haven Gold Mining Co.* (1882) 20 Ch.D. 151 (C.A.).
[84] *Re Medical Battery Co.* [1894] 1 Ch. 444.

the management of the company's business, and that confidence is not maintained or the petitioner is excluded from the management.

From about 1945 E. and N. were partners in a carpet dealing business with an equal share in the management and profits. In 1958 they formed a private company to take the business over. E. and N. were the first directors and each held 500 £1 shares. The articles provided that shares could not be transferred without the directors' consent. Later, N.'s son, G., was appointed a director and E. and N. each transferred 100 shares to him. The company made good profits which were all distributed by way of directors' remuneration, i.e. no dividends were paid. After a disagreement between E. and N., with whom G. sided, N. and G. at a general meeting removed E. as director by ordinary resolution under section [303], and thereafter excluded him from the conduct of the company's business. E. petitioned for an order under section [122(1)(g) of the Insolvency Act 1986] that the company be wound up on the ground that it was just and equitable. *Held*, (by the House of Lords) that it was just and equitable that the company be wound up. After a long association in partnership, during which he had had an equal share in the management and profits, E. had joined in the formation of the company; the inference was indisputable that he and N. had done so on the basis that the character of the association would, as a mater of personal faith, remain the same; and E. had established that N. and G. were not entitled, in justice and equity, to make use of their legal powers of expulsion. Furthermore E. was unable to dispose of his interest in the company without the consent of N. and G.: *Ebrahimi v. Westbourne Galleries Ltd* [1973] A.C. 360.

*Per* Lord Wilberforce at pp. 374, 375: ". . . there has been a tendency to create categories or headings under which cases must be brought if the [just and equitable] clause is to apply. This is wrong. Illustrations may arise but general words should remain general and not be reduced to the sum of particular instances."

And at p. 379: "The words [just and equitable] are a recognition of the fact that a limited company is more than a mere legal entity, with a personality in law of its own: that there is room in company law for recognition of the fact that behind it, or amongst it, there are individuals, with rights, expectations and obligations *inter se* which are not necessarily submerged in the company structure. That structure is defined by the Companies Act and by the articles of association by which shareholders agree to be bound. In most companies and in most contexts, this definition is sufficient and exhaustive, equally so whether the company is large or small. The 'just and equitable' provision does not . . . entitle one party to disregard the obligation he assumes by entering a company, nor the court to dispense him from it. It does, as equity always does, enable the court to subject the exercise of legal rights to equitable considerations; considerations, that is, of a personal character arising between one individual and another, which may make it unjust, or inequitable, to insist on legal rights, or to exercise them in a particular way.

It would be impossible, and wholly undesirable, to define the circumstances in which these considerations may arise. Certainly the fact that the company is a small one, or a private company, is not enough. There are very many of these where the association is a purely commercial one, of which it can safely be said that the basis of association is adequately and exhaustively laid down in the articles. The superimposition of equitable considerations requires something more [than the fact that the company is a small one, or a private company], which typically may include one, or probably more, of the following elements: (i) an association formed or continued on the basis of a personal relationship, involving mutual confidence—this element will often be found where a pre-existing partnership has been converted into a limited company; (ii) an agreement, or understanding, that all, or some (for there may be 'sleeping members'), of the shareholders shall participate in the conduct of the business; (iii) restriction on the transfer of the members' interest in the company—so that if confidence is lost, or one member removed from management, he cannot take out his stake and go elsewhere."

*Ebrahimi v. Westbourne Galleries* was applied in *Re A. & B.C. Chewing Gum Ltd,*[85] where the petitioners held one-third of the company's shares on the basis that they should have equal control with the two individual respondents, who were brothers and directors of the company and owned the other two-thirds of the shares. To achieve equality of control, the articles were altered so as to provide, *inter alia*, that the petitioners could appoint and remove a director representing them, and that decisions at board meetings should be unanimous. The petitioners, the respondents and the company also signed and sealed a shareholders' agreement setting out the way in which the day to day business was to be conducted. The respondents refused to recognise the petitioner's removal of their director and the appointment of another in his place. This was not a case of one side making use of its legal rights to the prejudice of another—the petitioners were excluded from their legal and contractual rights. Their right to management participation was repudiated.

Weinberg and Rothman were the sole shareholders in and directors of a company, with equal rights of management and voting power. After a time they became bitterly hostile to one another and disagreed about the appointment of important servants of the company. All communications between them were made through the secretary. The company made large profits in spite of the disagreement. *Held,* mutual confidence had been lost between W. and R. and the company should be wound up: *Re Yenidje Tobacco Co. Ltd* [1916] 2 Ch. 426 (C.A.).

[85] [1975] 1 W.L.R. 579.

Whether it is just and equitable to wind up a company depends on facts which exist at the time of the hearing and a petitioner is confined to heads of complaint set out in his petition.[86]

It is a matter therefore for the petitioner to establish mutual confidence and/or entitlement to management participation. If he can establish neither, then the matter will be left to be dealt with under the company's articles,[87] or possibly by a petition under section 459,[88] post. Such confidence or entitlement may be shown either by the very nature of the company and the relationship between the member/directors, as in a quasi-partnership company similar to that in the Ebrahimi case, supra, or by representations being made to the petitioner to a similar effect.[89] The remedy is even available to someone who is part contingent creditor and part contingent shareholder, i.e. a co-venturer with capital at stake who has a right to take shares, and who has been wrongfully excluded from the management he was intended to have, although it will not be available if he is pursuing a separate action for damages based on the same facts.[90] There is no bar to a petition by a shareholder who is guilty of misconduct if that is not the cause of the breakdown in confidence.[91]

If the petitioner can establish that the affairs of the company are not being managed in a proper manner then if the petition is not due to be heard for some time, the court will appoint a receiver[92] to manage the company's affairs to preserve the status quo and avoid any prejudice to either side. That jurisdiction is exercised by analogy with partnership law.[93]

## Alternative remedies

If, in the case of a contributories' petition, the court is of opinion that it is just and equitable that the company should be wound up and some other remedy, e.g. accepting an offer to purchase his shares, or seeking an order under sections 459–461,

---

[86] Re Fildes Bros. Ltd [1970] 1 All E.R. 923.
[87] Re A Company (1988) 4 BCC 80.
[88] Re A Company, ex p. Estate Acquisition and Development Ltd. [1991] BCLC 154.
[89] Tay Bok Choon v. Tachansan Sdn. Bhd. (1987) 3 BCC 132 (P.C.).
[90] Re A Company (1987) 3 BCC 575.
[91] Vujnovich v. Vujnovich (1989) 5 BCC 740 (P.C.).
[92] Under s.37 of the Supreme Court Act 1981.
[93] Re A Company [1987] BCLC 133.

*post*, is available to the petitioners, the court *must* nevertheless make a winding up order unless it is of the opinion that the petitioners are acting unreasonably in not pursuing the other remedy: Insolvency Act 1986 section 125(2).

In *Re A Company*,[94] Warner J. decided that where the petitioner had a potential claim under section 459, that did not make it unreasonable for him to maintain a claim for a winding up order since it was not plain and obvious that the relief that he would get at the hearing would be relief under section 459. The question would be resolved by the judge at the hearing. Even if the winding-up petition was damaging to the company it did not follow that a petitioner claiming his rights as a quasi-partner was being unreasonable in preventing a petition. The position is even clearer where the court has already refused an application under section 459.[95]

With regard to a bona fide offer being made by the other members under the articles for the petitioner's shares, *i.e.* at a valuation by an independent valuer, the Court of Appeal in *Virdi v. Abbey Leisure Ltd*,[96] overruling the judge below and other earlier decisions, decided that this was not an automatic reason for striking out the winding up petition. There was nothing unreasonable in the petitioner refusing to accept the risk that a valuer's decision might apply a discount for his minority shareholding, since the machinery in a winding up to determine claims against the company was preferable to their worth being estimated by an accountant. If the essence of the decision to allow petitions based on equitable considerations in *Ebrahimi v. Westbourne Galleries Ltd*[97] was that the company's constitution, *e.g.* as to dismissal of a director, might be overriden, then it could be likewise equitable to ignore the share valuation provisions in the articles. Equally, where there are no proper accounts to enable the share valuation provisions to operate, an offer to purchase the petitioner's shares will not be a bar to the petition being brought.[98]

## ALTERNATIVE REMEDY FOR UNFAIRLY PREJUDICIAL CONDUCT

[94] (1989) 5 BCC 18.
[95] *Vujnovich v. Vujnovich* (1989) 5 BCC 740.
[96] [1990] BCLC 342.
[97] [1973] A.C. 360, *ante*.
[98] *Re Wessex Computer Stationers plc.* [1992] BCLC 366.

Section 210 of the 1948 Act, now repealed, provided that any member who complained that the affairs of the company were being conducted in a manner oppressive to some part of the members, including himself, could petition for an order under that section. That section suffered from several drawbacks however,[99] and was repealed in 1980 and replaced by what are now sections 459 to 461 of the 1985 Act.

Under section 459 any member[1] of the company can petition the court for an order on the ground that the affairs of a company are being or have been conducted in a manner which is unfairly prejudicial to the interests of its members generally or of some part of the members (including at least himself) or that any actual or proposed act or omission of the company (including an act or omission on its behalf) is or would be so prejudicial.[2]

The reference to all of the members being affected, as distinct from some part of the members, was added by a 1989 Act amendment, to avoid confusion caused by conflicting decisions on whether if all the members were affected a petition would lie.[3]

If the company is a small private company all the members should be joined as respondents since they may well be affected by the petition. This might not be the case in a larger company, however.[4] Unlike a derivative action the petitioner cannot ask for an indemnity against costs[5] but the court may in appropriate circumstances either appoint a receiver[6] or grant an interim injunction to protect the petitioner,[6a] pending a full hearing of the petition.

---

[99] For details see the twelfth edition of this work.
[1] This includes registered shareholders and those with a perfect transfer of shares to them in equity: *Re Quickdome Ltd* [1988] BCLC 370, but not a beneficiary under a trust: *Re A Company* [1986] BCLC 39. A creditor cannot petition under s.459. The Secretary of State may, however, do so following an investigation, *post*, s.460. Executors of members may also bring a petition: s.459(2). A person who has assented to registration as a shareholder is a member for the purpose of presenting a petition: *Re Nuneaton Borough Association Football Club Ltd* (1989) 5 BCC 377.
[2] s.459(1). This remedy is not available to an employee but only to members: *Re A Company* [1986] BCLC 391.
[3] *Re A Company* [1988] 1 W.L.R. 1068, *cf. Re Sam Weller Ltd* (1989) 5 BCC 810.
[4] *Re A Company* (1987) 3 BCC 375.
[5] *Ante*. p. 407. *Re A Company* [1987] BCLC 82.
[6] *Re A Company* [1987] BCLC 133.
[6a] *Safinia v. Comet Enterprises Ltd* [1994] BCC 883; *Rutherford, Petitioner* [1994] BCC 867.

A majority shareholder can bring a petition if the board and the minority shareholders act together to prejudice him, but not if the board have been dismissed.[7]

## Meaning of unfairly prejudicial conduct

The alleged conduct may be past, present or future.[8] It may be by an act or omission and be by an agent (*e.g.* the directors). There is no statutory definition of what is "unfairly prejudicial" conduct. It is clearly wider than oppression and is no longer allied to the rules for winding up so that there is no compelling reason for the courts to insist that such conduct must be continuous.

### *Management Exclusion Cases*

The section only applies to members of the company and at first it seemed that this might prevent a member bringing a petition in another capacity. Thus in *Re A Company*,[9] the judge rejected a petition by the executors of a will for infant shareholders who wished to sell their shares to release funds for the beneficiaries. Although the directors had refused to consent to the sale (it was a private company) the petition failed because the conduct did not affect the petitioners *qua* shareholders but as executors. The judge also thought that no petition could be brought unless the act complained of had affected the value of the petitioners' shareholding.

In that case, the judge justified the restriction *qua* shareholder, by giving the example of a shareholder who lives next door to company property which is developed in a way detrimental to his property. However, suppose the conduct affects a shareholder as an employee or director? In the classic case we have been dealing with in the previous section of the exclusion of a director from management in a company formed on the basis of management participation, can such an exclusion amount to unfairly prejudicial conduct for the purposes of a section 459 petition? In *Re Westbourne Galleries Ltd*[10] the petitioner failed under section 210

---

[7] *Re Baltic Real Estate Ltd* [1993] BCLC 498.
[8] See, *e.g. Re Kenyon Swansea Ltd* (1987) 3 BCC 259.
[9] [1983] BCLC 126. See also *Re Carrington Viyella plc, The Financial Times,* February 16, 1983.
[10] [1973] A.C. 360, *ante,* p. 413.

of the 1948 Act (even though he succeeded in winding up the company). Would he have succeeded under section 459?

In *Re A Company*,[11] Vinelott J. said that he thought it unlikely that such persons were intended to be excluded from section 459, even though it would not strictly affect his rights as a shareholder. In *Re R.A. Noble & Sons (Clothing) Ltd*[12] Nourse J. adopted the following observations of Slade J. in *Re Bovey Hotel Ventures Ltd*,[13] as to the scope of "unfairly prejudicial" conduct: (1) all cases successful under section 210 of the 1948 Act would fall within section 459, and section 459 could include cases which would not have succeeded under section 210; (2) it would be sufficient for a member to show that the value of his shareholding had been seriously diminished or at least seriously jeopardised by a course of conduct by those who had *de facto* control of the company; (3) the test of unfairness is objective—there is no need to show any conscious knowledge on the part of the controller that it was unfair, or any other evidence of bad faith. It would be a question of whether a reasonable bystander would regard it as unfairly prejudicial.

Nourse J. then accepted that exclusion from management participation could amount to unfairly prejudicial conduct in cases such as *Re Westbourne Galleries*, even though the value of the petitioner's shareholding would not have been seriously diminished. Financial hardship of that type was not necessary. However, in *Coulson, Sanderson and Ward Ltd v. Ward*,[14] Slade L.J. considered that mere exclusion from management participation would not necessarily found a petition under section 459 since what was being complained of was the acts of the directors *inter se* and not the conduct of the affairs of the company.

In *Re A Company*,[15] Hoffmann, J. considered that exclusion from a "legitimate expectation" of taking part in a company's long term management would be unfairly prejudicial, and in *Re A Company*[16] he said that in each such case the question was whether the terms on which the relationship came to an end were unfairly prejudicial to any of the participants. Similarly, in *Re Ringtower Holdings plc*,[17] Peter Gibson J. accepted that if man-

---

[11] [1983] BCLC 151, 158.
[12] [1983] BCLC 273.
[13] Unreported, July 31, 1981
[14] *Financial Times*, October 18, 1985.
[15] [1986] BCLC 376.
[16] [1986] BCLC 362.
[17] (1989) 5 BCC 82.

agement participation was a legitimate expectation then its demise could found an unfairly prejudicial petition. In *Re A Company, ex parte Estate Acquisition and Development Ltd*[18], Mummery J. considered that dismissal of a director, alteration of the company's constitution and lack of information was sufficient even in a company which was not a *Westbourne Galleries* type.

## Other Cases — "affected as a shareholder"

The initial question to be answered is whether the petitioner is being affected as a shareholder. In *Re A Company*[19] Hoffmann J. allowed a petition to proceed where the directors of a private company had made an inaccurate statement to their shareholders in recommending acceptance of a bid from another company owned by them. It was unfair conduct because it affected the shareholders' right to sell their shares to a higher bidder and it affected them *qua* members because one of the interests of a shareholder was in being able to sell his shares at the best price. The judge rejected the argument that it only affected them in their capacity as vendors of the shares. On the other hand, a petition was rejected where the shareholder was seeking to protect his interests as the company's landlord which were in conflict with his interests as a shareholder.[20]

In some cases the judges have adopted the "legitimate expecta-tion" approach adopted by Hoffmann J., *supra,* to answer this question. Thus in *Re Blue Arrow plc,*[21] Vinelott J., although taking into consideration the wider equitable rights of the peti-tioner, rejected a petition by the president of a company when the articles were altered to allow her to be removed by a majority of the directors since she had no legitimate expectation that this would not happen on the company becoming a public company. Similarly, in *Re Posgate & Denby Agencies Ltd,*[22] the non-voting shareholders were held to have no legitimate expectation as to a resolution to sell off some of the company's assets and in *Jaber v. Science and Information Technology Ltd,*[23] one shareholder was held to have no such interest in the voting rights of others. In *Re*

[18] [1991] BCLC 154.
[19] [1986] BCLC 382.
[20] *Re J.E. Cade Ltd* [1992] BCLC 213.
[21] [1987] BCLC 586.
[22] [1987] BCLC 28.
[23] [1992] BCLC 764.

*Kenyon Swansea Ltd,*[24] attempts by the majority shareholders to alter the articles to regain control was held to be contrary to the legitimate expectation of the petitioner as to control.

A variation on this approach was applied in *Re Tottenham Hotspur plc,*[25] where there was a dispute between a minority shareholder and the controlling shareholder of a public company as to the former's dismissal as chief executive of the company. The dismissed chief executive was held to have no legitimate expectation of remaining in control since there was nothing which indicated to the other shareholders that the company was to be governed by anything other than its constitution, so that the board could dismiss him.

*Unfair and prejudicial conduct relating to the affairs of the company*

In most cases it is, however, a question of whether particular actions concerning the conduct of the company's business can be regarded as both unfair and prejudicial. In *Re D.R. Chemicals Ltd,*[26] whilst the action of a majority shareholder/director in allotting shares to himself to increase his shareholding from 60 per cent to 96 per cent was not only a breach of the pre-emption rules of the Companies Act[27] but was also a "blatant case" of unfairly prejudicial conduct; the fact that after that date the minority director/shareholder was paid no remuneration was not since he took no further part in the running of the company. Similarly, in *Re Ringtower Holdings plc*[28] late presentation of accounts was regarded as non-prejudicial and where pre-emption provisions in the articles were deleted and the company re-registered as a private company as part of a management buy-out by the majority, this was not unfair to the minority since the offer was available to them even though it might be prejudicial since they would be locked into the company if they refused the offer.

In general, allegations of mismanagement by the majority will not suffice—the shareholders must take that risk. In certain cases where there is serious mismanagement causing economic harm to

---

[24] [1987] BCLC 514. See also *Re Elgindata Ltd* [1991] BCLC 959.
[25] [1994] 1 BCLC 655.
[26] (1989) 5 BCC 39.
[27] *Ante*, p. 148.
[28] (1989) 5 BCC 82. See also *Re A Company* (1989) 5 BCC 792.

the company's business a petition might be brought, *e.g.* where the controllers refuse to remove an inept director, but it has been said that it is usually necessary to show misuse of corporate assets.[29] Thus, allegations of breach of fiduciary duties by the directors will have to show that they have exceeded their powers or have acted in an illegal or ulterior manner or have acted contrary to the articles in a material way.[30] However, in another case,[30a] the judge granted a petition where there were several continued examples of serious mismanagement which were causing substantial financial harm to the company and to the interests of the minority.

Where a parent company withholds payments to its subsidiary, that will not usually be considered to be conduct relating to the affairs of the subsidiary unless the two companies are in effect managed as one for financial purposes. Even then, it will not be unfair if such conduct saves the holding company which, if it had collapsed, would have destroyed the subsidiary.[31]

The conduct complained of must be unfair to the petitioner[32] and it must relate to the way in which the affairs were conducted or be attributable to an act or omission on the part of the company and not to the acts of a shareholder carried out in a personal capacity outside the course of the company's business, *e.g.* as a creditor.[33] Thus there can be no petition based on shareholder disputes as to voting arising from a shareholders' agreement as distinct from the effect of a resolution passed by such votes. The former are private affairs between shareholders.[33a] Similarly, if the only complaint is the actions of the company's auditors in valuing shares on a share transfer.[34]

If the conduct of the controller is prima facie "above board" it may still, because of surrounding circumstances, be "unfairly prejudicial" for the purposes of section 459.

L owned one third of the shares of a company and was a director. He was removed from his directorship by the other two shareholders and

---

[29] *Re Elgindata Ltd* [1991] BCLC 959. See also *Re A Company, ex p. Burr* [1992] BCLC 724.
[30] *Re Saul D. Harrison & Sons plc* [1994] BCC 475.
[30a] *Re Macro (Ipswich) Ltd* [1994] 2 BCLC 354.
[31] *Re A Company, ex p. Nicholas* [1993] BCLC 366.
[32] *Re Piccadilly Radio plc* (1989) 5 BCC 692.
[33] *Re A Company* [1987] BCLC 141.
[33a] *Re Unisoft Group Ltd* (No. 2) [1994] BCC 766.
[34] *Re Castleburn Ltd* [1991] BCLC 89.

presented a petition under section 459. An emergency general meeting of the company was then called to increase the company's capital and to give the directors power to allot the new shares. The majority shareholders only intended to issue the shares *pro rata* by way of a rights issue. L sued for an injunction to prevent this rights issue. Harman J. granted the injunction. Although the proposed rights issue was prima facie fair since it would not alter the balance, it might in certain circumstances amount to unfairly prejudical conduct *e.g.* (i) if it was known that the dissenting shareholder could not afford to take up the offer and this was the reason for making it, or (ii) if the dissenting shareholder was engaged in litigation and the offer was designed to deplete his available funds. The judge also said that when a section 459 petition had been presented the status quo between the parties should be preserved until the hearing except where a change was absolutely essential: *Re A Company*[35]

In deciding whether to grant a petition under section 459 the conduct of the petitioner is relevant only to the extent either that it might make the conduct of the controllers although prejudicial not unfair, or that it might affect the remedy which the court may make. There is no general rule, as with the old section 210, that the petitioner must come "with clean hands."[36]

X owned 250 and Y Ltd 750 shares in a company which ran degree courses. Y Ltd appropriated the students to its own courses and X was dismissed as a director and teacher. He set up another college and took several intending students with him. Nourse J. held that such an act was not a bar to his petition—on the facts there was no justification for Y Ltd's action: *Re London School of Electronics*.[37]

## Procedural aspects

It has been held that a petition can be brought against a former controller of a company for unfairly prejudicial conduct whilst he was a member.[38] Nor is it a bar that some of the shares are the subject of disputed ownership.[39] On the other hand a single petition covering a group of companies has been rejected on the basis that a separate petition must be brought for each company.[40]

A petitioner is not entitled to an indemnity against costs as in a derivative action[41] and in general costs will follow the result of the

[35] [1985] BCLC 80.
[36] *cf.* derivative actions, *ante*, p. 401.
[37] [1986] Ch. 211.
[38] *A Company* [1986] 1 W.L.R. 281.
[39] *Re Garage Door Associates Ltd* [1984] 1 W.L.R. 35.
[40] *Re A Company* [1984] BCLC 307.
[41] *Re A Company* [1987] BCLC 82, see above p. 407.

petition, although a reduction may be made on a successful petition if some heads prove to have been unsuccessful.[42] In general, no order will be made if the company is under the control of an administrative receiver unless the complaint relates to prevention of the petitioner selling his shares prior to the appointment.[43] A company other than the one directly involved may be joined as a party if it is directly involved in the transactions complained of[44], but this is a matter for the court's discretion.[44a]

## Interface with section 371 orders

In general, the courts will act to prevent changes to the company's constitution or assets pending the hearing of the petition[45] but the ordinary business of the company must be allowed to proceed. In this context a question can arise whereby during the existence of a section 459 petition the court is asked to order a meeting under section 371 because the necessary quorum for a meeting cannot be obtained, usually due to the dispute. This is particularly difficult if the purpose of the meeting is to appoint new directors of the company. In *Re Opera Photographic Ltd*,[46] the existence of a section 459 petition was held not to be a bar on the court making a section 371 order and this was followed in *Re Whitchurch Insurance Consultants Ltd.*[47] In that case the section 459 petition was presented on the eve of the hearing of the section 371 petition and the position may be different if the section 371 petition is presented some time after that under section 459. Thus in *Re Sticky Fingers Restaurant Ltd*[48] the court in those circumstances made the order under section 371 on the proviso that any director appointed by the meeting should undertake not to interfere with the section 459 petitioner's management rights pending the outcome of that petition. In *Harman v. BML Group plc*,[49] the existence of a section 459

---

[42] *Re Elgindata Ltd (No. 2)* [1993] BCLC 119.
[43] *Re Hailey Group Ltd* [1993] BCLC 459.
[44] *Re BSB Holdings Ltd* [1993] BCLC 915.
[44a] *Re Little Olympian Each-Ways Ltd* [1994] 2 BCLC 420.
[45] See *e.g. Re Mountforest Ltd* [1993] BCC 565.
[46] [1989] 1 W.L.R. 634.
[47] [1993] BCLC 1359.
[48] [1992] BCLC 84.
[49] [1994] 2 BCLC 674.

petition was regarded as a factor to be taken into account and the Court of Appeal took notice of the fact that the allegations related to misappropriations by those in control who were petitioning under section 371.

## Involvement of the company

The courts will also grant an injunction against the company being involved in the petition. This is designed to prevent the majority/respondents from dissipating the company's assets in what is essentially a shareholder dispute.[50] This rule may be relaxed to allow the company to be represented at the time when the judgment is given so as to have an input into the consequential orders which may be made[51]; but no other costs should be charged to the company and, if they are, an assets valuation will be amended to protect the petitioner.[52] The company may apply to the court for permission to be involved and in *Re A Company*[53] the court held that there was a rebuttable presumption that the company should not be involved and it would have to show that it was necessary or expedient in the company's interests to do so. Advance approval would require the most cogent evidence of compelling circumstances although it was not an automatic bar that the majority and the board were the same people.

## Available remedies — section 461

If the court is satisfied it may make such order as it thinks fit.[54] No specific request need be made in advance.[55] However, the section provides five possible orders[56] which the court may make.[57]

---

[50] *Re Milgate Developments Ltd* [1993] BCLC 291.
[51] *Re A Company, ex p. Johnson* [1992] BCLC 701.
[52] *Re Elgindata Ltd* [1991] BCLC 959.
[53] [1994] 2 BCLC 146.
[54] s.461(1). This can include refusing the specific relief sought where that is inappropriate or there is a preferred alternative: *Re Full Cup International Trading Ltd*, February 3, 1995.
[55] This was required under the former section 210.
[56] For interim orders see p. 427, *post*.
[57] s.461(2).

(1) an order regulating the affairs of the company in the future[58];

(2) an order to restrain the doing or continuing of an act or to rectify any omission[59];

(3) an order authorising civil proceedings to be brought in the name and on behalf of the company by such persons and on such terms as the court may direct[60];

The respondent to a petition argued that the petitioner was too emotionally involved and vindictive to be given control of any litigation. The Court of Appeal still authorised proceedings to be brought but subject to certain conditions: (i) protection of creditors; (ii) the control of the litigation to be solely the affair of the petitioner's solicitor to the entire exclusion of the petitioner; (iii) no other legal proceedings to be commenced without legal opinion in support; and (iv) no direct communication between the petitioner and respondent: *Re Cyplon Developments Ltd.*[61]

(4) an order altering the company's memorandum or articles. This will have automatic effect without any resolution of the company usually required for such alterations.[62] Such alterations may not be re-altered without the court's consent.[63]

(5) an order providing for the majority to buy out the minority or a purchase of the minority's shares by the company itself.[64] In the latter case it will arrange for the reduction of capital accordingly.

In making an order as to the purchase of shares the court has very wide powers. In certain situations the court will order that

---

[58] This order could be made under s.210 and was in *Re H.R. Harmer Ltd* [1959] 1 W.L.R. 62 (C.A.). In practice such orders usually now merge with those under (5) below to provide a solution: see, *e.g. Re A Company* (1989) 5 BCC 792; but see also *McGuinness v. Bremner plc*, 1988 S.L.T. 891 (O.H.) where such an order was made under this head alone.

[59] This was new in 1980. An instance occurred in *Whyte, Petitioner*, 1984 S.L.T. 330, in which the court pronounced orders restraining a company from holding a meeting, and from passing a resolution removing a director and replacing him with another, and restraining two shareholders from moving or voting in favour of such resolutions.

[60] This was new and intended to alleviate the rule in *Foss v. Harbottle, ante.*

[61] Unreported, March 3, 1982.

[62] s.461(4).

[63] s.461(3).

[64] This is an exception to s.143, *ante*, Chap. 10.

the petitioner buy out the controller's shares,[65] but that is unusual. Usually the issue is one of the purchase of a minority shareholder's shares. That raises two questions. By what method are those shares to be valued and at what date? As to the former it appears that when the shareholding is in a management participation company (*i.e.* an incorporated partnership such as that in *Re Westbourne Galleries Ltd*[66]) so that the shares were taken up initially and are still held by the shareholder as part of the management agreement, then the sale is in effect one from an unwilling vendor. The shares should therefore be valued pro rata according to the value of the shares as a whole. On the other hand where the shareholding has simply been acquired as a minority shareholding it should be valued at a discounted value as a minority shareholding.[67] Similarly where the petitioner has chosen to accept the ending of the management participation agreement and to remain as a minority shareholder his shares will be valued at the discounted price.[68] The court will adopt special valuation rules where the company is in a special positon, *e.g.* a football club where the valuation depends upon prestige rather than profits.[69]

Although the date of valuation is prima facie the date of the purchase order[70] this is not a general rule and if the value of the shareholding has been affected by the unfairly prejudicial conduct, the valuation date can be the date when the conduct began[71] or the date of the bringing of the petition.[72] The court has no power to make an interim order for payment pending an order for the purchase of the shares except where the only dispute is as to the valuation and the interim order is on the lowest possible contended valuation.[73]

---

[65] *Re Bovey Hotel Ventures Ltd*, Unrep. June 10, 1982 (C.A.); *Re Nuneaton Borough AFC Ltd (No. 2)* [1991] BCC 44.

[66] *Ante*, p. 413.

[67] *Re Bird Precision Bellows Ltd* [1985] 3 All E.R. 523 (C.A.); *Re London School of Electronics* [1986] Ch. 211; *Re Ghyll Beck Driving Range Ltd* [1993] BCLC 1126; *Re Macro (Ipswich) Ltd* [1994] 2 BCLC 354.

[68] *Re D.R. Chemicals Ltd* (1989) 5 BCC 39.

[69] *Re A Company* (1989) 5 BCC 792.

[70] *Re D.R. Chemicals Ltd.*, *supra*.

[71] *Re OC (Transport) Services Ltd* [1984] BCLC 251.

[72] *Re London School of Electronics*, *ante*; *Re Cumana Ltd* [1986] BCLC 430 (C.A.).

[73] *Re A Company* (1987) 3 BCC 41; *Ferguson v. Maclennan Salmon Co. Ltd*, 1990 S.L.T. 658.

A copy of any order requiring a company to alter its memorandum or articles must be filed with the registrar within 14 days.[74]

### Effect of offer to buy out the petitioner

If there is a breakdown in relations between director/shareholders so that one of them brings a petition under section 459 on the basis of unfairly prejudicial conduct, the most likely order that the court will make is that one side, usually the majority shareholders, buy out the other. As we have seen such an order will provide for the method and date of the valuation of the shares. In several cases, however, the majority will have already made an offer to purchase the petitioner's shares under the terms of the company's articles and the court is then faced with the problem as to whether such an offer, providing usually for valuation by an independent valuer such as the company's auditors, in effect settles the matter and accordingly no court order is necessary.[75]

In *Re A Company*[76] the articles actually required the dismissed director to offer his shares to the other shareholders. The majority intended to invoke this provision and on that basis Hoffmann J. refused to allow a section 459 petition based on that dismissal to continue. The articles had made provision in advance for what was to happen if there was a breakdown in relations. As in all such cases it was clear that one party had to leave and on the facts that had to be the petitioner on the terms of the articles. The judge did not, however, confine this principle to cases where the petitioner was obliged to sell his shares, but extended it to all cases where there is a dispute leading to a section 459 petition except where the majority have been guilty of bad faith or plain impropriety or the articles provide an arbitrary or artificial method of valuation.

> "It is almost always clear from the outset that one party will have to buy the other's shares and it is usually equally clear who that party will be. The only real issue is the price of the shares . . . . Not many such petitions go to full hearing. They are usually settled by purchase of the petitioner's shares at a negotiated price. But the presentation

---

[74] s.461(5).

[75] No interest is payable on such an agreement unless expressly agreed: *Harrison v. Thompson* [1992] BCLC 833.

[76] [1987] 1 W.L.R. 102.

of such a petition is a powerful negotiating tactic . . . . In these circumstances it seems to me that if the articles provide a method for determining the fair value of a party's shares, a member seeking to sell his shares upon a breakdown of relations with other shareholders should not ordinarily be entitled to complain of unfair conduct if he has made no attempt to use the machinery provided by the articles . . . . I therefore do not consider that in the normal case of breakdown of a corporate quasi-partnership there should ordinarily be any 'legitimate expectation' that a member wishing to have his shares purchased should be entitled to have them valued by the court rather than the auditors pursuant to the articles.[77]

This approach was initially followed in several cases. In *Re A Company*,[78] such an offer was held to render the section 459 petition inappropriate, and the exact words of Hoffmann J. quoted above were applied by Peter Gibson J. in *Re A Company*,[79] by Hoffmann J. again, *Re A Company*[80] and Judge Paul Baker QC in *Re Castleburn Ltd.*[81] In the latter case it was also said that if the valuers make a mistake the petitioner has a remedy to attack the valuation without resorting to a section 459 petition.

On the other hand the court would order a valuation under section 461 if the valuer under the articles cannot be seen to be wholly independent of the directors and to have no connection with the unfairly prejudicial conduct.[82] Nor did an offer to purchase some shares prevent a petition where the petitioner claimed to be entitled to other shares in the company.[83]

However, a change occurred when the Court of Appeal in *Verdi v. Abbey Leisure Ltd*,[84] in rejecting the idea that an offer under the articles would automatically bar a winding up petition on the just and equitable ground[85] and reversing Hoffmann J. on that point, refused either to confirm or reject the idea that it would automatically bar an unfairly prejudicial petition. Following that decision, Harman J. in *Re A Company ex parte Holder*[86] decided that an offer to purchase was no bar where the section

[77] [1987] 1 W.L.R. 102, 110.
[78] (1987) 3 BCC 624.
[79] (1988) 4 BCC 80.
[80] (1989) 5 BCC 218.
[81] [1991] BCLC 89.
[82] *Re Boswell & Co. (Steels) Ltd* (1989) 5 BCC 145.
[83] *Re A Company* (1989) 5 BCC 18.
[84] [1990] BCLC 342.
[85] *Ante*, p. 416.
[86] [1991] BCLC 597.

459 petition was a management exclusion case, even though the articles included a compulsory share purchase procedure. The petitioner, he said, has no real right to challenge the auditors' valuation or to make representations to him.

## Joint petitions for a just and equitable winding up and the alternative remedy

In practice many petitions based on management exclusion cases seek either a just and equitable winding up under section 122 of the Insolvency Act 1986 (*ante*) or relief under section 459 to 461, as alternatives. Prior to 1980 it was generally easier to obtain a winding up order (*e.g. Re Westbourne Galleries Ltd, ante*). This may still be the position in some cases today because of the different bases of the two remedies, *e.g.* conduct which is not unfair may amount to a breach of mutual confidence. Thus in *Re R.A. Noble and Sons*,[87] Nourse J. refused to grant a petition under section 459 on the grounds that objectively the management exclusion had not been unfair since it was partly due to the petitioner's disinterest. The judge did, however, make a winding up order since the exclusion had been the substantial cause of the breakdown in mutual confidence. Thus for a winding up the question is whether the management exclusion was a substantial cause of the subjective breakdown of the underlying equitable obligation of mutual trust whereas for an alternative remedy petition the exclusion must amount to unfairly prejudicial conduct affecting the petitioner *qua* member.[88] Similarly in *Jesner v. Jarrad Properties Ltd*,[89] conduct by the controller of two companies in using the assets of one to fund the other was held not to be unfair to the minority shareholders since both companies were owned by the same people, but a winding up order was granted on the basis of breach of underlying management rights.

The Chancery Division has warned in a Practice Direction[90] that a petition under section 122(1)g should only be used as an alternative to a section 459 petition if that is either the preferred relief or possibly the only relief available.[90a]

---

[87] [1983] BCLC 273. See also *Coulson Sanderson & Ward Ltd v. Ward, The Financial Times,* October 18, 1985; *Teague, Petitioner,* 1985 S.L.T. 469 (O.H.) (provisional liquidator appointed) and *Re A Company* (1989) 5 BCC 18.

[88] *Re A Company* [1990] BCC 221.

[89] [1993] BCLC 1032, 1994 S.L.T. 83.

[90] Chancery 1/90 [1990] BCLC 452.

[90a] Sometimes the court will direct a winding up rather than a purchase: see *Re Full Cup International Trading Ltd,* February 3, 1995.

## INVESTIGATIONS AND POWERS TO OBTAIN INFORMATION

Statutory provision is made for a number of forms of inspection.[91] These comprise investigation of a company's affairs, investigation of the ownership of a company, investigation of share dealings, and inspection of companies' books and papers.

### Investigations of a company's affairs

*Appointment of inspectors*

1. In the case of a company with a share capital, *on the application of not less than 200 members or of members holding not less than one-tenth of the shares issued, or on the application of the company*, the Secretary of State *may* appoint one or more inspectors to investigate the affairs of the company and to report on them. The application must be supported by evidence showing that the applicant or applicants have good reason for requiring investigation. Security, not exceeding £5,000, for the costs of the inquiry, may be required by the Secretary of State (for Trade and Industry): section 431.

An inspector is usually a Queen's Counsel, a Chartered Accountant or an official of the Department of Trade and Industry. In serious cases two inspectors will be appointed.

2. The Secretary of State *shall* appoint an inspector or inspectors *if the court by order,*[92] *declares that an investigation ought to be made*: section 432(1).

3. The Secretary of State *may on his own initiative*[93] appoint inspectors if it appears—

(i) that a company's affairs are being or have been conducted with intent to defraud its creditors or the creditors of any other person or otherwise for a fraudulent or unlawful purpose or in a manner which is unfairly prejudicial to part of its members, or that any actual or proposed act or

---

[91] *e.g.* the investigation into the affairs of House of Fraser Holdings plc, after the disputed take-over of that company.

[92] The procedure in England is to apply to the Companies Court by originating motion under R.S.C., Ord. 102, r.4. For Scotland, see R.C. 189.

[93] It is not improper for inspectors to be appointed where criminal investigations are proceeding at the same time: *Re London United Investments plc* [1992] BCLC 285.

omission of the company is or would be so prejudicial or that it was formed for a fraudulent or unlawful purpose; or

(ii) that the promoters or the person managing its affairs have been guilty of fraud, misfeasance or other misconduct towards the company or its members; or

(iii) that the members have not been given all the information as to the company's affairs which they might reasonably expect: section 432(2).

Inspectors appointed under this head may be appointed on the basis that any report they may make is not to be for publication. In such a case the usual rules as to availability and publication (*post*) will not apply: section 432(2A).[94]

If the Secretary of State appoints inspectors under these heads the company has no right to state its case before the inspectors are appointed. The only requirement is that the decision to appoint is made in good faith.[95]

*Powers of inspectors*

1. An inspector may, if he thinks it necessary, investigate any other body corporate which is or has been either the company's subsidiary[96] or holding company[96] or a subsidiary of its holding company or a holding company of its subsidary: section 433(1).

2. He may call for the production of documents[97] by past or present officers and agents (including bankers, solicitors and auditors) of the company or a related company, whose duty it is to produce to the inspector all documents of or relating to the company or related companies which are in their custody or power, to attend before the inspector when required and to give the inspector all reasonable assistance. These powers extend to persons other than officers or agents if the inspectors consider

---

[94] This is intended to speed up investigations to decide whether any offences have been committed. It is also a result of the House of Fraser Holdings plc investigation, and the unsuccessful attempt by Lohnro plc to have the report published before the Secretary of State was willing to do so: see (1989) 5 BCC 633 (H.L.).

[95] *Norwest Holst Ltd v. Department of Trade* [1978] 3 All E.R. 280.

[96] *Ante*, p. 48.

[97] Documents include information held in an electronic form, *e.g.* on a computer, and the inspectors may require such information in a legible form: section 434(6).

that they are or may be in possession of any information which they believe to be relevant to the investigation[98]: section 434(1)(2).

3.   The inspector may examine any person on oath for the purposes of an investigation: section 434(3).

If an officer or agent refuses to perform his duties under section 434 the inspectors may certify that refusal to the court which may punish him as if he were in contempt of court: section 436. The privilege against self-incrimination does not apply and the officer or agent must answer the questions of the inspectors unless their questioning becomes unfair or oppressive.[99]

A solicitor or barrister need not disclose a privileged communication made to him, except as regards the name and address of his client, and a banker need not disclose any information which is confidential by virtue of banking business relating to his customers other than the company unless either the customer consents or the Secretary of State authorises the disclosure: section 452.

An answer given by a person to a question put under powers given by section 434 (or section 446) may be used in evidence against him: section 434(5). This is so despite the provisions of the Police and Criminal Evidence Act 1984.[1]

In general all evidence to an inspector is admissible against him in both subsequent criminal and civil proceedings. This includes unsworn evidence. Section 434(5) is not limited to public interest proceedings brought by a public authority. Thus the section permits the evidence to be used in subsequent proceedings by the company or its liquidator to redress wrongs done to the company, *e.g.* against the company's auditors.[2]

4.   An inspector may at any time, and, if directed to do so, must inform the Secretary of State of any matters coming to his knowledge as a result of their investigation: section 437(1A). If matters have come to light which have led to the affairs being placed in the hands of the appropriate prosecuting authority the Secretary of State may direct the inspector either to take no further steps or to proceed only as directed by him. In such a case

---

[98] This could include partners and members of unincorporated associations not covered by s.433, *supra.*
[99] *Re London United Investments plc* [1992] BCLC 285.
[1] *R. v. Seelig* [1991] BCLC 869.
[2] *London and County Securities Ltd v. Nicholson* [1980] 3 All E.R. 861.

no final report will be made unless either the inspectors were appointed by a court order or the Secretary of State so directs: section 437(1B).

It has been held that the inspectors' function is investigatory and not judicial but they must, in view of the consequences which may follow from their report, act fairly and, before they condemn or criticise a person, give him a fair opportunity to answer what is alleged against him.[3] It is sufficient for the inspectors to put to witnesses what has been said against them by other persons or in documents to enable them to deal with those criticisms in the course of the inquiry; it is not necessary for the inspectors to put their tentative conclusions to the witnesses in order to give them an opportunity to refute them.[4]

It has been said[5] that the considerations which are to be borne in mind in respect of an inquiry under the Companies Act are:

(a)  it is a very special kind of inquiry. It is not a trial. There is no accused, prosecutor, no charge. It is simply an investigation;

(b)  there is no one to present a case to the inspector. There is no "counsel for the Commission." The inspector has to do it all himself;

(c)  the investigation is in private. This is necessary because witnesses may say something defamatory of someone else, and it would be quite wrong for it to be published without the party affected being able to challenge it;

(d)  the inspectors have to make their report. They should state their findings on the evidence and their opinions on the matters referred to them. They should make it with courage and frankness, keeping nothing back. Before they condemn or criticise a person they must act fairly by them.

---

[3] *Re Pergamon Press Ltd* [1971] Ch. 388 (C.A.), where the persons who were required to give evidence were not entitled to see the transcripts of evidence of witnesses. In *Testro Bros. Pty. Ltd v. Tait* (1963) 109 C.L.R. 353, the majority of the High Court of Australia held that the inspector need not, before making a report on the company's affairs, give the company an opportunity of answering or explaining matters which, if unanswered or unexplained, might give rise to adverse findings or comment in the report.

[4] *Maxwell v. Department of Trade and Industry* [1974] 1 Q.B. 523 (C.A.).

[5] *Per* Lord Denning M.R. in *Maxwell's* case, above, at p. 533.

*Inspectors' report*

The inspectors may make interim reports, and on the conclusion of the investigation they must make a final report to the Secretary of State.

The Secretary of State may send a copy of a report to the company's registered office, and, if he thinks fit, may furnish a copy on request and on payment of the prescribed fee to any member of the company or other company dealt with in the report, or to any person whose conduct is referred to in the report, or to the auditors of the company, or to the applicants for the investigation, or to any other person whose financial interests appear to be affected by it, *e.g.* creditors. He may also order the report to be printed and published. Where the appointment was under section 432 in pursuance of a court order, a copy *must* be furnished to the court: section 437. Section 437 has no application where the inspectors were appointed under section 432 on the basis that their report would not be published.[6]

In exercising his decision as to publication the Secretary of State must act reasonably and according to relevant considerations. He is entitled to withhold publication in the public interest if publication would inhibit a criminal investigation and/or prejudice the fair trial of anyone subject to such investigation.[7]

*Proceedings on inspectors' report*

Section 124A of the Insolvency Act 1986 provides that if it appears to the Secretary of State from the inspectors' report, or from any information obtained under an investigation,[8] that it is expedient in the public interest that the company be wound up, he may present a petition that it be wound up by the court if the court thinks it just and equitable that the company be wound up.[9] No evidence of fraud or misfeasance is necessary.

In addition a minority shareholder may use an inspector's report to support his own petition to wind up the company on the just and equitable ground under section 122(1)(g) of the 1986 Act.[10]

[6] *Ante*, p. 432.
[7] *R. v. Secretary of State for Trade and Industry, ex p. Lonrho plc* [1989] 1 W.L.R. 525 (H.L.).
[8] *Post*, p. 441.
[9] *Ante*, p. 409.
[10] *Re St. Piran Ltd* [1981] 3 All E.R. 270.

If from the report, etc., it appears that civil proceedings ought in the public interest to be brought by any company, section 438 empowers the Secretary of State to bring such proceedings in the name and on behalf of the company. The Secretary of State must indemnify the company against costs or expenses incurred by it in connection with any such proceedings. If civil proceedings are properly brought under this section and there is no evidence to show that the company will be able to pay the defendant's costs if the defence is successful, the defendant is fully protected by the indemnity provision in the section and security cannot be ordered under section 726.[11]

Under section 460 the Secretary of State may bring a petition for an alternative remedy consequent on a report.[12]

## Expenses of investigation

The expenses of an investigation of a company's affairs are defrayed in the first instance by the Secretary of State but the following persons are liable to repay him:

(1) any person convicted on a prosecution instituted as a result of the investigation, or ordered to pay the costs of proceedings brought by virtue of section 438, *ante*, may in the same proceedings be ordered to repay;

(2) any company in whose name proceedings are brought is liable to repay to the extent of money or property recovered by it as a result of the proceedings,

(3) a company dealt with by an inspectors' report, where the inspectors were appointed otherwise than of the Secretary of State's own motion and except where it was the applicant, is liable except so far as the Secretary of State otherwise directs;

(4) the applicants for the investigation, where the inspector was appointed under section 431, *ante*, or section 442(3), *post*, are liable to such extent as the Secretary of State may direct: section 439.

## Extension of Secretary of State's powers of investigation

The investigation powers apply to all companies incorporated outside Great Britain which are carrying on business in Great

---

[11] *Selangor United Rubber Estates Ltd v. Cradock* [1967] 1 W.L.R. 1168.
[12] *Ante*, p. 417.

Britain or have at any time carried on business therein, subject to any adaptations the Secretary of State may specify by statutory instrument: section 453. Sections 431, 438, 442 to 445 and 446 do not apply to such companies, however.

**Investigation of the ownership of a company**[13]

*Appointment of inspectors*

1.   Where he considers that there is good reason to do so, the Secretary of State (for Trade and Industry) *may* appoint one or more inspectors to investigate and report on the membership of a company, for the purpose of determining the true persons who are, or have been, financially interested in the success or failure of the company, or able to control or materially influence its policy: section 442(1). The scope of the investigation may be defined either as to time or as to the matters to be investigated: section 442(2).

2.   Unless the application is vexatious, the Secretary of State *must* appoint an inspector, on the application, with regard to particular shares or debentures, of those members who can apply under section 431[14] for an investigation of the company's affairs provided the applicants give security as to costs not greater than £5,000. The appointment shall not exclude from the scope of the investigation any matter stated by the applicants unless the Secretary of State is satisfied that it would be unreasonable to investigate it. The Secretary of State may, however, refuse to appoint inspectors if the powers to require information as to persons interested in shares (*post*) will be sufficient: section 442(3).

*Powers of inspectors. Inspectors' report*

An inspector appointed under section 442, above, has the same powers as an inspector appointed to investigate the affairs of a company under sections 431 and 432. Section 437 applies to the report of inspectors appointed under section 442.[15]

---

[13] *e.g.* the investigation, by Mr J. B. Lindon Q.C. of the membership of the Savoy Hotel Limited, June 14, 1954.

[14] *Ante*, p. 431.

[15] *Ante*, pp. 435 *et seq.*

In addition, the sections apply in relation to all persons whom the inspector reasonably believes to be or to have been financially interested in the success or failure of the company or related company, or able to control or materially influence its policy. However, the Secretary of State may furnish the company or any person with an abbreviated copy of the report if he is of the opinion that there is good reason for not divulging part of it: section 443(3).

*Expenses of investigation*

The expenses of an investigation under section 442 are defrayed initially by the Secretary of State but may be recovered in the same way as in an investigation into a company's affairs: section 439, *ante.*

*Power to require information as to persons interested in shares, etc.*

Where it appears that there is good reason to investigate the ownership of any shares or debentures of a company, and that it is unnecessary to appoint an inspector for the purpose, the Secretary of State (for Trade and Industry) may require any person whom he reasonably believes to have or to be able to obtain any information as to the present and past interests in the shares or debentures and the names and addresses of the persons interested therein and of any persons who act or have acted for them in relation to the shares of debentures to give them such information.

A person is deemed to have an interest in a share or debenture if he has a right to acquire or dispose of it or any interest therein, or to vote in respect thereof, or if his consent is necessary for the exercise of any right of other persons interested therein, or if such other persons can be required or are accustomed to exercise their rights in accordance with his instructions.

Failure to give information required under this section, or making a statement known to be false in a material particular, or recklessly making a statement false in a material particular, is punishable by imprisonment or a fine or both: section 444.

*Powers to impose restrictions on shares, etc.*

If the Secretary of State has difficulty in finding out the relevant facts about any shares or debentures, he may direct that the shares or debentures shall be subject to restrictions: section 445.[16] The restrictions prevent transfers and agreements to transfer, the exercise of voting rights, the issue of further shares or debentures in right of the shares or debentures or to the holder thereof, including an agreement to transfer such rights, and, except in a liquidation, payment or agreement to transfer payment of any sums due from the company on the shares or debentures, whether in respect of capital or otherwise, *e.g.* payment of a dividend: section 454.[17]

If an order is made, any person aggrieved may appeal to the court for the order to be lifted. The court may only lift an order if it is satisfied: (i) that all the relevant facts about the shares have been disclosed and that no unfair advantage has accrued to anyone by the earlier failure to disclose; (ii) the shares are to be transferred for a valuable consideration[18] and the court approves the transfer; or (iii) if the restrictions unfairly affect the rights of third parties, when a partial exemption can be given: section 456(1A), (3).

Where an order has been made, either the Secretary of State or the company may apply to the court for a further order that the shares be compulsorily transferred free from some or all of the restrictions. The proceeds of a compulsory transfer are to be paid into a separate fund against which the owners can claim, subject to the payment of costs.

Contravention of such restrictions renders the person or company concerned liable to penalties, although a prosecution in England can be instituted only by or with the consent of the Secretary of State: sections 455 and 732.

### Investigation of share dealings

Section 446 provides that if it appears to the Secretary of State (for Trade and Industry) that sections 323[19] or 324[20] or 328(3)–(5)[21] (these sections being concerned with penal-

---

[16] Exceptions can be made to protect third party rights: s.445(1A).
[17] This includes payment on a take-over bid: *Re Ashbourne Investments Ltd* [1978] 2 All E.R. 418.
[18] This will include, *e.g.* accepting a take-over offer of shares in the offeror company. It is no longer restricted to sales for cash.
[19] *Ante*, p. 322.
[20] *Ante*, p. 319.
[21] *Ante*, p. 320.

isation of dealing in options by, and notification of interests of, directors or their spouses or children) may have been contravened, he may appoint one or more competent inspectors to investigate and report to him.

Sections 434 to 437,[22] which impose on officers and agents the duty to assist inspectors, apply with one or two modifications. Thus section 446 applies, *e.g.* to any individual who is, or an officer of a company which is, an authorised person under the Financial Service Act 1986 (see Chapter 19, *post*).

Section 452[23] (savings for lawyers and bankers) applies.

The expenses of such an investigation are dealt with in the same way as with other investigations: section 439, *ante*.

## Inspection of a company's books and papers

This is dealt with in sections 447 to 451 as follows—

### *Power of Secretary of State to require production of documents*

Section 447 provides that the Secretary of State (for Trade and Industry) may, if he thinks there is good reason to do so, require a company to produce such documents[24] as may be specified.

Without prejudice to any lien he may have, production of documents may be required from any person who appears to be in possession of them to any officer or other competent person.[25] Copies of extracts may be taken, and explanations may be required from such person or from present or past officers or employees of the company. If the documents are not produced, the person required to produce may be required to state, to the best of his knowledge and belief, where they are: section 447.

Nothing in that section compels a lawyer to produce a document containing a privileged communication made by or to him: section 452.

Non-compliance with a requirement to produce documents or provide an explanation or make a statement renders the company or person concerned liable to imprisonment or a fine or both.

---

[22] *Ante*, p. 433.
[23] *Ante*, p. 433.
[24] Documents include information stored on computers and any copies required must be given in a legible form.
[25] Thus such low-key investigations may be undertaken by private firms.

Where a person is charged with failing to produce documents it is a defence for him to prove that they were not in his possession or under his control and that it was not reasonably practicable for him to produce them: section 447.

If a person provides or makes an explanation or statement which he knows to be false, or recklessly provides or makes a false explanation or statement, he is liable to imprisonment or a fine or both: section 451.

## Entry and search of premises

If a justice of the peace, or in Scotland a justice of the peace or a sheriff, is satisfied, on information on oath, or in Scotland on evidence on oath, laid by or on behalf of the Secretary of State or anyone authorised, that there are reasonable grounds for suspecting that there are on any premises any documents, in any form, of which production has been required under any investigation provision, and which have not been produced, he may issue a warrant authorising any constable and any other named person and other constables to enter and search the premises and take possession of any documents either appearing to be such or relevant to the investigation or to take steps to preserve them, or to take copies of them or to require any person named in the warrant to provide an explanation of them or state where they may be found.

A similar warrant may also be issued if the justice of the peace etc., is satisfied on information under oath that there are reasonable grounds for believing that an offence has been committed (punishable with at least two years' imprisonment), that there are premises on which documents relevant to that offence are kept, that the Secretary of State could require such documents and that such documents might not be produced but might be tampered with.

Any documents of which possession is taken may be retained for three months or, if within that period there are commenced criminal proceedings (being proceedings to which the documents are relevant), until the conclusion of the proceedings.

Penalties are imposed for obstructing the exercise of a right of entry or search, or of a right to take possession of documents section 448.

**Provision for security of information**

No information or document obtained under section 447, *ante*, may, without the previous written consent of the company, be published or disclosed, except to a competent authority (including the Secretary of State (for Trade and Industry), his officer, an inspector appointed under the Act, the Lord Advocate, the Director of Public Prosecutions, any constable and any procurator fiscal, any designated authority under the Financial Services Act 1986,[26] the City Panel on Takeovers and Mergers,[27] the Treasury or an officer thereof), unless the publication or disclosure is required, *inter alia*:

(1)   with a view to the institution of, or for the purposes of, any criminal proceedings or an application for the disqualification of a director[28];

(2)   for the purpose of the examination of any person by an inspector appointed under the Act in the course of his investigation;

(3)   for the purpose of enabling the Secretary of State to exercise his functions under the Companies Act, the Criminal Justice Act 1993, the Insurance Companies Act 1982, the Insolvency Act 1986 and the Financial Services Act 1986;

(4)   for the purposes of any disciplinary proceedings against public servants for misconduct, etc.

Publication or disclosure of any information or document in contravention of the section is punishable by imprisonment or a fine or both: section 449.

The Secretary of State may disclose any information obtained under any of the investigation sections to certain other bodies concerned in financial regulation, *e.g.* the Bank of England and overseas regulatory authorities; and in any other case where it is not restricted by the section concerned: section 451A.

**Penalisation of destruction, etc., of company documents**

Section 450 provides that an officer of a company or an insurance company, who destroys, mutilates or falsifies, or is

[26] Chap. 19, *post.*
[27] Chap. 31, *post.*
[28] *Ante*, p. 376.

privy to the destruction, etc., of a document affecting or relating to the property or affairs of the company is guilty of an offence unless he proves that he did not intend to conceal the state of affairs of the company or to defeat the law. Similarly if he fraudulently parts with, alters or makes an omission in, any such document. The penalty is imprisonment or a fine or both.

## Investigation to assist overseas regulatory authorities

The Companies Act 1989 introduced new powers to allow the Secretary of State to compel the divulging of information and documents "for the purpose of assisting an overseas regulatory authority which has requested his assistance in connection with inquiries being carried out by it or on its behalf": section 82 C.A. 1989. These powers are designed to enable the U.K. to comply with its obligations under various conventions on the mutual co-operation between countries relating to financial markets. As such they apply equally to the investigations into insider dealing set out in Chapter 19.

An overseas regulatory authority is one which is concerned with functions similar to those of the Secretary of State with regard to companies, financial services, insurance companies, to the Bank of England or any other U.K. regulatory authority (see Chapter 19, *post*), or to the control of insider dealing, companies or financial services: section 82 C.A. 1989.

The Secretary of State, or his agent or other competent person, cannot exercise these powers unless he is satisfied that the assistance requested is for the purposes of its regulatory functions, and may take into account when making his decision whether he would be given reciprocal help of this nature, the seriousness of the matter, the public interest and above all whether the alleged breach relates to a law which has no close parallel in the U.K. or to an asserted jurisdiction which is not recognised by the U.K. Finally, the Secretary of State may require the overseas authority to contribute towards the costs incurred.

The powers exercisable by the Secretary of State are similar to those given to inspectors appointed under section 432 (company investigation) and 442 (company ownership). Thus they include powers to require the production of documents, the giving of evidence on oath and to require such assistance as the person concerned is reasonably able to give: section 83 C.A. 1989. The standard exemptions for professional privilege are included by section 84, and section 85 imposes criminal sanctions for failure to comply or the giving of false or misleading information.

The restrictions on the disclosure of information so obtained are broadly similar to those relating to domestic investigations under section 449: sections 86 and 87 C.A. 1989.

# Chapter 19

# INVESTOR PROTECTION

COMPANIES operate their finances largely through the medium of shares and debentures, and public companies, in particular, rely on the marketability of those securities. Company law is, however, for the most part concerned with the legal aspects of shares and debentures from the company's angle—its rights and obligations *vis-à-vis* the issuing and redemption, etc. of company securities, and with the rights of the holders of those investments *vis-à-vis* the company, *e.g.* voting rights. However, there is another area of law which applies to company securities simply because they are investments—the law relating to investor protection. This area of the law is concerned to regulate the conduct of those engaged in the investment industry, either as advisers, market makers or in the marketing process, to regulate the conduct of the markets in various types of investment, including insurance, and to prevent abuses of the system by those with restricted or "inside" knowledge.

Four aspects of the law on investor protection are relevant to company law. Since shares and debentures are investments, regulation of the terms on which they are advertised and, if appropriate, quoted on the Stock Exchange, falls within this area. The legal framework for such issues was the subject of Chapter 7. Second, the classical UK take-over by one company of another involves the offeror company making an offer for some or all of the issued shares of the target company. This is an area where orderly conduct of the market and equal treatment of shareholders are regarded as being of paramount concern. The rules relating to such take-overs are the subject of Chapter 31.

This chapter is concerned with the other two areas. First it outlines the general system of regulation of the investment industry, since some of those concerned will be involved in the marketing and market making etc. of company securities. It should be stressed that this is merely an outline of what is a complex area and a subject in its own right distinct from company law. The second part deals with the law relating to insider dealing—*i.e.* the process of dealing in shares or other securities with special "inside" knowledge of their potential value. This is particularly relevant to company law and is now contained in Part V of the Criminal Justice Act 1993. The more general rules on investment can be found in the Financial Services Act 1986 which created a new framework for investor protection.

## CONTROL OF THE INVESTMENT INDUSTRY

### The Financial Services Act 1986

To a large extent the control of the investment industry has, until recently, been largely ignored by the law. Certain areas, such as banking and insurance have always been regulated to some degree but the law relating to the marketing and dealing in investments was patchy and inadequate. The Prevention of Fraud (Investments) Act 1958 and its satellite rules, the Licensed Dealers (Conduct of Business) Rules 1983 (formerly of 1960), applied in practice to very few dealers and were often found to be wanting. Other financial centres, such as New York and Paris, created statutory regulatory authorities to deal with the area of investor protection.

In the United Kingdom, Professor Gower was commissioned to write a report, the Review of Investor Protection.[1] In due course a white paper "Financial Services in the United Kingdom"[2] was published and the resultng legislation is contained in the Financial Services Act 1986. The 1958 Act and its machinery (most of its criteria were dispensed with by 10 General Permissions to issue circulars etc.) were repealed. The solution for the United Kingdom was to impose a statutory form of self-regulation upon the investment industry which is almost but not quite a contradiction in terms.

*All references to sections in this part of this chapter are to the Financial Services Act 1986, unless otherwise stated.*

### Initial control on investment personnel

Section 3 provides the central plank in the new system of regulation. No person shall carry on, or purport to carry on,

[1] 1984 Cmnd. 9125.
[2] 1985 Cmnd. 9432.

investment business in the United Kingdom unless he is either an authorised person or an exempted person. Schedule 1 elaborately defines the concepts of investment and investment business for this purpose. There are 11 classes of investments, including shares and debentures. Investment business includes dealing, arranging deals, managing or advising on investments—although certain activities, *e.g.* employee share schemes, are excluded. Breach of section 3 is a criminal offence,[3] and there are civil penalties on deals made in breach—*e.g.* the contract is voidable and money paid is recoverable.[4]

*Authorised persons*

Authorised persons only may carry on an investment business. There are in fact five ways a person may be so authorised.

(1) By being a member of a recognised self-regulating-organisation (SRO). SROs are organisations recognised as such for the purpose of the Act which have their own core rules and codes of conduct which can be enforced on their members.[5] SROs must apply for recognition and their rules and procedure(s) must be of a sufficiently high standard as to ensure an adequate level of protection for investors, bearing in mind the nature of the investment business, the kinds of investors and the costs of compliance.[6] If necessary their rules can be altered by the court. The SRO most closely connected with corporate securities is the Securities and Futures Authority (S.F.A.).

Traditionally, dealings on the Stock Exchange centred round jobbers, *i.e.* market makers, and brokers who act as intermediaries between the investor and the jobber. Since 1986, however, that distinction has broken down, and multi-media financial institutions have arisen which can be advisers, dealers and market makers at the same time. Special rules have had to be devised to prevent the obvious conflicts of interest.

(2) By being a member of a recognised professional body.[7] In effect such recognised professional bodies, *e.g.* The Institute of Chartered Accountants, are equivalent to SROs for this purpose and subject to a similar process of recognition, etc.

[3] s.4. See also s.200 which provides offences relating to false claims and the supply of false information in relation to authorisation, etc.
[4] ss.5, 6. See *e.g. SIB v. Pantell SA (No. 2)* [1992] BCLC 58.
[5] See *e.g. R. v. LAUTRO Ltd, ex p. Ross* [1992] BCLC 34.
[6] ss.7–14, and Sched. 2.
[7] ss.15–21 and Sched. 3.

(3) By being an authorised insurance company,[8] registered friendly society,[9] or the operator or trustee of a recognised collective investment scheme (unit trust).[10]

(4) By direct authorisation.[11] Any person or company can apply for direct authorisation. The grant, refusal or withdrawal of such authorisation is subject to an appeal to the Financial Services Tribunal established by the Act.[12]

(5) By being authorised in another member state of the European Union.[13]

## Exempted persons

There are five categories of exempted persons or institutions which would otherwise be required to be authorised to conduct investment business. These categories can be extended or restricted by regulations.[14] The exempted persons are:

(1) The Bank of England[15];

(2) recognised investment exchanges.[16] These include the Stock Exchange and other financial exchanges. It should be remembered that members of these exchanges will need to be authorised persons, only the exchanges themselves are exempt;

(3) Lloyd's and their underwriters are exempt for the purpose of insurance business carried on there.[17] This aspect of the securities industry is governed by Lloyd's itself under a separate statute;

(4) listed money market institutions, approved by the Bank of England and the Treasury[18];

(5) appointed representatives, *i.e.* employees etc. of employers who take responsibility for them (*e.g.* insurance salesmen)[19];

(6) various public officials exercising statutory functions, *e.g.* the Official Receiver.[20]

---

[8] s.22.
[9] s.23.
[10] s.24. See p. 450, *post.*
[11] ss.25–30.
[12] See p. 450, *post.*
[13] ss.32–34.
[14] s.46.
[15] s.35.
[16] ss.36–41 and Sched. 4.
[17] s.42.
[18] s.43 and Sched. 5.
[19] s.44.
[20] s.45.

## Subsequent control of investment business

Following changes made by the Companies Act 1989, the SIB (to whom overall control of the system has been delegated, *post*) promulgates general principles which may give rise to disciplinary proceedings only and requires SROs to adopt those for similar purposes. Beneath those, there are various rules laid down by the SIB governing, *e.g.* the conduct of business, which are designated as core rules to be adopted by all SROs. Below that second tier the SROs themselves have codes of practice, breach of which does not in itself constitute a breach of a rule but is evidence of such a breach. This three tier system provides the control of those authorised by the SROs.[21] These changes were made in an attempt to simplify the various rule books. There is some flexibility built into the system.

Section 47 of the Act creates criminal offences for deliberately or recklessly making a misleading statement or forecast and for deliberately engaging in misleading practices as to the market or value of an investment. This has been explained in Chapter 7 above. Rules can be made to allow cancellation of an investment agreement,[22] for the notification of certain events,[23] for indemnity[24] and as to the handling of client's money.[25] Unsolicited investment calls are also controlled and can amount to a criminal offence.[26] There is also provision for the establishment of a compensation fund to protect investors in the event of an investment business being unable to meet any claims under the Act.[27]

Investment advertisements are also strictly controlled and limited to those made by authorised and exempt persons.[28] In general those which may be made by way of exemption from that general rule are those related to offers of listed and unlisted securities which require a prospectus[29] and other offers which are made to or between experts. Prohibited persons may not be

[21] ss.47A, 63A, 63B, 63C.
[22] s.51.
[23] s.52.
[24] s.53.
[25] s.55.
[26] s.56.
[27] s.54. See *SIB v. FIMBRA* [1991] BCLC 815.
[28] ss.57, 58. For the powers of the court in the case of a breach, see *SIB v. Vandersteen Associates N.V.* [1991] BCLC 206.
[29] See Chap. 7, *ante.*

employed in connection with an investment business.[30] There are various sanctions for breach of the principles, rules or prohibitions including the making of public statements as to misconduct, injunctions, restitution orders and actions for damages.[31] No action for damages lies in the case of a breach of a principle, however, and in all cases such an action will only be available to private investors.[32]

In addition there are various powers of intervention against those directly authorised. These include a restriction of business, dealing with assets, vesting assets in a trustee (that can apply to SROs if they request it) and the requirement to maintain assets in the jurisdiction.[33]

## Unit trusts

Unit trusts (*i.e.* trusts which make investments and which themselves sell their beneficial units as investments) and overseas open-ended investment companies are referred to in the Act as collective investment schemes. Such schemes may not be promoted in the U.K. unless they are authorised unit trusts or recognised overseas schemes, or the promotion is to an authorised person or a professional investor.[34] Open-ended investment companies are not allowed under U.K. company law since no company may purchase all its own shares.[35]

## Financial Services Tribunal, information, audit and fees

The Financial Services Tribunal was created to hear appeals relating to direct authorisation and the disqualification of prohibited persons. It only relates to appeals from individuals and not dissatisfied SROs. It is seen as a judicial rather than a regulatory body. The Act provides for its constitution, jurisdiction and procedure.[36]

There is a register of all directly authorised persons, SROs, recognised professional bodies and exchanges, authorised unit

[30] s.59.
[31] ss.60–62.
[32] s.62A.
[33] ss.64–71.
[34] ss.75–95.
[35] *Ante,* Chap. 10.
[36] ss.96–101.

trusts and recognised schemes and prohibited persons. The register is open to inspection. In addition there are powers to obtain information and for investigation and to carry out audits on those engaged in an investment business.[37] There are also powers to charge fees, both initial and periodical, to assist in the costs of administration.[38]

**Administration of authorisation and control**

Although the Financial Services Act refers to the powers of recognition and control being in the hands of the Secretary of State, in fact the unique feature of the structure set up by the Act is that the Secretary of State is able to delegate most of his powers in this respect to a private sector company. The Act specifically provides for such delegation, with appropriate safe-guards and caveats, to the Securities and Investments Board Ltd (SIB). SIB has in fact most of the general principle and rule-making powers and is concerned with direct authorisation, recognition and control of bodies such as SROs.[39]

Certain powers are, however, retained by the Secretary of State, largely those relating to extending exemption from the Act, overseas aspects, the Tribunal and powers of investigation. He also retains control of whether to bring a prosecution under the Act (jointly, in England, with the Director of Public Prosecutions).[40]

INSIDER DEALING

**Introduction**

Part V of the Criminal Justice Act 1993 deals with certain forms of insider trading and makes them criminal offences.[41] Provisions to regulate dealings in a company's shares came about because of widespread concern prior to 1980 about the misuse of

---

[37] ss.102–111.
[38] ss.112, 113.
[39] ss.113–118.
[40] s.201.
[41] This Act replaced the provisions first introduced in sections 68–73 of the Companies Act 1980 and consolidated into the Company Securities (Insider Dealing) Act 1985.

confidential information by officers of the company, in particular, but also by their associates, their families and friends to whom information about the company had been relayed by them, or the misuse by others outside the company such as accountants, auditors and bankers who might equally have access to restricted information about the company which would affect the value of its shares on the market.

Insider dealing occurs where an individual or organisation buys or sells securities while knowingly in possession of some piece of confidential information which is not generally available and which is likely, if made available to the general public, to materially affect the price of these securities. So, for example, there is insider trading where a company director knows that the company is in a bad financial state and sells his shares in it knowing that in a few days' time this news will be made public together with an announcement of a cut in dividend payment. Likewise, the director would be insider dealing if, on being informed, before it was generally known by the public, that the company has discovered oil or gold on its own land, he bought more shares in the company in the not unrealistic expectation of an increase in their market value as a result of the subsequent public announcement.

## Ethical and legal objections

The moral or ethical reasons[42] for prohibiting such activities is that the use of insider information is clearly unfair to those who deal with the insider. One of the difficulties, however, is that in many cases it is seen as a victimless crime in that it is difficult to identify those who have lost by the insider dealing where, as the law currently requires, it takes place on a Stock Exchange dealing.

From the point of view of company law, perhaps a more significant reason for attempting to regulate insider trading by law is that the insider with access to confidential information is thereby in a potential conflict-of-interest situation. For example, he may be in such a position within the company as to be able to dictate or at least influence when the public disclosure of price-sensitive information is to be made. In that situation his decision

---

[42] There are some economic arguments in favour of the practice.

and his own desire to trade advantageously in the company's shares may conflict; in other words the best interests of the company may wrongly take second place to his own self interest. Directors are duty bound, subject to the exceptions contained in section 309 of the Companies Act 1985 and section 187 of the Insolvency Act 1986,[43] only to act bona fide in the best interests of the company as a whole.[44]

Furthermore, such unethical conduct is likely to bring not only the reputation of the company concerned but also that of the securities market in this country into disrepute with the possible risk of a consequent adverse investment effect. For this reason in particular, the Financial Services Act 1986 extended the scope of the provision aimed at preventing the abuse of information obtained by persons in their official capacity in connection with the new regulation of the securities and investment industry, and provided the innovation of investigations into suspected insider dealing. In turn the Companies Act 1989 allowed for investigations at the request of overseas regulators since insider dealing may well take place on an international scale.

**Methods of control**

Given that it is recognised as wrong for a director or another to deal in a company's shares knowing of some development which will affect the price of the shares and to which other members or the public generally are not privy, then the question arises how to put an end to such unethical activity. The universal condemnation of this malpractice has produced differing solutions for its eradication.

In the United States of America, which has been in the forefront of the attack on insider trading, the solution adopted is to make the insider disgorge his ill-gotten gains to the company itself or to the individual with whom he dealt.

---

[43] The first of these enjoins directors in the performance of their functions to have regard to the interests of the company's employees as well as those of its members (but without providing employees with any legal sanction for failure to do so). The latter section now permits a company to make provision for the benefit of its employees or ex-employees on the cessation or transfer of the whole or part of its business even if it is not in the best interests of the company and permits a liquidator to make over assets to employees in satisfaction of the amount decided to be provided to them in such circumstances.

[44] *Hutton v. W. Cork Rly.* (1883) 23 Ch.D. 654, C.A.; *Re Lee Behrens & Co.* [1932] Ch. 46; *Evans v. Brunner Mond & Co.* [1921] 1 Ch. 359; *Parke v. Daily News* [1962] Ch. 927; and *Re Roith* [1967] 1 W.L.R. 479.

In the United Kingdom on the other hand the approach has been to progress from a few disparate provisions of the Companies Act and prohibitions contained in various self-regulatory codes to making certain instances of insider dealing a criminal offence. These offences were first created in 1980 partly at the request of the Take-over Panel who acknowledged that their self-regulatory code was inadequate to control the practice. The current provisions are set out in Part V of the Criminal Justice Act 1993, incorporating changes required by the EU insider dealing directive.[45] These are dealt with in detail below but two general points should be noted at this stage. First, the offences do not apply to private share deals and, second, there are no civil consequences of a transaction being a criminal offence. The option for that in the directive was not adopted in this country.

Prior to the creation of the criminal offences by the 1980 Companies Act, the only statutory restrictions on insider trading by company officers were the prohibitions on option dealings by directors and the requirement that a register of their share dealings and the dealings of their spouses and children be maintained and available for inspection by an interested person.[46] These 1967 statutory provisions were ineffective because although they purported to create a legal duty or obligation to disclose share dealings, yet they provided no remedy for failure to comply with the Act's requirements.

Also by that time there were sanctions conceived and imposed by the Stock Exchange Authorities and the City Panel under the City Code on Take-overs and Mergers.[47] These, however, are only an extra-statutory form of self-regulation and open to criticism because they have no legal backing.[48] Despite that, these bodies have devised strict rules, for example, relating to the disclosure of director's personal interests in shares in relation to certain profitable transactions such as take-over bids; for absolute secrecy before any significant announcement is made, and for regulating dealings by insiders in the shares while negotiations continue.[49] In theory any breach of the rules, at the Panel's direction will be investigated by it or the Stock Exchange

---

[45] Dir. 89/592/EC [1989] O.J. L334/30.
[46] See Chap. 15, *ante*.
[47] See Chap. 31, *post*.
[48] They rely on private reprimand, public censure or the withdrawal of access to the facilities of the securities market.
[49] The City Code on Take-overs and Mergers.

Authority, and improprieties chastised or corrected by appropriate action.

## Civil liability

At common law officers of a company have always been freely permitted to hold and deal in the shares of their company. The only sanction which the common law imposed was to make actionable the use of certain confidential information belonging to the company. Such information included industrial or trade secrets and details concerning customers.[50] The misuse of such information by directors, whether it occurred during the course of, or after the termination of, corporate office, was actionable.

The reason why the common law imposed no clear prohibition on the use of insider information in share dealings stems largely from the decision in *Percival v. Wright*.[51] In this case where directors had purchased a member's shares in the knowledge that there was a ready buyer for all the shares of the company at a higher price than they paid him, it was held that the transaction could not be set aside for the director's failure to disclose the negotiations which were already taking place at a higher price. There was said to be no duty to disclosure because there was no fiduciary relationship between the directors and individual shareholders. The directors' duty was owed by the company alone. It followed that the ordinary rules of contract applied. Subsequently in the case of *Allen v. Hyatt*[52] the courts did recognise special but very limited circumstances in which a duty might be owed by directors to individual shareholders. In that particular case the directors had profited through share purchases from members and were held accountable to them because they had purported to act as agents for the members by inducing the latter to give them purchase options over each member's shares supposedly to facilitate a proposed amalgamation. Unless some special relationship of this type could be shown so as to establish a legal duty to disclose all relevant information, the officer retained his profit without adverse legal consequences.[53]

---

[50] See *British Industrial Plastics v. Ferguson* [1938] 4 All E.R. 504; *Cranleigh Precision Engineering Ltd v. Bryant* [1965] 1 W.L.R. 1293; *Measure Bros v. Measures* [1910] 1 Ch. 336, [1910] 2 Ch. 248; *Printers & Finishers Ltd v. Holloway* [1965] 1 W.L.R. 1.
[51] [1902] 2 Ch. 421.
[52] (1914) 30 T.L.R. 444.
[53] See, *e.g. Munro v. Bogie* [1994] 1 BCLC 415.

## PART V OF THE CRIMINAL JUSTICE ACT 1993

The criminal offences concerned with insider dealing are contained in Part V of the Criminal Justice Act 1993. These replace the former offences contained in the Company Securities (Insider Dealing) Act 1985[54] which was repealed by the 1993 Act. The new provisions incorporate the requirement to implement the EU directive on insider dealing,[55] together with other changes in the light of experience with the former provisions.

*In this section references to sections and Schedules are to the Criminal Justice Act 1993 unless otherwise stated.*

### The three offences

Section 52 creates three separate offences, each of which may only be committed by an individual and within the United Kingdom.[56]

The offences, which must be proved by the prosecution beyond all reasonable doubt, are:

(i)   where an insider[57] deals in securities[58] to which the inside information[59] relates (the dealing offence): section 52(1);

(ii)  where an insider[57] encourages another person[60] to deal in such securities,[58] knowing or having reasonable cause to believe that the other would do so (the encouraging offence): section 52(2)(a);

(iii) where an insider[57] discloses the inside information to another person,[61] otherwise than in the proper performance of the functions of his employment, office or

[54] See the previous edition of this work.
[55] Dir. 89/592/EC [1989] O.J. L334/30.
[56] S.62 requires either that the person committing the offence be within the U.K. at the relevant time or that the transaction takes place in the U.K. Where the offence is communicating information to another it is sufficient that the recipient be within the U.K. at the relevant time.
[57] Defined below.
[58] *ibid.*
[59] *ibid.*
[60] Not necessarily an individual.
[61] *ibid.*

profession (the disclosure offence): section 52(2)(b). There is no definition of what is meant by "proper" in this context and as with many other areas this will have to be settled by a judge and jury at the trial.

The dealing and encouraging offences can only be committed if the dealing actually takes place on a regulated market[62] or the person dealing is either a professional intermediary or relying on such a person. A professional intermediary is defined in section 59 to mean a person carrying on a business of dealing in securities and who holds himself out to the public as such. The effect of these restrictions is that private off-market transactions are not covered by the Act.

No offence can be committed by a person who is acting on behalf of a public sector body[63] in pursuit of monetary policies or policies with respect to exchange rates or the management of the public debt: section 63(1).

## The penalties and civil consequences

On conviction of any of the three offences an individual can be sentenced to a maximum of seven years imprisonment on indictment or six months on a summary conviction, together with a fine. No prosecution can be brought without the consent of either the Secretary of State for Trade and Industry or the Director of Public Prosecutions: section 61.

Section 63 provides, however, that no contract shall be void or unenforceable simply because of the fact that an offence was committed. Thus there are to be no civil consequences of an offence of insider dealing. This is intended to protect market transactions and the option to provide a civil remedy allowed for in the directive has not been adopted. The wording of section 63 is different from its predecessor in the 1985 Act which provided that no contract was to be void or voidable as a consequence of an offence. Thus the courts were able to hold that a contract was

---

[62] These are defined in article 9 of the Insider Dealing (Securities and Regulated Markets) Order 1994 (S.I. 1994 No. 187) including all the relevant stock exchanges and investment exchanges in the E.U. and Austria, Finland, Iceland, Norway, Sweden and Liechtenstein. Those regulated by the U.K., for jurisdictional purposes are set out in article 10 of the Order, principally the U.K. part of the International Stock Exchange of the U.K. and the Republic of Ireland.

[63] As defined in s.60(3)(b).

nevertheless unenforceable by the insider.[64] That is no longer possible so that in theory at least a criminal will be able to enforce a contract which was the subject of his crime.

The three offences each involve consideration of one or more of four concepts: securities, dealing, insider and inside information. It is necessary, therefore, to examine each of these in turn.

*Securities*

The dealing or information being communicated must relate to securities which are covered by the Act. These are defined in section 54 as those within Schedule 2 to the Act subject to any conditions for specific types of security as the Treasury may prescribe.[65] In general the list in Schedule 2 corresponds to that in Schedule 1 to the Financial Services Act 1986. For our purposes this includes shares and debentures issued by companies. The condition required for these to be securities to which the Act applies is that they must be officially listed within the European Economic Area[66] or to be admitted to, quoted on, or regulated by a regulated market within that area.[67]

*Dealing*

The dealing and encouraging offences require a definition of what amounts to dealing. Section 55 therefore provides that a person deals in securities if he acquires or disposes of them either as principal or agent, or if he procures their acquisition or disposal by another person who may, but does not need to be under his control. Agreements to acquire or dispose of securities, to create securities or ending an agreement which created a security are all caught by the section.

*Insiders*

All three offences can only be committed by individuals who are insiders. These are called by the Act "persons who have

---

[64] *Chase Manhattan Equities Ltd v. Goodman* [1991] BCLC 897.
[65] See the Insider Dealing (Securities and Regulated Markets) Order 1994 (S.I. 1994 No. 187).
[66] The E.U. and certain other European countries, including Austria, Norway and Sweden.
[67] See n. 62 *above*.

information as insiders". Under section 57 an individual can only be in that position if the information he has is inside information and he knows both that it is inside information and that he has it from an inside source. The concept of inside information is discussed below. The information will be deemed to have come from an inside source in relation to corporate securities in any of three situations. In other words people caught by these situations are potential insiders, who may or may not be actual insiders depending upon their knowledge. No one else can be an insider. The situations are:

(i) information gained by being a director, employee or shareholder[68] of the company (issuer of securities) which has issued the shares or debentures in question;

(ii) information gained by access to it through the individual's employment, profession or office. Note that there is no requirement, as previously, that the person be connected with the relevant company through his employment, *etc.* Thus individuals, such as financial journalists, can now be temporary potential insiders;

(iii) information which an individual has obtained directly or indirectly from a person within (i) or (ii) above. These people are known as "tippees" from primary insiders. Because of the word "indirectly", this liability can extend to sub-tippees, *i.e.* a tippee's tippee, although of course in all cases the requisite degree of knowledge must also be proved. Under the previous law the House of Lords held that a tippee could be regarded as obtaining information even if he did not actively seek the information but was merely a passive recipient of it.[69]

Thus potential insiders are those directly connected with the company in question, those who come across the information professionally and tippees from any of those. To make them actual insiders, and so liable for any of the three offences, it must be shown that the potential insider knows both that it is inside information and came from an inside source.

*Inside information*

The concept of inside information is therefore crucial to the definition of an insider and thus to the offences themselves. The

---

[68] Shareholders as such were not potential insiders under the previous Act.
[69] *Attorney-General's Reference (No. 1 of 1988)* [1989] A.C. 971.

definition, which is largely taken from the directive, is in section 56. There are four requirements:

(i)   the information must relate to particular securities or to a particular company or its business but not to securities generally or companies generally;
(ii)  it must be specific or precise;
(iii) it must not have been made public; and
(iv)  it must be such that if it were made public it would be likely to have a significant effect on the price or value of any securities, which are then known as price affected securities.

Many of these concepts are undefined and will have to be decided on by a jury after judicial guidance in each case. When, for example, does a rumour cease to be rumour and become specific or precise?

The only factor which is defined, non-exhaustively, in the Act is when information is deemed to have been made public and so is no longer insider information. Section 58 states that inclusion of the information on records to which the public have access and publication of it in accordance with the rules of a regulated market,[70] such as the information service of the Stock Exchange, will be sufficient. Since the section also makes it clear that such information is to be treated as being made public even if it is communicated to a section of the public for a fee and can only be accessed by observation, it is thought that this will include computer-linked market information systems such as TOPIC. If that is correct, the position is different from the previous law where it was agreed that time had to be allowed for the market to digest the information before it could be regarded as being in the public domain.

**The defences**

Section 53 provides specific defences to the three offences. With regard to the dealing and encouraging offences there are three defences which must all be proved by the defendant on the balance of probabilities.[71] The specified defences are:

[70] See n. 62, *above*.
[71] Thus it is not for the prosecution to prove that the defence is not applicable if the defendant simply raises the matter. This confirms the decision in *R. v. Cross* [1991] BCLC 125 on the previous, different, wording.

(i)   that the defendant did not at the time expect the dealing, by himself or another, to result in a profit or the avoidance of a loss. It is not for the prosecution therefore to show a profit motive but for the defence to show that there was none;

(ii)  that at the time the defendant reasonably believed that the information was widely enough known (although not made public) so as not to prejudice the other parties to the dealing. This is intended to save certain City transactions such as underwriting, *etc.*;

(iii) that the defendant would have dealt (or encouraged another to deal) in the securities even if he had not had the inside information. This may protect, *e.g.* a takeover bidder or possibly a trustee who under his duty as a trustee to do the best he can for the beneficiaries was obliged under trust law to deal. There is no specific defence for such conflict of duty situations,[72] however, as under the previous law.

The section provides for two defences, again to be proved on the balance of probabilities by the defendant, for the disclosure offence:

(i)   that the defendant did not expect that any person (the tippee) would deal as a result of such disclosure; and

(ii)  that, even if the defendant did expect another to deal, he did not expect a profit or avoidance of a loss to arise from such a dealing using inside information.

Schedule 1 to the Act also contains three general defences, available in respect of all three offences: for market makers; those acting reasonably with market information; and those involved in price-stabilisation transactions under section 48 of the Financial Services Act 1986. These defences are outside the scope of company law.

**Investigations into insider dealing**

When the offence of insider dealing was first made law by the Companies Act 1980 no provision was made or mechanism

---

[72] These could include liquidators, executors and administrators among others.

included whereby alleged or suspected abuse of insider information might be investigated by a regulatory body other than the
police. Despite the fact that this was a serious drawback to any
effectiveness that the legislation might have had, no amendment
was made to rectify that weakness until the Financial Services
Act 1986 empowered the Secretary of State to appoint investigators into what appears to him to be a contravention of Part V of
the Criminal Justice Act 1993. In investigating alleged insider
dealing the investigators have been provided with wide powers[73]
similar to those vested in an inspector appointed under the
Companies Act 1985.[74] The investigators are empowered to
require any person who may be able to give information concerning the sale or purchase of securities to disclose it; to produce
documents; to attend before the investigators and be questioned
on oath by them subject only to legal professional privilege and a
more limited exception in the case of bankers.[75] The evidence
provided may be used in evidence against that person or any
other person where it discloses prohibited insider dealings.

The Secretary of State may vary the terms of the investigation
and direct the inspectors to take no further steps. Any person
convicted of an offence as a result of an inquiry may be required
to contribute towards the costs of the inquiry.

If a person fails to co-operate with an investigation conducted
under 177 of the Financial Services Act 1986 then he may become
liable for the special penalties provided by section 178 of that
Act. Section 178 authorises the investigators to certify that failure
to the court which may inquire into the facts and if it decides that
there is no reasonable excuse for the non-cooperation it may
punish that person as if he had committed a contempt of court.[76]
Alternatively the court may direct that the Secretary of State may
use the powers given to him under section 178(3). These powers
entitle the Secretary of State to cancel that person's authorisation
to carry on investment business; to disqualify him from becoming
authorised or to impose on him any number of restrictions or
prohibitions in relation to the carrying on of investment business.

[73] Financial Services Act 1986, s.177.
[74] Companies Act 1985, Part XIV, ss.431–453, *ante*, p. 431.
[75] A journalist has no such exemption: see *Re an Inquiry under the Company
Securities (Insider Dealing) Act 1985* [1988] A.C. 660.
[76] The penalty for this common law offence is entirely at the discretion of the
court and may result in imprisonment and/or a fine. A journalist has no defence
to such an action on the grounds of public interest: *Re An Inquiry etc., ante.*

Although the Secretary of State is also empowered to revoke the previous penalty notice such a revocation does not necessarily revive any authorisation held by that person prior to the original penalty notice.

# Chapter 20

# ACCOUNTS

## INTRODUCTION

### The case for mandatory disclosure of financial information

WHEN the original legislation was passed in the 1850s enabling limited liability companies to be set up merely by registration, the intention was primarily to provide a minimum framework which would facilitate economic development in a manner consistent with *laissez-faire* capitalism.[1] The view which implicitly seems to have been taken was that companies would find it in their own interests to disclose a certain amount of reliable information, so reducing uncertainty in the minds of creditors, shareholders and other interested parties. This in turn might be expected to lower companies' financing costs. To the extent that they might be reluctant to disclose information voluntarily, it would be up to both the individuals dealing with a company, its officers and agents, and to its members to protect their interests by making appropriate contracts with the parties concerned. The justification for intervention in this process could only exist if it were perceived that the benefits to society that might be expected to result would more than offset the costs of complying with any regulations imposed.

Against this background, it is hardly surprising that in the latter half of the nineteenth century disclosure requirements were minimal, the view in particular being taken that record-keeping and the preparation of financial statements for a company were

---

[1] See Hadden, T., *Company Law and Capitalism* (2nd ed., 1977), Chap. 1 and *passim*. The idea has been given a new lease of life recently with the development of the economic theory of agency: see, for instance, Beaver, W. H., *Financial Reporting: An Accounting Revolution* (2nd ed., 1989), Chap. 2 and *passim*; and Bromwich, M., *Financial Reporting, Information and Capital Markets*, (1992).

really a domestic matter, of concern only to the directors and shareholders, unless the rights of third parties were directly affected.[2] As a result the only guidance in accounting matters in the early legislation was to be found in the model articles given in Table A.[3] At the same time, the non-interventionist philosophy was reflected in a number of decisions concerning the payment of dividends by companies, the overall view apparently being that the courts should not in general interfere in the business decision-making process unless there were good grounds for believing that the rights of certain interested parties were being prejudiced—a laudable policy given the fact that from an economic viewpoint there is no necessary connection between profit, however calculated, and the distribution decision.[4]

### The introduction of filing requirements

Towards the end of the nineteenth century views about mandatory disclosure gradually began to change. The formal accounts were beginning to be used for purposes (such as a basis for assessing income tax liabilities) which were different from those apparently originally intended. Moreover, specific examples of inequality of information and manipulation of data arose, and at a time when one third of new companies failed within a short space of time,[5] the view that unsecured creditors had insufficient information on which to base their decisions gained a certain currency. The result was that the statutory audit was introduced in 1900, and in 1908 the 10,000 businesses in the newly created "public" class of company were required to file their balance sheets. However, the 30,000 or so "private" concerns were still exempt from this provision.

[2] See In *Re Spanish Prospecting Co. Ltd* [1911] 1 Ch. 92;*Edwards v. Saunton Hotel Co. Ltd* (1943) 1 All E.R. 176; *Young v. Brownlee & Co. Ltd,* 1911 S.C. 677.
[3] See Edey, H.C. and Prot Panitpakdi, "British Company Accounting and the Law 1844–1900" in *Studies in the History of Accounting,* eds. Littleton, A.C. and Yamey, B.S., (1956), pp. 356–379. (In fact, under the original 1856 Act what became Schedule A from 1862 onwards was designated as Schedule B.)
[4] See *post,* Chap. 22; French, E.A., "The Evolution of the Dividend Law of England" in *Studies in Accounting* (3rd ed., 1977), eds. Baxter, W.T. and Davidson, S., pp. 306–331; and Morris, R.C., "Distribution Policy: An Economic Rationale", *Accountancy* (October 1992), pp. 80–82.
[5] See Shannon, H.A., "The Limited Companies of 1866–1883", *Essays in Economic History* (ed. Carus-Wilson E.M.) (1954) Vol. 1.

By 1925 the numbers of companies registered had risen to around 95,000 (of which some 85,000 were private), but the 1929 Companies Act nevertheless did not extend the duty to file accounts to private companies, nor did it substantially expand the disclosure requirements for company financial statements. The climate of opinion began to change in the 1930s, it being increasingly recognised that the affairs of the modern corporation are often of interest to a much wider constituency than just the existing body of shareholders.[6] The gradual shift in opinion was given added impetus by the Royal Mail debacle[7] and the creation of the Securities and Exchange Commission in the United States, events which forced lawyers and accountants in Great Britain to question the accepted wisdom in relation to the disclosure of a company's financial affairs.

The result was that the Cohen Committee[8] on company law reform of 1945 was charged with considering the needs of the public as well as shareholders and creditors. It recommended that so-called reserve accounting should be outlawed; that the pre-paration of group accounts (where appropriate) should be man-datory; and that for the first time companies should be required to prepare for the benefit of their shareholders an income statement worthy of the name. By that time there were some 200,000 registered companies, of which over 90 per cent enjoyed private status, and the 1948 Companies Act required some of these (a small proportion, described as "non-exempt") to file their annual accounts for the first time.

### The extension of filing requirements to all companies

The Jenkins Committee[9] on company law reform, reporting in 1962, favoured further compulsory disclosure, and it proposed that exempt private companies (which comprised some 75 per cent of the 400,000 or so companies then registered) should also be made to file their financial statements, the purpose being to benefit unsecured creditors. A requirement to this effect was included in the 1967 Companies Act, and this led to a rapid increase in the annual number of company searches, which rose

[6] See Hadden, op. cit., passim.
[7] R. v. Kylsant [1932], 1 K.B. 442.
[8] (1945) Cmnd. 6659.
[9] (1962) Cmnd. 1749.

from 600,000 in 1960 and 1.3 million in 1969 to 2.6 million in 1980. By 1985 the number of searches had further risen to 3.1 million and by the early 1990s to over 4 million per annum.

The 1967 Companies Act also greatly extended the disclosures which had to be made in the income statement, in notes to the accounts, and in the directors' report (*e.g.* turnover, hire charges, movements in fixed assets and segmental analysis of activities).

**The growth of regulation based on annual accounts**

As indicated previously, companies and unincorporated businesses had effectively been required to prepare annual accounts for income tax purposes since the latter half of the nineteenth century. But the 1960s and the 1970s witnessed an upsurge in activity aimed at regulating the ways in which companies publicly reported their financial affairs, most of it of a quasi-legal nature. Thus successive governments between 1965 and 1979 attempted to monitor and control price increases, first through the National Board for Prices and Incomes (1965–1971) and later through the Price Commission (1973–1979). These bodies (like the Monopolies Commission and the Restrictive Trade Practices Court before them) relied heavily on accounting information, which for the Price Commission had to be prepared following certain specified rules. Meanwhile, companies had for many years been required to keep detailed records to ensure PAYE, national insurance contributions and excise duties were properly accounted for, and the introduction of the value added tax in 1973 made this even more necessary. Another influence was the system of government contract pricing, which since the First World War had relied in part on published accounting indicators, and which had to be reformed following the discovery of certain abuses. In addition, powers were taken in the Industry Act 1975, which meant that— until the legislation was extensively revised at the end of the decade—certain companies could be required to disclose supplementary information to ministers and to trade unions.

Even in the nineteenth century companies had to consider the direct "economic consequences" of what they reported in their financial statements in terms of what they might involve in cash payments (*e.g.* with regard to corporate taxation and profit sharing contracts). However, by the 1960s and 1970s interest in the accounting and business community had for many years been much more closely focused on the "signalling properties", primarily for the 2,000 or so British listed companies, for which it was important to try to indicate to investment analysts the trend in permanently sustainable earnings, but also with respect to the much larger number of unlisted public and private companies trying to influence the opinions of third parties, such as credit suppliers and bank lenders. The economic consequences of such signals for companies are indirect in the sense that they only affect their costs of capital, as reflected in their relative share prices and borrowing costs, but the necessary information can be conveyed to interested parties by alternative means (*e.g.* in the chairman's report, press releases, or presentations to stockbrokers and institutional investors).[10]

## Conflicting objectives: the advent of accounting standards

One of the effects of the advent of new regulations in the late 1960s and the 1970s was to exacerbate conflicts of interest between different parties with respect to the information reported in company financial statements. This development in turn was largely responsible for the leading accountancy bodies setting up the Accounting Standards Committee (ASC) in 1969, and over the next 20 years it issued a number of mandatory statements concerning the preparation and publication of companies' annual accounts, two of the most important relating to the preparation of supplementary flow of funds and current cost accounting statements, the latter following the publication of a lengthy government report on the matter.[11] The ASC's efforts were backed up by the statements of the International Accounting Standards Committee (IASC), set up in 1973, and the London Stock Exchange's *Listing Agreement,* published in 1972, the latter applying to British quoted companies.[12] Elsewhere, the

[10] For a discussion of the economic consequences phenomenon and its role in moulding financial reporting practice, see Watts, R.L. and Zimmerman, J.L., *Positive Accounting Theory* (1986).

[11] (1985) Cmnd. 6225. With an abatement of the general rate of inflation and a lack of interest in such supplementary data on the part of analysts (who presumably estimate the likely impact of relative price changes on future sustainable permanent cash flow earnings by referring to other sources of information), the over-complicated standard (SSAP 16) requesting listed and other large companies to publish supplementary current cost accounting statements was withdrawn in September 1986.

[12] The *Listing Agreement* was superseded by the *Listing Rules* in 1993.

OECD and the United Nations have both published disclosure guidelines concerning the activities of international concerns.

**Harmonisation within the European Union**

Another major factor, of more direct relevance to changes introduced in the Companies Acts 1980 and 1981, was the EU's attempts to harmonise accounting regulations within the Common Market countries, the avowed aim being to encourage the efficient allocation of capital within the European Union. These two Acts incorporated most of the accounting and disclosure proposals contained in the EU's Second and Fourth Council Directives, dealing respectively with capital maintenance and distributions; and individual company accounts. Similarly, the Companies Act 1989 implemented the requirements of the Seventh and Eighth Council Directives, the former relating to group accounts and the latter to eligibility for appointment as a company auditor.

**The creation of the Financial Reporting Council**

The opportunity was also taken when framing the 1989 Act to reform the institutional framework for setting accounting standards. The process is supervised by a broadly based Financial Reporting Council (FRC), which guides the work of three subsidiary bodies: the Accounting Standards Board (ASB), the Urgent Issues Task Force (UITF), and the Financial Reporting Review Panel (FRRP). The ASB is recognised by the Accounting Standards Regulations 1990[13] as the delegated authority empowered to establish accounting standards under section 256 of the 1985 Act. It publishes Financial Reporting Standards (FRSs), which have to be applied by companies when preparing their statutory accounts.[14] For its part, the UITF publishes brief "abstracts" which deal with matters of immediate concern but which are not covered by accounting standards. As for the monitoring role, the FRRP is recognised by the Companies Order 1991[15] as the delegated authority empowered to examine *prima facie* defective accounts and require their amendment.

[13] S.I. 1990 No. 1667.
[14] The ASB has adopted the SSAPs established by its predecessor body, the ASC, until such time as it issues new standards to supersede them.
[15] S.I. 1991 No. 13.

What was perhaps surprising about the creation of the new supervisory framework in 1990 was the lack of debate beforehand about the economic rationale for requiring greater disclosure by companies—particularly as further regulation seems to imply an increasing degree of market failure. After all, the data contained in a set of published accounts are only part of a much wider information set available to decision makers, be they shareholders, potential investors, creditors or employees—and there is an impressive amount of empirical evidence suggesting that financial and other markets are efficient in obtaining and processing information perceived to be relevant.[16] Moreover, although the gradual extension of liability for professional negligence has been checked by the decisions in *Caparo Industries plc v. Dickman*[17] and *Galoo Ltd v. Bright Grahame Murray*,[18] it had been stretched through *Hedley Byrne v. Heller*[19] and subsequent cases to offer protection to third parties. Consequently, there was even more reason to question the validity of extending disclosure requirements, particularly since the costs of complying with the regulations were—and are—far from negligible. Rather surprisingly this did not seem to be a matter which greatly concerned lawyers and accountants, and it is only recently that discontent amongst businessmen has at last led the government and the accountancy profession to question the wisdom of the policies being pursued.[19a]

### The structure of the chapter

It is against this complex background that the current legislative rules should be viewed. In what follows, the text follows the structure of Part VII of the Companies Act 1985, "Accounts and Audit", and accordingly this chapter deals with:

(1)  the accounting records which must be kept by a company;
(2)  the reference period for which accounts must be prepared;
(3)  the regulations for laying them before the company in general meeting and filing copies with the Registrar of Companies;

---

[16] See, for instance, Beaver, *op. cit.*, especially Chaps. 5–6.

[17] [1990] 2 A.C. 605.

[18] *The Times*, January 14, 1994.

[19] [1964] A.C. 465. The issues raised by these cases are discussed later: see pp. 589–590.

[19a] Early in 1995 the professional accountancy bodies in the U.K. proposed that "small" companies (see below, pp. 488–489) should be exempt from the majority of accounting standards. If agreed, this would provide wider scope for the interpretation of what does and does not constitute "a true and fair view" (see below, pp. 485–487).

(4) the form and content of the annual accounts;
(5) the accounting principles which must be applied in their preparation;
(6) the regulations concerning group accounts;
(7) the directors' report;
(8) the auditor's report;
(9) a note on special requirements for banking and insurance companies;
(10) the powers of the Secretary of State to alter the accounting requirements of the Act;
(11) some brief details of other accounting and disclosure regulations; and finally
(12) the question of whether the inclusion of a debt in a signed balance sheet amounts to an acknowledgement of its existence by the company.

The position with regard to disclosure requirements for different types of company has become so complex in recent years that it may be helpful at the outset to try to summarise the situation. The decision table in Figure 1 therefore attempts to do this, indicating the pages where each main issue is dealt with.

## ACCOUNTING RECORDS

Section 221 of the Companies Act 1985 requires every company to ensure that adequate accounting records are kept, sufficient to show and explain its transactions. Moreover, they must be such as to disclose with reasonable accuracy, at any time, the financial position of the company, and also enable a balance sheet and profit and loss account to be prepared so as to give a true and fair view of the company's financial position and profit or loss. Parent companies are equally required, in relation to subsidiaries to which the provisions of section 221 do not apply, to take reasonable steps to ensure such undertakings keep sufficient accounting records so that the group accounts give a true and fair view.

In particular, the accounting records must contain:

(a) entries from day to day of all monies received and expended, with details of transactions, and
(b) a record of assets and liabilities.

In addition, a company dealing in goods must keep statements of stock held at the end of each financial year and of stocktakings

**Figure 1**

from which the year-end statements are made up, as well as records of all goods sold and purchased (other than in ordinary retail trade transactions), showing goods, buyers and sellers so as to allow identification. However, there is no requirement to keep statements of work in progress.[20]

Section 222 requires that the accounting records must be open for inspection by the officers of the company at all times, but there is no express statutory provision authorising the court to compel inspection. However, it was held in *M'Cusker v. M'Rae*[21] that the Court of Session may, on the petition of a director presented to the *nobile officium*, ordain a company to make the accounting records available for inspection by the director and by a named accountant on his behalf.

If the accounting records are kept outside Great Britain, such accounts and returns must be kept in Britain as will disclose the position of the business at intervals not exceeding six months and will enable the directors to ensure that any balance sheet or profit and loss account prepared by them gives a true and fair view of the company's financial position and profit or loss.

The accounting records must normally be kept for a minimum period of three years for a private company, or six years for a public company. However, the Taxes Management Act 1970 effectively requires a six year retention period, and in order to cover against possible actions for negligence under the Limitation Act 1980 (as amended) the retention period would have to be as long as fifteen years.

Failure to keep accounting records as required is an offence for which officers of the company are liable, the penalty being imprisonment and/or a fine.

A shareholder has no right to inspect the books of account of the company unless one is given to him by the articles. In this regard Table A, article 109 (S.I. 1985 No. 805), provides that: "No member shall (as such) have any right of inspecting any accounting records or other book or document or the company except as conferred by statute or authorised by the directors or by ordinary resolution of the company."

---

[20] Advice on the interpretation of the provisions of section 221 is given in a statement published by the Institute of Chartered Accountants in England and Wales, "Accounting Records".

[21] 1966 S.C. 253. See also *Conway v. Petronius Clothing Co. Ltd* [1978] 1 W.L.R. 72.

For the purposes of the Companies Act, accounting records need not be kept in bound books, so long as adequate safeguards are taken to prevent their falsification and the records are capable of being reproduced in a legible form (sections 722–723; S.I. 1985 No. 724).

## ACCOUNTING REFERENCE PERIODS

Section 223(1)–(2) of the Companies Act 1985 provides that the directors of a company must prepare accounts based on an *accounting reference period* for its *financial year*.[22] This commences on the day after the date to which the last accounts were prepared and ends on the last day of the company's normal financial year. However, in order to accommodate natural week ends, the directors may at their discretion move such reference dates by up to seven days before or after the last day of the company's normal financial year.

The *accounting reference date,* which under section 224(1) determines the accounting reference period, is either chosen by the company itself, giving notice of such date in prescribed form to the Registrar of Companies (section 224(2)); or, failing that, it will be March 31, for companies incorporated prior to the implementation of the Companies Act 1989, and for those incorporated thereafter the end of the month in which the anniversary of its incorporation falls (section 224(3)). Where the company opts to choose the date, prescribed notice must be given within nine months of incorporation, and the reference period must be not less than six nor more than eighteen months (section 224(2)(4)), while the period covered by the profit and loss account must begin with the first day of that accounting reference period and end not more than seven days before, or more than seven days after, the reference period, as the directors may determine (section 223(2)).[23]

Section 225 of the 1985 Act makes provision for alteration of the accounting reference period. Under its terms notice may be given to the Registrar in prescribed form at any time during the

---

[22] Corresponding requirements for overseas companies are contained in s.701.

[23] DTI returns show some 40 per cent of companies have March 31 year ends and another 20 per cent December 31 year ends. However, for listed companies about 40 per cent have December 31 year ends and 20 per cent March 31 year ends; and some 15 per cent avail themselves of the concession to vary the year end date by up to 7 days.

accounting reference period specifying a new accounting reference date, the effect of which will be to alter the current and
subsequent accounting reference periods of the company. This
may be done after the end of a reference period so as to change
the date by which the accounts would normally be laid and filed
only if the company is a holding or subsidiary company and the
change is made in order that the accounting reference dates of
the companies may coincide or if an administrative order under
Part II of the Insolvency Act 1986 is in force. However, the
change cannot be made in any case if the period allowed for
laying and delivering accounts in relation to the previous accounting reference period has expired.

Notice under section 225 must state whether the new period is
to be shorter or longer than the current reference period, and in
any case extension is not possible if a current period plus the
extension is more than 18 months in duration, except where an
administrative order under Part II of the Insolvency Act 1986 is
in force. Moreover, not more than one extension will generally
be allowed within a period of five years except to bring the
reference periods of holding and subsidiary companies into line.

## LAYING THE ACCOUNTS BEFORE THE COMPANY IN GENERAL MEETING AND FILING THEM WITH THE REGISTRAR

Except where advantage is taken of the provisions in sections
252–253 of the 1985 Act (see *post,* pp. 479–480) and/or the
Companies Act 1985 Regulations 1994[24] (see *post,* p. 491), a
company's directors must lay before the company in general
meeting in respect of each financial year copies of its accounts
and the directors' and auditors' reports. Failure to do so within
the periods specified in section 244 renders the directors liable to
fines (section 241 of the Companies Act 1985).

A company's directors are also required to deliver copies of the
accounts and directors' and auditors' reports to the Registrar of
Companies within the time intervals specified in section 244.
Where documents are in a foreign language they must be
accompanied by a certified English translation. Failure to comply
with these provisions render the directors liable to fine and, for
continued contravention, to a daily default fine. Moreover, if

---

[24] S.I. 1994 No. 1935.

they still fail to file the accounts and reports within 14 days of receiving a notice requiring them to do so, the court may make a direction ordering them to make good the default within a specified time, in which case it can also order them to bear the costs. However, it will be a defence to show that all reasonable steps were taken to ensure compliance (section 242 of the Companies Act 1985).[25]

In addition to the liability incurred by directors when accounts are not filed, a civil penalty can be imposed on the company. The size of this depends on whether the company is public or private, and it escalates according to the length of the delay (section 242A of the Companies Act 1985).

Where a parent company has an unconsolidated subsidiary which is either registered and operates outside Great Britain, or is an unincorporated business, the subsidiary will not be liable to file its individual accounts with the Registrar. In such circumstances, copies of the subsidiary's latest accounts (*i.e.* for a period ending not less than 12 months before the parent company's year end) have to be filed, together with the auditors' report. Where appropriate these will be its group accounts. Moreover, where necessary a certified English translation must be included. Exemptions from these requirements are available where such a business does not prepare or publish its accounts elsewhere, or where its activities are so different from those of the rest of the group that consolidation would be inappropriate (section 243 of the Companies Act 1985).

The periods allowed for laying and delivering a company's accounts and the directors' and auditors' reports are normally 10 months after the reference period for a private company and seven months for a public company, although if either has interests outside the U.K. the directors can give notice to the Registrar and claim a further three months' extension. Certain modifications are allowed where companies are in their first accounting reference period or where they shorten their accounting reference periods; moreover, the Secretary of State has powers to extend the period for laying and delivering accounts by giving notice in writing.

[25] At the time of an adverse report by the Public Accounts Committee in May 1984, no less than 58 per cent of active companies were failing to file their accounts on time. Following an advertising campaign and the introduction of a tougher enforcement policy, whereby over 80,000 defaulting companies were fined in the year to March 31 1994, the compliance rate has risen to over 95 per cent.

The modified rules for a company in its first reference period are that, where such a reference period is greater than 12 months in length, the accounts must nevertheless be laid and delivered within 22 months of its date of incorporation if it is a private company, or 19 months if it is a public company, but both subject to a three months' extension if it has overseas interests. However, this is subject to the proviso that there should always be a minimum allowed period of three months between the end of the reference period and the last date for laying and delivering accounts. Where a company's reference period is shortened under section 225,[26] the period allowed for laying and delivering the accounts is that which expires later of:

(a)  the period normally allowed, and
(b)  three months from the date of the notice of the change in the accounting reference period given under section 225 (section 244 of the Companies Act 1985).

It should be noted, however, that quoted companies are required by the London Stock Exchange's *Listing Rules* to issue their annual reports and accounts within six months of the end of the financial period to which they relate.

**Abbreviated and shortened accounts**

*Filed individual accounts*

Section 246 of the Companies Act 1985 offers concessions to small and medium sized private companies or groups, as defined in sections 247–249 of the Act, permitting them to file abbreviated financial statements with the Registrar of Companies (see *post*, pages 481; 488–490; 515–516; 542; 547), though it should be noted that these concessions do not affect the information that must be provided to members of the company. It is estimated that some 90 per cent of all registered companies qualify as small companies (Cmnd. 9794, para. 8.5). However, many of the 1.1 million companies registered at March 31, 1994, can be regarded as "inactive", only about half being registered for VAT. Nevertheless, in the year ending on that date, 762,800 had filed financial statements, of which

[26] *Ante*, pp. 474–475.

43.0 per cent submitted full accounts, 40.5 per cent abbreviated small sized company accounts, 0.6 per cent abbreviated medium sized company accounts, and 2.1 per cent group accounts. A further 13.8 per cent were classified as dormant. Research indicates that most of the companies filing abbreviated accounts appear to be larger "small" entities, which are apparently able to afford the luxury of preparing two different sets of accounts and can perhaps ignore the potential information requirements of their creditors that might be satisfied by a close scrutiny of their detailed financial statements.

*Shortened accounts*

The concessions relating to the filing of abbreviated accounts do not directly affect the information to be provided to members of a company, except with respect to the provision of group accounts (see below, pp. 490–491). However, the Companies Act 1985 Regulations 1992[27] reorganised Schedule 8, and the opportunity was taken to permit companies qualifying as small to lay a slightly simplified set of financial statements before members in general meeting. This is achieved in what are now colloquially referred to as "shortened" accounts by amalgamating some of the more detailed balance sheet headings[27a] and removing various requirements that small companies should disclose certain information in notes to their accounts and in their directors' reports (Sched. 8, Part I, Section A).

*Exemptions from having a statutory audit*

Under the Companies Act 1985 Regulations 1994[28] any company which qualifies as small under section 246 and whose annual turnover and balance sheet totals respectively do not exceed £90,000 and £1.4 million is exempt from the statutory audit requirement (see *post*, p. 491).

**Approval by directors**

A company's annual accounts have to be approved by its board of directors, and the balance sheet and the copy delivered to the

[27] S.I. 1992 No. 2452.
[27a] See p. 496.
[28] S.I. 1994 No. 1935.

Registrar must be signed on their behalf by one of their number. Moreover, every copy of the balance sheet which is laid before the company in general meeting or which is otherwise circulated and published must state the name of the signatory. Failure to observe these requirements renders the company and its defaulting officers liable to a fine. Equally, directors who approve the accounts without taking reasonable steps to ensure that they comply with the requirements of the Companies Acts or to prevent their being approved knowing that they do not comply are liable to a fine (section 233 of the Companies Act 1985).

Special provisions apply where shortened accounts are presented to shareholders and where abbreviated accounts are delivered to the Registrar (see *post,* pp. 478 and 490).

Section 711 of the 1985 Act provides that the Registrar must cause to be published in the *Gazette* notice of the receipt by him of any document delivered by a company in pursuance of section 242, *i.e.* its annual accounts, including the directors' and auditors' reports, and (where relevant) the group accounts.

Directors of an unlimited company are not required to deliver accounts and annexed reports to the Registrar unless a connected company has limited liability (section 254 of the Companies Act 1985).

**Dispensing with the obligation to lay accounts**

A private company may by elective resolution in accordance with section 379A dispense with the laying of its annual accounts and the directors' and auditors' reports before the company in general meeting. Such a resolution relates to the financial statements for the year in which it is made, and the election carries over to subsequent financial years. However, the financial statements still have to be circulated to members, and references in the Act to the laying of accounts are therefore to be interpreted in such circumstances as referring to the documents so circulated (section 252 of the Companies Act 1985).

Where an election is in force dispensing with the requirement to lay annual accounts and the directors' and auditors' reports before a company in general meeting, copies of these statements must be sent to members at least 28 days before the period allowed for laying and delivering accounts, together with a notice of their rights to require the laying of accounts and annexed reports before a general meeting. Failure to do so renders the

company and its officers liable to fines. An objecting member or
auditor must inform the company within 28 days of the accounts
being circulated, and the directors must then convene a general
meeting within 21 days, failing which the objecting party may do
so himself. Such a meeting must be held within three months.
Where an objecting party has to convene a meeting, he may
recover reasonable expenses from the company (section 253 of
the Companies Act 1985).

**Revision of defective accounts and reports**

Where a company's annual accounts and/or directors' report do
not comply with the provisions of the Companies Acts, the
directors may voluntarily revise them. Where the financial statements have been laid before the company in general meeting or
delivered to the Registrar, the revisions need only deal with the
corrections and consequential effects.

The Secretary of State is also empowered to give notice to a
company's directors dictating respects in which he believes the
financial statements laid before the company or delivered to
the Registrar may not comply with the Act's requirements. The
notice must specify a period up to one month, in which time the
directors must either explain satisfactorily the accounts or prepare revised financial statements, failing which the Secretary of
State may apply to the court. Moreover, the same actions can be
applied against revised accounts (section 245A of the Companies
Act 1985).

In the meantime regulations have been published in 1990[29]
concerning the revision of defective accounts under section 245;
while under sections 245B and 245C of the 1985 Act and the
Companies Order 1991[30] the Financial Reporting Review Panel is
empowered to apply to the court for a declaration that the
accounts are in breach of the Acts and for an order requiring
directors to prepare revised financial statements. Such an order
may give directions with respect to the audit, the revision of the
directors' report or summary financial statement, steps to be
taken by directors to bring the making of the order to the notice
of those likely to rely on the defective accounts, and any other
pertinent matters. The court may also order that some or all of

[29] S.I. 1990 No. 2570.
[30] S.I. 1991 No. 13.

the directors approving defective accounts should be liable to pay all or part of the costs of the action. Such proceedings can also be applied against revised accounts.

## The right to receive accounts

The general rule under section 238 of the 1985 Act is that a copy of a company's annual accounts, together with copies of the auditors' and directors' reports, must be sent to every member, debenture holder, and other person entitled to receive notice of general meetings at least 21 days before the date of the meeting at which they will be laid.[31] If all the members entitled to attend and vote so agree, a shorter time will suffice. Failure to comply renders the company and every officer in default liable to a fine.

Under section 239 any member or debenture holder is entitled to a copy on demand without charge. Failure to comply within seven days with such a demand renders the company and every officer in default liable to a fine and, for continued contravention, a daily default fine.

## Publication of financial statements

Section 240 sets out the requirements concerning the publication of a company's accounts. It distinguishes between a company's "statutory" and "non-statutory" accounts, the former being defined as the full individual or group accounts (including "shortened" accounts[32]) properly delivered to the Registrar. However, statutory accounts also include abbreviated individual or group accounts where properly filed under sections 246–249.[33] Such statutory accounts must be accompanied by the relevant auditors' report.

Where non-statutory[34] accounts are published, a statement must accompany them indicating:

(a) that they are not the statutory accounts;
(b) whether statutory accounts for the year in question have been delivered to the Registrar; and

---

[31] However, it is only necessary to send a copy to one joint holder.
[32] *Ante,* p. 478.
[33] Prior to the Companies Act 1989 abbreviated accounts were known as "modified" accounts. For the requirements with respect to filing accounts, see p. 475.
[34] Prior to the Companies Act 1989 these were known as "abridged" accounts.

ACCOUNTS

482

(c) whether the auditors have made a report on the statutory
accounts, and if so whether or not it was qualified.

The non-statutory accounts must not be published with the
auditors' report relating to the statutory accounts (section 240(3)
of the Companies Act 1985).

A company which is obliged to prepare group accounts must
not publish its individual accounts without also publishing its
group accounts (section 240(2) of the Companies Act 1985).

A company which contravenes these requirements and any
defaulting officers are liable to be fined.

Non-statutory accounts include preliminary announcements
made by quoted companies subject to the London Stock
Exchange's *Listing Rules*. Other summarised financial statements
qualifying as non-statutory accounts would appear to be the
simplified statements often circulated by large companies to their
employees, but not the summary financial statements circulated
to their shareholders by listed companies (see *post*).

**Summary financial statements**

A listed company need not send its members copies of its
annual accounts and the directors' and auditors' reports, as
required by section 238, *ante*. Instead, it can send them a
summary financial statement, although those wishing to receive
the full accounts must be sent them (section 251 and S.I. 1990
No. 515).[35]

The Act provides that the summary financial statement must be
derived from the company's annual accounts and the directors'
report in accordance with the Companies Regulations 1990.[36]
Moreover, it must include statements:

(a) indicating that it only contains summarised financial
information;
(b) by the auditors as to whether the information given is
consistent with the full accounts and the directors' report;
(c) whether the full auditors' report is qualified, and if so
include that full report; and

[35] The regulations for banks and insurance companies appear in S.I. 1992 No.
3075.
[36] S.I. 1990 No. 515.

(d) whether the full auditors' report contains a statement concerning the accounting records and/or the adequacy of the information and explanations received, and if so include such statements in full.

Failure to observe these conditions renders the company and every defaulting officer liable to a fine.

## THE ANNUAL ACCOUNTS

Neither the law nor the accountancy profession has satisfactorily defined the role and purpose of the annual accounts of a company, though the traditional view is that they primarily represent "a stewardship record". Thus, the Jenkins Committee expressed the opinion that "a profit and loss account is an historical record. It shows as the profit or loss the difference between the revenue for that period covered by the account and the expenditure chargeable in that period".[37]

Unfortunately the only objective historical record of a company's affiars is afforded by its cash account—any attempt to measure profit inevitably involves valuation, either of the business itself as a going concern, or (more usually) of the individual net assets it owns. Yet experience seems to suggest that what potential users want, above all, is a measure of profit, even though this must inevitably involve an element of subjectivity in its calculation. The traditional accounting approach, substantially influenced no doubt by the needs of the auditing side of the accountancy profession, has been to value the net assets according to a reasonably flexible set of conservatively biased rules, the overall effect of which is to delay the recognition of profit through time. However, when there is a significant systematic rise in prices over a given period the expenses (representing assets used up) that are matched against current revenues can give rise to a misleadingly inflated profit figure, thus defeating the accountants' aim to exercise prudence in determining the income figure. Another result is that the asset values in a balance sheet are even less likely to approximate to current market values (if indeed that is what is deemed desirable) than might be the case in a period when increases in the general price level are relatively small.

[37] (1962) Cmnd. 1749, para. 333.

In practice most classes of user of financial statements are well aware of the shortcomings of conventional accounts, and certainly for listed companies they seem primarily to look upon published profit figures as one amongst several signals they receive concerning a company's relative performance and its likely future prospects. In such circumstances the main purpose of the profit calculation would therefore appear to be to enable users of the accounts to compare reported outcomes against what was expected, and this is even true for unquoted companies where alternative sources of information (except at the wider industry level) are rather more limited. Where the reported income and other accounting figures are used not as one of a number of signals of likely future performance, but rather as the basis of a particular calculation (such as a share of profits, the liability to corporation tax, or a restriction under a debt convenant), the interested parties must specify more carefully the exact accounting conventions that are to be adopted in preparing the company's relevant annual financial statements.

The Accounting Standards Board is currently reviewing these issues and has published a draft Statement of Principles. This examines the objective of financial statements, the qualitative characteristics of financial information, the presentation of financial information, the elements of financial statements, the recognition of items in financial statements, measurements in financial statements (including the use of current market values), and the reporting entity.

It is against this background, then, that the statutory disclosure requirements contained in the Companies Acts (and most specifically in the Companies Act 1985, Sched. 4) should be seen. They establish a basic minimum of information which must be disclosed and be subjected to audit, thus increasing its credibility in the eyes of the reader and so hopefully reducing his uncertainty about future likely outcomes. Many companies will disclose more, either in the statutory accounts themselves and in supplementary statements demanded by the ASB (such as the cash flow statement) and by London Stock Exchange requirements (which *inter alia* provide that listed companies should publish half-yearly interim accounts); or, alternatively, by other means (*e.g.* for quoted companies through the chairman's report, press releases, or news leaked onto the market via stockbrokers' reports; and for unquoted companies by disclosing relevant information directly to bank managers, other major creditors and employee representatives).

## Basic principles

Section 226 of the Companies Act 1985 requires the directors of a company to prepare for each financial year its "individual accounts" (*i.e.* its end year balance sheet and a profit and loss account). Likewise, section 227 requires the directors of a company which is a parent company (see *post*) to prepare group accounts (see p. 529 *et seq.*). These sections establish two basic principles with regard to a company's or group's financial statements: first, that in so far as they are prepared under these sections of the Act they must comply as to their form and content with the provisions of Schedules 4 and 4A to the Act; and, second, that the balance sheets and profit and loss account and notes thereto must give a true and fair view of the company's or group's financial position and its profit or loss for a given period.

Since the responsibility for preparing the accounts falls on the directors, a shareholder is not entitled to bring proceedings to require certain information to be included in the accounts.[38]

Where a company does not trade for profit, the financial statements will include an income and expenditure account instead of the profit and loss account, together with the balance sheet and notes to the accounts (section 262(2)).

For the purpose of determining whether group accounts should be prepared, a parent undertaking is essentially defined in relation to a subsidiary if:

(a) it holds a majority of the voting rights;
(b) it is a member of the subsidiary and has power to appoint or remove a majority of its directors; or
(c) it can exert a dominant influence over the subsidiary (*e.g.* by virtue of a contract) or the companies are managed on a unified basis (section 258 of the Companies Act 1985).

Further guidance on the interpretation of these terms is given in Schedule 10A, which deals with such matters as voting rights, powers to appoint and remove a majority of directors, and rights to exercise a dominant influence.

Where a group relationship exists, the parent company must prepare group as well as individual company accounts, and they will generally be in the form of consolidated accounts comprising:

[38] *Devlin v. Slough Estates Ltd,* (1982) 126 S.J. 623.

(a) a consolidated balance sheet dealing with the state of affairs of the parent company and its subsidiary undertakings, and

(b) a consolidated profit and loss account dealing with the profit or loss of the parent company and its undertakings (section 227(1)–(2) of the Companies Act 1985).

However, where a parent undertaking prepares a consolidated profit and loss account, it need not publish a separate individual profit and loss account as long as it discloses how much of the consolidated profit or loss has been dealt with in the company's individual accounts and that it is taking advantage of this exemption (section 230 of the Companies Act 1985).

The requirement for the individual and group financial statements to give a true and fair view is an overriding one, so where information additional to the minimum specified in the Acts is necessary for the financial statements to give a true and fair view, such extra information must be included in those statements.[39] Likewise, where the circumstances are such that strict compliance with a requrement of the Act would not result in a true and fair view, the company must depart from that requirement, full particulars of the reasons for the departure and its effect being disclosed in the notes to the accounts (sections 226(4)–(5) and 227(5)–(6) of the Companies Act 1985; Sched. 4, para. 15).

Despite the fact that it is an overriding requirement that the financial statements should give "a true and fair view" of a company's financial affairs, the exact meaning of the phrase is unfortunately far from clear, a matter which was highlighted in the early 1980s by the presence of an alternative current cost set of accounts in the annual reports of most listed companies.[40] However, it seems that adherence to normal accounting practice

---

[39] A complication has arisen with the introduction of S.I. 1992 No. 2452, which permits "shortened" accounts to be presented to shareholders of small companies (*ante,* p. 478). As a result, small companies may omit some important information when preparing such accounts that would normally be included in a full set of accounts in order for them to reflect "a true and fair view." Such a view is still specifically deemed to be given as long as the directors have done nothing more than taken advantage of the exemptions available to them. Yet, unless there are grounds for qualification, auditors are no longer required to report on the truth and fairness of shortened small company financial statements, although they must consider whether such a view is given.

[40] Such supplementary statements were required to be published at that time under an accounting standard then in force: see p. 526.

would be *prima facie* evidence of giving a true and fair view. Thus the claim that accounts were misleading because they included property at original cost rather than at current market value was rejected by the courts because normal practice had been followed.[41]

More recently, the status of accounting standards[42] in helping to clarify the meaning of the phrase has been examined in the case of *Lloyd Cheyham and Co. Ltd v. Littlejohn and Co.*[43] There Woolf J. considered the evidential role of such standards and held that:

> "while they are not conclusive . . . and they are not . . . rigid rules, they are very strong evidence as to what is the proper standard which should be adopted . . ."

Nevertheless, it is clear that the "true and fair view override" cannot be used with impunity, as was demonstrated in the *Argyll Foods* case.[44] There the company wished to record "economic substance" at the expense of "legal form" and chose—with the agreement of its auditor—to consolidate into its group financial statements for the year ending December 1974 the accounts of a company, even though it did not acquire full control until after the group's balance sheet date. In so doing it was in breach of the Companies Act and Statement of Standard Accounting Practice (SSAP) 14. The magistrates who heard the case decided that the accounts did not show a true and fair view, and subsequently the Department of Trade and Industry (which had brought the prosecution) issued a statement interpreting the decision as confirming its view that the "true and fair view override" is confined to the disclosure requirements of the Companies Acts and that it does not enable companies to depart from the other provisions (*e.g.* definitions) in the Acts. In such circumstances it would seem appropriate where necessary to indicate the underlying economic substance in notes to the accounts or in supplementary pro-forma statements.

The figures included in the annual accounts have been given added significance as a result of sections 39–45 of the Companies

---

[41] *Re Press Caps Ltd* [1949] Ch. 434.

[42] See *post,* p. 516 *et seq.*

[43] [1986] PCC 389.

[44] Unfortunately the case is not reported, but the issues, evidence and decision have been examined at some length by Ashton, R.K., "The Argyll Foods Case: A Legal Analysis," (1986) *Accounting and Business Research,* Vol. 17, No. 65, pp. 3–12.

Act 1980 (now sections 263–281 of the 1985 Act), which prescribe that distributable profit is generally the aggregate of accumulated realised net profits as reported in the latest audited (or, if relevant, interim) accounts. Moreover, a public company can only pay a dividend if the net assets (after payment of the dividend) at least equal its capital plus any reserves not available for distribution (see *post*, chapter 22). Apart from introducing the problem of deciding which profits are actually realised and which are not—a somewhat arbitrary distinction and a matter anyway of some dispute amongst accountants[45]—such rules cannot ensure the protection of unsecured creditors, while at the same time they may possibly inhibit the efficient workings of the capital market.

### Large, medium, and small sized companies

*Size criteria*

Although the directors of private companies have always had to prepare statutory accounts to lay before their shareholders in general meeting, prior to 1967 most were exempted from the need to file these financial statements with the Registrar of Companies. However, under the provisions of the Companies Act put on the statute book in that year, this dispensation ceased to operate, and, apart from exemptions for special classes of business (like banks and insurance and—at that time—shipping companies), the only concessions were for companies below a certain size which were permitted not to disclose details of turnover and directors' remuneration, the criteria (set in terms of the size of the amounts involved) being altered from time-to-time by statutory instrument. Exemptions were also granted in relation to a turnover criterion permitting companies not to disclose in their directors' reports the value of exports, the average number of employees and their aggregate remuneration, and turnover and pretax profit or loss by each class of business. It was the view of the Bolton committee of enquiry on small firms that these concessions did not seriously prejudice the work of credit agencies and the interests of unsecured creditors.[46]

---

[45] Section 262(3) of the 1985 Act merely says that "realised" profits and losses are "such profits or losses of the company as fall to be treated as realised in accordance with principles generally accepted . . . with respect to the determination for accounting purposes of realised profits or losses." See *post*, p. 596.

[46] (1972) Cmnd. 4811, Chap. 17.

Using a size criterion to determine the extent of disclosure in the accounts filed with the Registrar of Companies was a principle established by section 5(1) of the Companies Act 1981, and now confirmed in section 246 of the 1985 Act. Briefly, while all limited companies (other than investment companies and companies engaged in banking and insurance—see *post*, pp. 549–550) must prepare and lay detailed accounts before their members in general meeting in accordance with one or other of a set of prescribed forms of financial statement given in Schedule 4 to the Act (section 241),[47] medium and small sized non-public companies can avail themselves of concessions whereby they need only *file* "abbreviated" accounts (*ante*, p. 477).

In order to qualify for this exemption, small or medium sized companies or groups must neither be nor include public companies, banks, insurance companies or authorised persons under the Financial Services Act 1986 (section 246(3)–(4) of the Companies Act 1985).

A company qualifies as small or medium sized where it meets the criteria described below:

(1) in its first financial year; or
(2) subsequently in the current and previous years; or
(3) it was so qualified in the previous financial year.

The qualifying criteria are that it should meet at least two of three conditions concerning annualised turnover, balance sheet totals and the average weekly number of employees as follows:

|  | Small sized | Medium sized |
|---|---|---|
| (1) annualised turnover | ≤£2.8m | ≤£11.2m |
| (2) balance sheet total | ≤£1.4m | ≤£5.6m |
| (3) average weekly number of employees | ≤50 | ≤250 |

(section 247 of the Companies Act 1985, as amended).

The concessions available to qualifying small and medium sized private companies are summarised below on pp. 515–516.

---

[47] Small companies may however present "shortened" accounts to shareholders (*ante*, p. 478), in which case the balance sheet must include a statement that they are taking advantage of Part A of Schedule 8 to the 1985 Act and giving the grounds which entitle them to do so.

However, a parent company will not qualify unless it meets the conditions necessary to exempt it from the need to prepare group accounts under section 249, described below.

## Filing abbreviated accounts

In order to file abbreviated accounts, a qualifying small or medium sized company must obtain a report from its auditors stating whether in their opinion the company is entitled to the exemptions (Schedule 8, paragraph 24(1)). The directors must also append to the filed accounts a statement indicating that advantage is being taken of the exemptions and the grounds for doing so (Schedule 8, paragraph 23). The abbreviated accounts must also be accompanied by a signed special auditors' report stating that in their opinion the company is entitled to the exemptions and that the accounts have been properly prepared in accordance with the provisions of Schedule 8. Included in this report will be the audit report required under section 235, which refers to the full accounts (Schedule 8, paragraph 24(2)–(4)).

## Exemptions from presenting and filing group accounts

A parent company of a group which qualifies as a small or medium sized group need not prepare group accounts, either for delivery to the Registrar or for presentation to the shareholders at a general meeting. To take advantage of this exemption, the company's auditors must provide the directors with a report stating that in their opinion the company is entitled to do so, and this must be attached to the company's individual accounts. However, a group is not eligible for the exemption if any of its members are public companies, banks, insurance companies or authorised persons under the Financial Services Act 1986 (section 248 of the Companies Act 1985).

To qualify as a small or medium sized group and thus be eligible not to prepare group accounts, it must meet the criteria:

(1)  in its first financial year; or
(2)  subsequently in the current and previous years; or
(3)  it was so qualified in the previous financial year.

The qualifying criteria are that it should meet at least two of the conditions concerning annualised turnover, balance sheet totals and the average weekly number of employees as follows:

|                                          | Small sized |        | Medium sized |         |
|------------------------------------------|-------------|--------|--------------|---------|
|                                          | Net         | Gross  | Net          | Gross   |
| (1) annualised turnover                  | ≤£2.8m      | ≤£3.36m | ≤£11.2m     | ≤£13.34m |
| (2) balance sheet total                  | ≤£1.4m      | ≤£1.68m | ≤£ 5.6m     | ≤£ 6.72m |
| (3) average weekly number of employees   | ≤50         |        | ≤250         |         |

(Net means after set-offs required by Sched. 4A when consolidated accounts are being prepared, and gross means before those set-offs: section 249 of the Companies Act 1985, as amended).

## Exemption from the statutory audit

Under the Companies Act 1985 Regulations 1994,[48] a company which qualifies as small under section 246 and whose annual turnover and balance sheet totals respectively do not exceed £90,000 and £1.4 million is exempt from the statutory audit requirement. Small companies whose annual turnover is in the range £90,000—£350,000 and whose balance sheet totals do not exceed £1.4 million are also exempt from the statutory audit requirement, but under section 249A their accounts must be examined by a reporting accountant who will prepare a *compilation report* on them (see *post,* p. 577–578).

## Form and content of accounts[49]

### 1. General rules

The approach adopted in the EU's Fourth Council Directive (on which the first Schedule to the 1981 Act and now the fourth Schedule to the 1985 Act are substantially based) was essentially prescriptive in nature, reflecting the influence of continental Europe. Thus, Section A of Part I of the fourth Schedule to the 1985 Act establishes the general rules in relation to the form and content of full individual company accounts, indicating that one of the prescribed formats (four for the profit and loss account and two for the balance sheet) must be used (paragraph 1) and be adhered to year by year unless there are special reasons justifying

---

[48] S.I. 1994 No. 1935.
[49] In the remainder of this chapter, paragraph refeences are to the fourth Schedule to the 1985 Act, unless otherwise indicated.

a change (paragraph 2). However, some flexibility is allowed. Thus, where necessary, directors may give greater detail than prescribed (paragraph 3(1)) or adapt the formats to reflect the special nature of a company's business (paragraph 3(3)). Moreover, certain items (indicated in the model statements by Arabic numerals) can be combined if the combination facilitates an assessment of the company's performance or position (paragraph 3(4)). Comparative figures for the previous accounting period are also to be shown (paragraph 4), but individual items may not be set off against each other (paragraph 5).

## 2. Balance sheet

Section B of Part I of the fourth Schedule to the Companies Act 1985 sets out two alternative formats of balance sheet, the contents of which are in fact identical. The first (reproduced below) equates net assets to the aggregate of the share capital and reserves, and is thus not dissimilar to the vertical layout commonly used in the United Kingdom before the 1981 Act came into effect. Not surprisingly it is therefore the most widely used layout, particularly for larger companies. The second format equates assets against claims, a method of presentation more commonly used in continental European countries.

### Balance sheet—Format 1

A *Called up share capital not paid*

B *Fixed assets*

 *I* **Intangible assets**
   1    Development costs
   2    Concessions, patents, licences, trade marks and similar rights and assets
   3    Goodwill
   4    Payments on account

 *II* **Tangible assets**
   1    Land and buildings
   2    Plant and machinery
   3    Fixtures, fittings, tools and equipment
   4    Payments on account and assets in course of construction

### *III* Investments
    1    Shares in group undertakings
    2    Loans to group undertakings
    3    Participating interests
    4    Loans to undertakings in which the company has a participating interest
    5    Other investments other than loans
    6    Other loans
    7    Own shares

## *C Current assets*

### *I* Stocks
    1    Raw materials and consumables
    2    Work in progress
    3    Finished goods and goods for resale
    4    Payments on account

### *IV* Debtors
    1    Trade debtors
    2    Amounts owed by group undertakings
    3    Amounts owed by undertakings in which the company has a participating interest
    4    Other debtors
    5    Called up share capital not paid
    6    Prepayments and accrued income

### *III* Investments
    1    Shares in group undertakings
    2    Own shares
    3    Other investments

### *IV* Cash at bank and in hand

## *D Prepayments and accrued income*

## *E Creditors: amounts falling due within one year*

    1    Debenture loans
    2    Bank loans and overdrafts
    3    Payments received on account
    4    Trade creditors

5   Bills of exchange payable
6   Amounts owed to group undertakings
7   Amounts owed to undertakings in which the company has a participating interest
8   Other creditors including taxation and social security
9   Accruals and deferred income

*F Net current assets (liabilities)*

*G Total assets less current liabilities*

*H Creditors: amounts falling due after more than one year*

1   Debenture loans
2   Bank loans and overdrafts
3   Payments received on account
4   Trade creditors
5   Bills of exchange payable
6   Amounts owed to group undertakings
7   Amounts owed to undertakings in which the company has a participating interest
8   Other creditors including taxation and social security
9   Accruals and deferred income

*I Provisions for liabilities and charges*

1   Pensions and similar obligations
2   Taxation, including deferred taxation
3   Other provisions

*J Accruals and deferred income*

*K Capital and reserves*

*I*   **Called up share capital**

*II*   **Share premium account**

*III* **Revaluation reserve**

## IV Other reserves
1 Capital redemption reserve
2 Reserve for own shares
3 Reserves provided for by the articles of association
4 Other reserves

## V Profit and loss account

Preliminary expenses, issuing expenses and commissions, and research expenditure are not permitted to be treated as assets in a company's balance sheet (Schedule 4, paragraph 3(2)). Intangible assets, such as patents and trade marks, can however be included if they were either acquired for valuable consideration or were created by the company itself. Similarly, only goodwill acquired for valuable consideration can be shown as an asset in a balance sheet, but its cost must be written off systematically over a period which must not exceed its estimated useful economic life (paragraph 21). The amount of each item to be shown under the head "Debtors" must be split between those amounts receivable within one year of the balance sheet date and those receivable later than that; and in determining the amount to be shown under "Net current assets", amounts shown as "prepayments and accrued income" have to be taken into account.

As regards claims, where there are debenture loans these have to be split between convertible and non-convertible loans; and the amounts of allotted and paid-up share capital have also to be shown separately. Payments received on account for orders must be shown under creditors unless disclosed as a deduction from stocks of finished goods.

A "participating interest" is an interest held by an undertaking in the shares of another undertaking which it holds on a long-term basis. Moreover, such a holding must be for the purpose of securing a contribution to its activities by the exercise of control or influence arising from or related to that interest. Normally a holding of 20 per cent of a company's shares, including convertibles and options, will give rise to the presumption of there being a "participating interest" unless the contrary is shown (section 260 of the Companies Act 1985).

A provision is "any amount retained as reasonably necessary for the purpose of providing for any liability or loss which is either likely to be incurred, or certain to be incurred but uncertain as to amount or as to the date on which it will arise" (Schedule 4, paragraph 89).

A company will normally only hold its own shares where it has acquired them by forfeiture or surrender. Where it purchases or redeems its own shares they must be cancelled (sections 146 and 160(4)).

For the rules relating to share premium and capital redemption reserve accounts, see chapters 9–10.

As indicated previously (pp. 477–478; 488–490), medium and large sized companies have to file a full balance sheet, but small companies need only submit an abbreviated statement, duly signed by a director, that discloses only those items that are preceded by a letter or a Roman numeral. However, the aggregate amounts of debtors and creditors have to be divided between amounts receivable or payable within one year and those receivable or payable beyond that period. Details can be disclosed either in the balance sheet itself or in the notes to the accounts (Schedule 8, paragraph 17).

The following balance sheet items may be combined together by a small company if it presents "shortened" accounts to its shareholders:

| | |
|---|---|
| B I | 1, 2 and 3 |
| B II | 2, 3 and 4 |
| B III | 1 and 3 |
| | 2 and 4 |
| | 6 and 7 |
| C I | 1, 2 and 3 |
| C II | 2 and 3 |
| | 4, 5 and 6 |
| C III | 2 and 3 |
| E | 6 and 7 |
| | 1, 3, 5, 8 and 9 |
| H | 6 and 7 |
| | 1, 3, 5, 8 and 9 |
| I | 1, 2 and 3 |
| K IV | 1, 2, 3 and 4 |

## 3. Profit and loss account

Of the four profit and loss account formats given in the fourth Schedule to the 1985 Act, the first two (reproduced below) are presented in a vertical form (and are therefore probably the most likely to be used in the United Kingdom), while the third and fourth show expenses on the left and income on the right. Formats 1 and 3 classify expenses by function, whereas formats 2 and 4 classify them by type. Format 1 is the layout most commonly used by large companies.

### Profit and loss accounts—Format 1

1 Turnover
2 Cost of sales
3 Gross profit or loss
4 Distribution costs
5 Administrative expenses
6 Other operating income
7 Income from shares in group undertakings
8 Income from participating interests
9 Income from other fixed asset investments
10 Other interest receivable and similar income
11 Amounts written off investments
12 Interest payable and similar charges
13 Tax on profit or loss on ordinary activities
14 Profit or loss on ordinary activities after taxation
15 Extraordinary income
16 Extraordinary charges
17 Extraordinary profit or loss
18 Tax on extraordinary profit or loss
19 Other taxes not shown under the above items
20 Profit or loss for the financial year

### Profit and loss accounts—Format 2

1 Turnover
2 Change in stocks of finished goods and in work in progress
3 Own work capitalised
4 Other operating income
5 (a) Raw materials and consumables
   (b) Other external charges
6 Staff Costs:
   (a) wages and salaries
   (b) social security costs
   (c) other pension costs

7   (a) Depreciation and other amounts written off tangible and intangible fixed assets
    (b) Exceptional amounts written off current assets
8   Other operating charges
9   Income from shares in group undertakings
10  Income from participating interests
11  Income from other fixed asset investments
12  Other interest receivable and similar income
13  Amounts written off investments
14  Interest payable and similar charges
15  Tax on profit or loss on ordinary activities
16  Profit or loss on ordinary activities after taxation
17  Extraordinary income
18  Extraordinary charges
19  Extraordinary profit or loss
20  Tax on ordinary profit or loss
21  Other taxes not shown under the above items
22  Profit or loss for the financial year

Where the format classifies expenses by function (*i.e.* formats 1 and 3) the amounts to be shown under cost of sales, distribution costs and administrative expenses are to include depreciation charges and provisions for diminution in the value of assets. However, the amounts of any such charges or provisions for both tangible and intangible fixed assets must be disclosed separately in the notes to the financial statements. In addition, any interest or similar charges payable to group companies must be shown separately.

Apart from the above, whichever format is adopted the following items must be disclosed separately in the profit and loss account:

(i)   profit or loss on ordinary activities before taxation;
(ii)  the aggregate amount of any dividends paid or proposed; and
(iii) movements to or from reserves (Schedule 4, paragraph 3(6), (7)).

Large sized companies have to choose one of the four profit and loss account formats and file the full version. However, medium sized companies are permitted to file an abbreviated statement. Effectively, the following items can be combined and be shown as one item, "gross profit or loss":

    (a)  where expenses are classified by function—turnover, cost of sales, gross profit or loss and other operating income; and

    (b)  where expenses are classified by type—turnover, change in stocks of finished goods and work in progress, own work capitalised, other operating income, raw materials and consumables, and other external charges (Schedule 8, paragraph 21).

The directors of a small company are exempted from having to file a profit and loss account (Schedule 8, paragraph 18). However, there are no concessions in the regulations relating to "shortened" accounts with respect to profit and loss account disclosures.

Various accounting standards affect the calculation and presentation of items in the profit and loss account, and they can be accommodated either in the notes or in the body of the statement as supplementary disclosures. These standards are either those published by the Accounting Standards Board (ASB), referred to as Financial Reporting Standards (FRSs); or those which it inherited from its predecessor body, the Accounting Standards Committee (ASC) and which it has yet to replace, referred to as Statements of Standard Accounting Practice (SSAPs).

The most inportant in this respect are probably the standards delaing with earnings per share (SSAP 3, as revised by FRS 3), which requires listed companies to show this figure on the face of the statement itself; on associated companies (SSAP 1, as modified by an interim statement by the ASB and FRS 2), which requires partial consolidation of associated companies' profits; on accounting for subsidiary undertakings (FRS 2), which deals with the methods of consolidation; on reporting financial performance (FRS 3) (which *inter alia* indicates the restricted circumstances when extraordinary items arise and how and where they should be disclosed); on taxation (SSAPs 8 and 15), which indicate how current and deferred tax charges should be disclosed; on foreign currency translation (SSAP 20); on accounting for leases and hire purchase contracts (SSAP 21); on segmental reporting (SSAP 25); on accounting for acquisitions and mergers (FRS 6); and on accounting for goodwill (FRS 7). In addition, FRS 1 requires all except the smallest of companies to publish a supplementary cash flow statement (see *post,* p. 528); FRS 4 deals with accounting for capital instruments (such as deep discount bonds, convertible debt, participating preference shares, stepped interest bonds and minority interests); and FRS 5—on reporting the substance of transactions—indicates how "off balance sheet financing" should be reflected in financial statements.

## Notes to the financial statements

Much of the information which was required to be disclosed either in the accounts or in the directors' report between 1967 and 1981, but which cannot be accommodated in the model formats given in the fourth Schedule to the 1985 Act, has to be revealed in notes to the financial statements, which themselves form an integral part of the accounts. These notes may be contained in the accounts themselves or in a separate document annexed to the accounts (section 261 of the Companies Act 1985). Most of the details of items which are to be disclosed in note form are given in the fourth Schedule, paragraphs 35–38, and in the fifth and sixth Schedules. However, items in the model statements required by the fourth Schedule which are preceded by Arabic numerals can also be relegated to a note if necessary (Schedule 4, paragraph 3(4)). Conversely, items required to be shown in notes may, where feasible, be shown on the face of the accounts (Schedule 4, paragraphs 3(1) and 35).

## 1. General notes

The accounting policies used by a company must be disclosed, in particular indicating the depreciation and foreign currency translation methods employed (paragraphs 36 and 58(1)), a requirement which substantially meets the conditions of SSAP 2. There must also be a statement indicating whether the accounts have been prepared in accordance with applicable accounting standards[50] and giving particulars of any material departure from such standards and the reasons for it (paragraph 36A).

Other accounting standards relevant in this context are group accounts (FRS 2), associated companies (SSAP 1, as amended by the ASB), the treatment of government grants (SSAP 4), accounting for value added tax (SSAP 5), depreciation (SSAP 12), research and development (SSAP 13), stocks and work in

[50] See *post,* pp. 516–518.

progress (SSAP 9), taxation (SSAPs 8 and 15), foreign currency translation (SSAP 20), accounting for leases (SSAP 21), accounting for acquisitions and mergers (FRS 6), fair values and goodwill in acquisition accounting (FRS 7), and accounting for pension costs (SSAP 24). A number of draft standards—financial reporting exposure drafts (FREDs)—have also been published which are relevant in this context, *e.g.* on related party disclosures (FRED 8).

Corresponding amounts for the previous financial year (adjusted if necessary to make them comparable), have to be given for all items disclosed in the notes, except for movements on reserves, provisions, fixed asset and depreciation accounts; loans and other transactions with directors and officers of the company under the sixth Schedule to the Act; and information on subsidiaries and significant shareholdings that has to be disclosed under Parts I and II of the fifth Schedule to the Act: *i.e.* in terms of the labels used immediately below on pp. 502–509 for balance sheet items: (B), (C), (D)(ii)–(iv), and (I) (Schedule 4, paragraph 58).

## 2. *Balance Sheet*

The following details must be disclosed by way of notes:

(A) SHARE CAPITAL AND LOAN STOCK

(i) Authorised share capital and the number and nominal value of each class of shares allotted (paragraph 38).

(ii) Where redeemable shares (either preference or equity) have been allotted, the notes must disclose the earliest and latest dates of redemption, whether the company is obliged to redeem them or merely has the option to do so, and whether any premium is payable on redemption, and if so the amount (paragraph 38).

(iii) Where shares or debentures have been allotted during the year, the reasons for making the issue, the classes of securities involved and the amount/number issued or allotted, and the aggregate nominal value and the consideration received for each class. Moreover, in respect of debentures particulars must be disclosed of any redeemable debentures the company has power to reissue, and the nominal amount and book value

of any debentures held by a nominee or trustee of the
company (paragraphs 39, 41).

(iv) Where options or similar rights exist in relation to shares,
the number, description and amount of the shares involved,
the period during which the right is exercisable, and the price
payable have to be disclosed (paragraph 40).

FRS 4 on accounting for capital instruments indicates procedures for dealing with deep discount bonds, stepped interest
bonds, options, etc. In the meantime, the UITF has issued two
abstracts dealing with disclosure of directors' share options and
issuer call options.

(B) RESERVES AND PROVISIONS[51]

The aggregate amounts of each reserve and provision (including any material amount included in the category "other provisions") at the beginning and end of the financial year must be
disclosed, together with details of movements to and from such
reserves and provisions during the year (paragraph 46). In
addition, the amount of any provision for deferred taxation other
than the amount of any provision for other taxation must be
disclosed separately (paragraph 47); while under the terms of
SSAP 15 the balance on the deferred tax account has to be shown
separately.[51a] Other requirements in relation to the presentation
of tax liabilities in the balance sheet and profit and loss account
and accompanying notes are to be found in SSAP 8.

(C) FIXED ASSETS[52]

For each item under this heading, both tangible and intangible
assets, and also for long-term investments, the notes must
disclose in respect of cost or valuation the aggregate amounts at
the beginning and end of the year, the amounts of any acquisitions, disposals and transfers, and the effect of applying the
alternative accounting valuation rules (see *post,* pp. 526–528).

[51] "Provisions" are defined in Sched. 4, paras. 88–89: see above, p. 495.
[51a] In October 1994 the IASC issued a proposal, E49, for a revised International
Accounting Standard on deferred tax. This would require that full provision should
be made for future tax, whereas SSAP 15 only requires provisioning for tax payable
in the foreseeable future. The ASB therefore released a discussion paper, "Accounting for Tax", in March 1995, which—in line with its own Statement of Principles—
favours a switch to full provisioning. This would generally have significant effects on
the accounts of U.K. listed companies, lowering reported profits in the short term
and increasing the nominal gearing shown in their balance sheets.
[52] "Fixed assets" are defined in s.262(1), Companies Act 1985.

In addition, details must be given of the cumulative amounts of provisions for depreciation or for the diminution in the value of assets at both the beginning and end of the financial year, and the amounts of any additions, reductions through asset disposals, and any other adjustments to such provisions made during the year (paragraph 42).

Where a fixed asset (other than listed investments) has been revalued, the notes must disclose the year in which the assets were severally valued and the several values; and in the years of each valuation the names or qualifications of the valuers and the bases of valuation (paragraph 43). Land and buildings must be divided among freeholds, long leaseholds (*i.e.* those with more than 50 years of lease unexpired at the year end) and short leaseholds (paragraphs 44, 83).

The UITF has published two abstracts respectively dealing with the presentation of long term debtors in current assets; and transfers from current assets to fixed assets.

(D) INVESTMENTS

Certain details of investments must be disclosed, regardless of whether they are shown as fixed or current assets.

*(i) Listed investments*

The following information must be shown with respect to listed investments: their amount, split between investments listed on a recognised stock exchange, together with their quoted value (and estimated market value where this is higher) if it (or they) differ from the value(s) shown in the balance sheet; and unlisted investments. The latter category includes securities traded on the Unlisted Securities Market (USM) and the over-the-counter (OTC) market, but there is no requirement (as there was under paragraph 5A of the second schedule to the 1967 Act) to disclose either the directors' valuation of the unlisted securities or other information relating to them (paragraphs 45 and 84).

*(ii) Holdings in subsidiary undertakings*

For companies required to prepare group accounts, the following information must be disclosed in respect of all subsidiary undertakings of the parent company at its year end: their names; the countries in which they are incorporated (and, if in Great Britain, the country of registration) or, if they are unincorporated, their principal places of business; whether they are included in consolidated group accounts and, if not, the reasons why not; how they qualify as subsidiaries under section 258 of the Act, except where this is a result of majority holdings of voting shares; and the proportions of each class of a subsidiary's shares held by the parent company and by the group as a whole.

With respect to each subsidiary not included in consolidated accounts, the aggregate of its year end capital and reserves and the profit or loss as shown in its last accounts must be disclosed, except where:

(a) the investment is dealt with by the equity consolidation method;

(b) the investee company is not required by the Act to deliver a copy of its accounts and does not publish them elsewhere;

(c) the holding is less than half the nominal value of the subsidiary's shares; or

(d) it is immaterial (Schedule 5, paragraph 17).

With respect to all subsidiaries, the parent company's directors must give reasons when their financial year ends differ from that of the parent company. They must also disclose the dates of the subsidiaries' most recent year ends, either for each subsidiary or the earliest and latest of such dates if there are several whose financial years do not coincide with that of the parent. Qualifications in auditors' reports on subsidiary undertakings' accounts, or material disclosures in such accounts which have avoided such qualifications, must also be revealed by the parent company if not disclosed in the group accounts (Schedule 5, paragraphs 18–19).

Details must also be disclosed of shares and debentures in the parent company held by subsidiary undertakings (Schedule 5, paragraph 20).

Similar disclosures must be made by a company which has subsidiary undertakings but is not required to prepare group accounts (Schedule 5, paragraphs 1–6). However, in such circumstances the company has to disclose the reason why it is not preparing group accounts and, if the reason is that all the subsidiaries fall within the exemptions specified in section 229, a statement for each subsidiary indicating which exclusion applies (Schedule 5, paragraph 1(4)–(5)).

### (iii) Joint ventures

A company which is required to prepare group accounts, and which accounts for an undertaking as a joint venture using the method of *pro rata* proportional consolidation, must disclose:

— the undertaking's name;
— its principal place of business;
— the basis of its joint management;
— the proportion of its capital held by undertakings included in the consolidation; and,
— where its financial year does not coincide with that of the company, its most recent year end (Schedule 5, paragraph 21).

### (iv) Associated undertakings

A company which is required to prepare group accounts, and which has an undertaking included in the consolidation that is an associated undertaking, must disclose the following in respect of such an associated undertaking:

— its name;
— the country in which it is incorporated (and, if in Great Britain, the country of registration) or, if it is unincorporated, its principal place of business; and
— the proportions of each class of the associate's shares held by the parent company and by the group as a whole (Schedule 5, paragraph 22).

### (v) Other significant holdings

Companies, whether required to prepare group accounts or not, must make additional disclosures with respect to companies in which they hold:

(1) more than 10 per cent of the nominal value of any class of share; or

(2) the amount invested as shown in the investor company's individual accounts exceeds 10 per cent of its assets.

The additional information concerning investee companies which must be disclosed (if it is not otherwise given) is:

— their names;
— the countries in which they are incorporated (and, if in Great Britain, the country of registration) or, if they are unincorporated, their principal places of business; and
— the proportions of each class of the investee company's shares held (Schedule 5, paragraphs 7–9; 23–24).

For holdings in excess of 20 per cent of the shares in an undertaking, the aggregate amount of the investee company's year-end capital and reserves and of its annual profit or loss must also be disclosed, except where:

(a) the investment is dealt with by the equity consolidation method;

(b) the investee company is not obliged to deliver a copy of its accounts and does not publish them elsewhere; and the holding is less than half the nominal value of the undertaking's shares;

(c) it is immaterial; or

(d) the investor company is exempt from preparing group accounts as its accounts are included in the financial statements of a larger group (Schedule 5, paragraphs 9 and 25).

Similar criteria are to be applied in respect of a group (rather than just the parent company) where this is relevant (Schedule 5, paragraphs 26–28).

*(vi) Stock Exchange Listing Rules*

In addition to the above, the London Stock Exchange's *Listing Rules* require, for all investments in which there is a participation of 20 per cent or more, disclosure of the countries in which the investee *operates*.

(E) CREDITORS

For each item under heading *H* in format 1 of the balance sheet (p. 494, *ante*) and its equivalent in format 2, the following must be disclosed:

  (i) Amounts payable (other than by instalments) more than five years hence.
  (ii) The aggregate amount of any instalments payable five or more years hence.
  (iii) The terms of payment and any applicable rate of interest.
  (iv) The aggregate figure for secured creditors and the nature of securities given.
  (v) The amount and period of any arrears of fixed cumulative dividends (paragraphs 48, 49, 85).

(F) GUARANTEES AND FINANCIAL COMMITMENTS

Under paragraph 50 of the fourth Schedule the following items must be disclosed:

  (i) The amount of third party liabilities secured by charges on the company's assets.
  (ii) The amount, nature and security provided (if any) in relation to any contingent liability. (SSAP 18 requires additional disclosures for such items.)
  (iii) The aggregate of capital expenditure (a) contracted for, and (b) authorised by the directors but not contracted for.
  (iv) Pension commitments (a) provided for, and (b) not provided for. (Further guidance on how this should be done is given in SSAP 24.)
  (v) Any other commitments relevant to a proper understanding of the company's affairs.

Commitments undertaken on behalf of:

  (a) subsidiaries of the company; and

(b)  parent or fellow subsidiary undertakings

must be stated separately both from each other and from the company's other commitments (paragraph 59A).

(G) DIVIDENDS

The aggregate amount of proposed dividends has to be disclosed (paragraphs 3 and 51).

(H) LOANS MADE FOR THE PURCHASE OF A COMPANY'S SHARES

Details of any outstanding loan made for the purpose of acquiring the company's shares under sections 153(4) or 155 of the Act (see *ante,* chapter 11) must be disclosed in aggregate for each item in which they are included (paragraph 51).

(I) CREDIT TRANSACTIONS WITH DIRECTORS AND OFFICERS OF THE COMPANY

Under Parts II and III of the sixth Schedule to the Act, particulars must be disclosed in notes to the accounts of any material credit transaction or arrangement with a director, shadow director, connected person or officer other than a director which are permitted under sections 330–338. Under paragraphs 22 and 29 of the sixth Schedule, the information to be disclosed is generally:

(i)   The fact that the transaction, loan, arrangement or agreement was made or existed during the financial year; and

(ii)  The name of the director or connected person; and/or the number of officers concerned.

With regard to directors and connected persons, the value of credit transactions has to be disclosed, as well as the nature of any material interest; while for loans and similar arrangements the following details must be given:

(i)   Principal and interest at the beginning and end of the financial year, the maximum amount of the liability during the year, interest due but not paid, and related bad debt provisions; and

(ii) The liability of the company or its subsidiaries under guarantees or security and other similar arrangements at the beginning and end of the year, the maximum potential liability, and expenses or liabilities incurred in discharging the guarantee or security arrangement (Schedule 6, paragraph 22(2)).

With regard to officers other than directors, disclosure must be made of loans and other equivalent arrangements in terms of the aggregate amounts outstanding at the end of the year, together with the number of persons concerned, under the following headings:

(i) Loans or security therefor and similar arrangements;
(ii) Quasi-loans or security therefor and similar arrangements; and
(iii) Credit transactions or security therefor and similar arrangements (Schedule 6, paragraph 29).

Such disclosures also apply when the company is a recognised bank or, for groups of companies, where the holding company or a subsidiary is a recognised bank (Schedule 9, Part IV).

Exemptions from the disclosure requirements for directors, connected persons and officers of the company are permitted on a number of grounds, most notably in relation to service contracts and where the values of the items or interest are small (generally if they do not exceed £5,000 in aggregate at any time during the year for each director; or, for officers other than directors, £2,500) (Schedule 6, paragraphs 17–21, 23–26, 29(2)).

In addition to the above requirements, directors' interests in shares of group companies and in material contracts with the company or its subsidiaries have to be disclosed in the directors' report, either as a result of statutory requirements or in order to meet the rules of the London Stock Exchange.

## 3. *Profit and loss account*

(A) SEGMENTAL ANALYSIS

(i) Where, in the opinion of the directors, a company has carried on two or more classes of business which differ substantially the notes must for each class show the turnover and the pretax profit or loss. Turnover in this context means revenues from ordinary activities net of trade discounts, VAT and other duties. (This treatment of VAT is consistent with the terms of SSAP 5). In determining the source of turnover or of profit or loss the directors are to have regard to the way in which the company's activities are organised (paragraphs 55 and section 262(1) of the 1985 Act).

(ii) Where, in the opinion of the directors, a company has supplied goods and services to two or more geographical *markets* the turnover must be disaggregated by *destination* (paragraph 55). SSAP 25, paragraph 34, requires that a geographical analysis of turnover and contribution to trading results by *origin* (*i.e.* by manufacturing etc. *operations* abroad) should also be disclosed.

(iii) Segmental information need not be disclosed if the directors are of the opinion that its publication would be detrimental to the company's best interests, but if this is the case the fact that such an analysis is being withheld must be stated (paragraph 55(5)).

SSAP 25 and International Accounting Standard (IAS) 14 indicate that in addition the segment assets employed should be disclosed.

(B) OTHER SOURCES OF INCOME

Income from listed investments and, where it comprises a substantial part of the company's revenue, net rents from land must be disclosed (paragraph 53). (Before the Companies Act 1981 there was also a requirement to disclose income from unquoted investments).

(C) EXTRAORDINARY ITEMS

Particulars must be disclosed of prior year transactions included in the profit and loss account; extraordinary items (gross and net of associated tax); and exceptional items (*i.e.* those which arise as a result of the ordinary activities of the business but are abnormal by virtue of their size or incidence) (paragraph 57).

Further guidance on the treatment and presentation of extraordinary items was given in an accounting standard, SSAP 6, but far reaching changes were introduced in another standard, FRS 3, in November 1992. This requires a profit and loss account to show separately: the results of continuing operations (including the results of acquisitions); the results of discontinued operations; profits or losses on the sale or termination of an operation; costs of fundamental reorganisation or restructuring; profits or losses on the disposal of fixed assets; and extraordinary items. The latter are restrictively defined as material items possessing a high degree of abnormality which arise from events or transactions that fall outside the ordinary activities of the reporting entity and which are not expected to recur. Other exceptional items should be disclosed in notes to the accounts, except where disclosure in the profit and loss account is necessary to give a true and fair view.

FRS 3 also requires that a new "primary" statement should be presented of equal prominence to the usual financial statements, showing the total of recognised gains and losses and their components. Moreover, where there is a material difference between the result as disclosed in the profit and loss account and the result on an unmodified historical cost basis, a note of the historical cost profit or loss for the period is to be presented.[53] Further, a note should be given reconciling the opening and closing totals of the shareholders' funds over the period under review.

FRS 3 additionally requires that the earnings per share (EPS) figures for listed companies, covered by the requirements of SSAP 3, are to be calculated after accounting for minority interests, extraordinary items and preference dividends. However, this does not meet the needs of investment analysts and the financial press, and listed companies are now publishing a second EPS figure calculated on an alternative basis.

(D) TAXATION

The notes must disclose the amounts of the charges to both United Kingdom corporation and United Kingdom income taxes, together with a note of the gross amount of the former before any double taxation relief, and details of any overseas taxation borne. Moreover, the tax associated with any extraordinary item must also be shown separately. In addition, the basis of the United Kingdom corporation tax charge must be disclosed,

---

[53] The application of historical cost and "alternative" accounting valuation rules are discussed below, pp. 519–528.

together with details of any special circumstances that affect any liability to taxation (paragraph 54).

Further requirements concerning the calculation and disclosure of taxation are given in SSAPs 8 and 15 (although the latter is subject to review by the ASB in 1995.[53b])

(E) SPECIFIC EXPENSES

Under paragraph 53 of the fourth Schedule details of the following must be disclosed:

(i) Interest on loans outside the group, analysed between (a) bank loans, overdrafts and other loans repayable either in a lump sum within five years, or by instalments with the last instalment payable within that period; and (b) any other loans.

(ii) Hire charges for plant and machinery. (SSAP 21 covers the treatment of leased assets.)

(iii) Amounts set aside for the redemption of (a) share capital and (b) loans.

In addition, under section 390A(3)–(4) of the 1985 Act, auditors' remuneration (including expenses) must be disclosed in a note to the accounts, distinguishing between amounts payable for audit and non-audit work (see *post*, p. 572).

(F) EMPLOYEES AND THEIR REMUNERATION

Details must be disclosed of the following:

(i) The average number of employees in the financial year, found by summing the number of employees (both full- and part-time) week-by-week and dividing by the number of weeks in the period. This figure is then broken down into such categories of employee as the directors select, having regard to the company's organisation (paragraph 56). (The data are to relate to all employees, not just to those working in the United Kingdom, as was the requirement under section 18 of the 1967 Act.)

(ii) In so far as they are not disclosed in the profit and loss account, the aggregate amount of each of the following:

[53b] See footnote 51a, p. 502.

    (a) wages and salaries payable;

    (b) social security costs, including contributions to state run pension schemes; and

    (c) other pension costs incurred, comprising contributions to a private pension scheme by the company, any other sums set aside for that purpose, and any pension payments (paragraphs 56 and 94).

(iii) Under section 232 of the Act and paragraphs 1, 7–9 of the sixth Schedule:

    (a) directors' emoluments;

    (b) directors' pensions;

    (c) compensation payments to directors for loss of office; and

    (d) sums paid to third parties in respect of directors' services.

(iv) Under section 232 of the Act and paragraphs 2–5 of the sixth Schedule, where the total emoluments of all the directors exceed £60,000 in the year in question, the emoluments of the chairman, the highest paid director (if other than the chairman), the number of directors who did not receive emoluments, and the number of directors who received emoluments in the following bands: £0 up to £5,000; over £5,000 and up to £10,000; over £10,000 and up to £15,000; and so on, the bands rising by increments of £5,000. It is only necessary to show those bands for which there are entries, and for these purposes emoluments include amounts waived as well as paid.

(v) Under section 232 of the Act and paragraph 6 of the sixth Schedule the number of directors who have waived rights to receive emoluments and the aggregate amount of those emoluments.

    The Stock Exchange's *Listing Rules* also require that particulars of any arrangement whereby a director has waived or agreed to waive emoluments should be disclosed.

For the purposes of (iii)–(v), above, "emoluments", where relevant, refers to remuneration from a group of companies and includes fees and percentages, expenses allowances so far as charged to United Kingdom income tax, and the estimated money value of any other benefits received otherwise than in cash

(Schedule 6, paragraph 1). In addition, for (iii) it includes contributions paid in respect of a director under a pension scheme (Schedule 6, paragraphs 1 and 2). The amounts to be brought into account for a financial year are the sums receivable in respect of that year, whenever paid, or, in the case of sums not receivable in respect of a period, the sums paid during that year. With regard to remuneration, the details given in the parent company's accounts must relate to the emoluments etc. of its directors or employees from all sources, including subsidiaries. (Schedule 6, paragraphs 10–11).

For the purposes of (iv)–(v), above, such disclosure is not required of a company which is neither a subsidiary nor a parent company if the aggregate amount of the emoluments disclosed as a result of (iii), above, does not exceed £60,000 (Schedule 6, paragraph 2).

## 4. Other notes

Certain other information has to be disclosed in notes to the financial statements (or sometimes on the face of the accounts themselves) in order to comply both with the provisions of the Companies Act 1985 on accounting principles and rules (discussed below) and with provisions of various accounting standards and (for quoted companies) the London Stock Exchange's *Listing Rules*. Moreover, as indicated above (p. 486), where there is a departure from strict compliance with a requirement of the Act to ensure the financial statements reflect a true and fair view, the reasons for the departure and its effect have to be disclosed in a note to the accounts (paragraph 15). In this context, the professional accountancy bodies in the British Isles suggest a material difference between reported and distributable profits should be disclosed in a note (see *post*, chapter 22).

Under paragraphs 11 and 31 of the fifth Schedule, a company which is a subsidiary must state the name and country of incorporation of its ultimate parent company. In addition, under paragraphs 10 and 30, it must give similar details relating to the parent company of both the largest group for which group accounts are drawn up and of which it is a member and also the smallest such group. In so doing, if the parent is incorporated in Great Britain, it must also disclose its country of registration; and if the parent undertaking is unincorporated, its principal place of business.

Companies are also required to disclose certain particulars where they have made arrangements during a year which attract merger relief (Schedule 5, paragraphs 10 and 29: see *post*, p. 538).

## 5. Abbreviated financial statements

Under section 246 and paragraphs 21–22 of the eighth Schedule to the Act, the directors of a *medium size*[54] private company may omit from the statements that they file with the Registrar of Companies the statement indicating that their accounts have been prepared in accordance with applicable accounting standards,[55] as well as detailed information concerning their trading operations (see *ante,* pp. 498–499) and turnover and pretax profit by line of business and geographical market (*i.e.* profit and loss account note (A) on pp. 509–510, *ante*).

The concessions offered to *small size*[55a] private companies under paragraphs 17–20 of the eighth Schedule are more far reaching. Thus of the items which may be disclosed in notes as listed above, only the following have to be disclosed:

1. General notes:          Accounting policies, including in particular the bases of foreign currency translations.

2. Balance sheet:[56]      (A) Share capital and loan stock: items (i) and (ii), and in so far as it relates to shares (but not to loan stock) (iii).

                           (C) Fixed assets, but only in respect of categories preceded by letters and Roman numerals.

                           (E) Creditors, items (i), (ii) and (iv).

                           (I) Transactions with directors and officers of the company.

---

[54] See *ante,* pp. 488–489 for the requirements for a private company to qualify as medium or small sized; and p. 490 for the requirement that a statement should be included above the directors' signatures indicating the company is entitled to benefit from the disclosure exemptions. See *post,* p. 542 for the concession concerning the directors' report; and p. 490 on the requirement to attach a "special" auditors' report to the accounts.

[55] See *post,* pp. 516 *et seq.*

[55a] See footnote 54, above.

[56] The letters and Roman numbers correspond to the items referred to above on pp. 501–509.

| 3. Profit and loss account: | None |
|---|---|
| 4. Other notes: | None of those required by Schedule 4 to the 1985 Act (*e.g.* relating to accounting principles and rules, except in so far as they can be interpreted as accounting policies), nor those required under Schedule 6, Part I, disclosing the remuneration of directors, or under Schedule 5 concerning subsidiaries in respect of alignment of their year ends, qualifications in their audit reports, the holdings of shares in the parent company, and arrangements attracting merger relief. |

Comparative amounts for previous years must still be given where appropriate for such items as are disclosed in notes.

## ACCOUNTING PRINCIPLES AND RULES

Prior to 1981 successive Companies Acts gave little guidance as to what accounting principles and rules should be followed in preparing the annual accounts of companies. However, the view taken by the Cohen and Jenkins Committees on company law reform, reporting respectively in 1945 and 1962, was that in general the traditional historical cost convention used by accountants was appropriate, and it was largely left to the professional accountancy bodies themselves to formulate such rules as they deemed necessary.[57] The supposed inadequacy of such rules was highlighted in the late 1960s in a number of instances referred to the City Panel on Take-Overs and Mergers (see chapter 31), and this led to the creation of the Accounting Standards Committee (ASC) in 1969, whose avowed aim was to codify the different practices and narrow the choice between them. In the 20 years that followed, the ASC succeeded in deflecting much of the criticism formerly directed at the accountancy profession, and while it provided a useful framework for codifying conventions and agreeing standard forms of presentation, it did not greatly

---

[57] (1945) Cmd. 6659, and (1962) Cmnd. 1749, respectively; the relevant paragraphs are 98 for Cohen and 333 for Jenkins.

change the substance of accounting practice. Only in relation to current cost accounting, on which its hand was forced by the report of the government-appointed Sandilands Committee,[58] did it take a new initiative, and even then in this respect the requirement under SSAP 16 that listed companies should publish supplementary current cost financial statements was quietly dropped in 1986, the standard eventually being withdrawn in 1988.

In the circumstances, it was perhaps not surprising that in the late 1980s there was considerable debate about the ways in which accounting standards should be promulgated and be monitored. As a result, a report was published in September 1988, and this led to the creation of the more broadly based Financial Reporting Council, which under a new section of the 1985 Act, s.265 (inserted by section 19 of the Companies Act 1989), sets and polices standards via three subsidiary bodies (see *ante*, p. 469).

In addition, the Companies Act 1989 inserted another new section into the 1985 Act, s.257, which empowers the Secretary of State to alter by statutory instrument the regulations concerning the contents of annual accounts either laid before a company in general meeting or filed with the Registrar.

In the meantime, while the ASC was developing standards in the 1970s, the EU was itself addressing the question of identifying so-called accounting principles which could be consistently applied within the European Union, and its ideas were included in its Fourth Council Directive of 1978. For the most part these related to the historical cost convention, widely applied in a particularly conservative manner in most continental countries, largely to delay profit recognition for tax purposes. However, it was necessary to accommodate current (replacement) cost accounting, used for over 40 years by some major companies in the Netherlands, and also the practice whereby many major listed companies in the United Kingdom had taken to revaluing all or some of their fixed assets, partly it seems as a way of signalling to the public changes in managerial expectations. Moreover, it was also regarded as providing a framework within which any new form of current price level or current cost system of accounting could be accommodated—a matter of some importance since there were moves afoot in the late 1970s to introduce such

[58] (1975) Cmnd. 6225.

systems in various continental countries as well as in the United
Kingdom.

The result was that Part II of the first Schedule to the 1981 Act
was divided into three sections: 1, accounting principles; 2,
historical cost accounting rules; and 3, alternative accounting
rules; and this now constitutes Part II of the fourth Schedule to
the 1985 Act.

## 1. Accounting principles and conventions

Paragraphs 10–15 of the fourth Schedule to the 1985 Act
reiterate the four so-called principles or concepts contained in
SSAP 2 which, so long as they are consistent with the statements
presenting a true and fair view, are supposed to underlie the
preparation of annual accounts: going concern concept, consis-
tency concept, accruals concept, and prudence doctrine.

The *going concern concept* implies that the net realisable values
of fixed assets will not normally be the relevant values to use in
the accounts—indeed, they will only be appropriate where liquidation is envisaged.

*Consistent application of accounting policies,* both within a set
of accounts and over time, is necessary to try to ensure com-
parability from year to year and reduce opportunities to manipulate results. As a result the user should have a better chance of
being able to identify the permanent (as opposed to transitory)
element in profit, which should improve his forecasting ability.

The *accruals concept* requires that revenues and expenses
reported should relate to the financial year in question, regardless
of when cash is actually received or spent.

In practice, however, accounts rarely take the accruals
principle to its logical conclusion, preferring to apply the *prudence doctrine,* which SSAP 2 (but not the 1985 Act) indicates
should prevail where there is conflict between the two. Paragraph
12 of the Schedule specifies two rules in relation to the prudence
doctrine:

(a) that only realised profits should be included in the income
statement (though section 262(3) of the 1985 Act defines
such profits only in terms of best accounting practice at
the time); and

(b) that all liabilities and losses that have arisen and are likely
to arise should be taken into account.

Moreover, they must be included even when they only become apparent after the end of the accounting year, which is consistent with the terms of SSAP 17 on accounting for post balance sheet events.

Paragraph 14 of the Schedule indicates that each asset and liability must be valued separately. Since an asset is undefined this might technically cause problems—for instance, where a machine is owned, is it the machine itself or its component parts that constitute(s) the asset(s)? However, the main purpose of the requirement seems to be to try to ensure that assets which may reasonably be regarded as separate (such as different lines of stock) are valued on an individual rather than a group basis. In fact, the standard on stock valuation, SSAP 9, requires use of the individual item valuation basis, though for tax purposes the group basis remains acceptable.[59]

Paragraph 15 of the Schedule permits directors to depart from any of the principles referred to above if their application is consistent with the overriding requirement of sections 226 and 227 to present a true and fair view. However, particulars of such a departure, the reasons and the effect must be disclosed.

## 2. Historical cost accounting rules

### (A) FIXED ASSETS

Section 262(1) of the 1985 Act defines fixed assets as those assets intended for use on a continuing basis, and the basic rule is that they should be shown at either the purchase price or production cost (the meaning of which terms is discussed below), net of any depreciation or diminution in value (paragraph 17). The latter applies where a fixed asset is wasting in nature and has a limited useful economic life, the cost (net of estimated scrap value) being written off "systematically" over such life (paragraph 18).

Additional depreciation *may* be provided for fixed asset investments in respect of a decline in value (paragraph 19(1)), and *must* be for any fixed asset (including a fixed asset investment) where such decline in value is expected to be permanent (which is consistent with the terms of SSAP 12 on depreciation) (paragraph

[59] *IRC v. Cock, Russell and Co.* [1949] 29 T.C. 387.

19(2)). The basis of such valuation is not defined, but under the going concern concept it will presumably normally be current value in use. Charges for additional depreciation, and amounts written back if such provisions are deemed no longer necessary, must be separately disclosed in the profit and loss account itself or in the notes thereto. Moreover, as regards the former, a distinction must be drawn between charges made under paragraph 19(1) and those under paragraph 19(2).

(B) INTANGIBLE FIXED ASSETS

(i) The original amount at which acquired goodwill is shown in the accounts must be written off "systematically" over a period chosen by the directors which must not exceed its useful economic life. The period, and the reasons for choosing such a period, must be disclosed in a note (Schedule 4, paragraph 21).

The amount attributed to purchased goodwill is the difference between the fair value of the consideration given and the fair value of the separable net assets acquired. Prior to 1994 the accounting standard on goodwill, SSAP 22, required that purchased goodwill, including that arising on consolidation, should either be written off immediately against reserves or be amortised through the profit and loss account over its estimated useful economic life. However, FRS 7 requires that the fair values of an acquired entity's assets and liabilities should not be increased or decreased by changes that result from the acquirer's intentions for future actions involving the acquired entity. Consequently, the fair values attributed to the acquired entity's liabilities should not include provisions for its future operating losses, or for reorganisation and integration costs expected to be incurred as a result of the acquisition. The fair values of monetary assets and liabilities should be based on the amounts expected to be received or paid, discounted where appropriate to their present values. By contrast, the fair values of separately identifiable non-monetary assets should normally be measured at the lower of replacement cost and recoverable amount at the date of acquisition. However, recoverable amount in such circumstances should reflect the condition of the asset at the acquisition date, but not any impairments resulting from subsequent events.

Under the 1985 Act, the amount written off goodwill year by year has to be disclosed in the profit and loss account, but where it is written off immediately against reserves on acquisition (which is currently the preferred method) such disclosure would not appear to be necessary. However, SSAP 22 (and now FRS 7) require that the amount of goodwill recognised as a result of any acquisitions during the year should be shown separately for each acquisition where material, even where it is written off immediately to reserves. Moreover, movements in goodwill must be shown in a note to a group's consolidated accounts (Schedule 4A, paragraph 14: see *post,* pp. 534 *et seq*).

The appropriate treatment of goodwill on a disposal has been determined by the UITF in an abstract. Moreover, the immediate write-off to reserves of purchased goodwill is not a recognised loss for the purpose of inclusion in the statement of recognised gains and losses required to be presented under FRS 3 (see *supra,* p. 511).

The ASB examined four methods of accounting for purchased goodwill in a discussion paper released in December 1993: capitalisation and amortisation over a predetermined life; capitalisation and amortisation, subject to an annual review; immediate elimination of purchased goodwill against reserves; and transfer of purchased goodwill when it arises to a separate goodwill write-off reserve.

(ii) Paragraph 20 permits development costs to be "capitalised" (a term defined in section 262(1) of the 1985 Act) and be shown in the balance sheet, and then only in "special circumstances". Where this is done, notes must disclose the reasons for capitalising such development costs and the period over which they are being written off. Development expenditure is defined in SSAP 13 (though not in the Act): it is essentially identifiable expenditure related to a specific project which can reasonably be expected to be recovered in the future, and upon capitalisation is to be amortised on a systematic basis. Where such expenditure is capitalised a further note to the accounts will generally be required by section 269 and paragraph 20 to indicate that such unamortised expenditure is not being treated as a realised loss in calculating distributable profits and the justification for such treatment (which under section 262(3) of the 1985 Act is likely to be that it is consistent with accepted accounting principles and practice).

The Act does not specifically refer to research expenditure, which, however, is distinguished from development expenditure in SSAP 13 as expenditure which cannot be related to a specific project and cannot reasonably be expected to be recovered in the future. The accounting standard requires that such expenditure should be written off immediately against revenues in the profit and loss account, and this would appear to be consistent with the intention of the Act, given its specific use of the word "development".

The reason for such interest in the treatment of intangible assets appears to be that debt covenants frequently contain clauses which specifically refer to a maximum ratio of debt to assets so as to provide the lender with a margin of security. This seems to encourage companies to engage on the one hand in off balance sheet financing (a topic which is the subject of a standard on leasing, SSAP 21, and a more general one, FRS 5) so as to reduce the face value of debt; and on the other to capitalise spending by creating or maintaining intangible assets, such as goodwill. A recent manifestation of the latter has been the practice of some large companies of putting brands into their balance sheets, a move which has been the subject of critical comment by the professional accountancy bodies. The matter is dealt with in the ASB's December 1993 discussion paper, which argues that purchased intangibles are inseparable from purchased goodwill and should therefore be subsumed in one figure.

It should perhaps be noted that attempts to engage in off balance sheet financing and/or to put intangible assets into a balance sheet are not costless to companies. When lenders see what is happening they will presumably respond by raising the cost of borrowing in the future, which will in part reflect their distrust of the company's management.

(C) CURRENT ASSETS

    (i)    Current assets are defined in section 262(1) of the 1985 Act as any assets not intended for use on a continuing basis in the company's activities.

Initially it must be established whether an asset is owned by a company. This is a matter of some relevance in the case of stocks, which are sometimes the subject of a reservation of title clause: *i.e.* ownership of the goods remains with the supplier until a given event occurs. In fact, the law is clear that a supplier can reserve title where goods are "unmixed" (*i.e.* they have not been transformed in any way), although the contract must be carefully worded.[60] However, where goods are mixed, a clause will only be effective if it is registered as a charge.[61] In practice, if there is doubt about ownership, the "economic substance" will be reflected by recording the goods as stock, but showing in the accounts either a provision against the liability or (if the likelihood of having to return the goods is remote) a note of the contingent liability.[61a]

Generally, current assets are to be valued at the lower of, on the one hand, purchase price or production cost (the meaning of which is discussed below); and, on the other, net realisable value (paragraphs 22–23). This is slightly more restrictive than accounting practice prior to the Companies Act 1981, when the rule was the lower of original cost and market value at the balance sheet date, the latter in some circumstances being capable of interpretation for stocks, both for tax and financial reporting purposes, as replacement cost rather than net realisable value.[62]

Accounting practice in showing debtors net of a bad debts provision is consistent with this rule. Small companies may well determine such provisions in relation to specific debts, as is required for calculating the company's liability to corporation tax.[63] However, larger companies

---

[60] *Aluminium Industrie Vassen BV v. Romalpa Aluminium Ltd* [1976] 2 All E.R. 552.

[61] *Re Peachdart Ltd* [1983] 3 All E.R. 204; *Modelboard Ltd v. Outer Box Ltd (in liquidation)* [1993] BCLC 623.

[61a] A similar problem concerning title to goods arises under ss. 16–18 of the Sale of Goods Act 1979: see *Re Ellis Son and Vidler Ltd; Re Stapylton Fletcher Ltd* [1994] BCLC 681.

[62] *B.S.C. Footwear Ltd v. Ridgway* [1971] T.R. 121; SSAP 9.

[63] Income and Corporation Taxes Act 1988, s.74.

may well prefer to use general bad debt provisions for financial reporting purposes.

Where the going concern assumption is reasonable, accounting practice is generally to value work-in-progress at cost, since net realisable value (which would usually be far lower) is irrelevant in such circumstances. Moreover, it is also common practice, in line with the terms of SSAP 9, for profits to be recognised gradually over the period of long-term contracts, although so as to ensure these are "realised" they have to be included in the turnover and debtors figures.

Paragraph 23 of the fourth Schedule indicates that where an asset has been written down to net realisable value, but such value has subsequently risen, even if not fully up to cost again, the amount of the provision so made and no longer required must be written back.

(ii) Under paragraph 27 of the fourth Schedule, the purchase price or production cost of each class of stocks and similar fungible items (that is, assets where individual units—such as shares held—are indistinguishable from each other), may be determined using the most appropriate of any one of four methods: first in first out (FIFO), last in first out (LIFO), weighted average cost, and any similar method. In addition, paragraph 25 (referred to below) effectively permits use of the base stock method for stocks of raw materials and consumables. LIFO and base stock methods are not acceptable for tax purposes in the United Kindom[64] and in such circumstances, because of the need to keep a second set of stock records, it is generally impractical to use the former for financial reporting purposes. Moreover, SSAP 9 suggests that neither LIFO nor base stock methods provide reasonable approximations to the cost of stocks. Nevertheless, some companies (notably in the sugar and base metal industries) continue to use the base stock method, and overseas subsidiaries of many British companies often use LIFO to obtain certain tax advantages, thus securing nominal qualification in the auditors' report for the group accounts as they do not technically comply with the terms of SSAP 9.

[64] The relevant cases are, respectively: *Minister of National Revenue v. Anaconda American Brass Ltd* [1956] A.C. 85; and *Patrick v. Broadstone Mills* [1953] 33 T.C. 44.

(iii) As discussed under D(ii) below, where stocks and work-in-progress are valued at production cost, the latter *may* include a reasonable proportion of manufacturing over-heads. Presumably these can comprise either just variable or both variable and fixed overhead costs. Tax law is fairly flexible on this matter,[65] but SSAP 9 in fact *requires* that for financial reporting purposes a reasonable propor-tion of manufacturing overheads (including a proportion of fixed costs) should be included in the valuation of stocks and work-in-progress.

(iv) Whatever method of stock valuation is used, any *material difference* between the purchase price or production cost and the "relevant alternative amount" must be shown in a note to the accounts. Such "relative alternative amount" will normally be replacement cost at the balance sheet date, but an acceptable approximation very often will be a value based on the most recent purchase price or produc-tion cost (paragraphs 27(3), (4), (5)).

(D) PURCHASE PRICE AND PRODUCTION COST

(i) Purchase price is defined in paragraph 26(1) of the fourth Schedule and section 262(1) of the 1985 Act as the actual price paid for an asset, including expenses incidental to its acquisition.

(ii) Production cost is the sum of (a) the purchase price of raw materials and consumables used; and (b) direct production costs incurred (but, in the case of current assets, excluding distribution costs); plus (c) other costs that *may* be included, being a reasonable proportion of indirect costs in so far as they relate to the period of production. These latter may include interest on bor-rowed capital, where appropriate, but if this is the case, the fact and the amount involved must be disclosed in a note (paragraph 26).

(iii) Where there is no record for an asset of its original purchase price or production cost, or of related expendi-ture, the earliest value ascribed to it may be used instead,

---

[65] *Ostime v. Duple Motor Bodies* [1961] 39 T.C. 537.

but this fact must be disclosed in the accounts or the notes thereto (paragraphs 28 and 51(1)).

(iv) Paragraph 25 permits tangible fixed assets and stocks of raw materials and consumables to be shown at a fixed quantity and fixed value where they are constantly being replaced and (a) their overall value is not material to the assessment of the company's state of affairs; and (b) their quantity, value and composition is not subject to material variation.

(v) Under paragraph 24, where an amount owed to a creditor is greater than the value of the asset received, the difference may be treated as an asset rather than an expense, analogous to acquired goodwill. However, it must be written off by "reasonable amounts" each year and must be completely written off before repayment of the debt. Any such asset in the balance sheet must be disclosed either in the statement or in the notes thereto. There is no reference to systematic amortisation in these provisions, as there is in relation to acquired goodwill, nor apparently is it necessary to indicate the period over which the asset is being written off.

## 3. Alternative accounting rules

If they so determine, companies may adopt any of the alternative accounting rules outlined in Section C of Part II of the fourth Schedule to the 1985 Act. Such rules only apply to the main financial statements, which as a result can be prepared not only in terms of the historical cost convention, but can instead be modified to take into account selective revaluations or be completely re-stated in current cost terms.

The ASC introduced a standard on current cost accounting in 1980 (SSAP 16) which permitted the listed and very large companies to which it applied to present current cost accounts either as supplementary statements (which became the usual practice) or as the main financial statements. Only in the latter case did the alternative accounting rules apply to the current cost accounts prepared so as to comply with SSAP 16. Following considerable opposition to the experiment, the ASC withdrew the standard in 1988, but the ASB has nevertheless indicated approval for the underlying current cost accounting concept in its "Statement of Principles". In the meantime, SSAP 16 provides guidance to any companies preparing current cost accounts. In fact, the standard is followed by utility companies—*e.g.* in the electricity industry—which publish a second set of *regulatory accounts* as current cost financial statements. These better reflect underlying economic costs and thus give some indication whether the companies' monopoly power is being exploited to earn abnormally high profits.

The alternative rules outlined in the fourth Schedule (paragraphs 31–34) are as follows:

(i) Intangible assets, other than goodwill, may be shown at current cost.

(ii) Goodwill (for which current cost has no clear meaning) should be shown at its cost of acquisition, less amortisation, unless it is written off immediately.

(iii) Tangible fixed assets may be stated either at their market values on the dates they were last valued or at current cost. (The latter could either be the second-hand value or the current cost new less notional depreciation.)

(iv) Fixed asset investments may be stated either at their market values on the dates they were last valued or at a value determined on an appropriate basis given the company's circumstances, in which case the method and reasons for using it must be disclosed. (Such a basis might be the equity "net assets" basis appropriate for accounting for associated companies under SSAP 1.)

(v) Current asset investments and stocks may be stated at their current costs.

(vi) As regards wasting fixed assets, depreciation should be based on the revalued amounts, not the purchase price or production cost. The charge to the profit and loss account can either be that based on the current value or just be the historical cost charge. However, in the latter case the difference between the two must be disclosed either in the accounts or in the notes thereto. This would appear to allow such differences to be debited or credited direct to the revaluation reserve.

(vii) Accumulated unrealised holding gains arising from revaluations which result from application of the alternative accounting rules must be credited to a revaluation reserve, and this must be shown separately in the balance sheet. Amounts can only be transferred from the revaluation reserve to the profit and loss account where the amount in question

(a) was previously charged to the profit and loss account;

(b) represents a realised profit; or

(c) is applied wholly or partly in paying up bonus shares allotted to members of the company.

Otherwise the balance of the reserve has to be reduced where there is no longer any justification for its existence (*e.g.* where there has been a subsequent decline in the value of an asset previously revalued upwards).

An explanation of the tax effects of increases or reductions in the revaluation reserve (such as the tax that would be payable if the asset were sold at its revalued amount) must be disclosed in a note to the accounts.

(viii) Where alternative rules are applied the notes must state the items affected, the basis of valuation of each balance sheet item, and (with the exception of stocks) for each of the latter items, including provisions separately, either the corresponding amount under the historical cost convention or the differences between the two sets of figures. Alternatively the basis of valuation, and the corresponding amount or differences, can be disclosed on the face of the balance sheet rather than in notes.

A draft accounting standard issued in 1990 (ED 51) suggests that the directors of a company should adopt a clear policy when deciding to revalue fixed assets on a selective basis. Consequently they should identify different classes of asset which they might wish to revalue and then reappraise those values on an agreed basis. Moreover, another draft standard (ED 55) suggests that current asset investments for which there are readily observable market values should be "marked to market".

**Non-statutory requirements**

The most important additional disclosure required of companies by the ASB is a cash flow statement under FRS 1, although this does not apply to small companies eligible to file abbreviated accounts. The standard gives considerable guidance with respect to definitions and the way in which cash transactions in a period should be summarised.

Other accounting standards which require companies to make additional disclosures include SSAP 3 on earnings per share for listed companies (as amended by FRS 3); SSAP 15 on deferred taxation; SSAP 17 on post balance sheet events; SSAP 18 on contingent liabilities; SSAP 19 on investment properties (as amended by the ASB); SSAP 21 on leases and hire purchase contracts; and SSAP 24 on pension commitments. In addition, FRED 8 and International Accounting Standard (IAS) 24 on related party disclosures; and IAS 23 on capitalisation of borrowing costs give further guidance on matters which should be disclosed in a company's financial statements.

Amongst the requirements imposed on quoted companies by the London Stock Exchange's *Listing Rules* are provisions for the publication of half-year and preliminary profit statements. The former (which is incidentally the subject of an EU Council Directive) may be important in terms of the requirement of section 272 that for a public company the declaration of an interim dividend should be related to accumulated realised profits, determined if necessary in interim accounts. These should be prepared on a basis consistent with the requirements of the Act with regard to a company's statutory annual accounts (see *post,* chapter 22).

Other matters referred to in the *Listing Rules* include under its, paragraph 12.43 disclosure in the annual report of reasons for any significant departure from standard accounting practice; an explanation of a substantial difference (*i.e.* 10 per cent or more) between trading results and any profit forecast made by the company; details of loans repayable in less than a year, in periods between one and two years and between two and five years, and beyond five years; and a statement as to whether or not for tax purposes the company is a close company (*i.e.* is under the control of a limited number of people).

## GROUP ACCOUNTS

Some users of accounting statements may only be interested in the financial affairs of the particular *legal entity* with which they are dealing, most obviously unsecured creditors. However, others (such as existing and potential shareholders) may be rather more interested in the affairs of an *economic entity,* since those are likely to be more relevant for their decision making needs. Such an entity can extend as far as a colluding group of companies

between which there are no formal legal links; or it may exist
where companies are tied together economically in a joint
venture arrangement or even sometimes by the existence of a
long term contract.

This latter notion of a group, where undertakings are managed
on a central and unified basis, is essentially the view taken in
Germany and adopted in the EU's Seventh Council Directive on
company law harmonisation. The traditional British view is
somewhat narrower, section 736 of the Companies Act detemin-
ing the existence of a group where the holding company either
controls the composition of the board of directors of a subsidiary,
or controls more than half its voting rights. However, the
Companies Act 1989 inserted a new section 258 into the 1985 Act
which introduces new criteria for determining whether a company
should prepare group accounts. Essentially this adopts the
broader view taken in the EU's Seventh Directive, the critical
element being whether "a parent company" exercises a dominant
influence (see *ante*, pp. 485–486).[66]

The advantage to a user of financial statements of having
access to a set of group accounts, however the term "group" is
defined, is that the statements can be prepared so as to eliminate
the often sizeable internal, intra-group transactions and show a
more complete picture of the group financial structure. However,
the preparation of full consolidated accounts may of necessity
mean some particularly interesting piece of information will be
lost—for instance, the fact that one subsidiary has been operating
at a loss may no longer be apparent. Nevertheless, the potential
significance of group accounts has long been recognised, and
many large public companies in the United Kingdom began
publishing them on a voluntary basis in the 1920s, long before
their preparation was made compulsory in the 1948 Companies
Act. Moreover, it is interesting that several large economic
entities, most notably Unilever and Royal Dutch-Shell, publish
joint venture accounts as well as the strictly legal accounts for
their British participant companies, and it is these supplementary
statements which are accorded most prominence in the group
annual reports and which are critically scrutinised by professional
financial analysts.

[66] See Chap. 2, *ante,* for further discussion of the contents of ss.736, 736A and
736B.

## General requirements

### (i) The accounts of the parent company

As indicated above (pp. 485–486), a parent company must prepare its individual accounts for its shareholders. One reason for this is that the dividend declared by a parent company must be based on these accounts and not on the group accounts (see *post*, p. 595). The fourth Schedule balance sheet formats include various headings which are appropriate for individual parent and subsidiary companies—*viz.* those on pp. 492–495, *ante*, marked as *B III* 1, 2; *C II* 2; *C III* 1; *E* 6; and *H* 6. In addition, under paragraph 59 a parent company and a subsidiary undertaking must disclose separately under the above headings the amounts owed to and from, and any interests in, a parent company or any fellow subsidiary, or any subsidiary. Set-offs cannot normally be used in making such disclosures, and amounts owing also have to be analysed between those due within one year and those not.

### (ii) Group accounts

By section 227 of the 1985 Act, where at the end of its financial year a company is a parent company, its directors must prepare a consolidated profit and loss account and balance sheet. Such accounts must give a true and fair view of the group's position and profit or loss, so far as concerns the members of the company, and comply with the provisions of Schedule 4A concerning the form and content of group accounts. However, if there is a conflict, either sufficient additional information must be disclosed to ensure a true and fair view is given, or there must be departure from the requirements of Schedule 4A, explaining the reasons for such action and its effect.

Under section 228, sub-groups need not prepare group accounts if the immediate parent undertaking of the sub-group prepares audited group accounts under the law of an EU member state and the subsidiary undertaking is wholly owned by the sub-group parent, or it holds more than 50 per cent of the shares and there is no request by a minority holding either half the remaining shares or 5 per cent of the total shares for such sub-group accounts to be prepared. However, exemption from the obligation to prepare group accounts is conditional also on the company indicating that it is taking advantage of the concession; stating the name of the parent and its country of incorporation (or, if it is unincorporated, its principal place of business); delivering copies of the group accounts and auditors' report (if necessary with an English translation) to the Registrar; and not having securities listed on a stock exchange within the EU.

Under section 229, subsidiary undertakings *may* be excluded from consolidation where:

(1) their inclusion individually or collectively would not be material in giving a true and fair view;
(2) long term restrictions hinder the parent's right to manage;
(3) the information required for the preparation of group accounts cannot be obtained without disproportionate expense or undue delay; and
(4) the interest of the parent is only temporary.

In addition, they *must* be excluded from consolidation where their activities are so fundamentally different that such accounts would not give a true and fair view. In such circumstances, they should be included in the consolidated financial statements using the equity method[67] (Schedule 4A, paragraph 18).

FRS 2 goes further than section 229 and *requires* exclusion from consolidation in cases (2) and (4) listed above. Further, it indicates that under case (2) the investment should be carried at its original cost, if the restriction existed at its acquisition date; or at the equity value[67a] at the date at which the restriction arises if that is subsequent to acquisition. With respect to exclusions on ground (4), the investment should be treated as a current asset and be valued accordingly at the lower of cost and net realisable value. Subsidiary undertakings excluded because of the fundamentally different nature of their activities should be recorded in the consolidated financial statements using the equity method.[67b] FRS 2 also indicates the disclosures that should be made for subsidiary undertakings excluded from consolidation.

Under Schedule 4A, group accounts must be prepared so far as possible to comply with the provisions of Schedule 4 as if the

[67] See p. 539.
[67a] See p. 539.
[67b] See p. 539.

undertakings included in the consolidation were a single group (Schedule 4A, paragraph 1(1)). For such purposes, as already mentioned (*ante*, p. 531), dealings with or interests in, on the one hand, a parent undertaking or fellow subsidiaries; and, on the other, subsidiaries, must be shown separately in aggregate (Schedule 4, paragraph 59). For this, unconsolidated subsidiaries are to be regarded as part of the group (Schedule 4A, paragraph 1(2)). Moreover, the formats for accounts under Schedule 4 are to be modified to include an item for "minority interests" (Schedule 4A, paragraph 17).

Where a parent company is treated as an investment company,[68] the group is to be similarly treated (Schedule 4A, paragraph 1(3)).

For the purpose of consolidation, the accounts must incorporate in full the information contained in the individual accounts of the undertakings included in the consolidation. However, if the financial year of a subsidiary does not coincide with that of the parent,[69] the group must deal with the subsidiary's state of affairs at the end of its financial year ending last before that of the parent company's, providing it is within three months of the latter. Otherwise, interim accounts must be used (Schedule 4A, paragraph 2). Moreover, the parent company should try to apply standard accounting rules when undertaking a consolidation. If it does not, it should disclose this in a note (Schedule 4A, paragraph 3). Likewise, any differences between the accounting rules used in preparing a parent company's individual accounts and its group accounts should be disclosed in a note (Schedule 4A, paragraph 4).

Where an acquisition takes place in a financial year, the name of the undertaking acquired must be disclosed in a note, stating whether the combination has been accounted for using the acquisition or merger methods of accounting.[70] In addition, details of the fair value of the consideration given must be disclosed, giving details in the case of an acquisition of the book values and fair values of the assets and claims and of the goodwill. Similarly, details of any adjustments made, in particu-

---

[68] See pp. 548-549. Under section 255A, banking and insurance groups are defined as where the activities of the parents or groups are predominantly in banking or insurance. Such groups are subject to special accounting and disclosure requirements: see *post*, pp. 549–550.

[69] See p. 475.

[70] See *post*.

lar to the consolidated reserves, must be given where the merger method is used. Further, the profit or loss of the undertaking acquired must be stated for the period from the beginning of its financial year up until the combination and for its previous financial year (Schedule 4A, paragraph 13). The parent company must also show movements in the goodwill figure shown in the group accounts (Schedule 4A, paragraph 14).

Where there has been a disposal of an undertaking in the year that significantly affects the figures shown in the group accounts, the name of the undertaking and the amount of profit or loss attributable to it must also be disclosed in a note (Schedule 4A, paragraph 15).

Additional guidance on how those provisions should be implemented is given in FRSs 2, 6 and 7 and UITF Abstract 3.

**Methods of consolidation**

There are several different ways of preparing consolidated accounts, some of which have already been referred to above. It may therefore be helpful to examine them briefly with the aid of some examples.

Let it therefore be assumed there are two companies, X and Y, whose summarised balance sheets at December 31, 1994, are as shown in Figure 2.

|                       | X          | Y          |
|-----------------------|-----------|-----------|
| Net assets            | £5,000,000 | £2,000,000 |
|                       |           |           |
| Ordinary £1 shares    | 1,500,000 | 500,000   |
| Distributable reserves | 3,500,000 | 1,500,000 |
|                       | £5,000,000 | £2,000,000 |

**Figure 2**

*(i) The acquisition method.*

First, let it be supposed that X acquires for cash the entire share capital of Y at December 31, 1994, the cash being part of its net assets of £5 million. The going concern value of Y is agreed as £3 million. The consolidated balance sheet would generally be shown as in Figure 3(a), though in practice the net assets would be added together line-by-line for each different asset and liability category identified. It can be seen that goodwill is created as an asset: it represents the difference between the going concern value of Y at the date of acquisition and the book value of the net assets acquired by the X group. It can also be seen that the pre-acquisition profits of Y, the subsidiary, are no longer free for distribution. Only the post-acquisition profits of the subsidiary will be added in to the group's free reserves.

Now let it be supposed that the consideration given to acquire Y was not cash, but instead was new shares issued by X. It is now necessary to value the consideration given and received. If the shares of X and Y are both quoted this may be relatively easy to assess, though depending on the dates chosen there may be slight differences in the total values of the shares issued and acquired. However, where the companies are unquoted it will be necessary either to assess the value by appraisal or to use the nominal value of the shares given as consideration. The latter gives rise to a problem which will be discussed below. For the moment, let it be assumed here that 750,000 new shares are issued in X to acquire the entire share capital of Y, the one third stake in the new combined enterprise and its future earning power being regarded by both parties as acceptable consideration. Given a market price of £4 per £1 nominal share unit in X, the consolidated balance sheet appears as in Figure 3(b).

|  |  | X Group |  | X Group |
|---|---|---|---|---|
| Goodwill | (£3m–£2m) | 1,000,000 | (£3m–£2m) | 1,000,000 |
| Other net |  |  |  |  |
| assets | (£5m–£3m;+£2m) | 4,000,000 | (£5m+£2m) | 7,000,000 |
|  |  | £5,000,000 |  | £8,000,000 |
| Ordinary share capital (X only) |  | 1,500,000 | (£1.5+£.75m) | 2,250,000 |
| Share premium |  |  | (£3m–£.75m) | 2,250,000 |
| Distributable reserves |  |  |  |  |
| (X only at date of acquisition) |  | 3,500,000 |  | 3,500,000 |
|  |  | £5,000,000 |  | £8,000,000 |
|  |  | (a) |  | (b) |

Figure 3

The method of consolidation shown in Figure 3 is known as the *acquisition method*, reflecting the "parent company approach" to group consolidation, and it is that which has been most commonly used in the United Kingdom. Moreover, it can easily be adapted to allow for a situation where less than the entire equity in a subsidiary is acquired. Thus in the case of 3(b), above, let it now be assumed that only three quarters of the share capital in Y is acquired for an issue of 562,500 shares in X, the value of the transaction being assessed at £2.25 million. The consolidated balance sheet is then as shown in Figure 4, the goodwill only relating to the majority stake acquired. The minority interest comprises the outside shareholders' stake in a subsidiary's share capital and both its pre- and post-acquisition reserves.

|  |  | X Group |
|---|---|---|
| Goodwill | (£2.25m – $^3/_4$ × £2m) | 750,000 |
| Net assets |  | 7,000,000 |
|  |  | £7,750,000 |
| Ordinary share capital (X only) | (£1.5m+£.5625m) | 2,062,500 |
| Share premium | (£2.25–£.5625m) | 1,687,500 |
| Distributable reserves (X only at acquisition) |  | 3,500,000 |
| Minority interest | ($^1/_4$ × £2m) | 500,000 |
|  |  | £7,750,000 |

**Figure 4**

It would technically be possible, without altering the basic technique, to allow the accounts to reflect a wider entity concept than the parent company approach by showing a notional goodwill figure for the *whole* group (here presumably £750,000 × 4/3 = £1 million) and crediting the appropriate share (here £250,000) to the minority interest, but this is never done in practice.

The above examples should have made it clear that the goodwill figure has little economic significance. It merely measures the *historical* difference between the going concern value of *part* of the group (typically the majority share in a subsidiary) and the corresponding book value at the date of purchase. Going concern values, even for parts of businesses, change from day-to-day as expectations of future likely outcomes alter; moreover, goodwill as such has no separate existence from the business as a whole, as do most other assets which appear in balance sheets.

Schedule 4A, paragraphs 7–9, indicate that it is the acquisition method of consolidation as there described which must be applied under the 1985 Act, except where specific conditions described below exist. The main requirement is that at the date of acquisition, the net assets of the company acquired must be included in the consolidated balance sheet at their fair value.

### (ii) The merger method.

A very different approach to consolidation, known as the *merger method* avoids some of the problems identified above, and it is probably more appropriate if it is deemed necessary to try to reflect a wider entity concept than the narrow parent company approach. Quite apart from avoiding the creation of goodwill on acquisition, it also has the advantage of bringing all or some of the preacquisition profits of the technical subsidiaries into the group balance sheet as distributable reserves.[71] It is therefore particularly attractive where two companies of more or less equal size merge their activities.

To illustrate the technique, return to the facts used to derive the consolidated balance sheet in Figure 3(b). If it is argued that the value of the shares issued is their par value of £750,000, only £250,000 (the difference between the par values of shares issued and acquired by X) of the pre-acquisition profits of Y has to be regarded as non-distributable. The consolidated balance sheet would then appear as in Figure 5.

|  |  | X Group |
| --- | --- | --- |
| Net assets | (£5m+£2m) | £7,000,000 |
|  |  |  |
| Ordinary share capital (X only) | (£1.5m+£.75m) | 2,250,000 |
| Distributable reserves | (3.5m+(£1.5m–£.25m)) | 4,750,000 |
|  |  | £7,000,000 |

**Figure 5**

Merger accounting more closely reflects the economic entity group concept than the acquisition method, and although some

---

[71] This is largely for presentational purposes, since only the parent company can distribute profits as dividends to its shareholders, not the group. However, where merger relief as described below is given, pooled group accounts show the effective position from an overall perspective.

British listed companies applied it from the late 1960s onwards, there was doubt about its validity in view of the decision in *Head (Henry) & Co., Ltd v Ropner Holdings Ltd*,[72] concerning the need to establish a share premium account (see *ante*, chapter 9). The decision in that case was confirmed in *Shearer v. Bercain Ltd*,[73] which was widely regarded by the accountancy profession as closing the door on the merger method of consolidation. However, the 1981 legislation, in what has become sections 131–134 of the 1985 Act, provided relief to *individual companies* from what is now section 130, making it legitimate to use the approach as long as the necessary conditions are met—the main one is that the acquiring company should secure at least 90 per cent in nominal value of each class of the share capital of the company being taken over (see *ante*, chapter 9).

An accounting standard, SSAP 23, was issued in 1985 relating to *groups*, which indicated four conditions that had to be met before the group *might* use either the merger or acquisition method of accounting for consolidation purposes. If any of the four conditions were not met, the group *had* to use the acquisition approach.

FRS 6, issued in 1994, has modified the rules so that they better reflect the substance of a combination. Essentially the standard *requires* that merger accounting should be used for any business combination which meets the following criteria:

(i) No entity in the combination is portrayed as either the acquiring or acquired entity.

(ii) All parties to the combination should participate in establishing the management structure for the combined entity, with decisions being reached by consensus rather than by virtue of voting rights.

(iii) The relative sizes of the combining entities should not be so great that one party effectively dominates the combined entity.

(iv) No material proportion of the fair value of the consideration received should be in the form of non-equity shares or in equity shares with restricted rights.

(v) No equity shareholders of the combining entities should retain a material interest in the future performance of merely a part of the combined entity.

[72] [1952] Ch. 124.
[73] [1980] 3 All E.R. 295.

By contrast, paragraph 10 of Schedule 4A prescribes that the parent company must hold at least 90 per cent of the relevant shares as a result of offering its or its subsidiary's equity shares; and that the fair value of consideration other than equity shares given does not exceed 10 per cent of the value of the shares issued.

Where a company takes advantage of the merger relief provisions of the Act under section 130, it must under paragraphs 10 and 29 of Schedule 5 disclose as a note to its accounts the name of the company, details of the shares allotted and of those received or cancelled in exchange, the accounting treatment adopted, and the effect on any group profit and loss account for the year of including preacquisition profits or losses of the merged subsidiary. Moreover, where the group sells directly or indirectly shares and/or assets in the merged company within 2–3 years of the merger, and in so doing makes a profit included in the income statements, such a profit has to be disclosed.

*(iii) The proprietary methods.*

A third approach to consolidation is the proprietary approach, which eliminates recognition of the outside interest in both the balance sheet and the profit and loss account and is usually applied where the ownership stake is 50 per cent or less. The concept can be implemented in one of two ways: either

(a) by *proportional consolidation,* where income, assets and liabilities are separately added in to the holding company's accounts on a *pro rata* basis item by item; or

(b) by the *equity method of consolidation,* where an investment is shown in the group balance sheet *pro rata* to its current net asset value, the net changes each year usually being dealt with in the profit and loss account.

Both methods were accommodated within the EU's Seventh Council Directive, but proportional consolidation, not uncommon on the Continent, is rarely practised by British companies, although its use is not unknown. The equity method has long been used in the United States to account for joint ventures and for subsidiaries not fully consolidated, and since the early 1970s it has been employed in Britain to account for associated companies, an accounting standard on the subject (SSAP 1) being issued in 1971. However, it should be noted that there is more than one way of showing the equity value of an investment in a consolidated balance sheet. Thus the Seventh Directive implied that the goodwill (or premium) on acquisition should be shown separately, although this only became standard British practice in 1982, when SSAP 1 was revised.

Paragraph 19 of Schedule 4A indicates that where an undertaking is jointly managed with one or more independent third parties, it may be accounted for by the method of proportional consolidation. Paragraph 20 indicates that an associated company is one in which an undertaking has a participating interest and exercises a significant influence. This is normally presumed if it holds over 20 per cent of the voting rights. In such circumstances, the equity method of accounting is to be used, with the standard format of accounts modified accordingly and with goodwill being treated as under the acquisition method (Schedule 4A, paragraphs 21–22).

Further guidance on the application of these procedures is given in FRS 2 and the ASB's interim statement "Consolidated accounts"; and in the ASB's August 1994 discussion paper "Associates and Joint Ventures".

## Unrealised intra-group profits

One further point relating to consolidated accounts, which is of some relevance in relation to distributable profits as defined in sections 263–281 of the 1985 Act, concerns the treatment of unrealised inter-company profits. Briefly, if one member of a group sells goods to another, such goods as are in stock at the balance sheet date will potentially include an element of unrealised profit. This can logically be eliminated in one of two ways:

(a) adopting a "single entity" approach and treating the transactions as though they had never taken place: this means writing back the unrealised profit against the company which sold the goods, with the minority interest in the selling company bearing its appropriate share; or,

(b) adopting a "separate entity" approach, in which case any unrealised profit must be written back against the company which holds the goods, with the minority interest in that company (if any) again bearing its appropriate share.

In practice, British companies in the past tended either to write back the whole of the unrealised profit regardless against the majority's profits; or, eliminate the majority's profit only against the company which sold the stock.[74]

Paragraph 6 of Schedule 4A merely states that intra-group debts and claims and intra-group transactions should be eliminated when group accounts are prepared; and that unrealised profits may be eliminated "in proportion to the group's interest in the shares of the undertakings". However, FRS 2 requires elimination in full.

## DIRECTORS' REPORT

**Introduction**

Before the Companies Act 1981, legislation permitted any item otherwise required to be disclosed in the accounts or notes thereto to be shown instead in the directors' report, though corresponding figures for the previous year had to be given and the item was still subject to audit. Moreover, certain additional matters were required to be dealt with in the report. Several are now dealt with directly in notes to the accounts: contracts with the company (except service contracts) in which a director has an interest, new issues of shares and debentures and the reasons therefor, directors' options to subscribe for the company's securities, turnover and profit or loss before tax of different classes of activity, and the average weekly number of United Kingdom employees and their total remuneration for the year.

This shift in emphasis reflects the approach of the EU's Fourth Council Directive towards the directors' report, where the intention was that it should merely supplement the financial details given in the accounts with certain narrative information about the company's activities and its future prospects.

In 1993 the FRC, the Hundred Group of Financial Directors and the London Stock Exchange issued a statement on the inclusion of an "Operating and Financial Review" (OFR) in the annual reports of large companies. This statement is persuasive rather than mandatory, and the OFR is similar to reviews published by U.S. companies to comply with Securities and

---

[74] See Egginton, D.A., "Unrealised Profit and Consolidated Accounts," *Accountancy* (May 1965), pp. 410–415.

Exchange Commission requirements. The statement identifies a number of matters that could helpfully be dealt with in an OFR: *e.g.* identification of factors which have affected past performance and which are likely to affect future trading; aspects which are particularly subject to uncertainty; the impact of exchange rates on profitability; a discussion of the enterprise's capital structure; a summary of investment plans; and so on.

**Disclosure requirements**

The statutory requirements for disclosure in a directors' report are described below. However, small size companies[75] do not have to file such a report with the Registrar, and certain concessions are available to them reducing the amount of detail that has to be included in reports submitted to shareholders.[76] Failure to comply with the statutory requirements makes the offending directors liable to a fine, although it is a defence to prove that all reasonable steps were taken to secure compliance.

Briefly, the items requiring disclosure in the directors' report may be summarised as follows:

(i)  A fair review of the development of the business of the company and its subsidiaries during the financial year ending with the balance sheet date, and of their position at the end of it (section 234(1)(a)).

(ii)  Amount recommended to be paid by way of dividend (section 234(1)(b)).

(iii)  Amount proposed to be carried to reserves (section 234(1)(b)).

(iv)  Names of directors at any time during the year under review (section 234(2)).

(v)  Principal activities of the company and its subsidiaries and significant changes in those activities (section 234(2)).

(vi)  Significant changes in the company's or its subsidiaries' fixed assets (Schedule 7, paragraph 1(1)).

(vii)  An indication of the difference between the book amount and the market values of land and buildings if, in the opinion of the directors, the difference is of

---

[75] For the definition of "small," see *ante,* pp. 488 *et seq.* The exemption is given in Sched. 8, para. 20, to the 1985 Act.

[76] Under para. 15 of Schedule 8 to the 1985 Act, as revised by S.I. 1992 No. 2452.

such significance that it should be drawn to the attention of the members or debenture holders (Schedule 7, paragraph 1(2)).

(viii) Interests of directors and their immediate families at the beginning and end of each year in shares or debentures of the company or its group undertakings, if such information is not shown in a note to the accounts. Details of options granted or exercised are also to be disclosed (Schedule 7, paragraphs 2, 2A, 2B). The London Stock Exchange's *Listing Rules* also require disclosure of any changes in such holdings between the financial year end and a date within one month of the notice of the annual general meeting being issued.

(ix) Details for a company or group of its U.K. charitable and political contributions where in aggregate they exceed £200, as follows:

|  | £ |
|---|---|
| U.K. charitable organisations | xxx |
| Political donations of over £200 each: | |
|     U.K. political organisations (by party, etc.) | xxx |
|     Individuals (by name) | xxx |
|     Others under £200 each (total) | xxx |
|  | xxx |

"Giving money for political purposes" is defined as giving, directly or indirectly, a donation or subscription to —

(1) a political party in the United Kingdom; or
(2) a person who, to the company's knowledge, is carrying on, or proposing to carry on, activities which can at the time reasonably be regarded as likely to affect public support for such a political party.

Money given for charitable purposes to a person ordinarily resident outside the United Kingdom is ignored. "Charitable purposes" means exclusively charitable purposes (Schedule 7, paragraphs 3–5).

(x) Particulars of any important events affecting the company which have occurred since the end of the year (Schedule 7, paragraph 6(a)). SSAP 17 additionally requires disclosure in the accounts and in the notes thereto of events which require adjustment to the accounting figures and those which do not.

(xi) An indication of future likely developments in the business of the company and of its subsidiaries (Schedule 7, paragraph 6(b)).

(xii) An indication of the activities (if any) of the company and its subsidiaries in the field of research and development (Schedule 7, paragraph 6(c)). SSAP 13 requires disclosure in the accounts or notes thereto of deferred development expenditure at the beginning and end of the year, movements during the year, and the accounting policy adopted.

(xiii) In respect of purchases of its own shares during the year by the company, the number and nominal value of the shares; the percentage of called-up capital so purchased; the aggregate consideration paid; and the reasons for such purchase. In respect of other acquisitions of its own shares, either directly by the company, or by persons with financial assistance from the company where the company has a beneficial interest in the shares, or where such shares are made subject to a charge: the maximum number and nominal value held at any time during the year, and percentage of called-up capital; the amount of any charge; the number and nominal value disposed of or cancelled during the year, and the percentage of called-up capital; and the consideration received in respect of disposals (Schedule 7, paragraphs 7–8).

(xiv) For companies where the weekly average number of employees in the United Kingdom during the financial year exceeded 250, a statement of the company's policy in respect of applications for employment from disabled persons; employees who have become disabled; and training, career development and promotion of disabled persons (Schedule 7, paragraph 9).

(xv) For companies of such classes as may be prescribed by regulations made by the Secretary of State, a statement as may be so prescribed about the arrangements in force for securing the health, safety and welfare at work of the company and its subsidiaries, and for protecting other persons against risks to health and safety arising out of, or in connection with, the activities at work of those employees (Schedule 7, paragraph 10). (To date no statutory instruments have been issued prescribing such regulations.)

(xvi) Where during the year a company has had on average more than 250 employees in the United Kingdom, a statement describing action taken to introduce, maintain or develop arrangements aimed at providing relevant information to those employees, consulting them or their representatives on a regular basis, encouraging their involvement in the business, and making them more aware of the financial and economic factors affecting its performance (Schedule 7, paragraph 11).

(xvii) Where appropriate, the directors' report should disclose the fact that the company has purchased insurance policies on behalf of its officers and/or auditors against liabilities in relation to the company (Schedule 7, paragraph 5A).

## Approval by the board and by the auditors

Under section 234A, the directors' report must be approved by the board, and both it and the copy delivered to the Registrar must be signed on the board's behalf by a director or the secretary. Moreover, the name of such a person must appear on each copy laid before the company in general meeting or otherwise circulated or published. Failure either to sign the report or to show the name of the signatory on circulated copies renders the company and its defaulting officers liable to a fine.

Under section 235(3) the auditor has a statutory duty to consider whether or not the information contained in the directors' report is consistent with the financial statements. Moreover, he is required to draw attention in his report to any inconsistency between the two for the year in question.

## Stock Exchange regulations

Under London Stock Exchange regulations the following information not directly relating to items disclosed elsewhere in the financial statements has to be detailed by a listed company's directors: reasons for departing from standard accounting practice; explanations of significant differences (*i.e.* 10 per cent or more) between outcomes and any forecasts made; interest capitalised during the year and the amount and treatment of related tax relief; particulars regarding equity shares issued for cash other than *pro rata* to existing equity shareholdings, unless specifically authorised; details of any participation by a parent company in any vendor consideration placing; short biographical notes on each non-executive director; substantial holdings (*i.e.* 3 per cent or more) in the company's shares, etc., and indicating if there is no such interest; whether or not the company is a close company for tax purposes; particulars of any agreement to waive dividends; directors' interests in contracts with the company; contracts between the company and substantial shareholders; a statement indicating compliance with the Code of Best Practice on corporate governance (the "Cadbury Code") (see *post*, pp. 557–558); and related party transactions.[77]

## AUDITORS' REPORT[78]

Section 235(1) of the 1985 Act requires that, where a company is required to have a statutory audit,[79] its auditors should make a report to its members on all accounts laid before the company in general meeting, stating whether they comply with the Companies Act and give a true and fair view. The auditors must also state the fact if: proper accounting records have not been kept and branch returns have not been obtained; the financial statements are not in agreement with the accounting records; full information and explanations regarded as necessary for the audit have not been obtained; or information relating to the year given in the directors' report is inconsistent with the financial statements (sections 237 and 235(3)).

The report should also include details of directors' emoluments and loans if not disclosed as required by Schedule 6 to the 1985

[77] Related party transactions are also covered in FRED 8 and IAS 24.
[78] This topic is dealt with in more detail in Chap. 22.
[79] For exemption from the requirement to have a statutory audit, see p. 491.

Act (section 237(4)); and, if the report is qualified, indicate whether the qualification is material in determining whether a distribution can lawfully be made (section 271(3), (5)).

Auditors belonging to the main professional accountancy bodies in the United Kingdom — which is the vast majority — are also required by those bodies to refer in their reports to any breaches of accounting standards. This has meant that in recent years audit qualifications for listed companies have become more common, though empirical research seems to suggest that the investing public is able to distinguish between material and merely technical qualifications.[80]

Auditors are also required to make special reports where shortened accounts are presented to shareholders by small companies; where abbreviated accounts are filed by small or medium-sized companies; where a parent company is exempted from the obligation to prepare group accounts; and when listed companies circulate summary financial statements.

Under section 240, the auditors' report must not be published with non-statutory accounts, although the latter must be accompanied by a statement indicating that such a report has been made on the statutory accounts and whether or not it is qualified.

## SPECIAL CLASSES OF COMPANY

### Dormant companies

Under section 250 of the 1985 Act a dormant company — which is one in which no significant accounting transaction occurred during the period in question — need not have appointed auditors and hence need not file an auditors' report with the accounts (see *post*, p. 567). Instead, the directors must include a statement immediately above their signatures on the balance sheet to the effect that the company was dormant throughout the relevant period. To qualify for such exemption the company must meet the following three conditions:

(i) it was not required to prepare group accounts during the previous financial year;

---

[80] Firth, M., "Qualified Audit Reports: Their Impact on Investment Decisions" *The Accounting Review* (July 1978), pp. 642–650. See pp. 575–576, *post,* for the nature of audit qualifications.

   (ii)  it was classed as a small company during the previous
        financial year; and
  (iii)  it has been dormant since the end of the previous financial
        year.

## Investment companies

Companies qualify for special treatment if they are investment
companies within the meaning of section 266 of the 1985 Act and
were not during the year prohibited from making a distribution
under section 265 (Schedule 4, paragraph 73: see *post*, pages 601–
602).

An investment company is defined under section 266 as being a
public company which has given notice in the prescribed form to
the Registrar of Companies of its intention to carry on business
as an investment company and:

  (a)  invests its funds in a portfolio of securities for the benefit
      of, and to spread risk for, its shareholders;
  (b)  fulfils the condition that none of its individual investments
      exceeds 15 per cent in value of its total investments;
  (c)  whose memorandum and articles prohibit a distribution of
      its capital profits; and
  (d)  which retains no more than 15 per cent of its income
      available for distribution in an accounting reference
      period.

In addition, under section 351(1)(c) an investment company
must indicate its status on its letter heads and on its order forms;
while under paragraphs 71–73 of Schedule 4 and paragraph 1(3)
of Schedule 4A the requirements with regard to the contents of
its accounts are subject to modification from those generally
applicable to other companies.

The conditions outlined above substantially coincide with those
demanded of an approved investment trust if it is to secure tax
and other privileges, although it would for these purposes also
have to be resident in the United Kingdom, not be a "close"
company and have its shares listed on a recognised stock
exchange. The latter requirement would in fact subject it to
various other conditions contained in the London Stock
Exchange's *Listing Rules* — *e.g.* no more than 20 per cent of the
group's assets could be invested in any one company; and it

would have to disclose supplementary information with its accounts, including a summary of its 10 largest investments and an analysis of realised and unrealised surpluses, with a separate statement of profits and losses analysed between listed and unlisted investments.

The provisions of the 1985 Act are adapted in three ways for investment companies:

(i) revaluations of investments need not be credited or debited to the revaluation reserve;

(ii) where the value of fixed asset investments is written down, such a debit need not be passed through the profit and loss account if it is either charged against a reserve to which investment revaluations have been credited, or shown as a separate item under "other reserves";

(iii) disclosure must be made in a note of any distribution reducing the company's net assets to less than the aggregate of its called-up capital and undistributable reserves (which can arise if it chooses to apply the asset ratio test for distribution rather than the capital maintenance criterion: section 264)[80a] (Schedule 4, paragraphs 71–72).

Under section 267 the Secretary of State is empowered to make regulations under a statutory instrument to extend the provisions of sections 265 and 266 to other investment companies, including those whose asset holdings are in the form of land. However, as yet no regulations have been made under this section.

## Banking and insurance companies

Between 1948 and 1991 banks and insurance companies did not have to prepare and publish financial statements in the full form required of other companies by the Companies Acts.[81] However, to implement an EU banking directive, the concessions to banks were effectively removed with the execution of the Bank Accounts Directive Regulations 1991[82] and the Companies Act

---

[80a] See *post*, pp. 599–602.

[81] In fact, many of the privileges were removed from the large clearing banks by S.I. 1970 No. 327.

[82] S.I. 1991 No. 2704.

1985 Regulations 1991[83], new sections 255 and 255A–D being inserted into the 1985 Act. At the same time, a very detailed Schedule 9 was substituted, the former Schedule 9 being renumbered as 9A and applying only to insurance companies. This in turn was replaced by another very detailed schedule when the Companies Act 1985 Regulations 1993[84] was implemented in order to comply with an EU insurance companies directive.

The broad effect of the concessions formerly available was to enable qualifying companies to conceal movements on reserve and fixed asset accounts, and for banks and insurance companies this was normally justified on the grounds that it was desirable not to undermine public confidence in such financial institutions. Yet the very fact that members of the public, as depositors or policy holders, have a direct interest in the financial affairs of such concerns has led successive governments to develop alternative means of monitoring their financial viability. In the case of banks and discount houses, the control machinery is informally operated and modified as the need arises by the Bank of England, although from 1979 the relationship between the Bank and the institutions it supervises has been formalised by the Banking Act of that year and has been further strengthened by the Banking Act 1987. Insurance companies are subject to the Insurance Companies Act 1982, and the Department of Trade and Industry also requires certain very detailed returns to the made.[85] For long term business (mainly life assurance) the conventional profit and loss account has relatively little significance, and more attention has to be paid to the actuarial report,[86] balance sheet, and other supplementary statements than to the income (*i.e.* flow of funds) account. For short term business (*i.e.* for one year contracts concerning fire, theft, motor and similar insurance) the rules are slightly different and have been tightened up in recent years following the collapse of Fire, Auto and Marine in 1966 and Vehicle and General in 1971, though again detailed returns have to be filed.[87]

[83] S.I. 1991 No. 2705.
[84] S.I. 1993 No. 3246.
[85] Most recently governed by S.I. 1983 No. 1811: The Insurance Companies (Accounts and Statements) Regulations 1983, as amended by S.I. 1988 No. 672.
[86] The significance of the actuarial valuation is in fact acknowledged in section 268 of the Companies Act 1985, which recognises actuarial surpluses or deficits as the appropriate measure of realised profits or losses available for distribution.
[87] Insurance Companies Acts 1974 and 1982, and various Statutory Instruments, including S.I. 1983 No. 1811, as amended.

POWERS OF THE SECRETARY OF STATE TO ALTER THE
ACCOUNTING REQUIREMENTS OF THE ACT

Under section 257 of the Act the Secretary of State can alter,
add to or otherwise modify by statutory instrument the requirements relating to financial statements and annexed reports.
Moreover, he also has powers under section 700 to exempt
oversea companies from certain requirements.

OTHER ACCOUNTING AND DISCLOSURE REGULATIONS

In recent years, there has been lengthy debate on the wider
aspects of corporate accountability, in particular as they affect
employees and society as a whole. A number of large companies
have responded by including in their annual reports Value Added
Statements, Employment Reports, Statements of Money
Exchanges with Government and Transactions in Foreign Currency, and (less commonly) Statements of Corporate Objectives
and Future Prospects. Some have also produced special reports
outlining the skills of their workforces and their contributions to
society.

As regards specific interest groups, the government most
obviously requires accounting information from companies to
assess their corporation tax liabilities. However, employee representatives are also empowered to receive information under
sections 181–185 of the Trade Union and Labour Relations
(Consolidation Act) 1992 (which effectively embodies sections
56–57 of the Industrial Relations Act 1971). If certain grounds for
exemption do not apply, an employer is obliged by this section to
disclose to trade union representatives material information relevant to collective bargaining procedures, and indeed any information relevant to collective bargaining which would be "in
accordance with good industrial relations practice". The
Advisory Conciliation and Arbitration Service (ACAS) has published a code to try to establish what constitutes such good
practice, and it suggests relevant data should include work
schedules, orders, market share, productivity figures, relevant
cost structures, transfer prices, government financial assistance,
intra-group loans and interest charged.[88]

---

[88] "Disclosure of Information to Trade Unions for Collective Bargaining" (1977),
   para. 11.

In several Continental countries legislation has established alternative means through which relevant information can be communicated to employee representatives, the most obvious being works councils and board representation. Works councils have their informal counterparts in many British companies, but they do not enjoy the same legal status. It is EU policy to encourage the creation of such councils throughout the Community, and this applies to British companies operating on the Continent, though not in the U.K. itself because of the opt-out clause in the Maastricht Treaty.

## ACKNOWLEDGMENTS OF DEBTS

Finally, there is the question of whether or not the inclusion of a debt in the balance sheet amounts to an acknowledgment of that debt by the company.

In *Jones v. Bellgrove Properties Ltd*,[89] it was held that a statement in a balance sheet "To sundry creditors £7,638", the balance sheet being signed by the company's agents, a firm of chartered accountants, was an acknowledgment, within the meaning of section 24(2) of the Limitation Act 1939[90] of a debt of £1,807 owed to a shareholder and included in the £7,638. Consequently the right of action to recover the debt was by section 23(4) of the 1939 Act deemed to have accrued on the date of the acknowledgment and the action was not barred by the six-year limitation period fixed by section 2(1) of the 1939 Act.

The *Jones* case was distinguished in *Re Transplanters (Holding Co.) Ltd*[91] (where the directors had made the acknowledgment in favour of one of themselves) and considered in *Good v. Parry*.[92] But in *Consolidated Agencies Ltd v. Bertram Ltd*,[93] where a section of the Indian Limitation Act 1908, which was similar to, but not identical with, section 23(4) of the 1939 Act, was construed, it was held that the word "acknowledgment" meant

---

[89] [1949] 2 K.B. 700 (C.A.).
[90] Not applicable to Scotland: any similar question arising in Scotland would be governed by the Prescription and Limitation (Scotland) Act 1973. The provisions of the Limitation Act 1939 are now included in the Limitation Act 1980.
[91] [1958] 1 W.L.R. 822.
[92] [1963] 2 Q.B. 418 (C.A.). For there to be an acknowledgment the debt must be quantified in figures or it must be liquidated in the sense that it is capable of ascertainment by calculation or by extrinsic evidence without further agreement of the parties.
[93] [1965] A.C. 470 (P.C.).

acknowledgment of a debt existing at the date of signature and, since the balance sheet was signed many months after the year to which it related, it was not an acknowledgment of such an existing debt but an acknowledgment of a past debt as at the date when the balance sheet was made up. It was said that the *Jones* case was rightly decided on its facts[94] and that it is questionable whether a signature on a balance sheet, which must of necessity be made some time after the date to which the balance sheet has been made up, can amount to an acknowledgment of an existing debt.

However, in *Re Gee & Co. (Woolwich) Ltd*[95], the *Consolidated Agencies* case was distinguished and it was held that a balance sheet, duly signed by the directors, is capable of being an effective acknowledgment of the state of the company's indebtedness as at the date of the balance sheet, so that the cause of action should, in an appropriate case, be deemed to have accrued at that date, being the date to which the signature of the directors relates. On the facts of the *Gee* case, the acknowledgment was effective even though it was made by the directors in favour of one of themselves, because it was sanctioned by every member of the company.

---

[94] No question arose there as to the date to which the acknowledgment related, although it was taken to be the date of the annual general meeting.
[95] [1975] Ch. 52.

# Chapter 21

# AUDITORS

## Introduction

### The rationale of a statutory audit

Reference to the *auditors' report* and its content has already been made in chapter 20 (see above pages 546–547), and the position of the auditors has become a very important one. In particular, it has become increasingly recognised that where there is inequality of information between parties, it is generally desirable, both as between the parties concerned and from a wider social perspective, that the accounts should be attested by an independent third party. This is necessary to avoid a breakdown in the market mechanism in two sets of circumstances.

First, a prospective purchaser of a company's shares will require information before he commits himself to the transaction — just as a person buying a second-hand car will want to ensure he is not about to acquire a "pup". Economists have demonstrated that in the absence of reliable information, the market mechanism will become unstable and at the limit no trading will take place. There are various ways to combat this — *e.g.* by offering guarantees and warranties; or by having an independent third party validate information. It is largely for this latter reason that disclosure of attested information is required in the primary share markets when a prospectus or listing particulars are published. But of course a prospective purchaser of a company's shares in the secondary markets will also want similar, reliable information.

The second situation arises where a "principal" (*e.g.* a shareholder) attempts to assess the performance of his "agent" (*e.g.* a manager) but has to rely on information given to him by the latter. The manager is clearly in a position to manipulate the data, and it is largely to counteract this that the device of a statutory audit has been developed.

As will be described below, the auditor is given wide powers by sections 389A, 391A, 392, 392A, and 394 of the Companies Act 1985, being able to enforce them by qualifying his report and, in an extreme case, by refusing to certify the accounts.

But just as it is important for readers of financial statements to have a guarantee that they have been properly prepared under an accepted set of conventions, it is also necessary for them to be able to rely on the word of those persons who certify them as having been so produced. This means, of course, that auditors should be recognised as fit and proper persons to carry out the duties of their office. Traditionally, the market response to situations where the public wishes to purchase quality services (*e.g.* in medicine, architecture, law or accountancy) is for practitioners to organise themselves into professional bodies, which then set minimum standards for members. Self-regulation along these lines can be very successful, but the position of professional bodies frequently enables them to restrict entry and exploit their monopoly power, making it necessary for central governments to intervene to try to redress the balance.

Prior to the Companies Act 1989 a person could only be appointed as an auditor of a company if he was a member of a professional body recognised by the Secretary of State (*i.e.* the Institute of Chartered Accountants in England and Wales; the Institute of Chartered Accountants of Scotland; the Institute of Chartered Accountants in Ireland; and the Chartered Association of Certified Accountants — section 389(1)(a) of the Companies Act 1985, now repealed). However, Part II of the 1989 Act, concerned with eligibility of company auditors, has introduced the provisions of the EU's Eighth Council Directive on company law harmonisation into British legislation. As a result two types of statutory supervisory body now exist: Recognised Supervisory Bodies (RSBs), of which all company auditors must be members; and Recognised Qualifying Bodies (RQBs), which offer appropriate professional qualifications that are the prerequisite for membership of an RSB. In practice, the same organisation can simultaneously be an RSB and an RQB, enabling the main professional bodies of public accountants to fulfil both functions.

Within the British context, the overall impact of Part II of the 1989 Act has not greatly altered the position already achieved under self-regulation with regard to the qualification of auditors, except to impose a more elaborate regulatory framework. This in turn has imposed greater compliance costs on those involved — directly on auditors and indirectly on the customers for their services — while at the same time the authorities are continuing for the most part to rely on competition in the market place to ensure that professional bodies do not over-exploit their monopoly power.

### The growth of regulation

The new institutional structure introduced by the 1989 Act has reinforced the regulatory complexities with respect to company accounting and the statutory audit. Studies have shown that for two thirds or more of the one million companies on the register the entire share capital is owned by the directors, which means that the reporting-to-shareholder function is effectively redundant for such businesses. The 1989 Act partly addressed this matter by introducing an "elective regime" for private companies. As a result, under section 252 of the 1985 Act they can by unanimous resolution dispense with the holding of annual general meetings and the laying of accounts and reports before such meetings (see *ante*, pp. 479–480).

However, this concession did little to reduce the administrative burden on small companies, and it was for this reason that legislation was introduced in 1994 to exempt about half of all companies from having to have a statutory audit (see *post*, pp. 577–578). Instead, only the largest "small" companies will have to have their accounts attested, and then frequently by means of a less demanding examination culminating in a *compilation report*.

Unfortunately the new regulations have spawned a new plethora of guidelines from the accountancy profession. Moreover, attested accounts will still have to be prepared for the Inland Revenue and banks. And, indeed, if companies do not publish reliable information, they are likely to find suppliers will be less prepared to advance credit. In the circumstances, the new measures seem unlikely to deliver the hoped for savings in administrative time and effort.

### Closing the "expectation gap"

At the other end of the scale there has been increasing concern, both amongst institutional investors and the general public, that the largest companies are not being run by directors in the best interests of either their shareholders or society in general. This has caused concern amongst the accountancy professional bodies as the public often seems to expect more from the audit then is legally required (*e.g.* with respect to directors' stewardship, future prospects and risks, fraud, internal controls and interim reporting; independence, in as much as auditors are perceived as being too closely identified with the interests of a company and its directors since they are directly employed by those parties; the audit report, which is often seen as uninformative, failing to disclose material findings, issues and concerns arising from the audit; an apparent lack of real competition between audit firms, despite moves by companies to put their audits out to tender — a move which itself threatens the quality and rigour of audits; and the threat of litigation — important at a time when the number of claims against the Big Six auditing firms rose from just three in 1982/83 to 210 a decade later, with the average size of the three largest claims increasing 12.5 times over the 10 years).

The profession has attempted to address these problems by elaborating the audit report and by revising the guidelines for conducting audits (see *post*, pp. 574–575).

### Corporate governance

Public concern has also been expressed at a perceived lack of accountability of the directors of the largest public companies, both to their shareholders and to society in general. In an attempt to improve the situation, the Cadbury Committee published a report at the end of 1992 entitled "The financial aspects of corporate governance", which contains a Code of Best Practice endorsed by the London Stock Exchange. This deals with four matters: the board of directors; non-executive directors; executive directors; and reporting and controls.

In terms of financial reporting, the Code requires that all listed companies should have audit committees, the aim of which is to strengthen the independence of the external auditor and reinforce the position of internal auditors. The Code also affects the position of the auditors in a number of other respects, including the following: interim announcements should be subject to review by a company's auditors; the accountancy profession should draw up guidelines for the rotation of audit partners;

directors should report on the effectiveness of their system of
internal financial control; directors should state in their report
that the business is a going concern, indicating the assumptions
on which they base their judgement, and the auditors should
report on such a statement; and companies should publish a
statement indicating that they have complied with the Code, but
only after it has been the subject of review by the auditors.

The auditor's statement of compliance with the Code is separate from the audit of financial statements, and this should be
made clear in their report to shareholders.

## Outline of the chapter

This chapter deals with the following matters: the professional
qualifications of auditors; the appointment of auditors; vacation
of office by auditors; the legal position of auditors; remuneration
of auditors; the auditors' report; the powers of auditors; and the
duties of auditors, including their legal liability both to shareholders and to third parties.

## PROFESSIONAL QUALIFICATIONS OF AUDITORS

## Supervisory bodies and professional qualifications

### Recognised supervisory bodies

A Recognised Supervisory Body (RSB) is a body established in
the United Kingdom which maintains and enforces rules as to:

(a)  the eligibility of persons seeking appointment or acting as
     company auditors; and
(b)  the conduct of company audit work

which are binding on persons seeking appointment or acting as
company auditors, either because they are members of that body,
or because they are otherwise subject to its control (section 30(1)
of the Companies Act 1989).

Bodies wishing to become RSBs have to apply to the Secretary
of State for recognition, and the conditions for granting or
revoking recognition are specified in Schedule 11 to the 1989 Act.

Prospective RSBs must submit their rules to the Secretary of State, but he may refuse to recognise a body if he is of the view that there are other bodies controlling the profession which have been, or are likely to be, recognised (Schedule 11, paragraphs 1–3). RSBs have to ensure that only individuals with appropriate qualifications and firms controlled by qualified persons are eligible for appointment as company auditors (paragraphs 4–5), and their rules must be such that only "fit and proper persons" can be so appointed (paragraph 6). The Secretary of State has so far recognised as RSBs the three institutes of chartered accountants in the British Isles,[1] the Chartered Association of Certified Accountants, and two much smaller professional bodies.

An RSB's rules are required to ensure that company audit work is conducted properly and with integrity and independence; that certain technical standards are applied; and that procedures exist for ensuring eligible persons maintain an appropriate level of competence (paragraphs 6–9). Prior to 1991 guidance as to how audit investigations should be undertaken was given in an Auditing Standard and a series of Auditing Guidelines published by the Auditing Practices Committee (APC). Since then it has been superseded by a more broadly based body, the Auditing Practices Board (APB), whose aim is to establish standards that can be adopted by RSBs. To this end it has published 28 Statements of Auditing Standards (SASs).

Legislation further requires that an RSB's rules should deal with monitoring and enforcement of compliance with its rules; admission and expulsion of members; the grant and withdrawal of eligibility for appointment as company auditors and disciplinary procedures; the investigation of complaints against its members and the body itself; and the provision by eligible persons of indemnity insurance and similar arrangements to meet claims arising from company audit work (paragraphs 10–13). The Councils of the three Institutes of Chartered Accountants in the British Isles therefore published a revised *Guide to Professional Ethics* in 1992, which deals with a number of these matters.

RSBs must also have rules requiring eligible persons to comply with sections 35 and 36 of the 1989 Act, respectively dealing with disclosure of auditors' names in a register and information about firms eligible for appointment as company auditors; have satisfac-

---

[1] *Ante*, p. 555.

tory arrangements for meeting the costs of complying with their
rules; and be able and willing to promote higher standards of
integrity in company audit work.

Under section 47 of the 1989 Act and Schedule 14, an RSB's
rules and other guidance have to be submitted to the Director-
General of Fair Trading before recognition is granted so that he
can assess whether they will restrict or prevent competition.
However, RSBs and their officers, employees and members of
their governing bodies are exempted from damages in respect of
their discharging their statutory duties or failing to do so, unless
it can be shown they have acted in bad faith. This effectively
prevents them being joined in any action taken against auditors
for negligence (section 48 of the Companies Act 1989).

To monitor the activities of auditing firms, the chartered
institutes formed a Joint Monitoring Unit in 1992. This identified
10,200 firms on the register. Of these, only 160 audited the
accounts of listed companies — and only 20 of these were
auditors to more than 5 listed companies. In fact, 90 per cent of
firms had 4 or fewer partners, and 68 per cent were sole
practitioners.

*Professional qualifications*

Effectively the 1989 Act requires that auditors should hold an
appropriate qualification. Usually this will be granted by a
Recognised Qualifying Body (RQB), approved by the Secretary
of State, but transitional arrangements provide that persons who
were qualified as auditors immediately before January 1, 1990,
continue to be eligible. Such provisions extend, first, to members
of one of the professional bodies recognised under section
389(1)(a) of the 1985 Act[2] and to students who have commenced
their training before January 1, 1990, and who qualify before
January 1, 1996, as long as their training is approved for this
purpose by the Secretary of State (section 31(1), (4)–(5) of the
Companies Act 1989).[3]

In order to offer recognised professional qualifications and
become an RQB, a body must be approved by the Secretary of

---

[2] *Ante*, p. 559.
[3] There were also provisions covering persons eligible for appointment as auditors
immediately before January 1, 1990, to enable them to continue to be treated as
qualified (section 31(2)–(3)).

State (section 32 of the Companies Act 1989). The procedure for recognition is similar to that for an RSB, and the conditions for granting, refusing and revoking recognition are laid down in Schedule 12 to the Act, paragraphs 1–3. Basically, the qualification must only be open to persons who have attained university entrance level or have a sufficient period of professional experience (*i.e.* at least seven years in a professional capacity in finance, law and accountancy). Periods of theoretical instruction, up to a maximum of four years, can count towards the necessary experience (Schedule 12, paragraphs 4–6). Those who seek recognition must also pass an examination, which tests theoretical knowledge and the ability to apply it in practice, and they must have completed at least three years practical training.

However, certain exemptions are available for those who have passed equivalent examinations or who have obtained relevant practical experience. The subjects to be covered under the examination syllabus are defined by the Secretary of State by statutory instrument (S.I. 1990 No. 1146), and the practical training must be given by persons approved by an RQB. In fact, at least two thirds of it must be with a fully qualified auditor, a substantial part being on company audit work (Schedule 12, paragraphs 7–8). In addition, the RQB must have rules and arrangements to ensure compliance with its regulations and procedures for ensuring the effective monitoring of continued compliance with such requirements (Schedule 12, paragraph 9).

The Secretary of State may declare a professional qualification obtained outside the United Kingdom to be "an approved overseas qualification" under section 31(1) of the 1989 Act, which enables persons so qualified to audit the accounts of British companies. However, in considering whether or not to make such a declaration, the Secretary of State may take into account reciprocal arrangements for persons professionally qualified in the United Kingdom to audit overseas; and he may require additional qualifications to ensure an adequate knowledge of law and practice in the United Kingdom relevant to the audit of accounts. He may also withdraw recognition of an overseas qualification after a specified date if he is no longer satisfied that there is equivalent competence or there are inadequate reciprocal arrangements (section 33 of the Companies Act 1989).

## Registers and fees

Under section 35 of the 1989 Act, the Secretary of State is empowered to make regulations through a statutory instrument requiring that a register be kept of all individuals and firms eligible for appointment as company auditors and of the qualified persons responsible for company audit work on their behalfs. The register will give the names and addresses and indicate the relevant RSB. The regulations may require further information to be disclosed on the register, and the Secretary of State can impose further obligations on the RSBs, on persons eligible to be company auditors, and on anyone charged by one or more RSBs to keep the register. The regulations may also include provisions concerning the availability of the register for public inspection, for copies of entries being made available, and for appropriate fees to be charged for such services.

Similarly, under section 36 of the 1989 Act, the Secretary of State is empowered to make regulations through a statutory instrument requiring an RSB to make available to the public information about firms which are eligible under its rules to act as statutory auditors. The information to be disclosed will be the names and addresses of all directors and shareholders, if the firm is a company; or of all partners, if it is a partnership. The regulations may require further information to be disclosed, and the Secretary of State can impose further obligations on the RSBs, on persons eligible to be company auditors, and on anyone charged by one or more supervisory bodies to keep such information. The regulations may also include provisions concerning the availability of the information for public inspection, for copies of information being made available, and for appropriate fees to be charged for such services. However, the regulations may make different provisions for different types of information.

Regulations under sections 35 and 36 of the Companies Act have been brought into force by statutory instrument.[4]

Section 45 of the 1989 Act provides for the payment of fees by applicants for recognition and of periodical fees payable by RSBs and RQBs. The regulations are set by statutory instrument, and the fees are paid into the consolidated fund.

Section 46 of the 1989 Act enables the Secretary of State, by order made by statutory instrument, to set up a body corporate

[4] S.I. 1991 No. 1566.

to exercise his functions under Part II of the Act, concerning the eligibility for appointment as a company auditor. The order can delegate some or all of the Secretary of State's powers, except those preventing restrictive practices (section 47 and Schedule 14) and those determining his relations with such a delegated body. If such a delegation order is made, the Secretary of State is still able concurrently to exercise his power to call for relevant information from an RSB or RQB under section 38 and to give directions so that such bodies should comply with EU and other international obligations under section 40. Moreover, the delegated body will only be able to refuse or withdraw approval of an overseas qualification because of lack of reciprocity under section 33(3) with the consent of the Secretary of State. Provision is also made for the revocation in whole or in part of the delegation order or for its variation under a further order made by statutory instrument. The status, constitution and proceedings of a delegated body and the exercise by it of functions transferred by the Secretary of State are detailed in Schedule 13 to the Act.

The Secretary of State is empowered to require RSBs and RQBs both to notify him in writing of specified events and to disclose such information as he may reasonably require. He can also, as an alternative to revoking recognition, apply to the court for an order directing an RSB or RQB to take the necessary steps to meet particular requirements and obligations, and he may also require such bodies to avoid actions that would be incompatible with international commitments (sections 37–40 of the Companies Act 1989).

**Penalties for offences**

A person or a partner or officer of a corporate body who supplies false or misleading information in relation to Part II of the 1989 Act, concerning eligibility for appointment as a company auditor, is liable to imprisonment and/or a fine. Similar penalties can be imposed where a person not on the register of auditors holds himself out as a registered auditor or where a body corporate which is not recognised as an RSB or RQB holds itself out as such. Proceedings, where necessary against an unincorporated body, must commence within 12 months of evidence coming to the notice of the prosecuting party, but action cannot be initiated more than 3 years after the offence took place (sections 41–44 of the Companies Act 1989).

## Eligibility of partnerships

Prior to the 1989 Act, partnerships and corporate bodies could not be appointed as auditors, only individuals. However, to bring British law into line with that in a number of EU countries and to limit the liability of individuals (though not of firms) in professional indemnity claims, section 25 specifically provides that a firm may be appointed as a company auditor. Where this is the case, when the membership of a partnership changes, a succeeding practice will be eligible for appointment, so long as the members and the business are substantially the same as before. Provision is also made for the situation where part of a practice is taken over by another partnership or person eligible for appointment (section 26 of the Companies Act 1989). This clarifies the fact that in English law the appointment is of the partnership itself and not the individual partners; and that the appointment will continue despite the routine cessations of partnerships when members join and leave. The position has always been different in Scotland where partnerships have a separate legal personality.

Where a corporate body is appointed as an auditor, it is necessary to ensure that the individuals responsible for the work hold appropriate qualifications and that the firm is controlled by qualified persons. Consequently, RSBs are required to have rules which deal with these matters and ensure that there are no potential conflicts of interest (paragraphs 4–5, 7, Schedule 11 to the Companies Act 1989).

## Ineligibility because of lack of independence

The 1989 Act also defines the circumstances in which a person is ineligible for appointment as a statutory auditor on the grounds of lack of independence — *viz.* if he is an officer or employee of the company or of a parent or subsidiary undertaking, or a partner or employee of such a person. A person may also be ineligible if there is a connection between him or any associate of his and the group of companies, the nature of such a connection being specified in regulations made by the Secretary of State (section 27 of the Companies Act 1989). Further advice on these matters is given in the professional bodies' *Guide to Professional Ethics*.

### Appointment of an ineligible auditor

Acting as a statutory auditor when ineligible is an offence, and the guilty party is liable on conviction to a fine and on summary conviction to a fine not exceeding the statutory maximum. In the case of continued contravention, the person will be liable on a second or subsequent summary conviction to a fine of up to one tenth of the statutory maximum for each day on which the offence is continued. However, it is a defence to show that there was no knowledge and no reason to believe that the person concerned was ineligible. In this context, a person may either be ineligible or become ineligible. In the latter case, he should vacate office and give notice in writing to the company that he has resigned because of ineligibility (section 28 of the Companies Act 1989).

Where a company audit has been carried out by an ineligible person, the Secretary of State may direct that an eligible person be appointed, either to undertake a second audit or to review the first audit and report whether a second audit is needed. When such a direction is given, a copy will be sent to the Registrar of Companies, and the company must comply within 21 days. On receiving any report on the possible need for a second audit, the company must forward a copy to the Registrar within 21 days. Failure to comply with these provisions is an offence, liable on summary conviction to a fine not exceeding the statutory maximum; and in the case of continued contravention, on a second or subsequent summary conviction to a fine of one tenth of the statutory maximum for each day on which the offence takes place. Moreover, the company is entitled to recover costs incurred complying with these provisions if the ineligible person knew he was ineligible (section 29 of the Companies Act 1989).

## APPOINTMENT OF AUDITORS

Except where a company:

(a)  is dormant;

(b)  is a private company electing to dispense with the laying of accounts; or

(c)  is exempt from having to have a statutory audit (see *post*, pp. 577–578)

auditors will be appointed at a general meeting where the company's accounts are laid (section 384 of the Companies Act

1985). Moreover, except again where a private company elects to dispense with the laying of accounts, a company must appoint an auditor at each general meeting where accounts are laid until the next such meeting. However, the first auditors may be appointed by the directors before the first general meeting at which accounts are laid, or — failing action by them — by the company in general meeting (section 385 of the Companies Act 1985).

Where a private company has elected in accordance with section 252 to dispense with the laying of accounts[5] and is not exempt from statutory audit requirements, auditors must be appointed by the company at a general meeting held within four weeks of accounts for the previous year being sent to members under section 238[6]; or, where such a meeting was held, the conclusion of a general meeting at which accounts for the previous year were laid. Such auditors hold office until the next date at which an appointment falls due. In the case of the first auditors of a private company taking advantage of an election under section 252, the directors (rather than the company in general meeting) can exercise the power of appointment, failing which the company in general meeting will appoint (section 385A of the Companies Act 1985).

Private companies may by elective resolution under section 379A opt to dispense with the obligation to appoint auditors annually, in which case the existing auditors will, so long as the election continues, be deemed to have been reappointed unless the company either is a dormant company or a resolution is passed ending the appointment (section 386 of the Companies Act 1985).

Where no auditors are appointed, a company shall within a week of the term of such an appointment elapsing give notice to the Secretary of State so that he can fill the vacancy. Failure to give such notice renders the defaulting company and officers liable to be fined (section 387 of the Companies Act 1985).

A company's directors or the company in general meeting are empowered to fill a casual vacancy for the office of auditor. Where this is done by the company in general meeting, special notice is required, as it is when an auditor appointed to fill a casual vacancy by the directors is subject to reappointment by the company in general meeting. Copies of such notice have to be

---

[5] *Ante*, pp. 479–480.
[6] *Ante*, p. 481.

sent to the auditor concerned and to his predecessor if he resigned (section 388 of the Companies Act 1985).

A company which is dormant under the provisions of section 250 of the 1985 Act[7] is exempt from the obligation to appoint auditors (section 388A(1) of the Companies Act 1985).

To qualify as dormant, during the period in question the company must not have engaged in any significant accounting transaction other than the receipt of monies for its shares from subscribers to the memorandum of association. It may then pass a special resolution exempting itself from the obligation under section 384 to appoint auditors. Such a special resolution may be passed either at an extraordinary general meeting held before the first general meeting where the accounts would normally be laid, so long as the company has been dormant since its formation; or at a general meeting where the accounts would normally be laid.

In order to take advantage of the dormant company provisions, steps will have to be taken to change the company's articles where they require it to appoint an auditor (as, indeed, would generally be the case for any company adopting Table A prior to the current form, which took effect from July 1, 1985).

Where a company ceases to be dormant, the directors may appoint auditors to hold office until the next meeting at which accounts are to be laid. Alternatively, if the company elects under section 252 to dispense with laying accounts, they may either appoint auditors within 28 days of the annual accounts being sent to members under section 238; or, if a shareholder gives notice requiring the laying of accounts at a general meeting, at the beginning of that meeting. If the directors fail to exercise such powers, they may be exercised by the company in general meeting (section 388A(2)–(5)).

## VACATION OF OFFICE BY AUDITORS

### Removal and resignation of auditors

A company may, by ordinary resolution, remove an auditor before his period of office has expired and notwithstanding any agreement with him. Where he is so removed, the company must

---

[7] See *ante*, pp. 547–548, for the necessary conditions.

give notice in a prescribed form within two weeks, failing which both it and the defaulting officers are liable to a fine and, for continued contravention, a daily default fine. An auditor so removed retains his rights to compensation or damages in respect of the termination of his appointment; and he is also entitled under section 390 of the 1985 Act to receive all communications relating to general meetings when his term of office would normally expire or at which it is proposed to appoint his successor, and to attend and be heard at such meetings (section 391 of the Companies Act 1985).

Special notice is required for a resolution removing an auditor or appointing his successor, and such notice must be forwarded to the parties concerned. The auditor who is being removed or who is resigning may make representations of reasonable length to the company which, if requested, must circulate them with the resolution, failing which the auditor may require them to be read out at the meeting. However, application may be made to the court by the company or other aggrieved party, and if such representations are deemed to be needlessly defamatory they need not be circulated or be read out at the meeting. In such circumstances, the court may require the auditor to pay some or all of the costs involved (section 391 of the Companies Act 1985).

An auditor may resign by depositing notice in writing at a company's registered office, but under section 394 it must be accompanied by a statement indicating whether or not there are any special circumstances leading to such action. The auditor's period of office ends when such notice is lodged, unless it specifies another date. The company must deliver a copy of the notice to the Registrar within a fortnight of its being lodged at the registered office, failing which the company and its defaulting officers are liable to a fine and, for continued contravention, a daily default fine (section 392 of the Companies Act 1985).

When an auditor's resignation letter is accompanied by a statement of circumstances leading to such action, as required by section 394, he may deposit a signed requisition calling on the directors to convene an extraordinary general meeting to receive such a statement and other explanations he may wish to give. He may also request the company to circulate a written explanation of reasonable length concerning the circumstances before such a meeting is convened, or before a meeting at which his term of office would normally have expired. The company must indicate in the notice of the meeting that such a statement has been made and circulate it to members of the company. The directors must convene a meeting within three weeks of the requisition being lodged, and it must be held within four weeks of the date of the notice of the meeting being given. Failure to do so renders every director who did not take reasonable steps to secure compliance liable to a fine. If the statement is not circulated, the auditor may require it to be read out at the meeting. However, application may be made to the court by the company or other aggrieved party, and if such representations are deemed to be needlessly defamatory they need not be circulated or be read out at the meeting. In such circumstances, the court may require the auditor to pay some or all of the costs involved (section 392A of the Companies Act 1985).

Where a private company by section 386 has elected to dispense with the annual appointment of an auditor, any member can deposit up to one notice in writing, in each financial year, at its registered office proposing that the appointment shall be terminated. The directors must then hold a general meeting within four weeks at which a resolution shall be put concerning the termination of the auditor's appointment. If the decision is to end the appointment, the auditor shall be deemed not to be reappointed when next he would be. Moreover, if notice was lodged within a fortnight of the accounts being circulated, any deemed reappointment that has taken place will be invalid. Where the directors fail to take steps to convene a general meeting within a fortnight of a member depositing notice, he may himself convene such a meeting, being reimbursed by the company for his expenses. The company in turn may then recoup them from the defaulting directors. However, no compensation or damages are payable directly as a result of such termination of appointment, although an agreement between the company and the auditor may still provide for compensation for loss of office (section 393 of the Companies Act 1985).

### Statement by a person ceasing to hold office as auditor

A person who for any reason has ceased to hold office as auditor is required to deposit at the company's registered office within specified periods a statement detailing any circumstances connected with his departure which he considers should be brought to the members' or creditors' attention. Where the auditor considers there are no such circumstances, the statement should indicate that fact. However, where there are such circumstances, the company must either send copies of the statement to those persons entitled to receive copies of the accounts under section 238[8]; or alternatively apply to the court, in which case the auditor must be informed. For his part, the auditor must send a copy of his statement to the Registrar within four weeks of depositing it with the company, unless he receives notice within three weeks that the company has applied to the court. If the court is satisfied that the auditor is needlessly using his statement for defamatory purposes, it will direct that copies of it should not be circulated and may order the auditor to pay some or all of the costs involved. Moreover, the company will have to circulate another statment indicating the effect of the court's order. If, however, the court is not satisfied that the auditor's statement is vexatious, the company must circulate it within 14 days and notify the auditor, who will then send a copy to the Registrar within a week of being so informed (section 394 of the Companies Act 1985).

The specified periods within which a statement under section 394 should be deposited at a company's registered office are as follows:

— resignation: to be deposited together with the notice of resignation forwarded to the company under section 392.
— failure to seek reappointment: to be deposited not less than 14 days before the end of the time allowed for next appointing auditors.
— in any other case: to be deposited within 14 days of the auditor ceasing to hold office (section 394(2) of the Companies Act 1985).

An individual auditor or a partnership acting as auditors are guilty of an offence if they breach the provisions of section 394, although it is a defence to show all reasonable steps were taken to comply. For its part, the company and every defaulting officer is liable to a fine; and, for continued contravention, a daily default fine.

[8] *Ante*, p. 481.

## THE LEGAL POSITION OF AUDITORS

The auditor is not a person included in the definition of "officer" in section 744 of the 1985 Act. However, he is an officer of the company for the purpose of a misfeasance summons under section 212 of the Insolvency Act 1986[9] and for the purpose of offences under sections 206–211 and 218 of that same Act[10] (which sections also are concerned with offences by officers of companies in liquidation). An auditor is presumably an officer for the purpose of the Theft Act 1968, [11] s.19, *ante*,[12] which is concerned with false statements by an officer of a body corporate, but an auditor appointed *ad hoc* for a limited purpose (*e.g.* appointed by the directors for a private audit) is not an officer.[13]

Under section 434(4) an auditor is specifically identified as an agent of the company for the purpose of an investigation into its affairs,[14] and he may be examined on oath by an inspector. Otherwise the auditor is not (in the absence of a special contract) an agent of the company, and his normal certificate as to whether the accounts represent a true and fair view of the company's affairs under section 235 cannot constitute an acknowledgment by an agent for the purposes of the Limitation Act 1980.[15]

An auditor is treated in the same way as an officer by sections 310 (provisions relieving officers and auditors from liability) and 727 (relief of officers and auditors).[16]

There is no provision in the Companies Acts or in Table A to the effect that an auditor shall cease to hold office on becoming bankrupt or insane. His position in these respects should be compared with that of a director under section 302 and article 81 of Table A respectively.

---

[9] *Re London and General Bank* [1895] 2 Ch. 16 (C.A.). Section 212 of the Insolvency Act 1986 replaces s. 631 of the 1985 Companies Act; it is dealt with *ante*, p. 370.

[10] ss. 206–211 and 218 of the Insolvency Act 1986 replace ss. 624–629 and 632 of the 1985 Companies Act.

[11] Not applicable to Scotland.

[12] *Ante.*

[13] *R. v. Shacter* [1960] 2 Q.B. 252 (C.C.A.).

[14] *Ante.*

[15] *Re Transplanters (Holdings Co.) Ltd* [1958] 1 W.L.R. 822.

[16] *Ante.*

## REMUNERATION OF AUDITORS

The remuneration of the auditor of a company appointed by the directors or by the Secretary of State is fixed by the directors or by the Secretary of State, as the case may be. In any other case it is fixed by the company in general meeting or as the company in general meeting may determine. "Remuneration" includes sums paid by the company in respect of his expenses (section 390A).

The auditor's remuneration (including expenses paid by the company) must be shown under a separate heading in the profit and loss account (section 390A(3)–(4) of the Companies Act 1985).[17]

A company is also required under section 390B of the 1985 Act and by the Companies Act 1985 Regulations 1991[18] to disclose in a note to the accounts remuneration received by its auditors for non-audit work.[19] Such disclosures relate not only to the company's auditor but to his associates; and to associated undertakings of the company. The auditors are also obliged to supply the company's directors with the necessary information for inclusion in the note to the accounts.

## THE AUDITORS' REPORT[20]

### 1. Report addressed to the members

The auditors must report *to the members*[21] on the annual accounts to be laid before the company in general meeting during their terms of office (section 235(1) of the Companies Act 1985).

### 2. Content of the report

The report must state[22]:

  (a) whether in the auditors' opinion the annual accounts have been properly prepared in accordance with the Companies Act 1985;

---

[17] *Ante*, pp. 512 *et seq*.

[18] S.I. 1991 No. 2128.

[19] Remuneration includes benefits in kind and expenses.

[20] See also pp. 546–547, *ante*.

[21] The exact terms would normally be established in formal engagement letters, on the form of which professional guidance is available.

[22] In the case of banking and insurance companies, the auditor has to ensure that the accounts comply with, and reflect a true and fair view with respect to, the provisions of Schedules 9 and 9A rather than Schedule 4. See ss. 255 and 255A, *ante*, pp. 549 *et seq*.

(b) whether in their opinion a true and fair view is given—

    (i)   in the case of an individual balance sheet, of the state of affairs of the company at the end of its financial year;

    (ii)  in the case of an individual profit and loss account, of the profit or loss of the company for the financial year; and

    (iii) in the case of group accounts, of the state of affairs at the end of the financial year, and the profit and loss for the financial year, of the undertakings included in the consolidation as a whole, so far as concerns the members of the company (section 235(2) of the Companies Act 1985).

(c) whether, after due consideration, they are of the opinion that the information given in the directors' report for the financial year for which the annual accounts are prepared is inconsistent with those accounts (section 235(3) of the Companies Act, 1985).

If the auditors think that proper accounting records or returns have not been kept or received, or that the balance sheet and (unless framed as a consolidated profit and loss account) the profit and loss account are not in agreement with the accounting records and returns, they must state that fact in their report (section 237(2)).

Further, if auditors fail to obtain all the information and explanations which, to the best of their knowledge and belief, are necessary for their audit, they must state that fact in their report (section 237(3)).

If the requirements of Schedule 6 are not complied with in the accounts (*i.e.* concerning disclosure of chairman's and directors' emoluments, waived emoluments, pensions, and compensation for loss of office; and details of loans and other credit transactions favouring directors and officers), it is the auditors' duty to include in their report, so far as they are reasonably able to do so, a statement giving the required information (section 237(4)).

### 3.  Signing of the auditors' report

The auditors' report and the copy delivered to the Registrar must state the names of the auditors and be signed by them. Similarly, all copies of the report laid before the company in general meeting or otherwise circulated must state the names of the auditors, and the penalty for default of these provisions is a fine (section 236 of the Companies Act 1985).

### 4.  The duties of auditors in relation to the audit report

In preparing their report the auditors must carry out certain investigations, namely those which will enable them to form an opinion as to:

(a)  whether proper accounting records have been kept by the company and proper returns adequate for their audit have been received from branches not visited by them;

(b)  whether the company's individual accounts are in agreement with the records and returns (section 237(1)).

Guidance is given as to how such investigations should be undertaken in the APB's Statements of Auditing Standards (SASs). These deal with matters such as objectives and general principles of auditing; fraud and error; going concern; engagement letters; subsequent events; planning; audit materiality; quality control for audit work; audit risk assessment; auditing in an information systems environment; audit evidence; analytical procedures; audit of accounting estimates; audit sampling; management representations; overall review of financial statements; considering the work of internal audit; the relationship between principal auditors and other auditors; auditors' report on financial statements; reports to directors and management; and the auditors' right and duty to report to regulators in the financial sector.

Further advice is also available from professional bodies concerning the verification of debts; stocks and work-in-progress; the implications of goods sold subject to reservation of title; and ascertaining contingent liabilities.

The standard audit report required in the 1993 SAS "Auditors' reports on financial statements" is longer than has hitherto been customary, *inter alia* describing the respective responsibilities of directors and auditors; and the basis of the opinion expressed and the key features of the audit process. In addition, it indicates that auditors should draw attention to the inherent uncertainties that they consider to be fundamental. One result of this is that opinions expressed "subject to" (which was previous practice) are no longer permitted. The SAS also gives a number of examples of model "long form" audit reports, the wording of which is now normally followed.

The auditors perform their duty to the members by forwarding their report to the secretary. They are not responsible if the report is not put before the members.[23] However, in an Australian case it was held that they must pay due regard to the possibility of fraud and must warn the appropriate level of management promptly and without waiting for the general meeting to report to the shareholders.[24]

The articles cannot preclude the auditors from availing themselves of all the information to which they are entitled as material for their report.[25]

## 5. Qualified reports

The APB's 1993 SAS on "Auditors' reports on financial statements" indicates that such reports should contain a clear expression of opinion on the financial statements and on any further matters required by statute or other requirements applicable to the particular engagement.

A qualified opinion should be issued either when there is a limitation on the scope of the auditors' examination; or when the auditors disagree with the treatment or disclosure of a matter in the financial statements. However, in either case, in order to give a qualified opinion the effect of the matter should be material so that the financial statements do not give a true and fair view of the matters on which the auditors are required to report or do not comply with relevant accounting or other requirements.

An *adverse opinion*, stating that the accounts do not give a true and fair view, should be issued when the effect of a disagreement is so material or pervasive that the auditors conclude that the

---

[23] *Re Allen, Craig & Co (London) Ltd* [1934] Ch. 483.
[24] *Pacific Acceptance Corpn. Ltd v. Forsyth* (1970) 92 W.N. (N.S.W.) 29.
[25] *Newton v. Birmingham Small Arms Co. Ltd* [1906] 2 Ch. 378.

financial statements are seriously misleading. Where the effect of a disagreement is not so significant as to require an adverse opinion, an opinion should be expressed that is qualified by stating that the financial statements give a true and fair view except for the effects of the matter giving rise to disagreement.

A *disclaimer of opinion* should be expressed when the possible effect of a limitation on scope is so material or pervasive that the auditors have been unable to obtain sufficient evidence to support an opinion on the financial statements. However, where the auditors conclude that the possible effect of the limitation is not so significant to require a disclaimer, they should issue an opinion that is qualified by stating that the financial statements give a true and fair view except for the effects of any adjustments that might have been found necessary had the limitation not affected the evidence available to them.

## 6. Special audit reports

(A) BANKING AND INSURANCE COMPANIES

Banking and insurance companies prepare their accounts under the special provisions of Schedules 9 and 9A.[26] In their report, the auditors must state whether in their opinion the balance sheet and profit and loss account, and, if applicable, group accounts, have been properly prepared in accordance with the provisions of the 1985 Act and reflect a true and fair view.

However, the auditors of banks and insurance companies have a wider responsibility than in an audit of an ordinary commercial company, and under sections 39 and 47 of the Banking Act 1987 and 21A of the Insurance Companies Act 1982 they have a duty not only to report to members but to the relevant regulators as well (*i.e.* the Bank of England and the Department of Trade and Industry respectively).

(B) SMALL- AND MEDIUM-SIZE COMPANIES

If the company qualifies as a small- or medium-sized company and wishes to take advantage of the *filing* concessions available to it (see pp. 488 *et seq.*), the auditors must prepare:

[26] *Ante*, pp. 549–550.

(a) a signed report for the directors stating whether, in their opinion, the necessary conditions for such a privilege have been met; and

(b) a signed special report appended to the accounts, which is the usual report together with a statement that the company fulfils the special filing requirements (paragraph 24, Schedule 8 to the Companies Act 1985).

Special reports must also be made where a parent company is exempted under sections 248–249 of the Companies Act 1985 from the obligation to prepare group accounts (see pp. 490–491); and when a small company prepares *shortened accounts* (see p. 478) for presentation to its shareholders.

(c) SMALL COMPANY EXEMPTION FROM HAVING A STATUTORY AUDIT

Under S.I. 1994 No. 1935 any company which qualifies as small under section 246 (see pp. 488–489) and whose annual turnover and balance sheet totals respectively do not exceed £90,000 and £1.4 million is exempt from the statutory audit requirement. A company is also exempt from the statutory audit requirement but has to have a *compilation report* prepared if:

(i) it qualifies as a small company under section 246;

(ii) its annual turnover exceeds £90,000 but is not more than £350,000; and

(iii) its balance sheet total does not exceed £1.4 million.

The exemption applies to some 500,000 companies, or about half those registered. However, a small company is not exempt if ten per cent or more of its members demand a full statutory audit.

Where a company takes advantage of the exemption, its directors have to make a statement on its balance sheet which *inter alia* acknowledges the directors' responsibility for ensuring that proper accounting records are kept; and for preparing accounts which comply with the Companies Act 1985 and which give a true and fair view of the state of affairs of the company at the end of its financial year and of its profit or loss for that period.

A *compilation report* has to be prepared by a *reporting accountant*, who must be a member of one of the recognised professional bodies for auditors and be eligible for appointment either as a reporting accountant or as a company auditor under its rules. Such a reporting accountant is subject to the same independence requirement as statutory auditors.

The compilation report has to state whether, in the reporting accountant's opinion, the accounts agree with the accounting records; and whether, on the basis of the information in the accounting records, they have been drawn up in accordance with the provisions of the Companies Act 1985. He also has to certify that the company satisfies the conditions for exemption from the statutory audit requirement.

The APB has issued detailed guidance for reporting accountants in the form of a statement, "Audit exemption reports".

(D) SUMMARY FINANCIAL STATEMENTS

Another special report must be made when a summary financial statement is circulated by a listed company under the provisions of section 251. This should indicate:

(i) whether in the auditors' opinion such a statement
  (a) is consistent with its full accounts and the directors' report; and
  (b) complies with the requirements of section 251 and the regulations relating to summary financial statements; and
(ii) whether the auditors' report on the full accounts was qualified, and if so setting out that report together with further material necessary to understand the qualification.[27]

(E) PROFITS AVAILABLE FOR DISTRIBUTION

Under section 270(2) of the 1985 Act, in order to determine whether a company has profits available for distribution,[28] and (if it is a public company) under section 264(1) to confirm that a distribution will not reduce the amount of the company's net assets below the aggregate of its called-up share capital plus its

---

[27] However, if the full report is unqualified it must not be published with non-statutory accounts.
[28] *Post*, Chap. 22.

undistributable reserves, reference must be made to certain items in the company's *relevant accounts*. Under section 270(3) such accounts will normally be the company's latest audited financial statements laid before the company in general meeting, but where necessary interim accounts or initial accounts must be prepared — the former in the case where a distribution would exceed the amount distributable according to the latest audited financial statements, and the latter where a company proposes to make a distribution during its first accounting reference period or before the date on which it lays its first audited financial statements before the shareholders (section 270(4)).

Even private companies are requried to prepare interim or initial accounts, where appropriate, to enable directors to make a reasonable judgment as to the profits available for distribution. But, in addition, public companies must ensure that certain requirements are met with respect to thé relevant accounts (section 270(5)). With respect to the auditors, the annual accounts (where used as the relevant accounts) must be accompanied by the auditors' report required under section 235 (section 271(3)); while any initial accounts, where used, must be accompanied by a report of the auditors in which they state whether in their opinion they have been properly prepared (section 273(4)). Interim accounts, where used, need not be subjected to an audit. With regard to the annual or initial accounts, where the auditors' report is qualified, it must be stated in writing whether the qualification is material in determining the legality of the proposed distribution (sections 271(3), (4); 273(4), (5)).

In the case where the annual accounts are used as the relevant accounts, the statement will be laid before the shareholders in general meeting; whereas in the case where the initial accounts are used as the relevant accounts, the statement together with the accounts and audit report will merely have to be filed with the Registrar of Companies. It should be noted, incidentally, that a material qualification in this context can be either favourable or unfavourable in terms of the proposed distribution.

The professional accountancy bodies have in the past offered guidance in relation to the realised profits of an insurance company with long term business covered by section 268 of the Act (*e.g.* a life insurance company). In such circumstances the amount of distributable profits is effectively determined by an actuarial valuation.

## (F)  ACCOUNTANTS' REPORTS FOR CREDITORS

As mentioned above, the audit report is addressed to members of the company (*i.e.* its shareholders), for whose benefit indeed the statutory accounts are basically prepared. It is therefore the case that, except in specific circumstances where they are with the auditors' knowledge referring to the accounts and the auditors' report for a specific purpose (see *post*, pages 589–590), third parties cannot rely on them in helping to reach a particular decision. As was made clear in an investigation into the affairs of an Australian company,[29] this is even true of creditors, including debenture stock holders. It may therefore be necessary for such parties, with the company's approval, to commission their own audit (if necessary by different accountants from those employed by the company to undertake the statutory audit), and guidance on how such a second audit should be undertaken and the form of a report in such circumstances is given in an APC Audit Brief on "Reports to debenture and loan stock trustees".

## (G)  ACCOUNTANTS' REPORTS TO MANAGEMENT

A company's statutory auditors may similarly undertake specific investigations which exceed their responsibilities in respect of a company's statutory accounts and their report on them to the shareholders under section 235 — for example, with respect to the records, systems and internal control that have been examined in the course of the statutory audit. In such circumstances, the letters of engagement should clearly specify the extent of such supplementary investigations.

## (H)  REPORTS FOR PROSPECTUSES AND ON BID FORECASTS

Accountants will also be commissioned to write reports in connection with the issue of listing particulars or a prospectus (see chapter 7, *ante*), and professional guidance notes on the conduct of such investigations have been issued.

## (I)  SPECIAL REPORTS REQUIRED UNDER THE COMPANIES ACTS

Special reports are also required from auditors under company legislation in the following circumstances:

---

[29] See Stamp, E. "The Reid Murray Affair", *Accountancy* (August 1964).

*Companies
Act 1985*

- Re-registration of a private company as a
  public company . . . . . . . . s. 43(b)
- Allotment of shares by a public company
  otherwise than for cash . . . . . s. 103(1)
- Transfer of non-cash assets to a public company by a member of the company . . s. 104(4)(b)
- Redemption or purchase by a private company of its own shares out of capital . . s. 173(5)
- Financial assistance for acquisition of a
  private company's own shares . . . s. 156(4)

The nature and form of these reports is fully discussed in the
APC's Guideline, *Reports by auditors under company legislation
in the United Kingdom*, June 1989.

(J) AGREED VALUATIONS OF PRIVATE COMPANIES

As explained in chapter 13, articles of private companies often
provide that a member who wants to sell his shares must first
offer them to the existing members at a price to be fixed by the
auditors. Similar provisions are often applicable in the case of a
member's death. In such circumstances case law has established
grounds under which the valuation can be set aside and/or the
auditors may be liable in negligence.

(K) PRELIMINARY ANNOUNCEMENTS

From 1993 the *Listing Rules* of the London Stock Exchange
require that preliminary announcements of quoted companies'
annual results should be agreed with their auditors. The professional bodies have therefore issued guidelines for auditors dealing
with this matter.

## POWERS OF AUDITORS

(A) RIGHTS TO INSPECT BOOKS AND RECEIVE EXPLANATIONS

The auditors have a right of access at all times to the books and
accounts and vouchers of the company, and they are entitled to

require from the officers of the company such information and explanations as they think necessary for the performance of their duties as auditors (section 389A(1)). (This power is in part necessary to enable them to obtain particulars of the directors' emoluments, including expenses charged to tax and benefits in kind,[30] which may not be ascertainable from an examination of the books.)

The auditors cannot require the information to be furnished in any particular form or that it should be certified in some way, *e.g.* as by the board of directors. There is no power to require the information to be supplied in writing, but auditors can reasonably say that they are not in a position to perform their duties without making further inquiries if they are asked to act on unrecorded oral statements. If proper information is not given, the auditors' remedy is to qualify their report.

If an officer of the company makes a statement to the auditors which purports to convey any information or explanation which they are entitled to require, and it is misleading, false or deceptive in a material particular, he is guilty of an offence and liable on conviction to imprisonment or a fine or both.

(B)  RIGHTS TO ATTEND GENERAL MEETINGS

Auditors have the right to attend any general meeting of the company and to receive the same notices of general meetings as the members, and to be heard at any general meeting on any part of the business which concerns them as auditors.

Where for a private company those entitled to attend and vote at a meeting agree under section 381A a resolution in writing without holding a meeting, the auditors are entitled to receive all relevant communications and (under section 381B(2)) shall give notice within seven days if in their opinion the matter should be considered by the company in general meeting. They then have the right to attend such a meeting and be heard on matters which concern them as auditors (section 390 of the Companies Act 1985).

[30] *Ante.*

(c) RELIANCE ON THE WORK OF SUBSIDIARY COMPANIES' AUDITORS

The APB has published an auditing standard concerning the reliance than can be placed on the work of other auditors in respect of group financial statements.[31]

The consolidation of an overseas subsidiary's accounts may necessitate a formal qualification in the auditors' report. This can arise if in order to comply with the accounting requirements of the country in which it is registered, the subsidiary's financial statements have been prepared using accounting principles and conventions which are unacceptable in Great Britain. This is sometimes the case with U.S. subsidiaries which for tax purposes use the LIFO system to determine the cost of stocks.

British subsidiaries and their auditors are required to give the parent company's auditors relevant information and explanations, in default of which they will be liable to a fine and possible criminal proceedings. Parent companies are equally required to obtain relevant information and explanations from overseas subsidiaries for the benefit of their auditors (section 389A of the Companies Act 1985).

## Duties of Auditors

**General duties**

The duties of auditors depend on the terms of the articles as well as on the statutory provisions. However, Table A no longer gives any guidance on this point. Prior to the 1985 Act an article provided that auditors' duties should be regulated in accordance with what are now substantially sections 235, 237 and 389A–394A (excluding 390B and 393); and Schedule 8, paragraph 24.

The auditors' duties may be summarised as follows:

(1) They must acquaint themselves with their duties under the articles and the Act.[32]

(2) They must carry out their duties with respect to the auditors' report as outlined above. In addition, they must ascertain and state the true financial position of the

---

[31] For a survey of current practice in this area, see Moizer P., Turley, S. and Walker, D., "Reliance on Other Auditors: A U.K. Study", *Accounting and Business Research* (1986).

[32] *Re Republic of Bolivia Exploration Syndicate Ltd* [1914] 1 Ch. 139.

# 584    AUDITORS

company by an examination of the books. This examination must be not merely to ascertain what the books
show, but also to ascertain that the books show the true
financial position.[33]

This is exemplified in the following judgements:

"The duty of the auditor . . . [is] . . . not to confine himself
merely to the task of verifying the arithmetical accuracy of the
balance sheet, but to inquire into its substantial accuracy, and
to ascertain that it . . . was properly drawn up, so as to
contain a true and correct representation of the state of the
company's affairs": *per* Stirling J. in *Leeds Estate Co. v.
Shepherd* (1887) 36 Ch.D. 787 at p. 802.

An auditor "is not to be written off as a professional 'adder-
upper and subtractor'. His vital task is to take care to see that
errors are not made, be they errors of computation, or errors
of omission or commission, or downright untruths. To perform this task properly he must come to it with an inquiring
mind — not suspicious of dishonesty, I agree — but suspecting that someone may have made a mistake somewhere and
that a check must be made to ensure that there has been
none": *per* Lord Denning in *Fomento (Sterling Area) Ltd v.
Selsdon Fountain Pen Co. Ltd* [1958] 1 W.L.R. 45 (H.L.) at
p. 61.

The statutory duty of an auditor (*e.g.* to state whether in
his opinion a true and fair view is given by the balance
sheet and the profit and loss account) is a personal one,
and if he adopts the opinion of the company's accountant,
and he is sued by the company for wrongly stating that a
true and fair view is given, it has been held in Australia
that he has no cause of action against the accountant.[34]

(3) They must act honestly, and with reasonable care and
skill, as the following observations make clear:

"An auditor is not bound to be a detective, or . . . to
approach his work . . . with a foregone conclusion that there
is something wrong. He is a watchdog, but not a bloodhound.

---

[33] *Per* Lindley L.J. in *Re London and General Bank (No. 2)* [1895] 2 Ch. 673
(C.A.) at p. 682 *et seq.*
[34] *Dominion Freeholders Ltd v. Aird* [1966] 2 N.S.W.R. 293 (C.A.), distinguishing *Hedley Byrne & Co. Ltd v. Heller & Partners Ltd.* [1964] A.C. 465.

He is justified in believing tried servants of the company in whom confidence is placed by the company. He is entitled to assume that they are honest, and to rely on their representations, provided he takes reasonable care. If there is anything calculated to excite suspicion he should probe it to the bottom; but in the absence of anything of that kind he is only bound to be reasonably cautious and careful": *per* Lopes L.J. in *Re Kingston Cotton Mill Co. (No. 2)* [1896] 2 Ch. 279 (C.A.) at p. 288.

"It is the duty of an auditor to bring to bear on the work he has to perform that skill, care and caution which a reasonably competent, careful, and cautious auditor would use. What is reasonable skill, care and caution must depend on the particular circumstances of each case. An auditor . . . is not bound to do more than exercise reasonable care and skill in making inquiries. . . . He is not an insurer; he does not guarantee that the books do correctly show the true position of the company's affairs: . . . he must be honest — *i.e.* he must not certify what he does not believe to be true, and he must take reasonable care and skill before he believes that what he certifies is true. . . . Where there is nothing to excite suspicion very little inquiry will be reasonably sufficient. . . . Where suspicion is aroused more care is obviously necessary; but, still, an auditor is not bound to exercise more than reasonable care and skill, even in a case of suspicion . . .": *per* Lindley L J. in Re *London and General Bank (No. 2)* [1895] 2 Ch. 673 (C.A.) at p. 683.

If directors do not allow auditors time to conduct such investigations as are necessary in order to make the statements required to be contained in their report, the auditors must either refuse to make a report or make an appropriately qualified report. They are not justified in making a report containing a statement the truth of which they have not had an opportunity of ascertaining.[35]

Auditors cannot be relieved from liability for any breach of duty by any provision in the articles or any contract (section 310 of the Companies Act 1985), but in certain circumstances they may obtain relief from the court (section 727).[36]

In England the auditors can plead the Limitation Act after six years.[37]

---

[35] *Per* Pennycuick, J. in *Re Thomas Gerrard, ante,* at p. 477.
[36] *Ante,* pp. 414–416.
[37] *Leeds Estate Co. v. Shepherd* (1887) 36 Ch.D. 787.

## Specific duties

(A) GROUNDS FOR SUSPICION

It may be that entries in or omissions from the books ought to make the auditors suspicious. In such a case they must make full investigation into the suspicious circumstances, but they are not liable for "not tracking out ingenious and carefully laid schemes of fraud when there is nothing to arouse their suspicion".[38]

> B. was the managing director of the company and the senior partner of E. & Co., stockbrokers. E. & Co. owed £250,000 to the company, but on February 27, just before the close of the financial year, E. & Co. bought Treasury Bills for £200,000 and credited the company with them, thus reducing their debt to £50,000. The company's balance sheet accordingly showed an investment in Treasury Bills for £200,000 and a debt from E. & Co. for £50,000. On March 3, after the close of the financial year, E. & Co. sold the Treasury Bills and became debtors again for £250,000. This was done for three successive years. *Held*, although the transactions, when isolated, should have led the auditors to conslude that fraud had taken place, yet as they formed only one item in a large audit, there was no negligence on the part of the auditors: *Re City Equitable Fire Insurance Co. Ltd* [1925] Ch. 407 (C.A.).

(B) UNAUTHORISED BORROWING

If payments are made or sums borrowed by the company, the auditors should see that they are authorised and made in accordance with the articles and the Act.[39]

> "When it is [shown] that audited balance sheets do not [show] the true financial condition of the company and that damage had resulted, the onus is on the auditors to show that this is not the result of any breach of duty on their part": *per* Astbury J. in *Re Republic of Bolivia Exploration Syndicate Ltd* [1914] 1 Ch. 139 at p. 171.

(C) EXISTENCE OF SECURITIES

Auditors must satisfy themselves that securities owned by a company in fact exist and are in safe custody. This duty is discharged by their making a personal inspection of the securities

---

[38] *Per* Lopes L.J. in *Re Kingston Cotton Mill Co. (No. 2)* [1896] 2 Ch. 279 (C.A.) at p. 290.

[39] See *Thomas v. Devonport Corpn.* [1900] 1 Q.B. 16 (C.A.).

in question. If, however, the securities are in the possession of a person who in the ordinary course of his business keeps securities for his customers (*e.g.* bankers) and that person is regarded as trustworthy, the auditors may safely accept his certificate that the securities are in his custody.

> The auditor accepted the certificate of the company's stockbrokers that they held securities on the company's behalf. In fact they did not hold the securities and the company suffered heavy loss. *Held*, by Romer J., the auditor was negligent, as he should have inspected the securities and either insisted on their being put in proper custody or reported the matter to the shareholders[40]: *Re City Equitable Fire Insurance Co. Ltd* [1925] Ch. 407.

(D)   EXISTENCE OF CASH BALANCES

Auditors must check the cash in hand and also the balance at the bank, by inspecting the pass book (or bank statement) or obtaining a certificate from the bank.[41]

(E)   STOCKS AND WORK-IN-PROGRESS

Auditors are under no duty to take stock,[42] but this is part of the wider question of the auditors' duty as to the value of the assets. However, the auditor must consider the effect of a reservation of title clause, where it exists, particularly where the stocks are unmixed goods (see p. 523).

Auditors are entitled to take the values of stocks and work-in-progress from the manager or other responsible official of the company, unless they have any reason to suppose them inaccurate.

> The auditors accepted the certificate of J., the manager, a person of acknowledged competence and high reputation, as to the value of the stock-in-trade. This was grossly exaggerated, as a result of which dividends were paid out of cpaital. Had the auditors compared the amount of stock at the beginning of the year with the purchases and sales during the year, they would have been put on inquiry, but they did not do so. *Held*, the auditors were not liable, as they were entitled to rely on J.'s certificate in the absence of anything to excite suspicion: *Re Kingston Cotton Mill Co. (No. 2)* [1896] Ch. 279 (C.A.).

---

[40] The Court of Appeal expressed no final opinion on this point. In any event, the articles protected the auditors from liability.
[41] *Fox & Son v. Morrish, Grant & Co.* (1918) 35 T.L.R. 126.
[42] *Re Kingston Cotton Mill Co. (No. 2), ante.*

In *Re Thomas Gerrard & Son Ltd* [1968] Ch. 455 the facts were similar to those in the *Kingston Cotton Mill* case. In the *Gerrard* case the managing director, by altering the dates on invoices, had caused the price payable on purchases of stock made shortly before the end of each accounting period to be included in the outgoings of the succeeding period. On discovering this the auditor nevertheless accepted the explanation of the managing director, whom he believed to be of the highest integrity. Instead he should have examined the supplies' statements and where necessary have communicated with the suppliers. Further, after as far as possible ascertaining the precise facts, he should have informed the board. By not taking these steps he failed in his duty and was liable for *inter alia* the amount of the dividends paid. As Pennycuick J. commented (at p. 475): "The standards of reasonable care and skill are, upon the expert evidence, more exacting today than those which prevailed in 1896".

(F) FIXED ASSETS

The duty of the auditors as to the value to be placed on fixed assets has previously been discussed (pp. 519–522; 525–526). Apart from complying with the requirements of the fourth Schedule to the 1985 Act, if the auditors have formed an opinion that the assets are overvalued, they are bound to report it to the shareholders.

Auditors made a confidential report to the directors, calling their attention to the fact that the security for loans was insufficient, and that there was a difficulty with respect to realisation. They also reported that in their opinion no dividend should be paid for the year. In their report to the shareholders, however, they merely said that the value of the assets was dependent upon realisation. A dividend of seven per cent. was declared out of capital. *Held*, the auditors were guilty of misfeasance and liable to make good the dividend paid: *Re London and General Bank (No. 2)* [1895] 2 Ch. 673 (C.A.).

(G) POLICIES OF THE COMPANY

Auditors are not concerned with the policy of the company or whether the company is well or ill managed.

"It is no part of an auditor's duty to give advice, either to directors or shareholders, as to what they ought to do. An auditor has nothing to do with the prudence or imprudence of making loans with or without security. It is nothing to him whether the business of a company is being conducted prudently or imprudently, profitably or unprofitably. It is nothing to him whether dividends are properly or improperly declared, provided he dischages his own duty to the shareholders. His business is to ascertain and state the true financial position of the company at the time of the audit": *per* Lindley L.J. in *Re London and General Bank (No. 2)* [1895] 2 Ch. 673 (C.A.) at p. 682.

## Liability to third parties

Apart from the auditor's contractual duty of care to the company, he owes a duty of care to third persons with whom he is not in contractual or fiduciary relationship if, as a reasonable man, he knows that he is being trusted or that his skill and judgment are being relied on and he does not make it clear that he accepts no responsibility for information or advice which he gives.[43] For breach of this duty an action for negligence lies if damage results from the negligence.

The scope of this duty was defined originally as follows:

". . . to whom do these professional people owe this duty? I will take accountants, but the same reasoning applies to . . . others. They owe the duty, of course, to their employer or client; and also I think to any third person to whom they themselves show the accounts, or to whom they know their employer is going to show the accounts, so as to induce him to invest money or take some other action on them": per Denning L.J. in *Candler v. Crane, Christmas & Co.* [1951] 2 K.B. 164 (C.A.) at p. 180.

In subsequent cases on professional negligence three principles emerged. Thus in order for a claim by a third party to succeed, the event leading to a loss should be *foreseeable*; there should be *proximity* between the two parties (*i.e.* the third party should not be so remote that his interests would not reasonably have been considered at the time the supposedly negligent statement was made); and the supposedly defective advice had to be given as a normal part of the expert's business.

The question of proximity was left open. Should liability just extend to persons to whom auditors show the accounts and those to whom they knew the company would show them? Or should it also extend to a general class of persons whom the auditors ought reasonably to have foreseen at the time the accounts were prepared might rely on the accounts?

In two cases the latter, broader view of proximity was taken. Thus in *JEB Fasteners Ltd v. Marks, Bloom, & Co.,*[44] the account-

---

[43] *Hedley Byrne & Co. Ltd v. Heller & Partners Ltd* [1964] A.C. 465, disapproving *Candler v. Crane, Christmas & Co.* [1951] 2 K.S. 164 (C.A.). See also *Esso Petroleum Co. Ltd v. Marden* [1976] 2 All E.R. 5 (C.A.) and *Yianni v. Edwin Evans & Sons* [1981] 3 All E.R. 592.

[44] [1981] 3 All E.R. 289, affirmed [1983] 1 All E.R. 583.

ants knew at that time the audit certificate was issued that outside finance was needed by the company. Consequently, they ought to have foreseen that the accounts would be used by someone providing such finance (*e.g.* in the form of a take-over offer) and owed a duty accordingly. Nevertheless, it was held that they would only be liable if reliance on the accounts caused the other person loss. As a result, where for instance the take-over offer would have been made anyway, there would be no liability. A similar view was taken by the court in *Twomax Ltd v. Dickson, McFarlane and Robinson.*[45]

However, this view was rejected in another, landmark case (which also involved a take-over), *Caparo Industries plc v. Dickman.*[46] There in a House of Lords decision, the court preferred the narrow view of proximity as determing liability to third parties. Moreover, in a number of subsequent cases it is the narrow view that has prevailed.

Since then the court has also narrowed the potential third party liability of auditors by addressing the issue of *causation*. Thus in another case involving a take-over, *Galoo Ltd v. Bright, Grahame and Murray,*[47] it was held that negligence was not the dominant cause of the plaintiffs' loss, so consequently their case could not succeed.

What constitutes professional skill and judgment where a reporting accountant or auditor is potentially liable is an interesting point. For instance, it is quite possible — even likely, perhaps — that over time as a result of inflation, the conventional historical cost accounts of many companies might show an upward trend in profits, whereas under current cost accounting principles the trend might instead be downwards. Arguably the conventional accounts could therefore give a misleading impression to an interested party.[48] However, it would seem likely that adherence to generally accepted principles, as codified by the accountancy profession, would provide a reasonable defence in such circumstances — though in view of the jury's attitude in the Royal Mail case in relation to a prospectus, where accounting principles acceptable at that time were properly followed, it is not clear that this would be an adequate defence in a criminal prosecution.[49]

[45] [1982] S.C. 113.
[46] [1990] 2 W.L.R. 358. The case also failed on grounds of foreseeability.
[47] *The Times*, January 14, 1994.
[48] For historical and current cost accounting rules, see pp. 519 *et seq., ante.*
[49] *R. v. Kylsant* [1932] 1 K.B. 442 (C.C.A.): see p. 466. Potential criminal liability for auditors arises under ss. 17–20 of the Theft Act 1968.

# Chapter 22

# DIVIDENDS

## INTRODUCTION

From an ideal economic perspective, a listed company's distribution policy should be determined as part of the overall investment decision taken by its directors, since it should only retain those funds on which it is expected to earn a risk-adjusted return greater than can be earned elsewhere by its shareholders. At one extreme, therefore, a company which has identified many profitable investment projects would make no distributions at all. Shareholders wishing to secure a cash income for a particular year would either be able to sell off part of their holdings in order to realise some of the capital gain that will be reflected in the increasing value of their shares; or they could use the enhanced value as security on which to raise a loan. At the other extreme, a company which has identified no profitable projects to justify reinvestment should logically distribute all its funds, including capital invested in the past.

It can also be demonstrated that even the potential distortions introduced by the differential incidence of taxation can be substantially neutralised in the market, since certain types of investor prefer capital gains, while others will prefer dividend income. (Indeed, even the private investor may find the latter attractive if he is able to offset direct or indirect borrowing costs against such income.)

There are, however, a number of complicating factors. Thus, for instance, listed companies seem to use the time trend of dividends as a signal of future likely prospects—*e.g.* a cut in the proposed distribution may reflect the directors' pessimism; whereas an increase in the dividend may indicate their optimism.[1] In fact, a very large proportion of U.K. equities are held by pension schemes, which can only invest in shares carrying trustee investment status, a condition of which is that dividends must be paid regularly.

[1] For a readable discussion of the economic rationale for dividend payout policies, see Brealey, R. and Myers, S., *Principles of Corporate Finance* (4th. ed.)

Moreover, pension funds seek dividend income because of their tax status. A further matter to consider is that a company will need to expect to be able to offset Advance Corporation Tax (ACT) against its Mainstream Corporation Tax (MCT), otherwise a dividend payment will be expensive.

Likewise, the distribution policy for unlisted companies must take into account the fact that their shares are not readily marketable, and for private companies it may be preferable for tax purposes to distribute profits as directors' fees and salaries. However, for closely held companies (*i.e.* those whose shares are owned or controlled by a small group of persons), revenue law even deems that a certain amount of profits may be treated as distributed to shareholders, regardless of whether or not such dividend payments have been made.

But whatever the economic rationale may be, the law also has to take account of the existence of limited liability. Effectively this means the doctrine of (money) capital maintenance (see chapter 9) must be applied so as to try to ensure a company's resources are not distributed in such a way as to prejudice the interests of unsecured creditors; or, indeed, of one class of security holders at the expense of another. In fact, it is not possible to provide fully effective protection to creditors and others in this way, but the general philosophy of money capital maintenance has nevertheless been behind the development of the law relating to the distribution of dividends as it has evolved over the past 140 years or so, although it is noticeable that in many of the cases around the turn of the century judges went out of their way not to impose unreasonable restrictions which might potentially lead to a misallocation of resources within the economy.[2]

In view of the underlying rationale behind the law in this area, the realised profits test introduced by the Companies Act 1980, and confirmed in sections 263–281 of the 1985 Act (see below), can be viewed as a retrograde step. However, in practice it is unlikely to prove an effective constraint. In the rare cases in which companies might wish to distribute more than their accumulated realised profits, they could always convert unrealised gains into realised income by selling off assets (and, if necessary, buying or leasing them back); purchase their own

[2] See French, E.A., "The Evolution of the Dividend Law of England", *Studies in Accounting* eds. Baxter, W.T., and Davidson, S. (3rd. ed., 1977), pp. 306–331.

shares under section 162 (see chapter 10); or, as has happened on a number of occasions in recent years, apply to the court for a reduction of capital under section 135.

## THE NATURE OF A DIVIDEND

Technically a dividend is the share, received by a shareholder, of the company's profits legally available for dividend and divided among the members. Commercial companies are formed to earn profits for the shareholders out of which dividends can be paid,[3] and no express power to pay dividends is required in the memorandum or the articles. However, under section 281, provisions in the articles or memorandum may restrict either the amounts available for distribution or the circumstances in which a distribution may be made.

Sections 263(3) and 270(2) of the 1985 Act state that dividends must only be paid out of accumulated realised profits as reported in the statutory accounts.

Dividends must be distinguished from interest. Interest is a debt which, like all debts, is payable out of the company's assets generally. A dividend, however, is not a debt until it has been declared by the company, and dividends cannot be declared for payment out of the assets generally; they can be declared for payment only out of assets equivalent to the profits available for the purpose.

## PROFITS AVAILABLE FOR DIVIDEND

As mentioned above and in the discussion in chapter 9, it is a fundamental principle of company law that a company's sub-scribed money capital (*i.e.* issued share capital plus share premium) be maintained. Paid-up capital must not be paid to the shareholders except by leave of the court or under strictly defined circumstances. It must be spent only upon the objects defined in the memorandum. Any other expenditure is *ultra vires* and reduces the fund available for the company's creditors in satisfaction of their claims.[4]

---

[3] Under s.30(3)(b)(ii) of the 1985 Act, a company may be prohibited from paying a dividend.

[4] See, *per* Jessel M.R., in *Flitcroft's Case* (1882) 21 Ch.D. 519 (C.A.) at p. 533. However, in *Quayle Munro Limited Partners* 1991 G.W.D. 35-2104, the Court approved a scheme for the cancellation of a company's share premium account which had the effect of converting the account into "distributable profits".

W. guaranteed the preference dividends for three years and the company agreed to repay to W. on demand any sums paid by him under the guarantee. *Held*, the company's agreement was *ultra vires* and void, as it might involve capital being reduced otherwise than by expenditure on the company's objects: *Re Walters' Deed of Guarantee* [1933] Ch. 321.

The principle that a company's subscribed money capital must be maintained requires that a dividend[5] declared by a company should not be paid except out of accumulated realised profits. Prior to the 1980 Companies Act there were no statutory provisions governing the funds available for distribution to the shareholders as dividend. In the meantime, the courts for the most part took the view that they should not in general interfere in the business decision-making process unless there were good grounds for believing that the rights of certain interested parties were prejudiced. Unfortunately the decisions in a number of cases were nevertheless regarded by many accountants and lawyers as determining specific rules for distinguishing between on the one hand income, which could be applied for distributions, and on the other capital, which could not.

Hardly surprisingly, given that they resulted from the peculiar circumstances of each case, these rules proved difficult to interpret.[6] In the circumstances, accountants tended to follow a conservative interpretation of the law and for the most part took the view that only accumulated realised profits should be regarded as available for distribution. The Jenkins Committee made several recommendations which would clarify the position by providing a statutory code to this effect.[7] These were eventually given effect, together with the requirements of the EU's Second Council Directive on company law harmonisation, as sections 39–45 of the 1980 Companies Act, which have substantially become sections 263–281 of the 1985 Act. But apart from including provisions requiring that the fund from which distributions can be made should be the accumulated *realised* profits of a

---

[5] In money or kind: *post*, p. 608.

[6] *e.g.* the "rules" that before 1980 in England it was neither necessary to charge depreciation nor to make good past trading losses when determining distributable profits. In fact, the judgments in the main supporting cases (*Lee v. Neuchatel Asphalte Co.* (1889) 41 Ch.D. 1 (C.A.), and *Ammonia Soda Co. v. Chamberlain* (1918) 1 Ch. 266 (C.A.) respectively) seem to have been very much dependent on the particular circumstances of the cases. For a general discussion of this point, see French, *op. cit.*

[7] (1962) Cmnd. 1749, paras. 335–350.

company, the 1980 Act also provided that these should be those shown in its statutory accounts. This requirement effectively determines that a company's statutory accounts should therefore only report realised profits as income, even though it might well be that to reflect properly the directors' performance to a company's shareholders the profit figure reported in the financial statements should include unrealised gains.

Under section 263(2) of the 1985 Act, the rules apply to all *distributions* made by a company. A distribution is defined there as any payment of a company's assets to members of the company except:

(a)  an issue of bonus shares[8];
(b)  the redemption or purchase by a company of its own shares[9];
(c)  an authorised reduction of capital under section 135[10];
(d)  distributions on a winding-up.

Moreover, under section 263(1) such *distributions* may only be made out of the profits available for that purpose. In fact, there are two tests to ascertain such profits. The first, the *realised profits test*, applies to all companies; the second, the *net assets test*, only to public companies.

It should be noted that, with regard to a group, it is only the accumulated realised profits of the holding company that are available for distribution to shareholders of that company. Profits of a subsidiary can be transferred to the holding company by declaration of dividends by that subsidiary. However, any part of such revenue receivable by the holding company cannot be regarded by it as available for distribution to its shareholders if it represents a return of part of the purchase price shown in the accounts as being the consideration paid for the subsidiary. Under the acquisition method of consolidating the group accounts, this effectively means that only the subsidiary's post-acquisiton profits may be transferred for distribution, but under the merger method (where it is available—see pages 166–167 and chapter 20), all or some of the pre-acquisition profits may also be transferred for this purpose, depending respectively on whether

---

[8] *Post*, pp. 609 *et seq.*
[9] *Ante*, Chap. 10.
[10] *Ante*, Chap. 9.

the nominal value of shares issued by the holding company is less than or equal to the nominal value of the subsidiary company's shares acquired; or whether the nominal value of the shares issued is greater than the par value of shares acquired.

## THE REALISED PROFITS TEST

A company's profits available for distribution are its accumulated realised profits (so far as not already distributed or capitalised[11]) less its accumulated realised losses (so far as not already written off by a proper reduction of capital) (section 263(3)). There is no attempt to distinguish between income and capital profits or losses—the only criterion is whether they are *realised*. Unrealised profits, *e.g.* on a revaluation upwards of an asset in the accounts which produces a gain, cannot be used: the gain must be realised, *i.e.* the asset must effectively be sold at arm's length.

Prior to 1980 a decision in a Scottish case[12] was in line with this principle, but one in a case in England was not.[13] Similarly under the provisions of the 1985 Act, realised losses (*e.g.* previous trading losses) must be deducted before a dividend can be declared—again in line with the decision in a Scottish case,[14] but not with that in an English one.[15] Unrealised profits cannot be used to pay up debentures or any amounts unpaid on issued shares (section 263(4)).

The notion of what is and is not a *realised* profit is specifically referred to in section 263(3) and defined in section 262(3) in the following terms:

> "references to 'realised profits' and 'realised losses' . . . are to such profits or losses . . . as fall to be treated as realised profits, in accordance with principles generally accepted, at the time when the accounts are prepared, with respect to the determination for accounting purposes of realised profits or losses."

This is hardly illuminating, and the few cases in tax law dealing with the question of realisation are not necessarily relevant in this context. Given that the notion of what is and is not a realised

---

[11] *Post*, p. 609.
[12] *Westburn Sugar Refineries Ltd v. Inland Revenue* (1960) S.L.T. 297.
[13] *Dimbula Valley (Ceylon) Tea Co. Ltd v. Laurie* (1961) Ch. 353, 373.
[14] *Niddrie etc. Coal Co. Ltd v. Hurll* (1891) 18 R. 805.
[15] *Ammonia Soda Co. Ltd v. Chamberlain* (1918) 1 Ch. 266 (C.A.).

profit is a subtle one, which has caused some controversy amongst accountants, the professional accountancy bodies in the British Isles issued two technical releases in September 1982 to offer guidance on the issue. The first[16] reached three conclusions:

(i) Accounting standards[17] would constitute evidence of generally accepted accounting principles, and the profits calculated applying such standards should in general be regarded as "realised profits", even where the usual criteria for establishing "realisation" (such as receipt of cash, or the creation of a contractual obligation to pay a specific sum of money) are not met. This would mean, for instance, that the procedure of gradually recognising profits on long term contracts established in SSAP 9 (see *ante*, p. 524), and the inclusion in the profit and loss account of foreign currency translation gains and losses on net monetary items, where required by SSAP 20, would both give rise to "realised profits".

(ii) Where no accounting standard is applicable, a profit can be regarded as "realised" where the policy followed is consistent with the accruals concept and prudence doctrine outlined in SSAP 2 and Schedule 4 to the Act.

(iii) Where necessary a company must, in order for its accounts to show a true and fair view of its financial performance and position, depart from accepted accounting principles and include an unrealised profit in its income statement. However, where this is done, paragraph 15 of Schedule 4 requires that a note should be given with the accounts indicating the nature of the departure, the reasons for it, and the effect.

The second technical release[18] noted that accumulated profits and losses shown in the accounts may in fact differ from those available for distribution for a number of reasons (*e.g.* the application of the net assets test to the accounts of public

---

[16] TR 481: "The determination of realised profits and the disclosure of distributable profits in the context of the Companies Acts 1948 to 1981".

[17] The status of accounting standards has been examined in terms of clarifying the meaning of the phrase "a true and fair view" in the case of *Lloyd Cheyham and Co. Ltd v. Littlejohn and Co.* [1986] PCC 389: see pp. 487 and 516, *et seq.*

[18] TR 482: "The determination of distributable profits in the context of the Companies Acts 1948 to 1981".

companies, discussed below). The statement concludes that, in order to show a true and fair view, a material difference between reported and distributable profits should be disclosed in notes to the accounts.

Apart from these general considerations, realised profits and losses are, under section 280(3), all profits and losses, whether revenue (*i.e.* income) or capital, which are deemed to have been realised. It follows that when a company sells an undepreciated fixed asset (such as freehold land) which has been revalued in the accounts for consideration above its original cost, and the revaluation has been credited direct to reserves, the relevant part of the revaluation reserve has to be regarded as realised profit, even though it has never been credited to the profit and loss account.

Similar considerations relate to wasting fixed assets, although the provisions are more complex. Thus section 275 refers specifically to the question of depreciation provisions for such assets. Section 275(1) indicates that charges made to create or increase a depreciation provision in any one year are to be treated as realised losses, but under section 275(2) any additional depreciation charges made against an upward revaluation of the cost new of a similar asset do not have to be so treated, even though they will be reflected in the lower reported profit figure.

In applying this latter provision, when there is no record of the original cost of an asset, or it cannot be obtained without unreasonable expense or delay, the calculations of any loss or gain in respect of that asset may be based on the earliest available record of its value since its acquisition by the company (section 275(3)). However, under section 275(1) a provision for a loss in value of one fixed asset cannot be offset against revaluation gains on other fixed assets unless *all* the company's fixed assets are revalued at the same time. For this purpose the revaluation of all the company's fixed assets may exclude goodwill. Moreover, under section 275(4), (5) the valuation does not have to be formal: it is sufficient that the directors are satisfied, after *considering* the value of a fixed asset against the value of all the company's fixed assets; and that the aggregate value is not less than the aggregate value at which such fixed assets are stated in the accounts. But where the directors take advantage of such a procedure, they must disclose in the notes to the accounts:

(i) that they have considered the value of some of the company's fixed assets, without actually revaluing those assets;

(ii) that they are satisfied that the aggregate value of the fixed assets whose value has been considered is not less than their value as stated in the accounts; and

(iii) that the asset that has diminished in value is recorded in the accounts after providing for that decline in value (section 275(6)).

With regard to development costs, section 269 specifically requires that where they are capitalised and shown as assets in a company's accounts, they should nevertheless be treated as a realised loss for the purpose of calculating distributable profits, unless there are special circumstances, and the note required by paragraph 20 of Schedule 4 gives the reasons for treating such an item as an asset.

Under section 263(5), where a company's directors are unable to determine whether a profit or loss made before December 22, 1980, is realised or unrealised, they may treat the profit as realised and the loss as unrealised.

Finally, when a company makes a distribution of a non-cash asset (*e.g.* part of its undertaking on a de-merger) any element of unrealised profits (*e.g.* on a revaluation) represented by those assets may be regarded as a realised profit (section 276). However, to make such a distribution the company has to be so empowered by its articles. (Table A contains such a power in article 105: see below, page 608.) Moreover, the value attributed to the asset that is being distributed will have to be a fair value— *i.e.* generally its open market value in a transaction at arm's length.

## THE NET ASSETS TEST

The realised profits test applies to all companies. A public company, however, is subject to a second, net assets, test. This means that even if it has profits available under the realised profits test, a public company may only make a distribution if, first, at the time, the amount of its net assets is not less than the aggregate of its called-up share capital and its undistributable reserves; and, second, the amount of the proposed distribution will not lower the amount of those assets to less than that aggregate (section 264(1)).

The effect of the second test is that whereas a private company can make a distribution provided only that it has sufficient realised profits available, a public company can do so only if it has sufficient profits available after it has provided for any net unrealised losses.

## Net assets

A public company's net assets for this purpose are the aggregate of its assets less the aggregate of its liabilities, including any provision for liabilities or charges in the accounts (section 264(2)). Uncalled share capital[19] may not, however, be used as an asset for this purpose (section 264(4)).

## Called-up share capital and undistributable reserves

The net assets must be measured against the called-up share capital and undistributable reserves of the company. The called up share capital is the aggregate amount of the calls made on its shares, whether or not they have been paid; any amount paid without being called; and any instalments due on the shares.[20] It is therefore more than the amount necessarily received by the company (section 737).

The undistributable reserves are those set out in section 264(3) of the 1985 Act:

(a)   the share premium account[21];
(b)   the capital redemption reserve[22];
(c)   the excess of its accumulated unrealised profits over its accumulated unrealised losses, in as much as they have not previously been capitalised or written off, the only exception being a capitalisation resulting from a transfer of profits to capital redemption reserve on or after December 22, 1980; and
(d)   any other reserve which cannot be distributed either by law (*e.g.* a revaluation reserve created under the alternative accounting rules (Schedule 4, paragraph 34))[23] or by the company's memorandum and articles.

---

[19] *Ante*, p. 156.
[20] *Ante*, p. 156.
[21] *Ante*, pp. 164 *et seq.*
[22] *Ante*, p. 191.
[23] *Ante*, Chap. 20.

## INVESTMENT AND INSURANCE COMPANIES

It would be inappropriate to apply the rules outlined above to certain types of company, and this is recognised in sections 265–268 of the 1985 Act, which relate to investment companies and insurance companies with long-term (generally life assurance) business. Thus in the case of the former, it might well be that the value of the portfolio of an investment company may have fallen and be below the aggregate of its called-up share capital and undistributable reserves, yet still be well in excess of its liabilities to third parties. In such circumstances the Act provides alternative rules for determining distributable profits to the two generally available to public companies described above.

With regard to insurance companies, the natural time horizon of long-term insurance business stretches over a period of anything up to 40 years rather than 12 months. The appropriate procedure to determine the actuarial surplus is to apply compound interest to discount projected streams of premium and investment income to a present value, and to deduct from that figure the corresponding discounted present value of projected payments to meet anticipated claims. The increase in the surplus year-on-year is then the "profit".

### Investment companies

A company which qualifies under section 266 as an investment company (see *ante*, p. 548) can take advantage of the alternative test for assessing profits available for distribution outlined in section 265(1) and described below, but it must also satisfy the following conditions:

(a) its shares must be listed on a recognised stock exchange (section 265(4)(a));

(b) during the previous accounting reference period the company must not have distributed any of its capital profits, nor must it have applied any unrealised profits or any capital profits in paying up debentures or amounts unpaid on its issued shares (section 265(4)(a), (5)); and

(c) it must have given the necessary notice to the Registrar to qualify as an investment company under section 266 (section 265(6)).

Where these conditions are met, the alternative test of distributable profits prescribed under section 265(1) may be applied. This involves a realised profits test which, however, only applies to revenue and not to capital profits or losses; capital profits are thus excluded from the funds available for distribution. Moreover, for this purpose accumulated realised revenue profits are calculated as realised revenue profits less realised and unrealised revenue losses. The corresponding net assets test requires that the value of the assets must be at least one and a half times the aggregate of the company's liabilities (including provisions) both before and after the proposed distribution. However, where a distribution by an investment company reduces the amount of its net assets below the aggregate of its called-up share capital and distributable reserves, this fact must be disclosed in the notes to its financial statements (Schedule 4, paragraph 72(1)).[24]

Under section 267 the Secretary of State may extend and modify by statutory instruments the provisions of sections 265–266 to companies whose principal business consists of investing in portfolios of securities, land and other assets with the objective of managing such portfolios and spreading risk for the benefit of the shareholders.

## Insurance companies

For an insurance company which qualifies as such under the provisions of the Insurance Companies Act 1982, and which carries on long-term business, the profits and losses to be used in applying the general realised profits test described above on pages 596–599 are to be the result of amounts properly transferred to the profit and loss account of the company from surpluses or deficits on actuarial valuations. Moreover, any other profits or losses included in the company's profit and loss accounts are to be left out of account in applying the realised profits test (section 268).

## RELEVANT ACCOUNTS

In deciding whether a company has distributable profits, reference must be made to its accounts. Moreover, in assessing whether a proposed dividend can properly be made, its effect on such accounts must be evaluated. For this purpose, where

[24] *Ante*, Chap. 20.

successive distributions are to be made by reference to one set of accounts, the amounts of the distributions, paid and proposed, must be accumulated (section 274). Under section 270(2) the items to be referred to in the relevant accounts are:

(a) profits, losses and liabilities;
(b) provisions (including those for depreciation); and
(c) share capital and reserves (including undistributable reserves).

Section 270(3), (4) of the Act identifies the relevant accounts for this purpose. The general rule is that they are the company's *last annual accounts* prepared in respect of the last preceding accounting reference period[25] (section 270(3)). However, in two cases other accounts may be used: first, such accounts as are necessary to enable a reasonable judgment to be made to determine distributable profits—these are referred to as *interim accounts*; and second, if the distribution is proposed during the company's first year before any annual accounts are prepared, such accounts as are necessary for a reasonable judgment to be made. These are referred to as *initial accounts* (section 270(4)).

**Last annual accounts**

The requirement that the last annual accounts must have been properly prepared in all material respects and in accordance with the Companies Act applies to all companies (*i.e.* including banking and insurance companies) (section 271(2)). The auditors must have prepared either an unqualified report[26] on the accounts or, if it is qualified, they must state in writing whether their qualification is relevant to the matter of distributable profits. Finally a copy of any such statement must be laid before the company in general meeting (section 271(3)–(5)).

**Interim accounts**

A public company may only use interim accounts if they have been properly prepared in compliance with the format of accounts set out in section 226[27] and Schedule 4 to the Act in all

---

[25] *Ante*, Chap. 20.
[26] *Ante*, Chap. 21.
[27] *Ante*, Chap. 20. The reference in ss.272(3) and 273(3) is only to s.226, relating to individual company accounts, and not to s.229, relating to group accounts, since only the holding company and not the group can declare dividends.

material respects and have been signed by the directors as required under section 233 (section 272(2), (3)). A copy must be sent to the Registrar with a certified English translation if appropriate (section 272(4), (5)). Section 272 does not apply to private companies, which may therefore use any interim accounts.

## Initial accounts

A public company may only use initial accounts if they have been properly prepared in compliance with the format of accounts set out in section 226[27a] and Schedule 4 to the Act in all material respects and have been signed by the directors as required under section 233 (section 273(2), (3)). Further, there must be an auditors' report that the accounts have been so prepared and which is either unqualified, or, if qualified, accompanied by a statement that the qualification is irrelevant to the question of distributable profits (section 273(4), (5)). A copy of the accounts and the auditors' report must be sent to the Registrar with a certified English translation if appropriate (section 273(6), (7)). Section 273 does not apply to private companies, which may therefore use any initial accounts.

## Banking and insurance companies

The rules under sections 274–275 relating to distributions are modified for banking and insurance companies (in particular with respect to relevant accounts) by section 279 and Schedule 11.

## The consequences of an unlawful distribution

Under section 270(5), a breach of the requirements of sections 270–273 relating to the relevant accounts for determining distributable profits constitutes a breach of the test of distributability. Moreover, shareholders cannot agree to waive these requirements.[28] Section 277(1) further provides that any share-

---

[27a] *Ante*, Chap. 20. The reference in ss.272(3) and 273(3) is only to s.226, relating to individual company accounts, and not to s.229, relating to group accounts, since only the holding company and not the group can declare dividends.

[28] *Precision Dippings Ltd v. Precision Dippings Marketing Ltd* [1985] BCLC 385 (C.A.).

holder who receives a distribution which he knows, or has reasonable grounds to believe, has been paid in breach of the 1985 Act rules, must repay that amount to the company. This is expressly made in addition to the shareholders' existing liabilities set out below, but it does not apply in relation either to financial assistance given by a company to a person to help him purchase its shares in contravention of section 151, or to any payment made by a company in respect of the redemption or purchase by the company of shares in itself (sections 277(2)).

With regard to payments of dividends out of capital, it was established prior to the 1980 Act that directors who are knowingly parties to such payments are jointly and severally liable to the company to replace the amounts of dividends so paid, with interest, and ratification is impossible so as to bind the company.[29] In such a case they are entitled to be indemnified by each shareholder who received dividends, knowing them to be paid out of capital, to the extent of the dividends received.[30] A shareholder who has knowingly received a dividend paid out of capital cannot individually, or on behalf of the company, maintain an action against the directors to replace the dividends so paid, at any rate until he has repaid the money he has received.[31]

## PAYMENT OF DIVIDENDS

Dividends are paid in the manner laid down in the articles. Table A, article 102, provides:

> "Subject to the provisions of the Act, the company may by ordinary resolution declare dividends in accordance with the respective rights of the members, but no dividend shall exceed the amount recommended by the directors."

This relates to the final dividend, declared at the annual general meeting. As to an interim dividend, which is a dividend paid on some date between two annual general meetings of the company,[32] article 103 provides:

---

[29] *e.g.* where debts known to be bad were entered as assets in reports and balance sheets, so that an apparent profit was shown, and the shareholders, relying on these documents, declared dividends: *Flitcroft's Case* (1882) 21 Ch.D. 519 (C.A.). See also *Liquidators of City of Glasgow Bank v. Mackinnon* (1881) 9 R. 535.

[30] *Moxham v. Grant* [1900] 1 Q.B. 88 (C.A.).

[31] *Towers v. African Tug Co.* (1904) 1 Ch. 558 (C.A.); *Liquidators of City of Glasgow Bank v. Mackinnon* (1881) 9 R. 535.

[32] *Per* P.O. Lawrence J. in *Re Jowitt* [1922] 2 Ch. 442, at p. 447.

"Subject to the provisions of the Act, the directors may pay interim dividends if it appears to them that they are justified by the profits of the company available for distribution. If the share capital is divided into different classes, the directors may pay interim dividends on shares which confer deferred or non-preferred rights with regard to dividend as well as on shares which confer preferential rights with regard to dividend, but no interim dividend shall be paid on shares carrying deferred or non-preferred rights if, at the time of payment, any preferential dividend is in arrears. The directors may also pay at intervals settled by them any dividend payable at a fixed rate if it appears to them that the profits available for distribution justify the payment. Provided the directors act in good faith they shall not incur any liability to the holders of shares conferring preferred rights for any loss they may suffer by the lawful payment of an interim dividend on any shares having deferred or non-preferred rights."

Before recommending a dividend, directors should have a complete and detailed list of the company's assets and investments prepared for their information, and they should not rely for a valuation of these items merely on the opinion of the chairman or the auditors.[33]

In the absence of anything to the contrary in the articles,[34] a company cannot be compelled to declare a dividend and no action can be brought for its recovery until it has been declared.[35] In England, the declaration of a dividend creates a simple contract debt due from the company to the shareholder which will be barred in six years from the date of declaration.[36] In Scotland, the period of prescription is five years.[37] However, Table A, article 108, provides that:

"Any dividend which has remained unclaimed for 12 years from the date when it became due for payment shall, if the directors so resolve, be forfeited and cease to remain owing by the company."

When preference shares entitle the holder to receive out of the profits of the company for each year a fixed dividend, the "profits

---

[33] *Per* Romer J. in *Re City Equitable Fire Insce. Co. Ltd* (1925) Ch. 407 at pp. 471, 474.

[34] For articles which were interpreted as requiring the whole profits to be divided, see *Paterson v. R. Paterson & Sons Ltd*, 1917 S.C. (H.L.) 13; 1916 S.C. 452.

[35] *Bond v. Barrow Haematite Steel Co.* [1902] 1 Ch. 353.

[36] *Re Compania de Electricidad de la Provincia de Buenos Aires Ltd* [1978] 3 All E.R. 668. The *Listing Rules* of the London Stock Exchange require that any power taken in the articles of a listed company to forfeit unclaimed dividends should not be exercised until at least 12 years after declaration.

[37] Prescription and Limitation (Scotland) Act 1973, s.6.

of the company" are the profits available for dividend after setting aside such reserves as the directors think fit. If the whole of the profits are transferred to reserve, the preference share-holders are not entitled to any dividend.[38]

More generally, the rights of holders of preference and other special shares must be observed, since infringement of such rights will give aggrieved members the right to apply for an injunction or other relief. Moreover, if dividends are paid infringing such rights, any class of members which suffers will be able to take legal action against the company, while the directors who wrongly paid the dividends will be liable to replace the sum involved.

When the articles (*e.g.* Table A, article 103, above) give the directors power to pay interim dividends, a resolution by the company in general meeting requiring the directors to declare an interim dividend is inoperative.[39]

In English law, unless the articles otherwise provide, dividends are payable to the shareholders in proportion to the nominal amounts of their shares, irrespective of the amounts paid up.[40] Section 119(c), however, permits a company, if so authorised by its articles, to pay a dividend in proportion to the amount paid up on each share where a larger amount is paid up on some shares than on others. Table A, article 104, accordingly provides that:

> "Except as otherwise provided by the rights attached to shares, all dividends shall be declared and paid according to the amounts paid up on shares on which the dividend is paid. All dividends shall be apportioned and paid proportionately to the amounts paid up on shares during any portion or portions of the period in respect of which the dividend is paid; but, if any share is issued on terms providing that it shall rank for dividend as from a particular date, that share shall rank for dividend accordingly."

In Scots law, if articles provide that "the directors may . . . declare a dividend to be paid to the members in proportion to their shares" and define "shares" as shares in the nominal

---

[38] *Re Buenos Ayres Great Southern Ry. Co. Ltd* [1947] Ch. 384; *cf.* the Scottish case *Wemyss Collieries Trust Ltd v. Melville* (1905) 8 F. 143, in which transfer of a sum to reserve was, on an interpretation of the articles, held to be valid, although preference shareholders were thereby deprived of an additional non-cumulative dividend.

[39] *Scott v. Scott* [1943] 1 All E.R. 582.

[40] *Birch v. Cropper* (1889) 14 A.C. 525.

capital, dividends fall to be declared according to the nominal amounts of the shares, irrespective of the amounts paid up.[41] Where, however, there is no provision in the articles as to how dividends are to be paid, the common law principle applicable is that they are payable in proportion to the amounts paid up on the shares.[42]

The articles usually provide (as does Table A, article 106) that dividends payable in cash may be paid by a cheque sent through the post to the registered address of the shareholder, or to such persons and to such address as the shareholder may in writing direct. In the absence of such a provision in the articles, the company will have to issue a fresh dividend cheque to the shareholder should the cheque first sent be lost in the post.[43]

Unless power is given in the articles, dividends declared must be paid in cash, and a shareholder can restrain the company from paying them in any other way.

A company declared a dividend and passed a resolution to pay it by giving to the shareholders debenture bonds bearing interest and redeemable at par, by an annual drawing, over 30 years. The articles empowered the company to declare a dividend "to be paid" to the shareholders. *Held*, the words "to be paid" meant paid in cash, and a shareholder suing on behalf of himself and the other shareholders could restrain the company from acting on the resolution on the ground that it contravened the articles: *Wood v. Odessa Waterworks Co.* (1889) 42 Ch.D. 636.

Accordingly, if it is desired to have the power to pay dividends otherwise than in cash, the articles should give such power, as they usually do. Table A, article 105, provides:

"A general meeting declaring a dividend may, upon the recommendation of the directors, direct that it shall be satisfied wholly or partly by the distribution of assets and, where any difficulty arises in regard to the distribution, the directors may settle the same and in particular may issue fractional certificates and fix the value for distribution of any assets and may determine that cash shall be paid to any member upon the footing of the value so fixed in order to adjust the rights of members and may vest any assets in trustees."

[41] *Oakbank Oil Co. Ltd v. Crum* (1882) 10 R. (H.L.) 11; (1881) 9 R. 198.
[42] *Hoggan v. Tharsis Sulphur etc. Co. Ltd* (1882) 9 R. 1191.
[43] See *Thairlwall v. Great Northern Ry.* [1910] 2 K.B. 509.

## CREATION OF A RESERVE

Section 234 of the Act requires that in their report the directors should state the amount, if any, which they recommend should be paid as dividend and the amount, if any, which they propose to carry to reserves. The articles therefore often contain provisions dealing with the creation of a reserve, and indeed there was an article to this effect in Table A to the 1948 Act (article 117). However, no corresponding article exists in the 1985 Table A (S.I. 1985 No. 805). Yet even where no power to create a reserve is included in its articles, a company may nevertheless create one as this is a business question for the decision of the company itself.[44] "The general practice of companies certainly is not to divide the total available profits, but to carry forward a part to make provision for meeting current liabilities."[45] Moreover, a reserve may at any time be distributed as dividend or be employed in any other way authorised by the articles.[46] The fact that it has been used in the business does not show that it has been capitalised so as not to be available for dividend.[47]

## CAPITALISATION OF RESERVES

Capitalisation of a company's profits is defined in section 280 as relating either to the creation of bonus shares; or to the transfer of profits to capital redemption reserve. However, to be able to issue so-called "bonus" shares credited as fully or partly paid, a company has to be so empowered by its articles.

Table A, article 110, accordingly provides:

"The directors may with the authority of an ordinary resolution of the company—
(a) subject as hereinafter provided, resolve to capitalise any undivided profits of the company not required for paying any preferential dividend (whether or not they are available for

---

[44] *Burland v. Earle* [1902] A.C. 83 (P.C.). Scottish cases decided on the interpretation of articles were *Cadell v. Scottish Investment Trust Co. Ltd* (1901) 9 S.L.T. 299, affirming (1901) 8 S.L.T. 480 (O.H.) (power to carry forward profits to the next year instead of paying a larger dividend on deferred shares); and *Wemyss Collieries Trust Ltd v. Melville* (1905) 8 F. 143 (transfer of profits to reserve fund instead of paying additional dividend on preference shares).
[45] *Per* Lord M'Laren in *Cadell v. Scottish Investment Trust Co. Ltd* (1901) 9 S.L.T. 299 at p. 300.
[46] e.g. *Blyth's Trustees v. Milne* (1905) 7 F. 799.
[47] *Re Hoare & Co. Ltd* [1904] 2 Ch. 208 (C.A.).

distribution) or any sum standing to the credit of the company's share premium account or capital redemption reserve;

(b) appropriate the sum resolved to be capitalised to the members who would have been entitled to it if it were distributed by way of dividend and in the same proportions and apply such sum on their behalf either in or towards paying up the amounts, if any, for the time being unpaid on any shares held by them respectively, or in paying up in full unissued shares or debentures of the company of a nominal amount equal to that sum, and allot the shares or debentures credited as fully paid to those members, or as they may direct, in those proportions, or partly in one way and partly in the other: but the share premium account, the capital redemption reserve, and any profits which are not available for distribution may, for the purposes of this regulation, only be applied in paying up unissued shares to be allotted to members credited as fully paid;

(c) make such provision by the issue of fractional certificates or by payment in cash or otherwise as they determine in the case of shares or debentures becoming distributable under this regulation in fractions; and

(d) authorise any person to enter on behalf of all the members concerned into an agreement with the company providing for the allotment to them respectively, credited as fully paid, of any shares or debentures to which they are entitled upon such capitalisation, any agreement made under such authority being binding on all such members."

Scrip dividends became increasingly popular in the late 1980s and early 1990s as many companies had unrelieved Advance Corporation Tax because of their substantial overseas earnings. By making a bonus issue they were able to retain cash and invest it profitably within the business. However, changes implemented in the 1993 Finance Act have substantially reduced this advantage.

**Capitalising distributable reserves**

When a company capitalises its distributable reserves, it reduces at a stroke its accumulated realised profits available for dividend and issues in their place, to existing ordinary shareholders in proportion to their holdings, shares or loan stock credited as fully paid up. From an accounting viewpoint, the distributable reserves figure in the balance sheet is reduced and the share or loan capital accounts increased by an equivalent offsetting amount. As a result, other things being equal, the net effect on the value of an individual's holding in the company remains unchanged. The term "bonus" used to describe such issues is therefore misleading, and more appropriate descriptions are "capitalisation-", "scrip-" or "script-issues".

In practice, other things are not usually equal, and the effect will generally be to increase the value of a holding. Thus one reason for engaging in such an exercise is to provide more security for creditors (particularly to existing or prospective holders of loan stock), which alters the balance of risk bearing between them and the company's shareholders. Another is to achieve a subdivision of the equity capital, similar to that permitted under section 121 (see above, page 169): this can make the company's shares more marketable. Thus, for instance, if the market value per share of a company has risen to £20 as a result of its retention of profits over time to finance growth, it may be preferable to reduce this to nearer £5 per unit. Moreover, in practice listed companies tend to use capitalisation issues as a means of signalling to the investing public that the company's future prospects are encouraging, often indicating specifically that it is not the directors' intention to reduce the dividend per share *pro rata* to the increase in the number of share units in issue, and there is empirical evidence which confirms that this news content is appreciated by the market.[48] Capitalisation issues can also be used to credit partly-paid shares with a further amount paid up.

### Capitalising undistributable reserves

A company which by its articles could, prior to the 1980 Act, use a reserve resulting from the revaluation of capital assets to pay for bonus shares, may continue to do so (1980 Act, s.45(1), now section 278 of the 1985 Act). Such a reserve could arise on a revaluation of fixed assets made in good faith by competent valuers and not being likely to fluctuate in the short term.[49] Moreover, by sections 130(2)[50] and 170(4)[51] of the 1985 Act respectively, a share premium account and a capital redemption reserve can be used to pay for unissued shares of the company to be allotted to members as fully paid bonus shares.

---

[48] *e.g.* Firth, M.A., "An Empirical Investigation of the Announcement of Capitalisation Issues on Share Prices", *Journal of Business Finance and Accounting* (1977), 47–60.

[49] *Dimbula Valley (Ceylon) Tea Co. Ltd v. Laurie* [1961] Ch. 353.

[50] *Ante*, p. 165.

[51] *Ante*, p. 191.

If bonus shares are to be issued:

(1) There must be authority in the company's articles.[52]

(2) The company's nominal share capital must be sufficient.

(3) The members must resolve by ordinary resolution to capitalise profits or to apply the share premium account or the capital redemption reserve fund, and to issue bonus shares.[53]

(4) The shares must be allotted by the board in the proportions specified in the articles, usually the same proportions as those in which the members would have received a cash dividend.[54]

(5) A return of allotments and a contract between the members and the company (which may be signed on the members' behalf by the person authorised by the articles) must be delivered to the Registrar within one month after the allotment.[55]

---

[52] *Wood's case, ante*. See also Table A, article 110, *ante*.

[53] See Table A, article 110, *ante*.

[54] See Table A, article 110, *ante*.

[55] *Ante*, Chap. 8. The Jenkins Report (1962, Cmnd. 1749, para. 495) recommended that it should be enough to file a copy of the resolution authorising the issue of the shares credited as fully paid up.

# Chapter 23

## DEBENTURES

This chapter is concerned with the borrowing of money by a company where the borrowing is on debentures or on debenture stock, and with fixed and floating charges which a company may create over its property in order to secure the principal sum borrowed and interest thereon until re-payment. Thus the chapter deals with the relationship between a company and its creditors, which is also central to the following chapters up to chapter 29.

Perhaps the most important part of the chapter is that with regard to charges and the registration of charges, particularly registration with the Registrar of Companies under section 395. The system of registration was intended to be modified by the Companies Act 1989 but these changes have still to be brought into effect. Since there is some doubt as to whether they will ever be,[0] the unmodified provisions are considered in this edition.

## A COMPANY'S POWER TO BORROW MONEY

Prior to the substantial changes to corporate transactions contained in sections 35 and 35A and 322A of the 1985 Act as substituted by the 1989 Act[1] it was important to decide whether or not the company had the capacity, *i.e.* by virtue of an express or implied power, to borrow money, and it was possible for a loan to be *ultra vires* the company and so void.[2]

Following those changes, however, any borrowing is simply one type of transaction by a company and so its validity is now governed, as with all other corporate transactions, by the new

---

[0] The matter is still under discussion—a consultative document was issued by the DTI in November 1994.

[1] Chap. 6, *ante*.

[2] For the position prior to the 1989 Act changes see the 13th edition of this work at pp. 607–11.

# 614 DEBENTURES

provisions. It follows that unless the lender is either not acting in good faith[3] or is a director of the borrowing company[4] no question of invalidity can arise as a result of the company's constitution. Even if the lender is not acting in good faith or is a director, the transaction may still be ratified by the appropriate resolution. Ratification is also possible if the defect arises from a lack of authority on the part of those negotiating the loan on behalf of the company, if it arises under the general law of agency rather than from the company's constitution.[5]

## DEBENTURES AND DEBENTURE STOCK

A debenture is a document which creates or acknowledges a debt due from a company. Such document need not be, although it usually is, under seal,[6] it need not give, although it usually does give, a charge on the assets of the company by way of security, and it may or may not be one of a series.[7] Thus debentures may be (1) secured, or (2) unsecured. A debenture is always for a specified sum, *e.g.* £100, which can only be transferred in its entirety. As will be seen, debentures may be collaterally secured by a trust deed.[8] Convertible debentures, *i.e.* debentures which the holder has the right to convert, at stated times, into shares in the company, have already been mentioned.[9]

It may be helpful to mention here that some of the differences between shares and debentures are:

(1)  the holder of a debenture is a creditor, not a member, of the company; a shareholder is a member[10];

(2)  debentures may be issued at a discount; shares, in general, may not be[11];

(3)  a company may purchase its own debentures; it must not purchase its own shares except in accordance with specific procedures[12];

---

[3] So that s.35A cannot apply.
[4] Thus applying s.322A.
[5] *i.e.* because the agent has no authority to bind the company.
[6] N.B. the new provisions relating to the sealing of documents in ss.36A and 36B, *ante*, p. 101.
[7] See *Lemon v. Austin Friars Investment Trust Ltd* [1926] Ch. 1 (C.A.).
[8] *Post.* p. 616.
[9] See *Mosely v. Koffyfontein Mines* [1904] 2 Ch. 108, *ante* p. 159.
[10] *Ante*, p. 208.
[11] *Ante*, p. 158.
[12] *Ante*, Chap. 10.

(4) interest at the specified rate on debentures may be paid out of capital; dividends on shares must be paid only out of distributable profits.[13]

Section 744 defines "debenture" as including debenture stock, bonds, and any other securities[14] of a company whether constituting a charge on the assets of the company or not. A mortgage of land by a company is a debenture.[15] Debentures, including debenture stock, loan stock, bonds and certificates of deposit are investments for the purposes of the Financial Services Act 1986[16] and Part V of the Criminal Justice Act 1993[17]: see Chapter 19, *ante*.

Debenture stock is borrowed money consolidated into one mass for the sake of convenience. This is normally done by a trust deed,[18] which may give the trustees a charge on the company's property. Where there is no charge, debenture stock is commonly called unsecured loan stock. The main advantage of debenture stock is that it is transferable in fractional amounts, although the trust deed may specify the minimum fractional amount which can be transferred. Again, the debenture stockholders will be given simple debenture stock certificates instead of debentures.

## ISSUES OF DEBENTURES

Debentures are issued in accordance with the provisions of the articles, usually by a resolution of the board of directors.

When debentures have been issued, the prospectus[19] cannot be looked at to ascertain the contract, but if the contract was intended to be contained in the prospectus and the debenture together, or if the prospectus contains a collateral contract the consideration for which was the taking up of the debentures, the prospectus can be looked at.[20]

Debentures or debentures stock certificates must be completed and ready for delivery within two months after allotment or after

[13] *Ante*, Chap. 22. There are also tax differences between interest and dividends.
[14] "Securities," as used in s.744, does not include shares.
[15] *Knightsbridge Estates Trust Ltd v. Byrne* [1940] A.C. 613.
[16] Financial Services Act 1986, Sched. 1, para. 2.
[17] Criminal Justice Act 1993, Sched. 2.
[18] See note 8, above.
[19] This presumably also applies to listing particulars.
[20] *Jacobs v. Batavia and General Plantations Trust Ltd* [1924] 2 Ch. 329 (C.A.).

the lodging of a transfer, unless the conditions of issue otherwise provide: section 185.

There is no objection to the issue of debentures at a discount but when any commission, allowance or discount has been paid or made to any person in consideration of his subscribing or procuring subscriptions for debentures, particulars of the amount or rate of the commission or discount must be sent to the Registrar within 21 days. The omission to do this does not, however, affect the validity of the debentures. The deposit of debentures as security for a debt of the company does not, for this purpose, amount to the issue of debentures at a discount: sections 397(3) and 413(3).

A contract to take up debentures may be enforced by specific performance: section 195. This section provides an exception to the rule, laid down in *South African Territories Ltd v. Wallington*,[21] that specific performance will not be granted of a contract to lend money since damages are an adequate remedy for breach of such contract.

Apart from the section, an agreement to issue debentures made in consideration of an actual balance of money has the effect in English law of putting the lender in equity in the same position as if the debentures had actually been issued.

A syndicate agreed to sell goods to a company on the terms that, as part payment, £3,000 debentures charged upon all the company's assets were issued. On this agreement the syndicate allowed the company to remove the goods, which were subsequently taken in execution by F. *Held*, although no debentures were actually issued, the syndicate was in the same position as if they had been and so F. was entitled subject to the charge: *Simultaneous Colour Printing Syndicate v. Foweraker* [1901] 1 K.B. 771.

## TRUST DEEDS

Debentures and particularly debenture stock are usually secured by a trust deed.

### Contents of a trust deed

The main terms of a *debenture trust deed* are:

(1) a covenant by the company for payment to the debenture holders of the principal moneys and interest;

---

[21] [1898] A.C. 309.

(2) clauses giving the trustees a legal mortgage by demise of the company's freeholds and leaseholds, which are specified,[22] and a floating charge over the rest of the undertaking and property[23];

(3) a clause specifying the events on which the security is to become enforceable, *e.g.* default in the payment of interest or principal moneys, order made or resolution passed for winding-up, appointment of a receiver, cessation of business, breach of covenant by the company;

(4) a clause giving the trustees power to take possession of the property charged when the security becomes enforceable, to carry on the business and to sell the property charged and to apply the net sale moneys in payment of the principal and interest and to pay the balance to the company;

(5) power for the trustees to concur with the company in dealings with the property charged;

(6) covenants by the company to keep a register of debenture holders, to insure and to keep in repair the property charged;

(7) provision for meetings of debenture holders;

(8) power for the trustees to appoint a receiver when the security becomes enforceable;

(9) provision for serving notices on the debenture holders by post.

A *debenture stock trust deed*, in addition to containing the foregoing terms, constitutes a stock by acknowledging that the company is indebted to the trustees in a specified sum and provides for the issue of debenture stock certificates.

A trust deed usually contains a clause providing that the rights of the debenture holders against the company or any property charged by the deed may be modified or compromised by extraordinary resolution of the debenture holders.

## Liability of trustees

Trustees for debenture holders are in the same position towards their beneficiaries as any other trustees, and cannot

[22] In Scotland, security over specified heritable property would be created by the execution of a standard security which would be referred to in the trust deed.

[23] Fixed charges may also be taken over other assets, *e.g.* book debts of a company. See p. 629, *post.*

purchase the debentures, the subject of the deed, without making full disclosure of all the information relating to them which is in their possession.[24] Any provision in a trust deed, or in a contract with the holders of debentures secured by a trust deed, for exempting the trustees from, or indemnifying them against, liability for breach of trust where they fail to show the degree of care and diligence required of them as trustees, is void, except that the trustees may be released from liability by a release given after the liability has arisen; and a provision in a trust deed for the giving of such a release by a majority of not less than three-fourths in value of the debenture holders present and voting in person or by proxy at a meeting summoned for the purpose is not void: section 192. (Contrast section 310 ante[25] as regards officers and auditors.)

Section 727 (power of court to grant relief) ante[26] does not apply to the trustees although the Trustee Act 1925, s.61, and the Trusts (Scotland) Act 1921, s.32, do, and so in an appropriate case the court may relieve the trustees from liability.

**Right to copy of trust deed**

A debenture holder is entitled to require a copy of the trust deed on payment of the prescribed fee: sections 191, 356.

## REGISTERED DEBENTURES

Debentures or debenture stock may be payable to either (1) the registered holder; or (2) the bearer.

**Contents of a registered debenture**

Where there is a trust deed the usual form of debenture payable to the registered holder is a document issued under the seal of the company and containing two clauses. The clauses are as follows:

(a) the company, for valuable consideration received, covenants to pay the registered holder the principal sum on a specified day or on such earlier day as it becomes payable

---

[24] *Re Magadi Soda Co.* (1925) 41 T.L.R. 297.
[25] p. 365.
[26] p. 366.

under the indorsed conditions, and in the meantime to pay interest by equal half-yearly payments on specified dates at a specified rate;

(b) the debenture is said to be issued subject to and with the benefit of the conditions indorsed thereon.

The indorsed conditions usually include the following:

(i) the debenture is said to be one of a series, each for securing a specified sum;

(ii) the registered holders of all the debentures of the issue are said to be entitled *pari passu* to the benefit and subject to the provisions of the trust deed, the date of execution of which the parties to which are specified, and the charges conferred by the trust deed are recited.

This has the effect of putting all the debentures of the issue on an equal footing; in the absence of such a clause the debentures would rank according to the order in which they were executed[27]:

(iii) the company is empowered, at any time after a specified date, by giving not less than a specified number of months' notice, to pay off the principal moneys secured with interest to the date of payment;

(iv) provision is made for keeping a register of debenture holders at the registered office. We shall see that this will comply with section 190 and that a right of inspection is given by section 191[28];

(v) the company is not to be bound to recognise anyone as having any title to the debenture except the registered holder, or his personal representative, and is not to be bound to enter notice of any trust in the register.

Section 360, which provides that trusts are not to be entered on the register of members in England and Wales, does not apply to the register of debenture holders, and consequently such a clause is necessary. If the company does receive notice of a trust, the clause relieves it from the obligation of entering it on the register, but if it deals with the debentures as a trader, *e.g.* by advancing

[27] *Gartside v. Silkstone and Dodworth Coal, etc., Co.* (1882) 21 Ch.D. 762.
[28] *Post*, p. 622.

money on them, after notice of a trust, it will be bound by that trust[29];

(vi)    transfer of the debenture is provided for. Every transfer must be in writing, as will be explained later;

(vii)   equities or, in Scots law, rights of compensation, between the company and any person other than the registered holder are excluded. This will be explained later[30];

(viii)  the principal moneys and interest are made payable at the company's registered office or at its bankers.

If this clause is not inserted it is the company's duty to follow the usual rule and seek out its creditor and pay him.

F. held 18 £100 debentures repayable in June, 1913, in the M. Corporation. Before the date of redemption F. died, and her executors neglected to present the debentures to the company for payment. In June, 1916, the company was sued for principal and interest. *Held*, as the debentures contained no clause to the effect set out above, it was the company's duty to seek out the debenture holder and pay her; as this had not been done, the company was liable to pay the principal with interest until the date of actual payment: *Fowler v. Midland Electric Corpn.* [1917] 1 Ch. 656 (C.A.);

(ix)   the company is empowered to purchase any of the debentures of the issue at any time;

(x)    interest is made payable by warrant on the company's bank payable to the order of the registered holder and sent by post to his registered address;

(xi)   the principal moneys are made immediately payable if the company defaults in the payment of interest for a specified number of months, or if a winding up order is made or resolution passed, or if the security constituted by the trust deed becomes enforceable and the trustees enforce it.

The debenture holder is entitled to repayment of his principal on the company's going into liquidation, whether or not the date fixed for repayment has arrived.[31]

---

[29] *Bradford Banking Co. v. Briggs & Co.* (1886) 12 App.Cas. 29; *Mackereth v. Wigan Coal Co. Ltd* [1916] 2 Ch. 293.
[30] *Post*, p. 631.
[31] *Hodson v. Tea Co.* (1880) 14 Ch.D. 859.

Transfer of registered debentures

Registered debentures are transferred in the manner laid down in the indorsed conditions (which usually require a transfer to be in writing under the hand of the registered holder or of his personal representatives) or by a stock transfer under the Stock Transfer Act 1963. As in the case of a transfer of shares[32] it is unlawful for a company to register a transfer of debentures unless a "proper instrument of transfer" has been delivered to the company: section 183(1).

The company must have the debenture or debenture stock certificate ready for delivery within two months of the lodging of the instrument of transfer unless the conditions of issue otherwise provide or the transfer is to SEPON, *i.e.* on a transfer under the stock exchange procedure: section 185. If registration of a transfer is refused, notice of refusal must be given to the transferee within two months: section 183(5).

Registered debentures are in England choses in action, and in Scotland incorporeal moveable property to the assignation of which the rule *assignatus utitur jure auctoris* ('the assignee acquires no higher right than his cedent had") applies. They are not negotiable instruments, and consequently a transferee takes them subject to all claims which the company may have against prior holders at the date of the transfer.

After a receiver had been appointed and a winding up petitions had been presented, P., a debenture stockholder, transferred £10,000 debenture stock to X, who was registered as the owner. P, was also a director of the company and a claim was made against him for money had and received by him while a director. *Held*, X was not entitled to payment until the amount due from P. to the company had been ascertained and deducted: *Re Rhodesia Goldfields Ltd* [1910] 1 Ch. 239.

To avoid this result, the indorsed conditions usually provide that the principal and interest shall be paid to the registered holder without regard to any equities or rights of compensation existing between the company and any prior holder of the debenture. Such a clause amounts to a contract by the company that it will not rely on equities or rights of compensation, and its effect is to make the debentures more marketable.

A company was in liquidation. C., who had been a director of the company, transferred debentures to R. as security for a loan. The

[32] *Ante*, pp. 247 *et seq*.

debentures contained a clause similar to that set out above. It was then discovered that C. had been guilty of misfeasance and he was ordered to pay a sum of money to the liquidator in respect thereof. The liquidator refused to register R.'s transfer. *Held*, the right to transfer and to have the transfer registered was not affected by the winding up, and R. was entitled to payment without regard to C.'s debt to the company: *Re Goy & Co. Ltd* [1900] 2 Ch. 149.

A transferee cannot claim the benefit of such a clause unless either he is registered or the conditions specifically allow the holder to transfer the debenture free of equities.

B. held debentures containing a clause similar to that set out above. After a resolution for winding up had been passed he transferred them for value to C., who took without notice of any defect in B.'s title. Notice of transfer but no request for registration was given to the liquidator. C. claimed payment but the court found that B. had paid nothing for the debentures and had obtained them by misrepresentation. *Held*, notwithstanding the clause, C. took subject to the company's claim against B. *Re Goy & Co.*, *ante*, was distinguished on the ground that when the transfer in that case was sent for registration the company was not aware of and was not setting up any equities between itself and the transferor: *Re Palmer's Decoration and Furnishing Co.* [1904] 2 Ch. 743. Where the actual agreement specifically allowed the holder to transfer free of all equities it has been held that following such a transfer the issuing company is bound to register the transfer: *Hilger Analytical Ltd v. Rank Precision Industries Ltd* [1984] BCLC 301.

Section 184 (certification of transfers) *ante*[33] applies to transfers of debentures as well as to transfers of shares.

### Register of debenture holders

A company is not required to keep a register of debenture holders but there are provisions regulating those companies which do. A company registered in England must not keep its register of debenture holders in Scotland, and vice versa. The register must be kept at the registered office or at any other office of the company where it is made up or, if it is made up by an agent, it may be kept at the agent's office: section 190. Debenture holders and shareholders in the company may, without fee, inspect the register of debenture holders within limits laid down by the Secretary of State. Other persons may inspect the register on payment of a prescribed fee. A copy may be demanded on

[33] p. 249.

payment of the prescribed fee: section 191.[34] A computer may be used to keep the register of debenture holders: section 723.

## BEARER DEBENTURES

Debentures payable to bearer are in the same form as registered debentures except that they are expressed to be made payable to bearer and coupons for the interest are attached. The indorsed conditions are also in the same form with the necessary modifications for bearer, instead of registered, instruments.

Bearer debentures are negotiable instruments and consequently a transferee in good faith and for value takes them free from any defects in the title of a prior holder.

The B. Company owned some bearer debentures and kept them in a safe. The secretary fraudulently took them from the safe and deposited them with the bank, who took them in good faith and as security for advances to the secretary. *Held*, the debentures were negotiable instruments transferable by delivery and the bank was entitled to them as against the B. Company: *Bechuanaland Exploration Co. v. London Trading Bank* [1898] 2 Q.B. 658.

Bearer debentures are transferable by delivery and no stamp duty is payable on transfer. Interest is payable by means of the coupons which are cut off and presented for payment to the company's bankers when the date of payment arrives.

Debentures to bearer issued in Scotland are expressly declared by section 197 to be valid and binding notwithstanding anything in the Blank Bonds and Trusts Act 1696 (Scots Act 1696 c.25).[35]

## REDEEMABLE DEBENTURES

Debentures may be (1) redeemable at the option of the company, or (2) irredeemable or perpetual.

Sometimes debentures are issued on the terms that the company is bound to redeem a certain number each year by "drawings" (in which case, in effect, the numbers of the debentures to be redeemable are drawn out of a hat),[36] or that it may purchase,

---

[34] For the relevant limits and fees see the Companies (Inspection and Copying of Registers, Indices and Documents) Regulations 1991, S.I. 1991 No. 1998.

[35] *Ante*, p. 270.

[36] For difficulties which may arise from the company's inability to trace the holders to whom repayment is due, see *United Collieries Ltd v. Lord Advocate*, 1950 S.C. 458.

*e.g.* on the Stock Exchange, or that it is bound to set aside a sinking fund for redemption purposes on a specified date. When debentures have been so redeemed, section 194 empowers the company to reissue them or issue other debentures in their place, unless—

(a) the company, in its articles or otherwise, has contracted not to reissue them; or

(b) the company has shown an intention to cancel the debentures by passing a resolution to that effect, or by some other act.

On a reissue of redeemed debentures, the person entitled to them has the same priorities as if the debentures had never been redeemed: section 194. The date of redemption of the reissued debentures cannot be later than that of the original debentures.[37]

Reissued debentures are treated as new debentures for the purpose of stamp duty: section 194.

## PERPETUAL DEBENTURES

Debentures are not invalid merely because they are made irredeemable, or redeemable on the happening of a contingency, however remote, *e.g.* the winding-up of the company, or on the expiration of a period, however long, *e.g.* 100 years after the issue of the debenture, *i.e.* the legal or contractual date for redemption may be postponed, despite any rule of equity to the contrary: section 193.

In Scotland, the Conveyancing and Feudal Reform (Scotland) Act 1970, ss.11 and 18, conferred on the debtor in a standard security the right, which could not be varied by agreement, to redeem the security on giving two months' notice. The Redemption of Standard Securities (Scotland) Act 1971, however, amended the 1970 Act on this point by providing that the condition relating to the debtor's right of redemption might be varied by agreement. The 1971 Act also, for the avoidance of doubt, declared that the provisions of the 1970 Act relating to the standard security do not affect the operation of section 193.

---

[37] *Re Antofagasta (Chile) and Bolivia Ry. Co.'s Trust Deed* [1939] Ch. 732.

## CHARGES SECURING DEBENTURES

A charge on the assets of a company given by a debenture or a trust deed in order to secure money borrowed by the company may be either (1) a specific or fixed charge, or (2) a floating charge.

In practice many debentures are secured by both a fixed and a floating charge. Such charges are usually drafted to cover "all moneys" due by the company to the lender including contingent and future liabilities. In *Re Quest Cae, Ltd*[38] it was held that such wording only covered debts arising as a result of transactions between the company and the lender so that where the lender subsequently acquired loan stock issued by the company to a third party it was not protected by the charge. The debt had not arisen by virtue of a transaction between the company and the lender.

### Fixed charges (English law)

A fixed charge is a mortgage of ascertained and definite property, *e.g.* a legal or an equitable mortgage of a specified factory, and prevents the company from realising that property, *i.e.* disposing of it free from the charge, without the consent of the holders of the charge. It has been said in one case,[39] however, that a limited licence for the company to deal with the charged property may not be inconsistent with a fixed charge, depending upon the nature of the property charged and the degree of the licence to deal. Where a charge is on fixed plant and machinery it will only apply to those items physically attached to the company's premises and not to all a company's fixed, *i.e.* capital, assets.[40] The question of creating a fixed charge over the book debts or other moneys due to the company is considered below.[41]

### Floating charges (English law)

In *Re Yorkshire Woolcombers Association Ltd*[42] Romer L.J. said that if a charge has the three characteristics set out below it is a floating charge:

---

[38] [1985] BCLC 266.
[39] *Re Cimex Tissues Ltd* [1994] BCC 626.
[40] *Re Hi-Fi Equipment (Cabinets) Ltd* (1987) 3 BCC 478, not following *Tudor Heights Ltd v. United Dominions Corporation Finance Ltd* [1977] 1 N.Z.L.R. 532.
[41] *Post,* p. 629.
[42] [1903] 2 Ch. 284 (C.A.) at p. 295.

(1) it is a charge on a class of assets of a company, present and future;
(2) which class is, in the ordinary course of the company's business, changing from time to time;
(3) it is contemplated by the charge that, until the holders of the charge take steps to enforce it, the company may carry on business in the ordinary way as far as concerns the class of assets charged.

Thus a floating charge is an equitable charge on some or all of the present and future property of a company, *e.g.* the company's undertaking, *i.e.* all its property, present and future.[43] It is effective as to future property only when that property is acquired by the company. The company may, in the ordinary course of business, realise property which is subject to the charge. A floating charge will be valid even if the assets covered do not yet exist.[44]

However, when the security is enforceable, *e.g.* there is default with regard to payment of interest or repayment of the principal sum, and the debenture holders or the trustees enforce it, *e.g.* they appoint an administrative receiver of the property charged, the floating charge is said to crystallise; *i.e.* it becomes a fixed charge on the assets in the class charged at the time of crystallisation or, where the floating charge so provides, assets which come to the company after crystallisation.[45]

Crystallisation also occurs on the commencement of the winding-up of the company, even if it is a voluntary winding-up for the purpose of reconstruction,[46] or when the company ceases business.[47] The latter, which is a form of "implied automatic crystallisation" in that it needs no act or specific event to bring it about and so may be difficult for other creditors to judge, was disputed until 1986. In coming to his decision on this point, Nourse J. pointed out that cessation of business prevents a company from dealing with its assets and so there is no reason why the charge should not crystallise. The judge, however, rejected another such ground for implied crystallisation, *i.e.* on

---

[43] *Re Panama, etc., Royal Mail Co.* (1870) L.R. 5 Ch.App. 318.
[44] *Re Croftbell Ltd* [1990] BCC 781.
[45] *N. W. Robbie & Co. Ltd v. Whitney Warehouse Co. Ltd* [1963] 1 W.L.R. 1324 (C.A.); *Ferrier v. Bottomer* (1972) 126 C.L.R. 597.
[46] *Re Crompton & Co.* [1914] 1 Ch. 954.
[47] *Re Woodroffes* (*Musical Instruments*) *Ltd* [1986] Ch. 366.

the crystallisation of a second floating charge which is postponed to the relevant floating charge.[48]

It is possible that the charging deed may provide for crystallisation on a certain event, *e.g.* an attempt by the company to create another charge over the assets in the class charged, or simply by the giving of a notice to that effect. Such "express automatic crystallisation" is valid under English law following the decision of Hoffmann J. in *Re Brightlife Ltd*[49] The judge pointed out that floating charges were developed to enable companies to raise money without inhibiting their ability to trade, but this involved potential prejudice to other creditors who could suddenly find assets becoming subject to a charge on crystallisation without anyone else being aware. The appointment of an administrative receiver, administrator or liquidator were public acts, but the giving of a notice or the happening of an event would not be. The judge, however, considered that any restrictions on the contractual freedom of parties to a floating charge were matters for Parliament, and it would be "wholly inappropriate" for the courts to impose restrictions on the ground of public policy. The judge followed a decision of the New Zealand courts to a similar effect.[50]

The characteristics of a floating charge are therefore:

(1) it is an equitable charge on assets for the time being of the company[51];

(2) it attaches to the class of assets charged in the varying condition in which they happen to be from time to time,[51] *i.e.* it does not fasten on any definite property but is a charge on property which is constantly changing;

(3) it remains dormant, subject to any automatic crystallisation until the undertaking charged ceases to be a going concern, or until the person in whose favour it is created intervenes. His right to intervene may be suspended by agreement but if there is no agreement for suspension he

---

[48] But see as to priority *Griffiths v. Yorkshire Bank plc* [1994] 1 W.L.R. 1427, 1435.

[49] [1987] Ch. 200.

[50] *Re Manurewa Transport Ltd.* [1971] N.Z.L.R. 909; *cf. R. v. Consolidated Churchill Copper Corpn. Ltd* [1978] 5 W.W.R. 652. See also the Australian case of *Deputy Commissioner of Taxation v. Horsburgh* [1984] V.R. 773.

[51] *Per* Lord MacNaghten in *Governments Stock Investment Co. Ltd v. Manila Ry. Co. Ltd* [1897] A.C. 81, at p. 86. See *Re G. E. Tunbridge Ltd* [1994] BCC 563.

may intervene whenever he pleases after default.[52] When this happens the charge is said to "crystallise" and becomes fixed[53];

(4) although it is an immediate and continuing charge, until it becomes fixed the company can, without consent[54] deal with the class of assets in the ordinary course of business, *e.g.* it has been held that a company can sell all or any of its business or property for shares or debentures of another company if the memorandum gives it power to do so, and the debenture holders cannot prevent such a sale if the company remains a going concern[55]; similarly, a company with three businesses may sell one of the three.[56]

Where, before crystallisation of a floating charge over all the company's assets and undertaking, the company contracted to sell goods to a buyer to whom it owed money under a previous contract, and the goods were delivered after crystallisation, the company's right to sue for the debt due to it was embraced, when it arose, by the floating charge, but the debenture holder could not be in a better position to assert the rights under the previous contract than the company.[57]

The advantage of a floating charge from the *company's* point of view is that the company can give security for a loan to it by charging property which changes in the course of business and over which it is impracticable to create a fixed charge, *e.g.* the company's stock-in-trade. Further, until crystallisation the company can carry on business in the ordinary way.

A floating charge can be created only by a registered company not by a partnership or a sole trader. One reason is that such a charge created by a firm over chattels would be a bill of sale within the Bills of Sale Acts 1878 and 1882, and would have to be registered and, as a mortgage bill, would have to be in the statutory form and specify the chattels, which is impossible.

---

[52] See note 46, above.
[53] *Evans v. Rival Granite Quarries Ltd* [1910] 2 K.B. 979 (C.A.).
[54] Restrictions on the company's power of disposal do not, however, convert a floating charge into a fixed charge: *Re G. E. Tunbridge Ltd* [1994] BCC 563.
[55] *Re Borax Co.* [1901] 3 Ch. 326.
[56] *Re H. H. Vivian & Co. Ltd* [1900] 2 Ch. 654.
[57] *Rother Iron Works Ltd v. Canterbury Precision Engines Ltd* [1974] Q.B. 1 (C.A.) applied in *George Barker (Transport) Ltd v. Eynon* [1974] 1 W.L.R. 462 (C.A.).

From the *chargee's* point of view, an important advantage is that, upon crystallisation of the floating charge, the chargee obtains priority in the payment of debts over the ordinary unsecured creditors and the existence of such a charge entitles the chargee to veto any proposal for an administration order.[58] However, there are a number of disadvantages attached to a floating charge from the chargee's point of view. For example:

(1) As will be seen, a floating charge is postponed to certain other interests, especially the preferred creditors.

(2) A floating charge may be invalidated under section 245 of the Insolvency Act 1986, *post*.[59]

## Charges over book debts

Creditors, aware of these drawbacks to a floating charge, yet wishing to give the company the maximum flexibility in dealing with its assets, have faced a difficult problem in relation to using the company's book debts as security for a loan. Book debts are moneys owed to the company, which by their nature are constantly being created and paid off. Creditors have therefore attempted to create fixed charges over the company's book debts and this was accepted as a possibility by Slade J. in *Siebe Gorman & Co. Ltd v. Barclays Bank Ltd*[60] but in many other cases the attempt has failed, the resulting charge being construed, despite its wording, as a floating charge.[61]

The test which has been applied relates to what is to happen to the proceeds of the book debts (*i.e.* when the debt is paid to the company). Invariably the charge will require that those proceeds be paid into a designated bank account. If that account can only be operated under the instructions of the chargee then the charge will be regarded as a fixed charge since the company is precluded from dealing freely with those assets, which is one of the hallmarks of a floating charge.[62] Thus where the charge covers

---

[58] See Chap. 26, *post*.
[59] *Post*, p. 639.
[60] [1979] 2 Lloyds Rep. 142.
[61] See *e.g. Re Armagh Shoes Ltd* [1982] N.I. 59; *Re Brightlife Ltd* [1987] Ch. 200; *Re Permanent House (Holdings) Ltd* (1989) 5 BCC 151 and *Re G. E. Tunbridge Ltd* [1994] BCC 563.
[62] See *e.g. Re Keenan Bros Ltd* [1986] BCLC 242 (Ir); *Re Atlantic Medical Ltd* [1993] BCLC 386; *William Gaskell Group Ltd v. Highley* [1994] 1 BCLC 197. In the last case it was also held that an assignment of the charge did not destroy its fixed nature since the restrictions remained.

future income in the hands of the company arising from agreements deposited with the chargee from time to time, it will be a fixed charge.[62a] On the other hand if the company is not so restricted in operating the designated account then the whole charge will be construed as a floating charge, since freedom to deal with charged assets without the consent of the chargee is inconsistent with a fixed charge. The effect is that in such a case even outstanding book debts will only be covered by a floating charge with its vulnerability to the preferred creditors.[63]

The solution to the dilemma of creating a successful fixed charge over book debts without unduly restricting the company's ability to use the proceeds of such debts may have been found by the Court of Appeal's decision in *Re New Bullas Trading Ltd*[64] In that case the chargee took a fixed charge over the company's book debts with the usual requirements that the proceeds be paid into a designated account with the bank. The charge then provided that if the chargee gave instructions to the company as to the use of that account then the proceeds would continue to be subject to the fixed charge but that if no such instructions were given they were to become subject to a separate floating charge, which would then apply to cover the moneys in the account. In fact no such instructions were given. The judge had therefore construed the whole charge as a floating charge but the Court of Appeal decided that the terms of the charge should be given effect as they stood. Thus the unpaid book debts remained subject to a fixed charge and only the proceeds became subject to a floating charge. The Court of Appeal saw no reason why public policy should dictate otherwise. The company was free to use the proceeds because of an agreement between the parties which should be given effect to.

*Retention of title clauses*

Sellers, particularly of raw materials, frequently protect themselves by inserting into the contract of sale a retention of title or "*Romalpa*" clause whereby they seek to retain title to the

---

[62a] *Royal Trust Bank plc v. National Westminster Bank plc* [1995] BCC 128.

[63] *Re Brightlife Ltd* [1987] Ch. 200; *Re Permanent Houses (Holdings) Ltd* (1989) 5 BCC 151.

[64] [1994] 1 BCLC 485 (C.A.). This decision was, however, described as 'odd' by Jonathan Parker J. in *Royal Trust Bank plc v. National Westminster Bank plc* [1995] BCC 128, p. 139.

materials supplied until the buyer has paid for them. There have been many cases since the original decision in *Aluminium Industrie Vaassen BV v. Romalpa Aluminium Ltd*[65] that such a clause could have the effect of retaining the legal title to the goods. Some clauses have failed, *e.g.* because the raw materials have ceased to exist,[66] or because they have created a floating charge which has thus been declared void for non-registration under the Companies Act[67] or because they have created a charge over the book debts of the company, which again is void for non-registration.[68] The distinction is always one of construction of the particular clause—is the buyer conferring a charge on *his* goods or the proceeds of sale of those goods[69] in favour of the seller,[70] or is the seller retaining title to *his* goods to provide himself with a security.[71] It may be indicative of the former if the seller attempts to retain title to the goods into which the raw materials have been incorporated.[72]

A seller supplied yarn to some fabric manufacturers. He included a clause whereby the ownership of the yarn was to remain with the seller and if it was incorporated into other goods the ownership of these other goods was to remain with the seller, in either case until payment. The Court of Appeal held that the first part of the clause was a valid retention of title clause whereas the second created a floating charge. Since only the unused yarn was claimed the seller was allowed to succeed: *Clough Mill Ltd v. Geoffrey Martin* [1985] 1 W.L.R. 111 (C.A.).

### Priority of charges (English law)

A company which has created a floating charge cannot later create another floating charge over some of the same assets ranking in priority to or *pari passu* with the original charge unless the provisions of the original charge allow this.[73]

---

[65] [1978] 1 W.L.R. 676 (C.A.).
[66] *Borden (U.K.) Ltd v. Scottish Timber Products Ltd* [1981] Ch. 25.
[67] *Re Bond Worth Ltd* [1980] Ch. 228; *Stroud Architectural Systems Ltd v. John Laing Construction Ltd* [1994] 2 BCLC 276.
[68] *E. Pfeiffer Weinkellerei-Weineinkauf GmbH & Co. v. Arbuthnot Factors Ltd* [1988] 1 W.L.R. 150; *Re Weldtech Equipment Ltd* [1991] BCLC 393.
[69] *Tatung (U.K.) Ltd v. Galex Telesure Ltd* (1989) 5 BCC 325.
[70] *Re Peachdart Ltd* [1984] Ch. 131; *Specialist Plant Services Ltd v. Braithwaite Ltd* (1987) 3 BCC 119 (C.A.).
[71] *Hendy Lennox (Industrial Engines) Ltd v. Grahame Puttick Ltd* [1984] 1 W.L.R. 485; *Re Andrabell Ltd* [1984] BCLC 522.
[72] *John Snow & Co. Ltd v. D. B. G. Woodcroft & Co. Ltd* [1985] BCLC 54.
[73] *Re Automatic Bottle Makers Ltd* [1926] Ch. 412 (C.A.).

On the other hand, since a company which has created a floating charge can, without the consent of the holders of the charge, deal with the class of assets in the ordinary course of business, it follows that the company can, in the ordinary course of business, create a later fixed charge, legal or equitable, over specific assets and with priority over the floating charge,[74] unless the floating charge provides that the company is not to create any mortgage or charge ranking *pari passu* with or in priority to the floating charge, in which case any fixed chargee taking *with notice of this provision* will be postponed to the floating charge. In spite of such a provision the holder of a specific charge will obtain priority over a floating charge on all the company's property if:

(1) taking a legal charge, he obtains his charge without notice of the provision, even though he has notice of the debentures[75]—the maxim "where the equities are equal the law prevails" will apply; or

(2) taking an equitable fixed charge, he obtains the title deeds without notice of the debentures[76]—the maxim "where the equities are otherwise equal the earlier in time has priority" will not apply since the debenture holders left the title deeds with the company so as to enable it to deal with its property as if it was unincumbered so that the equities are not equal.

Further, registration of a floating charge under the Companies Act, *post*,[77] although constructive notice under certain circumstances of the charge, is not notice that the charge contains a provision prohibiting the creation of subsequent charges with priority over the floating charge.[78]

The following also have priority over a floating charge:

---

[74] *Wheatley v. Silkstone, etc., Coal Co.* (1885) 29 Ch.D. 715.
[75] *English and Scottish Mercantile etc. Co. Ltd v. Brunton* [1892] 2 Q.B. 700 (C.A.).
[76] *Re Castell & Brown Ltd* [1898] 1 Ch. 315.
[77] pp. 642, *et seq.*
[78] *Per* Eve J. in *Wilson v. Kelland* [1910] 2 Ch. 306 at p. 313; *Dempsey v. Traders' Finance Corpn.* [1933] N.Z.L.R. 1258 (C.A.); but see *Ian Chisholm Textiles Ltd v. Griffiths* [1994] 2 BCLC 291.

(1)  an execution creditor if the goods are sold by the sheriff,[79] or the company pays out the sheriff to avoid a sale,[80] or the creditor obtains a garnishee order absolute[81] (not a garnishee order nisi),[82] *before* crystallisation of the floating charge;

(2)  a landlord's distress for rent or a local authority's distress for unpaid business rates levied before crystallisation[83];

(3)  the rights of persons such as one who has sold goods to the company under a hire-purchase agreement by which the goods are still the property of such person[84];

(4)  the rights of preferential creditors: section 196, I.A. 1986 section 40.[85]

On the other hand a floating charge may not be postponed to the holder of a *Mareva* injunction over the assets. Such an injunction prohibits the company from removing its assets outside the United Kingdom. The holder of the floating charge may apply to have the injunction set aside and will succeed if the holders of the injunction are unsecured creditors.[86]

### Fixed securities and floating charges (Scots law)

Before 1961 any attempt by a Scottish company to create a floating charge was of no effect, since such a charge violated the principle of the common law expressed in the maxim *"traditionibus, non nudis pactis, dominia rerum transferuntur,"* i.e. "delivery, and not mere agreement, is required for the transfer of real rights."

---

[79] *Re Standard Manufacturing Co.* [1891] 1 Ch. 627 (C.A.).
[80] *Heaton and Dugard Ltd v. Cutting Bros. Ltd* [1925] 1 K.B. 655.
[81] *Evans v. Rival Granite Quarries Ltd* [1910] 2 K.B. 979 (C.A.).
[82] *Norton v. Yates* [1906] 1 K.B. 112.
[83] *Re Roundwood Colliery Co.* [1897] 1 Ch. 373 (C.A.); *Re ELS Ltd* [1994] BCC 449. It follows that where distress is levied after crystallisation the floating charge takes priority. However, where a floating charge crystallised before the company's landlord served a distress notice on the company's tenants which assigned their rents to the landlord, the chargee still took priority over the landlord, since the latter had notice of the crystallisation, which was an earlier assignment by the company to the chargee: *Rhodes v. Allied Dunbar Pension Services Ltd* [1988] BCLC 186.
[84] See *Re Morrison, Jones and Taylor Ltd* [1914] 1 Ch. 50 (C.A.).
[85] *Post*, Chap. 29.
[86] *Cretanor Maritime Co. Ltd v. Irish Marine Management Ltd* [1978] 1 W.L.R. 966 (C.A.).

"There is no principle more deeply rooted in the law than this, that in order to create a good security over subjects delivery must be given. If possession be retained no effectual security can be granted"; *per* Lord Shand in *Clark v. West Calder Oil Co. Ltd* (1882) 9 R. 1017 at p. 1033 (a case in which trustees for debenture holders to whom the company had assigned certain leasehold and moveable property in security were held to have no preference over the ordinary trade creditors of the company since no possession had followed on the assignation).

"The whole method of creating a floating charge . . . is absolutely foreign to our law": *per* Lord President Dunedin in *The Ballachulish Slate Quarries Co. Ltd v. Bruce* (1908) 16 S.L.T. 48 at p. 51 (an attempt to create a floating charge in English form on the uncalled capital and other assets of a company was held to give a debenture holder no valid security).

A company registered in Scotland and having a place of business and assets in England borrowed money under debentures which were in English form and by which the company purported to create a floating charge over its whole undertakings, property and assets. *Held*, that no valid and effectual floating charge had been created even over the company's assets in England: *Carse v. Coppen*, 1951 S.C. 233.

"It is clear in principle and amply supported by authority that a floating charge is utterly repugnant to the principles of Scots law and is not recognised by us as creating a security at all. In Scotland the term 'equitable security' is meaningless. Putting aside the rare and exceptional cases of hypothec, we require for the constitution of a security which will confer upon the holder rights over and above those which he enjoys in common with the general body of unsecured creditors of a debtor, (*a*) the transfer of the creditor of a real right in specific subjects by the method appropriate for the constitution of such rights in the particular classes of property in question, or (*b*) the creation of a nexus over specific property by the due use of the appropriate form of diligence. A floating charge, even after appointment of a receiver, satisfies none of these requirements": *per* Lord President Cooper at p. 239.

Floating charges were introduced to Scots law by the Companies (Floating Charges) (Scotland) Act 1961, but there was no power under that Act to appoint receivers. Subsequently, on the recommendation of the Scottish Law Commission,[87] the Companies (Floating Charges and Receivers) (Scotland) Act 1972 was passed with the twofold purpose of:

(1) re–enacting with substantial modification the provisions of the Act of 1961; and

---

[87] *Report on the Companies (Floating Charges) (Scotland) Act 1961*, (1970) Cmnd. 4336.

(2)  making it competent under Scots law for receivers to be
appointed.

The 1972 Act was consolidated by and appeared as sections 462
to 487 of the 1985 Act. Of these sections the first five (*i.e.*
sections 462 to 466) relate to floating charges and are still
applicable, but the remaining sections (*i.e.* sections 467 to 487)
relating to receivers were amended by the Insolvency Act 1985
and in their amended form have now been consolidated by the
Insolvency Act 1986, where they appear as sections 50 to 71.

Scottish floating charges and receivers have statutory definitions and statutory incidents which distinguish them in some
respects from their English common law originals. The term
"fixed security" is used in the statutory provisions to denote a
security other than a floating charge.[88]

**Floating charges (Scots law)**

The main characteristics of the Scottish floating charge are:

(1)  It is a charge created by an incorporated company[89] over
all or any part of the property (including uncalled capital)
which may from time to time be comprised in its property
and undertaking.

(2)  It may be created for the purpose of securing any debt or
other obligation (including a cautionary obligation)
incurred or to be incurred by, or binding upon, the
company or any other person. It is therefore possible, for
instance, for a subsidiary company to create a floating
charge over its own property to secure a debt due by its
parent company (another person), or for a subsidiary
company to guarantee a debt due by its parent company
and create a floating charge over its own property to
secure its liability under the guarantee.

(3)  It can be created by a Scottish company only by the
execution, under the seal of the company, of an instrument or bond or other written acknowledgment of debt or

---

[88] s.486.
[89] Floating charges may also be created by industrial and provident societies
registered in Scotland: Industrial and Provident Societies Act 1967, as amended
by the Companies (Floating Charges and Receivers) (Scotland) Act 1972, s.10.

obligation which purports to create a floating charge. There is no longer any statutory form as there was under the 1961 Act. An alternative to execution by the company itself is execution by an attorney who has been authorised for that purpose by writing under the company's common seal. Where the floating charge relates to heritable property in Scotland, it takes effect on that property even although the instrument creating it has not been recorded in the Register of Sasines or registered under the Land Registration (Scotland) Act 1979: section 462.

(4) On the commencement of the winding up or on the appointment of a receiver it attaches (provided it is not invalid under section 410 of the 1985 Act[90] or section 245 of the Insolvency Act 1986[91]) to the property then comprised in the company's property and undertaking. Where heritable property had been dispensed by a company and the disposition had been delivered to the purchaser but not recorded before the appointment of a receiver, the property was held still to be the company's property and therefore attached by the floating charge.[92]

References in the Act to the crystallisation of a floating charge are, in relation to a Scottish floating charge, construed as references to the attachment of the charge.[93]

(5) Once attached it has the same effect as if it were a fixed security over the property for the principal of, and any interest due or to become due on, the debt or obligation to which it relates. The security extends to interest stipulated for from the date of attachment until payment.[94]

(6) It is postponed to the rights of certain creditors[95]: section 463.

The instrument creating a floating charge may contain:

[90] *Post*, p. 650.
[91] *Post*, p. 639.
[92] *Sharp v. Thomson* [1995] BCC 57 (O.H.); for comment on this case see Robert Rennie, "Dead on Delivery," 1994 S.L.T. (News) 183.
[93] ss.419(4) and 420, inserted by C.A. 1989, s.104. These are not yet in force.
[94] *National Commercial Bank of Scotland Ltd v. Liquidators of Telford Grier Mackay & Co. Ltd*, 1969 S.C. 181, followed in *Royal Bank of Scotland Ltd v. Williamson*, 1972 S.L.T. (Sh.Ct.) 45, and given statutory force by s.463(4).
[95] *Post*, Chap. 29.

(a) provisions prohibiting or restricting the creation of any fixed security or any other floating charge having priority over, or ranking equally with, the floating charge[96]; or

(b) provisions regulating the order in which the floating charge is to rank with any other subsisting or future floating charges or fixed securities over the property or part of it: section 464.

A floating charge may be altered by an instrument of alteration: section 466.

The advantage of a floating charge from the *company's* point of view is that the company can give security for a loan to it by charging property such as stock-in-trade and other moveables which it would be impracticable to deliver to the lender. Until the floating charge has attached to the property the company can, in the ordinary course of business, realise any of its assets without the consent of the creditor who is entitled to the benefit of the floating charge.

From the *creditor's* point of view, the two disadvantages exemplified on page 629, *ante*, in relation to English law, apply also in Scots law, but for the protection of the creditor it is provided that a Scots company may be wound up by the court "if there is subsisting a floating charge over property comprised in the company's property and undertaking and the court is satisfied that the security of the creditor entitled to the benefit of the floating charge is in jeopardy." The security of the creditor is deemed to be in jeopardy "if the court is satisfied that events have occurred or are about to occur which render it unreasonable in the creditor's interests that the company should retain power to dispose of the property which is subject to the floating charge": Insolvency Act 1986, section 122.

**Priority of charges (Scots law)**

Where all or any part of a company's property is subject both to a fixed security and to a floating charge, the fixed security has

---

[96] For an example see *AIB Finance Ltd v. Bank of Scotland* 1993 S.C.L.R. 851 (clause in floating charge prohibiting creation of subsequent standard securities gave the holder of the floating charge and the receiver priority over the holder of the standard security).

as a general rule priority over the floating charge. This is always
so if the fixed security is one arising by operation of law (*e.g.* by a
statutory provision). If the fixed security is not of that nature
(*e.g.* is a standard security over heritable property under the
Conveyancing and Feudal Reform (Scotland) Act 1970), the
order of ranking may be regulated by provisions in the document
which creates the floating charge or in any instrument of alteration. Where the right to a fixed security has become a real right
before a floating charge has attached, the fixed security has
priority of ranking over the floating charge.

Where there are two or more floating charges, the charges as a
general rule rank with one another according to the time of their
registration with the Registrar,[97] and if received by the Registrar
by the same postal delivery they rank equally with one another.
Here again the order of ranking may be regulated by provisions
in the document creating a floating charge or in any instrument of
alteration. There is, however, the following statutory restriction
on the priority which may be obtained: where the holder of a
floating charge which has been registered receives a written
intimation of the subsequent registration of another floating
charge over the same property or part of it, the preference in
ranking of the first floating charge is restricted to security for:

(a) the holder's present advances;
(b) future advances which he may be required to make;
(c) interest due or to become due on advances within (a) and
    (b), above; and
(d) expenses or outlays reasonably incurred by the holder:
    section 464.

The following have priority over a floating charge:

(1) the rights of any person who has effectually executed
    diligence on the property or any part of it: section 463.
    The meaning of the phrase "effectually executed dili-
    gence" is uncertain: in *Lord Advocate v. Royal Bank of
    Scotland Ltd*, 1977 S.C. 177, it was suggested that arrest-
    ment only became "effectually executed diligence" when
    completed by an action of furthcoming and in *Armour*

[97] *Post*, p. 643.

*and Mycroft, Petitioners*, 1983 S.L.T. 453 (O.H.), the creditor conceded without argument that an inhibition laid after the granting of a floating charge but not followed by adjudication before the appointment of receivers was ineffectual;

(2) the rights of persons such as one who has sold goods to the company under a hire-purchase agreement by which the goods are still the property of such person;

(3) certain *un*secured but preferential debts: Insolvency Act 1986, section 175.[98]

## Avoidance of floating charges

To prevent those in control of insolvent companies from creating floating charges to secure past debts so as to gain priority over other unsecured creditors, section 245 of the Insolvency Act 1986 provides that floating charges created within 12 months prior to the presentation of a successful petition for a winding up[99] or for an administration order[1] are invalid unless the company was solvent immediately after the charge was created, except insofar as money was paid or goods or services supplied to the company or a debt of the company was reduced or discharged, in consideration of and at the same time as or after the creation of the charge, with interest if appropriate.

The position is different if the floating charge is created in favour of a person who is connected with the company. In such cases the ambit of the section is widened to catch floating charges created within two years prior to the winding-up or administration petition, as appropriate, and it is of no consequence that the company was solvent immediately after granting the charge.

The difficulty therefore is to establish whether money was paid, goods or services supplied or a debt reduced or discharged in consideration of the charge and whether that was at the same time as the creation of the charge. The value of any goods or services so supplied are to be valued at the cost which could reasonably be expected to be paid for goods or services supplied at that time in the ordinary course of business and on the same

---

[98] *Post*, Chap. 29
[99] This, and not the date of the winding up order is the relevant date: *Power v. Sharp Investments Ltd* [1994] 1 BCLC 111 (C.A.).
[1] *Post*, Chap. 26.

terms (apart from the granting of a floating charge) as those on which they were supplied to the company. Section 245 replaced section 617 of the Companies Act 1985 which invalidated floating charges created within a year of a winding-up except to the amount of any cash paid to the company in consideration and at the time of the charge (unless the company was solvent immediately after granting the charge).

Whether cash was paid at the time when the charge was created was a question of fact for section 617, and "a payment made on account of the consideration for the security, in anticipation of its creation and in reliance on a promise to execute it, although made some days before its execution, [was] made at the time of its creation within the meaning of the section."[2] Section 245, on the other hand, expressly requires it to be paid *at the same time as or after the creation of the charge*.

The question arises, therefore, as to whether the relaxed attitude of the courts under the former section has been preserved.

In *Re Fairway Magazines Ltd*,[3] Mummery J. considered that it had and that the advancing of the cash and the creation of the charge should be regarded as a matter of substance rather than form so that a month's gap between the two did not prevent the cash being paid to the company at the same time as the charge. In *Re Shoe Lace Ltd*,[4] on the other hand, Hoffmann J. considered that the wording between the old and new sections was sufficiently different to justify a new approach which he considered should be whether a reasonable businessman, having knowledge of the statute, would regard the money as having been paid at the same time as the charge.

The reasoning in both cases was, however, rejected by the Court of Appeal in the *Shoe Lace* case.[5] The Court of Appeal decided that the difference in wording was insufficient to justify a distinction from the old cases but that they had been wrongly decided in the first place. It followed that any gap between the advancement of the cash and the creation of the charge would invoke section 425.[6] A mere agreement to create a charge at the

---

[2] *Per* Neville J. in *Re Columbian Fireproofing Co. Ltd* [1910] 1 Ch. 758, at p. 765; *Re F. & E. Stanton Ltd* [1928] 1 Ch. 180.
[3] [1992] BCC 924.
[4] [1992] BCLC 636.
[5] Reported as *Power v. Sharp Investments Ltd* [1994] 1 BCLC 111 (C.A.).
[6] Although they did concede that a short break for coffee might not count!

time when the money was advanced would not be enough unless that agreement itself created an equitable charge.

The words "in consideration for the charge" in section 617 meant "in consideration of the fact that the charge exists."

A company created a floating charge to secure its overdrawn current account with its bank. *Held*: (1) Every payment made by the bank to the company after the creation of the charge was "cash paid to the company" and was made in consideration of the charge. Consequently the charge was not invalid against the liquidator, and the bank was a secured creditor as to such payments. (2) The rule in *Clayton's Case*[7] applied. Each payment by the bank after the date of the charge was a provision of "new money" and there was nothing to displace the presumption that payments in by the company after the charge should be set in the first instance against the company's debt to the bank at the date of the charge: *Re Yeovil Glove Co. Ltd* [1965] Ch. 148 (C.A.).

Section 245 of the Insolvency Act uses the phrase "so much of the consideration as consists of." *Quaere* whether *Re Yeovil Glove Co. Ltd* is still valid?

In *Mace Builders (Glasgow) Ltd v. Lunn*[8] it was held that the effect of section 617 was simply to render the charge invalid from the date of the winding-up so that where the charge was repaid prior to the winding-up the section had no effect. The wording of section 245 is not identical, however, and it may be that the position is now different.[9]

Payments made direct to the company's creditors, though made on the company's behalf, have been held not to be within the phrase "Cash paid to the company."[10] The question is one of substance, however.

D. was a director of the company and a partner in the firm of D. & Co. who supplied goods to the company. The company owed D. & Co. £1,954 and D. & Co. refused to supply any more goods until this debt was paid. In March D., who wished to save the company, agreed to lend the company £3,000 on the security of a floating charge if the company would, out of this sum, pay £1,954 to D. & Co. This was done. The company was insolvent at the time. In July the company went into liquidation. *Held*, the floating charge was valid, the whole £3,000 being cash paid to the company: *Re Matthew Ellis Ltd* [1933] 1 Ch. 458.

On the other hand, the cash must have been intended to benefit the company and not certain creditors or the directors.[11]

[7] (1816) 1 Mer. 572.
[8] (1986) 130 S.J. 839 (C.A.).
[9] See also *Re Parkes Garage* [1929] 1 Ch. 139.
[10] *Libertas-Kommerz GmbH v. Johnston*, 1977 S.C. 191 (O.H.).
[11] *Re Orleans Motor Co. Ltd* [1911] 2 Ch. 41.

An insolvent company granted a floating charge to Z. to secure £900.
The money was provided by D., for whom Z. was a nominee, and the
same day as it was paid to the company the company paid £350 each to
B. and S. for directors' fees and £200 to D., the amount guaranteed by
D. in respect of the company's overdraft. Within 12 months, the
company went into liquidation. *Held*, the charge was invalid, as its
object was to benefit B., S. and D. and not the company—in substance,
no cash was paid to the company: *Re Destone Fabrics Ltd* [1941] Ch. 319
(C.A.).

Cash was held not to be paid to the company where the
substance of the transaction was the substitition of a better
security for the company's debts.[12] It was also said that the
section would apply irrespective of the motives of the chargee.[13]
These decisions on whether cash has been paid to the company
have been applied to section 425.[14]

### Preferences and transactions at an undervalue

*Any* charge made by a company within *six* months[15] before the
commencement of winding-up, or presentation of a successful
administration petition is void if it is a preference of any of the
company's creditors, or, within a two year period, if it is part of a
transaction of an undervalue, or within a three year period, if it is
part of an extortionate credit transaction: Insolvency Act 1986,
sections 238–244, chap. 29, *post*.

## REGISTRATION OF CHARGES

Charges created by a company are required to be registered (1)
in the company's own register of charges, and (2) with the
Registrar of Companies. The statutory system of registration was
intended to be changed by the Companies Act 1989. However,
those changes have not yet been brought into force so the
unmodified system is set out in this edition. The modified system
is described in the previous (14th) edition.

### Registration in company's own register of charges

Section 407, applicable in England, provides that every *limited*
company must keep at its registered office a register of *all* charges

---

[12] *Re G. T. Whyte & Co. Ltd* [1983] BCLC 311.
[13] *ibid.*, *per* Nourse J., p. 317.
[14] *Re Fairway Magazines Ltd* [1992] BCC 924.
[15] Two years for persons connected with the company.

specifically affecting the property of the company and *all* floating charges on the undertaking or any property of the company. The register must give:

(a)  a short description of the property charged;
(b)  the amount of the charge;
(c)  the names of the persons entitled thereto, except in the case of bearer securities.

There is a corresponding provision for Scotland in section 422 but that section applies to *every* company and is not restricted to *limited* companies.

The omission to comply with section 407 or section 422 merely results in a fine on every officer who is knowingly a party to the omission. The validity of the charge is *not* affected.

*Every* company must keep a copy of every instrument creating a charge required to be registered under section 407, section 422, or under sections 395 and 400 (for Scotland, sections 410 and 416), *post*, at the registered office of the company. In the case of a series of uniform debentures a copy of one of the series is sufficient: sections 406 and 421.

These copies, and also the company's register of charges, are open to the inspection of any creditor or member of the company without fee for at least two hours each day during business hours. The register of charges *only* is similarly open to the general public on payment of a fee not exceeding five pence: sections 408 and 423.

**Registration with Registrar**

There are some differences between the registration requirements imposed on English companies by the Act and those imposed on Scottish companies originally by the, now consolidated, Companies (Floating Charges and Receivers) (Scotland) Act 1972.

*Registration in England*

Section 395 provides that prescribed particulars of certain specified charges *created* by companies registered in England, together with the instrument, if any, creating them, must be delivered to the Registrar within 21 days after their creation. The object of registration is to protect the grantee of the charge.[16]

[16] *Per* Bankes L.J. in *National Provincial Bank v. Charnley* [1924] 1 K.B. 431 (C.A.) at p. 442.

The charges to which section 395 applies are specified in section 396:

(a) a charge to secure an issue of debentures;
(b) a charge on uncalled share capital;
(c) a charge created or evidenced by an instrument which, if executed by an individual, would require registration as a bill of sale[17];
(d) a charge on any land or any interest therein;

The general rule is that a deposit of title deeds by a company to secure a debt, whether owed by the company or a third party creates an equitable charge on the land,[18] and not just a naked lien on the documents themselves, which charge is registrable under section 395 since it is contractual in nature even though created as a result of a presumption of law.[19]

(e) a charge on book debts of the company;

If a company which has entered into hire-purchase agreements for the disposal of its products deposits the agreements as security for advances, there is a charge on the company's book debts.[20] Whether a particular agreement amounts to a charge on book debts is a question of construction.[21]

A charge on future book debts is registrable under section 395. However, where the subject-matter of a charge at the date of its creation is the benefit of a contract which does not then comprehend a book debt, e.g. a contract of insurance, the contract cannot be brought within section 395 merely because it might ultimately result in a book debt.[22] The test is whether there is a

---

[17] See *Stoneleight Finance Ltd v. Phillips* [1965] 2 Q.B. 537 (C.A.). The transfer of goods by way of security is caught by this head: *Welsh Development Agency v. Export Finance Co. Ltd* [1991] BCLC 936, reversed on other grounds [1992] BCLC 148.

[18] But see *Re Alton Corporation* [1985] BCLC 27.

[19] *Re Wallis & Simmonds (Builders) Ltd* [1974] 1 W.L.R. 391, distinguishing *London and Cheshire Insce. Co. Ltd v. Laplagrene Property Co. Ltd* [1971] Ch. 499 (unpaid vendor's lien created by law not registrable). In *Wallis & Simmonds* there was no lien on the title deeds having a separate existence and the charge was void for non-registration.

[20] *Independent Automatic Sales Ltd v. Knowles & Foster* [1962] 1 W.L.R. 974.

[21] *Carreras Rothmans Ltd v. Freeman Matthews Treasure Ltd* [1985] 1 All E.R. 155; *Re Welsh Irish Ferries Ltd* [1985] 3 W.L.R. 610.

[22] *Paul & Frank Ltd v. Discount Bank (Overseas) Ltd* [1967] Ch. 348.

charge on future book debts as and when they arise or there is simply an assignment of a contingent contractual right[23];

(f)   a floating charge on the undertaking or property of the company;
(g)   a charge on calls made but not paid;
(h)   a charge on a ship or aircraft;
(i)   a charge on goodwill, on a patent or a licence under a patent, on a trademark or on a copyright or a licence under a copyright.

*Registration in Scotland*

For Scotland section 410, corresponding to sections 395–396, requires registration of prescribed particulars of certain specified charges created by companies, together with *certified copies* of any instruments creating the charges.

The section applies to the following charges:

(a)   A charge on land wherever situated or any interest therein. Hence registration with the Registrar in Scotland is required of a charge created by a Scottish company over heritable property in England.[24]
(b)   A security over the uncalled share capital.
(c)   A security over incorporeal moveable property of any of the following categories—
    (i)    the book debts of the company;
    (ii)   calls made but not paid;
    (iii)  goodwill;
    (iv)   a patent or a licence under a patent;
    (v)    a trademark;
    (vi)   a copyright or a licence under a copyright.
(d)   A security over a ship or aircraft.
(e)   A floating charge.

A security over incorporeal moveable property not falling within any of the categories specified (*e.g.* shares in other companies) does not require registration, and if particulars of such a charge have been registered the court will order their deletion from the register.[24a]

[23] *Re Brush Aggregates* [1986] BCLC 320.
[24] *Amalgamated Securites Ltd, Petitioners*, 1967 S.C. 56.
[24a] *Scottish Homes Investment Co. Ltd, Petitioner*, 1968 S.C. 244.

It is to be observed that a charge to secure an issue of debentures which is the first in the English list is absent from the Scottish list. "For some inscrutable reason no corresponding provision has been made in regard to Scotland."[25]

In the Companies (Floating Charges) (Scotland) Act 1961 no provision was made for re-registration of any instrument creating a charge,[26] or for registration of an instrument increasing the amount secured.[27] Consequently, if at a later date the amount secured by a fixed charge was to be increased, the security had to be re-created from the beginning, a "cumbersome and expensive" practice for which the Scottish Law Commission suggested a remedy.[28] The 1972 Act accordingly provided that where the amount secured by a fixed charge was increased, a further charge was to be held to have been created, and that the registration provisions applied to that further charge. The provision is now in section 414 of the 1985 Act.

A fixed charge on land cannot now be created in any form other than a "standard security" under the Conveyancing and Feudal Reform (Scotland) Act 1970. For the creation of a real right the standard security must be recorded in the Register of Sasines or registered in the Land Register of Scotland: 1970 Act, ss.9, 11; Land Registration (Scotland) Act 1979, ss.2, 3.

Section 410 provides that the date of creation of a floating charge is the date on which the instrument creating the floating charge is executed by the company, and the date of creation of any other charge is the date on which the right of the person entitled to the benefit of the charge becomes a real right, e.g. in the case of a standard security, the date of recording in the Register of Sasines.[29]

The registration provisions extend to any instrument of alteration under section 466 if the instrument:

(a) prohibits or restricts the creation of any fixed security or any other floating charge having priority over, or ranking equally with, the floating charge; or

---

[25] Per Lord President Clyde in the *Scottish Homes* case, above, at p. 248 (shares in other companies assigned to trustees in security for an issue of debenture stock).

[26] *Archibald Campbell, Hope & King Ltd, Petitioners*, 1967 S.C. 21.

[27] *Scottish and Newcastle Breweries Ltd v. Liquidator of Rathburne Hotel Co. Ltd*, 1970 S.C. 215 (O.H.).

[28] (1970) Cmnd. 4336, paras. 17, 18.

[29] See note 26, above.

(b) varies, or otherwise regulates the order of, the ranking of the floating charge in relation to fixed securities or to other floating charges; or

(c) releases property from the floating charge; or

(d) increases the amount secured by the floating charge.

## Registration in England and Scotland

In the case of a series of debentures containing, or giving by reference to another instrument, a charge to the benefit of which the debenture holders are entitled *pari passu*, it is sufficient if the following particulars are registered:

(a) the total amount secured by the series;

(b) the dates of the resolutions authorising the issue of the series and the date of the covering deed, if any, by which the security is created;

(c) a general description of the property charged;

(d) the names of the trustees, if any, for the debenture holders; and

(e) in the case of a Scottish floating charge, a statement of the restrictions, if any, on the company's power to grant further securities ranking prior to or equally with the floating charge;

together with the deed (or in Scotland a copy of the deed) creating the charge or, if there is no deed, one of the debentures (or in Scotland a copy of one of the debentures) of the series: sections 397, 413. The sections also require registration of the date and amount of each issue in the series but failure to do so does not affect the validity of the debentures.

Particulars of the amount, or rate per cent, of the commission, allowance or discount on an issue of debentures must be registered: sections 397, 413.

The register contains the following particulars:

(a) in the case of a series of debentures, the particulars set out *ante*;

(b) in other cases—

    (i) the date of the creation of the charge;

    (ii) the amount secured by the charge;

    (iii) short particulars of the property charged;

(iv) the persons entitled to the charge; and

(v) in the case of a Scottish floating charge, a statement of the restrictions, if any, on the company's power to grant further securities ranking prior to or equally with the floating charge: sections 401, 417.

It is the duty of the company to register the particulars required by section 395 or section 410. Registration, however, may be effected by any person interested in the charge and the registration fees may be recovered from the company: sections 399, 415.

On the registration of a charge the Registrar gives a certificate of registration which is conclusive evidence that the requirements of the Act as to registration have been complied with: sections 401(2)(b), 418(2)(c). The particulars delivered to the Registrar may incorrectly state the property charged, or the amount or date of the charge, but if a certificate is given, the grantee of the charge is protected.[30] The certificate is conclusive evidence that the Registrar has entered the particulars in the register and that the prescribed, *i.e.* accurate, particulars have been presented to him.[31]

In the course of its business in 1960 a company bought properties. R., a shareholder, advanced money for each purchase and the company undertook to execute formal mortgages on demand. In 1961 the directors and R. agreed that the company should implement its undertakings, and memoranda of deposit of title deeds purporting to charge some of the properties with payments to R. of certain sums on demand were signed but not dated on June 5, 1961. On July 11 the memoranda were registered with the Registrar, the date of execution being given as June 23. On August 4 the company went into voluntary winding-up. *Held*, the charges were not void since the certificate of registration was conclusive that all the requirements of the Act had been complied with within 21 days of execution, although the particulars submitted for registration incorrectly stated the date of the charges: *Re Eric Holmes* (*Property*) *Ltd* [1965] Ch. 1052, applied in *Re C. L. Nye Ltd* [1971] Ch 442 (C.A.).

The Registrar used to adopt the practice whereby if incorrect particulars of a charge were delivered for registration within the 21 day period he would register the charge after the 21 day

---

[30] This is equally true where the particulars are delivered late with the consent of the court under s.404, *post*: *Exeter Trust Ltd v. Screenways Ltd* [1991] BCLC 888.

[31] *Re C. L. Nye Ltd* [1971] Ch. 442 (C.A.).

period on the delivery of amended particulars. This practice was challenged in the courts and disapproved of by the Court of Appeal, who nevertheless refused to allow the Registrar's certificate to be challenged. No evidence could be adduced to challenge the correctness of his decision—he has jurisdiction finally and conclusively to determine any question of law or fact as to whether the requirements for registration have been complied with. Only the Attorney-General can challenge registration by means of judicial review since the Crown is not bound by the section.[32] Following that decision, however, the Registrar has changed his practice so that unless correct forms are submitted within the 21 day period registration will not be allowed without the court's permission under section 404 (or 420).[33]

To discover the exact terms of a charge one has to look at the document creating it (which document, or in Scotland a copy of which document, will have been filed), and not at the register.[34]

In England, a copy of the certificate of registration must be indorsed on every debenture or debenture stock certificate issued by the company and the payment of which is secured by the charge registered. The penalty of neglect is a fine: section 402. There is no corresponding provision for Scotland.

When the debt for which any registered charge was given is satisfied, in whole or in part, or part of the property charged is released or ceases to form part of the company's property, the Registrar enters a memorandum of satisfaction or release on the register. The company is entitled to a copy of the memorandum: sections 403, 419.

In Scotland the Registrar must not enter any such memorandum on the register unless either:

(a) the creditor entitled to the benefit of the floating charge, or a person authorised by the creditor, certifies as correct the particulars submitted to the Registrar with respect to the entry; or

(b) the court, on being satisfied that such certificate cannot readily be obtained, directs the Registrar to make the entry: section 419.

---

[32] *R. v. Registrar of Companies, ex p. Central Bank of India* [1986] Q.B. 1114 (C.A.).

[33] *Post,* p. 650.

[34] *Re Mechanisation (Eaglescliffe) Ltd* [1966] Ch. 20, following *National Provincial Bank v. Charnley* [1924] 1 K.B. 431 (C.A.).

The register is open to public inspection: sections 401, 417.

*Effect of non-registration*

If a charge which ought to be registered under section 395 or section 410 is not so registered:

(a) the company and every officer who is knowingly a party to the default, is liable to a default fine (sections 399, 415);

(b) the charge is, so far as any security on the company's property is concerned, void against the liqudiator and any creditor of the company, but without prejudice to the contract to repay the money secured, which becomes immediately repayable (sections 395, 410). The result is that the holder of the charge is reduced to the level of an *unsecured* creditor.

In March the company gave T, a legal mortgage of specific land to secure £500. The mortgage was not restricted. In December the company issued debentures secured by a floating charge on its undertaking and assets to J. to secure another £500. This charge was registered. *Held*, although J., when he took his security, had actual notice of T.'s mortgage, he nevertheless had priority over T.: *Re Monolithic Building Co.* [1915] 1 Ch. 643 (C.A.).

In order to secure repayment of a loan a company gave the lenders subcharges on properties and deposited deeds and documents (such as legal charges and charge certificates) "to the intent that" they might "be equitably charged." The charges were void for non-registration (as charges on land or on book debts) under what is now section 395. *Held*, the lenders had no common law lien on the documents. The deposit was merely ancillary to the equitable charge, and the contractual right to retention of the documents was lost when the charges were avoided. The contract had no independent existence apart from the charge: *Re Molton Finance Ltd* [1968] Ch. 325 (C.A.), applied in *Re Wallis & Simmonds (Builders) Ltd* [1974] 1 W.L.R. 391.

*Rectification of register*

Under section 404 for England and section 420 for Scotland the court may, on application by the company or any person interested, extend the time for registration or rectify the register if:

(a) the omission to register a charge within the required time or the omission or mis-statement of a particular with respect to a charge is—

(i)   accidental; or

(ii)  due to inadvertence[35] or some other sufficient cause; or

(iii) not of a nature to prejudice the creditor or share-holders; or

(b)  on other grounds it is just and equitable to grant relief.[36]

Sections 404 and 420 require the court to be satisfied with respect to certain matters before it orders an extension of time and, therefore, if serious issues of fact are involved it should arm itself with the best information and evidence available.[37] The section does not empower the court to grant interim relief.[38]

If, on an application for late registration, it is shown either that a liquidation of the company is imminent or has actually occured, the court is unlikely to order an extension of time. This was held to be a factor against the applicant in *Re Telomatic Ltd*[38] and in *Re Barrow Borough Transport Ltd*,[39] where the court refused an application where the company was in administration for the purpose of ensuring the company's survival but that had proved to be incapable of achievement. The company's liquidation was not merely imminent, it was inevitable. The court indicated that the same would apply if the administration had not included the survival of the company as one of its purposes. On the other hand, the imminence of a liquidation is not an absolute bar to a late registration order if there are other circumstances which justify it. Thus in *Re Braemar Investments Ltd*[40] the court made an order on the basis that the fault was that of the chargee's solicitors and the chargee had acted promptly on discovering the non-registration.

That case also shows that when a chargee discovers that, by mistake, he is unregistered he must apply without delay for an extension of time and not deliberately defer his application in

---

[35] See, *e.g.* *Re Chantry House Developments plc* [1990] BCLC 813.

[36] See, *e.g.* *Re Fablehill Ltd* [1991] BCLC 830, where the directors registered their own charge during the period of non-registration of the applicant's charge.

[37] *Re Heathstar Properties Ltd* [1966] 1 W.L.R. 993. In *Re Heathstar Properties Ltd (No. 2)* [1966] 1 W.L.R. 999, it was found that the omission to register was due to inadvertence and the time for registration was extended notwithstanding that an action was proceeding in which the validity of the charge was in issue.

[38] [1994] 1 BCLC 90.

[39] [1989] BCLC 653.

[40] [1990] BCLC 556.

order to see which course would be to his best advantage. Failure to do so will prejudice his application: *Victoria Housing Estates Ltd v. Ashpurton Estates Ltd.*[41]

It has been argued that the court will allow late registration where to do so would prevent one of its officers invoking the non-registration so as to benefit the other creditors unfairly. In *Re John Bateson*,[42] Harman J. regarded such a rule as strange and that in any event it could only apply if the court officer had acted in an unworthy manner. He also doubted whether a voluntary liquidator was an officer for this purpose.

Relief will usually only be granted "without prejudice to the rights of parties acquired prior to the time when [the charge is] actually registered."[43] This proviso protects rights acquired *against the company's property in the extension of time*,[44] so that a secured creditor whose charge is created and registered in such time will not lose priority.[45] This is equally true if the later chargee knew of the existence of the unregistered charge at the date of registration of the later charge since the system is based on registration and not upon the actual notice of the chargee.[46] The court always has a discretion in these matters, however, so that in *Re Fablehill Ltd*[47] the court applied the proviso to give priority to one later registered charge but not another, since the latter had been created by the directors of the company in their own favour with full knowledge that the applicant's charge was unregistered.

The effect of the proviso is different where the second charge is created and registered within the 21 day period allowed by section 395 for registration of the first charge, *e.g.* the second chargee's rights do not gain priority by reason of the proviso—such rights are acquired at the date of execution of the second charge.

On January 22 a company created two floating charges on its undertaking and property by issuing a first debenture to X to secure £10,000 lent by him to the company and a second debenture to Y to secure £5,000. The second debenture was registered on January 28, but,

---

[41] [1983] 3 All E.R. 665 (C.A.). See also *Re Telomatic Ltd* [1994] 1 BCLC 90.
[42] [1985] BCLC 259.
[43] *Re Joplin Brewery Co. Ltd* [1902] 1 Ch. 79.
[44] *Re Ehrmann Bros. Ltd* [1906] 2 Ch. 697 (C.A.).
[45] *Re Monolithic Building Co.* [1915] 1 Ch. 643 (C.A.), *ante.*
[46] *Re Telomatic Ltd* [1994] 1 BCLC 90.
[47] [1991] BCLC 830.

by mistake, the first was returned to X unregistered. On October 20, X applied under section 101 of the 1948 Act for an extension of the time allowed for registration and on October 28 the court ordered an extention to November 11 with a proviso that the order was "without prejudice to the rights of any parties acquired prior to the time when the said debenture is to be registered." Also on October 28, Y appointed a receiver under the second debenture. The first debenture was registered on November 5 and a receiver appointed thereunder on November 8. On November 9, the company went into a creditors' voluntary liquidation.

*Held*, (1) Y's rights under the second debenture were acquired at the date of its execution and not at the expiration of the 21 days allowed by section 395 for registration of the first debenture (February 12), when the first debenture being then unregistered became void, nor in the ensuing period, during which it remained void, between the expiration of the 21 days and the date of its actual registration, and accordingly such rights did not gain priority over the first debenture by reason of the proviso to the court order; (2) although the appointment by Y of a receiver crystallised his floating charge, Y did not thereby acquire rights but merely exercised a power acquired when the debenture was executed (*Watson v. Duff, Morgan and Vermont (Holdings) Limited* [1974] 1 W.L.R. 450).

Unsecured creditors with no charge on the company's property do not qualify for the purposes of the proviso. However, if the company has gone into liquidation there will be, as a general rule, no benefit in obtaining an extension of time, as the unsecured creditors will then have acquired rights against the property of the company.[48]

A clear case for the exercise of the court's power was held to have been made out where a Scottish company had failed to register a charge created over heritable property in England.[49] In a sheriff court case an extension of time was granted where there had been a misunderstanding as to which party was to effect registration.[50]

## Registration of charges existing on property acquired

If a company acquires any property which is already subject to a charge which, if created by the company, would have required

---

[48] *Re S. Abrahams & Sons* [1902] 1 Ch. 695.
[49] *Amalgamated Securities Ltd, Petitioners*, 1967 S.C. 56; contrast *Archibald Campbell, Hope & King Ltd, Petitioners*, 1967 S.C. 21, in which a prayer for extension was held inept under the 1961 Act where the instrument creating the charge had already been registered and the company was seeking to re-register it for the purpose of securing an additional sum; see now s.414.
[50] *M. Milne Ltd, Petitioners* (1963) 79 Sh. Ct. Rep. 105.

registration under section 395 or 410, *the company* must register particulars of the charge and a copy of the instrument creating or evidencing it within 21 days after the acquisition is completed. Default renders the company and every officer in default liable to a default fine (ss.400, 416) but the validity of the charge is not affected.

## Remedies of Debenture Holders

1. If a debenture confers no charge, a debenture holder is an ordinary unsecured creditor. Thus, if there is default in the payment of principal or interest he may (*a*) sue for the principal or interest and, after obtaining judgment, levy execution against the company,[51] or (*b*), as will be explained later,[52] petition either for an administration order or for the winding-up of the company by the court on the ground that the company is unable to pay its debts.

2. When a charge is conferred on the company's assets by way of security, and default is made in the payment of principal or interest, a debenture holder, or the trustees where there is a trust deed, may:

(a) sue for the principal or interest; or
(b) present a petition for an administration order; or
(c) present a petition for the winding up of the company; or
(d) exercise any powers conferred by the debenture or the trust deed, *e.g.* of appointing a receiver or administrative receiver of the assets charged, of selling the assets charged or of taking possession of the assets and carrying on the business; or
(e) if the debenture or the trust deed does not contain powers in that behalf, apply to the court for:
   (i) the appointment of a receiver or a receiver and manager; or
   (ii) an order for sale or foreclosure.

A debenture or trust deed will normally contain an express power to appoint a receiver or administrative receiver of, or to sell, the company's assets charged by way of security. If there is

[51] The Scots equivalent is "do diligence on the decree obtained."
[52] *Post*, Chaps. 26 and 27.

no express power there will be an implied power under the Law of Property Act 1925, s.101,[53] if the debenture or trust deed is under seal. Failing an express or an implied power, an application may be made to the court for the appointment of a receiver or an order for sale. A company's inability to pay its debts for the purpose of appointing a receiver is to be assessed at the date of appointment. Further, where the receiver is to be appointed by a deed, his appointment is not invalidated by an appointment in another manner—that operates as an agreement to perfect the power if necessary.[54]

Where the debenture is an "all moneys" debenture (*e.g.* one for all sums owed to a bank) the demand for payment need not specify the exact sum due and a receiver may be appointed once reasonable time to effect payment has passed.[55] Similarly a demand for an amount less than the full amount due will be sufficient for the appointment of a receiver, although there is no authority if the demand is excessive, *i.e.* for more than the amount due.[56]

In England, where there are numerous debentures of the same class, a *debenture holders' action* is usually brought. This is brought by one debenture holder on behalf of himself and all other debenture holders of the same class as himself. In it a claim may be made for:

(1) a declaration that the debenture holders are entitled to a (first) charge on the property of the company;
(2) if there is a trust deed, the enforcement of the trust;
(3) an account of what is due to the debenture holders;
(4) the enforcement of the charge by sale or foreclosure;
(5) the appointment of a receiver and manager.[57]

An order for foreclosure will only be made if all the debenture holders of the same class as the plaintiff are before the court. If the assets require immediate protection an application for the appointment of a receiver is made.[58]

In Scotland, prior to the Companies (Floating Charges and Receivers) (Scotland) Act 1972, there was no provision for the

[53] Not applicable to Scotland.
[54] *Byblos Bank S.A.L. v. Al Khudhairy, Financial Times*, November 7, 1986.
[55] *Bank of Baroda v. Panessar*, [1987] Ch. 335.
[56] *N.R.G. Vision Ltd v. Churchfield Leasing Ltd* (1988) 4 BCC 56.
[57] Palmer's *Company Precedents* (16th ed.), Pt. III, p. 498.
[58] *Re Continental Oxygen Co.* [1897] 1 Ch. 511.

appointment of receivers, and this constituted a major difference between Scots and English law in the remedies available to the holder of a floating charge and in the procedure for enforcing the security. On the recommendation of the Scottish Law Commission[59] receiverships were introduced to Scotland by the Act of 1972. Though based in general on the English model, the Scottish provisions form a distinct self-contained code and are given separate consideration below.

The various remedies are discussed in chapter 25, *post*.

---

[59] *Report on the Companies* (*Floating Charges*) (*Scotland*) *Act 1961*, (1970) Cmnd. 4336, para. 38.

# Chapter 24

# CORPORATE INSOLVENCY

The Insolvency Act 1985 enacted major changes to the legal regulation of both corporate and personal insolvencies. This process began in 1976 when the Department of Trade announced the setting up of a Review Committee on Insolvency Law and Practice, which was actually established in 1977, under the chairmanship of Sir Kenneth Cork, and thus became known as the Cork Committee. The final Report of that Committee (the Cork Report) led first to a Government White Paper, *A Revised Framework for Insolvency Law*[1] in 1984 and then the Insolvency Act 1985, which adopted some but by no means all of the Cork Committee's recommendations. The Insolvency Act 1985 directly affected companies, not only by introducing new concepts and controls but also by amending (or repealing) several sections of the Companies Act 1985 concerned with corporate insolvency. The interaction of the two Acts led to the consolidation of Parts XIX, XX and XXI of the Companies Act 1985 and the Insolvency Act 1985 into the Insolvency Act 1986.

The Insolvency Act 1986 is thus the major Act[2] which applies to this and the next five chapters. Chapter 25 deals with receivers and the concept, introduced by the Insolvency Act 1985, of an administrative receiver, usually appointed by a debenture holder as the most efficient way of protecting his security in the face of possible insolvency. Such appointments may or may not lead to the ultimate liquidation of the company. Chapter 26 deals with one alternative to the liquidation of an insolvent company—the making of an administration order. Such orders were also introduced by the Insolvency Act 1985. Chapters 27 to 29 are, on the other hand, concerned with liquidations, that is to say the effective demise of the company, which may in fact arise

---

[1] 1984 Cmnd. 9174.
[2] See also the Insolvency Act 1994 and the Insolvency (No. 2) Act 1994, *infra*, pp. 677, 710 and 786.

otherwise than on an insolvency. The majority of liquidations, however, are caused by such an eventuality. We have already discussed, in chapter 15, one other aspect of insolvency law introduced by the 1985 Insolvency Act, *i.e.* that in relation to the disqualification of directors of insolvent companies.[3]

The present chapter is concerned with three general matters. The new framework for corporate insolvency, the controls on insolvency practitioners involved in the various aspects of insolvency, *e.g.* as administrative receivers, liquidators, administrators etc., and a second alternative to the liquidation of an insolvent company—a voluntary arrangement, *i.e.* a composition with creditors.[4]

## THE NEW FRAMEWORK FOR INSOLVENCY

One of the two main themes of the Insolvency Act 1986 was to tighten up the controls on the abuses of the corporate insolvency system. These included less than scrupulous liquidators, dubious acts by directors of companies which they knew to be hopelessly insolvent, and the general updating of a system which in large dated from the Bankruptcy Act of 1914. The second aim of the legislation was to provide genuine alternatives to the drastic remedy of liquidation for an insolvent company, where such remedies would provide a better opportunity for the creditors to recover their debts and for the companies concerned to remain in existence. Measures designed to assist in the first aim include the regulation of insolvency practitioners,[5] the disqualification of directors' provisions (including the concept of wrongful trading)[6] and the many amendments to the laws relating to receiverships and liquidations, including the new statutory concept of an administrative receiver. To achieve the second aim the Act introduced the new administration procedure[7] and a simplified procedure for a composition with creditors.[8] The use of these "rescue" procedures has been low as compared to the number of insolvencies. The Insolvency Service of the Department of Trade has proposed reforms to make them more attractive.[9] These

[3] *Ante*, 377.
[4] For the other alternative see Chap. 26, *post*.
[5] *Post*, p. 659.
[6] *Ante*, pp. 377 and 367.
[7] *Post*, Chap. 26.
[8] *Post*, p. 661.
[9] Company Voluntary Arrangements and Administration Orders. A Consultation Document. October 1993; The Insolvency Act 1986. Revised proposals for a New Company Voluntary Arrangement Procedure 1995.

statutory provisions are supplemented by many rules and regulations.[10] In particular, the Insolvency Rules 1986[11] and the rules relating to Qualified Insolvency Practitioners.[12]

The Insolvency Act 1986 also retained and redefined the role of Official Receivers for England and Wales in all types of corporate proceedings.[13] In effect, although they are civil servants under the control of the Secretary of State, Official Receivers are also officers of the court and are attached to the High Court or to one or more county court having insolvency jurisdiction. They assume the functions and responsibilities specified in the Act or the Rules in those cases falling within the jurisdiction of the court to which they are attached. Deputy Official Receivers can be appointed and have the same status and functions as an Official Receiver.

By virtue of section 426 of the Insolvency Act 1986 the courts in each part of the United Kingdom are required to recognise and enforce orders made by the courts of all other parts of the U.K. in relation to insolvency law. Thus where property exists *e.g.* in Scotland, but the insolvency proceedings are taking place in London, all such property can be protected and claimed for the benefit of creditors.[14]

## INSOLVENCY PRACTITIONERS

Part XIII of the Insolvency Act 1986 subjects insolvency practitioners to proper regulations by ensuring that they are "qualified" within the terms of section 390. To act as an insolvency practitioner in relation to a company when not qualified to do so is a criminal offence under section 389. For this purpose "acting as an insolvency practitioner" means acting either as a liquidator,[15] administrator,[16] administrative receiver[17] or as the supervisor of a composition with creditors[18]: section 388.

---

[10] I.A. 1986, ss.411–413, 419.
[11] S.I. 1986 No, 1925 as amended. For Scotland see the Insolvency (Scotland) Rules 1986 (S.I. 1986 No. 1915, S.139) as amended.
[12] See Insolvency Practitioners Regulations 1990, S.I. 1990 No. 439 as amended.
[13] I.A. 1986, ss.399–401.
[14] This replaced a much narrower and more difficult provision in the Bankruptcy Act 1914.
[15] *Post*, p. 740.
[16] *Post*, Chap 26.
[17] *Post*, Chap. 25.
[18] *Post*, p. 666.

This offence is one of strict liability—the knowledge of the person concerned is irrelevant. It does not, however, apply to the Official Receiver. The Official Receiver does not come within the terms of section 388 and therefore escapes the qualification requirements of section 390 and the criminal penalty in section 389; the control exercised over such public officials within the Department of Trade and Industry is deemed sufficient safeguard.

Section 390 sets out the requirements for qualification. Only an individual can be qualified to act as an insolvency practitioner.[19] He must be currently authorised to act as an insolvency practitioner either by virtue of membership of a professional body recognised under section 391[20] or by a direct authorisation granted by a competent authority set up by the Secretary of State,[21] and must have provided the requisite security (or, in Scotland, caution) for the proper performance of his functions.[22]

Even if a person is so qualified to act he may be disqualified if (a) he is an undischarged bankrupt,[23] or (b) he is subject to a disqualification order under the Company Directors Disqualification Act 1986[24] or (c) he is a patient under the Mental Health Act 1983 or the Mental Health (Scotland) Act 1984.[25]

Most individuals will qualify by virtue of being members[26] of a recognised professional body who are permitted to act as such by the rules of that body. The bodies currently recognised by the Secretary of State include the established accountancy bodies, the Law Society and the Insolvency Practitioners Association. The intention is that the control exercised by such bodies over their members shall be equivalent to that exercised by the competent authority over those directly authorised by that body under sections 392 to 398 of the Insolvency Act 1986. For those who

---

[19] I.A. 1986, s.390(1).
[20] See Insolvency Practitioners (Recognised Professional Bodies) Order 1986, S.I. 1986 No. 1764.
[21] *ibid.*, s.390(2)(*b*).
[22] s.390(3); by means of a fidelity bond in the amount of £250,000 plus an additional sum varying with the value of the assets in relation to which he is to act in the particular case: Insolvency Practitioners Regulations 1990, r.12.
[23] See I.A. 1986, ss.278–282, and Bankruptcy (Scotland) Act 1985, ss.54–56.
[24] See *ante*, p. 373.
[25] *i.e.* someone who has been judicially assessed to be mentally incapable of managing and administering his affairs.
[26] This includes those who, although not members, are subject to the rules of a recognised body in the practice of their profession: I.A., s.391.

cannot qualify as qualified insolvency practitioners by virtue of membership of a recognised professional body, those sections of the Act allow a direct application to the competent authority appointed to deal with such matters.[27] The Secretary of State is the competent authority for this purpose and he must grant the application if satisfied that the applicant is a fit and proper person to be an insolvency practitioner and satisfies prescribed educational and experience requirements: section 393. Regulations set out the matters which he is to take into account and prescribe the educational and other requirements.[28] Such authorisation is for a maximum of three years and may be withdrawn earlier on his ceasing to comply with the section 393 requirements or where he was authorised by virtue of false, misleading or inaccurate information. There is a right to make representations before a refusal or withdrawal of authorisation and a right to appeal against an adverse decision to the Insolvency Practitioners Tribunal.[29]

Withdrawal of authorisation results in automatic vacation of office.

P was acting as liquidator in relation to a number of companies when his authorisation was withdrawn. It was held that, though no longer a liquidator, he was a proper person to apply to the court under s.108 of the Insolvency Act 1986 for a compendious appointment in relation to all the companies with which he had been concerned: *Re A. J. Adams (Builders) Ltd* [1991] BCC 62.

## VOLUNTARY ARRANGEMENTS—COMPOSITIONS WITH CREDITORS

Sections 1 to 7 of the Insolvency Act 1986 introduced a new procedure which enables an insolvent or potentially insolvent company to come to a legally binding arrangement with its creditors. If the procedure is complied with it binds creditors, even those who have not agreed to it[30] (I.A. 1986, s.5(2)) and so perhaps will avoid a liquidation. There are alternative methods of effecting such a scheme under sections 425 to 427[31] of the

[27] I.A. 1986, s.419. The fee is currently £200.
[28] Insolvency Practitioners Regulations 1990 (S.I. 1990 No. 439), regs. 4–8.
[29] I.A. 1986, ss.395, 396. This Tribunal is governed by Schedule 7 to I.A. 1986, and by the Insolvency Practitioners Tribunal (Conduct of Investigations) Rules 1986 (S.I. 1986 No. 952).
[30] See *infra*; p. 664.
[31] See *post*, Chap. 30.

Companies Act 1985 or section 110 of the Insolvency Act 1986[32] but these procedures were not designed expressly for the purpose of enabling an insolvent company to rationalise its affairs and proved to be cumbersome in practice for such a purpose. Schemes of arrangement under sections 425 to 427 require the court's involvement at every stage and the court's ultimate consent. Schemes of reconstruction under section 110 do not bind dissentient creditors.[33] The essence of the Insolvency Act scheme is to simplify both the procedure and the court's involvement whilst maintaining the ability to bind creditors to the scheme if the requisite procedure is complied with.

## Implementing a voluntary arrangement

Section 1 of the Insolvency Act 1986 allows either a liquidator or administrator of a company (if it is in liquidation[34] or subject to an administration order[35]) or, if there is no liquidator or administrator, the directors, to make a proposal to the company and to its creditors for a composition in satisfaction of its debts or a scheme of arrangement of its affairs, to be known as a voluntary arrangement.[36] This proposal must provide for some person who is qualified to act as an insolvency practitioner in relation to the company[37] to act as the *nominee* of the scheme, *i.e.* as trustee or otherwise for the purpose of implementing the scheme. It is a criminal offence for an unqualified person to act as a nominee.[38]

Where the nominee is not the liquidator or administrator, he must observe the formalities in section 2 of the Insolvency Act 1986 which involve the scrutiny by him of the soundness of the proposed arrangement and the submission of a report to the court stating whether in his opinion meetings of the company and of its creditors should be summoned to consider the proposal, and, if so, the date, time and place he proposes the meetings should be held. In effect he is required to state that the scheme is worth pursuing.

[32] *ibid.* See also administration orders, *post*, Chap. 26.
[33] I.A. 1986, s.111.
[34] See *post*, Chap. 27.
[35] See *post*, Chap. 26.
[36] For a discussion of the meaning of "scheme of arrangement" see *post*, Chap. 30.
[37] This is someone qualified by virtue of s.390 of the I.A. 1986 and not connected with the company so as to be in breach of the professional or regulatory rules.
[38] I.A. 1986, ss.388, 389.

No such report is needed where the nominee is the liquidator or administrator; proper scrutiny by such office holders is assumed. In such a case the liquidator or administrator may proceed directly by virtue of section 3(2) of the Insolvency Act 1986 to summon meetings of the company and its creditors to consider the proposal for such a time, date and place as he shall think fit. Following a positive report by a nominee other than a liquidator or administrator, under section 2 of the Insolvency Act, that nominee should call the meetings as stated in that report unless the court orders otherwise: I.A. 1986 section 3(1). Section 3(3) requires every creditor of the company of whose claim and address the nominee is aware to be given notice of the creditors' meeting. There is no requirement to hold separate meetings for separate classes of creditors[39] which is a feature of schemes of arrangements under sections 425 to 427 of the Companies Act 1985.[40]

## Consideration of a voluntary arrangement

It is for the two meetings convened by the nominee to decide whether to approve the proposed composition or scheme, with or without modifications. Any such modification is allowed, including a change in the nominee, subject to three limitations. First no modification is allowed if the proposal would thereby cease to comply with the terms of section 1 of the Insolvency Act, *i.e.* it would no longer be a voluntary arrangement as there defined: Second no modification can affect a secured creditor's rights to enforce his security without his consent,[41] and third no modification can interfere with the rights of a preferred creditor, either as against ordinary creditors or other preferred creditors, without his consent: I.A. 1986, section 3.[42] The Insolvency Rules 1986[43] regulate the conduct of the meetings and it is for the chairman to make a report of the result to the court and other prescribed persons: I.A. 1986, section 4.

---

[39] See *post*, p. 808.
[40] See *post*, Chap. 30.
[41] See *ante*, p. 654.
[42] Preferred creditors are defined in the same way as for a liquidation except that they are calculated by reference to the date of the approval of the proposal if there is no liquidation or administration order in force: I.A. 1986, s.387. See *post*, p. 793.
[43] For Scotland, the Insolvency (Scotland) Rules 1986.

If both the company and creditors' meetings approve the proposal in identical terms, the scheme or composition "takes effect as if made by the company at the creditors' meeting," and binds every person who in accordance with the rules had notice of, and was entitled to vote at, that meeting (whether or not he was present or represented at the meeting) as if he were a party to the voluntary arrangement": I.A. 1986, section 5(1), (2).

Creditors vote in accordance with the amount of their debt.[44] The Rules provide that a creditor is not entitled to vote in relation to an unliquidated amount except where the chairman agrees to put upon the debt an estimated minimum value.[45]

A claimed £900,000 against the company. The chairman valued the claim at £1 and allowed A to vote. A later claimed not to be bound by the arrangement. Held: She was not bound. She had not been entitled to vote because her agreement to the valuation of the claim had not been obtained as required by the Rules: *Saigol v. Goldstein* [1994] BCC 576.[45a]

The position is otherwise where a creditor claims a liquidated debt but the company disputes the amount or claims a set off. Here the creditor is entitled to vote in respect of the whole debt subject to his votes subsequently being declared invalid.[46] The chairman's decision on a creditor's entitlement to vote can be challenged by a creditor or member.[47]

Prior to approval, an individual creditor is free to bring proceedings to enforce his debt, realise his security, distrain for rent, etc.[48] Where a substantial creditor takes this course, the voluntary arrangement cannot succeed. While the benefits of a moratorium can be obtained by channelling the voluntary arrangement through the administration order procedure, this is costly and cumbersome for smaller companies. The lack of a moratorium has been identified as one of a number of barriers to

---

[44] Insolvency Rules 1986 (hereafter I.R. 1986), r.1.17(2).

[45] I.R. r.1.17(3).

[45a] But compare *Doorbar v. Alltime Securities Ltd* [1994] BCC 994 (individual voluntary arrangement). A creditor is entitled to vote if the chairman agrees to put a value upon the debt and estimates a realistic value. The creditor's consent to the valuation is not required.

[46] *ibid.*, r.1.17(6). *Re A debtor (No. 222 of 1990)*, [1992] BCLC 137 (individual voluntary arrangements); and see *Saigol v. Goldstein, supra.*

[47] I.R. 1986, r.1.17(5).

[48] In this respect the company voluntary arrangement differs from the voluntary arrangement available to individuals (see I.A. 1986, s.252) and from the administration order (see I.A. 1986, s.10 and *infra*).

the use of the company voluntary arrangement and proposals have been made to introduce a new type of arrangement incorporating a stay of actions and reduced formality.[49]

Once the arrangement is duly approved a supplier of gas, electricity and other public utilities cannot make it a precondition of any further supply that outstanding charges in respect of earlier supplies are met.[50]

If a proposal is approved and the company is in liquidation or subject to an administration order the court may stay the winding-up proceedings or discharge the administration order or give such directions as to their future conduct as will facilitate the scheme. No such order can be made within 28 days from the date when the court received the reports of the meeting since that is the period allowed for the meetings' approval to be challenged in the court,[51] or at any time when such a challenge is under consideration by the court: I.A. 1986, section 5(3), (4).

**Challenge to a voluntary arrangement**

Within 28 days of the report of the meeting having been made to the court, anyone who was entitled to vote at either meeting, the nominee or his replacement or the liquidator or administrator (if any) can challenge the approval of the scheme by an application to the court. This challenge can, however, only be made on one of two grounds: either that the scheme will unfairly prejudice[52] the interests of a creditor, member or contributory[53] of the company, or there has been some material irregularity at or in relation to either of the meetings: I.A. 1986, section 6(1), (2), (3).[54]

**Supervising an approved voluntary arrangement**

An approved scheme which is not subject to a challenge is then put into effect. At this stage the person carrying out the

[49] See *supra*, n.658.
[50] S.233 I.A. 1986 and see *post*, p. 678.
[51] See below.
[52] There is no definition of this but the words are used in section 459 of the Companies Act 1985 in relation to the protection of a minority shareholder generally, see *ante*, p. 417. And see *Re Primlaks (UK) Ltd (No. 2)* [1990] BCLC 234.
[53] This is the term used for a member once the company has gone into liquidation.
[54] Irregularities not challenged within 28 days cannot invalidate the approval: I.A. 1986, s.6(7).

nominee's functions is known as the *supervisor* (who must also be a qualified insolvency practitioner). The supervisor is under the control of the court and any interested party may apply to the court if his conduct is unsatisfactory and the court may make an order to give him directions as it thinks fit. In return the supervisor himself may apply to the court for directions and can petition for a winding-up or the making of an administration order. *In extremis* the court can replace the supervisor or appoint an additional one: I.A. 1986, section 7. Under the Insolvency Rules 1986[55] the supervisor must keep accounts and records and must report annually upon the progress of the arrangement.

[55] For Scotland, the Insolvency (Scotland) Rules 1986.

## Chapter 25

## RECEIVERS AND ADMINISTRATIVE RECEIVERS

### English and Scots law

The law relating to receivers has developed quite separately in England and Scotland and for that reason this chapter is divided into two parts, the first dealing with English law and the second with Scots law. The relevant statute law is also quite separate: sections 28 to 49 of the Insolvency Act 1986 apply only to English law and sections 50 to 71 of that Act apply only to Scotland. The two sets of provisions are mutually exclusive.[1] On the other hand section 72 of the Insolvency Act 1986 provides that a receiver appointed under a floating charge in one jurisdiction may exercise his powers in the other "so far as their exercise is not inconsistent with the law applicable there."

In *Norfolk House plc (in receivership) v. Repsol Petroleum Ltd,* 1992 S.L.T. 235 (O.H.), a receiver of an English company with heritable property in Scotland was enabled by section 72 to grant a valid disposition to purchasers; the effect of section 72 was said to bridge the transaction from the original English crystallisation of the floating charge to the appointment of the receiver in order to ensure that the receiver could exercise his powers under Schedule 1 to the Act in relation to Scottish heritable property untrammelled by Scottish conveyancing and property law.

### ENGLISH LAW

### Receivers and other officeholders

A receiver takes possession of the property of the company over which he is appointed and realises it for the benefit of the

[1] See I.A. 1986, ss.28 and 50.

debenture holder(s). Where the charged property includes a business, a *receiver and manager* is usually appointed to preserve the goodwill pending sale or the resumption of control by the company on discharge of the debt. A receiver should not be confused either with a liquidator or an administrator. A liquidator is appointed with the object of winding up the company and terminating its existence. An administrator is appointed with the object of saving a company from a winding up or obtaining a more advantageous realisation of its assets, and acts for the benefit of the company's creditors and shareholders generally,[2] whereas a receiver is usually appointed by a specific debenture holder to protect his security under a fixed or floating charge. A receiver may take possession of only part of a company's property[3] (*e.g.* of a specific asset secured by a fixed charge) but if he takes possession of the whole (or substantially the whole) of the company's property and was appointed by the holders of a charge which, as created, was a floating charge, he is known as an *administrative receiver*.[4] Most receivers will in fact be administrative receivers since the major creditors appointing them, *e.g.* the banks, usually take extensive fixed and floating charges as a security. Administrative receivers are subject to special rules and given special powers by the Insolvency Act 1986.

As mentioned in Chapter 23, a receiver can be appointed: (1) under an express or implied power contained in the debenture or trust deed; or (2) by an order of the court where there is no such power.

## Receiver appointed by the court

While the Insolvency Act refers to receivers appointed by the court, and certain of its provisions,[5] applicable to all receiverships, would seem to apply to them, it has little to say about them. It is accepted that the court may appoint a receiver when—

[2] See *post*, Chap. 26.
[3] I.A. 1986, s.29(1)(a).
[4] *ibid.*, s.29(2)(a). So long as his security extends to the whole or substantially the whole of the company's property, the fact that some other person has previously been appointed receiver of the part of the company's property under a charge having priority to the floating charge and that consequently he does not in fact have possession of the whole or substantially the whole of the company's property, does not prevent him from coming within the definition of an administrative receiver: s.29(2)(b).
[5] *e.g.* I.A. 1986, ss.30, 39, 40 and 41; C.A. 1985, s.405(1), see *infra*.

(1)  the principal or interest is in arrear[6]; or
(2)  the company is being wound up[7]; or
(3)  the security is in jeopardy.

A creditor obtained judgment against the company and was in a position to issue execution. There was no default in payment of debenture principal or interest. *Held*, the debenture holders with a floating charge on the undertaking and property of the company were entitled to the appointment of a receiver because the security was in jeopardy: *Re London Pressed Hinge Co. Ltd* [1905] 1 Ch. 576.

The security is in jeopardy when there is a risk of its being seized and taken to pay claims which are really not prior to the debenture holders' claims. Accordingly a receiver was appointed where the company's works were closed and creditors were threatening actions,[8] where execution was actually levied by a judgment creditor,[9] where a creditor's winding up petition was pending and compulsory liquidation was imminent,[10] and where the company proposed to distribute its reserve fund, which was its only asset, among its members.[11] Mere insufficiency of security is not jeopardy where the company is a going concern, is not being pressed by its creditors and there is no risk of its assets being seized by its creditors.[12]

Appointments by the court are infrequent and usually occur because there is no adequate power of appointment in the instrument of charge or there is some doubt as to the validity of the instrument or the appointment under it. The appointment is made on the application of the debenture holders. It is uncertain whether a receiver appointed by the court can fall within the definition of an administrative receiver. Where the company is being wound up by the court, the court can appoint the official receiver as receiver: I.A. 1986, section 32. A receiver appointed by the court is an officer of the court, not an agent of the company or of the debenture holders.[13-14] He is personally liable on contracts he enters into.

---

[6] *Bissill v. Bradford Tramways* [1891] W.N. 51.
[7] *Wallace v. Universal Automatic Machines Co.* [1894] 2 Ch. 547 (C.A.).
[8] *McMahon v. North Kent Ironworks* [1891] 2 Ch. 148.
[9] *Edwards v. Standard Rolling Stock Syndicate* [1893] 1 Ch. 574.
[10] *Re Victoria Steamboats Ltd* [1897] 1 Ch. 158.
[11] *Re Tilt Cove Copper Co.* [1913] 2 Ch. 588.
[12] *Re New York Taxicab Co.* [1913] 1 Ch. 1.
[13-14] See I.A. 1986, s.29(2).

B was appointed receiver and manager by the court. He gave a signed order for goods, with the words "receiver and manager" appended to his signature. *Held,* he was personally liable to pay for the goods: *Burt, Boulton and Hayward v. Bull* [1895] 1 Q.B. (C.A.).

However, he is entitled to an indemnity, out of the assets in his hands, for liabilities properly incurred.[15] He "supersedes the company which becomes incapable of making contracts on its own behalf."[16]

His appointment causes floating charges to crystallise and thus prevents the company from dealing with assets without his consent. To enable him to carry on the business of the company or to preserve the property of the company, the court can authorise the receiver to borrow money ranking in priority to the debentures.[17] The company's servants are automatically dismissed[18] (but they may be entitled to damages for breach of contract) although they may be employed by the receiver.[19] As an officer of the court he cannot sue or be sued without leave of the court[20] but such leave may be given to enable an action to be brought against him by a person at whose instance he was appointed.[21] Officers of the court have a duty to act not merely lawfully, but in accordance with the principles of justice and honest dealing.[22] His remuneration is fixed by the court.

Notice of his appointment must appear on invoices, business letters, orders for goods, etc.: I.A. 1986, s.39.

## Receivers appointed out of court

A body corporate is disqualified for appointment as receiver[23]: I.A. 1986, section 30. Also, an undischarged bankrupt is dis-

---

[15] *ibid.* Where he is appointed manager of the business pending its sale within a limited time, unless the time is extended, expenditure incurred outside that time will be disallowed: *Re Wood Green Steam Laundry* [1918] 1 Ch. 423.
[16] *ibid.*, n.14 at p. 260.
[17] *Greenwood v. Algesiras Rly. Co.* [1894] 2 Ch. 205 (C.A.).
[18] The tenure of directors and other officers is unaffected: *Re South Western of Venezuela Ry.* [1902] 1 Ch. 701.
[19] *Reid v. Explosives Co. Ltd* (1887) 19 Q.B. 264 (C.A.).
[20] *Viola v. Anglo American Cold Storage Co.* [1912] 2 Ch. 305; *Searle v. Choat* [1884] 25 Ch. 723 (C.A.).
[21] *L. P. Arthur Insurance Ltd v. Sisson* [1966] 1 W.L.R. 1384.
[22] *Re Tyler* [1907] 1 KB 865.
[23] An attempted appointment of a body corporate is a nullity, and the body corporate does not thereby become an agent for the purpose of the Law of Property Act 1925, s.109, and the Limitation Act 1980: *Portman Building Society v. Gallwey* [1955] 1 All E.R. 227.

qualified from acting as receiver or manager, unless he is appointed by the court: I.A. 1986, section 31. Persons subject to the various disqualification orders under the Company Directors Disqualification Act 1986[24] cannot act as receivers.

Since an administrative receiver, but not an ordinary receiver, is acting as an insolvency practitioner within section 388 of the Insolvency Act 1986, only a qualified insolvency practitioner may be appointed as such[25] and it is a criminal offence for anyone else so to act.[26]

### Time of appointment and defects in appointment

A receiver or manager is appointed when the document of appointment is handed to him or his agent provided that he accepts such an appointment by the end of the next business day after such receipt[27]; I.A. 1986, section 33. The person delivering the document to the receiver or his agent must be a person having authority to appoint and the circumstances must be such that it could fairly be said that he was appointing the receiver.[28]

If the appointment of a receiver is discovered to be invalid (*e.g.* the document of appointment was defective[29] or the charge has been set aside for non-registration) the court can order the person appointing the receiver to indemnify him against any liability which arises solely by reason of that invalidity: I.A. 1986, section 34. This section will not protect a receiver from liability arising from other causes, *e.g.* his negligence in managing the company's affairs, simply because his appointment was also invalid. The court has a complete discretion in cases where the section applies and it may well seek to establish where the blame for the invalidity lies.

### Effect of appointment of receiver

When a receiver is appointed:

[24] *Ante,* p. 373.
[25] *Ante,* p. 659.
[26] I.A. 1986, s.389.
[27] Administrative receivers must confirm in writing within 7 days: Insolvency Rules 1986, r. 3.
[28] *A. Cripps & Sons Ltd v. Wickenden* [1973] 1 W.L.R. 944, applying *Windsor Refrigerator Co. Ltd v. Branch Nominees Ltd* [1961] Ch. 375 (C.A.).
[29] But see *Byblos Bank S.A.L. v. Al Khudhairy, Financial Times,* November 7, 1986.

(1) Floating charges crystallise and become fixed. This prevents the company from dealing with the assets charged, without the receiver's consent.[30]

(2) When a receiver of the undertaking of the company is appointed, the directors' power of controlling the company is suspended but they may have a residual role to play. Thus, where a receiver decides not to get in or realise an asset, which it would be in the interests of the company and its other creditors to get in or realise, the directors have power to act on the company's behalf, so long as the interests of the debentureholders, *qua* debentureholders, are not threatened.

The assets in respect of which a receiver was appointed included an action for damages against the debentureholders who had appointed him. It was alleged that they had, in breach of contract, refused further finance causing the company to forfeit its interest in, and profit from, a joint venture. The receivers having refused to sue the debentureholders, the action was initiated by the directors on behalf of the company. *Held,* the action could continue: *Newhart Developments v. Co-operative Commercial Bank.*[31]

The directors cannot claim fees from the receiver unless he employs them, but they can still claim from the company any fees to which they are entitled.[32]

(3) On the appointment of a receiver by the court the company's employees are dismissed.[33] The company ceases to employ them because it is no longer carrying on business: the receiver may carry on the business but he is not the company's agent. In the case of a receiver appointed by the debentureholders and acting as the company's agent,[34] "the business is still the company's business carried on by the company's agent"[35] and therefore there will generally be no automatic dismissal of company employees. Automatic dismissal will however occur if, exceptionally, the receiver is acting as agent for the debentureholders or if the receiver, having transferred the business to a

[30] *Ante*, p. 625.
[31] [1978] 2 All E.R. 896. See also *Lascomme Ltd v. United Dominion Trusts* [1994] I.L.R.M. 227 (High Court of Ireland); *cf. Tudor Grange Holdings Ltd v. Citibank N.A.* [1991] 4 All E.R. 1.
[32] *Re South Western of Venezuela etc. Rly.* [1902] 1 Ch. 701.
[33] *Ante*, p. 670.
[34] Most debentures will provide that the receiver is to be the agent of the company and, as to administrative receivers, statute so provides: I.A. 1986, s.44 (1)(a).
[35] *Per* Dillon L.J. in *Nicoll v. Cutts* [1958] BCLC 322 (C.A.).

third party, ceases to act as the company's agent in that regard.[36] Further, a particular employee may be subject to automatic dismissal if continuance of his contract of employment is inconsistent with the receiver's role and functions.[37] Where employees are automatically dismissed, the company is liable for breach of contract. Where they are not dismissed, the company remains liable for remuneration, etc. arising. The receiver will not be liable[38] in the absence of novation or adoption.[39]

(4) Every invoice, order for goods or business letter which is issued by or on behalf of the company or the receiver and on which the company's name appears must contain a statement that a receiver has been appointed: I.A. 1986, section 39.

(5) Within seven days after the appointment, the person who made or obtained the appointment must give notice of the fact to the Registrar who must enter it in his register of charges: Companies Act 1985, section 405(1).

(6) When a receiver appointed under a power in an instrument ceases to act, he must give notice to the Registrar: Companies Act 1985, section 405(2).

(7) A receiver appointed under a power in a debenture has his remuneration fixed by agreement. The court may, however, on the application of the liquidator, fix the receiver's remuneration. Under this power the remuneration may be fixed retrospectively, and any excess paid before the making of the order must be accounted for: I.A. 1986, section 36. This power does not entitle the court to interfere with the receiver's right to be indemnified for disbursements which have been properly incurred.[40]

## Position of receiver other than administrative receiver

In the case of a receiver appointed under a power in a debenture or a trust deed the debenture usually provides[41] that he is to be the agent of the company. Consequently the debenture holder(s) or the trustees are not liable for his acts, though the company is. Through this agency the company can claim docu-

---

[36] *Re Foster Clark's Indenture Trusts* [1966] 1 W.L.R. 125.
[37] *Griffiths v. Secretary of State for Social Security* [1974] Q.B. 468.
[38] *Nicoll v. Cutts, supra.*
[39] See *infra*, I.A. 1986, ss.37, 44.
[40] *Re Potters Oils* [1986] 1 W.L.R. 201.
[41] If it does not, he is agent of the debentureholders who are answerable for his faults and omissions: *Re Vimbos* [1900] 1 Ch. 470.

ments brought into existence in the course of the receivership in discharge of the receiver's duties to the company but not otherwise.[42]

Contracts made by the company and current at the date of his appointment are not binding on the receiver personally, unless they become binding by novation,[43] or, in the case of contracts of employment, adoption: I.A. 1986, section 37(1), (2).[44] The receiver must, however, carry out the company's current contracts if not to do so would injure the company's goodwill,[45] but if the contracts can only be carried out by borrowing money ranking in priority to the debenture holders and are unprofitable, he need not carry them out.[46] As agent of the company, he is immune from personal liability for breach of such contracts or for inducing a breach of contract so long as his decision not to carry out the contract is bona fide and within his authority.[47]

Under section 37(1), (3) of the Insolvency Act 1986, a receiver appointed under a power in an instrument (other than an administrative receiver) is, to the same extent as if he had been appointed by the court, personally liable on contracts made by him in the performance of his functions except so far as they otherwise provide and on any contract of employment adopted by him in the performance of his functions. Nothing he does or does not do within 14 days of his appointment can be regarded as his adopting such a contract of employment. Section 37(1)(a) was in part a response to *Nicoll v. Cutts*[48] which decided that a receiver who merely continued a contract of employment on behalf of the company did not incur personal liability. The employee, in relation to post-receivership remuneration, had the status of an unsecured creditor. Now causing the company to continue the contract of employment amounts to adoption and results in personal liability.[49] The receiver is unable to avoid

[42] *Gomba Holdings U.K. Ltd v. Minories Finance Ltd* [1989] BCLC (C.A.).
[43] *Parsons v. Sovereign Bank of Canada* [1913] A.C. 160 (P.C.).
[44] See below.
[45] *Re Newdigate Colliery Ltd* [1912] 1 Ch. 468 (C.A.) and see *Airlines Airspares Ltd v. Handley Page Ltd* [1970] Ch. 193, and *Freevale v. Metrostore Holdings* [1984] Ch. 199.
[46] *Re Thames Ironworks Co. Ltd* (1912) 106 L.T. 674.
[47] *Lathia v. Dronsfield Bros. Ltd* [1987] BCLC 321.
[48] [1985] BCLC 322 (C.A.).
[49] See *Powdrill v. Watson, Re Leyland Daf Ltd, Re Ferranti International plc*, [1995] 2 All E.R. 65 (H.L) (relating to section 19 (administrators) and section 44 (administrative receivers)).

personal liability unilaterally, as by service of a notice.[50] The liability is restricted to liabilities incurred on the contract while he was receiver.[51] In respect of it he enjoys a right of indemnity against the company's assets under section 37(1)(b). The Insolvency Act 1994, which qualifies the liability of administrative receivers and administrators,[52] is not applicable to ordinary receivers within section 37. It may be that the liability could be excluded or modified by a contract with the employees but such a contract will not readily be implied.[53]   On the commencement of a winding up of the company the receiver ceases to be the company's agent and his authority to bind the company ceases[55] but his powers with regard to the property charged are unaffected[56] so that he may continue to use the company's name for the purpose of the realisation of its assets.[57] On a liquidation the receiver may well become the agent of the debentureholder who will then be liable for his acts.[58]

A debentureholder or mortgagee must exercise his power to appoint a receiver in good faith for the propose of obtaining repayment.[59] If he complies with this rule, it is irrelevant that the appointment of a receiver is disadvantageous to the company and its other creditors, because, for example, it causes unnecessary expense[60] or frustrates negotiations with a third party for additional funding.[61] Once appointed, a receiver owes a duty of good faith to the company but it is qualified by the recognition that the primary function of the charge is repayment of the debt. Thus, where he is appointed manager of a business, he manages in order to discharge the debt and not, as would its directors, in order to benefit the company.[62] Where he exercises a power of

---

[50] *ibid. cf. Re Specialised Mouldings Ltd*, February 13, 1987 (unreported) which gave rise to the practice, now know to be ineffective, of sending "Specialised Mouldings" letters opting out of personal liability.

[51] *Powdrill v. Watson, supra.*

[52] see *infra.*

[53] *Re Leyland Daf Ltd* 1994 BCC 658.

[55] *Gosling v. Gaskell* [1897] A.C. 575; *Thomas v. Todd* [1926] 2 K.B. 511.

[56] *Gough's Garages Ltd v. Pugsley* [1930] 1 K.B. 615.

[57] *Sowman v. David Samuel Trust Ltd* [1978] 1 W.L.R. 22.

[58] *American Express International Banking Corp. v. Hurley* [1985] 3 All E.R. 564.

[59] *cf. Downsview Nominees Ltd v. First City Corpn. Ltd* [1993] 3 All E.R. 626 (P.C.) where the appointment was made to prevent a subsequent encumbrancer enforcing his security.

[60] *Re Potter Oils Ltd (No. 2)* [1986] 1 All E.R. 890.

[61] *Shamji v. Johnson Matthey Bankers Ltd* [1991] BCLC 36.

[62] *Re B. Johnson & Co. (Builders) Ltd* [1955] 2 All E.R. 775, 790–91.

sale, he can give preference to the interests of the debentureholders regarding the time of sale[63] but he does owe a duty of
reasonable care to obtain the true value of the property at the
time he chooses to sell it.[64] This duty has been equated with a
duty of care in negligence[65] but it is now accepted that it is an
equitable duty only[66] and it is owed to a limited class, namely, the
company, subsequent encumbrancers and guarantors.[67]

A company in receivership cannot interfere with the receiver in
the proper exercise of his powers but, in *Watts v. Midland Bank
plc,*[68] Peter Gibson J. thought that it could maintain an action
against him for the proper performance of his duties and so
refused to allow a minority shareholder to bring a derivative
action[69] against him.

A receiver appointed out of court, or the person who
appointed him, may apply to the court for directions in any
matter concerning the performance of his functions: I.A. 1986,
section 35.[70] He must within one month of his first year of
appointment, every subsequent period of six months and on
ceasing to act, deliver to the registrar the requisite accounts of his
receipts and payments: I.A. 1986, section 38. Since the receiver is
usually the agent of the company he must produce full accounts
to the company when required to do so.[71] The court may order
the receiver to make any returns or give any notices which he is
by law required to give or make: I.A. 1986, section 41.[72]

## Administrative receivers

Section 44 of the Insolvency Act 1986 provides that an administrative receiver is deemed to be the agent of the company unless
and until it goes into liquidation[73] so that the company remains

---

[63] *Cuckmere Brick Co. Ltd v. Mutual Finance Ltd* [1971] 2 All E.R. 633 (C.A.).
[64] *ibid.* And see *Downsview, supra.*
[65] *e.g. in Knight v. Lawrence* [1991] 01 E.G. 105.
[66] *China & South Sea Bank Ltd v. Tan* [1980] 3 All E.R. 839 (P.C.); *Parker -
Tweedale v. Dunbar Bank, plc (No. 1)* [1990] 2 All E.R. 577 (C.A.);
*Downsview, supra.*
[67] *American Express International Banking Corp. v. Hurley* [1985] 3 All E.R. 564;
*Parker - Tweedale, supra.*
[68] [1986] BCLC 15.
[69] *Ante,* p. 400.
[70] This section also applies to administrative receivers.
[71] *Smiths Ltd v. Middleton* [1979] 3 All E.R. 843.
[72] This section also applies to administrative receivers.
[73] *American Express Banking Corp. v. Hurley* [1985] 3 All E.R. 564.

liable as principal on all contracts made by him. The section also provides that an administrative receiver is personally liable on all contracts he makes in carrying out his functions and on any contract of employment he adopts (*i.e.* allows to continue for more than 14 days after his appointment).[74] In respect of contracts of employment adopted on or after March 15, 1994, the administrative receiver's personal liability is limited to liabilities arising under the contract of employment[75] which fall within the definition of a "qualifying liability" (I.A. 1986, section 44, as amended by I.A. 1994, section 2)[76] being:

(a) a liability to pay a sum by way of wages or salary[77] or contribution to an occupational pension scheme,
(b) incurred while the administrative receiver is in office, and
(c) in respect of services rendered wholly or partly after adoption of the contract.[78]

Where the liability arises in respect of services rendered partly before and partly after the adoption, it is provided that only so much of it as relates to the post-adoption period qualifies.[79]

In respect of the section 44 liability, the administrative receiver is entitled to an indemnity out of the assets of the company and this is without prejudice to any indemnity he can claim under any express clause in his appointment or in an order of the court under section 34 of the Act.

An administrative receiver has the powers set out in Schedule 1 to the Insolvency Act 1986, subject to any contrary express terms in the relevant debenture; Insolvency Act 1986, section 42(1). Schedule 1 in fact states the powers given to an administrator appointed under an administration order and they are set out in the following chapter of this book. Section 42(2) of the Act

---

[74] In respect of liabilities incurred while he was reveiver. See *Powdrill v. Watson, Re Leyland Daf Ltd, Re Ferranti International plc* [1995] 2 All E.R. 65 (H.L.). See *supra*, p. 674.

[75] *cf.* liabilities arising by virtue of statute in relation to redundancy or unfair dismissal.

[76] See Current Law Statutes Annotated (David Milman).

[77] S.2(3) of the I.A. 1994 inserts into s.44 I.A. 1986 a new subsection, (2C), which includes within the definition of wages or salary amounts payable in periods of absence due to holidays and sickness and also amounts payable in lieu of holidays.

[78] S.2(3) of the I.A. 1994 inserting a new subsection, (2A), into s.44 I.A. 1986.

[79] S.2(3) of the I.A. 1994 adding a new section (2B) to s.44 of the I.A. 1986.

adapts those powers to an administrative receiver by making it clear that they only apply to the property actually covered by the charge under which he was appointed and not over the whole property of the company and not to property subject to a prior charge under which a receiver has been appointed.[80] Section 42(3) of the Insolvency Act 1986 provides that a person dealing with an administrative receiver in good faith and for value does not need to inquire whether the receiver is acting within his powers.

By virtue of section 43(1) of the Insolvency Act an administrative receiver can sell property[81] which is subject to a security having priority over the security of his appointor[82] free of that security if the court is satisfied that such a sale is likely to promote a more advantageous realisation of the company's assets.[83] The secured creditor whose security is thus overturned is protected by section 43(3) so that the net proceeds of sale must be used to discharge his debt together with, if the court regards such proceeds as less than the open market value of the property, such additional sums as are necessary to make good the deficiency.[84] The receiver must send an office copy of any court order under this section to the registrar within 14 days, with a fine in default.

## Supplies to administrative receivers

Supplies of gas, electricity, water and telecommunications requested by an administrative receiver are protected: I.A. 1986, section 233.[85] Supplies of other goods and services are not protected,[86] and the supplier is entitled at common law to stipulate for payment in full of pre-receivership arrears before making further supplies.[87] Such a demand is not a breach of article 86 of the Treaty of Rome which prohibits abuse of a dominant position.[88]

---

[80] I.A. 1986, sections 233, 234, 235, 236 and 237 apply to administrative receivers. See *infra* pp. 740 *et seq*.
[81] Being property in relation to which he is the receiver or would be the receiver but for the appointment of a receiver by a prior chargee: I.A. 1986, s.43(7).
[82] I.A., s.43(2).
[83] Following a recommendation of the *Cork Report* paras. 1510-1513; *cf.* I.A. s.15, *post*, p. 705.
[84] If there is more than one charge on the property they are to be repaid in order of priority: I.A. 1986, s.43(4).
[85] See, *infra* p. 740.
[86] Whether requested by an administrative receiver or an ordinary receiver.
[87] *Leyland Daf Ltd v. Automotive Products, plc* [1993] BCC 389.
[88] *ibid.*

Where an administrative receiver himself contracts for post-receivership supplies, he will incur personal liability and will be entitled in respect of it to an indemnity out of the company's assets.[89] Where he merely continues the company's contract, he incurs no personal liability.[90] Thus he is not personally liable to pay rent or hire charges under an existing lease or hire-purchase agreement, even where he uses the land or goods. Such amounts are a company liability and "it is to the company that, along with other creditors, the lessor and the owner of the goods must look for payment".[91]

## Duties of administrative receiver

On appointment an administrative receiver must forthwith inform the company of his appointment and publish that fact in the Gazette and a newspaper appropriate for ensuring that it comes to the notice of the companies creditors: Insolvency Rules 1986, r. 3.2(3). Within 28 days of his appointment he must send a notice of his appointment to all the creditors of the company[92] so far as he is aware of their addresses. There are fines in default: I.A. 1986, section 46.

He must also obtain "forthwith" a statement of the company's affairs from some or all of the officers of the company (past or present), its promoters (if they acted within the year prior to his appointment), its employees (if they are in his opinion capable of giving the information required and are either current employees or have been employed within the preceding year) and the officers of any company which is (or has been within the previous year) an officer of the company concerned. Such a statement must be made within 21 days of being asked for, with a fine in default. Such persons are entitled to be paid their reasonable expenses by the administrative receiver.[93] The receiver may

---

[89] I.A. 1986, s.44. Such indemnity, together with his renumeration and any expenses properly incurred by him is charged on any property of the company in his custody or under his control at the time he vacates office in priority to any security held by the person who appointed him: I.A. 1986, s.45. Similar provisions apply to ordinary receivers: I.A. 1986, s.37.

[90] in the absence of novation.

[91] *Per* Nicholls L.J. in *Re Atlantic Computer Systems plc* [1992] 1 All E.R. 476 at p. 486. Unlike in the case of an administration or liquidation, such amounts are not treated as a prior charge on the assets, but, if not paid, the lessor or owner is free to take legal proceedings. *cf.* I.A. 1986, ss.11, 130.

[92] Unless the court otherwise directs, not the shareholders.

[93] Insolvency Rules 1986, r. 3.7(1).

excuse any person from the obligation or extend the time limits although the court may intervene and exercise the power on his behalf: I.A. 1986, section 47.

Statements submitted under section 47 must be verified by affidavit and contain particulars of the company's assets, debts and liabilities, the names and addresses of its creditors, any securities held by them and when they were given and such further information as may be prescribed. Similar statements are required to be given to an administrator.[94]

Within three months of his appointment, unless the court allows an extension, an administrative receiver must report to the registrar, the trustees for secured creditors and all secured creditors of whose addresses he is aware; I.A. 1986, section 48(1). This report must include details of the events leading up to his appointment, any dealings of his with company property and his carrying on of the company's business, the amounts of principal and interest payable to those debenture holders who appointed him and the amounts payable to preferential creditors, and the amount (if any) likely to be available for the payment of other creditors. It must also include a summary of the statements of affairs submitted to him under section 47 together his comments: I.A. 1986, section 48(5). It need not include anything "which would seriously prejudice the carrying out by the administrative receiver of his functions": I.A. 1986, section 48(6).

In addition, within three months an administrative receiver must also either send a copy of his report to all the company's unsecured creditors (of whose addresses he is aware) or publish an address to which they may write for copies to be sent to them free of charge. In either case he must also summon a meeting of the unsecured creditors on not less than 14 days' notice, before which he must lay a copy of the report. The court may dispense with such a meeting if the report states that the receiver intends to apply for such an order and the other requirements as to publicity are complied with at least 14 days before the application: I.A. 1986, section 48(2), (3). Such a meeting may appoint a committee, which may summon the receiver to attend before it and to give it such information as is reasonable, provided it gives him 7 days' notice: I.A. 1986, section 49. If the receivership is overtaken by a winding up, the report must be sent to the liquidator within 7 days: I.A. 1986, section 48(4). The administrative receiver must provide annual and final accounts of his receipts and payments to the Registrar of Companies, the company, the person who appointed him and each member of the creditors' committee (where there is one).[95]

These provisions replaced more limited ones in the Companies Act 1985 and reflect the Cork Committee's intention that creditors should be more aware and receivers more accountable.

### Preferential payments

A receiver appointed to enforce a charge which, as created, was a floating charge, must pay the preferential debts[96] in priority to any claims arising out of the charge under which he was appointed. This obligation applies even if the charge had crystallised prior to the appointment of a receiver, but it does not apply to a charge which as created was fixed. Creditors relying on a floating charge are thus deferred to the preferential debts but they are entitled to have the consequent depletion of assets made good out of assets available for the payment of general creditors: I.A. 1986, section 40.[97]

### Vacation of office by receiver

An administrative receiver may only be removed from office by an order of the court although he may resign on giving due notice. In addition he must vacate his office if he ceases to be a qualified insolvency practitioner. When he does give up office he must inform the registrar within 14 days and is subject to a fine in default: I.A. 1986, section 45. Any administrative receiver must also vacate his office if an administration order is made: I.A. 1986, section 11(1)(b).

When any receiver vacates office any remuneration, expenses or indemnity to which he is entitled at that time take priority over any security held by the person who appointed him: I.A. 1986, sections 11(4), 37(4), 45(3). Where the expenses of a receiver

---

[95] *Gomba Holdings U.K. Ltd v. Homan* [1986] 1 W.L.R. 1301; I.R. 1986, r. 3.32(1).

[96] See section 386 and Sched. 6, I.A. 1986. *Post,* p. 793. In this case the periods mentioned in Schedule 6 run from the appointment of the receiver or the taking of possession.

[97] See also s.196 Companies Act 1985.

appointed by the court exceed the assets in his hands, he is not entitled to recover them from the person who appointed him or the company.[98]

## Scots Law

The reasons for the introduction of the office of receiver to Scotland by the Companies (Floating Charges and Receivers) (Scotland) Act 1972[99] were:

(a) to enable the fortunes of a company to be revived and thus prevent unnecessary liquidation;

(b) to strengthen the rights of a holder of a floating charge by making it possible for him to take possession of and realise the security without liquidation; and

(c) to lessen the difficulties which could arise from the difference between Scots and English law where a group of companies included both Scottish and English companies.[1]

This Act was consolidated into the Companies Act 1985 and then, after amendments made by the Insolvency Act 1985 the general purpose of which was to standardise the English and Scottish provisions, into the Insolvency Act 1986. References are to sections of the 1986 Act, except when there is a statement to the contrary.

A receiver may be appointed by either the holder of a floating charge or the court on the application of the holder of a floating

---

[98] *Evans v. Clayhope Ltd* [1988] BCLC 238 (C.A.).

[99] A petition for the appointment of a judicial factor *ad interim* on the affairs of a limited company is competent at common law: *Fraser, Petitioner,* 1971 S.L.T. 146. (O.H.) (appointment made in a "position of chaos requiring urgently to be dealt with"). In *Weir v. Rees,* 1991 S.L.T. 345 (O.H.), a judicial factor *ad interim* was appointed where all the directors had been removed and the company was controlled by the secretary and the manager who were amongst the directors who had been removed, and who did not have the confidence of the majority of the members of the company. Where both a liquidator and a receiver were appointed, the receiver was held (*i*) to be entitled to take control of the property to satisfy the debt of the holder of the floating charge and (*ii*) to be primarily liable for the payment of the fixed securities and preferential debts of the company: *Manley, Petitioner,* 1985 S.L.T. 42 (O.H.). In *McGuinness v. Black (No. 2),* 1990 S.L.T. 461 (O.H.), there were circumstances in which the appointment of a judicial factor was preferred to the appointment of a provisional liquidator.

[1] *Report on the Companies (Floating Charges) (Scotland) Act 1961,* (1970) Cmnd. 4336, paras. 37, 38.

charge: section 51. The term "holder of the floating charge" is sufficiently widely defined as to include, in the case of a series of debentures, the trustees acting for the debenture holders under a trust deed, or, if there are no such trustees, specified majorities of the debenture holders: section 70.

## Appointment by holder of floating charge

A receiver may be appointed by the holder of the floating charge on the occurrence of any event which, by the instrument creating the charge, entitles the holder to make that appointment, and, in so far as the instrument does not provide otherwise, on the occurrence of any of the following:

(a) expiry of 21 days after the making of a demand—which is unsatisfied—for payment of the whole or part of the principal sum secured;

(b) expiry of two months during which interest has been in arrears;

(c) making of an order or passing of a resolution to wind up the company;

(d) appointment of a receiver by virtue of any other floating charge created by the company: section 52(1).

The appointment is made by means of an "instrument of appointment," validly executed by the holder of the charge or by a person having his written authority. A copy, certified in the manner prescribed by the Receivers (Scotland) Regulations 1986 (S.I. 1986 No. 1917 (S. 141)) to be a correct copy, must be delivered by the person making the appointment to the Registrar within seven days of its execution, and the Registrar enters particulars of the appointment in the register of charges. The receiver is regarded as having been appointed on the date and at the time when the instrument of appointment is received by him provided he accepts the appointment by the end of the business day next after such receipt (either by him or on his behalf).[2] A docquet signed by the receiver stating when he received the instrument of appointment is conclusive evidence of that fact.[3] As from the date of the receiver's appointment the floating charge,

---

[2] The Regulations make special provision for joint receivers.
[3] *Secretary of State for Trade and Industry v. Houston* 1993 GWD 30–1861.

subject to sections 410 to 414 of the Companies Act 1985 and section 245 of the 1986 Act, attaches to the property and takes effect as if it were a fixed security. Failure without reasonable excuse duly to register the certified copy of the instrument of appointment attracts a fine but does not affect the validity of the appointment: section 53.

In the case of a floating charge which covers the whole of the property from time to time comprised in the company's undertaking (an "all-assets" floating charge), any property which comes into the company's hands after the receiver's appointment will be attached and be available, if need be, for realisation by the receiver.

A receiver appointed to a company under an "all-assets" floating charge discovered that, before his appointment, the company had sold part of its stock-in-trade to a loan creditor and that the purchase price had been set off against the amount then due to that creditor. The receiver persuaded the creditor to return the stock to the company and allowed the debt to be correspondingly reinstated. The receiver then realised the assets of the company, including the restored stock. A liquidator was thereafter appointed, and he contended that the repurchased stock should not have been regarded as attached by the charge under what is now section 53. *Held,* it was not relevant to inquire whether particular assets were or were not comprised in the company's undertaking at the date of the receiver's appointment; the question was whether the instrument creating the floating charge covered the assets in question, and as the instrument in this case was expressed to cover assets whenever they came to be comprised in the company's undertaking, the reacquired stock was attached and available for realisation by the receiver: *Ross v. Taylor,* 1985 S.C. 156.

The interpretation of the phrase "as if the charge was a fixed security" in section 53 must take into account the definition of "fixed security" in section 70. The definition provides that "fixed security" means any security, other than a floating charge, which on the winding up of the company in Scotland would be treated as an effective security over the property.

Joint receivers were appointed by a bank over the whole of a company's property. The following day another creditor of the company purported to arrest in the hands of a third party a sum owing to the company. *Held,* because, by the appointment of the receivers, the floating charge had attached to, *inter alia,* the debt purported to be arrested, that debt had to be treated as if it had been attached as a fixed security, *i.e.* as if there had been an assignation of the debt in security in favour of the holders of the floating charge, followed by due intimation

of the assignation to the third party; the liability of the third party to pay
the debt to the company had therefore disappeared and the debt could
not be effectively arrested: *Forth & Clyde Construction Co. Ltd v.
Trinity Timber & Plywood Co. Ltd,* 1984 S.C. 1.

## Appointment by court

The circumstances in which a receiver may be appointed by the
court are the same as those for an appointment by the holder of
the floating charge (*ante,* p. 683) except that for paragraph (*d*)
there must be substituted:

(*d*)  where the court is satisfied that the position of the holder
of the charge is likely to be prejudiced if no appointment
is made: section 52(2).

The application to the court for the appointment is by petition,
which must be served on the company. A certified copy of the
court's interlocutor making the appointment must be delivered by
or on behalf of the petitioner to the Registrar within seven days
of the date of the interlocutor or such longer period as the court
may allow, and the Registrar enters particulars of the appointment in the register of charges. The receiver is regarded as
having been appointed on the date of the interlocutor, and as
from that date the floating charge attaches to the property and
takes effect as if it were a fixed security. Failure without
reasonable excuse duly to register the certified copy of the
interlocutor attracts a fine but does not affect the validity of the
appointment: section 54.

## Who can be appointed receiver

The following are disqualified from being appointed as
receiver:

(*a*)  a body corporate;
(*b*)  an undischarged bankrupt; and
(*c*)  a Scottish firm: section 51(3).

It is permissible to have joint receivers: section 51(6).

Where there are two or more floating charges, the same person may be appointed receiver by virtue of both or all of them: section 56(7).

## Powers of receiver

A receiver has the powers, if any, conferred on him by the instrument creating the floating charge, and in addition he has the extensive powers listed in Schedule 2 to the Act in so far as these are not inconsistent with any provision contained in the instrument creating the charge: section 55(1), (2). The statutory powers are such as to place the receiver in a position corresponding to that of an administrative receiver in England, and include the following powers:

(a) to take possession[4] and dispose of the company's property;

(b) to raise or borrow money and grant security over the property;

(c) to appoint agents and professional persons such as a solicitor and an accountant and to employ and dismiss employees;

(d) to bring or defend legal proceedings in the name and on behalf of the company[5],

---

[4] It is a matter of controversy whether this empowers a receiver to take proceedings in his own name against debtors to the company without having acquired an assignation of the debts from the company: *McPhail v. Lothian Regional Council*, 1981 S.C. 119 (O.H.), not followed in *Taylor, Petitioner*, 1982 S.L.T. 172 (O.H.). Funds consigned in court as a condition of recall of arrestment and inhibition on the dependence were held not to fall within the company's property in *Hawking v. Hafton House Ltd*, 1990 S.L.T. 496 (O.H.).

[5] In *Imperial Hotel (Aberdeen) Ltd v. Vaux Breweries Ltd*, 1978 S.C. 86 (O.H.), it was held not competent for the directors to raise actions in connection with the property which was within the receivership, but in *Shanks v. Central Regional Council*, 1987 S.L.T. 410 (O.H.), it was observed that, while the *Imperial* case was applicable to *most* situations, it did not mean that an action brought by a company in receivership was inherently incompetent or necessarily a fundamental nullity: it could not be held that directors were not empowered in any circumstances to deal in any way, including the raising of proceedings, with assets which were the subject of the floating charge.

(e) to refer questions to arbitration;
(f) to insure the company's business and property;
(g) to use the company's seal and execute documents, including bills of exchange and promissory notes, in the name and on behalf of the company;
(h) to carry on the company's business or any part of it;
(i) to grant or accept a surrender of a lease and to take on leases;
(j) to make any arrangement or compromise on behalf of the company;
(k) to call up any uncalled capital of the company;
(l) to establish subsidiaries of the company and to transfer to subsidiaries the business of the company or any part of it or any of the property;
(m) to change the situation of the company's registered office;
(n) to present or defend a petition for the winding up of the company; and
(o) to do all other things incidental to the exercise of his other powers.

The receiver may require to exercise only some of these wide statutory powers of management. It is a matter for his discretion as to which powers he will exercise and when he will exercise them. The company, through its directors, cannot normally interfere with the exercise by the receiver of his discretion by, for instance, raising actions which the receiver considers should not be raised but, where a receiver in the exercise of his discretion does not pursue an asset such as a claim for damages, the directors are entitled, and may be bound by their duty to other creditors, to vindicate the asset.[6]

The receiver has a duty of care to beneficiaries of the company's pension scheme, which he must not terminate without first giving adequate notice. Failure to do so may make him liable in damages to the beneficiaries.[7]

---

[6] *Imperial Hotel (Aberdeen) Ltd v. Vaux Breweries Ltd*, and *Shanks v. Central Regional Council, supra.*
[7] *Larson's Executrix v. Henderson*, 1990 S.L.T. 498 (O.H.), a case in which the receiver was held to have given adequate notice.

The exercise by the receiver of his powers is subject to the rights of persons who have effectually executed diligence[8] before his appointment and to the rights of persons who hold a fixed security or floating charge with prior or equal ranking: section 55(3).

A person dealing with a receiver in good faith and for value is not concerned to inquire whether the receiver is acting within his powers: section 55(4).

## Precedence among receivers

Where there are two or more floating charges, a receiver may be appointed by virtue of each charge, but the receiver whose charge has priority of ranking is entitled to exercise the statutory powers to the exclusion of any other receiver. Where two or more floating charges rank equally and two or more receivers have been appointed by virtue of these charges, the receivers are deemed to be joint receivers. The powers of a receiver whose charge has a ranking postponed to that of another charge by virtue of which a receiver has later been appointed are, from the date of the later appointment, suspended so far as is necessary to enable the second-mentioned receiver to exercise his statutory powers, and they revive when the prior floating charge ceases to attach to the property: section 56.

## Agency and liability of receiver for contracts

A receiver is deemed to be the agent of the company in relation to the property attached by the floating charge[9] and in

[8] An arrestment which has not been followed by a decree of furthcoming is not an "effectually executed diligence" for this purpose: *Lord Advocate v. Royal Bank of Scotland Ltd*, 1977 S.C. 155; nor is a landlord's hypothec for rent: *Cumberland Development Corporation v. Mustone*, 1983 S.L.T. (Sh. Ct.) 55. The *Royal Bank* case was distinguished in *Iona Hotels Ltd (in receivership), Petitioners*, 1991 S.L.T. 11 and the *Cumberland* case was not followed in *Grampian Regional Council v. Drill Stem (Inspection Services) Ltd (in receivership)* 1994 S.C.L.R. 36 (Sh. Ct.).

[9] This presumption was held to be rebuttable in *Inverness District Council v. Highland Universal Fabrications*, 1986 S.L.T. 556 (O.H.) (landlords seeking payment from receiver personally for occupation of premises after his appointment). In an application of this statutory provision receivers who carried on the company's business in licensed premises owned by the company were held not liable for rates since it was the company which remained in rateable occupation of the premises during the receivership: *McKillop, Petitioner*, 1994 GWD 18–1103 (O.H.).

relation to any contract of employment adopted by him in the carrying out of his functions: section 57(1) and (1A) (inserted by Insolvency Act 1994, s. 3(1) (2)).

He is personally liable on any contract entered into by him in the performance of his functions, except in so far as the contract otherwise provides, and, to the extent of any qualifying liability, on any contract of employment adopted by him in the carrying out of those functions: section 57(2) as amended by Insolvency Act 1994, section 3(1) (3).

A contract of employment is, by section 57(2A), inserted by Insolvency Act 1994, s. 3(1) (4), a "qualifying liability" if:

(a) it is a liability to pay a sum by way of wages or salary or contribution to an occupational pension scheme,

(b) it is incurred while the receiver is in office, and

(c) it is in respect of services rendered wholly or partly after the adoption of the contract.

However, where the sum payable as a qualifying liability is payable for services rendered partly before and partly after the adoption of the contract, the liability extends only to the sum payable for services rendered after the adoption of the contract: section 57(2B), inserted by Insolvency Act 1994, section 3(1) (4).

A receiver who is personally liable under section 57(2) is entitled to be indemnified out of the property in respect of which he was appointed: section 57(3).

As regards contracts of employment, nothing which is done or omitted within 14 days after his appointment is to be taken as an adoption of the contract by the receiver: section 57(5).

Contracts entered into by or on behalf of the company before the receiver's appointment continue in force, subject to the terms of the contract, after the appointment: section 57(7)[10]; but the receiver does not, merely by his appointment, incur personal liability on such contracts.

The provisions of section 57 do not limit any right to indemnity which the receiver would have apart from them, nor do they limit his liability on contracts made or adopted without authority: section 57(6).[11]

---

[10] See *Myles J. Callaghan Ltd v. City of Glasgow District Council*, 1988 S.L.T. 227 (O.H.).

[11] In *Hill Samuel & Co. Ltd v. Laing*, 1988 S.L.T. 452 (affirmed 1989 S.L.T. 760), a receiver who had recommenced business was held not to be exempted from personal liability by a clause in the debenture, that being a contract between the chargeholder and the company to which the receiver was not a party.

Contracts entered into by a receiver whose powers are later suspended under section 56, *ante,* continue in force, subject to the terms of the contract, after that suspension; section 57(7).[12]

A receiver has been held to be a joint occupier with the company of the company's premises for the purposes of the Explosives Act 1875, s. 23, which requires the occupier of every factory to take precautions against accidents by fire or explosion.[13]

## Remuneration of receiver

The remuneration to be paid to a receiver is fixed by agreement between the receiver and the holder of the floating charge, but where there has been no such agreement or the remuneration fixed is disputed by the receiver, the holder of any floating charge or fixed security, the company or the liquidator, it may be fixed instead by the Auditor of the Court of Session: section 58.

## Preferential payments and distribution of moneys

The Act provides that where a company is not at the time of the receiver's appointment in course of being wound up the debts which would be preferential payments in winding up[14] must be paid out of any assets coming into the receiver's hands in priority to claims of the holder of the floating charge. This applies only to debts which have been intimated to the receiver or have become known to him within six months after he has advertised for claims in the Edinburgh Gazette and in a local newspaper. Payments made in accordance with these provisions must be recouped as far as may be out of the assets available for ordinary creditors: section 59.

The moneys received by the receiver are distributed in the following order:

---

[12] See *Macleod v. Alexander Sutherland Ltd*, 1977 S.L.T. (Notes) 44 (O.H.) (decree of implement refused). For judicial comment on the receiver's position in general and on the distinction between receivership and liquidation, see *Lord Advocate v. Royal Bank of Scotland Ltd*, 1977 S.C. 155, and *Taylor, Petitioner*, 1982 S.L.T. 172 (O.H.).

[13] *Lord Advocate v. Aero Technologies Ltd (in receivership)*, 1991 S.L.T. 134 (O.H.).

[14] See note 96, above.

(a)  to the holder of any fixed security which ranks prior to or
     equally with the floating charge, persons who have effec-
     tually executed diligence on any part of the property,
     creditors to whom the receiver has incurred liability, the
     receiver himself in respect of his liabilities, expenses and
     remuneration, and preferential creditors entitled to pay-
     ment under section 59, *ante*;
(b)  to the holder of the floating charge in or towards satisfac-
     tion of the debt secured by the floating charge; and
(c)  to any other receiver, to the holder of a fixed security
     over the property, and to the company or its liquidator,
     according to their respective rights and interests.

Where there is doubt as to the persons entitled to a payment,
or where a receipt or discharge of a security cannot be obtained
for a payment, the receiver must consign the amount in a bank of
issue in Scotland in name of the Accountant of Court for behoof
of the person entitled to it: section 60.

**Cessation of appointment**

A receiver may, on application to the court by the holder of
the floating charge, be removed from office by the court on cause
shown. He may resign his office on giving the prescribed notice.
In addition he must vacate office if he ceases to be a qualified
insolvency practitioner.

Where at any time a receiver vacates office, his remuneration,
any expenses properly incurred by him and any indemnity to
which he is entitled out of the company's property must be paid
out of the property which is subject to the floating charge and has
the priority provided for in section 60, above.

Except where the cessation of a receiver's appointment is due
to his death or removal by the court, he must give notice of the
cessation to the Registrar within 14 days. Where the receiver has
been removed by the court, the duty to give such notice lies on
the holder of the floating charge. The Registrar enters the notice
in the register of charges. Default in complying with the requirement as to notice makes the receiver or the holder of the charge
as the case may be liable to a fine.

If, on the expiry of one month after cessation of a receiver's
appointment, no other receiver has been appointed, the charge
then ceases to attach to the property and becomes again a
floating charge: section 62.

## Powers of court

Under the Act the court may exercise certain powers in relation to receiverships, whether the receiver has been appointed by the holder of the floating charge or by the court:

(a)  The court may give directions in connection with the performance by the receiver of his functions. The application to the court may be made either by the receiver or by the holder of the floating charge: section 63(1).

(b)  The court may, on the application of the holder of the floating charge, remove the receiver on cause shown: section 62, *ante*.

(c)  Where the property which is subject to the floating charge is also subject to another security or burden or is affected by diligence, and the receiver wishes to sell or dispose of the property but is unable to obtain the necessary consent of the other parties, the court may, on the application of the receiver, authorise the sale or disposal of the property free of the security or burden or diligence.

However, where there is a fixed security over the property ranking prior to the floating charge, the court must not authorise the sale or disposal unless it is satisfied that this would be likely to provide a more advantageous realisation of the company's assets than would otherwise be effected. In such a case the court must impose the condition that the net proceeds of the disposal be applied to discharge the sums secured by the fixed security, together with, if the court regards such proceeds as less than the open market value of the property, such additional sums as are necessary to make good the deficiency.

Within 14 days of the granting of the authorisation the receiver must send a certified copy of the authorisation to the Registrar, and if without reasonable excuse he fails to comply with that provision he is liable to a default fine.

Where a sale or disposal has taken place under such court authorisation, the receiver must grant to the purchaser or disponee an appropriate document of transfer or conveyance, which, when recorded, intimated or registered as the case may be, has the effect of disencumbering the property of the security affecting it, and freeing the property from the diligence executed upon it.[15]

These provisions do not prejudice the right of any creditor of the company to rank for his debt in the winding up of the company: section 61.

(d) Where the appointment of a person as a receiver by the holder of a floating charge is discovered to be invalid (whether because of the invalidity of the instrument or otherwise), the court may order the holder to indemnify the person appointed against any liability which arises solely on account of the invalidity of the appointment: section 63(2).

(e) If the receiver makes default in delivering the documents or giving the notices which are required of him, *post*, the court may order him to make good the default within a specified time. Application to the court for this purpose may be made by any member or creditor of the company or by the Registrar. Similarly, if the receiver fails, on the liquidator's request, to render proper accounts of receipts and payments and to pay over the proper amount to the liquidator, the court may, on the liquidator's application, order the receiver to make good the default within a specified time: section 69.

### Requirements as to notification and information

When a receiver is appointed:

(a) Every invoice, order for goods or business letter which is issued by or on behalf of the company or the receiver or the liquidator and on which the company's name appears must contain a statement that a receiver has been appointed: section 64.

(b) The receiver must forthwith send to the company and publish notice of his appointment: section 65(1).

(c) The receiver must forthwith require a statement of the company's affairs to be submitted to him by some or all of the officers of the company (past or present), its promo-

[15] An example of a sale authorised by the court where inhibiting creditors had refused consent occurred, under the 1972 Act, in *Armour and Mycroft, Petitioners*, 1983 S.L.T. 43 (O.H.).

ters (if they acted within the year prior to his appointment), its employees (if they are in his opinion capable of giving the information required and are either present employees or have been employed within the preceding year) and the officers of any company which is (or has been within the previous year) an officer of or in the employment of the company concerned. Such a statement must be submitted within 21 days of its being asked for, with a fine in default. The receiver may excuse any person from this obligation or extend the time limits, and if the receiver has refused to exercise such powers, the court may do so.

A statement submitted under these provisions must be verified by affidavit and show particulars of the company's assets, debts and liabilities, the names and addresses of its creditors, the securities held by them and the date when they were given and such further information as may be prescribed: section 66.

(d) Within three months of his appointment, unless the court allows an extension, a receiver must send to the Registrar, the holder of the floating charge by virtue of which he was appointed and to any trustees for secured creditors of the company and (so far as he is aware of their addresses) to all secured creditors a report as to the events leading up to his appointment, his disposal of any property of the company and the carrying on by him of any business of the company, the amounts of principal and interest payable to the holder of the floating charge by virtue of which he was appointed and the amounts payable to preferential creditors, and the amount, if any, likely to be available for the payment of other creditors. The report also includes a summary of the statement of affairs submitted to the receiver under section 66 and of his comments, if any, on it.

The receiver must also, within three months (or longer if the court allows) after his appointment either send a copy of the report to all unsecured creditors of whose addresses he is aware, or publish a notice stating an address to which unsecured creditors should write for copies of the report to be sent to them free of charge. In either case he must summon a meeting of the unsecured creditors on not less than 14 days' notice and must lay a copy of the report before that meeting. The court may dispense with such a meeting if the report states that the receiver intends to apply for such an order and the other requirements as to publicity are complied with at least 14 days before the application.

If the company has gone or goes into liquidation, the receiver must send a copy of the report to the liquidator, at latest within seven days after the liquidator's appointment: section 67.

(e) The meeting of creditors summoned under section 67 may establish a committee ("the creditors' committee"), and that committee may, on giving at least seven days' notice, require the receiver to attend before it and furnish it with such information as to the carrying out by him of his functions as it may reasonably require: section 68.

Penalties are imposed for failure to comply with the requirements of sections 64 to 67.

# Chapter 26

# ADMINISTRATION ORDERS

THE Insolvency Act 1985 introduced an entirely new concept into U.K. company law—the administration order.[1] It is intended to provide an alternative to a liquidation for companies unable to pay their debts, either by rehabilitating the company and continuing it as a going concern or by providing a better way of either realising its assets or affecting a scheme or compromise with its creditors. It is therefore a form of "company rescue." An administrator is appointed by the court to control all the company's assets in an attempt to achieve the purpose of the administration order and as such he has different aims from that of an administrative receiver[2] appointed under a floating charge. Nevertheless the administrator is modelled on such receivers and many of the provisions relating to the two concepts are similar. If an administration order is made the company has a breathing space from any winding-up orders, appointment of receivers or other financial processes (*e.g.* enforcement of a hire purchase agreement). The procedure is, however, subject to the veto of any creditor who has validly appointed an administrative receiver prior to the consideration of the petition by the court—he must consent before the court can make such an order.

### Power to make an administration order

The court may only make an administration order if it is satisfied that the company is or is likely to become unable to pay its debts[3] and that such an order would be likely to achieve one or more of the following purposes:

---

[1] See the *Cork Report,* Chapter 9.
[2] *Ante,* p. 668.
[3] As defined in I.A. 1986, s.123. See *post,* p. 715.

(a) the survival of the company, and the whole or any part of its undertaking as a going concern;

(b) the approval of a voluntary arrangement with creditors[4];

(c) the sanctioning of a scheme of arrangement under section 425 of the Companies Act 1985[5]; and

(d) a more advantageous realisation of the company's assets than would be effected on a winding up.

No such order can be made after a company has gone into liquidation or if it is an insurance company[6] or an authorised institution within the Banking Act 1987[7]: I.A. 1986, s.8. The court will only make an order if the purpose specified, or, if several are relied upon, one at least of them, has a real prospect of being achieved. Thus in *Re S.C.L. Building Services Ltd*[8] the creditor sought an order relying upon purposes (a), (b) and (d) but the order granted was limited to (d)—the only purpose likely to be achieved. The court has jurisdiction to make an order where, though the company cannot meet its debts as they fall due, it has a surplus of illiquid assets over liabilities.[9] Any order must specify the purpose or purposes for which it was made and can subsequently be varied.[10-11]

## Application for an administration order

A petition for an administration order can be made by the company, the directors[12], the creditors, the clerk of a magistrates court,[13] or any combination of those people. It must be supported

---

[4] *Ante,* p. 661.

[5] *Post,* p. 808.

[6] As defined in the Insurance Companies Act 1982, ss.1, 96(1).

[7] ss.8–12.

[8] (1989) 5 BCC 746; *Re Consumer Industrial Press Ltd* [1988] BCLC 177 suggested that achievement of the purpose had to be "more likely than not" but this interpretation has been criticised in *Re Harris Simons Construction Ltd* [1989] BCLC 202, *Re Primlaks* [1989] BCLC 734 and *Re Rowbotham Baxter Ltd* [1900] BCLC 397.

[9] *Re Business Properties Ltd* (1988) 4 BCC 684; though it will not exercise its jurisdiction if the creditor was adequately secured, see *Re Imperial Motors U.K. Ltd* [1990] BCLC 29.

[10-11] I.A. 1986, s.18. See, *e.g. Re Ives Windings* [1987] 3 BCC 643.

[12] Acting collectively as a board. *Re Equiticorp International* ((1989) 5 BCC 599): petition by a single director authorised by a resolution at a board meeting at which he was not present, held, to be properly presented.

[13] In exercise of the power under s.87A Magistrates Courts Act 1980 (enforcement of fines on companies).

by affidavit and it may be accompanied by an independent report on the company's affairs.[14] Notice of the petition must be given to anyone entitled to appoint an administrative receiver[15] and other prescribed persons.[16] Once presented a petition cannot be withdrawn except with leave of the court: I.A. 1986, s.9(1)(2). In cases of urgency, an administration order can be made upon an undertaking by the petitioner to present a petition forthwith[17] or the time for service of notice can be abridged.[18]

In the period between the presentation of the petition and the date when the court either makes the order or dismisses the petition, section 10(1) of the Insolvency Act 1986 imposes a freeze on important aspects of the company's affairs so that the purpose of any order made can be achieved. In particular no resolutions for the voluntary winding up of the company nor any compulsory winding up order can be made; no steps may be taken to enforce any security against the company or to repossess any goods under a hire purchase agreement or similar arrangement[19] without the court's consent; and "no other proceedings" can be commenced or enforced against the company or its property without such consent.[20] However, the presentation of a petition does not prevent a winding-up petition being presented[21] nor the appointment and activities of an administrative receiver: I.A. section 10(2).

*Effect of appointment of an administrative receiver*

The role played by administrative receivers in the past was the model upon which the administration order procedure was based

[14] I.R. 1986, r. 2.1 & r. 2.2. The report should avoid disproportionate detail and expense and, in some circumstances, can be dispensed with: Practice Note (Administration Order Applications: Independent Report) Ch.D. [1994] 1 All E.R. 324.

[15] *i.e.* the holder of a floating charge within I.A. 1986, s.29(2): *ante,* p. 668.

[16] I.R. 1986, r.2.6 and 2.6A and, for Scotland, I.(S.)R. 1986, r.2.2(1).

[17] *Re Cavco Floors* [1990] BCC 589; *Re Shearing & Loader Ltd* [1991] BCC 232.

[18] *Re Gallidoro Trawlers* [1991] BCLC 441.

[19] These are conditional sale agreements under s.189(1) of the Consumer Credit Act 1974, chattel leasing agreements as defined in s.251 of the I.A. 1986, and retention of title agreements as defined in s.251: I.A. 1986, s.10(4).

[20] Where a commercial lease to a company provided that an irritancy should be incurred on the appointment of an administrator, service by the landlords of a notice of irritancy was held not to be a "legal process" requiring the leave of the court: *Scottish Exhibition Centre Ltd v. Mirestop Ltd (No. 2)* 1994 GWD 15–917 (O.H.).

[21] Though its advertisement may be restricted until the hearing of the petition for an administration order: *Re A Company No. 001992 of 1988* [1989] BCLC 9.

and therefore nothing in the new procedure is intended to undermine the position of an administrative receiver. Thus, although in general the administration order procedure gives companies a breathing space during which its creditors cannot enforce their rights, it does not prevent debentureholders exercising a right to appoint an administrative receiver. As we have seen, anyone presenting an administration petition must notify those with such a right who may then appoint such a receiver at any time prior to the court's decision. If he has already done so at the date of the petition the freezing period between the petition and order does not start to run until the debenture holder has consented to an administration order being made: I.A. 1986, section 10(3). On the other hand if he has not already appointed an administrative receiver but does so at any time before the making of an order the court must dismiss the petition unless either the debenture holder consents to an order being made or the debenture itself is invalid under the various controlling sections of the Insolvency Act[22]: I.A. 1986, section 9(3).

Thus, being able to appoint an administrative receiver gives a debentureholder an effective veto on the making of an administration order. It has been held that a debentureholder can appoint an administrative receiver where, though his security includes a charge which as created was a floating charge,[23] the company has no assets which could fall within that charge and it was granted merely to confer the right to appoint an administrative receiver and thus veto an administration order: *Re Croftbell*.[24] To exercise the veto the debentureholder has to appoint an administrative receiver before the administration order is made.[25] If he fails to do so, the court is free to make the order without his consent and thereafter the administrator can dispose of the charged property without his consent.[26]

*Court's discretion*

Subject to the existence of an administrative receiver the court on hearing a petition for an administration order may dismiss it,

---

[22] I.A. 1986, ss.238-240, 242-243, 245. See Chap. 29, *post*.
[23] See I.A. 1986, s.29(2).
[24] [1990] BCC 781.
[25] He is precluded from doing so afterwards by s.11(3)(b) I.A. 1986.
[26] See s.15(1) and (3) I.A. 1986.

adjourn the hearing conditionally or unconditionally, make the order or make any interim order it thinks fit, *e.g.* restricting the powers of the directors: I.A. 1986, section 9(4), (5). Where the company is in deadlock, the appropriate remedy is winding up and the court will not make an administration order.[27] If shareholders oppose a petition presented by the company, little weight will be given to their views if their reasons are linked to their aspirations as creditors.[28] An order can be made despite the opposition of creditors but it will not be appropriate to do so where creditors owed substantial sums are unlikely to vote in favour of the measures necessary to achieve the purpose of the administration.[29] Administration is a short term solution and should not be used where the company is hopelessly insolvent and the purposes of the order can only be achieved over a lengthy period.[30]

### The effect of an administration order

If the court makes an administration order, section 11 of the Insolvency Act 1986 provides for certain consequences since the administrator will need to assume control of all the company's affairs and be given time in which to operate the proposed scheme and achieve the purpose stated in the order. The following are the consequences of such an order being made:

(1) any winding up petition is dismissed;
(2) any administrative receiver shall vacate office[31];
(3) any other receiver must vacate office if the administrator requires him to do so[32];
(4) whilst the order is in force, no resolution may be passed to wind up the company voluntarily and no administrative receiver can be appointed[33];

---

[27] *Re Business Properties Ltd* (1988) 4 BCC 684.
[28] *Re Chelmsford City Football Club* [1991] BCC 133.
[29] *Re Land and Property Trust Co. (No. 2)* [1991] BCLC 849.
[30] *Re Arrows (No. 3)* [1992] BCC 131.
[31] Such a receiver is protected as to his fees, expenses and indemnity: I.A. 1986, s.11(4).
[32] On vacation of office an administrative or other receiver is excused from any obligation to preferential creditors: I.A. 1986, s.11(5).
[33] Thus a floating charge holder who consents to the order being made loses his right to appoint such a receiver.

(5) whilst the order is in force, no steps may be taken to enforce any security over the company's property or to repossess any goods in the possession of the company under a hire purchase agreement,[34] without the consent of the administrator or the court: I.A. 1986, s. 11(1)(c). The right of an airport under section 88 of the Civil Aviation Act 1982 to detain an aircraft for non-payment of airport charges is a security within section 11(3)(c) and its exercise requires consent.[35] Goods subject to a hire purchase or leasing agreement are in the possession of the company even if it has sublet them to an end user[36] and the agreement has been terminated[37] and thus consent to re-possess is necessary. The court has a discretion whether to give consent for re-possession or to order the administrator to pay a rental as an expense of administration thereby conferring priority over the unsecured creditors. In exercising this discretion it must balance the purpose of the prohibition, which is to enable the company to achieve the object for which the administration order was made, against the purpose of the power to give leave, which is to relax the prohibition where it would be inequitable for it to apply.[38] If an administrator wrongfully refuses consent, as where he seeks to use the goods as a bargaining counter against the owner, quite apart from possible liability in conversion, the court will refuse him his release until he has paid a rental and compensation to the owner;[39]

(6) whilst the order is in force, no proceedings, execution or other legal process can be commenced, continued or

---

[34] Including a conditional sale agreement, a chattel leasing agreement and a retention of title agreement. See Note 19 above.

[35] *Bristol Airport v. Powdrill* [1990] 2 All E.R. 493.

[36] *Re Atlantic Computer Systems plc* [1992] 1 All E.R. 4769 (C.A.).

[37] *Barclays Mercantile Finance Ltd v. Sibec Developments Ltd* [1993] 2 All E.R. 195; *Re David Meek Access Ltd* [1993] BCC 175.

[38] *Re Atlantic Computer Systems plc* [1992] 1 All E.R. 476 (C.A.) (leave granted); *Re David Meek Access Ltd* [1993] BCC 175 (leave refused).

[39] *Barclays Mercantile Finance Ltd v. Sibec Developments Ltd* [1993] 2 All E.R. 195.

enforced against the company by its creditors[40] without the consent of the administrator or the court: I.A. 1986, section 11 (1)(d). The meaning of *other legal process* in section 11(3)(d) has been considered in a number of contexts. It has been held that the phrase imports a process which requires the assistance of the court and therefore consent is not needed to serve a contractual notice making time of the essence or terminating a contract on the ground of repudiatory breach.[41] By contrast, an employee of a company in administration does need consent to bring a claim for unfair dismissal in an industrial tribunal.[42] An originating application seeking an extension of time for registering a floating charge has been held not to require consent within section 11(3)(d) because it is not a proceeding against the company or its property.[43]

(7)  whilst the order is in force, all documents[44] issued by the company or the administrator must state that an administration order is in force together with the administrator's name and the fact that he is managing the company's affairs, business and property: I.A. 1986, section 12.[45]

(8)  suppliers of utilities cannot make it a pre-condition of further supplies, that charges outstanding for supplies before the administration order was made, are paid.[46]

The court will appoint an administrator who must be a qualified insolvency practitioner and there are provisions for filling any vacancy which might occur: I.A. 1986, section 13.

---

[40] The administration order does not prevent a competitor applying to the court to have the company's air transport licence revoked: *Air Ecosse v. Civil Aviation Authority*, 1987 S.L.T. 751. In *Scottish Exhibition Centre Ltd v. Mirestop Ltd (in administration)*, 1993 S.L.T. 1034 (O.H.), joint administrators of M. Ltd had been attempting to sell the company as a going concern, but after 18 months had failed to do so. The landlord obtained leave from the court to irritate M. Ltd's lease of its premises.

[41] *Re Olympia & York Canary Wharf Ltd* [1993] BCC 154; *cf. Exchange Travel Agency Ltd v. Triton Property Trust plc* [1991] BCC 341.

[42] Though only rarely should it be refused because the purpose of the employment protection legislation is the protection of employees. Proceedings brought without consent are not a nullity: *Carr v. British International Helicopters Ltd* [1993] BCC 855.

[43] *Re Barrow Borough Transport Ltd* [1989] 5 BCC 646.

[44] Invoices, orders and business letters.

[45] There is a fine in default of this section.

[46] I.A. 1986, s.233; *post,* p. 740.

The administrator has complete control of the company's affairs and is charged with carrying out the purpose or purposes specified in the order. In many respects he is similar to an administrative receiver and has similar powers and duties.

On the appointment of an administrator certain prior transactions may be challenged by him. These provisions also apply on a liquidation and are set out in Chapter 29, *post*.[47]

**Powers of an administrator**

By virtue of section 14(1) of the Insolvency Act 1986 an administrator has the power to do anything which is necessary for the management of the company's affairs, business or property. In particular he has the following powers specified in Schedule 1 to the Act.[48]

(i)     To take possession of, collect and get in the property of the company and, for that purpose, to take such proceedings as may seem to him expedient.

(ii)    To sell or otherwise dispose of the property of the company by public auction or private contract or, in Scotland, to sell, feu, hire out or otherwise dispose of the property of the company by public roup or private bargain.

(iii)   To raise or borrow money and grant security therefore over the property of the company.

(iv)    To appoint a solicitor or accountant or other professionally qualified person to assist him in the performance of his functions.

(v)     To bring or defend any action or other legal proceedings in the name and on behalf of the company.

(vi)    To refer to arbitration any question affecting the company.

(vii)   To affect and maintain insurances in respect of the business and property of the company.

(viii)  To use the company's seal.

(ix)    To do all acts and to execute in the name and on behalf of the company any deed, receipt or other document.

---

[47] p. 784.
[48] These are the powers which are also available to an administrative receiver.

(x)    To draw, accept, make and endorse any bill of exchange or promissory note in the name and on behalf of the company.

(xi)    To appoint any agent to do any business which he is unable to do himself or which can more conveniently be done by an agent and power to employ and dismiss employees.[49]

(xii)    To do all such things (including the carrying out of works) as may be necessary for the realisation of the property of the company.

(xiii)    To make any payment which is necessary or incidental to the performance of his functions.

(xiv)    To carry on the business of the company.

(xv)    To establish subsidiaries of the company.

(xvi)    To transfer to subsidiaries of the company the whole or any part of the business and property of the company.

(xvii)    To grant or accept a surrender of a lease or tenancy of any of the property of the company, and to take a lease or tenancy of any property required or convenient for the business of the company.

(xviii)    To make any arrangement or compromise on behalf of the company.

(xix)    To call up any uncalled capital of the company.

(xx)    To rank and claim in the bankruptcy, insolvency, sequestration or liquidation of any person indebted to the company and to receive dividends, and to accede to trust deeds for the creditors of any such person.

(xxi)    To present or defend a petition for the winding up of the company.

(xxii)    To change the situation of the company's registered office.

(xxiii)    To do all other things incidental to the exercise of the fore-going powers.

In addition the administrator has the power to remove or appoint any director of the company, thus enabling him to provide the company with a new management, and to call any

---

[49] An administrator proposing to dismiss an employee as redundant must comply with the trade union consultation requirements imposed by section 188 of the Labour Relations (Consolidation) Act 1992: *Re Hartlebury Printers Ltd* [1992] BCC 428.

meeting of the members or creditors; I.A. 1986, section 14(2). He does not have power to make distributions to members.[50] When in doubt as to his powers he can apply to the court for directions: I.A. 1986, s.14(3).[51]

In exercising his powers the administrator is the agent of the company[52] and his status overrides that of the directors: their constitutional powers cannot be exercised in such a way as to interfere with his powers without his consent, general or specific: I.A. 1986, section 14(4), (5). A person dealing with the administrator in good faith and for value is not concerned to inquire whether he is acting within his powers: I.A. 1986, section 14(6).

Section 15(1) of the Insolvency Act 1986 gives an administrator the power to sell any property subject to a floating charge free of that charge.[52a] The chargee retains his priority in respect of the proceeds of the disposal.[53] In addition the administrator can apply to the court for permission to dispose of property free of any other existing security and of goods free of any hire purchase agreement[54] on the grounds that such a disposal would be likely to promote the purpose (or purposes) specified in the administrative order: I.A. 1986, section 15(2). The proceeds of the disposal (together with any sums necessary to make that up to open market value) must be used to redeem the security: I.A. 1986, section 15(5). Notice of such application should be given to the security holder.[55] The fact that he disputes the valuation put upon the property by the administrator will not prevent the court making the order: so long as the company has ample funds to make up any deficiency between the valuation and the market value, the existence and extent of such deficiency can be determined subsequently under section 15(5) I.A 1986.[56] An office copy of the court's order must be sent to the registrar[57]: I.A.

---

[50] *Re Business Properties Ltd* (1988) 4 B.C.C. 684.
[51] See *e.g. Re Home Treat Ltd* [1991] BCC 165 (the court made an order validating the running of an *ultra vires* business).
[52] This is also the position of an administrative receiver but note that there is no provision imposing personal liability on an administrator though such liability could arise independently of statute if such was intended: see *ante*, p. 673.
[52a] See also subs (3). An administrative receiver requires the court's consent for this.
[53] I.A. 1986, s.15(4).
[54] This includes conditional sale agreements, chattel leasing agreements and retention of title agreements: I.A. 1986, s.15(9). See Note 19 above.
[55] I.R. 1986, r. 2.51(2) and I.(S).R. 1987, r.2.2(1) but note I.R. 1986, r. 7.4(6) which applies in cases of urgency.
[56] *Re A.R.V. Aviations Ltd* (1988) 4 B.C.C. 708.
[57] There is a fine in default: I.A. 1986, s.15(8).

1986, section 15(5), (7). In the application of section 15 to Scotland, the administrator must grant to the disponee an appropriate document of transfer or conveyance to enable the property to be effectively disencumbered or freed from the security: I.A 1986, section 16.

## Duties of an administrator

An administrator is an officer of the court and in accordance with *Ex p. James*[58] must do the "fullest equity". Thus, where he is found liable to pay over an amount as an expense of administration, and he has had that amount invested pending the outcome of the dispute, he is liable to pay over the amount together with the interest it has earned: *Powdrill* v. *Watson, Re Paramount Airways Ltd (No. 3)* [1994] BCC 172, 182, C.A. The administrator's duty does not extend to advising a creditor what steps he should take to safeguard his security.[59]

On appointment the administrator takes into his custody or control all the company's property: I.A. 1986, section 17(1). He owes a duty to take reasonable care to obtain a proper price for the company's property and in choosing the time to sell.[60] He is charged with the management of the affairs, business and property of the company under the direction of the court or in accordance with the approved proposals.[61] His first duty is to publish the fact that an administration order has been made to the registrar and other prescribed persons[62] within 14 days, and to all the creditors of whose addresses he is aware within 28 days. He must inform the company "forthwith". There are fines in default: I.A. 1986, section 21.

His other immediate task is to require a statement of affairs of the company by giving notice of that requirement to the company's officers and other relevant people. The statement must show the company's assets and liabilities, the names and addresses of its creditors, details of securities held by the persons making the statement and other prescribed information I.A. 1986, section 22. The detailed rules relating to this statement of

[58] (1874) 9 Ch.App. 609.
[59] *Re Sabre International Products* [1991] BCLC 470.
[60] In *Re Charnley Davies Ltd* [1990] BCLC 729.
[61] I.A. 1986, s.17(2) and see below.
[62] See I.R., r. 2.10, and I.(S.)R., r. 2.3.

affairs are the same as those applicable to the statement of affairs
to be submitted to an administrative receiver which are set out in
the previous chapter.[63]

The central element in the administration procedure is the
formulation of a plan, or proposals, by the administrator, for
the purpose of achieving the purpose or purposes specified in the
order. Section 23 of the Insolvency Act 1986 requires the
administrator to send these proposals to the registrar and
the company's creditors within three months of the order. He
must also send a copy to each member of the company (or
publish an address from which they may obtain a free copy)
within that time span. Finally he must lay a copy of his proposals
before a meeting of the company's creditors summoned on not
less than 14 days' notice: I.A. 1986, section 23.[64] They vote
according to the amount of their debts at the date of the
administration order and a resolution may be passed by a simple
majority in value present and voting.[65] Secured creditors can only
vote in respect of the balance, if any, of their debt after
deducting the estimated value of their security.[66]

If the administrator subsequently wishes to make substantial[67]
revisions of his proposals he must publish them to the creditors
and members and summon another creditors' meeting to approve
the revisions in the same way as the original proposals were
published and approved: I.A. 1986, section 25. Where the
original purposes are incapable of achievement and time is of the
essence, the court may dispense with the section 25 procedure
upon application by the administrator for directions under section
14(3).[68]

In principle the implementation of the proposals should be
postponed pending the outcome of the creditors' meeting.
However the administrator enjoys his powers from the date of
the order[69] and section 17(2)(a) merely provides that prior to the
creditors' meeting he must act in accordance with any directions

[63] *Ante,* p. 679.
[64] A trustee creditor can apportion the total debt in accordance with the voting
    interests of those whom he represents: *Re Polly Peck International plc* [1991]
    BCC 503.
[65] See I.R., r. 2.28(1) but see also r. 2.28(1A); for Scotland, see I.(S.)R., r.
    2.10(1).
[66] See I.R., r.2.24 *et seq.* and for Scotland see I.(S.)R., r. 7.9.
[67] This is a matter for the administrator himself to decide.
[68] *Re Smallman* [1989] BCLC 420.
[69] I.A. 1986, s.14

given by the court. In the absence of negative directions by the court he may, therefore, have power to take steps which would effectively pre-empt any decision at the creditors' meeting, *e.g.* sale of the undertaking. This could however expose him to proceedings under section 27[70] and jeopardise his subsequent release under section 20. Before taking such steps it would be advisable for the administrator to seek directions from the court under section 14(3) authorising the transaction. In *Consumer Industrial Press Ltd*,[71] Peter Gibbs J. opined that only in exceptional circumstances should the court make a direction which would render nugatory the requirement for a creditors' meeting. Where he is proposing, not a sale of the undertaking, but a sale of a single asset at a good price and time is short, no application for directions is required.[72]

After the creditors have approved the proposals he must act in accordance with those proposals or any subsequent revisions: I.A. 1986, section 17(2). He must summon a meeting of the creditors if he is requested to do so by one tenth in value of the company's creditors or the court: I.A. 1986, section 17(3).

## The administrator and the creditors

If the meeting of creditors approves the administrator's proposals without modifications the administrator is simply required to carry out his duties in the light of those proposals. If modifications are suggested by the meeting they cannot be approved unless the administrator consents. The result of the meeting must be published to the court, the registrar and other prescribed persons.[73] If the meeting rejects the proposals and no modifications can be agreed the court can discharge the administration order, adjourn the hearing or make any order or interim order it thinks fit: I.A. 1986, section 24. If the meeting approves the proposals (modified or otherwise) it may appoint a committee (the creditors' committee[74]) which may require the administrator to attend before it (on not less than seven days' notice) and to supply reasonable information as to his progress: I.A. 1986, section 26.

[70] See *infra*.
[71] (1988) BCC 72.
[72] *Re N.S. Distribution Ltd* [1990] BCLC 169.
[73] I.R., 1986, r. 2.30; I.(S.)R., r.2.17.
[74] See I.R., 1986, r. 2.32 and *Re Polly Peck International plc* [1991] BCC 503; for Scotland see I.(S.)R., r.2.15.

Any member or creditor of the company can petition the court under section 27 of the Insolvency Act 1986 if the administrator is acting in a manner which is unfairly prejudicial[75] to the interests of the creditors or members generally or of some part of its creditors or members (including the petitioners) or if any actual or proposed act or omission of the administrator is or would be so prejudicial. The court can make such order as it thinks fit. This may include an order regulating the administrator's future conduct, or requiring him to do or not to do something, summoning a meeting or discharging the administration order. On the other hand no such order may interfere with the implementation of an approved voluntary arrangement[76] or a sanctioned scheme of arrangement.[77] It may only interfere with the implementation of proposals approved under sections 24 and 25 of the Insolvency Act 1986 if the petition was presented within 28 days of such approval: this prevents disruption of the administrator's work when it is substantially underway.

An allegation of unlawful conduct is neither necessary nor sufficient; what has to be shown are "instances of management of the company's affairs in a manner unfairly prejudicial to the petitioner's interest."[78] Where an administrator has acted fairly and impartially and with proper regard for the interests of all the creditors (and members where necessary) conscientiously endeavouring to do his best, but through an oversight or inadvertence, has fallen below the standards of a reasonably competent insolvency practitioner in the carrying out of some particular transaction, it is a misuse of language to describe him as having managed the affairs of the company in a manner unfairly prejudicial to the creditors. A petition under section 27 is inappropriate therefore. The proper course is to discharge the administration order, put the company into liquidation and bring proceedings under section 212 of the Insolvency Act 1986.[79]

**Variation or discharge of an administration order**

Section 18 of the Insolvency Act 1986 entitles the administrator to apply to the court for the administration order to be dis-

---

[75] *cf.* C.A. s.459, *ante,* p. 417.
[76] *Ante,* p. 661.
[77] *Post,* p. 808.
[78] *Re Charnley Davies* [1990] BCC 605, *per* Millett, J. at p. 624.
[79] *ibid.*

charged or to be varied so as to specify an additional purpose. He may do this if either the original stated purposes have been achieved or cannot be achieved or he is requested to do so by a creditors' meeting. The court has wide powers on hearing such an application. If the order is discharged or varied the registrar must be informed with 14 days.

## Vacation of office and release

An administrator may be removed by the court and he may also resign in the prescribed circumstances[80] by giving notice to the court. He vacates his office if the administration order is discharged or he ceases to be a qualified insolvency practitioner.[81] On vacation of his office his remuneration and proper expenses are charged upon any property of the company in his custody or under his control at that time, and such charge has priority ahead of any security which, as created, was a floating charge. It does not have priority over debts and liabilities incurred while he was an administrator under contracts entered into by him, or a predecessor of his, in the carrying out of his or the predecessor's functions: I.A. 1986, section 19(5). This provision provides some encouragement to third parties to deal with a company in administration. Furthermore the charge has no priority over any sums payable in respect of liabilities incurred, while he was administrator, under contracts of employment adopted by him or a predecessor of his in the carrying out of his or the predecessor's functions to the extent that such sums constitute "qualifying liabilities". An administrator adopts a contract of employment if he causes the company to continue the employment for more than 14 days after his appointment: I.A. 1986, section 19(6).[82] Qualifying liabilities are defined in terms similar to those applicable to administrative receivers.[83]

A person who has ceased to be an administrator has his release, in case of death, when the prescribed notice is given[84] and in any other case at such time as the court may decide. A

[80] I.R., 1986, r. 2.53 and for Scotland I.(S.)R., r. 2.18 (ill-health, retirement, conflict of interest).
[81] *Ante*, p. 659.
[82] See *Powdrill v. Watson, Re Leyland Daf Ltd, Re Ferranti International, plc* [1995] 2 All E.R. 65 (H.L.) See *supra*, p. 674 and p. 677.
[83] See *supra*, p. 677.
[84] See I.R., r.2.54 and for Scotland, I.(S.)R., r. 2.19.

release may be withheld to enable the administrator's conduct to be investigated.[85] Once he has his release, the administrator is discharged from all liability in respect of his acts or omissions in the administration and otherwise in relation to his conduct as administrator, save in relation to proceedings under section 212 of the Insolvency Act 1986 (summary proceedings against delinquent office holders).[86]

## Adjustment of prior transactions

On the making of an administration order certain charges and other transactions involving the company may be set aside under sections 238 to 246 of the Insolvency Act 1986. These sections also apply on a liquidation and are dealt with in Chapter 29 below.

---

[85] *Re Sheridan Securities* [1988] 4 BCC 200.
[86] *Ante*, p. 371.

# Chapter 27

# WINDING UP BY THE COURT

*[N.B. References in this chapter are to sections of the Insolvency Act 1986 unless otherwise specified.]*

THIS chapter and the following three chapters deal with the winding up of a company, which is governed by the Insolvency Act 1986. That Act is a consolidation of parts of the Companies Act 1985 (itself a consolidation) and the Insolvency Act 1985. A winding up may be—

(1) by the court; or
(2) voluntary; (s.73).[1]

and there are two kinds of voluntary winding up, namely—

(a) a members' voluntary winding up; and
(b) a creditors' voluntary winding up (s.90).

It will be recalled that winding up by the court on the "just and equitable ground" was explained in Chapter 18. Chapter 29 (Contributories and Creditors; Completion of the Winding Up) is partly concerned with winding up by the court, as well as the present chapter. Chapter 28 is concerned with voluntary winding up.

Section 652 of the Companies Act 1985, which is explained in Chapter 29,[2] provides a method of dissolving a defunct company by striking it off the register without a winding up, and under section 427 of the Companies Act 1985, *post,*[3] the court may order dissolution without winding up where there is a compromise or an arrangement to facilitate a reconstruction or an amalgamation.

---

[1] A third form, winding up subject to supervision of the court, was abolished by the Insolvency Act 1985. In practice that form was not used.
[2] *Post,* p. 762.
[3] p. 802.

A company cannot in Scotland be sequestrated.[4]

In addition to the statutory provisions, section 411 of the 1986 Act provides for the making of rules governing the conduct of company liquidation and section 414 for fixing fees.[5] These rules, the Insolvency Rules 1986,[6] replaced the Companies Winding Up Rules 1949, as amended. The Rules are made by the Lord Chancellor with the concurrence of the Secretary of State. In relation to Scotland, rules can be made by the Secretary of State.[7]

## JURISDICTION TO WIND UP COMPANIES

### In England

To obtain a winding up by the court, a petition must be presented to the court having the necessary jurisdiction. Section 117 provides that the courts having jurisdiction are:

(1) the High Court, *i.e.* the Companies Court,[8] in the case of all companies registered in England;

(2) Where the paid-up share capital does not exceed £120,000,[9] the county court of the district in which the registered office is situated, provided that such county court has winding up jurisdiction.[10]

### In Scotland

The courts having jurisdiction are:

(1) the Court of Session, in the case of all companies registered in Scotland;

---

[4] *Standard Property Investment Co. Ltd v. Dunblane Hydropathic Co. Ltd* (1884) 12 R. 328; Bankruptcy (Scotland) Act 1985, s.6(2). A Scottish company could, however, be made notour bankrupt for the purpose of the statutory provisions relating to equalisation of diligences: *Clarke v. Hinde, Milne & Co.* (1884) 12 R. 347; see now section 185 of the Insolvency Act 1986, applying section 37(1) to (6) of the Bankruptcy (Scotland) Act 1985.

[5] Insolvency Fees Order 1986 (S.I. 1986, No. 2030).

[6] S.I. 1986 No. 1925.

[7] See S.I. 1986, No. 1915 (S.139).

[8] *Eastern Holdings v. Singer & Friedlander Ltd* [1967] 1 W.L.R. 1017.

[9] This amount can be varied by order.

[10] See Civil Courts Order 1983 (S.I. 1983 No. 713) as amended; s.117(4).

(2) where the paid-up share capital does not exceed £120,000,[11] the sheriff court of the sheriffdom in which the registered office is situated: section 120.

## GROUNDS FOR WINDING UP BY THE COURT

Section 122 provides that a company[12] may be wound up by the court if:

(1) the company has by special resolution resolved to be wound up by the court[13]; or

(2) in the case of a public company first registered as such, no certificate of ability to commence business has been issued and the company has been registered for more than one year[14]; or

(3) the company does not commence business within a year after its incorporation, or suspends business for a whole year[15]; or

(4) the number of members is reduced below two; or

(5) the company is unable to pay its debts; or

(6) the court is of opinion that it is just and equitable that the company should be wound up. This part of the section was explained in connection with statutory protection of the minority.[16] It should be added that the power to wind up a company under this part is not confined to cases in which there are grounds analogous to those mentioned earlier in the section[17]; or

(7) in the case of a Scottish company, there is subsisting a floating charge over property comprised in the company's property and undertaking and the court is satisfied that

---

[11] See note 9. The sheriff court has no jurisdiction to wind up a company limited by guarantee and not having a share capital: *Pearce, Petitioner*, 1991 S.C.L.R. 861 (Sh. Ct.)

[12] *i.e.* one formed or registered under the Companies Act 1985 or a former Companies Act: C.A. 1985, s.735, I.A. 1986, s.73.

[13] *cf.* s.84, *post*, p. 762 which is more commonly resorted to, under which a company may pass a special resolution to be wound up voluntarily.

[14] *Ante*, p. 153.

[15] *cf.* C. A. 1985, s.652, *post*, p. 802, under which a defunct company may be struck off the register and so dissolved without being wound up.

[16] *Ante*, p. 409.

[17] *Loch v. John Blackwood Ltd* [1924] A.C. 783 (P.C.); *Symington v. Symingtons' Quarries Ltd* (1905) 8 F. 121; *Baird v. Lees*, 1924 S.C. 83; *Ebrahimi v. Westbourne Galleries Ltd* [1973] A.C. 360.

the security of the creditor entitled to the benefit of the floating charge is in jeopardy.[18]

There is another, transitional, ground, *viz* that the company is an old public company, *i.e.* a pre-1981 public company which does not comply with the criteria for such a company[19] and did not re-register as a private company in 1981.[20]

### Ground (3): Company not carrying on business

The period of a year is fixed by section 122, *ante*, so as to give the company a reasonable time in which to commence or resume business, as the case may be.

A winding-up order will only be made on this ground if the company has no intention of carrying on business.[21]

A company was formed to build and use assembly rooms. Owing to a depression in trade in the neighbourhood, building was suspended for more than three years although the company intended to continue its operations when trade prospects improved. A shareholder presented a winding-up petition which was opposed by four-fifths of the shareholders. *Held*, the petition should be dismissed. Since the conduct of the majority was not unreasonable or something of which the minority had a right to complain, the wishes of the majority were not to be disregarded. It would have been different if business could not have been carried on or there was an intention to abandon the undertaking: *Re Middlesborough Assembly Rooms Co.* (1880) 14 Ch.D. 104 (C.A.).

If a company is formed to carry on business in England and abroad and has carried on business abroad, it will not be wound up merely on the ground that it has not started its business in England within the year if it intends to do so as soon as possible.[22] There is no need to wait a year if it is apparent within the year that the company cannot carry out the objects for which it was formed.[23]

### Ground (5): Company unable to pay its debts

This is the ground on which a petition for a compulsory winding up is usually presented.

[18] s.122(2), for the meaning of "in jeopardy" see *ante*, p. 637.
[19] *Ante*, p. 42.
[20] See the Companies (Consequential Provisions) Act 1985, ss. 1–9.
[21] *Re Metropolitan Rlwy. Warehousing Co.* (1867) 36 L.J. Ch. 827.
[22] *Re Capital Fire Insurance Association* (1882) 21 Ch.D. 209.
[23] *Re German Date Coffee Co.* (1882) 20 Ch.D. 169 (C.A.). (petition on the "just and equitable" ground).

A company is *deemed* to be unable to pay its debts if:

(a) a creditor by assignment or otherwise, to whom the company is indebted in a sum exceeding £750[24] then due has served on the company, by leaving it at the registered office,[25] a demand in the prescribed form[26] requiring the company to pay the sum so due, and the company has for three weeks thereafter neglected to pay the sum due or to secure[27] or compound for it to the creditor's satisfaction; or

(b) in England and Wales, execution issued on a judgment in favour of a creditor is returned unsatisfied in whole or in part; or

(c) in Scotland, the induciae of a charge for payment on an extract decree have expired without payment being made; or

(d) it is proved to the satisfaction of the court that the company is unable to pay its debts as they fall due; or

(e) if it is proved to the satisfaction of the court that, taking the company's contingent and prospective liabilities into account, the value of its assets is less than the amount of its liabilities: section 123.

A company has not neglected to pay a debt within (a), *ante,* if it bona fide and upon substantial grounds disputes the debt[28]. The

---

[24] This sum may be increased by order.

[25] The demand need not be served by an officer of the court (*Lord Advocate v. Traprain*, 1989 S.L.T. (Sh. Ct.) 99, but, if it is not, the court must have evidence that the person who served the statutory demand was duly authorised by the creditor (*Lord Advocate v. Blairwest Investment Ltd*, 1989 S.L.T. (Sh. Ct.) 97. A statutory demand by a person bearing to act for and on behalf of the creditor is sufficient service: *Lord Advocate, Petitioner,* 1993 S.L.T. 1324 (O.H.).

[26] See I.R. 1986, rr. 4.4–4.6; Form 4.1; and I.(S.)R. 1986, Sched. 5, Form 4.1(Scot), as amended by I.(S.) Amendment Rules 1987 (S.I. 1981 No. 1921 (S. 132)).

[27] The security must be a marketable security covering the amount of the debt: *Commercial Bank of Scotland Ltd v. Lanark Oil Co. Ltd* (1986) 14 R. 147.

[28] *Re London and Paris Banking Corporation* (1874) L.R. 19 Eq. 444 *Cunninghame v. Walkinshaw Oil Co. Ltd* (1866) 14 R. 87; *W. & J.C. Pollok v. Gaeta Pioneer Mining Co. Ltd*, 1907 S.C. 182. Where it is doubtful whether there is a bona fide dispute, the Scots court may sist the petition in order that the petitioners may constitute their debt: *Landauer & Co. v. Alexander & Co. Ltd*, 1919 S.C. 492. There were held to be substantial grounds for dispute in

creditor must prove that the demand was left at the company's registered office; if this can be proved, it does not matter whether it was left by the creditor personally or by an agent or employee. If it is put in the post, it is properly served if delivery is accepted or proved.[29]

The period of three weeks' neglect required in *(a)* above, has been held to be a period of three clear weeks, excluding the day of service of the demand for payment and the day of presentation of the petition.[30] A creditor will not rely upon a statutory demand where there is a risk of dissipation of the assets in the three-week interval. If available, he may use *(b)*, *(c)* or *(e)* above; otherwise he can employ the more general ground in *(d)* — that the company is unable to pay its debts as they fall due. Thus in *Taylor's Industrial Flooring Ltd v. M. H. Plant Hire Manchester Ltd*[31] it was held that if a debt was due and unpaid and could not be disputed on some substantial ground, the presentation of a petition under ground *(d)*, *supra*, was amply warranted even in the absence of a statutory demand. The Court of Appeal commented that the practice of prevaricating in the payment of due debts was to be discouraged. A company is also unable to pay its debts if its acceptances have been dishonoured[32] or it has informed a judgment creditor that it has no assets on which to levy execution,[33] or the petitioner has demanded the sum due to him without success,[34] or the company disputes a comparatively small amount but fails to pay a much larger outstanding balance due to the same creditor.[35] A company is not unable to pay its debts just because it is carrying on a losing business, if its assets exceed its liabilities.[36] However, a company may be unable to pay

---

*Walter L. Jacob & Co. v. FIMBRA*, 1988 S.C.L.R. 184 (Sh. Ct.). In *Craig v. Iona Hotels*, 1988 S.C.L.R. 130 (Sh. Ct.), the sheriff held that (1) where a company was in bona fide doubt as to the identity of a creditor, liquidation proceedings were not a legitimate means of enforcing payment and (2) the statutory demand for payment was defective because it was sent by recorded delivery post to, and not left at, the company's registered office.

[29] *Re A Company, (No 008790 of 1990)* [1992] BCC 11; *cf. Re A Company* [1985] BCLC 37.

[30] See *Re Lympne Investments Ltd* [1972] 1 W.L.R. 523.

[31] [1990] BCLC 216.

[32] *Re Globe, etc., Steel Co.* (1875) L.R. 20 Eq. 337; *Gandy, Petitioner*, 1912 2 S.L.T. 276.

[33] *Re Flagstaff etc. Co. of Utah* (1875) L.R. 20 Eq. 268; *Re Douglas Griggs Engineering Ltd* [1963] Ch. 19.

[34] *Stephen, Petitioner* (1884) 21 S.L.R. 764.

[35] *Blue Star Security Services (Scotland) Ltd, Petitioners*, 1992 S.L.T. (Sh. Ct.) 80.

[36] *Re Joint Stock Coal Company* (1869) L.R. 8 Eq. 146.

its debts under *(d)* where its assets exceed its liabilities if its assets are not presently available to meets its current liabilities. Where a company persistently fails or neglects to pay its debts until forced to do so, the court may find that it is unable to pay its debts under *(d)*: *Re A Company* [1986] BCLC 261.

While grounds *(b)—(d), supra,* do not require the petitioner's debt to be £750 or more, in practice, an order will not usually be made unless this condition is complied with, since there must be circumstances which justify an inference that the company is insolvent.[37] On the other hand, where a company refused to pay a debt of £35 on the ground that it was too small to be the foundation of a petition, an order was made.[38] The Scottish practice has been to apply to rule that "any creditor, whatever the amount of his debt, is entitled to a winding-up order, unless special circumstances exist for refusing it."[39]

## PERSONS WHO MAY PETITION FOR WINDING UP BY THE COURT

Subject as below, a winding-up petition may be presented by any of the following parties—

1    the company or its directors[40];
2    a creditor or creditors (including contingent and prospective creditors);
3    a contributory: section 124(1);
4    in England, where the company is already being wound up voluntarily, the official receiver (s.124(5));
5    the Secretary of State for Trade and Industry (Insolvency Act 1986, s.124(4)[41]; Insurance Companies Act 1982, s.54 and s.124A[42]; or
6    in England, in the case of a charitable company, the Attorney-General (Charities Act 1960, s.30.); and in Scotland the Lord Advocate (Law Reform (Miscellaneous Provisions) (Scotland) Act 1990, s.14(3));

---

[37] *Re Industrial Assurance Association* [1910] W.N. 245.
[38] *Re World Industrial Bank* [1909] W.N. 148.
[39] *Per* Lord Johnston in *Speirs & Co. v. Central Building Co. Ltd,* 1911 S.C. 330 at p. 333.
[40] All: see *Re Instrumentation Electrical Services* (1988) 4 BCLC 550—some or a majority will not do.
[41] If the case falls within s.122(1)(b) or (c), or 124A.
[42] Upon the grounds there set out.

7   In England, in the case of a banking company, the Bank of England (Banking Act 1979, s.18[43]).

## A creditor

A compulsory liquidation is usually initiated by a creditor's petition. A secured creditor may petition but will normally rely on his security so that the petitioner is almost always an unsecured creditor. Where a petitioning creditor's debt is disputed on a substantial ground the court will usually restrain the prosecution of the petition as an abuse of the process of the court, even if the company appears to be insolvent.[44] On the other hand, even if the company is solvent, a creditor whose debt is clearly established can present a petition if there is a persistent refusal to pay the debt,[45] and no bona fide defence.[46]

A creditor whose debt is presently due and who cannot obtain payment normally has a right as between himself and the company *ex debito justitiae* to a winding-up order,[47] even if the company is being wound up voluntarily[48] or is in receivership.[49] This is not displaced merely by showing that the company has appealed against the judgment giving rise to the debt,[50] or has a disputed claim against the petitioning judgment creditor which is the subject of litigation in other proceedings.[51] Where there is a cross-claim the matter is one for the discretion of the judge.[52] It is, however, an improper use of the court to present a petition on the basis of a debt which has never been demanded and for which no opportunity to repay has been given.[53] It is an abuse of the

---

[43] As amended by I.A. 1986, s.219.

[44] *Mann v Goldstein* [1968] 1 W.L.R. 1091. A creditor must show an interest in the winding up; a petitioner who has been paid in full after the presentation of petition no longer has such an interest: *Furmston, Petitioner*, 1987 S.L.T. (Sh. Ct.) 10.

[45] *Cornhill Insurance plc v. Improvement Services Ltd* [1986] 1 W.L.R. 114.

[46] *Re A Company (No. 0012209 of 1991)* [1992] 2 All E.R. 797.

[47] See *Re Chapel House Colliery Co.* (1883) 24 Ch.D. 259 (C.A.); *Gardner & Co. v. Link* (1894) 21 R. 967.

[48] *Re James Millward & Co. Ltd* [1940] Ch. 333 (C.A.); *Smyth & Co. v. The Salem (Oregon) Capitol Flour Mills Co. Ltd* (1887) 14 R. 441.

[49] *Foxhall & Gyle (Nurseries) Ltd, Petitioners*, 1978 S.L.T. (Notes) 29 (O.H.).

[50] *Re Amalgamated Properties of Rhodesia (1913) Ltd* [1917] 2 Ch. 115 (C.A.).

[51] *Re Douglas Griggs Engineering Ltd* [1963] Ch. 19; *cf. Re Fitness Centre (South East) Ltd* [1986] BCLC 518.

[52] *Re L. H. F. Wools Ltd* [1969] 3 All E.R. 882 (C.A.); *Re A Company (No. 006273 of 1992)* [1992] BCC 794.

[53] *Re A Company* [1983] BCLC 492.

process of the court to maximise pressure on the company by simultaneously serving the petition on the company and faxing notice to its bankers precipitating the disruption of the company's bank account and depriving it of the opportunity to consider its position.[54] The re-presentation of a dishonoured cheque suspends the creditor's right to payment and the presentation of a petition to wind up is in these circumstances an abuse of the process of the court.[55]

The *ex debito justitiae* rule applies only between the petitioning creditor and the company. As between the petitioning creditor and the other creditors he is invoking a class right and so it is improper for him to present a petition for some private purpose. On the other hand if the petition is genuinely for the benefit of the class of creditors, malice on his part will not make the petition improper.[56] As with all matters relating to winding up, the court may have regard to the wishes of the creditors or contributories of the company, as proved by sufficient evidence, and may, for the purpose of ascertaining those wishes, direct meetings to be called, and in the case of creditors regard must be had to the value of each creditor's debt: section 195. This gives the judge a wide unfettered discretion to decide whether to make the order or not. Once an administration order has been made, however, no winding-up order can be made and any such petition must be dismissed.[57]

Where the company is insolvent the views of the creditors alone, as the only persons interested, are considered. In other cases the views of the contributories are considered.[58] Where there are different classes of creditors the wishes of those particularly interested will be given most weight and, in particular, where the company's assets are not entirely charged in favour of debenture holders the wishes of the unsecured creditors will be primarily considered. Where the assets are entirely charged in favour of debenture holders, if the petition of an unsecured creditor is opposed by the debenture holders the petitioner is entitled to a winding-up order unless the opposing creditors can show that there is no reasonable possibility of the unsecured

[54] *Re Bill Hennessey Associates Ltd* [1992] BCC 386.
[55] *Ex. P. Medialite* [1991] BCLC 594.
[56] *ibid.*
[57] *Ante,* p. 700.
[58] If only a contributory opposes a petition it will usually be granted: *Re Camburn Petroleum Products Ltd* [1979] 1 W.L.R. 86.

creditors obtaining a benefit from a winding up.[59] The court must not refuse a winding-up order just because the assets of the company have been mortgaged to an amount in excess of those assets or there are no assets: section 125(1).

If the petition of an unsecured creditor is opposed by the majority in value of the unsecured creditors, although the court has a complete discretion under section 125(1), *ante,* to make or refuse an order and the fact of the majority opposition is not conclusive, if they oppose for good reason (*e.g.* because the assets exceed the liabilities and there are prospects of the company being able to continue business) their wishes will prevail in the absence of special circumstances making winding up desirable.[60] Similarly if the petition is opposed by a minority of creditors this will normally not prevent the order being made although the wishes of the minority may prevail in special cases.[61]

If a company is being wound up voluntarily a compulsory order will not usually be made if the majority of the creditors want the voluntary liquidation to continue.[62] Where there are special circumstances the court may give effect to the wishes of the minority.[63]

Any assignee of a debt or a definite part of a debt can petition,[64] even if a petition was presented in respect of the debt before the assignment.[65] A secured creditor can petition, and his security will not be prejudiced; the holder of bearer debentures can also petition.[66] It has been held that the holder of debenture stock secured by a normal trust deed cannot present a petition as he is not a creditor of the company,[67] the trustees being the proper persons to present the petition in such case.[68]

---

[59] *Re Crigglestone Coal Co. Ltd* [1906] 2 Ch. 327 (C.A.); *Gardner's case, ante.*

[60] *Re Vuma Ltd* [1960] 1 W.L.R. 1283 (C.A.); *Re P & J Macrae Ltd* [1961] 1 W.L.R. 229 (C.A.). See also *Re A. B. C. Coupler Co.* [1961] 1 W.L.R. 243, *Re Fitness Centre (South East) Ltd* [1986] BCLC 518.

[61] *Re Southard & Co. Ltd* [1979] 1 W.L.R. 1198 (C.A.).

[62] *Re Home Remedies Ltd* [1943] Ch. 1; *Re B. Karsberg Ltd* [1956] 1 W.L.R. 57 (C.A.); *Re J. D. Swain Ltd* [1965] 1 W.L.R. 909 (C.A.); *cf. Pattisons Ltd v. Kinnear* (1899) 1 F. 551, *Elsmie & Son v. The Tomatin etc. Distillery Ltd* (1906) 8 F. 434 and *Re Fitness Centre (South East) Ltd* [1986] BCLC 518.

[63] *Bell's Trustees v. The Holmes Oil Co. Ltd* (1900) 3 F. 23; *Bouboulis v. Mann, Macneal & Co. Ltd,* 1926 S.C. 637; *Re Southard & Co. Ltd* [1979] 1 W.L.R. 1198 (C.A.); *Re H.J. Tomkins & Son* [1990] BCLC 76 and see *post,* p. 775.

[64] See *Re Steel Wing Co.* [1921] 1 Ch. 349.

[65] *Perak Pioneer Ltd v. Petroleum National Bhd* [1986] 3 W.L.R. 105 (P.C.); *cf. Re Paris Skating Rink* (1877) 5 Ch.D. 959.

[66] *Re Olathe Silver Mining Co.* (1884) 27 Ch.D. 278.

[67] *Re Dunderland Iron Ore Co. Ltd* [1909] 1 Ch. 446.

[68] But see Palmer's *Company Law,* para. 14.312, n.45.

It has been held in England that a garnishor of a debt due from the company cannot petition, because he is not a creditor, a garnishee order only giving him a lien on the debt and not operating as a transfer of the debt,[69] and that a petition cannot be presented by a person with a claim against the company for unliquidated damages.[70] However, it may be that such persons can petition as "contingent or prospective creditors."[71]

## A contributory

The term "contributory" means every person liable to contribute to the assets of the company in the event of its being wound up. As we shall see, it includes the present members and certain past members of the company: I.A. 1986, section 79.[72] A holder of fully paid-up shares in a limited company is a contributory.[73]

By section 124(2) the right of a contributory to present a petition is limited to cases where:

(1) the number of members is reduced below two; or
(2) his shares, or some of them, were originally allotted to him or have been held by him, and registered in his name, for at least six months[74] during the 18 months before the commencement of the winding up, or have devolved on him through the death of a former holder: I.A. 1986, section 124.

The object of the latter provision is to prevent a person acquiring shares to qualify himself to present a petition to wreck the company.

---

[69] Re Combined Weighing Machine Co. (1889) 43 Ch.D. 99 (C.A.).
[70] Re Pen-y-Van Colliery Co. (1877) 6 Ch.D. 477.
[71] In Re A Company [1973] 1 W.L.R. 1566 it was pointed out by Megarry J. at p. 1571 that the Pen-y-Van case was decided on section 82 of the 1862 Act which, unlike the present section, says nothing about contingent or prospective creditors and it is very doubtful whether it is an authority for the proposition that a claim for unliquidated damages will not support a petition. See also Re Dollar Land Holdings plc [1993] BCC 823.
[72] Post, p. 777.
[73] Re National Savings Bank Association (1866) L.R. 1 Ch.App. 547; Walker and Others, Petitioners (1894) 2 S.L.T. 230 and 397 (O.H.).
[74] See Re Gattopardo Ltd [1969] 1 W.L.R. 619 (C.A.), where an order was made that a name be entered on the register of members but the company was not a party to the proceedings and therefore was not bound to register the individual as a shareholder, and so the six months' period did not commence when the order was made.

A shareholder whose calls are in arrear can petition, but he must first pay the amount of the call into court.[75] A person to whom shares have been allotted can petition even though the shares have not been registered in his name, unless there is a bona fide dispute as to the allotment.[76] A person who is not an original allottee cannot petition unless he has been registered as a shareholder.[77] A registered shareholder has *locus standi* to petition notwithstanding that he is disputing the beneficial ownership of other shares. However, the court may order that the petition should not be advertised until the dispute has been settled.[78]

In the case of the holder of a share warrant the shares are not "registered in his name," so that unless, *e.g.* he is an original allottee, he cannot petition.[79]

The trustee in bankruptcy of a bankrupt shareholder, where the trustee is not on the register of members, is not a contributory and cannot petition.[80] It seems that the personal representative of a deceased shareholder is a contributory.[81]

A person who may be required to repay an amount to an insolvent private company following a payment out of capital by that company for the purchase or redemption of its own shares under section 76,[82] may petition to wind up the company on

[75] *Re Diamond Fuel Co.* (1879) 13 Ch.D. 499 (C.A.).
[76] *Re J.N. 2* [1978] 1 W.L.R. 183.
[77] *Re Quickdrome* (1988) BCLC 370 (mere agreement to acquire shares).
[78] *Re Garage Door Associates Ltd* [1984] 1 W.L.R. 35.
[79] *Re* Chitty J. in *Re Wales Wynaad India Gold Mining Co.* (1882) 21 Ch.D. 849, at p. 853.
[80] *Re H. L. Bolton Engineering Co. Ltd* [1956] Ch. 577 (s.82(2), by which the trustee represents the bankrupt shareholder, does not come into effect until a winding-up order is made.) In the Scottish case *Ker, Petitioner* (1897) 5 S.L.T. 126 (O.H.), a trustee in bankruptcy was held entitled as a contributory to petition for the removal of a liquidator and for a supervision order. The trustee on a sequestrated estate in Scotland can present a petition without registering his title to the shares since the whole estate, including the capacity to take proceedings, vests in the permanent trustee by virtue of the act and warrant: Bankruptcy (Scotland) Act 1985, s.31(1), (8) and *Cumming's Tr. v. Glennrinnes Farms Ltd*, 1993 S.L.T. 904 (O.H.).
[81] See *Re Norwich Yarn Co.* (1850) 12 Beav. 366; *Re Cuthbert Cooper & Sons Ltd* [1937] Ch. 392, at p. 399, where Simonds J. assumed, without deciding, that such a personal representative is a contributory, *per* Wynn-Parry J. in *Re H. L. Bolton Engineering Co. Ltd* [1956] Ch. 577, at p. 582; and *Re Meyer Douglas Pty. Ltd* [1965] V.R. 638, where Gowans J. pointed out at p. 655 that in *Re Norwich Yarn Co.* the statutory definition of "contributory" included not only every member, but also every other person liable to contribute, whether as an heir, devisee, executor or administrator of a deceased member. See also *Re Bayswater Trading Co. Ltd* [1970] 1 W.L.R. 343, and *Howling's Trustees v. Smith* (1905) 7 F. 390.
[82] *Ante,* p. 195, *post,* p. 778.

either the just and equitable or insolvency grounds, but no others: section 124(3).

The court will not, as a rule, make an order on a contributory's petition unless the contributory alleges and proves a financial interest in the winding up. A member's liability to contribute to the assets of the company on a winding up will suffice for this purpose. A holder of fully paid shares however will have to show, at least to the extent of a prima facie case, that there will be assets for distribution among the shareholders,[83] or that the affairs of the company require investigation in respects which are likely to produce a surplus of assets available for such distribution.[84] However, where a contributory's petition is based on the just and equitable ground[85] and alleges a failure by the company to supply accounts and information about its affairs, so that he cannot tell whether there will be a surplus for contributories,[86] a surplus need not be shown. The jurisdiction of the court to order the winding up of a company on the just and equitable ground on a contributory's petition is very wide and depends upon a full investigation of the facts at the hearing. A contributory may rely on a report by Department of Trade and Industry inspectors to support his petition.[87]

A petition by a contributory is uncommon. Such a petition which is opposed by the majority of the contributories will not be granted except where the conduct of the majority is something of which the minority have a right to complain.[88]

The right of a contributory to petition cannot be excluded or limited by the articles.

The articles provided that no winding-up petition could be presented without the consent of two directors, or unless a resolution to wind up was passed at a general meeting, or unless the petitioner held one-fifth of the share capital. None of these conditions was fulfilled. *Held,* the restrictions were invalid and a petition could be presented: *Re Peveril Gold Mines Ltd* [1898] 1 Ch. 122 (C.A.).

---

[83] *Re Rica Gold Washing Co.* (1879) 11 Ch.D. 36 (C.A.); followed in *Re Expanded Plugs Ltd* [1966] 1 W.L.R. 514; *Black v. United Collieries Ltd* (1904) 7 F. 18, *per* Lord Trayner at p. 20.

[84] *Re Othery Construction Ltd* [1966] 1 W.L.R. 69, considering *Re Haycraft Gold etc., Co* [1900] 2 Ch. 230 and *Re Newman and Howard, post.*

[85] *Ante,* p. 409.

[86] *Re Newman and Howard Ltd* [1962] Ch. 257.

[87] *Re St. Piran Ltd* [1981] 3 All E.R. 270.

[88] *Re Middleborough Assembly Rooms Co.* (1880) 14 Ch.D. 104 (C.A.), *ante,* p. 715; *Galbraith v. Merito Shpg. Co. Ltd,* 1947 S.C. 446; *Re Tivoli Freeholds Ltd* [1972] V.R. 445; *Re St. Piran Ltd* [1981] 3 All E.R. 270.

## The Official Receiver

The official receiver can petition for a winding up by the court when a company is already in voluntary liquidation in England. An order will only be made if the court is satisfied on a balance of probabilities,[89] that the existing liquidation cannot be continued with due regard to the interests of the creditors or contributories: section 124(5). The fact that a liquidator must now be a qualified insolvency practitioner and, in a creditors' voluntary winding up, his powers are restricted prior to the creditors' meeting, may reduce the occasions upon which this can be shown.

## The Secretary of State for Trade and Industry

Where a petition for compulsory winding up is presented by the Secretary of State after he has reached the conclusion, as a result of investigations, that it is expedient in the public interest to wind up the company compulsorily,[90] his conclusion, without being decisive, ought to be given appropriate weight by the court; where there are circumstances of suspicion it is highly desirable that the winding up be by the court; and the passing of a resolution for voluntary winding up shortly before the petition is presented ought not to be allowed to put the voluntary winding up in an entrenched position which can only be demolished if the Secretary of State can show that voluntary winding up would be markedly inferior to compulsory winding up.[91]

A report of inspectors appointed by him is prima facie evidence on which the court may act in deciding to make a winding-up order on a petition by the Secretary of State.[92] The Secretary of State's petition is in his own capacity and not that of a notional creditor.[93] Where the petition is subsequently withdrawn, the company is liable for the costs if the petition was properly presented.[94]

---

[89] *Re J. Russell Electronics Ltd* [1968] 1 W.L.R. 1252.
[90] See I.A. 1986, s.124A and p. 435, *ante.*
[91] *Re Lubin, Rosen and Associates* [1975] 1 W.L.R. 122.
[92] *Re Armvent Ltd* [1975] 3 All E.R. 441.
[93] *Re Highfield Commodities Ltd* [1985] 1 W.L.R. 149.
[94] *Re XYLLYX (No. 2)* [1992] BCLC 378; *cf. Re Secure & Provide plc* [1992] BCC 405.

## PETITION FOR WINDING UP BY THE COURT

In England the winding-up petition must be in one of the forms specified in the Insolvency Rules 1986.[95]

Unless the court otherwise directs, the petition must be advertised in accordance with the rules.[96] The rules require the advertisement[97] to appear not less than seven clear days after the petition has been served on the company and not less than seven clear days before the day fixed for the hearing. This gives the company the opportunity to discharge, or dispute, the debt or apply for validation of its transactions under section 127 before the advertisement appears.[98] The court will restrain the issue of the advertisement if the detriment to the petitioner from an injunction is outweighed by the potential harm caused to the company from the advertisement,[99] if the petition is an abuse of the process of the court,[1] or if the debt is bona fide disputed.[2]

In England it has been held (in a case where the Secretary of State presented the petition on the ground that winding up was expedient by reason of matters referred to in a report of inspectors appointed to investigate the affairs of the company) that when grave charges are levelled against individuals in a petition, the court will not be satisfied with merely prima facie evidence. The petitioner must, if practicable, prove facts by the evidence of witnesses who have first-hand knowledge of the matters on which they give evidence.[3] However, in a later case it was held that the report of inspectors stands in a wholly different position from the ordinary affidavit evidence and represents the conclusions of a statutory fact-finding body, after hearing oral evidence and examination of books. The court is entitled to look at the report and accept it not as hearsay evidence but as material

---

[95] S. I. 1986 No. 1925, r. 12.7(1); forms 4.2 & 4.3. For Scotland see S.I. 1986 No. 2298 (S. 170) and 1986 No. 2297 (S. 169).
[96] Unless the court otherwise directs, in the Gazette: I.R. 1980, r.4.11.
[97] In determining whether a petition has been advertised an informal communication, *e.g.* a fax to the company's bank can be regarded as an advertisement: *Re Bill Hennessey Associates Ltd*, 1993 BCC 386; *cf. SN Group plc v. Barclays Bank plc*, 1993 BCC 506.
[98] *Re Bill Hennessey Associates Ltd, ibid.*
[99] *Re A Company (No. 009080 of 1992)* [1993] BCLC 269.
[1] *Re A Company (No. 0012209 of 1991)* [1992] 2 All E.R. 797.
[2] *Ex p. Avocet Aviation* [1992] BCLC 869 (costs awarded against petitioner on an indemnity basis).
[3] *Re A. B. C. Coupier Co. (No. 2)* [1962] 1 W.L.R. 1236; not followed in *Re Travel & Holiday Clubs Ltd, post.*

of a different character. At least where the report is not challenged by the company, the court does not have to be satisfied anew by evidence of the ordinary nature as to the facts found in the report.[4]

After the presentation of a petition (which has not been struck out or dismissed[5]) an application may be made to the court for the appointment of a *provisional liquidator*: I.A. 1986, s.135.[6] The applicant must provide a deposit or security for the appointee's remuneration.[7] In England the appointment may be made at any time before the making of a winding-up order, and the person usually appointed is the official receiver. In Scotland the appointment may be made at any time before the first appointment of liquidators: section 135. An appointment is made if the assets are in jeopardy,[8] or to avoid possible prejudice.[9]

The provisional liquidator takes all the company's property into his custody or under his control (s.144), and after his appointment no legal proceedings can be commenced or continued against the company without leave of the court: section 130(2). An interpleader summons to which the company is made respondent is a proceeding against the company[10]; so also is distress levied on the company's property by the Commissioners of Customs and Excise for non-payment of VAT.[11] In one case the court gave leave to proceed to a person who had an unimpugnable right to a claim for specific performance of an agreement to sell property belonging to the company.[12] Leave will

---

[4] *Re Travel & Holidays Clubs Ltd* [1967] 1 W.L.R. 711, where it was said (at p. 716c) that it is undesirable that inspectors who have conducted an enquiry should have to give evidence of their findings upon which they would be liable to be cross-examined. This case was followed in *Re S.B.A. Properties Ltd* [1967] 1 W.L.R. 799. And see *Re Allied Produce* [1967] 1 W.L.R. 1469.

[5] *Re A Company* [1973] 1 W.L.R. 1566.

[6] Directors who improperly oppose the application may be ordered to pay the costs thrown away personally: *Gamelstaden plc v. Brackland Magazines Ltd* [1993] BCC 194.

[7] I.R. 1986, rr. 4.27 & 4.28.

[8] *e.g. Levy v. Napier*, 1962 S.C. 468, in which a deferred shareholder whose petition was opposed by the controlling ordinary shareholders averred that he was apprehensive that the proceeds of the sale of the company's business and assets were being depleted to his prejudice. See also, *Ex p. Nyckeln Finance Co.* [1991] BCLC 539 (where there was a real chance of assets being dissipated by being distributed otherwise than rateably between the creditors).

[9] *e.g. McCabe v. Andrew Middleton (Enterprises) Ltd*, 1969 S.L.T. (Sh. Ct.) 29.

[10] *Eastern Holdings v. Singer & Friedlander Ltd* [1967] 1 W.L.R. 1017.

[11] *Re Memco Engineering Ltd* [1986] Ch. 86.

[12] *Re Coregrange Ltd* [1984] BCLC 453.

be given to enable a person to enforce a debt against the company under an existing contract which the liquidator chose to continue for the benefit of the liquidation or a debt under a new contract with the liquidator entered into for the purposes of the liquidation.[13] The appointment of a provisional liquidator has the same result as the making of a winding-up order in that the board of directors of the company becomes *functus officio* and its powers are assumed by the liquidator,[14] but notwithstanding the appointment the board has some residuary powers, *e.g.* it can instruct solicitors and counsel to oppose the petition and, if a winding-up order is made, to appeal against it.[15] The board can also act in interlocutory proceedings, including a motion to discharge the provisional liquidator.

The court may also, after the presentation of a petition (which is still subsisting[16]) and before a winding-up order has been made, on the application of the company or of any creditor or contributory, stay or restrain any pending legal proceedings against the company: section 126. Section 126 is an exception to the rule that proceedings pending in the Supreme Court cannot be restrained by injunction. The object of sections 126 and 130(2) is "to put all unsecured creditors upon an equality, and to pay them *pari passu*."[17]

### Withdrawal of petition

A petitioner can apply to the court for leave to withdraw his petition so long as he does so at least five days prior to the hearing and satisfies the court that the petition has not been advertised, that no notices (whether in support or in opposition) have been received by him with reference to the petition, and that the company consents to an order being made.[18]

### Hearing of petition

The company and any creditor or contributory may attend the hearing of the petition. For this purpose a person is a creditor if

---

[13] *Re Atlantic Computer Systems plc* [1992] 1 All E.R. 476, C.A.
[14] *Post*, p. 735.
[15] *Re Union Accident Insce. Co. Ltd* [1972] 1 W.L.R. 640.
[16] See note 5, above.
[17] *per* Lindley L.J. in *Re Oak Pits Colliery Co.* (1882) Ch.D. 322 (C.A.) at p. 329.
[18] I.R. 1986, r. 4.15 and see Practice Direction [1987] 1 All E.R. 107.

he is a creditor for a present debt, a prospective debt or a contingent debt. Whether a person is a contingent creditor depends on circumstances existing at the date of the hearing.[19]

On the hearing of a petition the court may dismiss it, or adjourn the hearing conditionally or unconditionally, or make any interim order, or any other order that it thinks it fit: section 125(1).[20] The court may have regard to the wishes of the creditors or contributories: section 195.[21] When exercising its discretion to adjourn the hearing of a petition for the winding up of an international bank, the court had to consider the interests of the creditors worldwide rather than the interests of one class of creditor within the jurisdiction; English law does not permit the court to erect a ring fence around assets or creditors in any one jurisdiction.[22]

When a judgment creditor[23] is deprived of the right *ex debito justitiae* to a winding-up order because his petition is opposed by the majority of the creditors, the fair practice is to make no order as to costs.[24] The same is true where the petitioning creditor is not a judgment creditor but his debt is undisputed.[25] *Aliter* if the petitioning creditor acted unreasonably in presenting or prosecuting his petition,[26] or the company is being wound up voluntarily and no evidence is filed on behalf of the petitioner beyond an affidavit verifying the petition.[27] In special circumstances costs may be awarded against one party, *e.g.* where the company failed to defend an action so that the plaintiff petitioned to wind up the company, on the petition being dismissed and the action set aside, the company was held liable for the costs of the petition.[28] However, where a petitioner was paid in full by the company, apart from his costs, the petitioner was unable to recover his

---

[19] *Re S.B.A. Properties Ltd* [1967] 1 W.L.R. 799.
[20] *Ante.*
[21] See also *Re Middlesborough Assembly Rooms Co.* (1880) 14 Ch.D. 104 (C.A.), and *Galbraith v. Merito Shpg. Co. Ltd*, 1947 S.C. 446.
[22] *Re Bank of Credit & Commerce International S.A.* [1992] BCC 83.
[23] Scots equivalent, a creditor who has obtained a decree.
[24] *Re R. W. Sharman Ltd* [1957] 1 W.L.R. 774; *Re A. B. C. Coupler Co.* [1961] 1 W.L.R. 243.
[25] *Re Sklan Ltd* [1961] 1 W.L.R. 1013.
[26] *Re A. E. Hayter & Sons (Porchester) Ltd* [1961] 1 W.L.R. 1008.
[27] *Re Riviera Pearls Ltd* [1962] 1 W.L.R. 722.
[28] *Re Lanaghan Bros. Ltd* [1977] 1 All E.R. 265. See also *Re M. McCarthy & Co. (Builders) Ltd (No. 2)* [1976] 2 All E.R. 339 and *Re Arrow Leeds Ltd* [1986] BCLC 538.

costs because he had not complied with the rules as to advertisement of the petition.[29]

When a winding-up order is made, it is usual to order the costs of (1) the petitioner, (2) the company, and (3) one set of creditors and one set of contributories, to be paid out of the assets. Any other creditor who wishes to appear does so at his own expense. As a general rule no order for costs will be made in favour of one creditor against another.[30]

A copy of the order must be sent by the company to the Registrar of Companies: section 130(1).

Section 711 of the Companies Act 1985 provides that the Registrar must cause notice of the receipt by him of the copy of the order to be published in the *Gazette*. The notice must state the company's name, a description of the document received and the date of receipt.

The court has power to stay a winding-up order either altogether or for a limited time,[31] on such terms and conditions as it thinks fit, if an application is made to it by the liquidator or (in England) the official receiver or any creditor or contributory. In England the court may require the official receiver to furnish a report on matters relevant to the application. A copy of any order made by the court under this provision must be sent to the Registrar: section 147. Such an order is not usually made unless all the creditors are paid or satisfied, but the court will have regard to commercial morality and not just to the interests of the creditors.[32] As a matter of practice a stay is never granted, and there are good reasons for the practice.[33]

An appeal from the making of a winding-up order in England may be brought within 4 weeks: R.S.C., Ord. 59, r. 4.[34] An order made by a Lord Ordinary in Scotland may be reviewed by the Inner House if a reclaiming motion is enrolled within 14 days: section 162.[35]

Where an order winding up a solvent company was made on a contributory's petition opposed by the company and another contribu-

[29] *The Shushella Ltd* (1982) 126 S.J. 577.
[30] *Re Esal (Commodities) Ltd* [1985] BCLC 450. This case also provides guidance for costs where an alternative scheme of arrangement under section 425 of the Companies Act 1985, *post* p. 814 is under consideration.
[31] See *Re Boston Timber Fabrications Ltd* [1984] BCLC 328.
[32] *Re Telescriptor Ltd* [1903] 2 Ch. 174.
[33] See, *per* Plowman J. in *Re A & B.C. Chewing Gum Ltd* [1975] 1 W.L.R. 579, at p. 592.
[34] See I.R. 1986, r. 7.47.
[35] *e.g. Levy, Petitioner,* 1963 S.C. 46.

tory, and the company appealed against the order, the company had to provide security for the costs of the appeal otherwise than from the company's assets. It would have been wrong, if the appeal failed, for the petitioner to be liable to bear any proportion of the costs of the appeal or of a liquidation. An order was made that security be provided by the directors or shareholders promoting the appeal: *Re E. K. Wilson & Sons Ltd* [1972] 1 W.L.R. 791 (C.A.).

## CONSEQUENCES OF A WINDING-UP ORDER

The consequences of the making of a winding-up order date back to an earlier date than that on which the order was actually made. This date is called the *commencement of the winding up* and is:

(1) the time of the presentation of the petition; or
(2) where, before the presentation of the petition, the company was in voluntary liquidation, the time of the passing of the resolution for voluntary winding up (s.129).

The consequences of a winding-up order are:

(1) Any disposition of the property of the company, and any transfer of shares or alteration in the status of the members, after the commencement of the winding up, is void unless the court otherwise orders: section 127.

The company is divested of beneficial ownership of its assets.[36]

The object of section 127 is to prevent, during the period which must elapse before a petition can be heard, the improper alienation and dissipation of the property of a company *in extremis*. However, where a company is trading, the court can sanction transactions in the ordinary course of business—otherwise the presentation of a petition, whether well- or ill-founded, would paralyse the company's trade.[37] Thus the court may sanction the continued operation of the company's bank account in the ordinary course of business, so long as there is no serious

---

[36] *Ayerst v. C & K (Construction) Ltd* [1976] A.C. 167.
[37] *Per* Lord Cairns in *Re Wiltshire Iron Co.* (1868) L.R. 3 Ch.App. 443, at p. 447; see also *United Dominions Trust Ltd, Noters,* 1977 S.L.T. (Notes) 56 (O.H.) (warrant to sell security subjects valid).

doubt as to the company's solvency.[38] Further in the case of a solvent company the court will normally sanction a disposition which the directors consider to be necessary or expedient in the interests of the company for reasons which an intelligent and honest man could reasonably hold.[39]

Between the date of the presentation of the petition and the making of a winding-up order X advanced £1,200 to the company to enable it to pay wages due to the staff and took a debenture as security. X knew, at the time of the issue of the debenture, of the presentation of the petition. *Held*, the debenture was valid: *Re Park, Ward & Co. Ltd* [1926] Ch. 828.

The court may order that a debenture taken after the commencement of the winding up is not void if the money is advanced, not for the payment of wages, but for the company's benefit to enable it to carry out its contracts and the lender has acted in good faith and with the honest intention of benefiting the company.[40] If however the disposition was made with a view to assisting the company's creditors, it will not be validated.[41]

Where the company has an overdraft on its bank account the court will freeze that account as at the date of the presentation of the petition by discontinuing all further dealings on the existing account and will require all subsequent dealings to be on a new and separate account.[42]

After the presentation of a petition property may safely be transferred or payment made *to* the company,[43] but payments made *by* the company in respect of debts previously incurred must be refunded by the recipient,[44] and property transferred is held by the recipient on trust for the company, unless an order under section 127 is obtained.[45]

After the commencement of winding up, a company paid for petrol delivered prior to that date. The payments, which were

[38] *Re A Company (No. 007532 of 1986)* [1987] BCLC 200.
[39] *Re Burton & Deakin Ltd* [1977] 1 W.L.R. 390.
[40] *Re Steane's (Bournemouth) Ltd* [1950] 1 All E.R. 21, applied in *Re Clifton Place Garage Ltd* [1970] 1 All E.R. 352 (C.A.).
[41] *Re Webb's Electrical* [1988] BCLC 332.
[42] *Re Gray's Inn Construction Co. Ltd* [1980] 1 W.L.R. 711 (C.A.).
[43] *Mersey Steel Co. v. Naylor, Benzon & Co.* (1882) 9 Q.B.D. 648 (C.A.); (1884) 9 App.Cas. 434; *Millar v. The National Bank of Scotland Ltd* (1891) 28 S.L.R. 884 (O.H.).
[44] *Re Civil Service and General Store Ltd* (1888) 57 L.J.Ch. 119; *M'Lintock v. Lithauer*, 1924 S.L.T. 755 (O.H.).
[45] *Re French's Wine Bar* [1987] BCLC 499.

made in good faith, in ignorance of the petition and were beneficial to the company and the unsecured creditors in that they were necessary to ensure further supplies, were validated by the court: *Denny v. John Hudson & Co. Ltd.*[46]

The word "disposition" in section 127 includes dispositions of a company's property whether made by the company or by a third party, or whether made directly or indirectly.[47] However where, prior to the petition, the company has entered into an unconditional contract capable of specific performance to sell its property the completion of the contract after the presentation of the petition is not a disposition of its property within section 127 because whatever interest the company has at that time gives it no control over the property. Leave is therefore not required: *Re French's Wine Bar.*[48]

The court may, under the section, authorise a disposition of a company's property after presentation of the petition notwithstanding that a winding-up order has not yet been made and will do so if the disposition will benefit creditors of the company if an order is made.[49]

Section 127 contains no express provision as to who can apply for the validation of dispositions. However, an applicant must have some discernible interest in the matter. The company can apply under the section. A shareholder has a sufficient *locus standi* to apply. A director may have a sufficient *locus standi.*[50]

The rule which makes transfers of shares and alterations in the status of members void operates for the benefit of the company and its creditors, not for the benefit of third parties, and so, in Scotland, an assignation of shares, if duly intimated to the company, cuts out a subsequent arrestment of the shares.[51]

(2) As regards English companies and such property of Scottish companies as is situated in England, any attachment, sequestration, distress or execution put in force

---

[46] [1992] BCC 110.
[47] *Re Leslie Engineers Co. Ltd* [1976] 1 W.L.R. 292. But see *Re Mal Bower's Macquarie Electrical Centre Pty. Ltd (in Liqdn.) etc.* [1974] 1 N.S.W.L.R. 254 to the effect that the section does not effect agencies such as a bank interposing between a company, as disponor, and the recipient of the property, as disponee.
[48] *ibid.* In *Site Preparations v. Buchan Developments Co.,* 1983 S.L.T. 317 (O.H.), a floating charge created after the presentation of a petition was held to be a disposition.
[49] *Re A. I. Levy (Holdings) Ltd* [1964] Ch. 19.
[50] *Re Argentum Reductions (U.K.) Ltd* [1975] 1 W.L.R. 186.
[51] *Jackson v. Elphick* (1902) 10 S.L.T. 146 (O.H.).

against the estate or effects of the company after the commencement of the winding up is void: section 128.[52] As regards Scottish companies and such property of English companies as is situated in Scotland, any winding up is, as at the date of its commencement, equivalent to an arrestment in execution and decree of furthcoming, and to a completed poinding, and also to a decree of adjudication of the heritable property of the company for payment of the whole of its debts: section 185.

In spite of its plain words, section 128 is subject to the provisions of section 126, *ante*, and section 130(2), *post*, the combined effect of which is that a creditor who wishes validly to proceed to execution can apply to the court for leave.[53]

In relation to Scotland, the effect of section 185 is to equalise diligence by depriving any creditor who does diligence after the commencement of winding up (or within 60 days before that date) of the benefit which his diligence would otherwise have given him. The section is not restricted by the provisions of section 130(2), *post*. Accordingly the court could not under section 130(2) sanction diligence contrary to section 185.[54] Section 185 has been held not to render ineffectual an arrestment executed within 60 days before the commencement of winding up but superseded, owing to payment of the debt, before that date.[55]

(3) After a winding-up order has been made or a provisional liquidator has been appointed, no action can be proceeded with or commenced against the company except by leave of the court: section 130(2).

The purpose of section 130(2) is to ensure that when a company goes into liquidation the assets are administered for the benefit of all the creditors.[56]

---

[52] A prior charging order nisi will not be confirmed after a liquidation: *Roberts Petroleum Ltd v. Bernard Kenny Ltd* [1983] A.C. 192.

[53] *Re Lancashire Cotton Spinning Co.* (1887) 35 Ch.D. 656 (C.A.); *The Constellation* [1966] 1 W.L.R. 272.

[54] *Allan v. Cowan* (1892) 20 R. 36; see also opinion of Lord Trayner in *Radford & Bright Ltd v. D. M. Stevenson & Co.* (1904) 6 F. 429 at p. 431.

[55] *Johnston v. Cluny Trustees*, 1957 S.C. 184.

[56] *Per* Widgery L.J. in *Langley Constructions (Brixham) Ltd v. Wells* [1969] 1 W.L.R. 503 (C.A.) at p. 508; *cf.* the effects of an administration order, *ante*, p. 701.

Notwithstanding the section, if a company in liquidation brings an action the defendant may, without leave of the court, set up a cross-demand for liquidated or unliquidated damages, but only as a set-off to reduce or extinguish the plaintiff's claim.[57]

Since "the court" is defined as "the court having jurisdiction to wind up the company" (Companies Act 1985, s.744), an action brought in a Scottish court against a company registered in England requires to be sisted until leave of the English court has been obtained.[58]

(4) On a winding-up order being made in England, the official receiver becomes the liquidator, and he continues to act until another person becomes liquidator. He also acts as liquidator during any vacancy: section 136(2), (3).

(5) On a winding-up order being made, the powers of the directors cease,[59] and are assumed by the liquidator. Some of the duties of the directors cease, too, *e.g.* as to the mode of keeping the company's accounting records under what is now sections 221 to 223 of the Companies Act 1985.[60] One of the duties which remains after the making of a winding-up order is the duty not to disclose confidential information.[61]

(6) On a winding-up order being made, the employees of the company are *ipso facto*, dismissed,[62] and may be able to sue for damages for breach of contract, but an employee who continues to discharge the same duties and receive the same wages as before may be held to have entered by tacit relocation into a contract of service with the liquidator.[63] Where a liquidator re-engaged employees in order to complete certain contracts and thereafter dismissed them on the ground of redundancy, the employees were held, for the purposes of the Redundancy Payments Act 1965, to have been continuously employed by one

[57] *Langley Constructions (Brixham) Ltd v. Wells, supra.*
[58] *Martin v. Port of Manchester Insce. Co. Ltd,* 1934 S.C. 143. And see *Coclas v. Bruce Peebles & Co. Ltd* (1908) 16 S.L.T. 7 (O.H.).
[59] *Fowler v. Broad's Patent Night Light Co.* [1893] 1 Ch. 724.
[60] *Ante,* Ch. 20.
[61] *Re Country Traders Distributors Ltd etc.* [1974] 2 N.S.W.L.R. 135.
[62] *Chapman's Case* (1866) L.R. 1 Eq. 346; *Laing v. Gowans* (1902) 10 S.L.T. 461 (O.H.), *ante,* Ch. 16.
[63] *Day v. Tait* (1900) 8 S.L.T. 40 (O.H.).

employer (*i.e.* the company) from the dates of their initial engagement by the company down to the dates of their dismissal by the liquidator.[64]

Every invoice, order for goods or business letter issued by or on behalf of the company or the liquidator, on which the company's name appears, must contain a statement that the company is being wound up: section 188.

## Appointment of special manager

Where either a company has gone into liquidation or a provisional liquidator has been appointed, the liquidator or provisional liquidator, as appropriate, may apply to the court for the appointment of a special manager of the company's business or property if the nature of that business or property or the interests of the creditors, members or contributories require it. The court may give the special manager such powers as it thinks fit. Such a person need not, however, be a qualified insolvency practitioner but must give such security (or in Scotland, caution) as is prescribed[65]: section 177. This power applies to all kinds of liquidation.

## PROCEEDINGS AFTER A WINDING UP

## Statement of company's affairs and investigation by the official receiver

Where the court has made a winding-up order or appointed a provisional liquidator the official receiver[66] may require a statement of affairs to be produced. The persons who may be required to make such a statement, it contents and the procedural aspects are the same as those on the appointment of an administrative receiver[67] or administrator[68]: section 131.

In England it is the duty of the official receiver after a winding-up order has been made to carry out two investigations: (1) if the

---

[64] *Smith v. Lord Advocate,* 1978 S.C. 259.
[65] I.R. 1986, rr. 4.206–4.210, I.(S.)R. 1986, rr. 4.69–4.73.
[66] In Scotland, the liquidator, or provisional liquidator, as appropriate.
[67] *Ante,* Chap. 25.
[68] *Ante,* Chap. 26.

company has failed, into the causes of the failure, and (2), in any case, into the promotion, formation, business dealing and affairs of the company. Consequently, he may make a report to the court, which is prima facie evidence of the facts stated in it in any proceedings: section 132. The official receiver is therefore bound under (2) to investigate all compulsory liquidations and not just those concerned with insolvency, but he need only make a report to the court if he thinks fit.

If the company has insufficient assets to cover the expenses of the liquidation and the official receiver is satisfied that no further investigation is required he may apply for an early dissolution, in which case his responsibilities cease. This procedure is dealt with in Chapter 29, *post*.[69]

### Public examination of officers

Section 133(1) provides that the official receiver[70] may at any time before the dissolution of the company apply to the court for the public examination of (a) anyone who is or has been an officer of the company; (b) has acted as liquidator, administrator, receiver, or manager of its property; or (c) anyone else who has been concerned or has taken part in the promotion, formation or management of the company.[71] A public examination serves to expose serious misconduct and to promote a higher standard of commercial morality.[72]

The official receiver must apply for a public examination if he is requested to do so by either one half of the creditors or three quarters of the contributories: section 133(2). Failure to attend without a reasonable excuse is a contempt of court: section 134. Questions as to the company's formation, promotion, management or as to the person's conduct of its affairs or dealings with that company may be put by the official receiver, liquidator, special manager,[73] any creditor who has tendered a claim or any contributory: section 133(3), (4). The person examined is not entitled to refuse to reply on the ground of self-incrimination.[74]

---

[69] p. 797.

[70] In Scotland, the liquidator.

[71] The jurisdiction is not confined to British subjects or to persons within the jurisdiction at the relevant time: *Re Seagull Manufacturing Co. (In liquidation)* [1993] BCC 241, C.A.; *cf., infra,* private examinations.

[72] Cork Report (1982), Cmnd. 8558, para. 656.

[73] *Ante,* p. 736.

[74] *Re Paget* [1927] 2 Ch. 85; *Bishopsgate Investment Management Ltd v. Maxwell* [1992] 2 All E.R. 856, 869–871, C.A.

**Appointment of a liquidator**

In England the official receiver becomes the first liquidator until another person is appointed. There are two ways in which such a successor may be appointed:

(1) Within 12 weeks of the winding-up order the official receiver must decide whether or not to summon separate meetings of the company's creditors and contributories so that they might choose a liquidator in his place. If he decides not to do so he must notify the court, creditors and contributories to that effect but he must summon the meetings if requested by one quarter in value of the creditors, and any notice to the creditors of his refusal to summon the meetings must refer to that obligation: section 136.

If such meetings are held, each meeting may nominate a liquidator and, in the event of a disagreement, the creditors' nominee is to be the liquidator of the company subject to an application by any creditor or contributory to the court for the appointment of the contributories' nominee or some other person: section 139. This is similar to the appointment of a liquidator in a creditors' voluntary winding up except that the directors as such cannot apply to the court.[75] If no person is chosen as liquidator by the meetings, the official receiver must decide whether to refer the question of the appointment to the Secretary of State: section 137(2).

(2) The official receiver always has the alternative of applying to the Secretary of State for the appointment of a liquidator rather than summoning the meetings of creditors and contributories. The Secretary of State has complete discretion whether to appoint a liquidator but if he does so, the liquidator must give notice of his appointment to the creditors or advertise his appointment as directed by the court: section 137(3), (4).

Where a winding-up order either follows the discharge of an administration order[76] or is made at the time of a voluntary arrangement,[77] the court may appoint the administrator or supervisor, as appropriate, as liquidator. In such cases the official receiver does not become the liquidator at all: section 140.

The liquidator is to be known by the style of "the liquidator" of the particular company unless he is also the official receiver,

[75] *Post*, p. 768.
[76] *Ante*, p. 709.
[77] *Ante*, p. 666.

where he is to be known as "the official receiver and liquidator" of the company: section 163.

In Scotland, a liquidator, referred to as the "interim liquidator" is appointed by the court at the time when the winding-up order is made. He must, within 28 days of the winding-up order, summon separate meetings of creditors and contributories to choose another person or himself to be liquidator, except that, if the ground for winding up is inability to pay debts, the interim liquidator need summon only a meeting of creditors. If at the meeting or meetings no person is appointed liquidator, the interim liquidator reports that fact to the court which makes the appointment: section 138.

The provisions of sections 139 and 140 apply to Scotland as in England.

## Liquidation committees

If meetings of creditors and contributories are summoned to choose a liquidator, they may also, in England, appoint a committee (of creditors and contributories) to be known as the liquidation committee. This committee then fulfils several functions in the liquidation procedure the main one being to sanction certain actions of the liquidator.[78] Its exact composition and functions are governed by the Rules.[79] Such a committee may alternatively be appointed by general meetings of creditors and contributories summoned by the liquidator (not the official receiver). The liquidator must summon such meetings if requested to do so by one tenth in value of the creditors. If there is no liquidation committee or the liquidator is the official receiver the functions of the committee are vested in the Secretary of State: section 141.

In Scotland a liquidation committee may be established by the meetings of creditors and contributories (or of creditors only) summoned under section 138: section 142.[80] The provisions of section 142 are the same as those of section 141 applicable to England except that where there is no liquidation committee, the

[78] See e.g. s.167, I.A. 1986.
[79] I.R. 1986, rr. 4.151-4.172A. As to its constitution and rights, see Re W & A Glaser Ltd [1994] BCC 199.
[80] For the committee's exact composition and functions, see I.(S.)R. 1986, rr. 4.40-4.59A.

functions of the committee are vested in the court, and that a liquidation committee may have conferred on it the powers and duties of commissioners in a sequestration.

## THE LIQUIDATOR AS OFFICE HOLDER

### Office holders

The Insolvency Act applies certain basic rules and gives certain common powers to office holders. These are an administrator appointed under an administration order,[81] an administrative receiver,[82] a liquidator and a provisional liquidator (in any form of winding up). All such persons must be qualified insolvency practitioners[83]: section 230. If any joint appointment is made the terms of the appointment must specify whether they are required to act together or may operate individually: section 231. The acts of an office holder are valid despite any defect in his appointment, nomination or qualifications[84]: section 232.

Administrative receivers and administrators have been the subject of Chapters 25 and 26 but it is convenient to deal with the provisions applicable to all office holders in one place. The following provisions apply therefore to both those earlier Chapters, this Chapter and Chapter 28 on voluntary winding up.

### Supplies by public utilities

Although the utilities, such as gas, water and electricity are unsecured creditors, they could exercise considerable power against an office holder by refusing to continue supplies unless their debts from the company were paid in full. If the company's business was continuing this would be a potent threat. The Cork Committee therefore recommended[85] that an office holder must be treated as a new customer with a statutory right to receive supplies independently of the company whose account is in arrears. This recommendation was accepted and is contained in section 233.

[81] *Ante,* Chap. 26.
[82] *Ante,* p. 667.
[83] *Ante,* p. 659.
[84] *cf.* C.A. 1985, s.285; *ante,* p. 115.
[85] Paras. 1451–1462.

The supplies affected are a public supply of gas, public supply of electricity, a supply of water by a water undertaker, or, in Scotland, a water authority and a supply of telecommunications services by a public telecommunications operator.[86]

Although they may not require outstanding bills of the company to be paid[87] before supplying the office holder, they may require a personal guarantee from him for any subsequent supplies.

This section also applies to the supervisor of a voluntary arrangement who is not an office holder for any other purpose.[88]

### Getting in the company's property

The court may order any person who possesses any property, books, papers or records apparently belonging to the company to transfer them to the office holder. If the office holder[89] seizes or disposes of property which does not belong to the company but which he reasonably believes he is entitled to take or deal with, he is not liable for any loss or damage except that caused by his own negligence and is entitled to a lien on the property to recover any expenses: section 234.

### Co-operation with the office holder—private examination

Any person who may be asked to furnish a statement of affairs[90] to an office holder (including the official receiver) must on request give such information concerning the company's affairs as the office holder may reasonably require and must attend on him when required to do so: section 235. Such private examinations are designed to assist the office holder to carry out his task quickly and effectively.

### Private examinations

The office holder[91] is given powers to apply to the court if there is insufficient co-operation under the provisions detailed above.

---

[86] I.A. 1986, s.233(5).
[87] Directly or indirectly, *e.g.* by insisting on a coin-operated meter supply so calibrated as to recoup the previous unpaid amounts.
[88] *Ante,* p. 665.
[89] This includes the official receiver.
[90] *Ante.*
[91] Including at any time, the official receiver.

On such an application the court may summon any officer of the company, any person known or suspected of possessing company property or supposed to be indebted to the company, or any person it thinks capable of giving information about the company's affairs, to appear before it and to submit an affidavit detailing his dealings with the company, or to produce any relevant documents: section 236.[92]

The principles upon which the court exercises its discretion under section 236 were set out in *British & Commonwealth Holdings plc v. Spicer & Oppenheimer*[93]. A balance must be struck between the requirements of the office holder and oppression of the examinee.

> "An application is not necessarily unreasonable because it is inconvenient for the addressee or causes him a lot of work or may make him vulnerable to future claims or is addressed to a person who not an officer or employee of, or contractor with, the company . . ., but all these factors will be relevant, together no doubt with many others."[94]

While the court can exercise its power to enable the office-holder to reconstitute the state of knowledge which the company should possess, the discretion is broader and may be exercised to provide the office-holder with any information he reasonably requires to carry out his functions.[95]

B.C. plc had taken over A. Ltd for £420 million and subsequently invested a further £117 million in it. Two years later A. Ltd became insolvent with a deficiency of £279 million. B.C. plc itself went into administration and its administrator sought an order under s. 236 requiring the auditors of A. Ltd to produce books and papers relating to certain audits and to the takeover. The House of Lords granted the order even though B.C. plc would not have been entitled to such information when solvent: *British & Commonwealth Holdings plc v. Spicer & Oppenheimer*.[96]

The court may examine a person on oath and he may be ordered to hand over property, or to pay amounts due, to the

---

[92] The jurisdiction is subject to territorial limitations: see s.237(3); *Re Seagull Manufacturing Co. Ltd* [1993] BCC 241, C.A.

[93] [1992] 3 W.L.R. 853, H.L.

[94] Lord Slynn, *ibid.*, p. 885.

[95] Compare *Joint Administrators of Cloverbay v. Bank of Credit & Commerce International S.A.* [1991] Ch. 90. See also *First Tokyo Index Trust Ltd v. Gould* [1993] G.W.D. 36-2298 (O.H.).

[96] [1992] 3 W.L.R. 853, H.L.

company: I.A. 1986, section 237. A person being examined under these provisions is not entitled to remain silent: the privilege against self-incrimination is impliedly abrogated by the statute in the interests of enabling the office holder more effectively to perform his investigative functions.[97] An order can be made even where the examinee has already been charged with a criminal offence but not so as to submit him to simultaneous proceedings.[98] It was recognised in *Re Barlow Clowes Gilt Managers Ltd*[99] that the secrecy of a private examination is important for the efficient functioning of the investigation, encouraging speedy, voluntary disclosure to the office holder. However, the ability of the office holder to ensure confidentiality is impaired by section 433 of the Insolvency Act 1986 which provides that a statement made, *inter alia*, under section 236 can be used in evidence against the person making it and also by section 2(3) of the Criminal Justice Act 1987 which authorises the Director of the Serious Fraud Office to request transcripts from the office holder (notwithstanding any assurances of confidence which may have been given and notwithstanding a direction of the court under section 168(3)[1] that access should be denied as being prejudicial to the conduct of the investigation: *Re Arrows Ltd (No. 4)*.[2]

## The Property of the Company in a Winding Up by the Court

### Custody of company's property

When a winding-up order has been made, or a provisional liquidator appointed, the liquidator must take into his custody or

---

[97] *Bishopsgate Investment Management Ltd v. Maxwell* [1992] BCC 214 (C.A.); An order made in favour of a company in the course of an action for an account of assets is outside the scope of the statutory exception and the director can claim the right to silence (*ibid.*); see also *Re Jeffrey S. Levett* [1992] BCC 137 (Vinelott J.); *Re Brook Martin & Co.* [1993] BCLC 328. The privilege against self-incrimination is not available to persons examined by the Director of the Serious Fraud Office exercising powers under s.2 of the Criminal Justice Act 1987; *Smith v. Director of the Serious Fraud Office* [1992] 3 W.L.R. 66 (H.L.).

[98] *Re Arrows (No. 2)* [1992] BCC 446.

[99] [1991] 4 All E.R. 385.

[1] and I.R. 1986, r.9.5(4).

[2] [1993] BCC 473 (C.A.); [1994] 3 All E.R. 814 (H.L.). The liquidator does not, at the same time, have to disclose to the person charged: *Re Headington Investments Ltd* (C.A.) [1993] BCC 500.

under his control all the property to which the company is or appears to be entitled. In Scotland, if and so long as there is no liquidator, all the company's property is deemed to be in the custody of the court: section 144.

Winding up does not, as does bankruptcy or sequestration, operate as a *cessio bonorum* or transfer of property; the company's property remains vested in it as before[3] unless, under section 145, the court makes an order vesting it in him in his official name. Section 234[4] and section 160[5] also contain wide powers to enable the liquidator to get the company's property into his custody.

### Restriction of rights of creditor as to execution or attachment where company being wound up in England

In the case of a company being wound up in England, section 183 provides that where a creditor has issued execution against the goods or lands of a company or has attached any debt due to it, and the company is subsequently wound up, he is not entitled to retain the benefit of the execution or attachment against the liquidator unless he completed the execution or attachment before the commencement of the winding up[6] or, if he had notice of a meeting at which a resolution for voluntary winding up was to be proposed, before such notice. A purchaser in good faith, under a sale by the sheriff, of goods on which execution has been levied acquires a good title to them against the liquidator. The section does not apply to a distress for rent by a landlord.[7]

An execution against goods is taken to be completed either by seizure and sale or by the making of a charging order,[8] and an attachment of a debt by receipt of the debt, and an execution against land by seizure, the appointment of a receiver or by the making of a charging order[8]: section 183(3)

Where a judgment creditor issued a writ of *fi. fa.* in respect of the judgment and the sheriff seized the company's goods and, after a

---

[3] *Per* Warrington L.J. in *Re H. J. Webb & Co. (Smithfield, London) Ltd* [1922] 2 Ch. 369 (C.A.), at p. 388; *Per* Lord President Inglis in *Queensland Mercantile etc. Co. Ltd v. Australasian Investment Co. Ltd* (1888) 15 R. 935 at p. 939; *per* Lord Hailsham in *Alexander Ward & Co. Ltd v. Samyang Navigation Co. Ltd,* 1975 S.C. (H.L.) 26 at p. 47.

[4] *Ante.*

[5] Applies to England only.

[6] *Ante,* p. 731.

[7] *Re Bellaglade Ltd* [1977] 1 All E.R. 319.

[8] Under section 1 of the Charging Orders Act 1979.

petition for a compulsory winding up had been presented (although this was unknown to the sheriff), sold them, when an order for winding up was made the sheriff had to hand over the proceeds to the liquidator[9]

The phrase "the benefit of the execution" does not refer to "the fruits of the execution" but to the charge conferred on the creditor by the issue of execution.

Where a creditor has issued a writ of *fi. fa.* against a company, money paid to the sheriff or his officers in order to avoid a sale and which remains in their hands at the commencement of the winding up is outside "the benefit of the execution" so that the liquidator is not entitled to such money as against the creditor.[10]

"The benefit of the attachment" means the right to take the necessary steps to complete it.

If a judgment creditor who has obtained a garnishee order obtains payment after receipt by him of notice of a meeting called for the winding up of the company, he must, subject to the court's discretion under section 183(2)(c), *post*, account to the liquidator for the money.[11]

By section 183(2)(c), the rights conferred by section 183(1), *ante*, on the liquidator may be set aside by the court in favour of the creditor. The basic scheme of the Insolvency Act is that in a winding up unsecured creditors rank *pari passu* and an execution creditor who has not completed his execution at the commencement of the winding up is for this purpose in the same position as any other unsecured creditor. Section 183(2)(c) gives the court a free hand to do what is right and fair according to the circumstances of the case,[12] but weighty reasons are necessary to justify the court in exercising its discretion.[13]

Where a judgment creditor of a company refrained from levying immediate execution because of a promise of payment by a director, there being no dishonesty by the director, and the execution was not completed before the commencement of the winding up, the court refused to set the liquidator's rights aside. To allow the creditor to retain the benefit of the execution would have been contrary to the basic scheme of the Acts and unfair to the other creditors. During the year

---

[9] *Bluston & Bramley Ltd v. Leigh* [1950] 2 K.B. 548.
[10] *Re Walkden Sheet Metal Co. Ltd* [1960] Ch. 170.
[11] *Re Caribbean Products (Yam Importers) Ltd* [1966] Ch. 331 (C.A.); overruling *Re Rainbow Tours Ltd* [1964] Ch. 66.
[12] *Re Redman (Builders) Ltd* [1964] 1 W.L.R. 541.
[13] *Re Caribbean Products (Yam Importers) Ltd, ante.*

before the winding up the company was keeping its general body of trade creditors at bay and there was no reason why one execution creditor who had not completed execution should be preferred to the other creditors whether or not they had obtained judgment or commenced execution.[14]

On the other hand, where before the action the company stalled the creditors' claims by promises and defended the action by disputing a debt already admitted, the liquidator's rights were set aside.[15]

### Duties of sheriff as to goods taken in execution

Section 184 provides that where goods are taken in execution in England and Wales and, before their sale or the completion of the execution, notice of the appointment of a provisional liquidator, of a winding-up order or resolution for voluntary winding up, is served upon the sheriff, he must, if required, deliver up the goods to the liquidator. The costs of execution are however a first charge upon them. Where goods are seized in respect of a judgment exceeding £500 the sheriff must deduct the costs of execution and retain the balance for 14 days and pay it to the liquidator if so required. The rights of the liquidator may be set aside in favour of the creditor as the court thinks fit.

### Scottish companies, and property of English companies in Scotland

As regards Scottish companies and such property of English companies as is situated in Scotland, section 185 applies section 37(1) to (6) of the Bankruptcy (Scotland) Act 1985 with the following effect[16]

  (a) The winding up is, as at the date of commencement, equivalent to an arrestment in execution and decree of furthcoming, and to a completed poinding, and no arrestment or poinding of the funds or effects of the company executed on or after the sixtieth day before that date is effectual as against the liquidator except to the limited

---

[14] See Note 12, above.

[15] *Re Suidair International Airways Ltd* [1951] Ch. 165.

[16] The phrase "date of commencement" in the following provisions in (a), (b) and (c) means the day on which the winding-up order *was made*. (In other contexts it is the date of presentation of the petition). See *Morrison v. Integer Systems Control Ltd*, 1989 S.C.L.R. 495 (Sh.Ct.) (refusal of recall of arrestments because outwith the 60-day period before the winding-up order).

extent that an arrester or poinder who is thus deprived of the benefit of his diligence is entitled to a preference for the expense bona fide incurred by him in his diligence.

C. brought an action of payment against a company and arrested the sum sued for in the hands of S., a debtor of the company. On the instructions of the company, S. paid the sum arrested to C. with the result that the arrestment was superseded. Later, but less than 60 days after the execution of the arrestment, an order was made for the winding up of the company, and the liquidator brought an action to recover the amount paid to C. *Held,* the only arrestments made ineffectual by section 185 were those which, but for it, would have been effectual at the commencement of winding up, and therefore the section did not apply to arrestments which had been withdrawn or superseded by payment of the debt before that date: *Johnston v. Cluny Trustees,* 1957 S.C. 184.

In *Commercial Aluminium Windows Ltd v. Cumbernauld Development Corporation,* 1987 S.L.T. (Sh. Ct.) 91, where an arrestment had been executed more than 60 days before the winding up, the liquidator defended an action of furthcoming made during the winding up. *Held,* that the arrestment was effectual, because the liquidator had by this statutory provision the equivalent of an arrestment *and decree of furthcoming.* Contrast *Lord Advocate v. Royal Bank of Scotland Ltd,* 1977 S.C. 155 (*ante,* p. 719): in receivership, an arrestment by itself was not "effectually executed diligence."

(b) The winding up is, as at the date of its commencement, also equivalent to a decree of adjudication of the heritable estates of the company for payment of the whole debts of the company, subject to any preferable heritable rights and securities which are valid and unchallengeable and subject to the limited right to poind the ground provided for in (c).[17]

(c) A poinding of the ground which has not been carried into execution by sale of the effects 60 days before the commencement of winding up is of no effect in a question with the liquidator unless the poinder holds a heritable security which is preferable to the right of the liquidator, in which case the poinding is available for the interest for the current half-year and for the arrears of interest for the preceding year, but for no more.

---

[17] For an instance of the application of provision (b), see *Turnbull v. Liquidator of Scottish County Investment Co. Ltd,* 1939 S.C. 5; on the interrelation of this provision and the Conveyancing and Feudal Reform (Scotland) Act 1970, s.24 (application to court for warrant to sell), see *United Dominions Trust Ltd, Noters,* 1977 S.L.T. (Notes) 56 (O.H.).

### Attendance of officers at meetings in Scotland

While the public examination which may be required in sequestration[18] has no place in the liquidation of a company, the court in the compulsory winding up of a Scottish company has power to require any officer of the company to attend any meeting of creditors or of contributories or of a liquidation committee for the purpose of giving information as to the trade, dealings, affairs or property of the company: section 157.

### Fraudulent trading

Section 213 provides that if in the winding up of a company it appears that business has been carried on with intent to defraud creditors or for any fraudulent purpose, the court, on the application of the liquidator, may declare that any persons who were knowingly parties to the fraudulent trading shall make such contributions to the company's assets as the court thinks proper.[19]

Fraudulent trading (so defined) is also a criminal offence under section 458 of the Companies Act 1985.[20] The criminal offence, unlike the civil penalties in the Insolvency Act, however, is not linked to a winding up.

In general it may be properly inferred that there is an intent to defraud creditors if a company carries on business and incurs debts when, to the knowledge of the directors, there is no reasonable prospect of the company being able to pay them.[21] It is not necessary to show that there was no prospect of the creditors *ever* being paid. It is enough that there is no reason for thinking that they will be paid as the debts fall due or shortly thereafter.[22]

The expression "parties to" the fraudulent trading in section 213(2) indicates no more than "take part in" or "concur in" and involves some positive steps. Mere omission by the secretary to give certain advice (that the company is insolvent and should cease to trade) is not being a party to carrying on the business in

---

[18] Bankruptcy (Scotland) Act 1985, s.45.
[19] Any order is in favour of the liquidator not an individual shareholder: *Re Esal (Commodities) Ltd* [1993] BCLC 872.
[20] There must be a finding of dishonesty for the criminal offence to be committed: *R. v. Cox* [1983] BCLC 169.
[21] *Re William C. Leitch Bros. Ltd* [1932] 2 Ch. 71.
[22] *R. v. Grantham* [1984] Q.B. 675.

a fraudulent manner.[23] However, a creditor who, knowing of the circumstances, accepts money fraudulently obtained by the company may be liable to repay it even if he took no part in the fraudulent trading itself.[24]

It is not fraudulent trading for a parent company to give promises of support to a subsidiary which are not implemented. The fraud of the parent company cannot be linked to the subsidiary, since to establish liability the fraudulent trading must be committed by someone carrying on the business, *i.e.* the subsidiary. In any event such general statements would not be sufficient to prove fraud.[25]

It is not fraudulent trading to intend to prefer one creditor to another even if all could not be paid in full,[26] nor to sell goods which prove to be defective knowing that liability for such defects might not be met.[27]

The court may charge the liability of a person declared liable under section 213 on any debt due to him from the company, or on any charge on any assets of the company held by him, or any company or person on his behalf, or certain assignees from him or such a company or person: section 215.

**Wrongful trading**

The difficulties of establishing the "fraudulent" element of fraudulent trading led to many directors who had carried on the business recklessly being exempt. The Insolvency Act introduced another concept, that of wrongful trading which is designed to apply to such cases. Wrongful trading, which applies only to directors and to insolvent liquidations, has been dealt with in Chapter 15, *ante.*[28] As far as directors are concerned wrongful trading will largely replace fraudulent trading. Fraudulent trading, however, remains for other persons and as a criminal offence for serious cases (wrongful trading is not a criminal offence).

[23] *Re Maidstone Buildings Provisions Ltd* [1971] 1 W.L.R. 1085, *R. v. Miles* [1992] Crim.L.R. 657.
[24] *Re Gerald Cooper Chemicals Ltd* [1978] Ch. 262.
[25] *Re Augustus Barnett & Son Ltd* [1986] BCLC 170.
[26] *Re Sarflax Ltd* [1979] Ch. 592.
[27] *Norcross Ltd v. Amos* (1981) 131 N.L.J. 1213. See also *Rossleigh Ltd v. Carlaw,* 1986 S.L.T. 204 in Scotland as to the knowledge required of the intent to defraud.
[28] *Ante,* p. 367.

## Summary remedy against delinquent directors etc.

This was explained in the chapter on directors.[29]

## Disclaimer in case of company wound up in England

Where any part of the property of a company which is being wound up is onerous property, the liquidator may on giving notice disclaim that property. Onerous property for this purpose is (a) any unprofitable contract; or (b) any other property of the company which is unsaleable or not readily saleable or is such that may give rise to a liability to pay money or perform any other onerous act: section 178(1)-(3).

A disclaimer operates to determine the rights and liabilities of the company in respect of the property disclaimed but does not, except for the purpose of releasing the company from liability, affect the rights or liabilities of any other person: section 178(4).

Thus, where an insolvent company is the original tenant under a lease, a disclaimer by the liquidator releases the future rent liability not only of the company but also its surety: otherwise, the surety, on fulfilling his guarantee to the landlord, could seek indemnity against the company: *Stacey v. Hill.*[30] The liquidator cannot disclaim any property if notice in writing is served on him by a person interested in the property, requiring him to decide whether he will disclaim or not, and he does not, within 28 days, or any longer period allowed by the court, give notice of disclaimer: section 178(5).

Any person injured by a disclaimer is deemed a creditor of the company to the extent of his loss or damage and may prove for that amount in the winding up: section 178(6).

Where the property is a leasehold, no disclaimer can take effect unless the liquidator has served a notice on every person claiming under the company as underlessee or mortgagee and either no application for a vesting order (see below) has been made by such a person within 14 days or, if such application has been made, the court nevertheless directs that the disclaimer shall take effect: section 179.

The court may, on the application of any person interested in the property,[31] or who is under an undischarged liability in

[29] *Ante,* p. 371.
[30] [1901]1 Q.B. 660; *Murphy v. Sawyer-Hoare* (1993) 27 E.G. 127. *cf. Warnford Investments v. Duckworth* [1978] 2 All E.R. 518.
[31] This includes a statutory tenant: *Re Vedmay* [1994] 10 E.G. 108.

respect of the disclaimer,[32] make an order for the vesting or delivery of the property to that person or his trustee, but only if it would be just compensation to the person subject to the liability. The effect of any such order must be taken into account in assessing any loss subsequently provable in the winding up: section 181. Where the property is a leasehold, such a vesting order cannot be made in favour of an underlessee or mortgagee, unless it is either (a) subject to the same liabilities and obligations as those to which the company was subject under the lease at the commencement of the winding up, or (b), if the court thinks fit, subject only to the same liabilities and obligations as if the lease had been assigned to that person at that date: section 182.

Any person who is, as against the liquidator, entitled to the benefit or subject to the burden of a contract with the company may apply to the court for an order rescinding the contract. The court may grant rescission on such terms as it thinks fit, including the payment of damages for breach of contract. Any damages payable to such a person under the order may be proved for in the liquidation: section 186.

The Insolvency Act widened the former disclaimer provisions in two major respects. First the consent of the court is no longer required. The discretion previously vested in the court is now vested in the liquidator and its exercise can only be challenged[33] on the grounds of *mala fides* or perversity.[34] Second the definition of onerous property has been widened to include unsaleable property.[35]

## Repudiation in case of company wound up in Scotland

By the common law of Scotland the liquidator may either adopt or repudiate current contracts, and if he repudiates them the company is liable in damages for breach of contract. If the liquidator does not within a reasonable time declare his intention to adopt a contract, he will be held to have abandoned it and to be liable in damages.[36]

---

[32] *e.g.* the tenant-company's surety, see *Re A.E. Realisations* (1985) [1987] BCLC 486.

[33] See I.A. 1986, s.168(5).

[34] *Re Hans Place Ltd* [1992] BCC 737; *Cavendish Offices & Houses Investments Ltd v. Adams* [1992] E.G. 107.

[35] *cf. Re Potters Oils Ltd* [1986] 1 W.L.R. 201 decided on the old law.

[36] *Crown Estate Commissioners v. Liquidators of Highland Engineering Ltd*, 1975 S.L.T. 58 (O.H.).

Where the company is bound under two separate contracts with the same party, the liquidator is entitled to adopt one and repudiate the other, and the other party to the contracts is not entitled to retain a sum due to the company under the contract adopted, either in security for the proper fulfilment of that contract by the company or in security for a claim for damages in respect of the contract repudiated.[37]

The main criticism of the common law in this connection was the possible uncertainty of the other contracting party as to his position. Following a recommendation of the Scottish Law Commission,[38] the Bankruptcy (Scotland) Act 1985, section 42, enables the other contracting party to require the permanent trustee to reach a decision within 28 days of receiving written notice. By section 169 of the Insolvency Act 1986 the liquidator has the same powers, subject to the rules, as a trustee on a bankrupt estate.

## THE LIQUIDATOR IN A WINDING UP BY THE COURT

The liquidator in a winding up by the court is an officer of the court.[39]

### Appointment

The liquidator is appointed in the manner already discussed.[40] He is an office holder[41] and as such must be a qualified insolvency practitioner.[42]

The court has appointed as liquidator a person resident beyond the jurisdiction of the court but such an appointment was only made where there was an adequate reason.[43]

Any person who gives, or agrees or offers to give, any member or creditor of the company any valuable consideration with a

---

[37] *Asphaltic Limestone Concrete Co. Ltd v. Glasgow Corpn.*, 1907 S.C. 463; see also *Gray's Trustees v. Benhar Coal Co. Ltd* (1881) 9 R. 225.

[38] *Report on Bankruptcy and Related Aspects of Insolvency and Liquidation*, 1982 Scot. Law Com. No. 68, para. 10.26.

[39] *Per* Megarry J. in *Re Rolls Razor Ltd (No. 2)* [1970] Ch. 576, 586.

[40] p. 738.

[41] *Ante*, p. 740.

[42] *Ante*, p. 659.

[43] *Brightwen & Co. v. City of Glasgow Bank* (1878) 6 R. 244 (appointment as joint liquidator of accountant resident in London refused); see also *Barberton Development etc. Ltd, Petitioners* (1898) 25 R. 654, and contrast *Liquidators of Bruce Peebles & Co. Ltd v. Shiells*, 1908 S.C. 692.

view to securing his own appointment or nomination, or to securing or preventing the appointment or nomination of someone else, as the liquidator, is liable to a fine: section 164.

## Resignation and removal

A liquidator may resign by giving notice to the court before the completion of the liquidation: section 172(6).

In Scotland leave to resign was granted to an official liquidator where it was stated that there was nothing to recover from the estate, and the liquidator's application was concurred in by substantially all the creditors and was unopposed.[44]

A liquidator must vacate his office on ceasing to be a qualified insolvency practitioner[45] and on the holding of the final meeting of creditors[46]: section 172(5), (8).

A liquidator may be removed either by the court or by a meeting of the creditors: section 172(2). Grounds on which a liquidator has been removed by the court include personal unfitness (due to, *e.g.* his character, his residence,[47] or his personal interest or involvement,[48]) insanity,[49] prosecuting a claim against the wishes of a majority of the creditors where the company is insolvent,[50] or failing to carry out his duties with sufficient vigour and displaying a relaxed and complacent attitude towards wrongdoing by the directors.[51]

On the other hand the court has refused to remove a liquidator merely because he is a shareholder and former director,[52] or because the majority of the creditors or of the contributories desire it.[53]

The meeting of the creditors to replace a liquidator may be called by the liquidator himself, the court or one quarter in value

---

[44] *Jamieson, Petitioner* (1877) 14 S.L.R. 667.
[45] *Ante*, p. 659.
[46] *Post*, p. 797.
[47] *Skinner, Petitioner* (1899) 6 S.L.T. 388 (O.H.) (residence in England of sole liquidator).
[48] *Lysons v. Liquidator of the Miraflores Gold Syndicate Ltd* (1895) 22 R. 605; *Re Corbenstoke (No. 2)* [1990] BCLC 60 (liquidator was the company's debtor).
[49] *Re The North Molton Mining Co. Ltd* (1886) 54 L.T. 602.
[50] *Re Tavistock Ironworks Co.* (1871) 24 L.T. 605.
[51] *Re Keypack Homecare* [1987] BCLC 409.
[52] *M'Knight & Co. Ltd v. Montgomerie* (1892) 19 R. 501; but see *Re Corbenstoke, ibid.*, where Harman J. considered it unlikely that a director would ever be a suitable person to act as liquidator.
[53] *Ker, Petitioner* (1897) 5 S.L.T. 126 (O.H.).

of the creditors. If the liquidator was appointed by the Secretary of State only the Secretary of State may remove him.

A vacancy in the office of the liquidator appointed by the court is filled in England by the official receiver: section 136(3).

## Duties

The functions of a liquidator are to secure that the assets of the company are got in, realised and distributed to the company's creditors and, if there is a surplus, to the persons entitled to it: section 143(1).

A liquidator must:

(1) in England, give all information, assistance and documents to the official receiver as he may reasonably require: section 143(2);

(2) take all the property of the company into his custody as soon as possible: section 144;

(3) in England, as soon as may be, settle a list of contributories,[54] collect the company's assets, apply them in discharge of its liabilities and distribute any surplus among the members according to their rights and interests in the company: sections 148, 154, 160.

In Scotland, he must perform such duties as will enable the court to exercise the functions mentioned: sections 148, 154.

The word "liabilities" excludes claims which are not legally enforceable. Thus it does not include arrears of tax claimed by a foreign state, even one which adheres to the Commonwealth.[55]

If the liquidator distributes the assets without making provision for the liabilities he is liable to pay damages to the unpaid creditors.

The company had a lease of premises expiring in 1938 at a yearly rent of £1,217 10s. The lease was assigned to M., and in 1933 the company went into voluntary liquidation. M. was insolvent and unable to pay the rent. The liquidator distributed the assets without making any provision for the company's liabilities under the lease. *Held,* the liquidator had committed a breach of his duty and was liable in damages to the lessor: *James Smith & Sons (Norwood) Ltd v. Goodman* [1936] Ch. 216 (C.A.).

---

[54] But see *post,* p. 778.
[55] *Government of India v. Taylor* [1955] A.C. 491; *cf. Clyde Marine Insurance Co. Ltd v. Renwick & Co.,* 1924 S.C. 113.

(4) In England, summon meetings of the creditors or contributories when directed by resolution of the creditors or contributories or requested in writing by one-tenth in value of the creditors or contributories: section 168(2). He may summon meetings on his own initiative whenever he wants to ascertain the wishes of the creditors or contributories: section 168(2).

In Scotland the committee or any member of it may apply to the court for an order on the liquidator to summon a meeting of creditors or contributories or both: R.C. 218M (Court of Session) and Sheriff Court Company Insolvency Rules 1986, Rule 30.

(5) Summon a final meeting in accordance with section 146.[56]

**Powers of the liquidator**

Section 167[57] provides that:
(1) The liquidator (including a provisional liquidator[58]) in a winding up by the court has power, *with the sanction of the court or of the liquidation committee:*

(*a*) To bring or defend actions and legal proceedings in the name and on behalf of the company.

It is a matter for his discretion whether he should litigate or not and so the court will not give guidance as to whether he should appeal to a higher court.[59] If the liquidator brings an unsuccessful action he is personally liable as to costs and these are not limited to the assets of the company.[60]

(*b*) To carry on the business of the company so far as may be necessary for beneficial winding up.

In *Liquidator of Burntisland Oil Co. Ltd v. Dawson* (1892) 20 R. 180, the court refused the liquidator's application to carry on

---

[56] *Post,* p. 797.
[57] and Schedule 4.
[58] *Wilsons (Glasgow and Trinidad) Ltd, Petitioners,* 1912 2 S.L.T. 330.
[59] *Note for Liquidator in Liquidation of S.S. "Camelot" Ltd* (1893) 1 S.L.T. 358 (O.H.).
[60] *Re Wilson Lovatt & Sons Ltd* [1977] 1 All E.R. 274.

the business for an indefinite period on the ground that the company's property could not then be sold except on ruinous terms but granted power to carry on for six weeks while the property was advertised for sale. However, in *M'Intyre, Petitioner* (1893) 30 S.L.R. 386 (O.H.) power was granted to carry on business until the time of the year when the company's property, which consisted of a hall let for public entertainments, could be sold to best advantage.

When a liquidator carries on the business of the company he does so as the company's agent[61] and is not personally liable on contracts which he enters into as liquidator.[62]

- (c)  To pay any classes of creditors in full.
- (d)  To make any compromise or arrangement with creditors.[63]
- (e)  To compromise all calls and liabilities to calls and other debts and liabilities.

If a liquidator does any of the acts listed without the necessary sanction of the court or the liquidation committee he is personally liable although the court may retrospectively sanction such an act.[64]

(2) On his own responsibility and *without obtaining any sanction,* the liquidator can;

- (a)  Sell the property of the company.
- (b)  Do all acts and execute, in the name and on behalf of the company, all deeds and documents, and use the company's seal therefor.
- (c)  Prove, rank and claim in the bankruptcy, insolvency or sequestration of any contributory.
- (d)  Draw, accept, make and indorse any bill of exchange or promissory note in the name and on behalf of the company.
- (e)  Raise money on the security of the company's assets.

---

[61] See *Smith v. Lord Advocate*, 1978 S.C. 259.

[62] *Stead, Hazel & Co. v. Cooper* [1933] 1 K.B. 840.

[63] This was held, in *Taylor, Noter,* 1993 S.L.T. 375, to extend to entering into a compromise with the trustee on the sequestrated estate of a director where the director's own assets and those of his two companies were so confused that it was impossible to identify the assets of each.

[64] *Re Associated Travel Leisure and Services Ltd (in Liquidation)* [1978] 1 W.L.R. 547.

(f)   Take out letters of administration to any deceased con-
      tributory and do any other act necessary for obtaining
      payment of money due from a contributory or his estate.
(g)   Appoint an agent to do business which he cannot do
      himself.
(h)   Do all such other things as are necessary for winding up
      the affairs of the company and distributing its assets.

The exercise of these powers is subject to the control of the
court and any creditor or contributory may apply to the court
with respect to such exercise: section 167(3). If, in England, any
person is aggrieved by any act or decision of the liquidator, that
person may apply to the court, which may make such order as it
thinks just: section 168(5).

In England the liquidator may apply to the court for directions
in relation to any particular matter arising under the winding up:
section 168(3). The right should be exercised in every case of
serious doubt or difficulty in relation to the performance by the
liquidator of his statutory duties. The omission to exercise it may
lead the liquidator into serious liabilities.[65]

Subject to the various statutory provisions the liquidator may
use his own discretion as to the management and distribution of
the company's assets: section 168(4).

In Scotland, the liquidator has (subject to the rules) the same
powers as a trustee on a bankrupt estate: section 169(2).

## Liability

A liquidator is not strictly speaking a trustee for the individual
creditors or contributories, his position being that of agent of the
company.

During a liquidation a claim was made by a contributory for damages
for delay in handing over to the contributory his proportion of the
surplus assets of the company. *Held,* in the absence of fraud, bad faith or
personal misconduct, an action for damages would not lie against the

---

[65] See *Re Windsor Steam Coal Co. (1901) Ltd* [1929] 1 Ch. 151, and *Re Home and
   Colonial Insurance Co. Ltd* [1930] 1 Ch. 102, *post.* The opinion was expressed
   in *Ross v. Smith,* 1986 S.L.T. (Sh. Ct.) 59, that the liquidator in Scotland was
   entitled to seek directions from the court in appropriate circumstances. The test
   to be applied was the same as that which applied to applications to the court by
   a liquidator in a voluntary winding up, *i.e.* the court had to be satisfied that the
   determination of the question would be "just and beneficial."

liquidator at the suit of a creditor or contributory, the proper remedy being an application to the court to control the liquidator in the exercise of his powers: *Knowles v. Scott* [1891] 1 Ch. 717.[66]

On the other hand, for breach of any of his statutory duties the liquidator will be liable in damages to a creditor or contributory for injury caused to them.

A liquidator distributed the assets of the company without paying X, a creditor, who had no notice of the liquidation. The books of the company showed X to be a creditor but the liquidator made no attempt to communicate with X beyond issuing an insufficient advertisement for creditors. The company was dissolved. *Held*, the liquidator was liable in damages to X. The duty of the liquidator was not merely to advertise for creditors but to write to those of whom he knew and who did not send in claims: *Pulsford v. Devenish* [1903] 2 Ch. 625.

A liquidator should make provision for contingent claims of which he has notice, *e.g.* where the company, having assigned a lease, is under a contingent liability for the rent,[67] or where he knows of possible claims by workmen for injuries not covered by insurance.[68]

If a liquidator applies the company's assets in paying a doubtful claim, which turns out to be unfounded, without taking proper legal advice or applying to the court for directions, he will be liable to refund the amount paid on a misfeasance summons taken out by a creditor or contributory.[69]

A liquidator, however, is not liable for admitting a proof of debt which is ill-founded, provided he exercises all due care beforehand. But a "high standard of care and diligence is required from a liquidator in a . . . winding up. He is of course paid for his services; he is able to obtain wherever it is expedient the assistance of solicitors and counsel; and, which is a most important consideration, he is entitled, in every serious case of

---

[66] cf. *Liquidator of Upper Clyde Shipbuilders Ltd,* 1975 S.L.T. 39 (O.H.), *per* Lord Grieve (Ordinary), p. 40.
[67] *James Smith & Sons (Norwood) Ltd v. Goodman* [1936] Ch. 216 (C.A.); *cf. Lord Elphinstone v. Monkland Iron etc. Co. Ltd* (1886) 13 R. (H.L.) 98.
[68] *Re Armstrong Whitworth Securities Co. Ltd* [1947] Ch. 673.
[69] *Re Windsor Steam Coal Co. (1901) Ltd* [1929] 1 Ch. 151 (C.A.); where the court refused to grant him relief under s.61 of the Trustee Act 1925 (s.32 Trusts (Scotland) Act 1921).

doubt or difficulty . . . to submit the matter to the Court and to obtain its guidance.[70-71]

H. Co. made a reinsurance agreement with L. Co. which was invalid. On H. going into liquidation, L. tendered a proof which the liquidator ultimately accepted for £89,100, on which £38,000 was paid to L. in dividends. On learning that he should have disallowed the claim, the liquidator sued L. but the claim was dismissed, as no mistake of fact on the part of the liquidator was made. A creditor took out a misfeasance summons. *Held,* the liquidator was negligent in admitting so large a proof without taking legal advice or applying for directions, and was liable to pay compensation to the company: *Re Home and Colonial Insurance Co. Ltd* [1930] 1 Ch. 102.

Where a liquidator has paid money to shareholders under an error in law, caused, *e.g.* by an underestimation of tax liability, he is not entitled to recover it under the *condictio indebiti,* there being no special relationship between the liquidator and the shareholders such as to take the situation outside the general rule.[72]

## Release (England)

When a liquidator ceases to hold office, the question is whether and when he can be released from his obligations. If the liquidator is the official receiver he can be released either by notifying the Secretary of State that the winding up is for all practical purposes complete or, if he is replaced by another liquidator, on giving notice to the court that he has been so replaced. If he is replaced by a liquidator appointed by the court, it is for the court to determine his release: section 174(2)(3).

If the liquidator is someone other than the official receiver his release takes effect as follows:

(a)   if he was removed by the creditors' meeting which did not resolve against his release, or if he has died, at the time when notice of removal or death is given to the court;

---

[70-71] *Per* Maugham J. in *Re Home and Colonial Insurance Co. Ltd* [1930] 1 Ch. 102 at p. 125. In *Macrae v. Henderson,* 1989 S.L.T. 523 (O.H.), the question was whether the liquidator owed a duty to guarantors or cautioners to take reasonable care in realising assets to maximum advantage. *Held,* the liquidator did owe the duty, but on the evidence the offer which the liquidator had refused was not a reasonable one, and the liquidator was assoilzied.
[72] *Taylor v. Wilson's Trustees,* 1975 S.C. 146.

(b) if the creditors' meeting voted against his release but removed him from office, or he ceases to be a qualified insolvency practitioner he must apply to the Secretary of State for his release;
(c) on resignation his release is governed by the rules[73];
(d) if he has vacated office having called the final meeting of creditors he is released at that time unless the meeting votes to the contrary, in which case (b) applies: section 174(4).

The effect of a release is to discharge the liquidator from all liability in respect of his acts or omissions as such: section 174(6).

### Release (Scotland)

Section 174 applies to Scotland with the following modifications:

(a) the provisions relating to the official receiver have no application;
(b) for references to the Secretary of State substitute references to the Accountant of Court: section 174(7).

## WINDING UP OF UNREGISTERED COMPANIES

Section 221(5) provides that an unregistered company may be wound up by the court[74] if—

(i) it is dissolved, or has ceased business, or is carrying on business only for the purpose of winding up its affairs; or
(ii) it is unable to pay its debts[75]; or
(iii) the court is of the opinion that it is just and equitable that the company should be wound up.

---

[73] I.R. 1986, r. 4.121.
[74] Such a company cannot be wound up voluntarily: I.A. 1986, s.221(4). For a petition by a member of an incorporated association for the appointment of a judicial factor, see *Munro v. Edinburgh District Trades Council Social Club,* 1989 G.W.D. 6–240 (O.H.).
[75] This will be deemed in the circumstances set out in ss.222–224.

The expression "unregistered company" includes any association or company[76] with the exception of, *e.g.*—

(i) a company registered under the Companies Acts or Joint Stock Companies Act; or

(ii) a railway company incorporated by Act of Parliament: section 220.

For the purpose of determining the court having jurisdiction in the winding up, an unregistered company is deemed to be registered in England or Scotland according to whether its principal place of business is situated in England or Scotland: section 221(2).

Section 227 extends section 126[77] (stay of proceedings against company) to proceedings against a contributory where the application to stay is by a creditor, and section 228 provides that where an order has been made for winding up an unregistered company, no action or proceeding shall be proceeded with or commenced against any contributory of the company in respect of any debt of the company, except by leave of the court.

The provisions of Part V of the Act (sections 220 to 229) with respect to unregistered companies are in addition to and not in restriction of the provisions with respect to the winding up of companies by the court, and the court or liquidator has the same powers in the case of unregistered companies as in the case of the winding up of companies formed and registered under the Act: section 229.

---

[76] While these words are very wide, they do not include an association which parliament could not reasonably have intended should be subject to the winding-up process: *Re International Tin Council* [1988] 3 All E.R. 257, 361 C.A. approving *Re St. James Club* (1852) 2 D & GM & G 383; See also *Re Witney Town Football & Social Club* [1993] BCC 874. The word 'company' includes those incorporated elsewhere than in Great Britain: *Re Normandy Marketing Ltd* [1993] BCC 879.

[77] *Ante*, p. 728.

# Chapter 28

# VOLUNTARY WINDING UP

*N.B. All references in this chapter are to the Insolvency Act 1986 unless otherwise stated].*

FROM the point of view of the company itself, a voluntary winding up has many advantages over a compulsory winding up, the chief being that there are not so many formalities to be complied with. In consequence the great majority of liquidations are voluntary liquidations. The Cork Committee, however, made several recommendations to prevent abuses in the system of voluntary liquidation and some of these were adopted by the Insolvency Act 1985, since consolidated into the Insolvency Act 1986.

## Initiation of voluntary winding up

Section 84 provides that a company may be wound up voluntarily:

(1) When the period, if any, fixed for its duration by the articles expires, or the event, if any, occurs, on the occurrence of which the articles provide that it is to be dissolved, and the company in general meeting passes a resolution (*i.e.* an *ordinary resolution*) to be wound up voluntarily.
(2) If it resolves by *special resolution*[1] to be wound up voluntarily.

A company can be wound up by special resolution without any reason being assigned.

---

[1] *Ante,* p. 304.

(3)  If the company resolves by *extraordinary resolution* that it
     cannot by reason of its liabilities continue its business and
     that it is advisable to wind up.

An extraordinary resolution is allowed here because time is of
the essence since the company is insolvent and a special resolution would normally require a longer period of notice.[2]

A resolution for voluntary winding up must be advertised in
the *Gazette* within 14 days after it is passed: section 85. In
Scotland, where failure to make timeous advertisement was due
to inadvertence and no prejudice had been suffered as a result of
the failure, the Court of Session, in the exercise of its *nobile
officium,* authorised the liquidator to make a belated advertisement, the expenses of the proceedings to be borne by the
liquidator personally.[3]

A voluntary winding up commences at the time of the passing
of the resolution: section 86.

### Kinds of voluntary winding up

A voluntary winding up may be either (1) a members' voluntary winding up; or (2) a creditors' voluntary winding up: section
90.

## MEMBERS' VOLUNTARY WINDING UP

A members' voluntary winding up takes place only when the
company is solvent. It is entirely managed by the members, and
the liquidator is appointed by them. No meeting of creditors is
held and no liquidation committee is appointed. To obtain the
benefit of this form of winding up, a declaration of solvency must
be filed: section 89.

### Declaration of solvency

This is a statutory declaration made by the directors or, if there
are more than two of them, by the majority, at a board meeting,
that they have made a full inquiry into the company's affairs and,
having done so, they have formed the opinion that the company

---

[2] *Ante,* p. 304.
[3] *Liquidator of Nairn Public Hall Co. Ltd, Petitioner,* 1946 S.C. 395.

will be able to pay its debts in full together with interest at the official rate[4] within a specified period not exceeding 12 months from the commencement of the winding up.[5] The declaration has no effect unless it is made within the five weeks immediately preceding the date of the passing of the winding-up resolution. It may even be made on that date providing that it precedes the resolution.

The declaration must be filed with the Registrar within 15 days of the passing of the resolution. Further, the declaration has no effect unless it embodies a statement of the company's assets and liabilities as at the latest practicable date before it is made: section 89. If there is something which can reasonably be described as "a statement of the company's assets and liabilities," then, even if it subsequently appears that there were errors and omissions, these will not prevent it from being a statement within section 89.[6]

A director making a declaration of solvency without reasonable grounds is liable to imprisonment for six months, or a fine or both. If the debts plus interest are not paid or provided for within the period stated, he is presumed not to have had reasonable grounds: section 89(5).

If a declaration is made in accordance with the section the winding up is a members' voluntary winding up: section 90.

### The liquidator

Unlike the liquidator in a winding up by the court, a liquidator in a voluntary winding up is not an officer of the court.[7] He is the agent of the company, but not of the individual members.[8] He is appointed, by the company in general meeting (s.91), and within 14 days he must give notice of his appointment to the registrar of companies and publish it in the *Gazette*: section 109.[9] He may be appointed at the meeting at which the resolution for voluntary winding up is passed. If there is no liquidator acting, the court may appoint one. The court may also, on cause shown, remove a liquidator and appoint another: section 108[10] Where a person had

---

[4] See s.251.
[5] See above.
[6] *De Courcy v. Clement* [1971] Ch. 693.
[7] *Per* Megarry J. in *Re Rolls Razor Ltd (No. 2)* [1970] Ch. 576, 586.
[8] See *Taylor v. Wilson's Trustees*, 1975 S.C. 146.
[9] This provision applies to all voluntary liquidations.
[10] This provision applies to all voluntary liquidations.

been appointed liquidator without his knowledge and he declined to act, it was held that the appointment was invalid and there was therefore no need to remove him.[11] Anyone subject to a disqualification order under the Company Directors Disqualification Act 1986 cannot act as a liquidator.[12] The liquidator is also an office holder under the Insolvency Act.[13] He must be a qualified insolvency practitioner[14] and has the powers and duties of an office holder.

If a vacancy occurs in the office of liquidator, whether by death, resignation or otherwise, the company at a general meeting, summoned by any contributory or by a continuing liquidator, may fill it: section 92.

Until a liquidator is appointed the directors cannot exercise their powers without the sanction of the court, except to dispose of perishable goods or goods which are likely to fall in value if not disposed of immediately and to do anything necessary for the protection of the company's assets: section 114. This provision was introduced following a recommendation of the Cork Committee to prevent dissipation of the company's assets prior to the appointment of a liquidator.[15] Failure to comply with section 114 is a criminal offence on the part of the directors and transactions effected are invalid.[16]

A special manager may also be appointed under section 177.[17]

## Vacation of office by or removal of a liquidator

Being an office holder, a liquidator must vacate office if he ceases to be a qualified insolvency practitioner.[18] He may resign by giving notice to the registrar. He vacates office on giving notice to the registrar of the final meetings held under section 94.[19]

---

[11] *Liquidator of Highland etc. Dairy Farms Ltd and Another, Petitioners,* 1964 S.C. 1.
[12] *Ante,* p. 373.
[13] *Ante,* p. 740.
[14] *Ante,* p. 659.
[15] s.114(4).
[16] *Re A Company (No. 006341 of 1992), ex p. B Ltd* [1994] BCLC 225. Where a third party deals in good faith with the directors, in circumstances where he does not, and could not be expected to, know of the limitation on the directors' authority (as where the resolution to wind up has been neither registered nor advertised) the transaction may be binding on the company by virtue of ostensible authority. Judge Paul Baker, Q.C. *ibid.*
[17] *Ante,* p. 736.
[18] *Ante,* p. 659.
[19] *Post,* p. 766.

He may be removed at any time by a general meeting of the company summoned for that purpose or by the court. If the liquidator has been appointed by the court (*e.g.* to fill a vacancy) he may be removed and replaced by a meeting of members holding not less than one half of the total voting rights, or by a general meeting of the company summoned by the liquidator or the court: section 171.

## Release of a liquidator

The liquidator is released at the time of the final meeting. If he has been removed from office his release operates from the date at which notice was given to the registrar in accordance with the rules,[20] unless the meeting resolves against his release in which case he must apply to the Secretary of State for his release. If the liquidator has resigned he is released in accordance with the rules. Such a release absolves him from all liability in relation to the winding up except for proceedings against him under section 212.[21]

## Conduct of liquidation

Subject to section 96,[22] within three months after the end of the first and every succeeding year of the liquidation, the liquidator must summon a general meeting of the company and lay before it an account of his acts and dealings and of the conduct of the winding up during the preceding year: section 93.

As soon as the affairs of the company are fully wound up the liquidator must call a general meeting of the company. This is done by advertisement in the *Gazette* at least one month before the meeting. At the meeting the liquidator must present an account of the winding up, showing how the winding up has been conducted and how the company's property has been disposed of. A copy of this account, together with a return of the holding of meeting, must be sent to the Registrar within a week after the meeting: section 94. It is not necessary for the affairs of the company to be fully wound up before the liquidator can validly make his return, only that they should be fully wound up so far as the liquidator is aware.[23]

---

[20] I.R. 1986, r. 4.144; I.(S.)R. 1986, r. 4.28A (inserted by Sched. 2).
[21] *Ante,* p. 371.
[22] *Post,* p. 767.
[23] *Re Cornish Manures Ltd* [1967] 1 W.L.R. 807.

If a quorum is not present at the final meeting, the liquidator must make a return that the meeting was summoned but no quorum was present, and this has the same effect as a return of the holding of the meeting: section 94(5).

The Registrar must publish in the *Gazette* notice of the receipt of the return (Companies Act 1985, s.711).

### Effect of insolvency on a members' voluntary winding up

If the liquidator is of the opinion that the company will in fact be unable to pay its debts in full (including interest) within the time specified by the directors in their declaration of solvency he must call a creditors' meeting within 28 days, giving them at least seven days' notice by post and advertising it in the *Gazette* and two local newspapers.[24] He must also supply the creditors with any information they might reasonably require in that period: section 95(1), (2).

The liquidator must lay before the meeting a statement of affairs set out in accordance with the rules,[25] showing, in particular, the company's assets, debts and liabilities, its creditors and their securities, together with the dates on which they were created: section 95(3), (4).

The effect of holding such a meeting is that the winding up proceeds as if the declaration of solvency had never been made; *i.e.* as a creditors' voluntary winding up: section 96.

## CREDITORS' VOLUNTARY WINDING UP

If no declaration of solvency is filed with the Registrar, a voluntary winding up is a creditors' voluntary winding up: section 90.

In such a case the company must summon a meeting of creditors[26] for a date not later than 14 days after the passing of the resolution to wind up the company. Notices of the meeting must be sent to the creditors at least seven days before the meeting. Notice of the meeting must also be advertised in the

---

[24] *i.e.* within the location of its principal place of business during the preceding six months.

[25] I.R. 1986, r. 4.34—CVL, I.(S.)R. 1986, r. 4.7 as substituted by Sched. 1.

[26] If the winding up has been converted to a creditors' winding up the creditors' meeting making such a decision under s.95, *supra*, is the creditors' meeting for this purpose: section 102.

*Gazette* and two local newspapers.[27] The notice must also state either the name and address of a person qualified to act as an insolvency practitioner in relation to the company who will provide such information as the creditors may reasonably request prior to the meeting or a place in the locality where on two business days prior to the meeting a list of the creditors' names and addresses will be available free of charge: section 98.

Management of such a winding up is shared by the members and creditors but in all cases the creditors have the ultimate control by virtue of the following provisions.

## Meeting of creditors

The meeting of creditors is presided over by one of the directors nominated for that purpose by the directors: section 99. The business of the meeting is:

(1) To receive a full statement by the directors as to the company's affairs, together with a list of the creditors, and details of any securities and other information required by the rules[28]: section 99.

(2) To appoint a liquidator: section 100, *post*.

(3) To appoint a liquidation committee: section 101, *post*.

## The liquidator

The creditors and the company at their respective meetings may nominate a liquidator and, if different persons are nominated, the person nominated by the creditors is the liquidator, subject to any order made by the court. If the creditors make no nomination the company's nominee is the liquidator. If different persons are nominated, any director, member or creditor of the company may, within seven days after the creditors' nomination, apply to the court for an order that the company's nominee be liquidator instead of or jointly with the creditors' nominee, or that some other person be liquidator: section 100.

Under this system of appointing a liquidator it is still possible for the company to appoint a liquidator elect for the 14 days before a creditors' meeting is required to be held. Prior to the

---

[27] See note 24 above.
[28] I.R. 1986, r. 4.34—CVL; I.(S.)R. 1986, r. 7.30 and Sched. 5.

Insolvency Act it was possible to delay the creditors' meeting for several weeks because of the decision in *Re Centrebind Ltd*[29] to the effect that whilst failure to call the meeting was a criminal offence, it did not invalidate the appointment of the nominated liquidator or his actions. This abuse, known as "centre-binding", whereby the company's assets were in fact unprotected and beyond the creditors' control, has been countered by many provisions, following recommendations of the Cork Committee.[30] These include the requirement that any liquidator be a qualified insolvency practitioner,[31] that until any liquidator is appointed the directors' powers are subject to the court's control[32] and the 14 day time limit within which the creditors' meeting must now be held.[33]

In addition where the company nominates a liquidator prior to the creditors' meeting his powers can only be exercised with the court's consent. He may, however, assume custody of the company's property, dispose of perishable goods and those likely to diminish in value unless disposed of, and protect the company's assets. He must attend the creditors' meeting and report to that meeting on the exercise of any of his powers in the meantime. He is also charged with the duty to apply to the court if the company or the directors fail to comply with the requirement *vis-a-vis* the creditors' meeting: section 166. This effectively prevents "centre-binding" since any liquidator acting in default can be fined and will be liable under section 212.[34]

Any vacancy, by reason of death, resignation or otherwise, in the office of a liquidator, other than a liquidator appointed by the court may be filled by the creditors: section 104.

A liquidator may vacate office by removal and be released from liability in the same way as a liquidator in a members' voluntary winding up, except that the function of the members' meetings are carried out by a meeting of creditors: sections 171, 173, *ante*.[35]

---

[29] [1967] 1 W.L.R. 377.
[30] Paras. 667–673.
[31] *Ante,* p. 659.
[32] s.114.
[33] *Post.*
[34] *Ante,* p. 371.
[35] p. 765.

## Liquidation committee

The creditors, at their first or any subsequent meeting, may appoint a liquidation committee of not more than five persons to act with the liquidator.[36] If they do so, the company in general meeting may appoint not more than five persons to act as members of the committee, but the creditors may resolve that these persons ought not to be members of the committee, and thereupon, unless the court otherwise directs, they cannot act on the committee: section 101.

## Conduct of liquidation

Within three months after the end of the first and every succeeding year of the liquidation the liquidator must summon a general meeting of the company and a meeting of creditors, and lay before the meetings an account of his acts and dealings and of the conduct of the winding up during the preceding year: section 105.

When the liquidation is complete, the liquidator must, by at least one month's notice in the *Gazette,* call final meetings of the company and the creditors, and present his account. Within a week after these meetings, a copy of the account and a return of the holding of the meetings or a return that no quorum was present thereat must be filed with the Registrar, who must publish it in the *Gazette* (Companies Act 1985, s 711).

## CONSEQUENCES OF ANY VOLUNTARY WINDING UP

The commencement of a voluntary winding up is the date of the passing of the resolution for voluntary winding up: section 86. Even if the company is subsequently wound up by the court, the commencement of the winding up is the date of the passing of the resolution: section 129.

The consequences of a voluntary winding up are:

(1) As from the commencement of the winding up the company must cease to carry on business except so far as is required for its beneficial winding up, although the

---

[36] *Post,* p. 774.

corporate state and powers continue until the company is
dissolved: section 87. Notification that the company is in
liquidation must be given on the company's documents on
which its name appears: section 188.[37]

(2) No transfer of shares can be made without the sanction of
the liquidator and any alteration in the status of the
members is void: section 88. A transfer of debentures
can, however, be made.[38]

(3) On the appointment of a liquidator the powers of the
directors cease except so far as the company in general
meeting or the liquidator (in a members' voluntary winding up), or the liquidation committee or, if there is no
such committee, the creditors (in a creditors' voluntary
winding up), sanction their continuance: sections 91(2)
and 103.

A voluntary winding up does not automatically operate as a
discharge of the company's employees[39]; it has been suggested
that it will do so if it takes place because the company is
insolvent.[40] In any event, the liquidator has power to terminate
contracts of employment and may do so by his conduct.[41]
Premature termination of a written fixed term agreement may
entitle the employee to damages.[42] When the terms of the
contract of employment are to be found in the articles, no
damages for breach of contract are recoverable.[43]

After the commencement of the winding up the liquidator may
continue the employment of the company's employees if required
to ensure a more beneficial winding up of the company.[44]

In England there is no statutory provision for the stay of
actions and other proceedings against the company in the case of
a voluntary winding up (cf. sections 126, 128, 130, ante[45]), but on
an application under section 112, post,[46] the court has a discretion

---

[37] Ante, p. 736.
[38] Re Goy & Co. Ltd [1900] 2 Ch. 149.
[39] Compare a winding up by the court; ante, p. 735.
[40] Fowler v. Commercial Timber Co. Ltd [1930] 2 K.B. 1 (C.A.), per Greer L.J.;
compare amalgamation, see Midlands Counties District Bank Ltd v. Attwood
[1905] 1 Ch. 357.
[41] Fowler v. Commercial Timber Co. Ltd, ibid.
[42] ibid.
[43] Re T. N. Farrer Ltd [1937] Ch. 352.
[44] cf. Day v. Tait (1900) 8 S.L.T. 40 (O.H.).
[45] Chap. 27, pp. 733, 734.
[46] p. 774.

to stay proceedings.[47] Executions will usually be stayed when it is necessary to ensure the distribution of assets among the creditors *pari passu*,[48] but actions will not be stayed when there is a dispute as to liability, or when no advantage will be gained, *e.g.* no expense will be saved, by a stay.[49]

In Scotland, the provision now in section 112 had been interpreted as not giving the court power to stay proceedings against the company,[50] and section 113 provides that, on the application of the liquidator of a Scottish company, the court may direct that no action or proceeding shall be proceeded with against the company except by leave of the court. Section 185 (relating to diligence in Scotland)[51] applies to voluntary, as well as to compulsory, winding up.

## DISTRIBUTION OF THE PROPERTY OF THE COMPANY IN A VOLUNTARY WINDING UP

The costs, charges and expenses properly incurred in a voluntary winding up, including the remuneration of the liquidator, are payable in priority to all other claims: section 115. The pre-liquidation expenses of a person who expected to be liquidator but was not, in the event, appointed, can be paid but only in so far as they were incurred to enable the company to pass the winding-up resolution. Expense incurred in collecting the assets was not recoverable: *Re Sandwell Copiers*.[52] The liquidator must then apply the property[53] of the company first in paying the preferential debts[54] and then in discharging the liabilities of the company *pari passu*. The liquidator has a duty to inquire into all claims against the company.[55] Even where the company is solvent, statute-barred debts cannot be paid unless the contributories consent.[56] Any surplus must then be distributed amongst the

---

[47] *Currie v. Consolidated Kent Collieries Corpn. Ltd* [1906] 1 K.B. 134 (C.A.).
[48] *Anglo-Baltic Bank v. Barber & Co.* [1924] 2 K.B. 410 (C.A.).
[49] *Cook v. "X" Chair Patents Co. Ltd* [1960] 1 W.L.R. 60.
[50] *Sdeuard v. Gardner* (1876) 3 R. 577.
[51] *Ante*, p. 734.
[52] [1988] BCLC 209.
[53] *Post*, Chap. 29.
[54] See s. 175, *post*, p. 793.
[55] *Austin Securities Ltd v. Northgate and English Stores Ltd* [1969] 1 W.L.R. 529 (C.A.) applying *Pulsford v. Devenish* and *Re Armstrong Whitworth Securities Co. Ltd, ante*, p. 758.
[56] *Re Art Reproduction Co. Ltd* [1952] Ch.89. The Scottish equivalent of "statute-barred" is "prescribed."

members according to their rights and interests in the company: I.A. 1986, section 107.

Provision may be made for employees on the cessation of business if it is approved by the members or otherwise in accordance with the articles either before or during the liquidation. Such payment must be made out of the assets available to the members: Companies Act 1985, section 719. Any exercise of this power is not subject to section 107: section 187.

A contracting out of the provisions of section 107 is contrary to public policy.[57] Section 107 does not, however, affect contracts which bona fide deprive the company of ownership prior to the winding up, e.g. the creation of a trust fund.[58] Such contracts may, however, be invalid under alternative provisions.[59]

## POWERS AND DUTIES OF THE LIQUIDATOR IN A VOLUNTARY WINDING UP

In every voluntary winding up it is the duty of the liquidator to pay the debts of the company and adjust the rights of the contributories among themselves.[60]

To enable him to do this, section 165[61] and Schedule 4 provide that he may *without sanction*:

(1) commence or defend legal proceedings on behalf of the company;
(2) carry on the company's business so far as it is beneficial for the winding up;

He may carry on the business of the company, if he reasonably thinks it is necessary for the beneficial winding up of the company. If he does

---

[57] *British Eagle International Air Lines Ltd v. Compagnie Nationale Air France* [1975] 1 W.L.R. 758 (H.L.), where the rules of the general liquidation prevailed over the International Air Transport Association clearing house arrangements and, despite such arrangements, the plaintiff company was entitled to recover the sums payable to it by other airlines for services rendered by it and not cleared through the I.A.T.A. system and vice versa.

[58] *Carreras Rothmans Ltd v. Freeman Matthews Treasure Ltd* [1985] Ch. 207.

[59] *Post,* Chap. 29.

[60] The duty to pay the company's debts is a fiduciary one and the liquidator of a Scottish company, no matter where he resides, can be called to account before the Court of Session; his duty continues despite the dissolution of the company, and the jurisdiction of the court is not brought to an end by dissolution: *Lamey v. Winram,* 1987 S.L.T. 635 (O.H.).

[61] Subject to s.166.

so, those to whom he incurs obligations are entitled to be paid in priority to the creditors at the commencement of the winding up: *Re Great Eastern Electric Co. Ltd* [1941] Ch. 241.[62]

(3) exercise all the general powers of a liquidator listed in Part III of Schedule 4, I.A 1986.

In a members' voluntary winding up, *with the sanction* of an extraordinary resolution of the company, and in a creditors' voluntary winding up, *with the sanction* of the court or the liquidation committee or (if there is no such committee) a meeting of the creditors, the liquidator may:

(1) pay any classes of creditors in full;
(2) make any compromise or arrangement with creditors;
(3) compromise all calls and liabilities to calls and other debts and liabilities: section 165, Schedule 4.

**Power to apply to court**

In a voluntary winding up the liquidator, or any contributory or creditor, may apply to the court to determine any question arising in the winding up or to exercise any of the powers which the court could exercise if the company were being wound up by the court: section 112.[63] This gives the liquidator in a voluntary winding up the same right to the guidance of the court as in a compulsory liquidation. For example, in England, if he is of opinion that fraud has been committed in the formation or promotion of the company or in relation to the company since its formation, he can obtain an order of the court for the public examination[64] of any promoter, director or other officer of the company concerned. Again, he can apply for an order for private examination.[65]

---

[62] *cf. Day v. Tait* (1900) 8 S.L.T. 40 (O.H.).
[63] For examples of applications under s.112, see *Liquidators of North British Locomotive Co. Ltd v. Lord Advocate*, 1963 S.C. 272 (O.H.), *Smith and Another, Petitioners*, 1969 S.L.T. (Notes) 94 (O.H.) (as to exercise of directors' discretionary powers under pension scheme) and *Liquidators of Highland Engineering Ltd v. Thomson*, 1972 S.C. 87 (O.H.) (as to provisional liquidator's right to retain funds to pay his remuneration and expenses).
[64] *Re Campbell Coverings Ltd (No. 2)* [1954] Ch. 225 and see *supra* p. 737 (Public Examination of Officers) and p. 741 (Private Examination).
[65] As in *Re Rolls Razor Ltd (No. 2)* [1970] Ch. 576.

In 1971 a company went into voluntary liquidation. In 1976 it became apparent that it might be liable for claims in tort for negligence during its operations. In 1979, after the liquidators had started preparing the final accounts, solicitors warned the liquidators of the possible claims. The liquidators applied for an order that they should distribute the final dividend to the members without regard to the claims on the basis of delay. Alternatively they sought an order that the claimants should bear the costs of the delay in distribution. Megarry V.-C. held that the test was whether in all the circumstances it was just to make either of the orders sought. Default or lack of diligence by either party was relevant and the court was less likely to facilitate a distribution among the members than among the creditors. In the circumstances, both orders would be refused: *Re R-R Realisations Ltd* [1980] 1 All E.R. 1019.

**Duty to report criminal offences**

If the liquidator thinks that any past or present officer, or any member, of the company has committed a criminal offence in relation to the company, he must report the matter, in an English winding up, to the Director of Public Prosecutions, and in a Scottish winding up, to the Lord Advocate. The matter may then be referred to the Department of Trade and Industry, who have the same powers of investigating the company's affairs as in an investigation into the affairs of a company under sections 431 or 432 of the Companies Act 1985: section 218.

## COMPULSORY LIQUIDATION AFTER COMMENCEMENT OF VOLUNTARY LIQUIDATION

A voluntary liquidation does not bar the right of any creditor or contributory to have the company wound up by the court: section 116. A creditor of a company in voluntary liquidation is not entitled *ex debito justitiae* as between himself and the company to a compulsory winding-up order and the views of the contributories must be taken into consideration,[66] unless the company is insolvent.[67] Even in such a case it had been said that the court will require reasons as to why the voluntary winding up is inappropriate: it is not inappropriate merely because the petitioner would prefer a different liquidator.[68] However, more recently it has been stated that a compulsory order should be made wherever

---

[66] *Re Surplus Properties (Huddersfield) Ltd* [1984] BCLC 89.
[67] *ibid.*, *Re James Millward & Co. Ltd* [1940] Ch. 333 (C.A.).
[68] *Re Medisco Equipment Ltd* [1983] BCLC 305, *per* Harman J.

the creditors would otherwise be left with a justifiable feeling of grievance that they had been prevented from having the company's affairs investigated by a liquidator who was not appointed by the directors.[69] There is no rule that the probity or competence of the liquidator must be attacked[70] but he must not only be independent but must be seen to be independent.[71] Further, the court is bound to have regard to the wishes of all the creditors,[72] and if the majority favour the continuance of the voluntary liquidation an order will not be made unless the petitioner can show special circumstances.[73] The court can, however, examine the motives of the creditors,[74] and, in particular, of those creditors who are also members.[75] Considerations of fairness and commercial morality should also be taken into account.[76] In the case of a financial company, the wish of the regulatory authority, based upon reasonable material, to have the sort of investigation which would follow on from a compulsory winding up may outweigh factors like inconvenience and expense.[77] A contributory must satisfy the court that the rights of the contributories will be prejudiced by a voluntary winding up: section 116. What the Secretary of State must show when he is the petitioner has been dealt with already.

When a voluntary winding up is superseded by a compulsory winding up, all proceedings in the voluntary winding up are deemed to have been validly taken unless the court, on proof of fraud or mistake, thinks fit to direct otherwise: section 129, *ante*.

---

[69] *Re M.C.H. Services* [1987] BCLC 535, Vinelott J.
[70] *Re Palmer Marine Services Ltd* [1986] 1 W.L.R. 573.
[71] *Re Lowestoft Traffic Services Ltd* [1986] BCLC 81: and see *H.J. Tomkins & Son* [1990] BCLC 76.
[72] *Re Home Remedies Ltd* [1943] Ch. 1; *Re Lowestoft Traffic Services Ltd* [1986] BCLC 81; *cf. Pattisons Ltd v. Kinnear* (1899) 1 F. 551 and *Elsmie & Son v. The Tomatin etc. Distillery Ltd* (1906) 8 F. 434.
[73] *Re B. Karsberg Ltd* [1956] 1 W.L.R. 47 (C.A.); *Re J.D. Swain Ltd* [1965] 1 W.L.R. 909 (C.A.); for special circumstances, see *Bouboulis v. Mann, Macneal & Co. Ltd*, 1926 S.C. 637: and see *Re H.J. Tomkins, ibid.*, where the court followed the wishes of creditors representing a majority in value, though not in number.
[74] *Re Falcon (R.J.) Developments* [1987] BCLC 437.
[75] *Re Palmer Marine Surveys Ltd* [1986] 1 W.L.R. 573.
[76] *ibid.* See also *Re Gordon & Breach Science Publishers Ltd* [1995] BCC 261.
[77] *Securities & Investments Board v. Lancashire and Yorkshire Portfolio Management Ltd* [1992] BCC 381.

## Chapter 29

## CONTRIBUTORIES AND CREDITORS: COMPLETION OF THE WINDING UP

*[N.B. References in this chapter are to sections of the Insolvency Act 1986 unless otherwise stated]*.

As soon as may be after a winding-up order is made, it is the duty of the liquidator in England to—

(1) settle a list of contributories;
(2) collect the company's assets and apply them in discharge of its liabilities: sections 148, 160.

In Scotland it is for the court to settle a list of contributories and to cause the assets of the company to be collected and applied in discharge of the company's liabilities; section 148. Section 160, which provides for delegation of the court's power to the liquidator, does not apply to Scotland.

### CONTRIBUTORIES

A contributory is a person liable to contribute to the assets of a company in the event of its being wound up: section 79. A fully paid-up shareholder in a company limited by shares falls within this definition.[1] Section 74 provides that on a winding up every present and past member is liable to contribute to the assets of the company to an amount sufficient for payment of its debts and liabilities, and the expenses of the winding up, and for the adjustment of the rights of the contributories among themselves. This is subject to certain qualifications, *post*, *e.g.* a past member is not liable to contribute if he ceased to be a member one year

---

[1] *Re Anglesea Colliery Co.* (1866) L.R. 1 Ch.App. 555, followed, *e.g.* in *Paterson v. M'Farlane* (1875) 2 R. 490.

or more before the commencement of the winding up[2]: section 74(2)(a).

Where a private company which has purchased or redeemed its own shares out of capital under section 170 of the Companies Act 1985 goes into liquidation within one year of such payment, and is found to be insolvent, the directors and the recipient are liable to contribute the amount of the payment to cover any insolvency. Such persons are not, however, governed by sections 76 or 79 and are not true contributories: section 76.[3]

### The list of contributories

The list of contributories is in two parts, the A list and the B list. The A list consists of the members of the company at the commencement of the winding up, *i.e.* present members. The B list consists of persons who were members within a year before the commencement of the winding up. The B list is often not settled at all, and is never settled unless it appears that the A contributories are unable to satisfy their contributions.[4] The list must distinguish between contributories who are liable in their own right and those liable as representatives of others[5]: section 148(3).

The court may dispense with the settlement of a list of contributories where it appears that it will not be necessary to make calls on or adjust the rights of contributories: section 148(2). The distribution of surplus assets among the contributories does not of itself involve an adjustment of the rights of the contributories among themselves and therefore no list need be settled.[6] The court should not exercise its discretion to dispense with a list of contributories if the company has a large number of shares held by a large number of shareholders.[7]

### Liability of contributories

The liability of a contributory in a company limited by shares[8] is qualified as follows—

---

[2] *Ante,* p. 731, this qualification does not apply to the winding up of an unlimited company which has re-registered as limited under s. 51 Companies Act 1985, see s. 77.

[3] *Ante,* p. 195.

[4] See s. 74(2)(c) IA 1986.

[5] See *post.*

[6] *Re Phoenix Oil, etc., Co.* [1958] Ch. 560.

[7] *Re Paragon Holdings Ltd* [1961] Ch. 346.

[8] See s. 74(3) for companies limited by guarantee.

(1) The liability of a contributory, whether on the A list or the B list, is limited to the amount unpaid on his shares: section 74(2)(d). Where shares are partly paid, a past member only has to contribute if the existing member has not paid up in full. Where there are several past members in the year before the winding up, all will appear on the B list but the primary liability will be on the latest trans-feror.[9] The fact that all debts have been paid does not necessarily absolve the holder of partly paid shares from his liability: a contribution may still be required to adjust the rights of the contributories amongst themselves.[10]

(2) B contributories are not liable to contribute in respect of any debt or liability of the company contracted *after* he ceased to be a member: section 74(2)(b).

The assets of the company, including the amount received from A contributories, are first applied *pari passu* in payment of the debts of the company, irrespective of the time when they were contracted.[11] The liability of the B contributories is therefore further restricted, because they are liable only for such of the company's debts contracted before they ceased to be members as have not been satisfied by the distribution of the company's other assets among the creditors generally. The B contributories may therefore not be fully called upon although the creditors are not paid in full.

The liquidator made calls on the B contributories of 5p a share in 1925, and 7½p a share in 1927. The amount so realised exceeded by about £10,000 the debts of the company contracted while the B contributories were members but the total of all the calls did not suffice to pay the creditors in full. The liquidator asked to retain the full amount of the calls on the B contributories as assets available for the creditors. *Held*, he could not retain the full amount, but must return the £10,000 to the B contributories: *Re City of London Insce. Co. Ltd* [1932] 1 Ch. 226.

B contributions are part of the general assets of the company, and are not to be applied, preferentially or exclusively, to the payment of debts incurred before the B shareholders ceased to be members.[12]

---

[9] *Humby's Case* (1872) 26 L.T. 936.
[10] *Re Anglesea Colliery Co.* (1866) L.R. 1 Ch. 555.
[11] *Morris' Case* (1871) L.R. 7 Ch.App. 200.
[12] *Webb v. Whiffin* (1872) L.R. 5 H.L. 711.

(3) B contributories are not liable to contribute unless it appears to the court that the existing members are unable to satisfy their contributions: section 74(2)(c).

Example: C and D are holders of £1 shares, 37½p. paid. C transfers his shares to X and D transfers to Y. Within a year the company is wound up, and is insolvent. X pays up his shares in full, but Y pays nothing. No contribution will be required from C. A contribution will be required from D.

A member cannot claim any dividend in competition with any other creditor not a member of the company: section 74(2)(f). For the purposes of this section the word "member" includes a past member.[13] This provision has been held in Scotland not to apply to dividends which have been carried to an account current between the company and a member.[14] In England the section has been applied to dividends due to a holding company but retained by the subsidiary for use in its business. The judge decided that the onus of proving that such sums were not due as dividends to a member was on the holding company. This could be done by an express or implied agreement which created a loan by the holding company of the money involved or recognition of that fact with the passage of time, but there was no such evidence in that case.[15]

The liability of a contributory creates a debt (in England of the nature of a speciality) accruing at the time when his liability commenced, but payable when a call is made; section 80.

If a contributory dies either before or after he has been placed on the list of contributories, his personal representatives are liable. They are not personally liable; they are liable in their representative character. In England, if they make a default in payment, proceedings may be taken for administering the estate of the deceased: section 81.

If a contributory becomes bankrupt, his trustee in bankruptcy represents him for all the purposes of the winding up and is a contributory accordingly. Calls already made and the estimated value of the bankrupt's liability to future calls may be proved against the estate.[16]

---

[13] *Re Consolidated Goldfields of New Zealand Ltd* [1953] Ch. 689.
[14] *Liquidator of Wilsons (Glasgow and Trinidad) Ltd v. Wilson's Trustees*, 1915 1 S.L.T. 424 (O.H.).
[15] *Re L. B. Holliday & Co. Ltd* [1986] 2 All E.R. 367.
[16] s. 82.

There are special provisions as to the liability of B contributories where a company has re-registered under section 49 or 51 of the Companies Act[17]: sections 77, 78.

## Calls on contributories

In England calls on contributories are made by the liquidator with the leave of the court or the sanction of the liquidation committee: section 160. In Scotland calls are made by the court: section 150.

Calls may be made either before or after the insufficiency of the assets has been ascertained. They are made for an amount necessary to satisfy the debts and liabilities of the company, and the costs of winding up, and for adjustment of the rights of the contributories among themselves. In fixing the amount regard is had to the probability that some contributories may fail to pay the call: section 150.

A debt due from the company to a contributory cannot be set off against calls, whether made before or after the winding up,[18] except—

(1) where all the creditors have been paid in full (s.149); or
(2) in the case of an unlimited company, where the debt is due to him on an independent dealing with the company and not due to him as a member in respect of dividend or profit (s.149); or
(3) where the contributory is bankrupt.[19]

A contributory on the list may be ordered by the court, at any time after the making of a winding-up order, to pay any money due from him to the company: section 149.[20] The court can also order the arrest of, and seizure of the movable personal property of, a contributory believed to be about to abscond or to remove his property with the object of evading payment of calls: section 158.

---

[17] *Ante,* Chap. 2.
[18] *Grissell's Case* (1866) L.R. 1 Ch.App. 528; *Cowan v. Gowans* (1878) 5 R. 581; this has been held to be so where a shareholder deposited money with the company against calls: *Millar v. Aikman* (1891) 28 S.L.R. 955 (O.H.).
[19] *Re Duckworth* (1867) L.R. 2 Ch.App. 578.
[20] The effect of s. 149 dies with the company when it is dissolved: *Butler v. Broadhead* [1975] Ch.D. 97.

## CREDITORS

The rules apply with regard to (1) the respective rights of secured and unsecured creditors, (2) debts provable, and (3) the valuation of annuities and future and contingent liabilities.

### Secured creditors

A secured creditor is one who holds some security for a debt due to him from the company, such as a mortgage, charge or lien. He must give credit for the realised or estimated value of his security unless he surrenders it. Thus he may—

(1) realise his security and prove,[21] as an unsecured creditor, for any balance due to him after deducting the amount realised; or
(2) value his security and prove, as an unsecured creditor, for any balance due after deducting the value of the security; or
(3) surrender his security and prove, as an unsecured creditor, for the whole debt; or
(4) where he is fully secured, rely on his security and not prove at all.

A secured creditor who has realised his security for less than the total amount of his debt, part of which is preferential,[22] can appropriate the proceeds of sale to that part of his debt which is not preferential, so that he can prove for the preferential part.[23]

If the creditor has made a mistake in the valuation of his security, he may amend it by application to the court. If he subsequently realises his security, the amount realised must be substituted for the amount in the proof.

### Proof of debts

The debts which are provable on a winding up, and the manner of proof, are governed by the Insolvency Rules 1986.[24] The

---

[21] The term used in Scotland is "claim".
[22] *Post,* pp. 793, *et seq.*
[23] *Re William Hall (Contractors) Ltd* [1967] 1 W.L.R. 948.
[24] r. 12.3 and rr. 4.73-4.99; I.(S.)R. 1986, r. 7.30 and Sched. 5.

liability must exist at the commencement of the winding up[25] but, subject to that, it may be present or future, certain or contingent, ascertained or sounding only in damages. The liquidator can estimate the value of any debt of uncertain amount[26] or, in difficult cases, he can apply to the court for directions: section 168(3).[27] It is no longer the case that in an insolvent winding up unliquidated claims in tort are excluded. Some claims can only be proved when those of all other creditors have been paid in full, with interest, e.g. those arising by virtue of restitution orders under sections 6 and 61 of the Financial Services Act 1986.[28] Statute-barred debts cannot be proved.[29]

If a debt is owed in foreign currency it must be paid at the rate of exchange prevailing at the commencement of the liquidation and not at the date of payment.[30]

Where there have been mutual credits, mutual debts or other mutual dealings between the company and one of its creditors, an account is taken of what is due from one to the other, and the balance of that account and no more can be claimed or paid.[31]

A Co. borrowed money from B Co. on the security of bills of sale charging some machinery and providing for its insurance against fire. The policies were in the name of B, and A paid the premiums. The machinery was destroyed by fire and the insurance amounting to £1,600 paid to B. A then went into liquidation. £744 was owing to B on the bills of sale at the date of the fire, so that B had £856 in hand, but A owed B £2,009 unsecured book debts. *Held,* B could set off the £856 against the £2,009: *Re H. E. Thorne & Son Ltd* [1914] 2 Ch. 438.

The holder of a life policy in an assurance company mortgaged the policy to the issuing company. On the company's going into liquidation the policy holder claimed to set off the value of the policy against his mortgage debt. *Held,* he was entitled to do so: *Re City Life Assurance Co. Ltd* [1926] Ch. 191.

---

[25] Community charges incurred by a property development company in respect of property which it has completed after its liquidation is not a provable debt (and neither is it an expense of liquidation): *Re Kentish Homes Ltd* [1993] BCC 212.
[26] I.R. 1986, r. 4.86; I.(S.)R. 1986, rr. 4.15, 4.16.
[27] Any person aggrieved can also apply: s.168(5).
[28] See S.I. 1987, No. 1919, Sch. 1, Pt. I, para. 143.
[29] *Re Art Reproduction Co. Ltd* [1952] Ch. 89; *Re Overmark Smith Warden Ltd, The Times,* March 22, 1982. In a compulsory winding up the limitation period is ascertained by reference to the date of the winding-up order not the petition: *Re Case of Taffs Well* [1991] 3 W.L.R. 731.
[30] *Re Lines Brothers Ltd* [1983] Ch. 1 (C.A.).
[31] I.R. 1986, r. 4.90; on mutuality see I. F. Fletcher. *The Law of Insolvency* (1990), p. 253. Note also *Re Norman Holdings Co. Ltd* [1990] 3 All E.R. 757 (a secured creditor who opts to rely upon his security rather than prove is not subject to r. 4.90).

This statutory set-off cannot be excluded by agreement between the parties.[32] It applies automatically, irrespective of the wishes of the parties, wherever there are mutual debts (or provable claims) between the company and a creditor, so that the liquidator cannot deal with the subject of such mutual cross-claims free of the right of set-off.[33] Where the company is entitled to set-off a claim against a preferential creditor[34] who is also a non-preferential creditor, the company's claim must be set-off rateably in proportion to the amounts of the preferential and non-preferential claims.[35] It has been held that directors who had guaranteed a loan to their company, had constituted themselves principal debtors with their company, and had lodged deposits with the lender as further security, could, when the lender went into liquidation, set-off the amount of the deposits against both their own and the company's debt.[36]

Interest is payable on all debts provable in the winding up, including interest which has accrued under the contract rate prior to the winding up. Post-winding-up interest is only payable, however, if there is a surplus after paying all debts (including pre-winding-up interest), and is paid before any surplus is returned to the contributories. The rate of post-winding-up interest is that specified by order made under section 17 of the Judgments Act 1838[37] on the commencement of the winding up, unless the contract itself provided for a higher rate of interest[38]: section 189. If interest is payable on a foreign currency debt it should be calculated with respect to the exchange rate at the date ot winding up and not when it is paid.[39]

## Adjustment of prior transactions

The Insolvency Act contains provisions which enable the liquidator to apply to the court to set aside certain prior transactions which are disadvantageous to the general body of

---

[32] *Rolls Razor Ltd v. Cox* [1967] 1 Q.B. 552 (C.A.).

[33] *Farley v. Housing and Commercial Development Ltd* [1984] BCLC 442.

[34] *Post*, p. 793.

[35] *Re Unit 2 Windows Ltd* [1986] BCLC 31.

[36] *High Street Services Ltd v. Bank of Credit and Commerce International S.A.* [1993] BCC 360, C.A.

[37] In Scotland see the Insolvency (Scotland) Rules 1986 (S.I. 1986 No. 1915 (S. 139)), r.4.66.

[38] Such a rate may be challenged by the liquidator under s.244, *post*, p. 791.

[39] *Re Lines Brothers Ltd (No. 2)* [1984] Ch. 438.

creditors. These provisions also apply where an administration order has been made.[40]

## Transactions at an undervalue and preferences in England

A transaction at an undervalue entered into by a company is a transaction whereby a company makes a gift to another person or enters into a transaction on terms which provide that the company either receives no consideration or significantly less consideration than the value of the consideration it provides, measured in money or money's worth: section 238(4).[41] However, this does not include transactions entered into by the company in good faith for the purpose of carrying on its business and at the time there were reasonable grounds for believing that the transaction would benefit the company: section 238(5). Further such a transaction must have taken place at a time when the company was unable to pay its debts[42] (or became unable to pay them as a result of the transaction) and also within two years prior to the commencement of the winding up.[43] If the transaction is with a person connected with the company the company is assumed to have been insolvent at the time unless the contrary is shown: section 240.

A company gives a preference to a creditor[44] if it does anything or suffers anything to be done which has the effect of putting the creditor into a position which, in the event of the company going into insolvent liquidation, would be better than the position he would have been in if that thing had not been done, and the company in doing that was influenced by a desire to produce that effect. Such a motive is presumed if the creditor is connected with the company; section 239. The preference must have been given at a time when the company was unable to pay its debts[45] (or became unable to do so as a result of the preference) and also within six months of the commencement of the winding up. The time limit is extended to two years if the creditor is connected with the company: section 240.

[40] *Ante*, p. 711.
[41] The creation of a security over the company's assets has been held not to be a transaction at an undervalue: *Re M.C. Bacon Ltd* [1990] B.C.C. 78.
[42] As defined in s. 123, *ante* p. 715.
[43] Or presentation of the petition for an administrative order.
[44] Including a surety or guarantee for any of its debts or liabilities.
[45] See Note 42.

Both transactions at an undervalue and preferences may be challenged by the liquidator who can apply for a court order to return the position to what it would have been if the company had not entered into the transaction or given the preference: sections 238, 239. The court can make any order it thinks fit[46] and section 241 gives it wide powers relating to the transfer of property, return of benefits received and release of any security. A charge may therefore be set aside under these provisions.[47] An order under section 238 or 239 may affect the property of, or impose an obligation on, any person whether or not he is the person with whom the company entered the transaction or to whom the preference was given. However, the position of such third parties is protected by section 241 (as amended by section 1 of the Insolvency (No. 2) Act 1994) which limits the orders which the court can make where a person has acted in good faith and for value. Lack of good faith is presumed if, at the time of the acquisition of the property or the receipt of the benefit, the person had notice of the relevant surrounding circumstances and the relevant proceedings[48] or was connected with, or an associate of, either the company, the person with whom the company entered the transaction or the person to whom the company gave the preference. The relevant surrounding circumstances are the fact that the transaction was at an undervalue or the circumstances which amounted to the giving of the preference.

In relation to preferences, in the past, a liquidator had to prove that the giving of the preference was accompanied by a dominant intention to prefer on the part of the company. Section 239(5) requires merely that the company be influenced by a desire to prefer, even if there was no dominant intention to do so. If, however, the company has no positive desire to prefer at all and the preference was given solely as a result of commercial pressure (*e.g.* to avoid the appointment of a receiver by the bank) or for proper commercial considerations, it is not subject to avoidance.[49]

---

[46] Even against a person resident abroad: *Re Paramount Airways Ltd* [1992] 3 All E.R. 7, C.A.

[47] A floating charge may also be attacked under s. 245, *ante*, p. 639.

[48] See s. 241(3B) and 241(3C).

[49] *Re M. C. Bacon Ltd* [1990] BCC 78; *Re Fairway Magazines Ltd* [1992] BCC 924; *Re Beacon Leisure Ltd* [1991] BCC 213; *cf. Re D.K.G. Contractors Ltd* [1990] BCC 903.

## Transactions in fraud of creditors

These are transactions at an undervalue (defined as in section 238, *supra*) entered into for the purpose of putting assets beyond the reach of creditors or otherwise prejudicing their interests: section 423. An order can be made, on the application of the liquidator,[50] restoring the position to what it would have been had the transaction not been entered into and protecting the interests of persons who are victims of the transaction. The court does not have to set aside the transaction but should seek both to restore the position and protect the victims so far as practicable. Unlike section 238, section 423 is subject to no time limits.[51]

## Gratuitous alienations and unfair preferences (Scots law)

In Scotland sections 242 and 243 relate, respectively, to the challenge of gratuitous alienations and unfair preferences.[52]

By section 242, once a winding up has commenced an alienation to which the section applies may be challenged by:

(*a*)   any creditor the debt to whom was incurred on or before the date of the commencement of the winding up; or

(*b*)   the liquidator.[53]

The section covers any alienation by which any part of the company's property has been transferred or by which any claim or right of the company has been discharged or renounced, provided the alienation has become completely effectual:

(*a*)   if it favours an "associate," on a day not earlier than five years before the commencement of the winding up; or

---

[50] or the administrator or victim.

[51] *Arbuthnot Leasing International Ltd v. Havelot Leasing Ltd (No. 2)* [1990] BCC 636; *Chohan v. Saggar* [1994] BCC 134.

[52] Formerly governed by the Bankruptcy Acts of 1621 and 1696, respectively. *Bank of Scotland, Petitioners*, 1988 S.L.T. 690, made it clear that gratuitous alienations by companies can be challenged at common law; the common law right had not been taken away but had been extended by sections 242 and 243. In this case there was held to be a prima facie case for an interim interdict. In *Bob Gray (Access) v. T.M. Standard Scaffolding*, 1987 S.C.L.R. 720 (Sh. Ct.) the liquidator was entitled to recover £6,000 paid by the debtor to a particular creditor under the 1696 Act.

[53] The liquidator does not require the sanction of the court to bring such an action, since s. 167 and Sched. 4, para. 4 (see p. 755, *supra*) relate to actions in the name and on behalf of the company, which an action under s. 242 is not: *Dyer v. Hyslop* 1994 S.C.L.R. 171 (Sh.Ct.).

(b)  if it favours any other person, on a day not earlier than two years before such commencement.

The definition of "associate" is incorporated from section 74 of the Bankruptcy (Scotland) Act 1985, a section which may be altered by regulations. By that section the term "associate" extends to husband, wife, relative (*i.e.* brother, sister, uncle, aunt, nephew, niece, lineal ancestor or lineal descendant), partner, employer, employee (any director or other officer of a company being treated as an employee of the company for this purpose), and the section has been amended by the Bankruptcy (Scotland) Regulations 1985 (S.I. 1985 No. 1925, para. 11) to provide for circumstances in which a company is an "associate" of another company.

On a challenge being brought within these provisions, the court must grant decree of reduction or for such restoration of property to the company's assets or other redress as may be appropriate, unless the person seeking to uphold the alienation establishes:

(a)  that immediately, or at any other time, after the alienation the company's assets were greater than its liabilities; or

(b)  that the alienation was made for adequate consideration; or

(c)  that the alienation was a reasonable alienation by way of a birthday, Christmas or other conventional gift or by way of a gift for a charitable purpose to a person other than an associate of the company.

A reduction under section 242 was granted in *McLuckie Brothers Ltd v. Newhouse Contracts Ltd,* 1993 S.L.T. 641 (O.H.): The company in question had disponed a partially completed housing development to N. Ltd for £300,000. At no time after the disposition did the company's assets exceed its liabilities. The issue was whether the price paid represented adequate consideration. The evidence showed that N. Ltd.'s director, who was a brother of the company's director, had purchased the site without its having been advertised and that the company's director had not checked the sum offered.

A challenge does not prejudice any right or interest acquired in good faith and for value from or through the transferee in the alienation.

Further, a liquidator has the same right to challenge a gratuitous alienation as a creditor has at common law. For a successful challenge at common law the challenger would require to prove that the company was absolutely insolvent at the date of the transaction (or was made so by the transaction) and continued to be absolutely insolvent at the date of the challenge, as well as that the transaction was gratuitous and to the prejudice of lawful creditors. While proof of these points would make a common law challenge more difficult, such a challenge is not restricted to alienations made to associates nor is it restricted to alienations made within two years prior to the commencement of winding up. For an example see *Stuart Eves Ltd (in liquidation) v. Smiths Gore,* 1993 S.L.T. 1274 (O.H.).

Section 243 applies to transactions entered into by a company which have the effect of creating a preference in favour of a creditor to the prejudice of the general body of creditors, provided the preference has become completely effectual not earlier than six months before the commencement of the winding up.

There are the following exceptions to the right of challenge under section 243:

(*a*) a transaction in the ordinary course of trade or business;
(*b*) a payment in cash of debts due, unless the transaction was collusive with the purpose of prejudicing the general body of creditors;
(*c*) a transaction by which the parties to it undertake reciprocal obligations[54] unless the transaction was collusive as under (*b*), above;
(*d*) any mandate granted by the company authorising an arrestee to pay over arrested funds to an arrester, where:

(i) there has been a decree for payment or a warrant for summary diligence; and
(ii) the decree or warrant has been preceded by an arrestment on the dependence of the action or followed by an arrestment in execution.

The challenge may be brought by:

(*a*) any creditor the debt to whom was incurred on or before the date of commencement of the winding up; or

---

[54] The consideration given must not be less than full value: *Nicoll v. Steelpress (Supplies) Ltd*, 1993 S.L.T. 533 (payment of £5,071 made by company in order to obtain the release of supplies worth £584).

(b) the liquidator.

On a challenge being brought, the court, if satisfied that the transaction challenged is one to which section 243 applies, must grant decree of reduction or for such restoration of property to the company's assets or other redress as may be appropriate.

A challenge does not prejudice any right or interest acquired in good faith and for value from or through the creditor in whose favour the preference was created.

As with gratuitous alienations, the liquidator has the same right to challenge a preference created by the debtor company as a creditor has at common law.

At common law the challenger must prove that—

(a) the debtor was insolvent at the date of the transaction and continuously thereafter down to the date of the challenge;
(b) the debtor was aware at the date of the transaction that he was insolvent;
(c) the transaction was voluntary and in satisfaction or further security of a prior debt; and
(d) the transaction was to the prejudice of the debtor's other creditors.[55]

At common law the following are recognised as exceptions and are not reducible unless there is proof of fraudulent contrivance between debtor and creditor[56]—(i) cash payments of debts actually due, (ii) transactions in the ordinary course of trade[57] and (iii) *nova debita*, namely, new debts arising out of new transactions.

A transaction is not "voluntary" if the debtor is doing "the very thing which he is bound to do",[58] such as implementing a prior obligation to grant a specific security provided that obligation is part of the original contract.[59]

---

[55] For a comprehensive review of the authorities see *Nordic Travel Ltd v. Scotprint Ltd*, 1980 S.C. 1.
[56] Mere knowledge on the creditor's part of the debtor's absolute and irretrievable insolvency at the time of payment is not enough: *Nordic Travel Ltd v. Scotprint Ltd, ante.*
[57] See *Nordic Travel Ltd v. Scotprint Ltd, ante.*
[58] *Taylor v. Farrie* (1855) 17 D. 639 at p. 649 (joint opinion).
[59] *T. v. L.*, 1970 S.L.T. 243 (O.H.).

The preference is equally challengeable whether conferred directly (*e.g.* where security is given to a creditor previously unsecured) or directly.[60]

An isolated and unprecedented assignation by an insolvent company cannot claim the protection afforded to transactions "in the ordinary course of trade," and is therefore reducible.[61]

## Avoidance of certain floating charges

As we have seen section 245 provides that certain floating charges created within 12 months prior to the liquidation are voidable unless new consideration was supplied by the creditor.[62] This provision operates in addition to sections 238 to 244 detailed above.

## Extortionate credit transactions

A transaction is an extortionate credit transaction if credit has been supplied to a company on terms which are extortionate (grossly exorbitant) having regard to the risk involved or it otherwise grossly contravenes the ordinary principles of fair dealing.[63] All credit transactions are presumed to be extortionate until the contrary is proved. The transaction must have been entered into within three years prior to the commencement of the winding up.

In such cases the liquidator may apply to the court for an order setting aside the transaction, varying its terms, for repayment of money or property held as security to the company or for the taking of accounts. This power may be used concurrently with the power to avoid a transaction at an undervalue: section 244.

## Unenforceability of liens

Under section 246 a liquidator can override any lien or other right to retain possession of any books, papers or records of the

---

[60] *Walkraft Paint Co. v. Lovelock*, 1964 S.L.T. 103 (O.H.) (mandates given by the company to certain of its debtors to pay the favoured creditor); *Walkraft Paint Co. Ltd v. James H. Kinsey Ltd*, 1964 S.L.T. 104 (O.H.) (cheque from company's debtor endorsed by company to the favoured creditor).

[61] *Walkraft Paint Co. Ltd v. James H. Kinsey Ltd, ante.*

[62] *Ante,* p. 639.

[63] *cf.* Consumer Credit Act 1974, ss. 137–139.

company in order to gain possession of them. The only exception is a lien on documents which give a title to property and are held as such.

## Order of application of assets

The effect of sections, 175, 176 and the rules is that in a winding up the assets of the company are applicable in the following order:

(1)   costs, charges and expenses properly incurred in the winding up,[64] including the remuneration of the liquidator;

(2)   the preferential debts;

(3)   debts secured by a charge which as created was a floating charge[65];

(4)   the ordinary unsecured debts;

(5)   post insolvency interest on debts;

(6)   deferred debts;

(7)   the balance (if any) to be returned to the contributories.

All liabilities belonging to a higher category must be paid for or provided for in full before any payment can be made in respect of liabilities of a lower category. None of this will affect creditors with a fixed charge (so long as it is valid and properly registered): they may simply pay themselves out of their security. In relation to any balance remaining unpaid, they rank as ordinary or preferential unsecured creditors.[66]

In the event of the assets being insufficient to satisfy the costs, charges and expenses incurred in the winding up, there is an internal order of priority: section 156 and Insolvency Rules 1986, rule 4.218.[67] Unless the court orders otherwise, the order of priority is:

---

[64] For example liabilities under contracts made or continued by the liquidator for the purposes of the winding-up: *Re Atlantic Computer Systems plc* [1992] 1 All E.R. 476.

[65] s.175(2)(b) and s.251; where necessary the property subject to the charge can be used to pay liabilities in categories (1) and (2). For the position where a fixed charge is made subject to a floating charge see: *Re Portbase Clothing Ltd* [1993] 3 All E.R. 829.

[66] See, *e.g. Re Mesco Properties* [1980] 1 W.L.R. 96.

[67] For Scotland, see I.(S.)R. 1986, r. 4.5(3) and (4); the words in r. 4.5(3) "without prejudice to any order of the court as to expenses" give the court a wide discretion: *Graham v. John Tullis & Son (Plastics) Ltd (No. 2)*, 1992 S.L.T. 514 (held unreasonable in the circumstances for the company to be required to bear the outlays and remuneration of the provisional liquidator).

(a) Fees and expenses properly incurred in preserving, realising or getting in the assets. The costs of an unsuccessful action to set aside a security under s. 239 cannot be regarded as incurred in realising or getting in the company's assets.[68]

(b) Costs of the *petition*[69] including costs of those appearing on the petition whose costs are allowed by the court.[70]

(c) Remuneration of the special manager (if any).

(d) Costs and expenses of any person who makes the company's statement of affairs.

(e) Charges of a shorthand writer appointed to take an examination.

(f) Disbursements of the liquidator.

(g) Costs of any person properly employed by the liquidator.

(h) Remuneration of the liquidator.

(i) Expenses of the liquidation committee.

Where the company is a lessee rent accrued due after the winding-up order is an expense of the liquidation if the liquidator retained the lease solely for the benefit of the liquidation, and not for the joint benefit of himself and the lessors.[71]

The *preferential debts* rank equally among themselves and must be paid in full, after the expenses of winding up, unless the assets are insufficient to meet them, in which case the preferential debts abate in equal proportions: section 175(2)(a).

By section 386 and Schedule 6 the preferential debts include:

(a) Value added tax, excise duty on beer, lottery duty and air passenger duty which is referable to the period of six months next before the relevant date.[72-73] Car tax, general

---

[68] *Re M. C. Bacon Ltd* [1990] 3 W.L.R. 646, 652.

[69] See *Re Bostels* [1968] Ch. 346.

[70] In *Re Bathampton Properties Ltd* [1976] 1 W.L.R. 168 the company's costs were increased by its unsuccessful and unjustifiable opposition to the petition, and only its costs down to and including the first hearing, when it could have consented were paid out of the assets.

[71] *Re A.B.C. Coupler & Engineering Co. Ltd (No. 3)* [1970] 1 W.L.R. 702; and see *Re Owner Enterprises Ltd* [1974] 1 W.L.R. 1460, where an intermediate lessee paid the arrears of rent and was held entitled to the lessor's rights by way of subrogation; such rent does not however fall within the para. (a) but para. (f), see *Re Linda Marie* [1989] BCLC 46.

[72-73] See *Re Liverpool Commercial Vehicles Ltd* [1984] BCLC 587. Formerly the period was 12 months and also included rates.

betting and other gaming duties which have become due within 12 months next before the relevant date.

The expression "the relevant date" means, when the company is being wound up compulsorily, the date of the appointment of a provisional liquidator or, if no such appointment was made, the date of the winding-up order; if the company is or was being wound up voluntarily, it means the date of the passing of the resolution for winding up: section 387. If the winding up follows the discharge of an administration order the "relevant date" is the date of the making of that order. There are equivalent rules for voluntary arrangements, administration orders and receiverships: section 387.

(b)  Sums due from the company to the Inland Revenue as deduction from the employees' salaries under PAYE for the period of 12 months next before the relevant date. The former preference given to arrears of corporation tax was repealed by the Insolvency Act.
(c)  Remuneration owed to an employee in respect of services rendered to the company within four months next before the relevant date, not exceeding £800 per claimant.[74]

In England a full-time company secretary is probably an employee,[75] but in Scotland there may be more doubt.[76] A managing director[77] is not an employee nor is a director as such. However, a director may, under power in the articles, be employed in a salaried position with the company and so be an employee. Thus, where a director could be, and was, employed as editor of a periodical, he was a preferential creditor.[78]

A chemist engaged two days a week at a salary to work on formulae for perfumiers is an employee.[79] A contributor, even a

[74] These include other sums payable to employees by virtue of s. 121 of the Employment Protection (Consolidation) Act 1978 and various other statutory benefits: see Sched. 6, para. 13.
[75] Cairney v. Back [1906] 2 K.G. 746. The former wording was "clerk or servant".
[76] Scottish Poultry Journal Co. (1896) 4 S.L.T. 167 (O.H.) (secretary and manager); Clyde Football etc. Co. Ltd (1900) 8 S.L.T. 167 (O.H.); Laing v. Gowans (1902) 10 S.L.T. 461 (O.H.). Quaere whether these still apply to the changed wording.
[77] Re Newspaper Proprietary Syndicate Ltd [1900] 2 Ch. 349.
[78] Re Beeton & Co. Ltd (1913) 2 Ch. 279.
[79] Re G. H. Morison & Co. Ltd (1912) 106 L.T. 731.

regular contributor, to a newspaper, although paid by a fixed salary, is not.[80]

(d) National Insurance contributions due from the company as class 1 or 2 payments under the Social Security Act 1975, for 12 months next before the "relevant date," and certain class 4 contributions due to the Inland Revenue for the preceding tax year.

(e) Accrued holiday remuneration in respect of any period of employment before the relevant date payable to an employee whose employment has been terminated before, on, or after that date.

(f) Debts due under Schedule 4 of the Pension Schemes Act 1993.

(g) Debts in respect of levies on the production of coal and steel, or any surcharge for delay, as imposed under the European Coal and Steel Treaty.[81]

In England if a landlord or other person has distrained on the company's goods within three months next before a winding-up order, the preferential debts are a first charge on the goods or the proceeds of the distress. The landlord or other person, however, has the same priority as the persons paid out of the proceeds: section 176. This section applies to anyone who has seized goods and is holding them for the purpose of sale at the time of the winding-up order.[82]

The ordinary debts rank and abate equally *inter se*.[83]

It may be mentioned here that a sum of money paid into a company's bank account for behoof of the company's employees and which is at the date of the liquidation "clearly distinguishable and capable of being disentangled from the company's own funds" do not form part of the company's assets but must be paid to the employees.[84]

---

[80] See Note 76, above.

[81] See S.I. 1987, No. 2093.

[82] *Re Memco Engineering Ltd* [1986] Ch. 86. The position is different in a voluntary winding up: *Re Herbert Berry Associates Ltd* [1977] 1 W.L.R. 1437 (C.A.).

[83] *Per* Lord Selbourne in *Black & Co.'s case* (1872) L.R. 8 Ch. 254 at p. 262. There is, however, no objection to an agreement whereby a creditor agrees to subordinate his debt and such agreements are accordingly valid: *Re Maxwell Communications Corp. plc (No. 2)* 1994 1 All E.R. 737.

[84] *Smith v. Liquidator of James Birrell Ltd*, 1968 S.L.T. 174 (O.H.).

Where a company fails to implement an agreement to purchase its shares under section 162 of the Companies Act 1985[85] or to redeem its shares under section 159 of that Act,[86] and the company subsequently goes into liquidation the vendor/shareholder may enforce the agreement as a creditor. This will not apply if at any time between the date for purchase or redemption and the commencement of the winding up the company could not have fulfilled its obligation out of distributable profits: Companies Act 1985, section 178.[87]

## COMPLETION OF WINDING UP BY THE COURT

When the liquidator has collected the assets and received the proofs of the creditors, he proceeds to divide the assets among the creditors.

If there is any surplus after the costs of the liquidation and the company's debts have been paid, the court must adjust the rights of the contributories among themselves and distribute any surplus among the persons entitled thereto: section 154. The section requires a court order before the liquidator can distribute surplus assets, whether or not an adjustment has to be made among the contributories.[88] It will be remembered that under normal articles preference shareholders are entitled to priority over ordinary shareholders in the return of capital.[89] Persons not registered as members but in possession of share certificates as collectors or scriptophilists are not beneficially entitled to the shares to which the certificates relate and have been excluded from a distribution of surplus assets.[90]

If the liquidation is not completed within a year after its commencement, the liquidator must send to the Registrar of Companies, at such intervals as may be prescribed, a statement in the prescribed form and giving prescribed particulars as to the position of the liquidation: section 192.[91]

---

[85] *Ante,* Chap. 10.
[86] *ibid.*
[87] *Ante,* Chap. 10.
[88] *Re Phoenix Oil, etc., Co. Ltd (No. 2)* [1958] Ch. 565, where a list of contributories was dispensed with and the register of members was seven years out of date.
[89] *Ante,* Chap. 12.
[90] *In re Baku Consolidated Oilfields Ltd* [1993] BCC 653.
[91] See I.R. 1986, r. 4.223.

## Final meetings and release of the liquidator

The holding of final meetings of the company or its creditors as appropriate in the case of a voluntary winding up has been dealt with already,[92] together with the release of the liquidator consequential upon such a meeting.[93]

In a compulsory winding up the liquidator, other than the official receiver, if he is satisfied that the liquidation is for practical purposes complete, must call a final general meeting of the creditors. The liquidator will then make his report to that meeting which must then decide whether to release him. He may also give notice of any final distribution of the company's property at the same time. If he cannot do so the meeting must be adjourned until he can do so. The costs of the final meeting must be covered by the company's assets and so the liquidator must retain sufficient for this purpose; section 146. The release of a liquidator consequential on this meeting has been dealt with above.[94]

## Early dissolution of company in England

If the company is in compulsory liquidation and the official receiver, who is automatically the first liquidator,[95] discovers that the realisable assets of the company will be insufficient to cover even the expenses of the winding up he may apply to the Registrar of Companies for an early dissolution of the company. Before he can do this, however, he must be satisfied that the company's affairs do not require any further investigation and he must give 28 days' notice of his intention to the creditors, contributories and any administrative receiver. Once such a notice is given the official receiver's duties are at an end, although any creditor, contributory, administrative receiver or even the official receiver himself, may apply to the Secretary of State for directions within three months on the grounds either that the assets are sufficient to cover the expenses, the company's affairs do merit further investigation or that an early dissolution would be inappropriate: sections 202, 203.

[92] *Ante,* p. 766.
[93] *ibid.*
[94] *Ante,* p. 759.
[95] pp. 735, 738.

If no such application is made the company is automatically dissolved three months after the Registrar receives the application. If the Secretary of State does give directions, those would be that the winding up should proceed as if no notice of early dissolution had been given and he may defer the date of dissolution as he thinks fit. Notice of such directions must be given to the Registrar of Companies by the applicant within seven days. There is an appeal from the Secretary of State's decision to the court: sections 202, 203.

This procedure was adopted on the recommendation of the Cork Committee.[96] Up to one third of companies in compulsory liquidation are likely to be subject to these provisions.

## Early dissolution of company in Scotland

If after a meeting or meetings under section 138 (which deals with appointment of a liquidator in a compulsory winding up in Scotland) it appears to the liquidator that the realisable assets of the company are insufficient to cover the expenses of the winding up, he may apply to the court for an order that the company be dissolved, and the court then makes an order for early dissolution under section 204 if it appears to the court appropriate to do so.

Within 14 days from the date of the order, the liquidator must forward a copy of the order to the Registrar of Companies, who immediately registers it, and, at the end of the period of three months from the day of that registration, the company is dissolved.

The court may, however, on an application made to it by any person who appears to the court to have an interest, order that the date of dissolution be deferred for such period as the court thinks fit. If such an order for deferment is made, the person who applied for it must, within seven days of the making of the order, deliver a copy of it to the Registrar of Companies.

## Dissolution of company

In the case of a compulsory winding up where either the liquidator gives notice to the Registrar that the final meeting has been held and that he has vacated office,[97] or the official receiver

---

[96] Paras. 649–651.
[97] *Ante,* Chap. 27.

gives notice that the winding up is complete, the registration of that notice begins a period of three months at the end of which the company will be automatically dissolved unless on the application of an interested party the Secretary of State defers that date.[98] There is an appeal to the court from any such decision: section 205.

In a voluntary winding up the three months' period ending with the automatic dissolution of the company begins with the registration of the liquidator's final account and return under either section 94 or section 106.[99] Otherwise the procedure is the same as on a compulsory winding up: section 201.

Subject to any order which may at any time be made by the court under sections 651 or 652 of the Companies Act 1985, any property vested in or held on trust for a company immediately before its dissolution (excluding property held by the company on trust for any other person) vests in the Crown as *bona vacantia*: section 654 of the Companies Act 1985. The Crown may disclaim such property by a notice signed in the case of property in England by the Treasury Solicitor (and in the case of property in Scotland by the Queen's and Lord Treasurer's Remembrancer). The effect of such disclaimer is much the same as if the property had been disclaimed under section 178, *ante*.[1] The notice of disclaimer must be executed within 12 months after the vesting of the property came to the notice of the Crown representative or, where any person interested in the property applies in writing to the Crown representative requiring him to decide whether he will disclaim, usually within three months after the application. The notice of disclaimer must be delivered to the Registrar of Companies and registered by him, and copies must be published in the *Gazette* and sent to persons who have given the Crown representative notice of their interest in the property: sections 656, 657 of the Companies Act 1985.

Where a company has been dissolved the court may make an order declaring the dissolution void. Such an order may be made on the application of the liquidator or of any other person who appears to the court to be interested: section 651 of the Com-

---

[98] In Scotland there can be no application to the Secretary of State to defer the date of dissolution if the winding-up order was made by the court, but the court can itself defer the date.

[99] *Ante*, Chap. 28.

[1] Chap. 27. See also *Allied Dunbar Assurance plc v. Fowle*, 1994 BCC 422.

panies Act 1985.[2] A solicitor acting on behalf of a client with a claim against the dissolved company, and having neither a financial nor a proprietary interest, is not a "person . . . interested" within section 651.[3] A liquidator de son tort, *i.e.* a person who has never been a duly appointed liquidator of the company but who has, without lawful authority, been carrying on the liquidation of the company, is.[4] So is a contributory in the liquidation.[5] The Inland Revenue may apply where an assessment for taxes has been made but the assessments were under appeal when the company was struck off the register under section 652 of the Companies Act 1985, *post*.[6]

As a general rule, the application cannot be made more than two years after the date of the dissolution. This has caused some hardship, *e.g.* to employees who contract an industrial disease which becomes apparent in later years, and special provision has now been made for such cases. An application for the purpose of bringing proceedings against the company for damages for death, personal injuries or funeral expenses can now be made at any time. No order will be made if the limitation period for such action under the Limitation Act 1980 (or the Prescription and Limitation (Scotland) Act 1973) has already expired but the court has power to extend such limitation period by the period between the dissolution and the order declaring the dissolution void: section 651(5) and (6) of the Companies Act 1985. Application can be made in relation to dissolutions occurring before the enactment, *i.e.* before November 16, 1989, so long as the dissolution was not more than two years (or, in the case of subsection (5) applications, 20 years) before that date.

When a dissolution is declared void, any property of the company which vested in the Crown under section 654 of the Companies Act 1985 remains the Crown's property. Instead the company will receive a cash payment equivalent to those assets. This payment will be either the sum the Crown received or the value of any property which has since been disposed of by the Crown. This provision allows the Crown to dispose of such

---

[2] As amended by Companies Act 1989, s. 141 and Sched. 24.
[3] *Roehampton Swimming Pool Ltd* [1968] 1 W.L.R. 1693.
[4] *Re Wood and Martin (Bricklaying Contractors) Ltd* [1971] 1 W.L.R. 293.
[5] *Re Thompson and Riches Ltd* [1981] 2 All E.R. 477.
[6] *Re Belmont and Co. Ltd* [1952] Ch. 10; followed in *Re Test Holdings (Clifton) Ltd* [1970] Ch. 285. As may the Secretary of State in performance of his statutory duties: *Re Townreach Ltd (No. 002081 of 1994)* [1994] 3 W.L.R. 983.

property without fear of a revival of the company: section 655 of the Companies Act 1985. An office copy of the order declaring the dissolution void must be delivered to the Registrar of Companies with seven days: section 651 of the Companies Act 1985. Such an order does not validate proceedings taken on behalf of the company between the dissolution and its avoidance.[7] Thus it does not revive a misfeasance summons issued, but not served, before dissolution.[8]

It is incompetent for the court to declare the dissolution void for a limited purpose only.[9]

The court has an absolute discretion whether to declare a dissolution void and the petition may be opposed, *e.g.* by the Official Receiver, the Treasury Solicitor or a third party whose position would be directly affected thereby.[10] The delay between the dissolution and the petition is a factor the court will take into account.[11] It is sufficient ground for the exercise of his discretion that some liability of the company may otherwise remain unpaid.

The company was the original tenant under a lease which it had assigned prior to its dissolution. The lease ultimately became vested in B.C.C.I. which became insolvent. The landlord sought therefore to have the company's dissolution declared void to enable the company to meet its contractual liability for rent (probably by making a claim against its immediate assignee under an indemnity covenant). *Held,* the company should be restored to the register. *Re Forte's Manufacturing Ltd* [1994] BCC 84.[12]

The discretion is also exercised to enable a liquidator to distribute overlooked assets, *e.g.* money wrongly paid to the Inland Revenue.[13] It was not exercised where the application had nothing to do with unpaid or undistributed assets but was "an attempt to play ontological ducks and drakes with the law relating to legacies"[14]:

A testatrix by her will gave a share of her residuary estate to a company but the company was dissolved before she died. An order was

[7] *Morris v. Harris* [1927] A.C. 252.
[8] *Re Lewis and Smart Ltd* [1954] 1 W.L.R. 755.
[9] *Champdany Jute Co. Ltd, Petitioners,* 1924 S.C. 209 (for the purpose of receiving a repayment from the Inland Revenue).
[10] *Re Forte Manufacturing Ltd* [1994] BCC 84.
[11] *per* Slade J. in *Re Thompson and Riches Ltd* [1981] 2 All E.R. 477, 488.
[12] See also *Re Spottiswoode, Dixon and Hunting Ltd* [1912] 1 Ch. 410.
[13] *Champdany case, ante.* And to enable a liquidator to grant a title to property of the company sold since dissolution: *M'Call and Stephen Ltd, Petitioners* (1920) 57 S.L.R. 480.
[14] *per* Hoffmann, L.J. in *Re Forte Manufacturing Ltd, supra* at p. 87.

refused because the share of residue did not belong to the company before dissolution. The next of kin therefore took the lapsed share as on a partial intestacy: *Re Servers of the Blind League* [1960] 1 W.L.R. 564.

In very special circumstances the Court of Session in the exercise of its *nobile officium* may declare a dissolution void, although the application has not been made within the two years.[15]

## DEFUNCT COMPANIES

By section 652 of the Companies Act 1985, if the Registrar of Companies has reasonable cause to believe that a company is not carrying on business or is not in operation, he may, after carrying out a specified procedure, strike the company's name off the register, after which it is dissolved and sections 654 to 657, *ante*, apply.

The procedure under section 652 is:

(1) The Registrar sends to the company by post a letter asking whether the company is carrying on business.

(2) If no answer is received within one month, he sends within the next 14 days a registered letter, stating that if no reply is received within one month a notice will be published in the *Gazette* with a view to striking the company's name off the register.

(3) If no satisfactory reply is received he sends to the company by post and publishes in the *Gazette* a notice, stating that unless cause is shown to the contrary the company will be struck off after three months.

(4) If cause is not shown to the contrary, he strikes the company off and publishes notice thereof in the *Gazette*, whereupon the company is dissolved.

Striking the company's name off the register does not affect the liability of any director or member of the company, and the company may still be wound up by the court. If the company is to be wound up, it should first be restored to the register under section 653 of the Companies Act 1985.[16]

---

[15] *Collins Brothers and Co. Ltd, Petitioners*, 1916 S.C. 620. Contrast *Kerr (Lord Macdonald's Curator Bonis) and Another, Petitioners*, 1924 S.C. 163, and *Forth Shipbreaking Co. Ltd, Petitioners*, 1924 S.C. 489.

[16] *Re Cambridge Coffee Room Association Ltd* [1952] All E.R. 112. *Alliance Heritable Security Co. Ltd, Petitioners* (1886) 14 R. 34; *Beith Unionist Association Trustees, Petitioners*, 1950 S.C. 1.

Section 653 provides that if the company, or any member or creditor thereof, feels aggrieved by the striking off the register, it or he may within 20 years, apply[17] to the court which, if satisfied that it is just that the company be revived, may order that the name of the company be restored to the register. A petition for restoration under the section should contain an outline explanation of why the company was struck off.[18] Upon an office copy of the order being delivered to the Registrar the company is deemed to have continued in existence as if its name had not been struck off.[19] The court may, by the order, give directions for placing the company and all other persons in the same position as nearly as may be as if the company had not been struck off. This provision should be compared with section 651, *ante*, as to the persons who may apply for a court order. A contributory may apply under either section although the time limits are different; 20 years under section 653 and two years under section 651.[20] The word "creditor" in section 653 extends to a plaintiff claiming damages under the Fatal Accidents Acts 1846 to 1959 and having therefore an unquantified claim against the company.[21]

To qualify as a "member or creditor" within section 653 an applicant for restoration must have been a member or creditor of the company at the date when it was struck off the register. However, the personal representative of a deceased shareholder has been held entitled to apply for restoration of a company's name to the register, and then for its winding up, even though he is not registered as a shareholder.[22]

On an application for restoration to the register, the court may only restore or refuse to restore and cannot, *e.g.*, impose a

---

[17] By petition: R.S.C., O. 102, r. 5; R.C. 189.

[18] Practice Note (Companies Court) [1974] 1 W.L.R. 1459.

[19] Thus, where the company's interest in a lease had vested in the Crown as *bona vacantia* and, the Crown having disclaimed it, the surety's liability for future rent had terminated, the effect of restoring the company to the register was that none of these events were deemed to have occurred: *Allied Dunbar Assurance plc v. Fowle* [1994] BCC 422. *Re Thompson and Riches Ltd* [1981] 2 All E.R. 477.

[20] *Re Harvest Lane Motor Bodies Ltd* [1969] 1 Ch. 457. In *Percy v. Garwyn Ltd* 1991 G.W.D. (O.H.) 2–80 P's petition for restoration of a dissolved company was granted since P had demonstrated an interest in having the company restored, *i.e.* to enable him to pursue a claim of damages for injuries suffered while employed by the company.

[21] *Re New Timbiqui Gold Mines Ltd* [1961] Ch. 319; *Re Aga Estate Agencies* [1986] BCLC 346.

[22] *Re Bayswater Trading Co. Ltd* [1970] 1 W.L.R. 343.

penalty (beyond costs) as a condition of restoration.[23] It may, however, make the restoration conditional on the company's filing such statutory returns with the Registrar as are necessary to bring the company's file up to date.[24]

The restoration of the company to the register under section 653 validates retrospectively all acts done on behalf of the company between its dissolution and its restoration.[25] In one English case, where the petition was that of a contributory and there were assets available for the shareholders or creditors, as the case might be, the court directed that, as regards creditors whose debts were not statute-barred at the date of dissolution, the period between dissolution and restoration to the register was not to be counted for the purposes of any Statute of Limitations.[26] Where, *e.g.*, a creditor petitions and there is no indication that other creditors might be unfairly affected by an order not containing a special provision as to the limitation of actions, no such provision will be inserted in the order.[27] In so far as the property of the company has passed to the Crown under section 651, *ante*, the provisions of section 655 apply and the Crown may validly dispose of those assets paying a cash sum in lieu on the company's revival, *ante*.

Where the company is in breach of its statutory obligations and at least one applicant is guilty of some default, the normal order for taxation of costs under R.S.C., Order 62, rule 28, should be on a common fund basis (instead of the usual order on a party and party basis).[28]

---

[23] *Re Brown Bayley's Steel Works Ltd* (1905) 21 T.L.R. 374; *Re Moses and Cohen Ltd* [1957] 1 W.L.R. 1007.

[24] *Healy, Petitioner* (1903) 5 F. 644, followed in *Charles Dale Ltd, Petitioners,* 1927 S.C. 130.

[25] *Tymans Ltd v. Craven* [1952] 2 Q.B. 100 (C.A.), applied in *Re Boxco Ltd* [1970] Ch. 442 (Legal charge created by a company after being struck off. Order for restoration made. Company put in same position retrospectively as if charge duly created and registered).

[26] *Re Donald Kenyon Ltd* [1956] 1 W.L.R. 1397. *Aliter* where the company is already in liquidation: *Re Vickers and Bott Ltd* [1968] 2 All E.R. 264n.

[27] *Re Huntingdon Poultry Ltd* [1969] 1 W.L.R. 204, distinguished *Re Donald Kenyon, ante* and *Re Rugby Auto Electric Services Ltd, ante.*

[28] *Re Court Lodge Developments Co. Ltd* [1973] 1 W.L.R. 1097.

# Chapter 30

# MERGERS AND DIVISIONS

NEITHER of the words "merger" and "division" has any definite general legal meaning.[1] A division is where a company transfers its assets to one or more new companies with substantially the same shareholders. The latter case is also known as a reconstruction. A merger is the amalgamation of two or more companies into one. This occurs, *e.g.* where a company acquires the assets of, or the shares in, two or more companies whose shareholders are issued with the appropriate number of shares in the new company. In this chapter the formal procedures which are available to achieve such divisions and agreed mergers, *i.e.* where all the companies, but not necessarily all the shareholders and creditors, concerned are in agreement, are set out. The alternative, an often contested form of merger, is usually referred to as a "take-over", *i.e.* the acquisition of a controlling interest in the shares in one company by another company. Such take-overs are the subject of chapter 31, *post*.

Both a merger and division in the sense used in this chapter may be effected (1) under section 110 of the Insolvency Act 1986, or (2) under sections 425 to 427A of the Companies Act 1985.[2] The latter procedure becomes more complex in certain mergers and divisions involving public companies, as a result of the implementation of the third and sixth EU directives[3] by Schedule 15B.

A scheme of arrangement under section 425 can also be used for purposes other than mergers and divisions, *e.g.* to effect a composition with creditors or a variation of class rights.

---

[1] There is a definition for some mergers and divisions of public companies as the result of the implementation of two EU directives. See p. 815, *post*.

[2] For examples of amalgamation see *Head (Henry) & Co. Ltd v. Ropner Holdings Ltd* [1952] Ch. 124. *Government Stock etc. Investment Co. Ltd v. Christopher* [1956] 1 W.L.R. 237; *Rights and Issues Investment Trust Ltd v. Stylo Shoes Ltd* [1965] Ch. 250; and *Clydesdale Bank Ltd, Petitioners*, 1950 S.C. 30.

[3] Adopted on October 9, 1978 [1978] O.J. L295/36, and December 17, 1982 [1982] O.J. L378/47, respectively. See p. 815, *post*.

## Mergers or Divisions under Section 110 of the Insolvency Act 1986

Under section 110 a company (1) which is in voluntary winding up; (2) may transfer or sell the whole or part of its business or property to another company, whether a company within the meaning of the Act or not; and (3) may, in the case of a members' voluntary winding up, pass a special resolution authorising the liquidator to receive as consideration cash or shares, policies or other like interests in the transferee company for distribution among the members of the transferor company according to their rights and interests in that company. The sanction of the court is unnecessary in a members' voluntary winding up. In the case of a creditors' winding up the liquidator's authority for (3) must come either from the court, or from the liquidation committee.

The sale may be to a foreign company.[4] However, it must be to a company and not to a speculator who hopes to form a company to take over the assets.[5]

### Procedure

The following procedure might be adopted under section 110 if a members' voluntary winding up is involved. A meeting of the transferor company is summoned in order to pass resolutions for reconstruction or amalgamation. At the meeting, resolutions are passed for the voluntary winding up of the company, the appointment of a liquidator, and giving authority to the liquidator to enter into an agreement with the transferee company on the terms of a draft submitted to the meeting.

The agreement typically provides that the transferee company shall purchase the assets of the transferor company, except a sum retained by the liquidator to discharge its liabilities, that the consideration shall be the allotment by the transferee company to the liquidator or his nominees of shares, fully or partly paid up, in the transferee company, that the liquidator shall give notice to the shareholders of the transferor company of the number of shares to which they are entitled, and the time within which they

---

[4] *Re Irrigation Co. of France* (1871) L.R. 6 Ch.App. 176.
[5] *Bird v. Bird's Patent, etc., Sewage Co.* (1874) L.R. 9 Ch.App. 358.

must apply, and that failure to apply for shares within that time shall preclude their rights to any shares.

A reconstruction scheme provided that shareholders in the old company should apply for shares in the new company within 10 days after being given notice requiring them to apply, and that the liquidator should dispose of all shares not applied for. On June 12 the liquidator sent out notices requiring application for shares in the new company to be made before June 25. P., a shareholder in the old company, applied on August 24. *Held*, P. was not entitled to an allotment of shares in the new company, or to any other relief: *Postlethwaite* v. *Port Philip, etc., Gold Mining Co.* (1889) 43 Ch.D. 452.

In the case of a creditors' winding up the necessary authority would come either from the court or from the liquidation committee.[6]

Instead of the liquidator being authorised to dispose of all shares not applied for by the members of the transferor company, an underwriting agreement may be made in respect to such shares.[7] If the agreement is silent as to the disposal of the proceeds of sale of the shares not applied for, the proceeds must be distributed among the members of the transferor company who have not applied for shares in the transferee company.[8]

Shares may be given directly to the members of the transferor company instead of being applied for in the manner explained above.

### Protection of dissentient members

A sale or arrangement under section 110 of the Insolvency Act 1986 is binding on all members of the transferor company, whether they agree to it or not: section 110(5). However, a member who (1) did not vote in favour of the special resolution, and (2) expressed his dissent from it in writing addressed to the liquidator and left at the registered office within seven days after the passing of the resolution, may require the liquidator either to abstain from carrying the resolution into effect or to purchase his interest at a price to be determined by agreement or arbitration: section 111 of the Insolvency Act 1986. Subsection 111(3) below shows that the election is that of the liquidator.

A transferee of shares whose transfer was not registered when the special resolution was passed may be entitled to have the register of members rectified and to dissent from the resolution.[9]

[6] *Ante*, Chap. 28.
[7] *Barrow v. Paringo Mines (1909) Ltd* (1909) 2 Ch. 658.
[8] *Re Lake View Extended Gold Mine Co.* [1900] W.N. 44.
[9] *Re Sussex Brick Co.* [1904] 1 Ch. 598 (C.A.).

If the liquidator elects to purchase the member's interest, the purchase money must be paid before the transferor company is dissolved, and be raised by the liquidator as is determined by special resolution: section 111(3). The agreement usually provides for the retention by the liquidator out of the assets of the transferor company of a sum to cover the interests of the dissentient shareholders.

The articles cannot deprive a member of his statutory right to the value of his shareholding if he dissents.[10]

## Protection of dissentient creditors

The liquidator must pay the creditors of the transferor company in the usual way in a winding up. If, however, the creditors conceive that they will be prejudiced by the transfer of all the company's assets to the transferee company, they may petition for a compulsory winding-up order. Section 110(6) of the Insolvency Act 1986 provides that the special resolution for reconstruction shall not be valid if, within a year, an order is made for winding up the company by the court, unless the court sanctions the resolution.

## Sale under power in memorandum

The memorandum of association may give power to a company to sell its undertaking for shares in another company. If, however, the whole of the undertaking is to be sold and the proceeds are to be distributed among the shareholders, the procedure laid down in section 110 of the Insolvency Act 1986, including the provisions for the protection of dissentient shareholders and creditors, cannot be excluded.[11]

# SCHEME OF ARRANGEMENT UNDER SECTION 425 OF THE COMPANIES ACT 1985

## Scope of the section

The Insolvency Act contains provisions whereby the administrator or liquidator may make an arrangement with a company's

---

[10] *Payne v. The Cork Co. Ltd* [1900] 1 Ch. 308.
[11] *Bisgood v. Henderson's Transvaal Estates Ltd* [1908] 1 Ch. 743 (C.A.); *cf. Waverley Hydropathic Co. Ltd, Petitioners*, 1948 S.C. 59.

creditors.[12] Those are not suitable for mergers or divisions, however. But under section 425 of the Companies Act 1985 a company can also enter into a compromise or arrangement with its creditors, and also its members, or any class thereof, without going into liquidation. Schemes of arrangement under section 425 have a wider potential than voluntary arrangements under the Insolvency Act and can be used for an agreed merger or division of two or more companies subject to the requirements of the section as to consent of the members and the court.

The proper way to distribute the assets of a company otherwise than strictly in accordance with creditors' rights has been held to be by a scheme of arrangement under section 425 which binds all creditors, and not by an agreement or compromise under section 167 of the Insolvency Act which would deprive non-assenting creditors of the court's protection and prevent them from expressing their views.[13]

Although this chapter is concerned primarily with mergers and divisions, schemes of arrangement can be used for many other purposes and therefore the following discussion involves all aspects of the procedure.

**Statutory requirements**

Section 425 provides that a compromise or arrangement will be binding on the company and the creditors or class of creditors or the members or class of members, as the case may be, if:

(1) The court, on the application in a summary way of the company or of any creditor or member of the company (or, if the company is being wound up, of the liquidator), orders a meeting of the creditors[14] or class of creditors, or of the members or class of members, to be summoned.

---

[12] ss.1–7 and 167. *Ante* Chap. 24.
[13] *Re Trix Ltd* [1970] 1 W.L.R. 1421. Voluntary arrangements under ss. 1–7 are, however, available for this.
[14] Creditors who cannot possibly benefit, *e.g.* because the company's assets are too low, need not be involved in the scheme: *Re British & Commonwealth Holdings plc (No. 3)* [1992] BCC 58; *Re Maxwell Communications Corp. plc* [1994] 1 BCLC 1.

(2) The compromise or arrangement is agreed to by a majority in number representing three-fourths in value[15] of
those present and voting either in person or by proxy at
the meeting.

(3) It is sanctioned by the court.

If the scheme involves the merger or division of one of more
public companies additional requirements are imposed.[16]

To effect a merger or division under this section, the scheme,
involving a transfer of one company's assets to another in return
for shares in that company, must therefore be approved by at
least 75 per cent of the members and creditors of the transferor
company, and by the court. The benefit is that, if the scheme is
approved, dissenting shareholders and creditors are bound by it.[17]
This is not possible under section 110 of the Insolvency Act, *ante*.

The word "company" in sections 425 and 426[18] means any
company liable to be wound up under the Act: section 425(6).
Thus it includes a company formed and registered under the 1985
Act, an existing company (in effect, a company formed and
registered under a previous Companies Act), or an unregistered
company.[19]

## Compromise or arrangement

The word "arrangement" has a very wide meaning, and is
wider than the word "compromise".[20] An arrangement may
involve debenture holders giving an extension of time for payment, accepting a cash payment less than the face value of their
debentures,[21] giving up their security in whole or in part,
exchanging their debentures for shares in the company[22] or in a
new company[23] or having the rights attached to their debentures

---

[15] In the case of creditors the value of their debt is the relevant criterion; see, *e.g.*
*Re Exchange Securities and Commodities Ltd* (1987) 3 BCC 48.

[16] See p. 815, *post*.

[17] s.425(2). For an example of the effect of such approval see *Barclays Bank plc v.
British & Commonwealth Holdings plc* [1995] BCC 19.

[18] *Post*.

[19] s. 220, I.A. 1986.

[20] *Re Guardian Assce. Co.* [1917] 1 Ch. 431 (C.A.).

[21] *e.g. The Philadelphia Securities Co. v. The Realisation etc. Corpn. of Scotland
Ltd* (1903) 11 S.L.T. 217 (O.H.).

[22] *e.g. Gillies v. Dawson* (1893) 20 R. 1119 (O.H.).

[23] *Re Empire Mining Co.* (1890) 44 Ch.D. 402.

varied in some other respect[24]; creditors may take cash in part payment of their claims and the balance in shares or debentures in the company; preference shareholders may give up their rights to arrears of dividends,[25] agree to accept a reduced rate of dividend in the future, or have their class rights otherwise varied[26] (the use of section 425 to vary class rights has already been dealt with[27]). Or the members of a company in liquidation may agree with the company to seek or not to oppose a stay of the winding up, whereunder the members will give up their existing right to have all the proceeds of the company's assets distributed among them and instead be remitted to their contractual rights under the articles.[28] It even includes a scheme whereby the shareholders transfer their shares to another company, since that affects the contractual arrangements between the shareholders and their company so that there is an arrangement between them.[29]

Section 425 itself provides that the expression "arrangement" includes a reorganisation of the share capital of the company by the consolidation of shares of different classes or by the division of shares into shares of different classes. The word "compromise" implies some element of accommodation on each side. It is not apt to describe a total surrender. Similarly, the word "arrangement" implies some element of give and take.[30]

Where an arrangement under section 425 is essentially a scheme for the purchase by an outsider of all the issued shares of a company the scheme will not be sanctioned unless that company consents. Such consent may be expressed by the members in general meeting or by the board of directors.[31] It cannot be used therefore for a contested take-over or merger. Even if the take-over or merger is an agreed one the court will not allow the provisions of section 428 to 430F, which require the outside

[24] e.g. *Wright & Greig Ltd, Petitioners* 1911 1 S.L.T. 353.
[25] e.g. *Balmenach-Glenlivet Distillery Ltd, Petitioners*, 1916 S.C. 639.
[26] *City etc., Trust Corporation Ltd, Petitioners*, 1951 S.C. 570
[27] *Ante*, p. 242.
[28] Per Megarry J. in *Re Calgary and Edmonton Land Co. Ltd* [1975] 1 W.L.R. 355 at p. 363.
[29] *Re N.F.U. Development Trust* [1972] 1 W.L.R. 1548.
[30] *Re Savoy Hotel Ltd* [1961] 3 All E.R. 646.
[31] But not all such cases will fail, see *Re National Bank Ltd* [1966] 1 W.L.R. 819; *The Singer Manufacturing Co. Ltd v. Robinow*, 1971 S.C. 11 (scheme to enable parent company to acquire remaining 7·3 per cent shareholding in subsidiary held competent).

purchaser to acquire 90 per cent of the shares before he may compulsorily acquire the remainder,[32] to be circumvented by the use of section 425 where the necessary resolution under section 425 can only be passed with the assistance of votes of the wholly-owned subsidiary of the offeror company.[33]

## Sanction by the court

It is the responsibility of the petitioners to see that the class meetings are properly constituted, and if they fail the court has no jurisdiction to sanction the arrangement.[34] In addition to the usual differentiations between classes of shareholders and creditors under the general law,[35] the court will be concerned that the class meetings called by the company are correctly defined. Thus the interests of a wholly-owned subsidiary of a company which is taking shares in another company under a scheme of arrangement, when that subsidiary holds shares in that other company, are different from those of the other ordinary shareholders in the other company. In such a case the subsidiary was held to be in a different class from the other ordinary shareholders and separate meetings had to be held to approve the scheme.[36] Separate class meetings are required whenever the parties are not all on an equal footing, e.g. where some creditors are secured and others unsecured.[37] It does not matter that there is only one member of the class.[38]

As to (1) ante, where a meeting of creditors or members is summoned under section 425, with every notice of the meeting there must be sent a statement explaining the effect of the compromise or arrangement and, in particular, stating any material interests of the directors in any capacity and the effect thereon of the compromise or arrangement in so far as it is different from the effect on the like interest of other persons. If the meeting is summoned by advertisement, a similar statement, or a notification of the place where such a statement may be obtained, must

[32] Re Savoy Hotels Ltd, supra.
[33] Re Hellenic & General Trust Ltd [1976] 1 W.L.R. 123.
[34] ibid.
[35] Ante, Chap. 29.
[36] See note 33, above.
[37] La Lainière de Roubaix v. Glen Glove etc. Co. Ltd, 1926 S.C. 91; cf. Re Heron International N.V. [1994] 1 BCLC 667.
[38] Re RMCA Reinsurance Ltd [1994] BCC 378.

be included. Where the compromise or arrangement affects the rights of debenture holders the statement must give the like explanation as respects the trustees of a deed for securing the issue of debentures as it is required to give as respects the directors: section 426.

Section 426 must be faithfully complied with; the court "has no discretionary power to dispense with the procedural requirements of section [426]."[39] Thus a scheme will not be sanctioned if the explanatory statement, while stating that the company's assets have been revalued, does not give the amount of the revaluation,[40] or if a copy of the petition[41] or a copy of the scheme[42] has been sent without any further explanation.[43] Material interests of directors must always be stated, even although those interests are in no way differently affected by the scheme from the interests of other persons.[44]

Where there is a change in the material interests of the directors or of any other material circumstances between the issue of the statement and the meetings to consider the scheme the court will nevertheless sanction the scheme, even though the meetings are not informed of the change, if it is satisfied that no reasonable shareholder would have altered his decision as to the scheme had he known of the changes.[45] The test is whether all material changes of circumstances which have come to the attention of the board between the issuing of the circular and the meeting have been disclosed to those entitled to vote at the meeting. A material change for this purpose is one which would be likely to affect a reasonable shareholder's voting intentions.[46]

As to (2) *ante*, "three-fourths in value of the members or class of members" in section 425 refers to the size of the stake which each member has in the company. "The purpose is to prevent a numerical majority with a small stake outvoting a minority with a

---

[39] *Per* Lord Guthrie in *The Scottish Eastern etc. Trust Ltd, Petitioners*, 1996 S.L.T. 285 at p. 288.
[40] *Re Dorman, Long & Co. Ltd* [1934] Ch. 635.
[41] *Rankin & Blackmore Ltd, Petitioners*, 1950 S.C. 218.
[42] *Peter Scott & Co. Ltd, Petitioners*, 1950 S.C. 507.
[43] The fact that some creditors have more background information than others is not fatal, however: *Re Heron International NV* [1994] 1 BCLC 667.
[44] *Coltness Iron Co. Ltd, Petitioners*, 1951 S.C. 476; contrast *Second Scottish Investment Trust etc., Petitioners*, 1962 S.L.T. 392.
[45] *Re Jessel Trust Ltd* [1985] BCLC 119; *Re Minster Assets plc* [1985] BCLC 200.
[46] *Re MB Group plc* (1989) 5 BCC 584.

large stake, *e.g.* to prevent 51 members with one share each
outvoting 49 members with 10 shares each."[47]

Any proper form of proxy may be used and it is not necessary
to its validity that it should be sent to the company's offices
before the meeting.[48] Directors who, pursuant to the court's
order, receive proxies must use them whether they are for or
against the scheme.[49]

As to (3) *ante*, before giving its sanction to a scheme of
arrangement the court will see "First, that the provisions of the
statute have been complied with. Secondly, that the class was
fairly represented by those who attended the meeting and that
the statutory majority are acting bona fide and are not coercing
the minority in order to promote interests adverse to those of the
class whom they purport to represent; and, thirdly, that the
arrangement is such as a man of business would reasonably
approve."[50]

An order sanctioning a compromise or arrangement under
section 425 has no effect until an office copy has been delivered
to the Registrar of Companies. A copy of the order must also be
annexed to every copy of the memorandum issued after the
making of the order: section 425(3).

The costs of the scheme may be borne by the company and
there may be one set of costs for opposing creditors but not for
any supporting creditors. In general, costs should be kept to a
minimum and one set of creditors should not be ordered to pay
the costs of another set of creditors.[51]

## Facilitating a division or a merger

In order to facilitate schemes of reconstruction and amalgamation, section 427 provides that when an application is made to the
court under section 425 for the sanctioning of a compromise or

[47] *per* Brightman J. in *Re N.F.U. Development Trust Ltd* [1972] 1 W.L.R. 1548 at
p. 1553.
[48] *Re Dorman, Long & Co. Ltd* [1934] Ch. 635; *La Lainière de Roubaix v. Glen
Glove etc. Co. Ltd*, 1926 S.C. 91.
[49] See note 44, above.
[50] *per* Astbury J. in *Re Anglo-Continental Supply Co. Ltd* [1922] 2 Ch. 723 at p.
736. See to the same effect *per* Lindley L.J. in *Re Alabama, etc. Rlwy. Co.*
[1891] 1 Ch. 213 (C.A.) at p. 238. For adoption in Scotland, see *per* Lord
President Dunedin in *Shandon Hydropathic Co. Ltd, Petitioners*, 1911 S.C.
1153 at p. 1155.
[51] *Re Esal (Commodities) Ltd* [1985] BCLC 450.

arrangement, where the compromise or arrangement is for the purposes of a scheme for the division of a company or the merger of two or more companies and the scheme involves the transfer of the whole or part of the undertaking or property of a company (called "a transferor company") to another company (called "the transferee company"), the court may make an order providing for the following matters:

(1)  The transfer to the transferee company of the whole or part of the undertaking and of the property or liabilities of a transferor company. An order so made cannot operate to transfer to the transferee company the benefit of a personal contract such as a contract of service between the transferor company and a person employed by it.[52] Further, a scheme under section 425, or an order under section 427 for giving effect to such a scheme, cannot transfer the office of executor from one bank to another; such an office of personal trust is incapable of assignment.[53]

(2)  The allotting by the transferee company of any shares, debentures, policies or other similar interests in such company to the appropriate persons.

(3)  The continuation by or against the transferee company of any legal proceedings pending by or against a transferor company.

(4)  The dissolution, without winding up, of a transferor company.

(5)  The provision to be made for persons who dissent from the scheme.

(6)  Any incidental matters.

An office copy of an order made under section 427 must be registered with the Registrar of Companies within seven days.

The word "company" in section 427 means a company within the meaning of the Act. Thus it means a company formed and registered under the Act or an existing company, in effect a company formed and registered under a previous Companies Act: section 735.[54]

---

[52] *Nokes v. Doncaster Amalgamated Collieries Ltd* [1940] A.C. 1014.
[53] *In the Estate of Skinner (Decd.)* [1958] 1 W.L.R. 1043.
[54] *cf.* s. 425(6), *ante.*

## Mergers and divisions of public companies—additional requirements

Following the implementation of the third and sixth EU directives on company law[55] by the Companies (Mergers and Divisions) Regulations 1987,[56] additional requirements to those already required by sections 425 to 427 are imposed where the scheme of arrangement falls within one of the following three categories as defined in section 427A.

### Case 1—Mergers by acquisition

Where a public company proposes to transfer all of its undertaking, property and liabilities to another public company (which has not been formed for that purpose) in return for shares in the transferee company to be held by the transferor shareholders.

### Case 2— Mergers by formation of a new company

Where two or more public companies propose to transfer all their undertakings, etc. to any type of company formed for that purpose, members of the transferor company receiving shares in the new company by way of total or part consideration.

Note that case 1 does not apply where the transferee company is specially formed to receive the assets, etc. of the transferor and that case 2 applies where the transferee company is a private company provided it was set up for the purpose of the merger.

### Case 3—Divisions

Where a public company proposes to divide all its undertaking, etc. between two or more companies which are either public companies or companies formed for the purpose of the division, members of the transferor company receiving shares in the transferee companies by way of total or part consideration.

In all these cases there is therefore an agreed arrangement involving a share exchange by the transferee company's share-

---

[55] Dir. 78/885 [1978] O.J. L295/36 and Dir. 82/891, [1982] O.J. L378/47.
[56] S.I. 1987 No. 1991.

holders. It is envisaged that the transferor company or companies will be dissolved after the scheme has gone through.[57]

Where section 427A applies the court cannot sanction a scheme unless the additional requirements specified in Schedule 15B have been complied with. These are somewhat complex since there are eight additional requirements for specified mergers and divisions with a further two for divisions alone, whilst at the same time there are seven different exemptions from some or all of these additional requirements. As a final complication, in three of these exemptions additional exemptions from parts of sections 425 and 426 are also included.

The following is a summary of the additional requirements and exemptions:

*The additional requirements*

(i)     In a case 1 or case 3 scheme there must be a meeting of each class of members of any transferee company not formed for the purpose of the merger or division. Section 425 already requires a meeting of the transferor company.

(ii)    The directors of all transferor and transferee companies[58] must draw up draft terms of the merger or division. These must include details of the companies involved, the share exchange ratio, the allotment of the new shares, the directors' benefits, and, in a division, the allocation of the shares.

(iii)   The draft terms must be delivered to the registrar who will publish a notice of receipt in the Gazette. This gives official notification of that receipt.[59]

(iv)    There must be at least one month's gap between such publication and the holding of any meeting[60] to consider the scheme.

(v)     The directors[61] must draw up a report consisting of the explanatory statement already required by section 426[62] together with the legal and economic grounds for the

---

[57] The new requirements do not apply if the transferor company is already in liquidation and so do not apply to reconstructions under section 110 of the Insolvency Act 1986, *ante*.

[58] Except those formed specifically for the purpose of the scheme.

[59] *Ante*, p. 64.

[60] Including one under s.425.

[61] Of all the companies.

[62] *Ante*, p. 813.

draft terms including the share exchange ratio, and in a division, the allocation arrangements.

(vi)   An expert's report must be drawn up for each transferor and transferee[63] company involved, dealing in particular with the share exchange ratio and any valuation problems. A statement as to the reasonableness of these must be included.

(vii)  The draft terms, directors' report, experts' report and the previous three years' accounts must be available for inspection for at least one month prior to any meeting required under section 425 or (i) above.

(viii) The memorandum and articles of any transferee company set up for the purpose of the scheme must be approved by an ordinary resolution of each transferor company involved.

(ix)   In a division the directors of the transferor company must report any material changes between the time when draft terms were adopted and any meeting, to that meeting and to the directors of the transferee company.

(x)    Following receipt of a report under (ix) the transferee directors must notify the change to any meetings of the transferee companies or send a notice to every member entitled to attend such meetings.

*Exceptions to the additional requirements*

(a)   The requirement to hold a meeting of the transferee company may be dispensed with if five per cent. of the transferee members could have required such a meeting and no such meeting has been requested, provided requirement (vii) has been complied with.

(b)   There need be no directors' or experts' reports in a case 3 scheme if all the relevant shareholders agree.

(c)   The court may decide that no meetings at all need be held (including ones held under section 425) in a case 3 scheme.

(d)   In a case 1 scheme where the transferor is wholly owned by the transferee company, the draft terms of the merger can omit all references to share exchange ratios etc., the

---

[63] Except those formed specifically for the purpose of the scheme.

directors' and experts' reports can be omitted and no explanatory circular under section 426 need be given.

(e)   Where exemption (d) applies the court may order that no meetings of either company be held, even under section 425.

(f)   In a division, where the transferor is wholly-owned by the transferee companies the court may dispense with the need for a meeting of the transferor company under section 425.

(g)   In a case 1 scheme, where the transferor is an 80 per cent. or more but not wholly owned subsidiary of the transferee company the court may dispense with a meeting of the transferee company.

## Chapter 31

## TAKE-OVERS

MOST mergers or take-overs, take place without a scheme of
arrangement under section 425 or a reconstruction under section
110 of the Insolvency Act 1986, but by the simple method of one
company acquiring a majority or the whole of the shares of
another company from its shareholders. In such a case it is usual
for the acquiring company (the offeror company) to make an
offer (called a take-over bid) to the shareholders in the other
company (the target or offeree company) to purchase their shares
at a stated price and to fix a time within which the offer is to be
accepted, with a condition that if a named percentage of the
shareholders do not accept the offer, the offer is to be void. The
offer is usually at a higher price than the current market price of
the shares as quoted on the Stock Exchange and it may be in cash
(*e.g.* £2 per share) or in kind (*e.g.* two of the offeror company's
shares for each of the target company's shares). There are many
economic reasons why such an offer is made. Sometimes more
than one take-over bid is made for the same company so that
there are rival bidders. As has already been seen[1] this form of
merger is the only practical form where the two companies do not
agree to the merger although it can also be used for agreed
mergers by way of an agreed bid.

### Statutory provisions

There is little in the Companies Act of specific relevance to
such take-overs. Section 428–430F are an exception to this in that
they allow an offeror who has received 90 per cent or more
acceptances to purchase the remaining shares compulsorily.
Those sections are considered in detail at the end of this chapter.
Other parts of the Act which are relevant include: the restrictions
on a company acquiring its own shares[2]; the restrictions on

[1] *Ante,* p. 812.
[2] See p. 184, *ante.*

companies giving financial assistance for the acquisition of their shares[3]; the rules on merger accounting relating to the share premium account[4]; and disclosure of interests by directors[5]. Aspects of the Financial Services Act also apply[6]. The public controls of mergers to avoid monopoly situations arising, which is outside the scope of this book, are contained in legislation both domestic and from the European Union. The most important controls on the conduct of take-overs are those set out in the City Code on Take-overs and Mergers and administered by the City Panel. This is a "voluntary" self-regulatory code to which all who deal in shares in public companies are subject. The City Code is dealt with below.

## Other relevant legal provisions

Various common law and equitable rules also play a part in the legal regulation of take-overs. The directors of both the offeror and target companies will continue to owe fiduciary duties to their companies.[7] The impact of these duties in a take-over situation has arisen where the target directors have entered into an agreement with an offeror company whereby they agree to recommend the bid to their shareholders but subsequently decide that a better offer has been made by another offeror and they recommend that bid instead.

In *Dawson International plc v. Coats Patons plc*,[8] the directors sought to excuse their breach of contract by claiming that to adhere to it would breach their fiduciary duty to their shareholders to act in their best interests. That proposition was rejected by the Scottish courts on the basis that their duties were owed to the company and not to the shareholders as sellers of their shares. The two were not necessarily the same. If the directors took it upon themselves to give advice to current shareholders they have a duty not to mislead and to give good advice but that is not a pre-existing duty which prevents them from entering into such an agreement. In a subsequent hearing[9]

---

[3] See p. 196, *ante*.
[4] See p. 164, *ante*.
[5] See p. 319, *ante*.
[6] See Chap. 19, *ante*.
[7] See Chap. 15, *ante*.
[8] (1989) 5 BCC 405.
[9] [1991] BCC 276.

the Court decided that there was no such agreement partly
because their statements had been made subject to the City Code
and thus could not amount to a legal agreement.

In England, the impact of the directors' fiduciary duties on
agreements by directors has been considered generally. Initially it
was held that if they broke such agreements because not to do so
would be contrary to their duties to the company at the time of
breach (e.g. because of subsequent events) then they would have
a defence[10], but in *Fulham Football Club Ltd v. Cabra Estates
plc*[11] the Court of Appeal decided that the test should be whether
at the time of the agreement the directors were acting bona fide
for the benefit of the company. If they were then the agreement
would be binding on them even if they now considered that to
implement it would be contrary to the company's interests.

The ordinary law of contract also applies to take-overs and
there have been occasions where parties have resorted to the law
of tort. Thus in *Lonrho plc v. Fayed*[12] claims were made involving
the torts of conspiracy and wrongful interference with trade,
alleging that false information was given by one potential offeror
to the Secretary of State causing him not to refer that offer to the
Monopolies and Mergers Commission which prejudiced the
chances of a rival offeror. Similarly, in *Lonrho plc v. Tebbit*[13] the
Secretary of State was held to owe a potential duty of care to that
second offeror in deciding whether or not to release them from a
monopolies' restriction.

## CITY CODE ON TAKE-OVERS AND MERGERS

The latest edition of the City Code was published in July 1993.
Unlike the early editions, this edition is in loose leaf form and
can be regularly amended.[14] It is administered by the City Panel
which was instituted by the Bank of England and contains
representatives of all the major City institutions, so that anyone
in breach of its provisions is liable to fall foul of his own
professional organisation and may suffer penalties in consequence. In particular the Stock Exchange is represented, and

---

[10] *John Crowther Group plc v. Carpets International plc* [1990] BCLC 460;
*Rackam v. Peek Foods Ltd* [1990] BCLC 895.
[11] [1992] BCLC 863.
[12] [1991] BCLC 779 (H.L.).
[13] [1993] BCLC 96.
[14] The first release to the July 1993 edition was issued in November 1993.

withdrawal of a licence to deal on the Exchange is a potent threat against those dealing in shares on a take-over. The City Panel is an autonomous body which also administers the Rules governing Substantial Acquisitions of Shares. Those Rules, dealt with below,[15] relate to the build-up of shares prior to a bid. The Panel also has a full-time executive, under a full time Director General, which is available for advice at any time during the course of the bid, not as to the merits of the offer but as to procedure and conduct.

## Administration of the Code

The Panel and the executive have the joint responsibility for the administration of the Code. In *R. v. Panel on Take-overs and Mergers, ex parte Guinness plc* Watkins L.J. expressed the function of the executive as follows[16]:

> "It is the executive which takes the lead in examining the circumstances of take-over bids and, if thought necessary, referring them to the Panel for consideration and adjudication according to the rules. Almost daily it is called upon to give advice and rulings, which mostly are accepted. . . . It acts as a sort of fire brigade to extinguish quickly the flames of unacceptable and unfair practice."[17]

If the executive or either of the parties considers that the matter is serious enough it will be referred to the Panel for a full hearing. This is a quasi-judicial affair and at the end the Panel may give a definitive ruling imposing either disciplinary sanctions or a course of action which the parties must adhere to.

There is only an automatic right of appeal from a decision of the Panel if disciplinary action is taken[18] or the dispute is as to the Panel's jurisdiction. In other cases there is only a right of appeal with the Panel's consent. Any appeal lies to the Appeals Committee with a former judge as chairman. That Committee will only interfere if it concludes that the Panel was wrong or, where the Panel's exercise of a discretion is being challenged, if either that power has been wrongly exercised or the Panel has misdirected itself.[19]

---

[15] p. 828.
[16] (1988) 4 BCC 325 (D.C.).
[17] See *e.g.* Panel statement on *British Coal Pension Funds/Globe Investment Trust plc* [1991] J.B.L. 67.
[18] Including a ruling as to exempt market status, *post*, p. 838.
[19] Appeal statement on *BAT Industries plc* [1990] J.B.L. 67.

## The City Panel and the Law

In 1987 a Canadian-based company, Datafin, became the first
party to challenge a Panel decision in the courts by way of an
application for judicial review. In the Court of Appeal it was
established that the Panel was subject to the process of judicial
review.[20] Lord Donaldson M.R., however, stressed that an application for judicial review should not be used as a ploy to hinder a
bid and that in general the Panel's decisions would remain
binding until otherwise directed. He considered that a challenge
could be made against the Panel acting as legislator if it made a
rule contrary to its own terms of reference; as interpreter of the
Code; and as a disciplinary body, but in that case the internal
appeals procedure should be used first.

The dispute in *Datafin* was as to the Panel's interpretation of a
particular rule. The Court of Appeal rejected the application on
the basis that a challenge would have to show that the Panel's
view was so far removed from the natural and ordinary meaning
of the words that no ordinary user of the market could reasonably be misled. In the case of an exercise of the Panel's discretion
the Court would only interfere in a totally inequitable case.

A second challenge to the Panel by way of judicial review was
mounted by Guinness plc on the basis of a breach of natural justice
in the Panel's proceedings. This too failed, the Court finding that
although the Panel had been inconsiderate and harsh there was no
procedural impropriety and no breach of the rules of natural
justice.[21] The Court of Appeal accepted again, however, that
judicial review could apply and Lord Donaldson M.R. suggested
the test as being whether something had gone wrong of a nature
and degree which required the intervention of the court.

The third challenge mounted against the Panel by way of
judicial review concerned a Panel executive's ruling that there
had been a breach of the Code and a proposed hearing of the
Panel to investigate this. This was challenged by the Fayed
brothers on two grounds. First, that the ruling would be prejudicial to civil litigation then in progress relating to the same matter,
and second that the hearing would rely on the report of DTI

[20] *R. v. Panel on Take-overs and Mergers, ex parte Datafin* [1987] Q.B. 815
(C.A.).
[21] *R. v. Panel on Take-overs and Mergers, ex parte Guinness plc* [1990] Q.B. 147
(C.A.).

inspectors which was hearsay evidence. This challenge was rejected by the Court of Appeal[22]. There was no general risk of prejudice to the civil litigation and the judge in that trial would not be unduly influenced by any decision of the Panel. Further, the Panel would be aware that the evidence before them was hearsay and take that factor into account.

That decision also raises the issue as to how the Code is viewed in legal proceedings in which it is raised.

In *Dunford & Elliott Ltd v. Johnson & Firth Brown Ltd*[23] one party to a bid sought an injunction to prevent the abuse of alleged confidential information in a take-over situation. Both Lord Denning M.R. and Roskill L.J. quoted the Code and used it as a guide to good commercial practice in an area where the court had a discretion. Again in *Re St. Piran Ltd*[24] the Court said that when considering whether to wind up a company on the just and equitable ground[25] the fact that the directors of a public company chose to flout the City Code or to ignore, without good reason, the consequent directions of the City Panel so that the minority shareholders were hurt by a withdrawal of the company's Stock Exchange quotation,[26] would be strong evidence in favour of granting the petition.

In *R v. Spens*[27] the question arose in a criminal trial as to whether the Code was a document which should be left to the jury to consider or quasi-legislation which was a matter for the judge to interpret for the benefit of the jury. The Court of Appeal had no doubt:

"As to the present case, our view is that the code sufficiently resembles legislation as to be likewise regarded as demanding construction of its provisions by a judge. Moreover, the code is a form of consensual agreement between the affected parties with penal consequences."

Further, as we have seen,[28] the court has held that statements made during the course of a bid did not amount to a binding legal agreement because they were made in the context of the oper-

[22] *R. v. Panel on Take-overs and Mergers, ex p. Fayed* [1992] BCLC 938.
[23] [1977] 1 Lloyd's Rep. 505 (C.A.).
[24] [1981] 3 All E.R. 270.
[25] *Ante*, p. 409.
[26] This effectively prevents the shares being sold.
[27] [1991] BCC 140.
[28] p. 821, *ante*.

ation of the Code to that bid.[29] On the other hand where a shareholder agreed to accept an offer unless a higher offer was announced by midnight on a certain date, the provisions of the Code were used to determine whether such an announcement had been so made.[29a]

In earlier times, however, the Court awarded injunctions preventing the Panel from issuing statements,[30] and the Panel had, on one occasion, a battle of words with the Department of Trade and Industry following an inspectors' report under section 432.[31]

## Scope of the code

The Code is applicable to all mergers and take-over transactions involving public companies and not just listed companies[32] and applies to all those involved whether as directors, advisers, offerors, offerees or in any other capacity. However, it only applies where a merger or take-over bid is concerned.[33] The Panel does not see itself as being concerned with the merits of a bid but as an instrument of investor protection.

The Code itself is divided into General Principles and Rules. The following is a summary of some of the more important parts of the Code. The references in this chapter to Panel decisions and statements are to *The Journal of Business Law* which monitors the Panel on a regular basis.

## General principles

There are 10 general principles concerned with the provision of adequate and timely information to the shareholders so that all are to be treated equally, and with the general responsibilities of the boards of directors of both the offeror and the offeree companies. The introduction to the general principles emphasises that the spirit as well as the precise wording of the Code must be

---

[29] *Dawson International plc.v. Coats Patons plc* [1991] BCC 276.
[29a] *Hasbro U.K. Ltd v. Harris* [1994] BCC 839.
[30] Panel statement on *Sandstar Ltd v. Graff Diamonds Ltd* [1979] J.B.L. 274.
[31] Panel statement of May 14, 1979 [1979] J.B.L. 364.
[32] Panel statement on *Chez Nico Restaurants Ltd* [1991] J.B.L. 352.
[33] Panel statement on *N.F.U. Development Trust* [1976] J.B.L. 162; *cf.* Panel statement on *Chaddesley Investments Ltd* [1979] J.B.L. 271. The Code does not apply to offers for non-voting non-equity capital.

observed. This enables the Panel to find that there has been a breach of the Code even though no specific provision was involved.[34]

The boards of both companies are required to act in the best interests of their respective shareholders. The offeree board should seek competent independent advice on receiving an offer and must not do anything to frustrate the offer without the general meeting's approval. In particular, rights of control must be exercised in good faith—minority oppression is "wholly unacceptable" (G.P.s. 1, 7 and 8).[35]

General Principle 3 provides that no offer should be announced unless the offeror has every reason to believe that it can, and will continue to be able to, implement the offer. This responsibility also applies to the offeror's financial advisers.[36]

General Principle 4 requires that the shareholders be put in possession of all the facts necessary for an informed judgment as to the merits of an offer and must have sufficient time to make an assessment and decision. No relevant information is to be withheld from them. No false market in shares is to be created—this can cause problems in relation to the disclosure of information about preliminary negotiations.[37] Rumour and speculation can drastically affect the quoted share price of a company (G.P. 6). The Panel have indicated that a false market usually involves an element of contrivance but it may also be caused by any step which results in a market price which is manifestly unrealistic.[38]

General Principle 9 relates to the responsibilities of the directors of the companies involved, in effect reminding them of their fiduciary duties to their company and warning them against entering into binding commitments which could restrict their freedom to advise shareholders.[39]

---

[34] Panel statement on *Mount Charlotte Investments v. Gale Lister & Co. Ltd* [1974] J.B.L. 310.

[35] Thus the offeree must not take any action to frustrate a bid or to prevent their shareholders considering it on its merits without shareholder consent. This includes taking legal action. See, *e.g.* Appeal Committee Statement on *BAT Industries plc* [1990] J.B.L.67.

[36] Panel statement on *Luirc Corp/Merlin International Properties Ltd* [1992] J.B.L. 105.

[37] Panel statement on *Rockwell International Corporation v. Wilmot Breedon (Holdings) Ltd* [1979] J.B.L. 387. Dealings in derivatives linked to the offeree company's shares must be approved in advance by the Panel: Statement on *Swiss Bank Corporation/Trafalgar House plc/Northern Electric plc*, March 3, 1995.

[38] Panel statement on *Gateway plc* 1990 J.B.L. 72.

[39] See p. 820. *ante.*

TAKE-OVERS

## The Rules

There are 38 rules currently in the Code. However, many of these are subdivided and are further amplified by notes.

### (1) *The approach, announcements and independent advice (Rules 1–3)*

An offer should be made first to the board of the offeree company or its advisers. The identify of the offeror if it is not the person making the bid should be disclosed at the outset and the offeree board is entitled to be satisfied that the offeror company will be in a position to implement its offer (either in cash or by shares) in full. The offeree board must circulate the independent advice it receives, usually from a merchant bank, to its share-holders. This independent advice must come from outside any financial conglomerate involved in the bid.

When a firm intention to make an offer is notified from a serious source a press notice must be issued immediately followed by a circular to the shareholders. More difficult is the announce-ment of approaches which may or may not lead to an offer. Too early an announcement may kill the offer, too late and the market will have reacted in advance with all the possibilities of insider dealing by those with insider information.[40] Accordingly, an announcement, together with a temporary halt in dealings on the Stock Exchange, is normally expected either when negotia-tions have reached a point at which a company is reasonably confident that an offer will be made for its shares or when negotiations are about to be extended to embrace more than a small group of people. The responsibility is on the offeree company to make the announcement.[41] However, the Code requires a statement from the potential offeror company where, prior to an approach, the offeree company is the subject of rumours and speculations or an untoward price movement, and there are reasonable grounds for concluding that it is the poten-tial offeror's actions which have led to the situation.[42] An

---

[40] *Ante*, Chap. 19.
[41] See Panel statement on *Dickinson Robinson Group Ltd/Royal Sovereign Group Ltd* [1978] J.B.L. 66; *Teachers (Distillers) Ltd/Allied Breweries Ltd* [1978] J.B.L. 67; and *Balfour Ltd/Aurora Holdings Ltd* [1979] J.B.L. 366.
[42] Panel statement on *Argyll Group plc/Distillers Group plc* [1986] J.B.L. 233.

announcement that a block of shares carrying over 30 per cent of the voting rights or that the board is seeking offers for the company will be treated as an announcement of a possible offer for the purposes of the Code. Offerors will usually be bound by so-called denial statements, *i.e.* that no bid is intended. Such statements must be clear and unambiguous.[43]

The formal announcement of an intention to make an offer must include any conditions to which the offer is subject including the conditions as to acceptance levels, the ability to achieve a quotation for the new shares and the authority to issue those new shares[44] if a share for share offer is being made. Thus where a requirement as to the giving of a proxy vote was included in the offer documents but not in the original announcement the former were held to be void.[45] If a formal offer is not forthcoming within 28 days after the announcement the offeror must be prepared to justify this to the Panel.[46] If necessary the Panel will take steps to enforce completion of the offer, *e.g.* by freezing the voting rights of shares already obtained.[47]

## (2) *Dealings and restrictions on the acquisition of shares and rights over shares (Rules 4–8)*

Rule 4 provides that no person, other than the offeror, may deal in the offeree company's shares if he is privy to confidential price-sensitive information[48] relating to the offer, between the time when there is reason to suppose that an approach or offer is contemplated and the public announcement. Nor should such persons make any recommendations to any other person as to dealing in the relevant securities. Together with Rule 2 relating to the announcement of a prospective offer, this provision is an attempt to inhibit insider trading by preventing both the leakage of information and dealings by the "informed". Despite this, prior to the criminalisation of insider dealing, a pattern emerged.

---

[43] Panel statement on *Storehouse plc* [1989] J.B.L. 518.
[44] See *ante* p. 147.
[45] Panel statement on *Bassishaw Investments Ltd/UDS Group plc* [1982] J.B.L. 329.
[46] Panel statement on *Combined English Stores Ltd/David Grieg Ltd* [1974] J.B.L. 312.
[47] Panel statements on *St. Martins Property Ltd/Hays Wharf Ltd* [1974] J.B.L. 312; *B.S.Q. Securities Ltd/Court Hotels (London) Ltd* [1976] J.B.L. 162.
[48] As defined by the Code. See also the Panel statement on *Johnson & Firth Brown Ltd/Dunsford & Elliott Ltd* [1977] J.B.L. 161.

There was a substantial price movement in the market price of shares in a company the reason for which became apparent when a take-over bid involving the company was subsequently announced. Subsequent investigations rarely brought to light any dealings by actual "insiders".[49]

If the offeror, potential offeror, or anyone acting in concert[50] with him purchases shares at above the offer price, then that price must be increased to the highest price, excluding stamp duty and commission, so paid. If 15 per cent or more of the shares of a class are acquired for cash, the offer must include a cash alternative, being the highest price paid for such shares. A cash alternative may also be required if the offeror cannot fulfil the paper offer.[51] When a revised offer is announced it should "whenever practicable" disclose the number of securities purchased and the price paid. Purchases by a financial adviser for discretionary clients must be cleared by the Panel unless he is an exempt fund manager (see below).

Voting rights are defined in the City Code as all voting rights attributable to the share capital of a company currently exercisable at a general meeting. This will include preference shareholders whose shares have acquired temporary voting rights through their dividends being in arrears during the entire course of an offer. It is not clear how this will operate if the preference shareholders lose their votes during the course of a bid.

Rule 8 requires dealings by parties to the offer and their associates either for themselves or for discretionary or non-discretionary clients, to be disclosed daily. This applies to dealings whereby an associate indemnifies a third party who has acquired relevant shares against any loss on the resale of those shares.[52] Such disclosure must now reveal the true identity of the person dealing, and in the case of an associate why such disclosure was necessary. Disclosure of dealings must also be made by a holder of one per cent of the shares in either

---

[49] See the Panel statements on *United Drapery Stores Ltd/William Timpson Ltd* [1973] J.B.L. 37; Panel statement on *G.K.N. Ltd/Miles Drew & Co. Ltd* [1974] J.B.L. 309; Panel statement on *Boots Co. Ltd* and *House of Fraser Ltd* [1975] J.B.L. 43; *cf.* the Panel decision on *P. R. Grimshawe & Co. Ltd, Grimshawe-Windsor Merger* [1973] J.B.L. 46 and *D. R. Lyons Co. Ltd* [1973] J.B.L. 451.

[50] As defined in the Code. See Panel statements on *United Newspapers plc/Fleet Holidays plc* [1986] J.B.L. 230 and *Chiltern Radio plc* [1995] J.B.L. 87.

[51] To avoid the problems such as those raised in the Panel statement on *St. Martins Property Ltd/Hays Wharf Ltd* [1974] J.B.L. 312.

[52] Panel statement on *Turner and Newall plc/AE plc* [1987] J.B.L. 140.

company. Further, any type of inducement to deal or refrain from dealing or for any connected person to bear any investment risk[53] must be disclosed if a party to the bid is involved. Disclosure is also required by intermediaries and they must warn their clients if dealings exceed £25,000 in any one account period.

In 1981 Rules governing Substantial Acquisitions of Shares were published.[54] These were originally framed for "dawn raids" of the type experienced in 1980 and apply to acquisitions giving a holding of between 15 and 30 per cent. The Rules, which are dealt with below, basically provide a seven day freeze on all offers to acquire more than a 15 per cent but less than a 30 per cent holding.

At the same time the City Code was amended by what is now Rule 5. Anyone who owns 30 per cent of the voting rights of a company may not increase his holding above 30 per cent prior to the first closing day[55] of an offer. Anyone who owns 30 per cent already, but less than 50 per cent, may not acquire more than two per cent prior to that time. There are four exceptions: acquisitions which immediately precede and are conditional on the announcement of an agreed bid; acquisitions from a single shareholder; where the offer has been recommended by the offeree board or declared unconditional; and where it is by way of acceptance of an offer. In one case the Panel has excused a breach of Rule 5 where the breach was due to inaccurate professional advice.[56]

Following the ending of single capacity on the Stock Exchange a new Rule 38 has been added to deal with the problems of multi-service financial organisations: see below.[57]

## (3) *The mandatory offer and its terms (Rule 9)*

Since January 1972 the Code has contained rules which require a compulsory bid to be made by a purchaser of shares who has amassed a significant holding of the shares without making a

---

[53] Following the Guinness plc revelations. See [1989] J.B.L. 520.
[54] These were revised in 1985 and 1988. See *post*, p. 840.
[55] The time limits in these Rules relate to midnight on the day in question and not to 3.00 p. m. as had been previously thought. Panel statement on *Arthur Bell & Sons plc/Gleneagles Hotels plc* [1984] J.B.L. 421.
[56] Panel statement on *Glanfield Lawrence plc/Gregory Securities Ltd* [1985] J.B.L. 47.
[57] p. 838.

formal offer. This has presented problems of enforcement, particularly in times of economic depression, and the present position, set out in Rule 9, is that anyone who, together with persons acting in concert,[58] has acquired 30 per cent or more of the voting rights by a series of transactions or who, owning between 30 and 50 per cent of such rights acquires one per cent of such voting rights within a period of a year, shall make an offer. The rule is activated by a relevant purchase by any one member of a group who have previously "come together" to obtain control of a company. The obligation extends to each of the principal members of a consortium if the facts so warrant. The Panel has drawn a distinction between a group acting to obtain control of a company (a "wide concert party") and those dealing with a community of interest in the purchase of a dealing profit. The latter, known as a "fan club," do not fall within this Rule but it may well be difficult to distinguish between them.[59]

The requirement to make a mandatory offer can extend to a situation whereby as the result of a successful offer, the offeror company has effected a change of control in another company owned in part by the target company. This is known as the "chain principle." It has been held not to apply to a joint venture company where the target company's holding in that company was deadlocked.[59a]

If the implementation of such an offer would require a resolution, then no purchases which would give rise to the offer shall be made.[60] The offer must be in cash of at least the highest price paid by the offeror in the previous year or have a cash alternative. The offer must be conditional on acceptances carrying 50 per cent of the voting rights and, if it does not become conditional, then no further shares may be purchased.[61]

---

[58] See *e.g.* Panel statement on *St. Martins Property Ltd/Hays Wharf Ltd* [1974] J.B.L. 312; *Ashbourne Investments Ltd* [1975] J.B.L. 44; *St. Piran Ltd (No. 1)* [1980] J.B.L. 270; *St. Piran Ltd (No. 2)* [1980] J.B.L. 358 and the preceding section of this chapter; *cf.* Panel statement on *Inoco plc/Petranol plc* [1986] J.B.L. 409.

[59] Panel statement on *Glanfield Lawrence plc/Bajou Ltd* [1985] J.B.L. 47.

[59a] Panel statement on the *British Land Company plc/Stanhope Properties plc*, March 7, 1995.

[60] Panel statement on *Manx & Overseas Investments Ltd* [1978] J.B.L. 184. See also Panel statement on *Rothmans International Ltd* [1981] J.B.L. 373.

[61] See [1980] J.B.L. 270; J.B.L. 358; Panel statement on *Westminster Property Group plc* [1983] J.B.L. 358; Panel statements on *Westminster Property Group plc* [1983] J.B.L. 491, and [1983] J.B.L. 492; and Panel statement on *Gilgate Holdings Ltd* [1980] J.B.L. 269.

## (4) *The voluntary offer and its terms (Rules 10–13)*

No offer which, if accepted in full, would result in the offeror having voting control can be declared unconditional unless acceptances are received or promised amounting to a total of 50 per cent of the voting rights of the equity share capital.[62] If 10 per cent or more of the shares of any class under offer are purchased by the offeror during the offer period or within 12 months prior to its commencement a cash alternative must be included in the offer of at least the highest price paid for those shares during that period, excluding stamp duty and commission, unless the Panel agrees to the contrary.[63] Failure to make such a cash alternative will make the offeror liable to compensate those who have suffered as a result.[64] Further if there is a possibility of a reference to the Monopolies and Mergers Commission or the European Commission then the offer must be subject to withdrawal on such a reference. Where there is a delay in deciding whether such a reference is to be made, the Panel has decided that the time limits for the bid[65] are suspended until after the decision not to make a reference has been announced.[66]

## (5) *Provisions applicable to all offers (Rules 14–18)*

Rule 14 requires comparable offers where there is more than one class of share capital involved[67] and Rule 15 states the appropriate offer for convertible securities etc. Rule 16 prohibits an offeror from entering into arrangements to make purchases of shares in the offeree company if such arrangements have attached thereto favourable conditions which are not extended to all shareholders. The Panel does, however, allow an exception if the payments can be justified commercially.[68]

---

[62] As to what can be counted as acceptances see [1986] J.B.L. 317 and [1990] J.B.L. 71. For difficulties in the counting process see Panel statement on *Blue Circle Industries plc/Britoil Qualcast plc* [1988] J.B.L. 323, and [1989] J.B.L. 69.

[63] See *e.g.* Panel statements on *Hillsdown Holdings plc/S & W Beresford plc* [1986] J.B.L. 407; and *International Marine Systems Ltd/Benjamin Priest Group plc* [1991] J.B.L. 351.

[64] Panel statement on *Guinness plc/Distillers Company plc* [1989] J.B.L. 520.

[65] Rules 30–34, *post.*

[66] See [1992] J.B.L. 314.

[67] See Panel statement on their usual practice in *Stead & Simpson plc* [1990] J.B.L. 72.

[68] Panel statement on *Mooloya Investments Ltd/Customagic Manufacturing Co. Ltd* [1979] J.B.L. 49.

Rule 17 is concerned with the announcement or failure to announce acceptance levels at critical times during the offer period.[69]

## (6) *Conduct during the offer (Rules 19–22)*

Rule 19 relates to the quality of and responsibility for information issued during the course of an offer, together with its distribution. In addition to the imposing of a standard of care equivalent to that required in preparing a prospectus (see Chap. 7, *ante*), it prohibits statements which whilst not factually inaccurate may mislead shareholders and the market or may create uncertainty.[69a] In particular, an offeror should not make a statement to the effect that it may improve its offer without committing itself to doing so and specifying the improvement.[70] Following an increase in newspaper advertisements made in connection with take-overs and the nature of the material used, Rule 19 restricts such advertisements to nine specific types, seven of which require Panel clearance in advance.[71] Special attention is paid to organised telephone campaigns,[72] including cold-calling, and media interviews and debates.

Copies of all documents must be sent at the time of release to the press to the Panel and the advisers to all the other parties involved in the offer, even outside office hours.[73] Statements made whilst an offer is being referred to the Monopolies and Mergers Commission or the European Commission must be capable of being substantiated if the offer is subsequently revived.

Rule 20 applies to the equality of the supply of the information subject to Rule 19. In particular all competing offerors are entitled to receive information given to one, favoured offeror, at least where there has been a public announcement of that

---

[69] For an interesting example of the crucial importance of such announcements see the Panel statement on *Burton Group plc/Debenhams plc* [1985] J.B.L. 231.

[69a] See, *e.g.* Panel statement on *Enterprise Oil plc/LASMO plc* [1995] J.B.L. 86.

[70] See [1984] J.B.L. 422.

[71] See Panel statements on *Imperial Group Ltd* [1986] J.B.L. 315 and on advertisements [1986] J.B.L. 318. See also Panel statement on graphs and diagrams [1985] J.B.L. 476.

[72] Following the Panel statements on *B.P.C.C. plc/John Waddingtons plc* [1983] J.B.L. 491.

[73] Panel statement on *European Leisure plc/Midsummer Leisure plc* [1991] J.B.L. 66.

offeror's existence. A less welcome offeror is required to specify the questions to which it requires answers.

Rule 21 provides that in the case of an actual or imminent offer, the offeree board must not, without approval of the members, issue shares or grant options or sell or otherwise dispose of material assets except under a pre-existing obligation.[74]

### (7) Documents from the offeror and the offeree board (Rules 23–27)

The rules elaborate General Principal 5 that all documents, etc. falling within these headings must be treated with the same standard of care as if they were prospectuses.[75] Amongst the minimum content of the information to be disclosed must be the social and employment consequences of the projected take-over, including the offeror's intention with regard to the continuance of the business. Rule 24 sets out the required contents of offer documents in some detail.

Rule 25 sets out the contents of the target company's response. In particular it requires that documents sent to shareholders of the offeree company recommending acceptance or rejection of offers must contain particulars of all service contracts over 12 months of any director or proposed director with the offeree company or any of its subsidiaries. Further, any amendment to such contract within six months of the date of the document must be stated; if there are no such amendments that should be stated. Rule 26 concerns the availability of documents for inspection and Rule 27 concerns the need to inform shareholders of material changes to the published information during a bid.

### (8) Profit forecasts (Rule 28)

This rule, together with its note occupies seven pages of the Code, which reflects the many problems encountered by the Panel in the area. Despite the hazard of forecasting, profit forecasts must be compiled with "care and objectivity" by the directors and checked on that basis by their financial advisers. It

---

[74] See, e.g. Panel statements on W. Henshall & Sons (Addlestone) Ltd/Bovbourne Ltd [1979] J.B.L. 46; Burton Group plc/Debenhams plc [1985] J.B.L. 231; IMI plc./Birmingham Mint Group plc [1991] J.B.L. 178.
[75] Panel statement on York Trust Ltd/Greenword and Batley Ltd [1978] J.B.L. 68.

is now mandatory to include in a forecast: taxation, extraordinary items and minority interests where these are expected to be significant. The Rule also defines a profit forecast for its own purposes.[76]

In one statement the Panel condemned the publication by an offeror of a profit forecast produced by the offeree company and sent to the offeror in confidence. This was based on the facts that the Panel did not feel it right to require the offeree to publish the forecast, that publication here was in breach of confidence and that what was made public was the profit forecast of another company on which the offeror was not in a position to obtain the reports acquired by the Code.[77]

### (9) *Asset valuations (Rule 29)*

This rule requires valuations to be supported by a named independent valuer (as defined) and lays down criteria for the valuer. It applies wherever a valuation is given "in connection with an offer" although this will not normally include the usual estimates for accounting purposes. The basis of valuation must be stated; in general this is to be open market value and there are special rules for land with development value.[78]

### (10) *Timing and revision (Rules 30–34)*

Rule 30 relates to the timing of the offer document and the offeree circular, 28 days from an announcement in the first case and 14 days from the offer document in the second. Rule 31 is concerned with the timing of the offer, specification of further closing dates and the well established rule that an offer must remain open for 14 days after being declared unconditional as to acceptances. No offer may be declared so unconditional after midnight on the 60th day after the posting of the offer based on acceptance up to 1.00 p.m. on that day.[79] The effect of this is to

---

[76] See Panel statements on *Guinness Peat/The Distillers Company* [1986] J.B.L. 316; *TI Group plc/Dowty Group plc* [1992] J.B.L. 599.

[77] Panel statement on *Yule Catto & Co. plc/Donald Macpherson Group plc* [1984] J.B.L. 425.

[78] The Panel cannot, however, prevent genuine disputes, *e.g.* as to property valuations: Panel statements on *BS Group plc/Scott's Restaurant plc* [1991] J.B.L. 350.

[79] See Panel statement on *Burton Group plc/Debenhams plc* [1986] J.B.L. 231.

limit any changes in an offer to the first 46 days since all revised offers must be kept open for 14 days. This includes the making of a "no increase" statement by the offeror.[80] Since no offer may be open for more than 60 days all such amendments are restricted to the first 46 days, including any purchase of shares which would trigger a mandatory bid under rule 9 since that would amount to a revised offer. This has caused many problems, in particular where there are competing offers still extant at the end of the 46 day period and an auction situation has in effect arisen.[81] The Panel may vary these time limits in exceptional cases.[82] Rule 34 gives the acceptor of an offer the right to withdraw his acceptance within 21 days of the first closing date of the offer unless it has then become unconditional.

## (11) *Restrictions following offers (Rule 35)*

Rule 35 provides that where an offer has not become unconditional in all respects the offeror (and persons acting in concert) may not within 12 months from the offer's withdrawal or lapse make a further offer or purchase shares if the offeror either falls within the mandatory bid rules or, if it holds 49 per cent but less than 50 per cent of the offeree shares. There are exceptions to this rule, *e.g.* where the subsequent offer is an agreed offer, or the original offer was referred to the Monopolies and Mergers Commission or the European Commission[83] and the Panel has a general power of dispensation.[84] The rule will be applied, however, even if there has been no formal offer but the target company has been subjected to a state of siege by a threatened offer.[85] If the offeror holds over 50 per cent of the offeree shares it cannot purchase shares at above the offer price for six months. Nor may it conclude special deals with favourable conditions during that period.

---

[80] Panel statement on *Siebe Gorman/Telecamit* [1984] J.B.L. 159.

[81] Panel statement on *Allianz Verischerungs A.G./Bat Industries plc/Eagle Star Holdings plc* [1984] J.B.L. 158.

[82] Panel statements on *Woolworth Holdings plc/Dixons plc; Emess Lighting plc/ Rotaflex plc* [1986] J.B.L. 410; and *Service Corporation International plc/Great Southern Group plc* [1995] J.B.L. 89; [1995] J.B.L. 90.

[83] Panel statement on *GC & C Brands/Irish Distillers Group plc* [1989] J.B.L. 150.

[84] Panel statement on *Severn Trent plc/Caird Group plc* [1991] J.B.L. 177.

[85] Panel statement on *Storehouse plc* [1989] J.B.L. 518.

## (12) *Partial offers (Rule 36)*

The Panel's consent is required for a partial offer. There are complex provisions governing these offers, *e.g.* an offer for 30 per cent or more requires 50 per cent approval.

## (13) *Redemption or purchase by a company of its own voting shares (Rule 37)*

Following the provisions of the Companies Act allowing companies to purchase their own shares the Code is concerned with the position whereby a shareholder will, as a result of such a purchase or redemption, come to hold shares which carry more than 30 per cent or more of the voting rights of that company, or to have increased the percentage of his holding by more than two per cent in the relevant 12 months period if he already holds 30 per cent or more. Rule 37 states that such a shareholder will not be obliged to make a mandatory bid if he only votes in favour of a resolution authorising the board to exercise the powers of purchase or redemption. However, when the board actually exercises the power, the Panel will examine the relationship between the board and the shareholder concerned.

## (14) *Dealings by connected exempt market makers (Rule 38)*

*Multi-service financial organisations—acting in concert.* With the repeal of the existing single capacity on the Stock Exchange, *i.e.* the separation of jobbers, brokers and corporate advisers, etc., it is now perfectly allowable for one financial organisation to perform all those functions, *i.e.* it can act as a market-maker, broker, investment adviser and corporate finance adviser. This has clear implications for the City Code since the same organisation may be acting as adviser to the offeror (or offeree), making investment decisions for its discretionary clients, providing information as brokers to other clients and making a market in the offeree company's shares. Opportunities to influence an offer clearly abound—for example, an adviser to an offeror may acquire offeree shares as a market maker, deal in those shares for it discretionary clients and influence others to deal.

*Market-making and other dealings as a principal.* The basic rule is that where one arm of a multi-service financial organisation is advising an offeror, any dealings by that organisation as principal (*i.e.* not as agent for its clients) in the offeree's securities will be presumed to be acting in concert with the offeror. This will affect the price to be paid, the mandatory bid rule and the possible obligation to make a cash offer, etc.

However, there is an exception to this presumption in the case of market-making only (and not for other dealings as principal) if the market maker arm of the organisation achieves the status of an *exempt market maker, i.e.* one which is recognised as such by the Panel who must be satisfied that an effective "Chinese Wall" system operates within the whole organisation, in particular separating the market making division from the corporate finance division.

Exempt market makers will, however, be subject to Rule 38 of the Code. Rule 38.1 provides that if they are connected with an offeror or offeree company they must not carry out any dealings with the purpose of assisting the offeror or offeree, as appropriate. An exempt market maker will be so connected if it is controlled by, controls or is under the same control as, the offeror, offeree, or any bank, broker, financial or other professional adviser to the offeree or offeror company. The sanction for a breach of this rule will be loss of exempt status—which may amount to exclusion from the market in practical terms.[86]

Rules 38.2 to 4 provide three restrictions on dealings with an exempt market maker where it is connected with the offeror or offeree.[87] These are: (i) a ban on dealings by the connected offeror (or concert parties) with the market maker during the offer period; (ii) a ban on assents of shares owned by the market maker to the offeror until the offeror has become or been declared unconditional as to acceptances; and (iii) the exempt market maker must not vote with shares in the connected offeror or offeree in the context of a take-over or possible take-over. Liability under (i) is on the offeror, under (ii) and (iii) on the market maker.

Finally rule 38.5 requires disclosure by the exempt market maker of dealings in relevant shares where there is a connected offeree or offeror company by noon on the next business day. This must include details as to amount, price, the nature of the connection and, if appropriate, the relevant overseas location.

---

[86] Panel statement on *Raine Industries plc/Tarmac plc* [1989] J.B.L. 67.
[87] See Panel statement on *Peachey Property Corporation plc/Estates Property Investment Co. plc* [1988] J.B.L. 325.

There is no presumption of acting in concert between fund managers and connected offerors before the involvement of the corporate finance arm has become public (although that situation may of course exist in fact). However, such fund managers may now apply for exemption from certain Code consequences which would otherwise follow once the connection with the offeror/offeree is public knowledge. Exemption is achieved by application to the Panel, the criteria being the existence of a "Chinese Wall" as with exempt market-makers. Rule 7.2 provides that the presumption is that a fund manager will be acting in concert with a connected offeror or offeree unless he is an exempt fund manager, thus bringing into play the consideration, mandatory bid and partial offer rules. No such presumption will apply to an exempt fund manager.

Where the exempt fund manager is associated with a party to a take-over it will not have to disclose its dealings in the relevant securities except privately to the Panel. One exception to this will arise where the associate status arises because the fund manager holds five per cent or more of the issued equity capital of an offeror or offeree company (*i.e.* under paragraph (6) of the definition of an associate in the Code).

## RULES GOVERNING SUBSTANTIAL ACQUISITIONS OF SHARES

The City Code on Take-overs only operates in a take-over situation and this effectively commences either on an offer being made or a 30 per cent holding of shares being amassed by one person or consortium.[88] In 1980, however, there was a series of "dawn raids" on the Stock Exchange whereby one person would acquire, in a matter of minutes, less than 30 per cent of the shares of a public company but nevertheless a significant amount. Such practices were considered undesirable for two reasons. First, the identity of the acquirer would often be disguised, *e.g.* by several linked companies each acquiring five per cent of the shares on behalf of an unnamed person, and, second, it was obvious that only a few shareholders benefited from being able to dispose of their shares on a "dawn raid" at above market value. This opportunity was not available to the other shareholders.

The first problem was countered by pressure on the Government which led to the rules on share disclosures by shareholders

---

[88] Rule 9, *ante.*

or groups owning originally five per cent, now three per cent, or more of the shares of a public company introduced by the 1981 Act.[89] The second problem, that of equal opportunity, was to be the subject of another self-regulatory code, the Rules Governing the Substantial Acquisition of Shares.[90] The City Panel[91] is responsible for administering this Code.

The Rules apply to acquisitions of listed shares in United Kingdom companies[92] within seven days amounting to 10 per cent or more of the voting rights in any one company and which take the purchaser's holding to 15 per cent or more of that company's voting rights but less than 30 per cent, at which stage the City Code will come into operation.[93] Purchase by two or more persons acting together by agreement or understanding are regarded as purchases by a single purchaser, including those held on a discretionary basis by a non-exempt fund manager (for the purposes of the City Code).[94] There are exceptions for purchasers from a single shareholder[95] if that is the only one in a seven day period and purchased in advance of an agreed bid.

Any acquisition caught by the Rules must now either follow the strict rules for partial bids set out in the City Code on Take-overs[96] or be acquired by means of a tender offer.[97] Under this procedure the buyer makes a firm offer to buy a specified number of shares for cash only either at a fixed price or up to a maximum price. Shareholders then offer their shares by tender, in the latter case at any price up to the maximum specified. Shareholders are bound by their tenders and the purchaser and his associates must not deal in the shares during the tender period of at least seven days. Tenders are to be advertised in two national newspapers and sent to the company and the Stock Exchange.

The effect of these rules is to check advances in shareholdings between 10 per cent and 30 per cent

---

[89] *Ante,* p. 222.
[90] Introduced on December 11, 1980; the latest version dates from July 1993.
[91] *Ante,* p. 823.
[92] Thus not to all public companies.
[93] Rule 9, *ante.*
[94] See, *e.g.* Panel statement on the *Norton Group plc* [1991] J.B.L. 352.
[95] See, *e.g.* Panel statement on *Timpson plc/Automagic Holdings plc* [1991] J.B.L. 65.
[96] Rule 36.
[97] See Panel statement on *Norton Opax plc* [1989] J.B.L. 148.

## Power to Acquire Shares of Shareholders not Accepting Take-Over Offer Accepted by Majority

Sections 428 to 430F of the Companies Act 1985 were substituted by section 172 and Schedule 12 to the Financial Services Act 1986. That Act repealed the original sections 428 to 430 which had consolidated the 1948 Act provisions. All these sections have had the effect of tidying up after a successful take-over offer, so that if an offeror has achieved a 90 per cent acceptance he may compulsorily acquire the remaining shares, or, alternatively, the minority may require such an offeror to buy them out.

### Scope of sections 428 to 430F

Before the powers conferred by these sections can be used there must be a take-over offer made by an offeror to acquire all the shares (or for all of a class of shares) of a company on the same terms,[98] except for those shares already owned by the offeror[99] at the date of the offer: section 428(1). The offer must be for all the shares (or class of shares) allotted on the date of the offer but it may also include shares allotted subsequently to the offer before a date specified by or determined in accordance with the offer: section 428(2). Where shareholders are invited to offer their shares to a person, that person is not making a take-over offer for the purposes of the sections and so cannot invoke the powers conferred by them.[1]

Any revised offer is not a new offer for the purpose of the timetable laid down in the sections provided that the original offer made provision for such a revised offer. If it did not, each revision counts as a fresh offer and the acceptance cannot be added together to achieve the 90 per cent threshold[2]: section 428(6).

The sections apply not only to an offeror but also to his associates, *i.e.* his nominees, members of the same group of

---

[98] A variation is allowed if it is necessary to comply with any foreign laws as to what consideration must be provided under the offer to shareholders resident abroad (*e.g.* in the USA): s.428(3), (4).

[99] These include shares he has contracted to buy but not those which he has contracted to buy in consideration of making the offer: s.428(5).

[1] *Re Chez Nico (Restaurants) Ltd* [1992] BCLC 192. That was not intended to be a general definition for other purposes, however.

[2] *ibid.*

companies or a company which is de facto controlled by the offeror or part of a consortium: section 430E(4)—(8). Thus in deciding whether an offer has been made for *all* the shares (or class of shares) the following are to be discounted:

(i) shares already owned by the offeror (s.428(1));
(ii) shares which the offeror has contracted to buy at the date of the offer except for acquisitions without consideration and, in England, by deed or only by virtue of having promised to make the offer (s.428(5)); and
(iii) shares already owned or contracted to an associate of the offeror at the date of the offer (s.430E(1)).

The remaining shares (or class) form the target against which the 90 per cent thresholds are to be judged.

## Joint offers

Section 430D allows joint offerors to take advantage of (or be subject to) the sections, provided they acquire the shares jointly and accept joint or several liability for other purposes. In general their rights under the section are joint rights whereas their obligations are joint and several (*i.e.* each is liable for the whole). Offeror is so construed unless the particular provision expressly states to the contrary. This section reverses the Privy Council decision in *Blue Metal Industries Ltd v. Dilley.*[3]

## Convertible securities

Problems arose with the original sections over convertible securities, *e.g.* debentures which can be converted into shares on a take-over offer being made. In *Re Simo Securities Trust Ltd*[4] some such debentures were converted into shares in the name of the offeror, others were converted into shares and then transferred to the offeror, and others were not converted at all. The Judge decided that those debentures which were converted could be counted towards the 90 per cent acceptance—those not converted were ignored. Now section 430F provides that all securities which are convertible into shares or entitle the holder

---

[3] [1970] A.C. 827 (P.C.).
[4] [1971] 1 W.L.R. 1455.

to subscribe for shares are shares for the purposes of the sections but they are to be treated as a separate class of shares separate from other shares. The effect of this is that such securities have a 90 per cent threshold of their own since each class of shares is treated separately by the new sections[5].

## Compulsory purchases by the offeror

If the offeror achieves a 90 per cent (in value) acceptance figure[6] he can serve a notice on those who have not accepted the offer that he desires to acquire their shares. The 90 per cent threshold applies to each class of shares separately so that each class is subject to a separate offer for this purpose: section 429(1), (2).

The 90 per cent threshold does not include shares to which the offer does not relate (*i.e.* shares already held or contracted to an offeror or his associates at the date of the offer). However, the offeror can count shares acquired by the offeror or his associates during the course of the offer otherwise than by acceptance of the offer (*e.g.* by market purchase) provided either that they have been so acquired for less than the offer price or that the offer price is revised upwards to the price paid[7]: sections 429(8), 430E(2).

To take advantage of the compulsory purchase power the 90 per cent threshold must be acquired within four months of the date of offer and the notice served in the prescribed manner within two months of achieving the threshold: section 429.

Provided that the notice has been validly served,[8] the offeror "shall be entitled and bound to acquire" the non-acceptor's shares "on the terms of the offer": section 430(2). If the offer provided for alternative consideration, *e.g.* cash or shares in the offeror company, the offeror must give the non-acceptors the same choice with six weeks in which to choose. Any notice must specify this choice, the time limit and which will be paid if no choice is initiated: section 430(3). If the non-cash consideration is

---

[5] See the next paragraph.

[6] *i.e.* acquired or contracted to acquire by offeror (plus associates).

[7] This adopts the principles of rule 4 of the City Code.

[8] The notice can be signed by a solicitor and a copy must be sent to the offeree company at the same time, together with a statutory declaration that the requisite conditions for its issue have been met. See *Re Chez Nico (Restaurants) Ltd* [1992] BCLC 192.

no longer available[9] the cash equivalent must be paid[10]: section 430(4).

The mechanics of the acquisition are that six weeks after the notice has been issued,[11] the offeror sends a copy to the offeree company and pays it the consideration due (or allots the shares, as appropriate) together with an instrument of transfer executed by a person nominated by the offeror. The offeree company must then register the offeror as owner of the shares. The offeree company must keep the consideration so received in a separate bank account on trust for the former shareholders. If they cannot be traced within 12 years after reasonable enquiries have been made at reasonable intervals, the money, etc. is to be paid into court: section 430(5)-(15).

If the offeror fails to achieve the necessary number of acceptances the court, on his application, may nevertheless allow him to acquire the remaining shares if the reason is that some shareholders have proved to be untraceable. The court can only do this, however, if the total acceptances plus untraceable shareholders amounts to the 90 per cent figure and the consideration is fair and reasonable. In making its decision the court must decide that it is just and equitable to allow such an acquisition having regard to the number of known shareholders who have rejected the offer: section 430C(5).

## Minority right to apply to the court to prevent acquisition

The offeror's right to acquire the non-acceptor's shares under section 429 is subject to the latters' right to apply to the court under section 430C. Within six weeks of receiving a notice of intent to acquire, any non-acceptor can apply to the court for an order (a) preventing the compulsory acquisition or (b) specifying different acquisition terms: section 430C(1). The effect of such an application is to freeze the compulsory acquisition process until the application has been disposed of: section 430C(2). No order for costs or expenses may be made against an applicant unless the application was improper or vexatious, or there has been unreasonable delay or conduct on his part: section 430C(4).

[9] From any of the joint offerors.
[10] This confirms the decision in *Re Carlton Holdings Ltd* [1971] 1 W.L.R. 918.
[11] Unless there is an application to the court by the dissentients—see below.

In *Re Britoil plc*.[12] the Court of Appeal ruled that an application will not be vexatious (and so will not incur a penalty in costs) if there is evidence justifying the court's looking at the offer to make sure it is fair. The fact that, of necessity, only a small minority of shareholders have not accepted the offer will not preclude the operation of section 430C(4).

The minority had a similar right to petition under the former sections although only to prevent an acquisition. The cases decided on the former sections are therefore of relevance.

Under the former sections the court decided that it would only make such an order if it was satisfied that the scheme was unfair to the general body of shareholders in the transferor company. There was normally a heavy burden of proof on the dissentients[13]—since the scheme has been approved by nine-tenths of the shareholders, prima facie it must be taken to be a fair one.[14] The test was one of fairness to the body of shareholders as a whole and not to individual shareholders, and it was not enough merely to prove that the scheme was open to criticism or capable of improvements.[15] It was not enough that the materials put before the shareholders were inadequate to enable them to form a just conclusion as to the acceptance or refusal of the offer.[16] Where there was a Stock Exchange quotation for the shares, prima facie that could be taken as the value of the shares.[17] The element of control of the transferor company, which would accrue to the transferee company from the acquisition of all the shares in the transferor company, was not taken into account in determining the value of the shares of a minority shareholder.[18] It was also held, however, that dissentient shareholders, who were not satisfied with the price offered, could not obtain an order for discovery so as to enable them to carry out an investigation into the value of the shares, unless there were special circumstances[19] but a more recent decision has established that discovery will apply unless the court is satisfied that it is unnecessary.[20]

---

[12] [1990] BCC 70 (C.A.).
[13] *Re Sussex Brick Co. Ltd* [1961] Ch. 289: *Nidditch v. The Calico Printers' Association Ltd*, 1961 S.L.T. 282.
[14] The onus is the other way round under s.425, *ante: per* Templeman J. in *Re Hellenic & General Trust Ltd* [1976] 1 W.L.R. 123, at pp. 130, 131.
[15] *Re Grierson, Oldham & Adams Ltd* [1968] Ch. 17.
[16] *Re Everite Locknuts Ltd* [1945] Ch. 220.
[17] See *Re Press Caps Ltd* [1949] Ch. 434 (C.A.).
[18] See note 14 above.
[19] *Re Press Caps Ltd* [1948] 2 All E.R. 638.
[20] *Re Lifecare International plc* [1990] BCLC 222.

However, if the dissentient shareholders showed that in substance the transferee company was the same as the majority holding in the transferor company the onus was on the majority to satisfy the court that the scheme was one which the minority ought reasonably to be compelled to fall in with.

A and B were the two shareholders, each holding 50 shares, in the transferee company which offered to purchase the shares in the transferor company in which there were three shareholders, A and B, who each held 4,500 shares and who accepted the offer, and C, who held 1,000 shares and who dissented. *Held*, that C, by showing that the transferee company was, for practical purposes, equivalent to the holders of nine-tenths of the shares in the transferor company who accepted the offer, had, prima facie, shown that the case was one in which the circumstances were special and the court ought to "order otherwise" within the meaning of section [430C], and the majority had not shown that there was some good reason in the interests of the company (*e.g.* the minority shareholder was acting in a manner highly damaging to the interests of the company) for allowing the section to be invoked for the purposes of enabling the majority to expropriate the minority: *Re Bugle Press Ltd* [196] Ch. 270 (C.A.).

This approach has been followed in two decisions on the new sections. In *Re Lifecare International plc*,[21] the dissentients were said to have a heavy burden of proof to discharge, especially where their directors took independent advice and recommended acceptance of the bid. In *Re Chez Nico (Restaurants) Ltd*,[22] on the other hand, where the offeror was an insider, as in the *Bugle Press* case, it was held that the burden of proof would be reversed, so that the offeror would need to show that the offer was fair. Since there had been breaches of the City Code in that case, that had not been discharged.

### Non-acceptor's right to be bought out by offeror

If the offeror has acquired 90 per cent in value of all the shares in a company (or all the shares of a class) any non-acceptor can require the offeror to acquire his shares: section 430A(1), (2). Note that this is not 90 per cent of shares subject to the offer but of all the shares, so that shares held by the offeror etc. at the date of the offer or contracted to him are included both in the total and the 90 per cent threshold.[23] This is different from the

[21] [1990] BCLC 222.
[22] [1992] BCLC 192.
[23] Associates are counted in for this purpose: section 430E(3).

threshold which enables the offeror to acquire the shares under section 429.

If the offer is still open for acceptances the shareholder can apply to be bought out by a written communication to the offeror.[24] Otherwise within one month of gaining his 90 per cent threshold (and not necessarily that for a compulsory purchase) the offeror must inform the non-acceptors of their rights to be bought out—unless he has already served a compulsory purchase notice: section 430A(3), (5). The offeror must give non-acceptors at least three months from the end of the offer period in which to apply to be bought out: section 430(4).

If a non-acceptor sends such a written communication the offeror is then "entitled and bound" to acquire the shares on the terms of the offer or such other terms as may be agreed: section 430B(1), (2). The provisions relating to alternative consideration under the offer are the same as for a compulsory purchase: section 430B(3), (4).[25]

In the case of any dispute any non-acceptor who has applied to be bought out can apply to the court to set the terms for the acquisition: section 430(3). Again such an applicant is protected as to costs: section 430C(4).

---

[24] To one of two or more joint offerors will suffice.
[25] *Ante,* p. 844.

# INDEX

Annual Return, 231–233
Arrangement,
  meaning, 810–811
Articles of Association, 78–89
  alteration, 83–89
    agreement as to, 88
    benefit of company, 85–87
    injunction to prevent, 88–89
    modification of rights clause, 84
    natural justice, and, 87
    voting powers of classes of shares,
      87–88
  binding contract, as, 80–83
  effect, 80–83
  inspection, 89
  rectification, 89
  registration, 79–80
Auditors, 554–590
  appointment, 565–567
  closing the "expectation gap",
    556–557
  corporate governance, 557–558
  duties, 583–590
  eligibility of partnerships, 564
  existence of cash balance, 587
  fees, 562–563
  fixed assets, 588
  general duties, 583–585
  grounds for suspicion, 586
  growth of regulation, 556
  ineligibility because of lack of
    independence, 564
  ineligible, appointment of, 565
  legal position, 571
  liability to third parties, 589–590
  penalties for offences, 563
  policies of company, 588
  powers, 581–583
  professional qualifications, 558–565
  rationale of statutory audit, 554–556
  recognised qualifying body, 560–561
  recognised supervisory bodies,
    558–560
  registers, 562–563
  reliance on work of subsidiary
    companies' auditors, 583
  removal, 567–569
  remuneration, 572
  resignation, 567–569
  rights to attend general meetings,
    582

Auditors—cont.
  rights to inspect books and receive
    explanations, 581–582
  securities, existence of, 586–587
  specific duties, 586–589
  statement by person ceasing to hold
    office, 569–570
  stocks, 587-588
  unauthorised borrowing, 586
  vacation of office, 567–570
  work-in-progress, 587–588
Auditors' Report, 546–547, 572–581
  addressed to members, 572
  content, 572–573
  duties of auditors in relation to,
    574–575
  qualified, 575–576
  signing, 574
  special, 576–581
    agreed valuations of private
      companies, 581
    banking and insurance companies,
      576
    bid forecasts, on, 580
    Companies Acts, under, 580–581
    creditors, for, 580
    management, to, 580
    preliminary announcements, 581
    profits available for distribution,
      578–579
    prospectuses, on, 580
    small and medium-sized
      companies, 576–577
    small company exemption,
      577–578
    summary financial statements, 578

Balance Sheet, 492–500
  Format 1, 492–495
  small company, 496
Banking Companies,
  accounts, 549–500
Bills of Exchange, 103
Brokerage, 145–146
Bubble Act 1720, 7
Business Names, 61–62

Calls,
  contributories, on, 781
Calls on Shares, 272–273